T0188969

Communications
in Computer and Information Science 1685

Editorial Board Members

Joaquim Filipe ⓘ
  Polytechnic Institute of Setúbal, Setúbal, Portugal
Ashish Ghosh
  Indian Statistical Institute, Kolkata, India
Raquel Oliveira Prates ⓘ
  Federal University of Minas Gerais (UFMG), Belo Horizonte, Brazil
Lizhu Zhou
  Tsinghua University, Beijing, China

More information about this series at https://link.springer.com/bookseries/7899

Juan Carlos Figueroa-García · Carlos Franco ·
Yesid Díaz-Gutierrez ·
Germán Hernández-Pérez (Eds.)

Applied Computer Sciences in Engineering

9th Workshop on Engineering Applications, WEA 2022
Bogotá, Colombia, November 30 – December 2, 2022
Proceedings

 Springer

Editors
Juan Carlos Figueroa-García [iD]
Universidad Distrital Francisco José de
Caldas
Bogotá, Colombia

Carlos Franco [iD]
Universidad del Rosario
Bogotá, Colombia

Germán Hernández-Pérez [iD]
National University of Colombia
Bogotá, Colombia

Yesid Díaz-Gutierrez [iD]
Universidad de La Salle
Bogotá, Colombia

ISSN 1865-0929   ISSN 1865-0937 (electronic)
Communications in Computer and Information Science
ISBN 978-3-031-20610-8   ISBN 978-3-031-20611-5 (eBook)
https://doi.org/10.1007/978-3-031-20611-5

© The Editor(s) (if applicable) and The Author(s), under exclusive license
to Springer Nature Switzerland AG 2022, corrected publication 2022
This work is subject to copyright. All rights are reserved by the Publisher, whether the whole or part of the material is concerned, specifically the rights of translation, reprinting, reuse of illustrations, recitation, broadcasting, reproduction on microfilms or in any other physical way, and transmission or information storage and retrieval, electronic adaptation, computer software, or by similar or dissimilar methodology now known or hereafter developed.
The use of general descriptive names, registered names, trademarks, service marks, etc. in this publication does not imply, even in the absence of a specific statement, that such names are exempt from the relevant protective laws and regulations and therefore free for general use.
The publisher, the authors, and the editors are safe to assume that the advice and information in this book are believed to be true and accurate at the date of publication. Neither the publisher nor the authors or the editors give a warranty, expressed or implied, with respect to the material contained herein or for any errors or omissions that may have been made. The publisher remains neutral with regard to jurisdictional claims in published maps and institutional affiliations.

This Springer imprint is published by the registered company Springer Nature Switzerland AG
The registered company address is: Gewerbestrasse 11, 6330 Cham, Switzerland

Preface

The ninth edition of the Workshop on Engineering Applications (WEA 2022) was focused on applications in computer science, computational intelligence, IoT, bioengineering, optimization and simulation. WEA 2022 was one of the flagship events of the Faculty of Engineering of the Universidad Distrital Francisco José de Caldas, the School of Engineering, Science and Technology of Universidad del Rosario and the Faculty of Engineering of the National University of Colombia.

WEA 2022 was held from November 30 to December 02 in hybrid mode due to the post-COVID-19 pandemic economic and travel restrictions. In total, 143 submissions were received from authors in 12 countries on topics like computer science, artificial intelligence, operations research/optimization, simulation systems and their applications. The peer review process for all submissions was rigorous where every paper was reviewed by one Program Committee member who assigned at least 3 external reviewers in a single blind manner, so as a result a total of 39 papers were accepted for oral presentation at WEA 2022. The Program Committee organized all the accepted papers into four different sections for clarity of presentation and to increase the impact of this volume published by Springer's Communications in Computer and Information Sciences (CCIS) series.

The Faculty of Engineering of the Universidad Distrital Francisco José de Caldas, the School of Engineering, Science and Technology of Universidad del Rosario and the Faculty of Engineering of the National University of Colombia made significant efforts to guarantee the success of the conference considering post-COVID-19 global economic effects.

We would like to thank all members of the Program Committee for their commitment to help in the review process and for spreading WEA 2022 call for papers and the team at Springer for their helpful advice, guidance and continuous support in publicizing the proceedings. Also, we would also like to thank all the authors for supporting WEA 2022 as without all their high-quality submissions the conference would not be possible. Finally, we are especially grateful to the IEEE Universidad Distrital Francisco José de Caldas Student branch, the Laboratory for Automation and Computational Intelligence (LAMIC) and GITUD research groups of the Universidad Distrital Francisco José de Caldas, the Algorithms and Combinatorics (ALGOS) research group of the Universidad Nacional de Colombia, the AVARC and CALPOSSALLE research groups of the Universidad de La Salle and the faculty staff of the School of Engineering, Science and Technology of Universidad del Rosario.

November 2022

Juan Carlos Figueroa-García
Carlos Franco
Yesid Díaz-Gutierrez
Germán Hernández

Organization

General Chair

Juan Carlos Figueroa-García   Universidad Distrital Francisco José de Caldas, Colombia

Technical Chairs

Elvis Gaona   Universidad Distrital Francisco José de Caldas, Colombia

Germán Hernández-Pérez   Universidad Nacional de Colombia, Colombia

Program and Track Chairs

Carlos Franco   Universidad del Rosario, Colombia

Yesid Díaz-Gutierrez   Universidad Santo Tomás de Aquino, Colombia

Germán Hernández-Pérez   Universidad Nacional de Colombia, Colombia

Publication Chair

Alvaro David Orjuela-Cañon   Universidad del Rosario, Colombia

Organizing Committee Chairs

Julio César Sandoval   Universidad de La Salle, Colombia

John Leonardo Vargas Mesa   Universidad del Rosario, Colombia

Plenary Speakers

Oscar Castillo   Tijuana Institute of Technology, Mexico

Yurilev Chalco-Cano   Universidad de Tarapacá, Chile

Alejandro Correa Bahnsen   Rappi, Colombia

Carmine Bianchi   University of Palermo, Italy

Luis C. Rabelo   University of Central Florida, USA

Program Committee

Adil Usman   Indian Institute of Technology at Mandi, India

Adolfo Jaramillo-Matta   Universidad Distrital Francisco José de Caldas, Colombia

Alvaro David Orjuela-Cañon	Universidad del Rosario, Colombia
Andres Gaona	Universidad Distrital Francisco José de Caldas, Colombia
Carlos Osorio-Ramírez	Universidad Nacional de Colombia, Colombia
De-Shuang Huang	Tongji University, China
Diana Ovalle	Universidad Distrital Francisco José de Caldas, Colombia
Elvis Eduardo Gaona-García	Universidad Distrital Francisco José de Caldas, Colombia
Fabián Garay	ESINF, Colombia
Feizar Javier Rueda-Velazco	Universidad Distrital Francisco José de Caldas, Colombia
Francisco Ramis	Universidad del Bío-Bío, Chile
Guadalupe González	Universidad Tecnológica de Panamá, Panama
Gustavo Puerto-Leguizamón	Universidad Distrital Francisco José de Caldas, Colombia
Gustavo Suárez	Universidad Pontificia Bolivariana, Colombia
Heriberto Román-Flores	Universidad de Tarapacá, Chile
I-Hsien Ting	National University of Kaohsiung, Taiwan
Jair Cervantes-Canales	Universidad Autónoma de México, Mexico
Jairo Soriano-Mendez	Universidad Distrital Francisco José de Caldas, Colombia
Javier Arturo Orjuela-Castro	Universidad Distrital Francisco José de Caldas, Colombia
J. J. Merelo	Universidad de Granada, Spain
Jose Luís Gonzalez-Velarde	Instituto Tecnológico de Monterrey, Mexico
Jose Luis Villa	Universidad Tecnológica de Bolívar, Colombia
Lindsay Alvarez	Universidad Distrital Francisco José de Caldas, Colombia
Mabel Frías	Universidad de las Villas "Marta Abreu", Cuba
Mario Enrique Duarte-Gonzalez	Universidad Antonio Nariño, Colombia
Martha Centeno	University of Turabo, Puerto Rico
Martin Pilat	Charles University, Czech Republic
Martine Ceberio	University of Texas at El Paso, USA
Miguel Melgarejo	Universidad Distrital Francisco José de Caldas, Colombia
Nelson L. Diaz Aldana	Universidad Distrital Francisco José de Caldas, Colombia
Paulo Alonso Gaona	Universidad Distrital Francisco José de Caldas, Colombia
Rafael Bello-Pérez	Universidad de las Villas "Marta Abreu", Cuba
Rodrigo Linfati	Universidad del Bio-Bio, Chile

Roman Neruda   Charles University and Czech Academy of
                                    Sciences, Czech Republic
Sebastián Jaramillo-Isaza   Universidad Antonio Nariño, Colombia
Sergio Rojas-Galeano   Universidad Distrital Francisco José de Caldas,
                                    Colombia
Vladik Kreinovich   University of Texas at El Paso, USA
Yurilev Chalco-Cano   Universidad de Tarapacá, Chile

Contents

Optimization

Simulation

Applications

Artificial Intelligence

Comparison of Higher-Order Approximations to Solve Dynamical Systems Using Interval Constraint Solving

Angel F. Garcia Contreras$^{(\boxtimes)}$ and Martine Ceberio

The University of Texas at El Paso, El Paso, TX 79968, USA
afgarciacontreras@miners.utep.edu

Abstract. Phenomena that change over time are abundant in nature. Dynamical systems, composed of differential equations, are used to model them. In some cases, analytical solutions exist that provide an exact description of the system's behavior. Otherwise we use numerical approximations: we discretize the original problem over time, where each state of the system at any discrete time moment depends on previous/subsequent states. This process may yield large systems of equations. Efficient tools exist to solve dynamical systems, but might not be well suited for certain types of problems. For example, Runge-Kutta-based solution techniques do not easily handle parameters' uncertainty, although inherent to real world measurements. If the problem has multiple solutions, such methods usually provide only one. When they cannot find a solution, it is not know whether none exists or it failed to find one. Interval methods, on the other hand, provide guaranteed numerical computations. If a solution exists, it will be found. Interval methods for dynamical systems fall into two main categories: step-based methods (fast but too conservative with overestimation for large systems) and constraint-solving techniques (better at controlling overestimation but usually much slower). In prior research, we developed a promising method that speeds up constraint-based techniques. In this article, we test that method with higher order approximations known as multi-step methods. We compared these approximations based on their accuracy when attempting to include the real solution. We share insightful experimental results.

1 Introduction

Phenomena that change over time are abundant. Their behavior can be modeled using dynamical systems that represent chronological change via differential equations. For some real life problems, we have analytical solutions that describe the behavior exactly. For many other problems, there is no such exact representation, so we use numerical approximations: we take the original problem, which is continuous over time, and we *discretize* it such that we get a series of discrete moments in time, and in which the system state at each discrete moment depends on previous and/or subsequent states. This relationship is described

© The Author(s), under exclusive license to Springer Nature Switzerland AG 2022
J. C. Figueroa-García et al. (Eds.): WEA 2022, CCIS 1685, pp. 3–18, 2022.
https://doi.org/10.1007/978-3-031-20611-5_1

through a state equation; depending on the desired granularity/precision for the approximation, discretization may generate a very large set of equations.

There are many tools that solve dynamical systems, but these might not be well-suited for certain types of problems. For example, a Runge-Kutta-based technique cannot easily handle a problem with uncertain parameter values obtained from real world measurements. Solutions are heavily reliant on an initial set of parameters. If a problem has multiple solutions, such methods can find *a* solution, but cannot identify *how many* solutions exist, or if the found solution is the best based on given criteria. If the method does not find a solution, it is unknown whether the problem has no solution, or method simply failed to find one.

We want to provide guaranteed numerical computations, which identify all solutions if they exist, and the certainty that our computations return no solution it means none exist. We use *interval-based computations* [13,14], as they provide the desired guarantees. When solving dynamical systems, there are two main categories of interval-based techniques: *step-based* methods that generate an explicit system of equations one discretized state at a atime, and *constraint-solving techniques* that solve the entire system of implicitly discretized equations. Step-based method are fast and have less computational overhead, so they have been widely studied in the past; however, on complex systems (either because they are simulating longer times or the differential system is very non-linear), the solution they find can lead to overestimated ranges. Constraint-solving techniques can better control the overestimation through the entire system at once, but this reduction comes at a computational time cost and may take considerably longer to produce a result.

In previous work [7,8], we introduced a heuristic approach that dramatically improves the computation time of constraint-solving interval techniques for dynamical systems, by solving smaller overlapping sub-problems. In this paper, we take a look at the algorithm's accuracy under a given discretization, then we analyze the performance and accuracy of discretizations with various degrees of complexity. Our results who that careful selection of the discretized form is essential in improving accuracy while also maintaining a reasonable computation time, as discretized forms with higher-complexity do not necessarily provide better solutions.

2   Background

2.1   Dynamical Systems

Dynamical systems model how a phenomenon changes over time. In particular, we are interested in continuous dynamical systems.

Definition 1. A continuous *dynamical system* is a pair (D, f) with $D \subseteq \mathbb{R}^n$ called a *domain* and $f : D \times T \to \mathbb{R}^n$ a function from pairs $(x, t) \in D \times T$ to $\mathbb{R}^n$.

Definition 2. By a *trajectory* of a dynamical system, we mean a function $x : [t_0, \infty) \to D$ for which $\frac{dx}{dt} = f(x, t)$.

To obtain the state equations of a dynamical system, we *integrate* its differential equations. The type of problems we are interested in often lack an exact integral, instead we use *numerical methods* that *approximate* the actual solution. These methods can provide good results, but as they are approximations their solutions always have a margin of error that must be included in the computation. This error can be minimized by the choice of numerical methods and by tweaking the method's approximation parameters.

2.2 Traditional Methods

Numerical methods to solve dynamical systems are usually classified in two general categories based on the type of approximation they make for the integral: explicit and implicit methods. In *explicit* methods, the state equation for a specific state involves the values of one or more previous states. This means that given an initial state, every subsequent state value can be obtained by evaluating each discretized equation in order, as each state equation already has the values it needs from previous evaluated equations. *Implicit* methods involve past and future states in their discretization. These equations cannot be solved by simple successive evaluation, but with search algorithms instead. The most common type of algorithm used is root-finding methods, such as Newton-Rhapson. Both types of methods are used to solve dynamical system problems, either separately or synergistically.

2.3 Interval Methods

An interval is defined as: $\boldsymbol{x} = [\underline{x}, \overline{x}] = \{x \in \mathbb{R} \mid \underline{x} \leq x \leq \overline{x}; \ \underline{x}, \ \overline{x} \in \mathbb{R}\}$.
Intervals represent all values between their infimum $\underline{X}$ and supremum $\overline{X}$. In particular, we can use them to represent uncertain quantities. We manipulate them in computations through the rules of interval arithmetic, naively posed as follows: $\boldsymbol{x} \diamond \boldsymbol{y} = \{x \diamond y, \text{ where } x \in \boldsymbol{x}, y \in \boldsymbol{y}\}$, where $\diamond$ is any arithmetic operator, and combining intervals always results in another interval. However, since some operations, like division, could yield a union of intervals (e.g., division by an interval that contains 0), the combination of intervals involves an extra operation, called the hull, denoted by $\square$, which returns one interval enclosure of a set of real values. We obtain: $\boldsymbol{x} \diamond \boldsymbol{y} = \square \{x \diamond y, \text{ where } x \in \boldsymbol{x}, y \in \boldsymbol{y}\}$.

We can extend this property to any function $f : \mathbb{R}^n \to \mathbb{R}$ with one or more interval parameters:

$$f(\boldsymbol{x_1}, \ldots, \boldsymbol{x_n}) \subseteq \square \{f(x_1, \ldots, x_n), \text{ where } x_1 \in \boldsymbol{x_1}, \ldots, x_n \in \boldsymbol{x_n}\}$$

where $f(\boldsymbol{x_1}, \ldots, \boldsymbol{x_n})$ represents the range of f over the interval domain $\boldsymbol{x_1} \times \ldots \times \boldsymbol{x_n}$, and $\square \{f(x_1, \ldots, x_n), \text{ where } x_1 \in \boldsymbol{x_1}, \ldots, x_n \in \boldsymbol{x_n}\}$ represents the narrowest interval enclosing this range. Computing the exact range of f over intervals is very hard, so instead we use surrogate approximations. We call these surrogates *interval extensions*. An interval extension F of function f must satisfy the following property:

$$f(x_1, \ldots, x_n) \subseteq F(x_1, \ldots, x_n)$$

Interval extensions aim to approximate the range of the original real-valued function. In general, different interval extensions can return a different range for f while still fulfilling the above property. For more information about intervals and interval computations in general, see [13, 14].

Step-based Interval Methods for Solving Dynamical Systems. These algorithms use explicit discretization explicit discretization schemes, such as Taylor polynomials or Runge-Kutta, that must be evaluated to provide a guaranteed enclosure that includes the discretization error at every step. The solvers implement interval evaluation schemes that reduce overestimation. For example, VSPODE [11] uses Taylor polynomials for discretization and Taylor models [1, 12] for evaluation; DynIBEX [6] uses Runge-Kutta discretization and evaluates its functions using affine arithmetic [9, 16].

Interval Constraint-Solving Techniques. The methods used to solve a dynamical system using explicit discretization do not work for implicit discretization. We need to solve the entire system. We can do this if we treat the state equations as a system of equality constraints and the dynamical system as an interval Constraint Satisfaction Problem (CSP):

Definition 3. An interval *constraint satisfaction problem* is a tuple $P = (X, D, C)$, X is a set of n variables $\{x_1, \ldots, x_n\}$, D is the Cartesian product of the variables' associated interval domains $D = x_1 \times \ldots \times x_n$, and C is the set of m constraints $C = \{c_1, \ldots, c_m\}$. [5]

The initial interval domain D represents the entire space in which a real-valued solution to the CSP might be found. With intervals, we want to find an *enclosure* of said solution. This enclosure X^* needs to be narrow: the differences between the infimum and supremum of all interval domains in X^* must be less than a parameter ϵ, representing the *accuracy* of the solution's enclosure. If the entire domain is inconsistent, it will be wholly discarded, which means that the problem has no solution.

An interval constraint solver attempts to find a narrow X^* through consistency techniques. *Consistency* is a property of CSPs, in which the domain does not violate any constraint. For interval CSPs, we want domains that are at least *partially consistent*: if they do not entirely satisfy the constraints, they may contain a solution. Figure 1 shows a visualization of the general concept behind contraction using consistency. Figure 1a shows the evaluation of a function $f(x)$ over an interval x, represented by the gray rectangle $y = f(x)$. This function is part of a constraint $f(x) = -4$, whose solutions are found in the domain of x; however, this interval is too wide, so it must be contracted. In this case, the range of $f(x) \geq -4.0$ can be discarded, which creates a new interval value for the range of $f(x)$, or y', which can be *propagated* to remove portions of x that are not consistent with y'. This creates the contracted domain x', which is a narrower enclosure of the solutions of $f(x) = -4$, as shown in Fig. 1b.

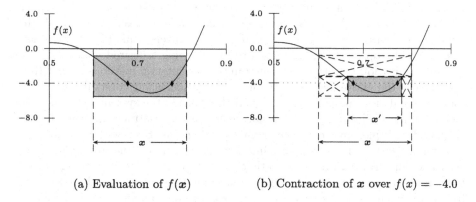

(a) Evaluation of $f(x)$ (b) Contraction of x over $f(x) = -4.0$

Fig. 1. Visual example of interval domain contraction

Contraction via consistency is just part of how interval constraint solver techniques find narrow enclosures of solutions to systems of constraints. For example, the constraint $f(x) = -4$ shown in Fig. 1 has two solutions enclosed inside the domain x', but we need the individual solutions.

Interval constraint solvers use a *branch-and-prune* algorithm. The "prune" part of the algorithm is achieved through contraction via consistency; when "pruning" is not enough to find the most narrow enclosure that satisfies the constraints, the algorithm "branches" by dividing the domain X into two adjacent subdomains by splitting the interval value of one of its variables through a midpoint $m(x) = \frac{x+\overline{x}}{2}$. These two new sub-boxes, $X_L = \{x_0, \ldots, [\underline{x_i}, m(x_i)], \ldots, x_n\}$ and $X_U = \{x_0, \ldots, [m(x_i), \overline{x_i}], \ldots, x_n\}$, are then processed using the same algorithm. This means that all sub-boxes are put in a queue of sub-boxes, as each sub-boxes and be further "branched" into smaller sub-boxes.

Interval constraint solvers such as RealPaver [10] and IbexSolve [3,4] solve systems of constraints. To solve a dynamical system, we need to generate all required state equations, and provide an initial domain containing all possible state values. While interval solvers can provide good results, when system are too large, they can be slow to find a reasonable solution. For large systems, there have been attempts at making them easier to solve, including generating an alternative reduced-order model [17], and focusing on a subset of constraints at a time [15].

Step-Based or Constraint-based? The solvers that use step-based interval methods (VSPODE, DynIBEX) work well, up to a point. As with non-interval approaches, there is an approximation error; however, due to the need for guaranteed computations, these methods compute an *enclosure* of each state plus its range of approximation errors. These bounds on the error can introduce a small amount of overestimation into the solution, which compounds after computing multiple states, each with their own bounded approximation error. Even when dynamically computing the step size between states (which helps reduce the overestimation), this additional range accumulates at every iteration. If the interval value of a state becomes too large, these solvers cannot compute a new step size and stop the simulation even before reaching a desired final state.

Our motivation behind using constraint-based interval methods is that they can explore the entire system. Solving a full system using interval constraint-solving techniques can explore multiple realizations of the system with a desired width for the enclosure. To potentially increase the contraction, each state is evaluated multiple times over one or multiple domains. Even with a static value of h for all states, implicit approximations used increase the approximation's accuracy. The drawback of these methods is tied to this particular strength: contractors need to evaluate each equation multiple times, and branch-and-prune-based solvers incorporate multiple contractors. Additionally, the "branching" process creates problems exponentially based on the number of variables; each sub-problem needs to be processed, including potential further sub-divisions, so the number of subproblems being generated becomes exponential. Thus, these techniques provide a strong computational guaranteed, with a trade-off of a considerably higher computation time.

Prior Work. In previous work [7,8], we showed a *Sliding Windows* scheme to improve the computation time to find a solution using interval constraint methods. The main idea of this type of algorithm is to take advantage of the structure in a dynamical system (specifically, an *initial value problem*) to create and solve subproblems made of subsets of *contiguous state variables* and their respective equations. We take the state variables $X_{\text{sub}} = \{x(j), \ldots x(j+w)\}$ with domains $\{\boldsymbol{x}(\boldsymbol{j}), \ldots, \boldsymbol{x}(\boldsymbol{j}+\boldsymbol{w})\}$, along the following set of state equations as a system of constraints C_{sub}:

$$g_i(x(j), \ldots x(j+w), t_i) = f(x(i), t_i, h), \; \forall i \in \{j, \ldots j+w\}$$

where function g_i is a discretization of $\frac{dx}{dt}$ at t_i. We call this subproblem $P_{\text{sub}} = (X_{\text{sub}}, C_{\text{sub}})$ a *window* of size w. Our technique aims to speed up the computation process of interval constraint solvers by sequentially creating and solving a series of subproblems with size w.

We can solve the first subproblem normally, as it is exactly an initial value problem. However, subsequent problems cannot be treated the same: if we took the last values of the previous problems as initial values, we would lose the trajectory created by the previous states.

The second element involves maintaining this trajectory by *transfering* multiple state values between subproblems. Solving the k-th subproblem $P_k = (X_k, C_k)$ yields a reduced domain X_k^* representing w states, from t_j to t_{j+N_k}. For the next subproblem, $P_{k+1} = (X_{k+1}, C_{k+1})$, we take the last o interval values of X_k^* and use them as the initial domain for the *first* o values of X_{k+1}:

$$\{x_{k+1}(1), \ldots, x_{k+1}(o)\} = \{x_k(w-o), \ldots, x_k(w)\}$$

We then solve subproblem P_{k+1} using interval constraint-solving techniques, yielding a new reduced domain used to repeat the process again. We call o the *overlap* between subproblem *windows* of size w. Figure 2 shows a graphical representation of how o states are transferred from one subproblem to the next.

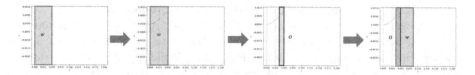

Fig. 2. Graphical plot of overlap transfer

With interval constraint solvers, a series of subproblems with a smaller number of variables is faster to solve than one with more variables: the number of subproblems generated from domain division is reduced, which speeds up the overall process.

3   Problem Statement and Experiments

Our first experiments with the Sliding Windows proved we could find solutions to dynamical systems in reasonable time using interval-based constraint solving techniques. These experiments were carried out with a simple approximation to the dynamical system called *backwards Euler*, which involves just two variables per state equation, and without bounding the approximation error. Existing step-based solvers use *high order approximations* that involve multiple prior variables while including techniques that bound the approximation error.

Without any changes, the backwards Euler discretization used in previous experiments with the Sliding Windows algorithm is not a perfectly accurate enclosure, as it does not bound the real solution. This motivates our next research question: how can we improve the enclosures of the approximations in the Sliding Windows algorithm?

To look for an answer, we took a look at the existing, step-based solvers. They use explicit discretization methods that result in polynomials with a more accurate approximation. VSPODE uses high-order Taylor polynomials, generating the coefficients using automatic differentiation of the original ODE. DynIBEX uses an interval-based version of Runge-Kutta, which uses intermediate points between states in its computation of a specific state. Both of these methods bound the approximation error by computing upper and lower bounds of the local truncation error on each step and add it to the discretized equations to guarantee an enclosure of the solution.

Without a computation of the bounds (for now), we want to find more accurate implicit approximations that work with the Sliding Windows algorithm. We focused on experiments in two main areas: *higher-order approximations* and *artificially-inflated enclosures*.

3.1 Higher-Order Approximations

In general, an approximate state equation that involves more states increases the accuracy of the approximation. Existing solvers apply this concept with explicit discretizations by creating *intermediate sub-states* that are computed on evaluation but not stored outside of finding the state for that equation. This kind of approach would be inefficient for Sliding Windows: if two main states share one or more points, they would have to be computed multiple times, unless we added them to our full set of states.

If adding new sub-states is not an option, the best alternative we have is to have approximations that involve *multiple existing states*; these type of approximations are known as *linear multistep methods*, and each state equation can involve multiple states from before or after the current state. For these experiments, we selected the *Adams-Moulton* method.

The Adams-Moulton Method. The Adams-Moulton method is the implicit version of the explicit Adams-Bashfort method [2]; in non-interval solvers, these two methods work together in a *predictor-corrector method*: the solver finds an "initial guess" to the complete behavior of the system using Adams-Bashfort as a slightly inaccurate predictor, then uses this behavior as an "initial point" to solve an Adams-Moulton approximation to "correct" the results and make them more accurate.

As we are working with interval constraint-solvers, and we want to test their accuracy on their own, we can use interval evaluation and constraint-solving on the Adams-Moulton method only. The general formula for this approximation is:

$$x_{n+s} = x_{n+s-1} + h \sum_{m=0}^{s} b_s f\left(x_{n+m}, t_{n+m}\right)$$

where t_i is a discrete time, x_i is a state variable at t_i, $f(x_i, t_i)$ is an ordinary differential equation s.t. $\dot{x} = f(x,t)$, and b_s is a unique coefficient. These coefficients are independent from x_i and t_i, and its value depends on the *order of the approximation* s, which represented the number of states involved in each state equation.

We believe that such a multi-step discretization method is a good fit for solving dynamical systems using interval constraint-solving techniques. Each state equation involves multiple state values, maintained naturally by the interval box that represents the entire set of states from the full problem – or, in the case of the Sliding Windows algorithm, an individual window.

A higher order approximation using Adams-Moulton means $s > 0$ ($s = 0$ is backwards Euler), which means each state equation will involve more terms and coefficients. This can impact the interval evaluation and contraction processes. Given the conditions of the Sliding Windows algorithm and these tests, we will also no include bounding the error in any way. This means we know in advance that our approximations will not bound the real solution, but we can use this lack of computational rigor to identify in advance potential issues with higher-order enclosures, such as excessive overestimation or inaccuracy.

We measure said inaccuracy by the *error* on each state enclosure, which we define as the distance between an interval state enclosure and the real solution outside its bounds. For each state enclosure $x_i = \left[\underline{x_i}, \overline{x_i}\right]$ and real solution x_i^*, the *error* in x_i is:

$$\tau(x_i) = 0 \qquad \text{if } x_i^* \in x_i$$
$$\tau(x_i) = \underline{x_i} - x_i^* \qquad \text{if } x_i^* < x_i$$
$$\tau(x_i) = x_i^* - \overline{x_i} \qquad \text{if } x_i^* > x_i$$

The first objective of the experiments is to use these metrics to explore the accuracy of various orders of Adams-Moulton discretizations. In particular, we focus on the Adams-Moulton discretizations of order $s = \{0, \ldots, 8\}$. While we are not including bounds on the approximation error, we can still attempt to replicate the impact of including these bounds into the process. We do this by manipulating the state enclosures using artificial intervals into the models given by the Adams-Moulton approximations.

The Adams-Moulton Method. To analyze the impact of the calculation of the approximation error, we created new models based on the systems generated by the Adams-Moulton method that introduce an "artificial bounding" that increases and changes the interval state enclosures. With this, we can explore how much the solution process of higher-order enclosures is changed by these additional bounds.

We explored two different types of enclosure manipulations:

– *Initial value inflation.* We change the initial value of the model by making it a "wider" interval enclosure.
– *State equation inflation.* We "naively" simulate a per-state bound on the error by adding a narrow $[-\Delta, +\Delta]$ interval, to examine the impact of an additional interval term.

3.2 Experiments and Results

We designed experiments along two axes: the *approximation level* and *type of enclosure manipulation*. We generated models for Adams-Moulton involving $s = \{0, \ldots, 8\}$, with $s = 0$ representing the Backwards Euler method examined in previous experiments. For enclosure manipulation, we settled on the following seven types:

- Case Base: The normal case, with no additional uncertainty added.
- Case All-A: Add to all state equations a constant $\delta = [-10^{-16}, 10^{-16}]$
- Case All-B: Add to all state equations a constant $\delta = [-10^{-8}, 10^{-8}]$
- Case All-C: Add to all state equations a constant $\delta = [-10^{-4}, 10^{-4}]$
- Case Ini-A: Add to all initial states a constant $\delta = [-10^{-16}, 10^{-16}]$
- Case Ini-B: Add to all initial states a constant $\delta = [-10^{-8}, 10^{-8}]$
- Case Ini-C: Add to all initial states a constant $\delta = [-10^{-4}, 10^{-4}]$

We ran each of the models with each of the enclosure manipulation types, for a total of 63 experiments using a three-species food chain model with Holling type II predator response function:

$$\frac{dm_1}{dt} = r_1 m_1 \left(1 - \frac{m_1}{K_1}\right) - a_{12} \left(\frac{m_1 m_2}{m_1 + A_1}\right) \tag{1a}$$

$$\frac{dm_2}{dt} = -d_2 m_2 + a_{21} \left(\frac{m_1 m_2}{m_1 + A_1}\right) - a_{23} \left(\frac{m_2 m_3}{m_2 + A_2}\right) \tag{1b}$$

$$\frac{dm_3}{dt} = -d_3 m_3 + a_{32} \left(\frac{m_2 m_3}{m_2 + A_2}\right) \tag{1c}$$

For the discretization, we used a step size of $h = 0.01$.

Comparison Metrics. Given that we are not bounding the approximation error, the enclosures found with the state equations and the Sliding Windows algorithm will not always enclose the solution at all discrete times. We designed a group of metrics with the intent of using them to compare the Adams-Moulton discretizations for $s = \{0, \ldots, 8\}$:

- *Time states until overestimation.* Number of states contracted before reaching a "window" of states whose interval width is beyond a certain threshold. We consider a state to be overestimating, when the supremum of a state is 10% above its midpoint. For these experiments, we set a goal of $t_f = 40.0$, or $N = 4000$ states, which represents the max value for this metric. We chose this target based on previous experiments [7,8] that showed existing solvers could reach this target number without leading to excessive overestimation.
- *Solution accuracy.* If the approximation was not perfectly accurate, it means that in our solution there were interval states that did not enclose the actual solution to the system. There are various ways to analyze the accuracy of the system:
  - *Coverage.* Defined as the percentage of states that enclose the solution. For example, if in a system of 100 states, the interval solution encloses the actual solution in 90 of those states, we say there is a coverage of 90%. A higher coverage is better in this metric; all solvers that bound the approximation error, such as VSPODE and DynIBEX, have a coverage of 100%.

- *Total accumulated error.* The sum of all errors across all states. States that provide an enclosure have an error of 0, states that do not enclosure the solution have an error equal to the linear distance from the closest bound to the real solution. The smallest this value is, the better is the result.
- *Total average error.* The average of the error across all states, including those that provide an enclosure to the real-based solution. The smallest this value is, the better is the result.
- *Coverage average error.* The average of the error across all states that do not enclose the real-based solution. The smallest this value is, the better is the result.

While these metrics might seem enough, we want discretizations that produce better enclosures to longer simulations. Interval methods struggle to produce tighter enclosures after a longer simulated time, particularly when the equations are complex (i.e. highly non-linear) or the simulated time is longer/has more states.

There is no guarantee that we will get narrow state enclosures for all $N = 4000$ states, and in fact it is more likely that we will not. Instead of using these metrics as-is, we use the "Time states until overestimation" metric to *weight* the accuracy metrics based on how close the model was to the desired goal of $N = 4000$ states without overestimation:

$$<\text{weighted metric}> = <\text{base metric}> \times \frac{<\text{states until overest.}>}{4000}$$

This creates four new metrics: *weighted coverage, weighted accumulated error, weighted average error,* and *weighted coverage average error.* Using these metrics we can compare the overall impact of each discretization in improving the quality of the solution (by increasing coverage/decreasing error). Table 1 shows the "Time states until overestimation" metric, while Tables 2, 3, 4 and 5 show the weighted metrics.

Table 1. Comparison of time states until overestimation

Disc	Base	All-A	All-B	All-C	Ini-A	Ini-B	Ini-C
$s=0$	4000	4000	2190	860	4000	4000	2980
$s=1$	4000	4000	2200	850	4000	4000	2970
$s=2$	4000	4000	2140	260	4000	4000	2940
$s=3$	4000	4000	2120	250	4000	4000	2820
$s=4$	4000	4000	2080	240	4000	4000	2560
$s=5$	4000	4000	2010	200	4000	4000	2040
$s=6$	3850	3870	1880	180	3880	2650	1630
$s=7$	2350	2300	1640	140	2330	1910	230
$s=8$	1290	1290	470	110	1280	1050	220

Table 2. Comparison of weighted coverage in the experiments.

Disc.	Base	All-A	All-B	All-C	Ini-A	Ini-B	Ini-C
$s=0$	0.0000	0.0000	0.4178	0.1880	0.0000	0.0008	0.0608
$s=1$	0.0000	0.0038	**0.4733**	0.2060	0.0000	0.0868	**0.7100**
$s=2$	0.0327	0.2460	**0.5138**	0.0635	0.0345	0.4198	**0.7298**
$s=3$	0.0330	0.2178	**0.4868**	0.0600	0.0343	0.2650	**0.6895**
$s=4$	0.2380	0.2558	**0.4778**	0.0578	0.2383	0.2943	**0.6260**
$s=5$	0.2855	0.2833	0.4605	0.0475	0.2878	0.4610	**0.4963**
$s=6$	0.3518	0.3568	0.4290	0.0425	0.3620	**0.5480**	0.3958
$s=7$	0.4590	0.4555	0.3710	0.0325	0.4558	0.4110	0.0478
$s=8$	0.2530	0.2530	0.0850	0.0250	0.2505	0.2163	0.0475

Table 3. Comparison of weighted total accumulated error in the experiments.

Disc.	Base	All-A	All-B	All-C	Ini-A	Ini-B	Ini-C
$s=0$	26.5617	26.5582	10.6833	22.0304	26.5617	26.5134	14.7647
$s=1$	0.5927	0.5896	0.2961	0.3136	0.5927	0.5482	0.1982
$s=2$	**0.0159**	**0.0148**	**0.0184**	0.0898	**0.0159**	**0.0113**	**0.0117**
$s=3$	0.0910	0.0850	0.0502	0.1432	0.0909	0.0705	**0.0301**
$s=4$	0.0691	0.0646	0.0449	0.1365	0.0691	0.0481	**0.0287**
$s=5$	0.0571	0.0575	0.0483	0.1677	0.0568	**0.0265**	0.0369
$s=6$	0.0401	0.0396	0.0506	0.1844	0.0396	**0.0365**	0.0443
$s=7$	0.0416	0.0425	0.0584	0.2386	0.0420	0.0511	0.3057
$s=8$	0.0750	0.0750	0.1983	0.3022	0.0756	0.0917	0.3039

Table 4. Comparison of weighted total average error in the experiments.

Disc.	Base	All-A	All-B	All-C	Ini-A	Ini-B	Ini-C
$s=0$	6.64e-03	6.64e-03	4.88e-03	2.56e-02	6.64e-03	6.63e-03	4.95e-03
$s=1$	1.48e-04	1.47e-04	1.35e-04	3.69e-04	1.48e-04	1.37e-04	6.67e-05
$s=2$	**3.97e-06**	**3.70e-06**	**8.60e-06**	3.45e-04	**3.97e-06**	**2.82e-06**	**3.98e-06**
$s=3$	2.27e-05	2.12e-05	2.37e-05	5.73e-04	2.27e-05	1.76e-05	1.07e-05
$s=4$	1.73e-05	1.61e-05	2.16e-05	5.69e-04	1.73e-05	1.20e-05	1.12e-05
$s=5$	1.43e-05	1.44e-05	2.40e-05	8.39e-04	1.42e-05	**6.61e-06**	1.81e-05
$s=6$	**1.04e-05**	**1.02e-05**	2.69e-05	1.02e-03	**1.02e-05**	1.38e-05	2.72e-05
$s=7$	1.77e-05	1.85e-05	3.56e-05	1.70e-03	1.80e-05	2.68e-05	1.33e-03
$s=8$	5.81e-05	5.81e-05	4.22e-04	2.75e-03	5.90e-05	8.74e-05	1.38e-03

Table 5. Comparison of weighted coverage average error in the experiments.

Disc.	Base	All-A	All-B	All-C	Ini-A	Ini-B	Ini-C
$s=0$	6.64e-03	6.64e-03	2.06e-02	2.04e-01	6.64e-03	6.63e-03	5.39e-03
$s=1$	1.48e-04	1.48e-04	9.64e-04	1.21e-02	1.48e-04	1.50e-04	1.52e-03
$s=2$	**4.11e-06**	**4.90e-06**	2.17e-04	1.50e-02	**4.11e-06**	**4.85e-06**	5.57e-04
$s=3$	2.35e-05	2.72e-05	2.90e-04	1.43e-02	2.35e-05	2.40e-05	4.85e-04
$s=4$	2.27e-05	2.17e-05	2.66e-04	1.52e-02	2.27e-05	**1.70e-05**	5.12e-04
$s=5$	2.00e-05	2.01e-05	2.87e-04	1.68e-02	**1.99e-05**	**1.23e-05**	6.71e-04
$s=6$	**1.64e-05**	**1.62e-05**	3.09e-04	1.84e-02	**1.63e-05**	7.96e-05	9.42e-04
$s=7$	8.10e-05	8.89e-05	3.74e-04	2.39e-02	8.28e-05	1.92e-04	7.84e-03
$s=8$	2.70e-04	2.70e-04	1.53e-03	3.02e-02	2.72e-04	4.96e-04	1.01e-02

Analysis of Results

States Until Overestimation. The behavior in Table 1 is as expected. Wider initial states, such as the ones in Cases *Ini-A, Ini-B and Ini-C*, lead to over-estimation happening earlier in the simulated set of states. This effect is more noticeable on the *All* Cases, as each state introduces more overestimation. The data we find most interesting is on the discretization complexity: as s increases, these models lead to earlier overestimation, which can be seen in Fig. 3. This suggests that under the conditions of the experiment it is preferable to use a lower complexity model to avoid overestimation. It is important to note that this might not be applicable in all scenarios: it is certainly possible that changes to the default constraint solver in Ibex, or even the implementation of a different constraint solver could lead to improvements with these higher complexity models.

Weighted Coverage. In general, coverage is a measure of how well a specific experiment managed to enclose the solution. In general, adding wider intervals to the models leads to better coverage, as seen in case *Ini-C*. Among the *All*

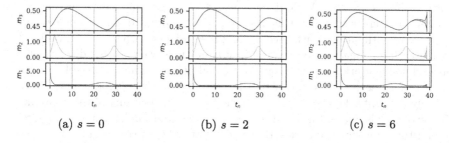

(a) $s = 0$ (b) $s = 2$ (c) $s = 6$

Fig. 3. Visual comparison of simulated results for Case Base.

cases, it is surprising that *All-B* gets better weighted coverage than *All-C*, a model that fails to get even close to the target of 4000 states.

We note that higher order approximations, such as $s=6$ and $s=7$ provide increasingly better coverage than lesser order ones on cases with low interval expansion, *Base*, *All-A* and *Ini-A*. This suggests that the bounds on the error in these higher order approximations needs to be as small as possible.

Weighted Accumulated Error. Weighted accumulated error is a good measure of how close each experiment was to the actual behavior of the system that we want our results to enclose as narrowly as possible. The high accumulated error in the $s = 0$ experiments is expected, as this is a very simple discretization and thus prone to high approximation error on each state. The most surprising results are the ones for $s = 2$, as they are consistently low across all categories. This suggests that the $s = 2$ discretization level might be overall closer to bounding the expected solution.

Weighted Average Error and Coverage Average. With this metric, we want to compare how close each state in the system might be to the expected solution. Similar to weighted accumulated error, the results for the $s = 2$ are also good: not only does the overall error is low across the whole set of states, but each state that fails to enclose the solution does so by a smaller amount than in other discretizations. This case also does well with weighted coverage average. Surprisingly, on these two metrics the $s = 6$ discretization also does well, with its major drawback being that none of the cases run under this discretization level reached the desired final narrow state of $N = 4000$.

4   Conclusions and Future Work

Based on the presented results, we find that, for the sliding windows heuristic, increasing the complexity of the discretization does not necessarily lead to better results. The simplest types of discretization such as backwards Euler, represented by the $s = 0$ Adams-Moulton discretization, is definitely the worst; once we increased the complexity, we started getting better results. The best results we obtained were with an Adams-Moulton discretization involving two prior state variables ($s = 2$). While it may seem that increasing it even further could produce better results, for this experiment we obtained diminishing returns, as the overestimation starts occurring progressively earlier as the value of s increases. This suggests that, under these conditions, we must use discretizations beyond a single prior variable, but also avoid using too many variables.

All of these results come with the caveat that these experiments are not entirely guaranteed enclosures, due to the lack of an enclosure of the approximation error. This is a natural future work: to seek and implement a technique to bound the approximation error that is compatible with constraint-solving techniques. We are also looking into other implicit discretization schemes beyond Adams-Moulton that could have smaller error, as well as different contractor settings and configurations that could either improve the computation time or provide better contraction with reduced overestimation. We also plan to incorporate these techniques with other dynamical systems such as boundary value problems, as well as comparing against other approaches that reduce computational complexity, such as reduced order modeling.

References

1. Berz, M., Makino, K.: Verified integration of odes and flows using differential algebraic methods on high-order taylor models. Reliable Comput. **4**, 361–369 (1998)
2. Butcher, J.C.: Numerical Methods for Ordinary Differential Equations. Wiley, Hoboken (2016)
3. Chabert, G.: Ibex - an interval-based explorer. Online slides (2007). https://agora. bourges.univ-orleans.fr/ramdani/gtmea/legacy/www2.lirmm.fr/ensemble/IMG/ pdf/slides_chabert.pdf
4. Chabert, G., Jaulin, L.: Contractor programming. Artif. Intell. **173**(11), 1079–1100 (2009)
5. Collavizza, H., Delobel, F., Rueher, M.: Comparing partial consistencies. Reliable Comput. **5**(3), 213–228 (1999)
6. dit Sandretto, J.A., Chapoutot, A.: Validated explicit and implicit Runge-Kutta methods. Reliable Comput. **22**(1), 79–103 (2016)
7. Garcia Contreras, A., Throneberry, G., Olumoye, O., Valera, L., Ceberio, M., Abdelkefi, A.: Interval-based solving techniques for large-scale dynamical systems. In: Proceedings of the 2020 International Design Engineering Technical Conferences & Computers and Information in Engineering Conference (IDETC-CIE) (2020)
8. Contreras, A.F.G., Ceberio, M.: Solving dynamical systems using windows of sliding subproblems. In: Figueroa-García, J.C., Díaz-Gutierrez, Y., Gaona-García, E.E., Orjuela-Cañón, A.D. (eds.) WEA 2021. CCIS, vol. 1431, pp. 13–24. Springer, Cham (2021). https://doi.org/10.1007/978-3-030-86702-7_2
9. Goubault, E., Putot, S.: Under-approximations of computations in real numbers based on generalized affine arithmetic. In: Nielson, H.R., Filé, G. (eds.) SAS 2007. LNCS, vol. 4634, pp. 137–152. Springer, Heidelberg (2007). https://doi.org/10. 1007/978-3-540-74061-2_9
10. Granvilliers, L., Benhamou, F.: Algorithm 852: realpaver: an interval solver using constraint satisfaction techniques. ACM Trans. Math. Software (TOMS) **32**(1), 138–156 (2006)
11. Lin, Y., Stadtherr, M.A.: Validated solutions of initial value problems for parametric odes. Appl. Numer. Math. **57**(10), 1145 (2007)
12. Makino, K., Berz, M.: Taylor models and other validated functional inclusion methods. Int. J. Pure Appl. Math. **4**(4), 379–456 (2003)
13. Moore, R.E.: Methods and applications of interval analysis. SIAM (1979)
14. Moore, R.E., Kearfott, R.B., Cloud, M.J.: Introduction to interval analysis. SIAM (2009)
15. Olumoye, O., Throneberry, G., Garcia, A., Valera, L., Abdelkefi, A., Ceberio, M.: Solving large dynamical systems by constraint sampling. In: Figueroa-García, J.C., Duarte-González, M., Jaramillo-Isaza, S., Orjuela-Cañón, A.D., Díaz-Gutierrez, Y. (eds.) WEA 2019. CCIS, vol. 1052, pp. 3–15. Springer, Cham (2019). https://doi. org/10.1007/978-3-030-31019-6_1

16. Rump, S.M., Kashiwagi, M.: Implementation and improvements of affine arithmetic. Nonlinear Theory Appl. Inst. Electron. Inf. Commun. Eng. (NOLTA-IEICE) **6**(3), 341–359 (2015)
17. Valera, L., Garcia, A., Gholamy, A., Ceberio, M., Florez, H.: Towards predictions of large dynamic systems' behavior using reduced-order modeling and interval computations. In: Proceedings for the 2017 IEEE International Conference on Systems, Man, and Cybernetics (SMC), pp. 345–350. IEEE (2017)

Globally Explainable AutoML Evolved Models of Corporate Credit Risk

Miguel Rodríguez[1(✉)], Diego Leon[2], Edwin Lopez[1], and German Hernandez[1]

[1] Universidad Nacional de Colombia, Bogotá, Colombia
{miarodriguezfo,edlopez,gjhernandezp}@unal.edu.co
[2] Universidad Externado de Colombia, Bogotá, Colombia
diego.leon@uexternado.edu.co

Abstract. Corporate credit ratings are one of the most relevant financial indicators in credit risk analysis. These are generated by different rating agencies which base their methodologies on the use of various financial variables of each company and the experience of their analysts; their impact on the market is of such importance that their mismanagement can trigger major financial crises such as the one that occurred in 2008. Along with this, the great importance of internal models for calculating credit risk and international regulations and agreements seek to have a level of explainability of the methods used to perform this risk management. This paper proposes the use of Automatic Machine Learning (AutoML) as a tool for the generation of a machine learning model that performs a prediction of corporate credit ratings using data from balance sheets, financial statements, and descriptive information about the company. The main contribution of this work lies in the development of the level of interpretability of each model as a second goal to be optimized with a global measure of explainability, allowing the generation of models that can better explain their results.

Keywords: AutoML · Interpretability · Credit risk · Machine learning · Artificial intelligence · Corporate credit rating · LIME

1 Introduction

After the global financial crisis occurred in 2008, known as the Subprime crisis, mainly caused by the wrong assignment of credit ratings to mortgages groups, in this case, the ratings indicated that these groups of mortgages were in investment grade, and investors were confident with this ratings, but actually, many of these mortgages had a higher risk, entering into default and starting the financial crisis. All this was due to the lack of a rigorous analysis by the rating agencies, and the lack of knowledge and history of this type of financial instrument [7].

Additionally, financial regulations such as the European GDPR, have started to require financial corporations that assign a credit rating to individuals with artificial intelligence to ensure that their models can give explanations regarding the final results and what criteria were taken into account for this. Along with

© The Author(s), under exclusive license to Springer Nature Switzerland AG 2022
J. C. Figueroa-García et al. (Eds.): WEA 2022, CCIS 1685, pp. 19–30, 2022.
https://doi.org/10.1007/978-3-031-20611-5_2

this, we also see agreements, such as those established in Basel II, where the emphasis is placed on strengthening the financial system by employing internal controls that help mitigate and manage risk. With this, Basel provides a structure in which banks can implement their internal systems for credit risk measurement, thus opening the possibility of using new techniques for its measurement. This makes it necessary to develop highly explainable models, contrary to the 'black box' normally resulting from the implementation of machine learning models.

As a use case of this work, corporate credit risk analysis will be analyzed, to generate a machine learning model able to predict the credit rating of a particular company based on different variables taken from its financial statements, balance sheets, and other fundamental characteristics of the company. This approach could be used to know in advance the credit ratings assigned by the different agencies or it could be used to implement an internal credit analysis system with its rating scale, obtaining also the explainability of the results obtained.

To achieve high performance and interpretability results, in this paper we propose the global interpretability as part of the optimization realized by automatic machine learning algorithms in search of the best model, for this purpose we modified the TPOT library that uses genetic algorithms, to use as a second optimization objective the level of global interpretability based on the proposed metric and compare it with the normal results.

1.1 Credit Rating

A credit rating is a formal and independent opinion that expresses the ability of a company or individual to fulfill its credit obligations. From the borrower's point of view, a credit rating is generally a requirement for the issuance of a public bond and access to certain lending structures [8]. Issuer default ratings (IDR) are assigned to corporate entities, sovereign entities, financial institutions, banks, insurers, leasing companies, and public financial entities such as local and regional governments. These ratings are indicators of the repayment probability according to the terms set in the debt issuance and express the risk in relative rating order, i.e., they are ordinal measures of credit risk and do not predict a specific frequency of default or loss. [2].

1.2 Automated Machine Learning

Given the high increase in the generation of large volumes of data, the use of machine learning techniques has attracted attention in different fields of industry to solve highly complex problems that require a certain level of expert knowledge. In most cases, the fields are not fully mastered by the data scientists who implement these solutions, generating a greater expenditure of time in the development cycle, where feature engineering, selection of the algorithm to be used, parameter optimization, error measurement, and others, must be performed [1].

To improve this process and achieve better performance without having expert knowledge during the process, automated machine learning or AutoML arises as a process to applying machine learning in real-world problems, from automating the feature engineering process to optimizing model parameters [10].

In general, the AutoML approach usually covers the entire machine learning flow, but it can also be used to cover only a part of the problem, where more focus may be needed to reach an optimal result, where the human resource may not have the expertise.

Within this process we can find the following sections [9]:

– Data engineering and data preprocessing.
– Model selection, hyperparameter optimization.

TPOT. Tree-based Pipeline Optimization Tool is an AutoML framework developed using strongly typed genetic programming (GP) to recommend an optimized analysis pipeline for the data scientist's prediction problem [3].

The goal of TPOT is to automate the building of ML pipelines by combining a flexible expression tree representation of pipelines with stochastic search algorithms such as genetic programming.

1.3 Machine Learning Interpretability

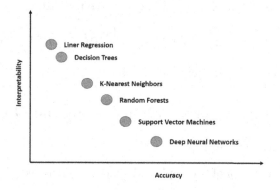

Fig. 1. Interpretability vs. Accuracy: The Friction that Defines Deep Learning [6]

The increase in the use of machine learning models in the search for complex solutions in different industries and fields has brought new challenges, mainly in those sectors in which a greater understanding of the decisions or outputs generated by models is needed, due to the great impact they have on society. For this reason, the models that solve these problems turn out to be complex algorithms that work as black boxes, which do not allow humans to understand the logic and internal operation to reach the result. Additionally, in some of the fields of application of these techniques, such as the health and financial sectors, regulations on the use and explainability of the models have arisen (Fig. 1).

LIME. (Local Interpretable Model-Agnostic Explanations)[1] [5] is an interpretability analysis method that explain a prediction of a complex ML model f around an instance x of the input space x with a good locally interpretable surrogate ML model $explanation_x^f$. Mathematically the surrogate ML model $explanation_x^f$ can be expressed as follows [4]:

$$explanation_x^f = \arg\min_{g \in G} \left\{ d_{N_x^\delta}(f, g) \right\}$$

The explanation is the local ML model g from a family of local interpretable models G (usually linear regression models or a decision trees) that minimizes the distance $d_{N_x}(f, g)$ in the neighborhood N_x^δ of radius δ of x in the input space of the model f. The distance measure how close are the predictions of a surrogate model g and f are in N_x^δ. Usually the distance is an estimation of a loss function L (e.g. mean squared error) on the neighborhood N_x^δ, commonly the loss functions used is the mean squared error between the explanation and f on a random sample of points $S_{N_x^\delta}$ of N_x^δ, so

$$d_{N_x}(f, g) = L_{N_x}(g, f) = MSE_{S_{N_x^\delta}}(g, f).$$

Some times a model complexity requirement is added to the explanation so this is not only close to f but also simple, in this case the distance becomes

$$d_{N_x}(f, g) = [L_{N_x}(g, f) + \Omega(g)] = \left[MSE_{S_{N_x^\delta}}(g, f) + \Omega(g) \right]$$

with $\Omega(g)$ a measure of complexity of $g \in G$.

2   AutoML with Interpretability as Second Goal

2.1   Global Interpretability

The *global intepretability* of a complex ML model f, denoted $GI(f)$, is defined as

$$GI(f) = \frac{1}{|T|} \sum_{x \in T} \left[MSE_{S_{N_x}^\delta} (explanation_x^f, f) \right]$$
$$= \frac{1}{|T|} \sum_{x \in T} \left[\frac{1}{|S_{N^\delta}|} \sum_{y \in S_{N^\delta}} |explanation_x^f(y) - f(y)|^2 \right]$$

where T is the training set, N_x^δ is the neighborhood of radius δ of x in the input space of f, S_{N^δ} is a random sample of points of N_x^δ, $explanation_x^f$ is a LIME surrogate ML model around x (in this paper linear regression models as local surrogates). Intuitively $GI(f)$ is a measure of how close in average are the local surrogates $explanation_x^f$ are to the global model f on the training examples, see Fig. 2.

---

[1] https://github.com/marcotcr/lime and https://lime-ml.readthedocs.io/en/latest/.

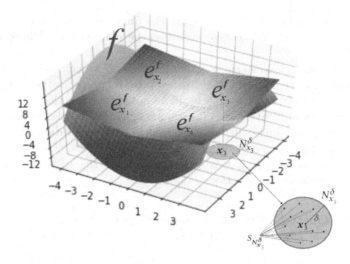

Fig. 2. A global ML model f with four LIME subrogated linear regression local models $e_{x_1}^f, e_{x_1}^f, e_{x_3}^f, e_{x_4}^f$ with $e_{x_i}^f = explanation_{x_i}^f$, fntuitively $GI(f)$ is a measure of how close are in average f and the local surrogates.

2.2 Implementation

To implement global interpretability as the goal of the AutoML process, in this paper we modified the AutoML implementation in LIME and TPOT libraries. TPOT uses genetic algorithms for the search for the best machine learning pipeline based on optimizing a defined score metric [in this paper we use accuracy] and the complexity of the pipeline as the second goal. In this evaluation function, we change the second goal with the global interpretability measure proposed.

As mentioned before, LIME gives us a level of local interpretability, then to get the global interpretability we add a function as follows:

```
Function global_explanation(data, predict_fn,
              num_features, num_samples,
              distance_metric, model_regressor):

   for i=0 to len(data):
       exp=lime.explain_instance(data[i])
       lime_pred=exp.model.predict(exp.neighborhood_data)
       tpot_pred=predict_fn(exp.neighborhood_data)
       score_list[i]=distance_metric(lime_pred,tpot_pred)

   return =  sum(score_list)/len(data)
```

Where the function receives as input the entire dataset, the predicted function of the model, the features to be explained, the number of samples to generate, the distance metric, and the model regressor. The function returns the global interpretability as the weighted average, based on the score given a defined distance metric.

With the global explanation function defined, no we can use it to calculate the value for each model generated in the AutoML process of TPOT, for this we use the result obtained to the evaluate_individual function of the TPOT library, with the modification, this function assigns the global explanation score as the second goal, which will be minimized in each generation with the new populations within the genetic algorithm.

The process of assigning this score to each of the models generated is described in the following function:

```
Function evaluate_individuals(TpotBase, population,
                features, target):

   for ind in population:
       trained_model = ind.get_model()
       global_interpr= global_explanation(features,
                            trained_model.predict_proba,
                            mean_squared_error,
                            linear)
       pred=trained_model.predict(features)
       inter_cv_score=prediction_score(pred,target)
       ind.fitness.values=(
           evaluated_individuals_[ind]["inter_cv_score"],
           evaluated_individuals_[ind]["global_interpr"],
       )

   return = population
```

Where the function receives as input the TPOT configuration of the experiment, a list of DEAP individuals, an array with the features or inputs, and a target list with the labels of each feature entered. This function returns a population with a calculated fitness.

This function is called in the genetic algorithm process performed by TPOT, there in each generation the algorithm selects the best models of the population based on the fitness calculated in the evaluate_individuals function, the goal is to minimize the global_interpr value and maximize the inter_cv_score (in this paper, the accuracy).

When the automatic learning process is completed with our modified library we can extract the total population of evaluated models with their performance and interpretability metrics calculated, where we can identify the Pareto front, or set of optimal solutions that solve the problem, with this we can validate not just a single final model, allowing as a final point to select the model that has a better fit to the requirements of the problem.

The modification explained in this paper was made only for the classification problem because of the nature of the use case presented, but can be extended to regression problems with a similar approach. The use of this global interpretability implies a high consumption of resources and time, due to the process that must be done in each of the samples and in each of the models to obtain its interpretability.

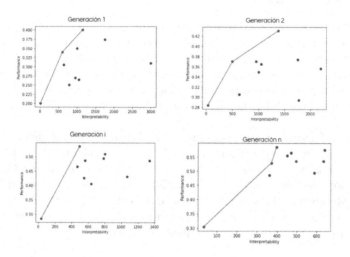

Fig. 3. Evolution of models by generation and Pareto front generated by training modified TPOT models with LIME

Figure 3 shows the evolution of the population in each of the TPOT generations, in each generation can be seen how the performance metrics (accuracy) and the level of interpretability are optimized, and how the optimal solutions are grouped in a Pareto front. In the end, in each trained generation the set of models is less dispersed and tends to cluster around the best values for the final generation.

3   Data

The process of assigning a credit rating to a particular company is mainly based on its descriptive information, financial statement information, balance sheets, and cash flows, among others, and depending on the rating agency these aspects may have more or less relevance in the model.

For the scope of this work, a group of companies belonging to the U.S. market will be analyzed. For the construction of the dataset used market[2] in the implementation, two different financial information platforms were used, which

---

[2] The training and testing data sets are available at https://github.com/miarodriguezfo/explanaible_automl.

are openly available for downloading the public financial information of each company through APIs:

– Financial Modeling Prep[3]
– SimFin[4]

3.1 Data Preparation

All the data was downloaded in separate files by type of report, this information was unified (using as the main key the Ticker of each company, which allows to identify each one within the set of files and remains over time), in the main file with the content of all the reports used, in the process of this unification the records in which the complete information of the reports (Description, Cash Flow, balance sheet, financial statement or rating) was not available were discarded.

For the information corresponding to the history of credit ratings, which is the target variable in the model to be built, as it is owned by each of the rating agencies, it was not available for massive download within the platforms used, so it was not possible to use the information from any of the three main rating agencies: Moody's Ratings, S&P Ratings, and Fitch. Instead, the rating provided by the Financial Modeling Prep platform was used, which is free to use and is defined with the following scale described in the Fig. 4.

Fig. 4. Rating scale provided by Financial modeling prep.

By to the nature of the problem presented and as explained in Sect. 1.1 Credit rating, the ratings to be predicted are characterized by a specific order, the original letter label is then converted to a numerical scale in which a lower degree of investment is related to a lower value, while the ratings that correspond to better investment grades are homologized to higher values as can be seen in the Fig. 4.

Another important point in the process of preparing the data, when analyzing the distribution of each of the classes, in the case of this rating, it was found that most are found within the A+ and A grades, while the number of records found in the lower grades are lower. For this reason, it was decided to unify the ratings below B- in a single category called "Default", this grouping does not affect the nature of the problem, a risk analyst would like to determine when a company becomes non-investment grade, regardless of how far down the scale it is on the scale.

---

[3] https://simfin.com/data/api.
[4] https://financialmodelingprep.com/developer/docs.

4   Results

Experiments in this section were run under the same random data split, where the train set was 70% of the entire dataset and the test the 30%. To have a reference value, a generalized linear estimator model has been generated that allows us to compare the performance of a basic model with the results generated by the AutoML iteration. In this case, the following result was obtained:

Dataset	Accuracy	Interpretability error
Test	0.4099	0.049

AutoML base experiments were performed with the TPOT and H2O libraries, using all the variables in our dataset, so that the machine learning process could find the most relevant features for the problem and evaluate these results against those obtained using interpretability as the objective in the optimization process.

As for the models generated by AutoML, the first, corresponding to the TPOT library reach its best performance with a configuration of 20 generations, populations of size 10, and performing 5 cross-validations, neighborhood radius radius $\delta =$, and 20 points in the random sample of points of the neighborhoods of the training data points achieving an accuracy of 74% over the test set.

Dataset	Accuracy	Interpretability error
Test	0.742654	0.0417

The final model generated from TPOT, which obtained the best performance after the experiments were performed was an ExtraTreeClassifier, with the following parameters:

```
ExtraTreesClassifier(bootstrap=False, criterion=
    "entropy", max_features=0.8500000000000001,
    min_samples_leaf=3,
    min_samples_split=7, n_estimators=200)
```

As we can see in the confusion matrix most of the predictions are on or very close to the diagonal, representing that the predictions are quite close to the actual label. In this initial experiment, the analysis of local interpretability of the predictions obtained by LIME was performed, which gives us the probability that a prediction belongs or not to a certain rating Fig. 5

Regarding the results obtained with the H2O library, the best performance obtained during the AutoML process was done employing an XGBoost model. In this case, we found that the generated model has better results than those presented by TPOT, reaching in this case 88% accuracy in the test set.

Dataset	Accuracy	Interpretability error
Test	0.8843	0.057

When interpretability was included as a second objective in the TPOT optimization process, we found the following result.

Dataset	Accuracy	Interpretability error
Test	0.7380	0.0367

The running time of this experiment with the addition of this modification grew exponentially because calculating the local interpretability on the entire training set for each model is computationally expensive. In our case reaching this level of accuracy took about 60 h of training.

The resulting models are much more complex than those found in the standard AutoML run, but allow us to give more accurate local explainability to the predictions for each instance evaluated. The best-resulting model during this experiment was an ExtraTressClassifier, as in the initial experimentation, but in this case in an ensemble, with a DecisionTreeClassifier, also applying transformations such as SelectPercentile and StackingEstimator.

```
Pipeline(steps=[('stackingestimator',
  StackingEstimator(estimator=
       DecisionTreeClassifier(criterion='entropy',
              max_depth=4,
              min_samples_leaf=17,
              min_samples_split=20,
              random_state=16))),
 ('selectpercentile', SelectPercentile(percentile=82)),
 ('extratreesclassifier',
  ExtraTreesClassifier(bootstrap=True,
     criterion='entropy',
     max_features=0.8500000000000001,
     min_samples_leaf=2, min_samples_split=3,
     random_state=16))])
```

In a second modification of the library, we explored the reason between the proposed interpretability error and the level of complexity or depth of the automatically generated model as a second objective, during this exploration we obtained the following result:

Dataset	Accuracy	Interpretability error
Test	0.654	0.046

In the final set of models obtained, it is observed in the behavior of the metrics that reaching a higher level of accuracy has an impact on the interpretability error presented, thus having a trade-off when selecting one or another model according to the needs of the problem, if it is necessary to have higher performance or if having a good level of interpretability is more important.

With this, we can arrive, in a longer time, at a model that in comparison has no performance loss concerning the simple model, but we have again in the level of interpretability of the final model since it has been optimized during the learning process. With this we can analyze the test set and determine its local interpretability, thus identifying the most relevant features in the model:

Fig. 5. Local explanation TPOT model

Features
IndustryID
Total assets
Total equity
Net Income
Net Income (Common)
Income (Loss) from continuing Operations
Net Income (Starting Line)
Pretax Income (Loss)
Total liabilites

When analyzing these characteristics we observe that they mostly correspond to the basic variables that build the analysis ratios used by rating agencies at the time of evaluating each company.

5   Conclusions

The use of auto ml-generated models facilitates the process of exploration of different models and algorithms and the optimization of their parameters, achieving good results in the final performance of the models, close to those previously generated by other authors with classical modeling, thus allowing the application of machine learning in different fields without having extensive prior knowledge.

Taking advantage of the evolution capacity of genetic algorithms in the optimization process of TPOT, the implementation of a global interpretability level as a second objective, given the ability to improve the explanatory capacity of complex models generated by AutoML, reducing the interpretability error according to the proposed metric.

Due to having global interpretability based on the local interpretability of each of the points of the data set, the use of this modification in the library implies greater use of computational resources and time.

6   Future Work

The next step in search of a better level of explainability in machine learning models generated through AutoML is to perform an initialized search in the optimization, including manually generated models that already have a good level of precision or accuracy, looking for close models that can be much more interpretable than the base model.

References

1. Elshawi, R., Maher, M., Sakr, S.: Automated machine learning: state-of-the-art and open challenges (2019). https://arxiv.org/abs/1906.02287v2
2. Fitch: Rating   definitions.   https://www.fitchratings.com/products/rating-definitions
3. Le, T.T., Fu, W., Moore, J.H.: Scaling tree-based automated machine learning to biomedical big data with a feature set selector. Bioinformatics **36**(1), 250–256 (2020)
4. Molnar, C.: Interpretable Machine Learning, 2 edn. (2022). http://christophm.github.io/interpretable-ml-book/
5. Ribeiro, M.T., Singh, S., Guestrin, C.: Why should i trust you?: explaining the predictions of any classifier (2016). Accessed 26 Sept 2019
6. Rodriguez, J.: Interpretability vs. accuracy: the friction that defines deep learning (2018). https://www.linkedin.com/pulse/interpretability-vs-accuracy-friction-defines-deep-jesus-rodriguez/
7. Rom, M.C.: The credit rating agencies and the subprime mess: greedy, ignorant, and stressed? Public Adm. Rev. **69**(4), 640–650 (2009)
8. Santos, K.: Corporate credit ratings: a quick guide, vol. 44, pp. 45–49 (2007). https://www.treasurers.org/ACTmedia/ITCCMFcorpcreditguide.pdf
9. Truong, A., Walters, A., Goodsitt, J., Hines, K., Bruss, B., Farivar, R.: Towards automated machine learning: evaluation and comparison of automl approaches and tools (2019)
10. Yao, Q., et al.: Taking human out of learning applications: a survey on automated machine learning (2018). https://arxiv.org/abs/1810.13306v4

Bioactivity Predictors for the Inhibition of *Staphylococcus Aureus* Quinolone Resistance Protein

Michael Stiven Ramirez Campos[1,2]([✉]) [iD], David Alejandro Galeano López[1,2] [iD], Jorman Arbey Castro Rivera[1,2], Diana C. Rodriguez[1], Oscar J. Perdomo[1] [iD], and Alvaro David Orjuela-Cañón[1] [iD]

[1] School of Medicine and Health Sciences, Universidad del Rosario, Bogotá D.C, Colombia
[2] Escuela Colombiana de Ingeniería Julio Garavito, Bogotá D.C, Colombia
michael.ramirez@mail.escuelaing.edu.co

Abstract. Antibiotic resistance is a problem that has been increasing in recent years due to the inappropriate use of antibiotics. However, more techniques to design new medicines are employed frequently nowadays. In addition, the application of artificial intelligence tools in discovering new drugs has proven to be a possible solution to this problem. This paper aims to show and analyze the results obtained from the use of machine learning techniques when two different sets of features: i) constructed from Lipinski's rules of five, and ii) fingerprints from biomolecular sequences, were used. Six regressors were implemented to predict the minimum inhibitory concentration (MIC) valuer to generate models that allow the identification of possible drugs. A specific case for inhibition of the *Staphylococcus Aureus* and its protein NorA was studied in problems associated to Quinolone antibiotic resistance. A dataset of 187 sequences extracted from ChEmbl repository was used for this purpose. The results show that both Lipinski rules and fingerprints were favorable for generation models that fit actual MIC values of the molecules. The feature sets used and the regressors selected allowed generating models that can predict the bioactivity of a molecule, constituting a tool that could be valuable in the generation of new antibiotics to combat the problem addressed.

Keywords: Fingerprint · Lipinski rules · Machine learning · Protein · Regression · Sequence · Staphylococcus aureus

1 Introduction

Antibiotics are medicines whose principal purpose is treating bacterial infection by inhibition of metabolic processes. Some antibiotics mechanisms to destroy bacteria are based on the ability to attack the cell wall, destroy proteins that are involved in the synthetization process, or the transportation of the precursors that form the cell wall. In addition, other antibiotics affect the cytoplasm, the protein, and nucleic acid synthesis [1]. These medicines can be administered orally or intravenously, and it is essential that

© The Author(s), under exclusive license to Springer Nature Switzerland AG 2022
J. C. Figueroa-García et al. (Eds.): WEA 2022, CCIS 1685, pp. 31–40, 2022.
https://doi.org/10.1007/978-3-031-20611-5_3

the patient sticks to the proposed dose treatment to avoid developing bacteria antibiotic resistance. However, it is important that the patient follow the recommendation of health-care professionals to take the pills, or any different presentation of the antibiotics because an erroneous treatment can develop resistance. Resistance to bacteria is a problem for the development of antibiotics. Every time bacteria mutate, they develop mechanisms for resistance to drugs, making it difficult to treat some diseases such as pneumonia, tuberculosis, septicemia, gonorrhea to name but a few [1].

One of the bacteria that commonly develop drug resistance is the *Staphylococcus Aureus*, this bacterium represents a real danger to public health since it is the first cause of nosocomial bacteremia in North America and Latin America and the second in Europe [2]. *Staphylococcus* is classified as a coccus and is characterized by infecting soft tissues such as skin, muscles, tendons, and blood vessels. This bacterium is also present in medical elements, being a cause of hospital infection. *Staphylococcus Aureus* is a colonizing agent on the skin; however, it can enter the body through cuts or orally and lodge in tissues, the bloodstream, or urine. The symptoms presented by patients with severe infections are fever, chest pain, fatigue, skin rashes and headaches [3]. The high mortality cases are directly related to the resistance to drugs such as penicillin and methicillin. This is due to the great virulence of the strain and resistance mechanisms such as biofilms, which are extracellular matrices used to adhere to the surface of the tissue and protect the bacteria as a barrier. Finally, this coccus is also resistant to quinolones, a drug that inhibits the topoisomerase enzyme that synthesizes DNA, the protein that makes it resistant to this is the Quinolone resistance protein NorA [4]. This study developed an algorithm to identify new components that can contribute with the inhibition of the Quinolone resistance protein NorA.

1.1 Related Works

An explanation about methods of machine learning related to the generation and evaluation for new drugs is detailed in [5]. Different approaches of this new branch of bioinformatics were based at the developed of quantities structure-activity (QSAR) models created in 1930. Then, a variety of mathematical strategy were associate to chemical and physical properties to evaluated biological responses. One of the derivate methods from QSAR is the virtual screening. There, an evaluation of a large set of candidates to select the smaller molecule with more probability of joining an objective drug and synthesizing a new medicine.

At the same time, the employment of artificial neural networks for property prediction by using features such as fingerprints and descriptors were analyzed in [5]. Good performance of the algorithms was obtained with multiple machine learning methods approaches to predict toxicity assays of different components.

An additional study, where the machine learning tool called AdvProp based on four modules was proposed and presented in [6]. Two based on graph–based methods, multilevel message neural network (ML- MPNN) and Wisfeiler Lehman subtree kernel and two sequence-based methods, contrastive – BERT and subsequence kernel were used. Two ways to represent the biomolecules digitally were implemented. First, by using graphs that show clearly the enhancement between atoms and keeping the molecular structures. Second representation was worked based on the simplified molecular input line entry specification (SMILES), where the sequences have a more extended history in bioinformatics. SMILES represent a sequences line using grammar rules which symbolize atoms and bonds. The AdvProp developed different tasks, including molecular properties prediction and drug discovery applications.

In [7], researchers used artificial neuronal networks (ANN) to predict molecules with antibacterial activity. ANN were trained with fingerprint vectors that were designed manually. Fingerprints represent the absence and presence of functional groups in the drug molecular structures. Models were trained to predict the inhibition of crop growth at the *Escherichia Coli* using a databank of 2335 sequences. Then, authors applied the results of the previous predictions to chemical libraries of 107 million molecules. This seeks to identify potential active molecules again *Escherichia Coli* bacterium. Finally, the results were classified according to the punctuations received and selected by the best candidate based on a threshold value. As results, they obtain a group of 23 predictions empirically probe and eight antibacterial compounds that are structural completely different. 51 molecules were identified with inhibitory activity, the molecules obtained most like helicine with similarity of 0.37 and metronidazole with similarity of 0.21.

According to the literature and the interest of studying the NorA protein, this study searches to analyze machine learning models for extraction and evaluation of molecular properties using the SMILES format. Six different regressor models such as gradient boosting regressor, random forest, multilayer perceptron, k nearest neighbors, and Bayesian regressor were employed. However, the algorithm that is intended to be developed has the purpose of predicting a characteristic corresponding to the minimum inhibitory concentration (MIC) as a characteristic to define the level of drug concentration of a drug to inhibit bacterial activity, finding the relation to the the most effective molecule to inhibit the microorganism as presented in [6].

2 Methodology

For the developing of new drugs, the MIC value is commonly used. This value is defined as the minimum concentration of antimicrobial (in μg/mL) that inhibits the visible growth of a microorganism after 24 h of incubation at 37 °C. This parameter allows knowing if a crop is sensitive or resistant to antibiotics. If the MIC value is less than 1 ug/ml means that the bacterium is sensitive, and if this is greater than 4 ug/ml, presents resistance [8].

For several years, different pharmacists used five rules that indicate if a component is bioactive and safe for humans. They are called Lipinski rules and were formulated by Cristopher A. Lipinski in 1997 based on the empirical observation of the behavior of oral drugs. These five rules represent parameters that a drug should accomplish to determine oral viability. These rules are molecular mass less than 500 Dalton, high lipophilicity (expressed as LogP less than 5), less than 5 hydrogen bond donors, less than 10 hydrogen bond acceptors, and molar refractivity should be between 40–130 [9].

2.1 Database

The ChEMBL database comprises bioactive molecules and information on their chemical, bioactive and genomic properties extracted from studies found in peer-reviewed literature in medicinal chemistry journals. These properties are related to drug properties, facilitating the characterization of these molecules in the drug discovery process [10]. ChEMBL contains information about two million two hundred thousand compounds, one million five hundred thousand molecules in the testing phase, eighty-four thousand documents related to ChEMBL molecules between patents and articles, and another amount of information in which fourteen thousand targets and fourteen thousand drugs are highlighted [11].

In this study, 187 compounds were identified as a potential targets to the Quinolone-resistant NorA protein. The structure of protein as was defined, with a length of 388 amino acids, all in SMILES format. The compounds were filtered by the type of bioactivity, in this case, MIC value was used for choosing the compounds. This classification showed that 34 compounds were classified as resistant and 51 as sensible.

2.2 Data Preprocessing

Based on the MIC value reported in [9, 12], the compounds were labeled in three different classes sensitive, indeterminate, or resistant. Compounds labeled as indeterminate were eliminated, considering that their interaction with the target specified above is inconclusive, thus reducing from 187 to 152 samples. MIC values were standardized using the -$log(MIC)$ function due to the better distribution of these values in terms of the regression training process.

2.3 Parameter's Calculation

The calculation of pre-established parameters followed the ligand-based drug design (LBDD) technique, which uses 2D (molecular fingerprints, topological descriptors, molecular properties) or 3D (pharmacophore, molecular properties, molecular shape) information to search for similarities to build or apply models for classification and/or prediction of biological activity.

Four of the five parameters of Lipinski's Rule of five considerations (molecular weight, octanol-water partition coefficient (*logp*), hydrogen bond donors, and hydrogen bond acceptors) were calculated from the SMILES format of each of the compounds remaining after preprocessing. Considering that the considered antibiotic is not orally administered, aspects related to his rule were determined as mentioned above. On the other hand, the structures of the compounds were coded to obtain their molecular fingerprint. In this case, a series of binary numbers characterize each compound's absent or present substructures [13]. Thus, two sets of characteristics were established: one set with the Lipinski descriptors and the other with the fingerprint of the molecules under study.

For the feature reduction stage only the set of features containing the fingerprints was considered, and a variance threshold was used to remove features from the dataset that had high redundancy.

2.4   Regression Algorithms

Taking into account the advantages of the machine learning (ML) algorithms, six regression methods were employed to determine the MIC value from 152 components. In this way, provide the approximation for future compounds that can be determined in laboratory.

In the present work, models based on Bayesian ridge regressor, support vector regressor (SVR), multilayer perceptron (MLP), gradient boosting regressor (GBR), random forest (RF), and k nearest neighbors (KNN) were implemented. For all methods, a search of hyperparameters based on grid was utilized to find the model with the best performance.

Each of these algorithms was chosen based on state of the art. Several papers demonstrated that machine learning models could successfully predict activity from chemical structures [13–16]. For the test set, 20% of the data from each of the feature set corresponding to 31 molecules were used. In addition, the cross-validation technique was performed using five folds inside the 80% for training. Each generated model was evaluated from the R-squared parameter that represents how close the estimated values are to a fitted regression line [17]. In addition, the mean absolute error (MAE) and the mean squared error (MSE) were employed to analyze the models. Finally, individual standard deviations were computing, providing an idea of the behavior of the implemented models,

3   Results

The results obtained from the test set was evaluated and visualized through two graphs (see Figs. 1 and 2) where the trend and variation of the pMIC value is shown. Table 1. exhibits the performance when Lipinski descriptors were employed. There mean R-squared value and its respective standard deviation are shown, giving an idea of the behavior of the implemented models. Table 2. visualizes the results when fingerprint information was used to train the models.

It is important to remember that the use of the two sets of features mentioned above, not only has the purpose of considering which model has better performance in the prediction, but also what type of features are the most suitable to generate models that allow to correctly predict the bioactivity of a molecule through the pMIC value.

Table 1. Regression results for the Lipinski descriptors set

Regressors	R^2 Score	MAE score	MSE score
Bayesian	1.0 ± 0.0	4.43e-10 ± 6.13e-11	2.58e-10 ± 6.33e-20
SVR	0.999 ± 1.164e-06	5.49e-03 ± 6.87e-04	4.38e-05 ± 7.84e-06
MLP	0.999 ± 6.20e-05	1.63e-02 ± 1.58e-02	2.34e-03 ± 2.59e-03
GBR	0.996 ± 8.265e-07	2.45e-02 ± 7.78e-04	7.06e-03 ± 6.68e-04
Random Forest	0.996 ± 1.250e-04	3.17e-02 ± 4.28e-03	4.67e-03 ± 1.54e-03

(continued)

Table 1. (*continued*)

Regressors	R^2 Score	MAE score	MSE score
KNN	0.822 ± 0.113	0.582 ± 0.153	0.988 ± 0.498

Table 2. Regression results for the fingerprint set

Regressors	R^2 Score	MAE score	MSE score
Bayesian	0.762 ± 0.082	0.860 ± 0.113	1.30 ± 0.303
SVR	0.745 ± 0.116	0.877 ± 0.267	1.55 ± 0.990
MLP	0.837 ± 0.019	$0.677 \pm 5.31e-02$	0.930 ± 0.127
GBR	$0.865 \pm 2.376e-03$	$0.620 \pm 2.31e-02$	$0.764 \pm 3.91e-02$
Random Forest	$0.866 \pm 3.786e-03$	$0.727 \pm 1.25e-02$	$0.822 \pm 2.44e-02$
KNN	0.720 ± 0.102	0.785 ± 0.138	1.355 ± 0.386

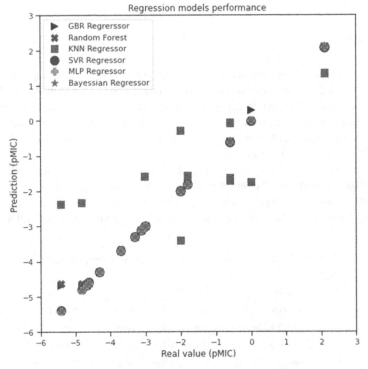

Fig. 1. Performance of each regression algorithm using the set of features obtained from the Lipinski descriptors.

On the other hand, Figs. 1 and 2 were obtained and show the real behavior of the pMIC values (standardized MIC) of the compounds and the behavior resulting from the prediction of the pMIC values performed by the machine learning models. Thus, the best performing model is the one whose behavior tends to be linear.

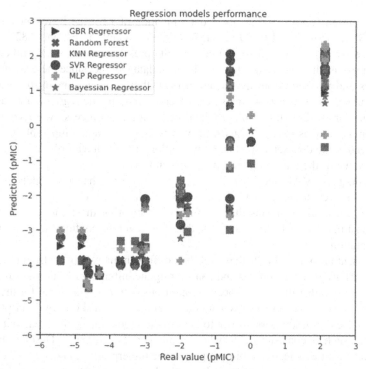

Fig. 2. Performance of each regression algorithm using the set of features obtained from the fingerprint.

4 Discussion

Considering the results obtained, a hypotheses could be that the expected results were achieved. As shown in Tables 1. and 2., and Figs. 1 and 2, the performance of all the algorithms have values near to 0.8 for the R-squared metric, and MAE and MSE small values, mostly. This represents results reasonably good, since the predictions made by the generated models closely aligned to the actual values. Similarly, it is essential to mention that the performance of the models trained using Lipinski's descriptors outperform some reported works where methods of higher complexity, such as ANN. As mentioned in [18], an R-squared value of 0.93 was obtained using an ANN model to predict the inhibition intervals of whole extracts of Turkey nuts against twelve bacterial species. Besides, this work documents the use of algorithms such as Levenberg-Marquardt (LM), resilient backpropagation (RP), and scaled conjugate gradient (SCG), where coefficients of determination of 0.7 for RP, 0.86 for LM, 0.7 for SCG and 0.81 for BR were obtained, respectively. On the other hand, in [16] SVR was used to predict the inhibitory activity of drugs that could be useful in therapies to combat Covid-19, a comparable overall performance was indicated according to the coefficient of determination reported to be 0.62.

In the present study, coefficients of determination of 1 for the Bayesian algorithm, 0.999 in SVR, 0.999 in MLP, 0.99 in GBR, 0.996 in random forest and 0.822 in KNN were achieved. As shown above, the coefficients presented in this study reflect more accurate models, this may be due to the volume of data worked, since there are not many sequences, and all of them may have a uniformity in their sequence making the prediction more accurate. Another aspect to take into account may be the regression parameters, which can change due to the employed data and the training process. Although different regression techniques have been used in both works, they are comparable since they draw a trend in the data set, allowing the prediction of the behavior of a variable, in this case, the value of the minimum inhibitory concentration.

Regarding the MAE and MSE, it is possible to affirm that the models generated show good scores since the best results showed values very close to zero in each of the two metrics, which means that the margin of error of these models is minimal, which constitutes a possible future tool that can generate confidence at the time of implementation.

It is essential to mention that an antibiotic differs in many aspects from other more conventional drugs. Based on this and considering the initial use of Lipinski rule, it was possible to prove that this set of specific conditions could be functional for the design of antibiotics, since the best results were obtained using Lipinski set of descriptors.

The molecular descriptors proved to help in the prediction of the bioactivity of the molecule, which is consistent with what is found in the literature. Despite obtaining good results, for the objective set in this project the fingerprints did not completely meet the expectations, since, as mentioned above, the Lipinski descriptors outperformed the fingerprints, both in the performance of the algorithms and in the computational time at the time of extracting the features.

5   Conclusion

The parameter's computation and selected algorithms allowed the generation of models that can predict the bioactivity of a molecule. This can be a valuable tool in generating new antibiotics to combat the growing problem of antibiotic resistance. Both Lipinski descriptors and fingerprints showed to be useful features for the objective of the present work. However, the use of Lipinski descriptors is recommended before the use of finger-prints, since as mentioned above these features have the facility to provide better results in less time, which means that the computational cost is lower when they are used.

Likewise, the proposed method is innovative, even though there is much literature involving the use of machine learning tools to predict the bioactivity of a molecule that can be used to combat antibiotic resistance This method used six different regressors and compared them in addition to obtaining results superior to those reported in the literature with methods of greater complexity, such as artificial neural networks.

Further work is needed to improve these models and results, using more data to generalize the proposed model. In this case, the model is only functional for those compounds that seek to inhibit the quinolone resistance protein NorA in *Staphylococcus Aureus*.

References

1. Kapoor, G., Saigal, S., Elongavan, A.: Action and resistance mechanisms of antibiotics: A guide for clinicians. J. Anaesthesiol. Clin. Pharmacol. **33**(3), 300 (2017)
2. Pasachova Garzón, J., Ramirez Martinez, S., Muñoz Molina y, L.: Staphylococcus aureus: generalidades, mecanismos de patogenicidad y colonización celular, Nova **17**(32), 25–38 (2019). https://doi.org/10.22490/24629448.3631
3. Encyclopedia, M., (MRSA), M.: Methicillin-resistant Staphylococcus aureus (MRSA): MedlinePlus Medical Encyclopedia. Medlineplus.gov. https://medlineplus.gov/ency/article/007 261.htm. Accessed 29 Jul 2022
4. Ng, E.Y., Trucksis, M., Hooper y, D.C.: Quinolone resistance mediated by norA: physiologic characterization and relationship to flqB, a quinolone resistance locus on the Staphylococcus aureus chromosome, Antimicrob. Agents Chemother **38**(6), 1345–1355 (1994). https://doi.org/10.1128/AAC.38.6.1345
5. Walters, W., Barzilay, R.: Applications of deep learning in molecule generation and molecular property prediction, Acc. Chem. Res. **54**(2), 263–270 (2020). https://doi.org/10.1021/acs.accounts.0c00699
6. Wang, Z., et al.: Advanced graph and sequence neural networks for molecular property prediction and drug discovery, Bioinformatics **38**(9), 2579–2586 (2022). https://doi.org/10.1093/bioinformatics/btac112
7. Stokes, J.M., et al.: A Deep Learning Approach to Antibiotic Discovery, Cell **181**(2), 475–483, (2020). https://doi.org/10.1016/j.cell.2020.04.001
8. Horna Quintana, G., Silva Diaz, M., Vicente Taboada, W., Tamariz Ortiz y, J.: Concentración mínima inhibitoria y concentración mínima bactericida de ciprofloxacina en bacterias uropatógenas aisladas en el Instituto Nacional de Enfermedades Neoplásicas, Rev. Med. Hered. **16**(1), 39 (2012). https://doi.org/10.20453/rmh.v16i1.862
9. Benet, L.Z., Hosey, C.M., Ursu, O., Oprea y, T.I.: BDDCS, the Rule of 5 and drugability, Adv. Drug Deliv. Rev. **101**, 89–98 (2016). https://doi.org/10.1016/j.addr.2016.05.007
10. Mendez, D., et al.: ChEMBL: towards direct deposition of bioassay data, Nucleic Acids Res. **47**(D1), D930–D940 (2019). https://doi.org/10.1093/nar/gky1075
11. Target: Quinolone resistance protein norA. (s. f.). EMBL- EBI: EMBL's European Bioinformatics Institutel EMBL'sEuropeanBionformatics Institute. https://www.ebi.ac.uk/chembl/target_report_card/CHEMBL5114/
12. Lima, A., Philot, E., Trossini, G., Scott, L., Maltarollo, V., Honorio, K.: Use of machine learning approaches for novel drug discovery. Expert Opin. Drug Discov. **11**(3), 225–239 (2016)
13. Yap, C.W.: PaDEL-descriptor: An open source software to calculate molecular descriptors and fingerprints, J. Comput. Chem. **32**(7) 1466–1474 (2011). https://doi.org/10.1002/jcc.21707
14. Patel, L., Shukla, T., Huang, X., Ussery, D., Wang, S.: Machine learning methods in drug discovery. Molecules **25**(22), 5277 (2020)
15. Serafim, M., et al.: The application of machine learning techniques to innovative antibacterial discovery and development. Expert Opin. Drug Discov. **15**(10), 1165–1180 (2020)
16. Kowalewski, J., Ray, A.: Predicting novel drugs for SARS-CoV-2 using machine learning from a >10 million chemical space. Heliyon **6**(8), e04639 (2020)

17. Probst, P., Boulesteix, A.L., Bischl y, B.: Tunability: Importance of Hyperparameters of Machine Learning Algorithms, p. 32
18. Kavuncuoglu, H., Kavuncuoglu, E., Karatas, S., Benli, B., Sagdic, O., Yalcin, H.: Prediction of the antimicrobial activity of walnut (Juglans regia L.) kernel aqueous extracts using artificial neural network and multiple linear regression. J. Microbiol. Methods **148**, 78–86 (2018)

Comparison of Named Entity Recognition Methods on Real-World and Highly Imbalanced Business Document Datasets

S. A. Moreno-Acevedo[1(✉)], D. Escobar-Grisales[1],
J. C. Vásquez-Correa[1,3,4], and J. R. Orozco-Arroyave[1,2]

[1] GITA Lab. Faculty of Engineering, University of Antioquia UdeA, Medellín, Colombia
santiago.moreno3@udea.edu.co
[2] Pattern Recognition Lab, Friedrich-Alexander-Universität Erlangen-Nürnberg, Erlangen, Germany
[3] Pratech group SAS, Medellin, Colombia
[4] Fundación Vicomtech, Basque Research and Technology Alliance (BRTA), Donostia-San Sebastián, Donostia, Spain

Abstract. Named Entity Recognition (NER) is a topic of natural language processing that has gained interest in the research community for its applications in different areas, especially industrial environments where the analysis of business documents is very important. Different methods proposed for NER are usually tested in benchmark databases, which gives several advantages to the evaluated methods including a large number of samples with a low number of entities to recognize, and an "artificially" created balance in the dataset. This paper compares and analyzes several models for NER on data collected from real business processes. In the addressed scenarios, the number of samples is limited and there is a large number of imbalanced entities in the documents. Two scenarios are considered for the proposed comparison: (1) a set of German legal documents from court decisions, and (2) a set of Spanish business documents related to the company's registration at the Colombian chamber of commerce. Both scenarios are evaluated using state-of-the-art methods such as conditional random fields, bidirectional long-short term memory networks, and Transformers. The results in both scenarios indicated that architectures based on Transformers outperformed architectures based on conditional random fields and recurrent neural networks. Additionally, we observed that the performance to accurately recognize certain entities highly depends on different criteria such as the number of available tokens per entity, the average length of the entities within the document, and most importantly on the semantic similarity that exists among tokens per entity and the rest of the document.

Keywords: Named entity recognition · Deep learning · Transformers · Bussines documents · Imbalanced data · Data features · Semantic analysis

© The Author(s), under exclusive license to Springer Nature Switzerland AG 2022
J. C. Figueroa-García et al. (Eds.): WEA 2022, CCIS 1685, pp. 41–53, 2022.
https://doi.org/10.1007/978-3-031-20611-5_4

1 Introduction

Named Entity Recognition (NER) is a topic of natural language processing that aims to identify and categorize key information within text data. Entities are predefined categories such as persons, places, organizations, dates, and others. Those categories are typically assigned to a set of tokens within the text document. In the NER context, a token is defined as a word in a sentence, and multiple sentences conform to a corpus. NER has been studied by the research community considering different applications like question-answering [19], financial news [7], and industrial environments [16], where business document analysis is required. Usually, the models used for NER are tested in general databases of different topics and with a large number of samples and generic entities [10,17]. In contrast, in real environments, there are many specific entities and some of them have very few samples available [11,12].

Different methodologies have been proposed for NER, and include rule-based techniques [8], unsupervised algorithms [21], supervised learning based on features [9], and others. The research community has started to use deep learning techniques recently [3,10,12]. Architectures such as Convolutional Neural Networks (CNNs) [11], Long-Short Term Memory units (LSTMs) [11], Bidirectional LSTMs (BiLSTMs) [10,11], and more recently, Transformer-based models [17] have enabled the development of more sophisticated methods of NER.

Most of the methods in the literature are tested in view of databases with a small number of entity types, many samples, and balanced classes. However, in real and productive environments such as in legal, financial, and government-related document analysis, a high number of entities with a few samples are usually available. Currently, some studies have been proposed to overcome such limitations as in [12], where the methodology introduced by the authors has two parallel models: one for entities with large amounts of samples, and another one for entities with a few samples. Besides these efforts, the evaluation of trained systems for NER considering data from real business processes has been poorly explored. To the best of our knowledge, data distributions have not been properly analyzed in NER models. The performance of NER systems for certain entities could be affected by multiple characteristics such as: single-token and multi-token entities, the number of tokens to represent the entities, and the semantic similarity between the interest entity and the rest of the document, which is usually higher in financial and legal documents than in other types of text data.

This study aims to compare and analyze the performance of different NER models using data collected from real environments, where the number of available tokens is limited, several entities with close semantic relationships should be recognized, and each entity can be composed of many words. Two scenarios are contemplated: (1) a benchmark corpus from German legal documents related to court decisions, and (2) a corpus with registration certificates in Spanish generated by the Colombian chamber of commerce. The first scenario provides a nearly ideal scenario with balanced data and a large amount of samples, while the second scenario constitutes a highly imbalanced dataset with a few samples. We considered five different methods of NER to perform the modeling of the documents. The methods are mainly different in the data representation layer based on classical, sequential, and attention approaches. Additionally, the classification layer is changed based on probabilistic and neural approaches. Results are analyzed according to performance of each model and an analysis of statistic and semantic features of the data is presented for entities with low performance.

The rest of the paper is as follows: Sect. 2 describes the different corpus used for this study. In Sect. 3, we explain the different implemented methods for NER. Section 4 includes the experiments and results along with an analysis of the performance obtained with the models in each scenario. Section 5 discusses the main insights obtained from the results. And finally, Sect. 6 contains the conclusions and future research resulting from this study.

2 Data

Two corpus are considered in this work: (1) a set of German legal documents extracted from 7 federal courts [11], and (2) business documents written in Spanish and consisting of company's registration forms generated by the Colombian chamber of commerce in Medellín (Colombia). Both datasets contain different defined entities such as names of persons, places, names of organizations, and others. Tables 1 and 2 summarize the information of both databases concerning the number of tokens and sentences per entity. In addition, we reported the average number of tokens in a segment, which is defined as an occurrence of consecutive matching words or tokens of the same entity. Figure 1 shows the histogram of the number of tokens per sentence in both corpus.

German: This corpus contains 750 German court decisions selected from the Federal Ministry of Justice and Consumer Protection. This set consists of 66,723 sentences with 2,157,048 tokens categorized in 19 entity types. The minimum number of tokens per entity is 160 and the entity type with the highest average number of tokens per segment is "Court decision", where each segment is composed of 15 tokens on average.

The original corpus was modify because some sentences were composed by a large number of tokens (1000 approximately), therefore all the sentences were limited to 120 tokens that corresponds to the maximum length of the 99 % of the sentences. Figure 1 (left) shows the distribution of the tokens by sentence.

Spanish: This corpus consists of a set of registration certificates from the Colombian chamber of commerce. The certifications contain entity types such as the company's name, company activity, registration date, among others. The corpus is formed with 126,198 tokens and 21 entity types. The minimum number of tokens per entity is 4. The entity type with the largest average number of tokens per segment is called "Limitations". In addition, this corpus shows a greater imbalance and a small number of tokens in comparison with the German database. Additional details are summarized in Table 2. Figure 1 shows that the

Table 1. Details of the data in the German dataset.

Entity type	Acronym	Tokens	Segments	Tokens per segment
Court decision	RS	194601	12846	15.15 ± 6.19
Law	GS	116934	18536	6.31 ± 4.23
Legal literature	LIT	38119	3085	12.36 ± 5.88
Contract	VT	15227	2864	5.32 ± 4.41
European legal norm	EUN	12520	1501	8.34 ± 9.71
Institution	INN	6872	2196	3.13 ± 2.63
Court	GRT	5981	3212	1.86 ± 1.58
Ordinance	VO	5238	796	6.58 ± 7.68
Regulation	VS	4702	610	7.71 ± 7.90
Organization	ORG	2771	1164	2.38 ± 1.56
Company	UN	2384	1058	2.25 ± 1.42
Person	PER	2262	1746	1.29 ± 0.65
Country	LD	1752	1429	1.23 ± 0.49
Judge	RR	1625	1519	1.07 ± 0.25
City	ST	772	704	1.10 ± 0.35
Brand	MRK	666	283	2.35 ± 1.38
Street	STR	265	136	1.95 ± 0.91
Landscape	LDS	231	198	1.17 ± 0.54
Lawyer	AN	160	111	1.44 ± 0.53

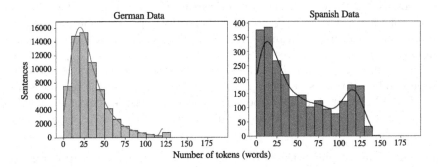

Fig. 1. Number of tokens (words) per sentence for German (left) and Spanish (right) corpus.

length of the sentences for this corpus is shorter and more unbalanced than the ones in the German corpus.

3   Methods

This study considers different methodologies for NER, based on two main paradigms: (1) Transformers and (2) Conditional Random Fields (CRF) combined with different deep learning models for feature extraction. These approaches have shown high performance for NER in different benchmark databases [10,11,17]. These approaches have become popular because the development of frameworks s such as FLAIR [1] that allows a fast implementation of models based on Transformers, and UKPLab-BiLSTM [15] that simplifies the building of architectures using BiLSTM and CRF techniques.

Table 2. Distribution of the classes in the Spanish dataset.

Entity type	Acronym	Tokens	Segments	Tokens per segment
Activity	ACT	4520	417	10.84 ± 6.20
Date	FCH	3704	1050	3.52 ± 1.85
Person	PER	1295	353	3.67 ± 1.17
Organization	ORG	846	261	3.24 ± 1.21
Limitations	LIM	615	11	55.91 ± 27.76
Type of document of identy	TDID	374	301	1.24 ± 0.64
Title registration date	TFMT	371	718	2.10 ± 1.11
Identity document	DID	326	288	1.13 ± 0.41
Title principal activity	TACTP	317	159	1.99 ± 0.21
Title name or business name	TNRS	259	103	2.51 ± 0.86
Legal representative position	CRL	254	123	2.06 ± 0.40
Title secondary activity	TACTS	171	86	2 ± 0.11
Title other activity	TACTO	166	83	2 ± 0
Organization type	TORG	91	23	3.96 ± 0.46
Substitute position	CAS	67	39	1.72 ± 0.85
Title state registration	TEMT	13	7	1.86 ± 0.64
Old organization type	TORGA	11	4	2.75 ± 1.30
Title effective date	TFV	9	6	1.50 ± 1.12
Title limitations	TLIM	5	4	1.25 ± 0.43
Title organization type	TTORG	4	4	1 ± 0
State of registration	EMT	4	2	2 ± 0

3.1   Models Based on Transformers

Different models based on Transformers have been proposed for NER. **FLERT** is one of them and it was introduced in [17], which has demonstrated a high capability to recognize named entities [2,17,20]. The model computes word representations using a multilingual pre-trained model based on RoBERTa [5]. The model is formed with 24 Transformer blocks, which include 16 self-attention heads, and a fully connected layer composed of 1024 units. RoBERTa was pre-trained with 2.5 TB of data from the cleaned Common Crawl corpus [18], which includes text data in 100 different languages and allows for computing text representations in multiple languages. Embeddings from RoBERTa feed a fully connected neural network that classifies the entities using a linear activation function. In this paper, we fine-tuned the RoBERTa model and modified the output layer according to the considered corpus (German and Spanish).

3.2 CRF

CRFs are stochastic models used to label and segment sequential data and also to extract information from documents [6]. We implemented and compared four methods based on CRF, considering different feature extraction approaches: (I) CRF with features (**CRF-F**), where words are represented according to the following questions: (1) Are all characters uppercase?, (2) Are all characters lowercase?, (3) Is the first character uppercase and the rest lowercase?, (4) Are all characters digits?, (5) Are all characters letters?, (6) Are all characters numbers? and (7) Is the word a title? or all the characters are lowercase/uppercase?. Each question represents a feature to be classified by the CRF. In addition, the feature extraction process considers two context words, one on each side. (II) The second approach is called **BiLSTM-CRF** because it uses word embeddings extracted from a word2vec model to feed BiLSTM layer before the CRF classifier. The BiLSTM-CRF model allows finding semantic features from the embeddings by itself. (III) The third model extracts a character embedding via an LSTM layer and concatenates the word embeddings from word2vec with the character embeddings before the BiLSTM layer from the previous model, forming a model known as **LSTM-BiLSTM-CRF**. (IV) Finally, we considered a **CNN-BiLSTM-CRF** model, which is similar to the LSTM-BiLSTM-CRF one but replaces the LSTM layer with a CNN.

In models where deep layers are used (i.e., models II, III, and IV), the representation of the words is obtained using pre-trained word2vec models based on the skip-gram architecture. The word2vec model for the German data considered the pre-trained model introduced in [13], which was trained with 116 million sentences and 648,462 tokens from different German corpus. The word2vec model for the Spanish corpus contemplated the pre-trained model from [4], which has 1,000,653 tokens and was pre-trained with 1.4 billion words obtained from the Spanish Billion Word Corpus.

4 Experiments and Results

We preserved the original configuration of the methods along the experiments. The Transformer model based on FLERT was fine-tuned with 20 epochs, a learning rate of 5×10^{-6}, and 128 context words (64 on each side), according to the configuration presented in [17]. For the CRF-F model, we used five words as the context window and the hyperparameters configuration proposed in [11]. Finally, the BiLSTM-CRF, LSTM-BiLSTM-CRF, and CNN-BiLSTM-CRF models used two BiLSTM layers using a dropout of 0.25, and 100 units for the hidden layer. An early stopping strategy was used to stop the training when the F1-score did not improve for 5 consecutive epochs [14].

The validation process consisted of a 10-fold and a 5-fold cross-validation strategies for the German and Spanish corpus, respectively. The decision about the number of folds was made based on the number of available samples in each corpus.

4.1   German

The left side of Fig. 2 shows the F1-scores obtained for the German corpus. High F1-scores are achieved for the 19 entities addressed in this dataset. In addition, Table 3 presents the results of each method, where F1-scores of up to 0.94 are obtained using the FLERT model.

4.2   Spanish

Details of the average results obtained for the Spanish corpus are reported in Table 4, notice that all models achieved lower F1-scores than those obtained with the German dataset. The right side of Fig. 2 shows the F1-scores obtained in each entity type. Note that entity types such as ACT, FCH, PER, ORG, and others achieve F1-scores between 0.75 and 0.8; however, other entity types like LIM, TORGA, TFV, TLIM, and others yield results close to 0. We observed a similar behaviour regardless of the model.

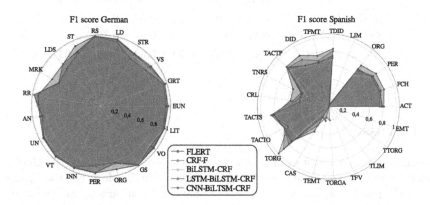

Fig. 2. F1-scores obtained per entity. (Right) German dataset and (Left) Spanish dataset.

4.3 Comparison

Although its high computational complexity, the model with higher performance in both datasets was FLERT. Results shown in Fig. 2 confirm the fact that a hand-crafted dataset allows finding better and consistent results (i.e., the case of the German corpus). Unfortunately, this is not the case when data captured in real environments are considered. In the Spanish corpus, approximately 52% of entity types have an F1-score above 0.75, 14% have an F1-score between 0.4 and 0.5, and 34% have an F1-score close to 0. These results reflect the unbalanced and complex distribution of the entities when real data are used.

Table 3. Results for German dataset.

Model	Precision	Recall	F1-score
FLERT	**0.94 ± 0.01**	**0.94 ± 00.1**	**0.94 ± 0.01**
CRF	**0.94 ± 0.01**	0.85 ± 0.02	0.89 ± 0.01
BiLSTM-CRF	0.91 ± 0.01	0.91 ± 0.01	0.91 ± 0.01
LSTM-BiLSTM-CRF	0.92 ± 0.01	0.92 ± 0.01	0.92 ± 0.01
CNN-BiLSTM-CRF	0.91 ± 0.01	0.92 ± 0.01	0.92 ± 0

Table 4. Results for Spanish dataset.

Model	Precision	Recall	F1-score
FLERT	0.47 ± 0.04	**0.54 ± 0.02**	**0.50 ± 0.02**
CRF	**0.52 ± 0.05**	0.45 ± 0.04	0.48 ± 0.04
BiLSTM-CRF	0.41 ± 0.02	0.42 ± 0.03	0.41 ± 0.03
LSTM-BiLSTM-CRF	0.44 ± 0.01	0.48 ± 0.01	0.45 ± 0
CNN-BiLSTM-CRF	0.45 ± 0.03	0.50 ± 0.03	0.46 ± 0.03

5 Discussion

The different models tested in this study yielded similar results in the German dataset according to the average F1-scores reported in Table 3. For the Spanish corpus the results are not satisfactory but still consistent among models as it is shown in Table 4.

Although the average results in Spanish were very low, we believe that the models based on Transformers are a good choice since the FLERT model was the one that showed better results in both datasets. The results observed with the Spanish dataset are not systematic. Some of the entity types yielded relatively high F1-scores while some others dropped down to almost zero. This behavior was model-independent and could be due to several factors including the reduced number of tokens available to train the model, the average length of the segments, or the semantic similarity between the tokens in each entity type. Further details about the analysis of these factors are shown below.

Number of Available Tokens: Figure. 3 shows the F1-score for the 10 entities with the lowest number of available tokens. The Spearman's correlation coefficient was computed and the results indicate a strong correlation between the number of available tokens and the F1-score. According to these results, entities with more than 90 tokens can be accurately recognized by the FLERT model, conversely, entities with a small number of tokens are not accurately modeled which limits the recognition of these entities.

Average Length of the Segments: This is a metric computed for each entity and it represents the number of tokens per segment for a given entity. The upper part of Fig. 4 shows the performance of the model for all entities, and the bottom part of the figure shows the average length of the segments in terms of number of tokens. The results show that LIM entity has an average length of 56 tokens and a very small F1-score, despite the high number of tokens. It seems like a high number of tokens in a segment for a given entity produces the model to fail in the process of recognizing the entities. This is likely because existing models are not able to correctly capture information from long segments where the dependencies require long contexts.

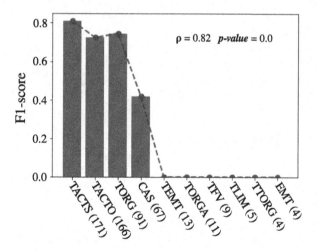

Fig. 3. F1-score for the 10 entities with the lower number of tokens for Spanish corpus.

Semantic Similarity: This factor has to do with the uniqueness of the terms used to name the entities in the corpus. Unfortunately, existing documents like those produced by companies, the court, chambers of commerce, and others, were not thought to generate consistent representations in terms of named entities. Given this fact, what language scientists have done is to associate unknown tokens to a kind of "trash" entity called OTHER. Semantic similarity is defined as the ratio between the number of unique tokens that appear in a given entity and also appear in the entity OTHER with respect to the total number of unique tokens in the given entity. When many words from the interest entity appear in the entity OTHER, the semantic similarity is high. This happens mainly due to labeling problems, when there is not enough information to generate additional entities consistent along the documents in the corpus. In the particular case of this study, the entity OTHER has a total of 126,198 tokens, while the number of tokens for other entities ranges between 4 and 4,520. With the aim to perform a deeper analysis of this aspect, we evaluated the Spearman's correlation between the semantic similarity of each entity and its F1-score (with FLERT). The result is shown in Fig. 5. Notice that entities with higher similarity are the ones with the lower F1-score, which suggests that entities in which there were a lot of tokens that also appeared in the OTHER entity, generates the performance of the model to decrease. This finding also suggest that the labeling process of document corpus should be performed paying special attention to the semantic similarity measure. Similar experiments were performed with the German database (not reported here) and we confirmed that all of the entities had semantic similarities of below 0.8 and F1-scores between 0.8 and 1.0, which is in agreement with the results presented in Fig. 2 (left).

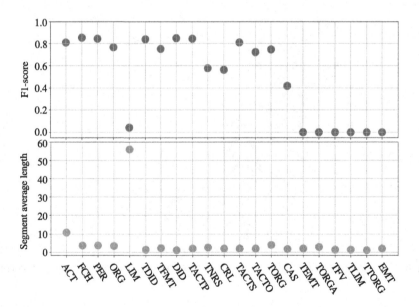

Fig. 4. Comparison of F1-score (up) and the average length of the segment (bottom) for each entity. The entities are sorted according to the number of tokens.

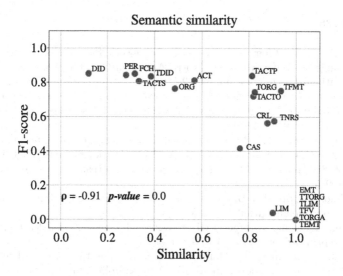

Fig. 5. Semantic similarity analysis.

6   Conclusion

This paper addressed the problem of classifying named entities in documents of two corpus. One with German court decisions selected from the Federal Ministry of Justice and Consumer Protection and the other one with registration certificates written in Spanish and provided by the Colombian chamber of commerce. Different methods including those based on CRFs, BiLSTMs and Transformers were tested for comparison purposes. The classification results obtained in the German database were systematically high, with F1-scores around 90% in classification of 19 entities. For the case of the Colombian corpus, the results were not satisfactory. After performing a detailed analysis of the results, we found that there were a subset of entities for which the F1-scores were nearly zero. Further analyses showed three factors as possible reasons to explain the poor results for these entities: a small number of tokens in the interest entity, a high average segment length, and a high semantic similarity. This last factor is of especial interest because it happens when there is a high number of tokens that belong to a given entity that are also present in an another entity called OTHER that is typically created for terms (tokens) without a stated entity. This fact reflects existing limitations in the labeling problems that need to be addressed with especial attention by the research community. For future experiments methods will be studied with the aim to find those that are robust against the aforementioned labeling problem, such upsample the entity types with few tokens or generate class weights to focus the model in those entities with few tokens.

Acknowledgments. This work was funded by CODI at UdeA grant PRG2017-15530, and the CCC dataset was provided by PRATEC group SAS.

References

1. Akbik, A., et al.: Flair: an easy-to-use framework for state-of-the-art NLP. In: Proceedings of Conference of the North American Chapter of the Association for Computational Linguistics, pp. 54–59 (2019)
2. Arkhipov, M., et al.: Tuning multilingual transformers for language-specific named entity recognition. In: Proceedings of Workshop on Balto-Slavic Natural Language Processing, pp. 89–93 (2019)
3. Bhatia, P., Arumae, K., Busra Celikkaya, E.: Dynamic transfer learning for named entity recognition. In: Shaban-Nejad, A., Michalowski, M. (eds.) W3PHAI 2019. SCI, vol. 843, pp. 69–81. Springer, Cham (2020). https://doi.org/10.1007/978-3-030-24409-5_7
4. Cardellino, C.: Spanish Billion Words Corpus and Embeddings, August 2019. https://crscardellino.github.io/SBWCE/
5. Conneau, A., et al.: Unsupervised cross-lingual representation learning at scale. arXiv preprint arXiv:1911.02116 (2019)
6. Finkel, J.R., Grenager, T., Manning, C.D.: Incorporating non-local information into information extraction systems by GIBBS sampling. In: Proceedings of Annual Meeting of the Association for Computational Linguistics (ACL 2005), pp. 363–370 (2005)
7. Jabbari, A., Sauvage, O., Zeine, H., Chergui, H.: A french corpus and annotation schema for named entity recognition and relation extraction of financial news. In: Proceedings of Language Resources and Evaluation Conference, pp. 2293–2299 (2020)
8. Kim, J.H., Woodland, P.C.: A rule-based named entity recognition system for speech input. In: Proceedings of International Conference on Spoken Language Processing (2000)
9. Krishnan, V., Manning, C.D.: An effective two-stage model for exploiting non-local dependencies in named entity recognition. In: Proceedings of International Conference on Computational Linguistics and 44th Annual Meeting of the Association for Computational Linguistics, pp. 1121–1128 (2006)
10. Lample, G., et al.: Neural architectures for named entity recognition. arXiv preprint arXiv:1603.01360 (2016)
11. Leitner, E., Rehm, G., Moreno-Schneider, J.: Fine-grained named entity recognition in legal documents. In: Acosta, M., Cudré-Mauroux, P., Maleshkova, M., Pellegrini, T., Sack, H., Sure-Vetter, Y. (eds.) SEMANTiCS 2019. LNCS, vol. 11702, pp. 272–287. Springer, Cham (2019). https://doi.org/10.1007/978-3-030-33220-4_20
12. Nguyen, T., Nguyen, D., Rao, P.: Adaptive name entity recognition under highly unbalanced data. arXiv preprint arXiv:2003.10296 (2020)
13. Reimers, N., et al.: Nested named entity recognition with neural networks (2014)
14. Reimers, N., Gurevych, I.: Optimal hyperparameters for deep LSTM-networks for sequence labeling tasks. arXiv preprint arXiv:1707.06799 (2017)
15. Reimers, N., Gurevych, I.: Reporting score distributions makes a difference: performance study of LSTM-networks for sequence tagging. In: Proceedings of Conference on Empirical Methods in Natural Language Processing, pp. 338–348. Copenhagen, Denmark, September 2017. http://aclweb.org/anthology/D17-1035
16. Schiersch, M., Mironova, V., Schmitt, M., Thomas, P., Gabryszak, A., Hennig, L.: A german corpus for fine-grained named entity recognition and relation extraction of traffic and industry events. arXiv preprint arXiv:2004.03283 (2020)

17. Schweter, S., Akbik, A.: Flert: document-level features for named entity recognition. arXiv preprint arXiv:2011.06993 (2020)
18. Wenzek, G., et al.: CCNet: Extracting high quality monolingual datasets from web crawl data. In: Proceedings of Language Resources and Evaluation Conference, pp. 4003–4012. European Language Resources Association, Marseille, France, May 2020. https://aclanthology.org/2020.lrec-1.494
19. Wongso, R., Suhartono, D., et al.: A literature review of question answering system using named entity recognition. In: Proceedings of International Conference on Information Technology, Computer, and Electrical Engineering, pp. 274–277. IEEE (2016)
20. Yan, H., et al.: Tener: adapting transformer encoder for named entity recognition. arXiv preprint arXiv:1911.04474 (2019)
21. Zhang, S., Elhadad, N.: Unsupervised biomedical named entity recognition: experiments with clinical and biological texts. J. Biomed. Inform. 46(6), 1088–1098 (2013)

Colombian Dialect Recognition from Call-Center Conversations Using Fusion Strategies

D. Escobar-Grisales[1]([envelope])[iD], C. D. Rios-Urrego[1][iD], J. D. Gallo-Aristizabal[1][iD],
D. A. López-Santander[1][iD], N. R. Calvo-Ariza[1][iD], Elmar Nöth[2][iD],
and J. R. Orozco-Arroyave[1,2][iD]

[1] GITA Laboratory Faculty of Engineering, University of Antioquia UdeA, Medellín, Colombia
daniel.esobar@udea.edu.co
[2] Pattern Recognition Lab, Friedrich-Alexander-Universität Erlangen-Nürnberg, Erlangen, Germany

Abstract. Automatic dialect recognition is a challenging problem with many applications in different fields. Particularly, in customer service, it is used to improve the interaction between customers and providers or to segment offers such that products and services are exposed to the group of greatest interest. This study proposes a bi-modal analysis to discriminate between two Colombian dialects ("Antioqueño" and "Bogotano") using text and speech signals generated in real call-center conversations. First, we evaluated uni-modal strategies considering classical and deep approaches to analyze speech recordings and their corresponding transliterations (text). Then, different fusion strategies were considered to combine the information from speech and text in different stages of the methodology. In early fusion, the uni-modal feature vectors are concatenated and used as input to generate a new model. In late fusion, the scores resulting from the uni-modal classifications are concatenated to form the features vectors to train a support vector machine to predict the dialect. Furthermore, a joint fusion strategy was tested to enhance the characterization process of one mode based on the information from the other one. The results indicate that bi-modal approaches using the late fusion strategy outperform uni-modal approaches by up to 9%. To the best of our knowledge, this is the first work of Colombian dialect recognition based on call-center conversations using a bi-modal approach. Future experiments will consider other fusion strategies where information from text and speech are synchronously merged to improve the dialect classification.

Keywords: Dialect recognition · Customer service · Speech analysis · Text analysis · Fusion strategies

© The Author(s), under exclusive license to Springer Nature Switzerland AG 2022
J. C. Figueroa-García et al. (Eds.): WEA 2022, CCIS 1685, pp. 54–65, 2022.
https://doi.org/10.1007/978-3-031-20611-5_5

1 Introduction

Dialects can be considered as linguistic characteristics of a community and such characteristics can be represented by variations in a phoneme, an utterance, and other changes when communicating (both orally and in writing). Therefore, dialect recognition can help in improving applications where automatic speech recognition is used, such as voice dialing, data entry, dictation, digital assistance, home automation, call routing, interactive voice response, call-centers conversations, and others [12]. Call-centers conversations are the main focus of this work, where different bi-modal approaches are considered for automatic dialect recognition in real scenarios. Customer service centers could use this information in order to improve marketing strategies.

Due to similarities or small changes in utterances within the same language, dialect recognition becomes a challenge that generates a greater difficulty than simply identifying a language [24]. This becomes even more challenging when we attempt to classify different dialects from the same country. Thus, works on automatic dialect identification have been done using information obtained from speech [11,27] and also from text [5,22]. Most works used common features for the analysis of text, such as Term Frequency-Inverse Document Frequency (TF-IDF) or Part Of Speech-Tagging (POS-tagging), as well as more modern representations such as Word2Vec and Bidirectional Encoder Representations from Transformers (BERT) [2,5,26]. In the case of speech-based studies, typical approaches are based on Mel-Frequency Cepstral Coefficients (MFCCs) along with prosody features [4,11].With the aim to improve results, the research community has introduced the use of multi-modal representations, e.g., considering information from text and speech or from video and speech, and among others. Multi-modal approaches have been mainly implemented in emotion recognition [14,16,20,23]. All of these studies reported improvements in the classification accuracy when several modalities were merged.

In the case of dialect recognition, a few papers combine text and speech to perform the classification. In [3], the authors performed the dialect detection among different types of Arabic dialects, including Egyptian, Leviathan, Gulf, and Moroccan. The authors used videos from YouTube and extracted their audios and corresponding transliterations. Embeddings of both speech and text were concatenated in an early fusion strategy, and the authors reported an improvement of 14% in the accuracy compared to the used of text and speech analysis independently. In [1] the authors compared text and speech signals to detect differences among 4 different sub-dialects (Sfax, Tuni, Souse, and Tataouine) from Tunisia in Africa. Results show that the speech embeddings were better than the text ones, concluding that speech-based systems were better for dialect identification. According to the authors' analyses, the reason is because there is a high overlap in the vocabulary used in these different sub-dialects, generating a reduction in the sensitivity of the text-based approaches. Fusion strategies were not performed in this study.

This work aims to classify between two dialects typically used in two different regions of Colombia, i.e., "Bogotano" and "Antioqueño". Instead of considering recordings extracted from public platforms like YouTube, where the content could have been acted or intentionally generated, in this study we considered recordings collected in a real call-center environment where customers from different regions of the country received attention from the service agents. We focused only on "Bogotano" and "Antioqueño" because these were the two dialects from which we were able to collect more recordings. The methodology introduced in this study is divided in two sections, the first part is based on extracting information from speech and text signals separately to perform the classification; and second, three different fusion strategies (early, joint, and late fusion) were applied with the aim to improve the classification results.

The rest of the paper is as follows: Sect. 2 gives a brief description of the data used for this work, Sect. 3 introduces the methods used in both, uni-modal and bi-modal approaches. Section 4 presents the results obtained in the different experiments. Finally, Sect. 5 contains the conclusions derived from this study and future experiments.

2   Data

Call-center conversations were collected from a Colombian pension administration company. These speech utterances were analyzed by a group of linguist experts, who generated manual transliterations of each conversation. They also assigned labels corresponding to Colombian dialects according to their perceptual judge. Customer dialects were labeled as "Bogotano" when the customer had an accent typical from the regions close to the Colombian capital, Bogotá, or as "Antioqueño" when the customer had a typical accent from the Colombian region of Antioquia. A summary of the metadata corresponding to this corpus is provided in Table 1. Notice that the average number of words per call, the average duration of the calls, and the number of male and female subjects are similar in both groups. Speech signals were normalized according to amplitude, transliterations were converted to lower case and punctuation marks were removed.

Table 1. Description of the database. **M**: Male. **F**: Female. **ND**: Non-defined. Values are reported in terms of mean ± standard deviation.

	Bogotano	Antioqueño
Samples	71	67
Average # words	202 ± 81	209 ± 103
Average duration [s]	509.4 ± 207.1	483.2 ± 267.7
Gender	M: 28; F: 41; ND: 2	M: 23; F: 41; ND: 3

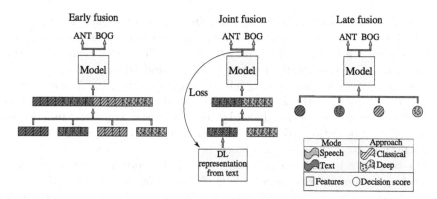

Fig. 1. Fusion strategies addressed in this work. ANT: Antioqueño, BOG: Bogotano, DL: Deep Learning.

3   Methods

The uni-modal methods considered in this work are based on those proposed in [6], where different classical and deep approaches were tested for dialect discrimination using speech and text, separately. For the multi-modal approach, different fusion strategies were addressed, Fig. 1 shows a general methodology that illustrates each fusion strategy. Early and late fusion aims to combine information from different stages from uni-modal architectures. Specifically, early fusion combines feature vectors extracted in each uni-modal model, while late fusion combines the decision score resulting from each uni-modal approach. In the joint fusion strategy a fine-tuning over the parameters of the text-based model is performed considering information of the deep model generated from the speech recordings. Further details about uni-modal methods and the fusion strategies are presented below.

3.1   Uni-Modal Approach

Speech and text signals were considered separately by using classical and deep approaches. The methods selected for each approach correspond to those that provided the best individual performance in [6]. For the classical approach, speech signals were modeled with MFCCs, Mean Hilbert Envelop Coefficients (MHECs), and prosody features based on pitch, energy, duration, and speech rate [15]. The transliterations were modeled considering word embedding models like Word2vec and bidirectional encoding such as BERT. The deep approach was applied using Convolutional Neural Networks (CNN) which were trained using each modality separately, i.e., spectrograms were used to train a CNN for speech, and embedding matrices were used to feed a CNN for text. Details of the models created for each modality are presented below.

Speech Features. In [6], the best performing feature of the classical approach was the MHECs extracted from the voiced segments of the recordings detected from the presence of the fundamental frequency. These coefficients constitute an alternative for noise-robust acoustic modeling and are capable of capturing information such as speaker identity and language structure [19]. The extraction of MHECs is based on the Hilbert envelope at the output of 32 Gammatone filters. Each feature vector is reduced by computing four statistical functionals: mean, standard deviation, skewness, and kurtosis. This is performed to create a fixed-length feature vector per utterance.

The best deep learning model obtained in [6] for speech analysis was based on spectrograms of the raw signal taking chunks of 500 ms length with a time-shift of 250 ms. The training and validation of this approach are based on the ResNet architecture [9]. In this case, we considered a ResNet model with six residual blocks and three main blocks with 16, 32, and 64 feature maps. Then an average pooling layer and a fully connected layer are added to reduce the output to 2 neurons. ReLu activations are considered in the hidden layers, and a Softmax activation function is used in the output. Since each participant had M number of spectrograms per audio, the final decision was made based on the mode computed over the M network predictions per speaker. The model was trained with a cross-entropy loss function and a stochastic gradient descent optimizer. Dropout and L2-regularization methods were optimized according to the accuracy in the development set.

Text Features. The classical method used in this work to model text was Word2Vec. According to [6], this model outperforms other approaches like BERT and BETO in the Colombian dialect recognition task. Word2Vec is a classical feature extraction method, where vector representations (embeddings) are obtained per word. These embeddings preserve semantic information between words and are context-independent, therefore there is only one embedding per word in the resulting representation [13]. The pre-trained model used in this work consists of 300 neurons in its hidden layer and it was trained by using a continuous skip-gram strategy with the Spanish Wikipedia corpus [18]. To obtain a fixed-length feature vector per subject, several statistical functionals are computed: average, standard deviation, kurtosis, skewness, maximum and minimum.

The text's deep approach consisted on representing the transliterations as an embedding matrix, this matrix is built from the embeddings of the words that compose the transliteration, these word-embeddings are calculated using an embedding layer. This matrix is used to feed a convolutional layer formed with three parallel convolutional filters. This allows the analysis of different n-gram relationships in the temporal dimension. We considered $2 \times d$, $3 \times d$, and $4 \times d$ filters, where d is the embedding dimension. These filters are used to map semantic relationships at different levels: bi-gram, tri-gram, and four-gram, respectively. The outputs of the convolutional layer are max-pooled and then concatenated, this part of the architecture is known as the feature extraction stage. The resulting vector from the feature extraction stage is later used as the input to the classification stage, composed of fully connected layers that make the final decision using Softmax activation function. In the same way as in [6] the weights of the architecture are pre-trained by following a transfer learning strategy based on a source model initially trained with the PAN17 corpus [17]. This allowed the creation of a deep text model despite the reduced amount of text available for the experiment.

3.2 Bi-Modal Approach

In general terms, data fusion is the combination of data from different modalities that provide separate views on a common phenomenon to solve an inference problem [8]. Depending on the level where the fusion is performed in a machine/deep learning approach, it is possible to distinguish three kinds of approaches: early fusion (low-level), intermediate/joint fusion, and late fusion.

Early Fusion. This fusion level is a typical method for fusing different modalities before making the final decision. For this type of fusion, features need to be extracted individually and then combined to create the input of the classifier or regressor. This allows to combine models with different sampling rates, otherwise, the process would be more complicated. In the fusion process for this study we considered the best unimodal feature vectors found in the classical speech and text approaches. For the case of the deep approach, we extracted an intermediate network representation from the two implemented CNNs. Particularly, we calculated the statistical average in the deep speech approach to obtain a statistical representation per participant.

Joint Fusion. This fusion strategy joints feature representations learned from an intermediate neural network layer with features extracted from other modalities. The new representation is used as the input to a classifier or regressor, as in the early fusion method. The main difference is that in the joint fusion, the loss is back-propagated to the feature extraction stage of the neural network, generating a loop that enables the finding of better feature representations based on multi-modal information. In this paper, the joint fusion strategy is implemented only with deep uni-modal models to take advantage of back-propagation property. Notice that, deep uni-modal models for speech and text have different resolutions. This is because the deep model for text generates a feature vector per subject, while in the case of speech it generates a feature vector by chunk. Thus, for the process of fine-tuning the text representations by considering the back-propagation of the loss with speech information, the average feature vector over the chunks produced per subject is considered. We used a concatenation to combine the information from text and speech models prior to the prediction stage, as in [21,25]. We did not consider the fine-tuning of the speech model based on text features because, according to [7], in tasks related to dialect recognition, the approaches based on CNNs taking short text sequences (text chunks with some words) show a lower performance compared to approaches where long text sequences are considered.

Late Fusion. This strategy is also known as decision level fusion. It uses the decision scores found on each modality to make a final decision. This technique is inspired by the methodology of ensemble of classifiers, and it is flexible because it allows the fusion of information with different sampling frequencies, data dimensionality, and unit of measurement [10]. In this work, two strategies for the classification stage in the late fusion were considered: the average of the scores obtained with the classifiers trained on each modality separately is computed to make the final decision, and a Support Vector Machine (SVM) is trained with those scores to maximize the separation between the two classes before making the decision.

4   Experiments and Results

Four experiments are presented in this work, the classification with the uni-modal approaches (baseline) and the three fusion strategies presented in Sect. 3.2 for the bi-modal approaches: early, joint, and late fusion. For all experiments, the parameters optimization was performed following a stratified 10 fold speaker-independent cross-validation strategy and test sets were normalized according to train sets. Notice that the same folds were used along all experiments to enable direct comparisons among models. In experiments where an SVM was implemented, we used a Gaussian kernel and the parameters of the classifier were optimized through a grid-search, where $C \in \{0.001, \cdots, 100\}$ and $\gamma \in \{0.0001, \cdots, 100\}$. Finally, the performance of the models was evaluated according to accuracy, sensitivity, specificity, and F1-score.

4.1   Uni-Modal Approach

Table 2 shows the results obtained with the uni-modal representations separately. These results are considered here as the baseline to evaluate the suitability of different methods to classify between "Antioqueño" and "Bogotano". Classical approaches to model speech (CS) and text (CT) are included along with the methods based on deep learning to model speech and text, namely DS and DT, respectively. Notice that the best individual result was obtained with the DS approach, with an accuracy of 76.9%. On the other hand, the CS approach yielded an accuracy of 52.4%, just above chance.

4.2   Bi-Modal Approach with Early Fusion

Different combinations of feature representations taken from the uni-modal approaches were considered: The combination of feature vectors from classical approaches for text and speech is denoted as CT + CS, the combination of feature vectors from deep approaches as DT + DS, and the combination of feature vectors from all approaches as: CT + CS + DT + DS. An additional experiment was performed considering only feature vectors from the three approaches that yielded acceptable results in the uni-modal experiments, i.e., CT + DT +

Table 2. Classification of dialects using uni-modal strategy. **CT**: Classical Text. **CS**: Classical Speech. **DT**: Deep Text. **DS**: Deep Speech. Values are reported in terms of mean ± standard deviation.

	CS	CT	DS	DT
Accuracy	52.4 ± 13.9	74.7 ± 11.1	**76.9 ± 8.8**	72.1 ± 13.0
Sensitivity	54.9 ± 27.3	78.3 ± 18.3	**67.0 ± 13.7**	68.4 ± 18.7
Specificity	53.0 ± 12.1	71.1 ± 11.4	**85.9 ± 10.1**	74.2 ± 14.0
F1-score	48.3 ± 19.5	74.5 ± 14.3	**76.5 ± 8.9**	68.8 ± 15.5

DS. Table 3 shows the results obtained with this fusion strategy. The best result was obtained when the feature vectors from CT, DT, and DS approaches were merged. This experiment yielded an accuracy of 79% and an F1-score of 78.5%. Besides, notice that sensitivity and specificity are well balanced, 77.1% and 80%, respectively, indicating that the resulting model is robust and does not have any bias towards any classes.

Table 3. Classification of dialects with early fusion strategies. **CT**: Classical Text. **CS**: Classical Speech. **DT**: Deep Text. **DS**: Deep Speech. Values are reported in terms of mean ± standard deviation.

	CT + CS	DT + DS	CT + DT CS + DS	CT + DT DS
Accuracy	68.1 ± 9.4	69.6 ± 9.3	76.8 ± 7.0	**79.0 ± 6.7**
Sensitivity	63.3 ± 16.1	71.4 ± 25.7	72.9 ± 21.7	**77.1 ± 18.0**
Specificity	72.3 ± 18.0	67.5 ± 11.4	80.0 ± 14.6	**80.0 ± 11.4**
F1-score	65.5 ± 11.4	68.6 ± 10.2	75.9 ± 7.6	**78.5 ± 7.3**

4.3   Bi-Modal Approach with Joint Fusion

Table 4 shows the results obtained when deep speech and text models are combined. Notice that these results are similar to those obtained in early fusion when only feature vectors from the deep learning models are considered (DT + DS). The joint fusion strategy allowed to fine-tune the feature extraction stage of the deep text model based on information extracted from the deep speech model. However, the results show that this additional information does not improve the accuracy of the individual deep model for text. To some extent, this result was expected due to the reduced number of samples available to train the deep learning architecture.

4.4   Bi-Modal Approaches with Late Fusion

In this fusion strategy, we continued with the same combinations of uni-modal models explored in early fusion but in this case, the decision scores of each uni-

Table 4. Classification of dialects using joint fusion strategy. **DT**: Deep Text. **DS**: Deep Speech. Values are reported in terms of mean ± standard deviation.

	DT + DS
Accuracy	70.3 ± 9.3
Sensitivity	69.3 ± 11.2
Specificity	80.5 ± 15.1
F1-score	72.6 ± 5.8

modal approach are considered. We implemented two methods to combine the decision scores of each model: (1) we use the average of the decision scores to classify between the dialects, and (2) we considered the decision scores obtained from each modality as features to train an SVM. Table 5 shows the results obtained with the different combinations. The best result is obtained when the decision scores from the classical text, deep text, and deep speech models (CT+ DT + DS) are combined to train an SVM. Note that, for all combinations, when the decision scores are used as input to the SVM, the results improved with respect to those obtained when the average score is used to classify the subject's dialect directly.

Table 5. Classification of dialects with late fusion strategies. **CT**: Classical Text. **CS**: Classical Speech. **DT**: Deep Text. **DS**: Deep Speech. **Avg. score**: Average score. **Acc.**: Accuracy. **Sen.**: Sensitivity. **Spe.**: Specificity. **F1**: F1-Score. Values are reported in terms of mean ± standard deviation.

	CT + CS		DT + DS		CT + CS + DT + DS		CT + DT + DS	
	Avg. score	SVM	Avg. score	SVM	Avg. score	SVM	Avg. score	SVM
Acc.	64.3±11.8	72.4± 8.5	81.9±11.4	82.6± 9.9	73.1± 9.4	83.4± 9.7	83.3± 9.3	**84.9± 7.5**
Sen.	59.8±20.1	70.7±17.9	88.0±11.5	89.3±12.1	78.2±15.6	89.3±14.7	84.9±11.5	**92.4±10.7**
Spe.	69.0±20.1	73.8±18.8	72.1±26.3	76.3±16.5	67.1±16.6	77.5±14.5	81.4±18.3	**77.5±11.3**
F1	60.4±16.7	70.9± 9.4	76.5±18.6	82.3±10.2	70.0±10.9	83.1± 9.9	81.3±13.5	**84.7± 7.6**

5   Discussion: Uni-Modal vs. Bi-Modal

The uni-modal approach showed that the most accurate model is based on deep speech representations. In the bi-modal approach, late fusion showed higher accuracies than those obtained with early and joint fusion. Particularly, the late fusion strategy with an SVM was the model that yielded the best results in this work. The experiments performed with late fusion strategies showed that the combination of decision scores from uni-modal deep learning models (DT + DS) is always better than the combination of decision scores from classical approaches (CT + CS). Additionally, we could also observe that feature vectors or decision scores taken from the classical speech approach did not contribute with information for the classification of dialects, conversely, when this app-roach was not considered, the resulting model in the bi-modal analysis yielded the highest accuracy.

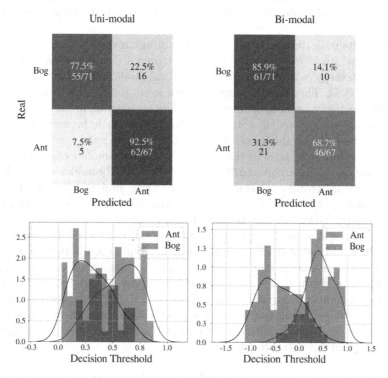

Fig. 2. Confusion matrices and distributions of the scores obtained with the best mod-els: uni-modal (left) and bi-modal (right).

Figure 2 shows the confusion matrices and the distributions of the scores obtained with the best uni-modal model (DS) and bi-modal model (late fusion strategy with SVM considering decision scores from the approaches CT + DT + DS). Notice that in the uni-modal approach, samples labeled as "Bogotano" are easier to classify compared to samples labeled as "Antioqueño", which is consistent with sensitivity and specificity reported in Table 2. On the contrary, in the bi-modal approach, the samples labeled as "Bogotano" are more easily recognized for the model. The superiority of the bi-modal approach is confirmed according to the area of the error shown as the overlap between the "Antioqueño" and "Bogotano" distributions.

6 Conclusions

This paper proposes a bi-modal analysis to automatically discriminate between two variants of the Spanish spoken in Colombia namely "Antioqueño" and

"Bogotano". Speech recordings and their corresponding transliterations obtained from real call-center conversations between customers and agents are considered. Benchmark uni-modal approaches are implemented, including classical and deep representations for text and speech analyses. Finally, the information extracted from the uni-modal models is combined using three fusion strategies: early, joint, and late.

The results indicate that it is possible to automatically discriminate between "Antioqueños" and "Bogotanos" with an accuracy of up to 84.9% following a late fusion strategy, where decision scores of uni-modal models are used as the input to an SVM. These results outperformed in up to 9.6% the best uni-modal result obtained when speech is modeled with deep learning methods. The early fusion strategies discussed in this work also showed an improvement of up to 3.7%. Conversely, the joint fusion strategy did not yield good results. The main reason for the low accuracies in this case is the limited amount of data available to fine-tune the deep architecture. In uni-modal and bi-modal approaches, a transfer learning strategy is used to overcome these limitations, but in the bi-modal approach this strategy was not successful because the base model never considered a modality different from text.

These results showed that information from text and speech are complementary, which could be used for the automatic discrimination between customers from Antioquia and Bogotá in call-center conversations. Given the existing cultural differences between these two regions, the results reported in this work will help in performing appropriate market segmentation and in improving customer support. Future experiments will include new fusion strategies, where information from text and speech can be synchronously merged to exploit the temporal information that could be complementary.

Acknowledgment. This work was funded by CODI at UdeA grant #PRG2017-15530.

References

1. Abdallah, N.B., et al.: Text and speech-based Tunisian Arabic sub-dialects identification. In: Proceedings of LREC, pp. 6405–6411 (2020)
2. Akhtyamova, L., et al.: Twitter author profiling using word embeddings and logistic regression. In: CLEF (Working Notes) (2017)
3. Al-Azani, S., El-Alfy, E.S.: Audio-textual arabic dialect identification for opinion mining videos. In: Proceedings IEEE SSCI, pp. 2470–2475 (2019)
4. Chittaragi, N.B., Koolagudi, S.G.: Acoustic features based word level dialect classification using SVM and ensemble methods. In: Proceedings of IC3, pp. 1–6 (2017)
5. Elfardy, H., Diab, M.: Sentence level dialect identification in Arabic. In: Proceedings of ACL, pp. 456–461 (2013)
6. Escobar-Grisales, D., et al.: Colombian dialect recognition based on information extracted from speech and text signals. In: Proceedings of ASRU, pp. 556–563 (2021)
7. Escobar-Grisales, D., et al.: Author profiling in informal and formal language scenarios via transfer learning. TecnoLógicas **24**(52), 212–225 (2021)

8. Hall, D.L., Llinas, J.: An introduction to multisensor data fusion. Proc. IEEE **85**(1), 6–23 (1997)
9. He, K., Zhang, X., Ren, S., Sun, J.: Identity mappings in deep residual networks. In: Leibe, B., Matas, J., Sebe, N., Welling, M. (eds.) ECCV 2016. LNCS, vol. 9908, pp. 630–645. Springer, Cham (2016). https://doi.org/10.1007/978-3-319-46493-0_38
10. Kuncheva, L.I.: Combining pattern classifiers: methods and algorithms. John Wiley & Sons (2014)
11. Lei, Y., Hansen, J.H.: Dialect classification via text-independent training and testing for Arabic, Spanish, and Chinese. IEEE Trans. Audio Speech Lang. Process. **19**(1), 85–96 (2010)
12. Li, J., et al.: Robust automatic Speech recognition: a bridge to practical applications (2015)
13. Mikolov, T., et al.: Distributed representations of words and phrases and their compositionality. In: Proceedings of NIPS. pp. 3111–3119 (2013)
14. Mittal, T., et al.: M3ER: multiplicative multimodal emotion recognition using facial, textual, and speech cues. In: Proceedings of AAAI, vol. 34, pp. 1359–1367 (2020)
15. Orozco-Arroyave, J.R., et al.: Neurospeech: an open-source software for Parkinson's speech analysis. Dig. Sig. Process. **77**, 207–221 (2018)
16. Pampouchidou, A., et al.: Depression assessment by fusing high and low level features from audio, video, and text. In: Proceedings of AVEC, pp. 27–34 (2016)
17. Rangel, F., et al.: Overview of the 5th author profiling task at pan 2017: gender and language variety identification in twitter. Working notes papers of the CLEF, pp. 1613–0073 (2017)
18. Reese, S., et al.: Wikicorpus: A word-sense disambiguated multilingual wikipedia corpus (2010)
19. Sadjadi, S.O., Hansen, J.H.: Mean Hilbert envelope coefficients (MHEC) for robust speaker and language identification. Speech Commun. **72**, 138–148 (2015)
20. Sebastian, J., et al.: Fusion techniques for utterance-level emotion recognition combining speech and transcripts. In: Proceedings of INTERSPEECH, pp. 51–55 (2019)
21. Spasov, S.E., et al.: A multi-modal convolutional neural network framework for the prediction of alzheimer's disease. In: Proceedings of EMBC, pp. 1271–1274 (2018)
22. Talafha, B., et al.: Multi-dialect Arabic BERT for country-level dialect identification. arXiv preprint arXiv:2007.05612 (2020)
23. Tao, F., Busso, C.: End-to-end audiovisual speech activity detection with bimodal recurrent neural models. Speech Commun. **113**, 25–35 (2019)
24. Torres-Carrasquillo, P.A., et al.: Dialect identification using Gaussian mixture models. In: Proceedings of ODYSSEY (2004)
25. Yala, A., et al.: A deep learning mammography-based model for improved breast cancer risk prediction. Radiology **292**(1), 60–66 (2019)
26. Zaharia, G.E., et al.: Exploring the power of Romanian BERT for dialect identification. In: Proceedings of VarDial, pp. 232–241 (2020)
27. Zhao, Y., et al.: Tibetan multi-dialect speech and dialect identity recognition. Comput. Mater. Continua **60**(3), 1223–1235 (2019)

Risk Automatic Prediction for Social Economy Companies Using Camels

Joseph Gallego-Mejia[1]([✉]) [iD], Daniela Martin-Vega[2] [iD],
and Fabio A. Gonzalez[1] [iD]

[1] Universidad Nacional de Colombia, Bogota, Colombia
{jagallegom,fagonzalezo}@unal.edu.co
[2] Universidad Distrital Francisco Jose de Caldas, Bogota, Colombia
dmartinv@correo.udistrital.edu.co

Abstract. Governments have to supervise and inspect social economy enterprises (SEEs). However, inspecting all SEEs is not possible due to the large number of SEEs and the low number of inspectors in general. We proposed a prediction model based on a machine learning approach. The method was trained with the random forest algorithm with historical data provided by each SEE. Three consecutive periods of data were concatenated. The proposed method uses these periods as input data and predicts the risk of each SEE in the fourth period. The model achieved 76% overall accuracy. In addition, it obtained good accuracy in predicting the high risk of a SEE. We found that the legal nature and the variation of the past-due portfolio are good predictors of the future risk of a SEE. Thus, the risk of a SEE in a future period can be predicted by a supervised machine learning method. Predicting the high risk of a SEE improves the daily work of each inspector by focusing only on high-risk SEEs.

Keywords: Machine learning · Random forest · Forecasting · Regression · CAMELS · Risk prediction

1 Introduction

Reviewing, monitoring and inspecting are important tasks for governments when evaluating social economy enterprises (SEEs). Social economy enterprises are a group of private or semi-private enterprises in which profit distribution and decision making are not related to the asset ownership of each member [8]. Governments have to inspect these SEEs and are responsible for categorizing and measuring companies that have medium-high risk and medium-high severity. Risk relates to the likelihood of a company going into financial failure, i.e., being unable to pay its debts. Severity measures the relative impact of a potential SEE bankruptcy within a relative area, e.g., a town, city or state. It should be noted that all SEEs cannot be inspected on-site due to limitations on the number of inspectors in a given time. Therefore, a good analysis finding medium-high risk

© The Author(s), under exclusive license to Springer Nature Switzerland AG 2022
J. C. Figueroa-García et al. (Eds.): WEA 2022, CCIS 1685, pp. 66–76, 2022.
https://doi.org/10.1007/978-3-031-20611-5_6

SEEs should be performed by supervisors without an on-site inspection. In this paper, we present a model that measures the future risk of financial failure of an SEE using: its financial history; operational reports; the CAMELS rating system, which is a system created in the U.S. to evaluate the overall condition of its banks; and macroeconomic indicators, such as the consumer price index.

This paper presents a novel model to predict the risk of financial failure of an SEE in the next period considering historical financial and operational data. This predictive model is built using machine learning models with the help of historical financial and operational data provided by each SEE. A preprocessing step was performed in order to clean and transform the raw data. This new prototype model shows the opportunities offered by machine learning for the decision making process. Our main hypothesis is that the new model will be a valuable tool for prioritizing which SEE requires inspection by government inspectors.

The rest of this paper is organized as follows. Section 2 reviews related work on bankruptcy prediction and the CAMELS system. Section 3 presents the description of the data. Section 4 presents the description of the proposed model. Section 5 presents the experimental evaluation of the proposed model. Section 6 presents the results and discussions achieved with the proposed model. Finally, Sect. 7 presents the conclusions.

2 Background and Related Work

Social economy enterprises are really important for healthy societies; they provide several jobs and sustain part of the economy. Assessing their performance and possible bankruptcy is a crucial task for governments. Therefore, several machine learning methods have been applied to predict bankruptcy [12,14,17]. These algorithms are based on financial figures such as balance sheet and income statements, company-specific variables and stock market data. In addition, for a more general evaluation of a company, it is necessary to evaluate the qualitative attributes of the company [16].

Several types of methods for predicting bankruptcy have been proposed in the state-of-the-art. In [5], the authors used decision trees to predict whether a given firm will go bankrupt in the following year. They showed that decision trees are better than logit regression. In [11], the authors built a model to predict the distress of a given company. They used logit, probit, multivariate discriminant analysis and artificial neural networks, showing that logit and probit are good, as they have explainable and understandable properties. In contrast, artificial neural networks performed well but had poor explainable and understandable properties. In [3], the authors evaluated 3,000 companies in Romania in eight categories, from AAA to D. They tried to predict their probability of downward transition from one year to the next. They used logit regression and artificial neural network and showed that artificial neural networks perform better than logit regression. In [18], the authors supplemented traditional data, such as financial figures, with quality data, such as a company sharing director or senior managers. With these relationships, a neighborhood prediction model was built. They showed that when quality data is combined with financial data, the performance of the algorithm increases. In [16], the authors evaluated four machine learning techniques: decision trees, neural networks, random forest, and logistic regression. They showed that the random forest outperforms the other methods for bankruptcy prediction.

Financial datasets pose various problems, for example, the ratio of bankrupt to non-bankrupt companies is imbalanced, i.e., there are more non-bankrupt companies. In this case, the algorithm cannot be evaluated with the accuracy metric alone and more robust metrics such as f1-score, precision or recall can be used. Therefore, in [20], the authors propose a comparison between three algorithms that deal with imbalance: probabilistic least-squares classification for outlier detection, an isolation forest, and a one-class support vector machine. They show that probabilistic least-squares classification (LSDA) outperforms the other two methods. The size of the company is also a really important factor to take into account. Another problem is to evaluate small, medium and large companies with the same model. In [9], the authors showed that firm size is a good predictor variable for the success or failure of a firm [5].

The CAMELS model was developed in the United States in 1991 to assess the overall performance of banks through capital adequacy, assets, management capacity, earnings, liquidity and sensitivity to market risk. This model gives the overall health and performance on a rating system between one and five, where one implies safe performance and five implies unsatisfactory performance, of the banking system, but can be used to evaluate other types of companies such as SEEs [1]. In [6], the authors developed an advanced CAMELs model with a Supervisory Risk Assessment and Early Warning Systems to evaluate banks over a two-year period. In [19], the authors developed a new method to calculate the probability of migrating from a low to a high level of risk based on CAMELS. In [2], the authors evaluate the possibility of predicting changes in bank ratings in the following years by showing that they could predict some variables such as capital adequacy, and leverage. In [4], the authors used the CAMELS system to evaluate the performance of Turkish banks in the period from 2001 to 2008, showing that a strong liquidity ratio signifies overall good health. In [13], the authors analyzed the development of the public and private bank sector in India. They showed that CAMELS is a good rating system for assessing bank performance. In [10], the authors evaluate several Indian banks using CAMELS and showing that 95% of the change is given by debt-to-equity ratio, loan-to-deposit ratio, income per employee, capital adequacy ratio, and total investment-to-total assets ratio.

3 Data Description

The Colombian government collects data from each SEE at regular intervals. Some companies have to send information monthly, others every six months. The type of data collected are total assets, total savers, total employees, total associates, financial portfolio per debtor, total income in the period, among others. Each company receives a risk label ranging from one to five, where one indicates low risk and five indicates high risk. The process of labeling each company is performed manually by an inspector. Note that the risk assesses the probability that a new company will default in the next period. In this work, the risk is the value we want to learn to predict with an automated algorithm.

To build the predictive model, we used historical data collected from each SEE provided by the government. The periodicity of the financial reports that each SEE has to submit to the Colombian government varies according to the number of employees, capital, assets, among others. However, all SEEs have to submit their financial reports every semester. For this reason, we selected a semi-annual periodicity for our proposed model. We use semi-annual periodicities from the first half of 2016 to the first half of 2019 (Table 1).

Table 1. Number of social economy enterprises (SEEs) that submitted financial information for four consecutive periods.

Consecutive periods	Numbers of SEEs that presented financial information
2016–1 al 2017–2	3287
2016–2 al 2018–1	2056
2017–1 al 2018–2	1999
2018–1 al 2019–1	2042

The data is very unbalanced due to intrinsic properties. The majority of companies belong to risk 2 or 3, with 46.6% and 51.8% respectively. There are a similar number of companies belonging to risks 1 and 4 with 0.2% and 0.1% respectively. Finally, risk 5 has the lowest number of companies with 0.03%. We used an oversampling technique for companies with risk 1, 4 and 5 and applied an undersampling to companies with risk 2 and 3. The method used to balance the data was SMOTE, which has good results in the literature [1].

4   Model Description

We proposed a supervised machine learning model. A supervised machine learning model takes an input data X and learns to predict an output $\hat{y}$ that is compared to the true value of y. In the present model, the input data is three consecutive periods of historical financial and operational data given by each SEE and the output prediction is the fourth consecutive period of the same historical data.

$$X_t = c + \sum_{i=1}^{p} X_{t-i} + \epsilon_t \qquad (1)$$

We transformed the data as follows: first, historical data from three consecutive periods of the same SEE were concatenated into a single row; second, historical data from the fourth consecutive period are selected as the period to be predicted; finally, we proposed a supervised machine learning model where the model learns a function that predicts the fourth consecutive period given the three consecutive periods. The Eq. 1 presents a mathematical notation of the model representation. Each company was characterized by a set of characteristics that change over time denoted X_t^j where t refers to time and j refers to the characteristic. For each SEE i, we have j features for consecutive periods $t-3$, $t-2$ and $t-1$. A supervised machine learning model predicts the risk for period t.

Furthermore, we hypothesize that the use of macroeconomic variables for each period can increase the power of the model. Therefore, we use the following macroeconomic variables: consumer price index, unemployment rate and gross domestic product.

5   Experimental Evaluation

We developed three slightly different models and compared them to an assessment metric. Our goal was to have a prediction model that could predict risk at each of the risk levels 1 to 5 according to the CAMELS risk model. For each model, we evaluated several regression models: random forest, support vector machines, logistic regression and neural networks.

5.1   Experimental Setup

Table 2. Data description: total number of data, number of training points and number of test points

Total	Training (70%)	Test (30%)
9383	6568	2815

Cross-validation with stratification according to SEE risk was used to select the best model. A 70–30 partition was used for cross-validation. Seventy percent of the data were used as training points and thirty percent were used as test points. The Table 2 shows the number of training and test data points. Each categorical variable was transformed as a dummy variable or one-hot encoding [7]. Eighty variables were used to build the model, such as total liabilities for the period, total deposits, total equity, among others. Table A shows the complete list of variables used. Three types of preprocessing tools were used for the ordinal variables: standardization, or mean removal and variance scaling; min-max scaling; and log-normal. The best result was obtained with log-normal preprocessing. We used four different supervised methods for this problem. The methods we used were: random forest, support vector machines (SVM), logistic regression and neural networks. The results presented in the following section are based on random forest. Random forest was selected because of its good performance compared to the other methods in terms of accuracy. Random forest is a supervised method that ensembles several trees. It uses a voting system to select which decision trees to use for the given problem [15]. A replication method was used to select the trees that the Random Forest considered. Support vector machines was trained using a Gaussian kernel. A random grid was used for hyper parameters tuning of each algorithm. The parameters that were optimized by the search were: number of neurons, number of hidden layers, number of iterations, γ-parameter, C complexity parameter, number of decision trees, maximum depth of each decision tree, number of openings in each node of the decision trees and the minimum number of openings in each leaf of the decision trees (Fig. 1).

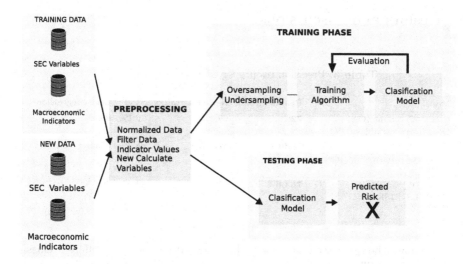

Fig. 1. Experimental setup

Three models were evaluated. The first model takes into account SEE variables, such as chart of accounts, number of debtors, number of employees, and legal nature, among others. In addition, this first model is naive and did not use feature extraction, which is commonly used in machine learning models. The second model used the variables of the first model and additionally the variation between two consecutive periods of several variables such as number of associates, number of employees, total assets, among others. The third model shows the addition of the CAMELS variables and macroeconomic indicators (MI).

As an evaluation measure, we used the precision of each risk class in a confusion matrix. We created a confusion matrix for each of the experiments. Each row of the confusion matrix corresponds to the actual risk value and each column corresponds to the risk predicted by the algorithm. The accuracy is calculated as the ratio between the companies with correct predicted risk i versus all companies belonging to risk i. The matrix allows visualizing the values at which the prediction algorithms make an error, i.e. the prediction model predicts that the risk is i but the actual risk is j. The evaluation equation is $\text{Accuracy}_{\text{risk}_i} =$ Number of companies that was predicted as risk i and the real risk is i / Number of companies predicted in risk i. The predicted model is expected to have the lowest possible error when comparing the predicted risk with the actual risk. For this experiment, it is important to consider prediction models that maximize accuracy when the risk is higher. Since high-risk SEEs are the main concern of the government. Those high-risk SEEs with medium-high severity may affect a large number of people and, consequently, may affect the country's economy. For the latter reason, the model needs to have high confidence in those SEEs that have high risk.

6   Results and Discussions

Table 3. Precision results for each proposed model

Model	Random forest	Neural networks	SVM	Logist regression
Chart of account (CA) + Descriptive variables (DV)	**72%**	69.3%	70.1%	65.5%
CA + DV + Variation between periods (VBP)	**70.95%**	68.3%	68.2%	63.5%
CA + DV + VBP + CAMELS/RISK + MI	**76.66%**	75.5%	74.5%	70.3%

Table 3 shows the precision result for each predicted model using different classification models. The best classification method in each model is random forest. Therefore, the following analysis uses only the random forest as a classification method. The first model achieved an overall accuracy of 72%. Table 4 shows the confusion matrix for the first proposed model. The fourth highest risk achieves only 9% accuracy. Most of the SEEs fall between risk two and three. However, the assumption for the following proposed models is that the accuracy for the fourth risk can be improved.

Table 4. Confusion matrix of the first model

	1	2	3	4	5
1	**14%**	79%	7%		
2		**80%**	20%		
3		33%	**67%**	1%	
4		7%	84%	**9%**	
5		100%			**0%**

The second proposed model did not improve accuracy. This model achieved only 70.95% accuracy. Table 5 shows the confusion matrix of the third proposed model. This third proposed model achieves an overall accuracy of 76.66%. In this case, our model can predict with 18% accuracy the fourth risk. In this model, we found that if the legal nature of the SEE is an employee fund or a cooperative, the risk of SEE increases. In addition, we found that the variation of past-due portfolio between consecutive periods is a good predictor of SEE risk. We selected the third model as the best because of its overall accuracy and good results in predicting the risk of the fourth period.

Table 5. Confusion matrix of the third model

	1	2	3	4	5
1	**25%**	75%			
2		**78%**	22%		
3		22%	**77%**		
4			82%	**18%**	
5		100%			**0%**

The proposed prediction model for the government showed good results in predicting the fourth risk of an SEE. This model could be improved if we add new variables and/or feature extractions. In addition, we could add more variables from the chart of accounts. In the proposed prediction model we did not take into account whether or not the government inspected the SEE. This information could help predict the real risk of some SEEs.

The current forecasting model could be improved if we took a larger data window than the last 10 years. A larger window has the risk of adding noise to the model, as the model could learn patterns that are not necessarily true with the current market dynamics. However, there are a large number of cyclical patterns within the economy, so using a larger window could be a good opportunity to improve the accuracy of the model.

7 Conclusions

Governments have to supervise and inspect social economy enterprises. These enterprises present different levels of risk depending on their management and finances. In this paper, we seek to extract knowledge from historical data provided by each social economy enterprise. The proposed best prediction model presented in Sect. 5 aims to show the impact that machine learning models can have on the management decision process. We show that we can build a prediction model using data stored on government servers. This model shows that using this data we can predict whether a social economy enterprise will enter a higher risk in the next period. The best machine learning method for this model is random forest. In addition, the model is very good at predicting the fourth risk. With this model, the government could improve the management of its inspectors. For future work, more accounting plan variables could be included. In addition, it could be included whether an SEE was previously inspected by the government.

Acknowledgements. This work was partially funded by "Contrato interadministrativo 232" between *Universidad Nacional de Colombia* and *Supersolidaria*.

A Variables Used

- Type of organization
- Whether it is a cooperative, fund or other type of organization.
- Type of company: Multi-active, employee funds.
- Type of supervision: 1,2,3.
- Group Niif of the organization
- Department of the organization
- Municipality of the organization
- Category of the organization
- Number of associates
- Number of employees
- Number of offices
- Number of correspondents
- Number of savers
- Number of debtors
- Total assets of the organization
- Client portfolio for the period
- Net client portfolio for the period
- Clients' consumer portfolio for the period
- Clients' housing portfolio for the period
- Total liabilities for the period
- Total deposits
- Total deposits in bank accounts
- Total CDT deposits
- Total contractual deposits
- Total permanent savings deposits
- Total equity
- Total social contributions
- Total surplus
- Total income for the period
- Total expenses for the period
- Total gross portfolio
- Total past due portfolio
- Total female members
- Total male members
- Consolidated risk rating
- Risk rating
- Camel rating
- Credit risk
- Liquidity risk
- Operational Risk
- Sarassoft risk

- Customer commercial portfolio for the period
- Clients' micro portfolio for the period
- Total investments of the organization
- Cash receivable under agreement
- Variation between two consecutive periods of employees
- Change between two consecutive periods in the number of offices
- Change in the number of savers between two consecutive periods
- Variation between two consecutive periods in the number of debtors.
- Change between two consecutive periods in total assets
- Variation between two consecutive periods of gross portfolio
- Variation between two consecutive periods of the consumer portfolio
- Variation between two consecutive periods of the housing portfolio
- Change between two consecutive periods for the commercial portfolio
- Change in micro portfolio between two consecutive periods
- Change between two consecutive periods in the investment portfolio
- Variation between two consecutive periods of covenants receivable
- Variation between two consecutive periods of liabilities
- Change in deposits between two consecutive periods
- Total capital of the organization
- Total assets of the organization
- Total administration expenses
- Total profitability of the organization
- Organization's liquidity
- Variation between two consecutive periods of associates
- Change between two consecutive periods in demand deposits
- Variation between two consecutive periods of CDT deposits
- Variation between two consecutive periods of contractual deposits
- Variation between two consecutive periods of permanent savings deposits
- Variation between two consecutive periods of shareholders' equity
- Variation between two consecutive periods of social contributions
- Variation between two consecutive periods of the surpluses
- Variation of income between two consecutive periods
- Change in expenses between two consecutive periods
- Variation between two consecutive periods of overdue accounts receivable
- Variation between two consecutive periods of female associates
- Variation between two consecutive periods of male associates
- Variation between two consecutive periods for other associates
- Risk weighting (variable to be predicted)

References

1. Chawla, N.V., Bowyer, K.W., Hall, L.O., Kegelmeyer, W.P.: Smote: synthetic minority over-sampling technique. J. Artif. Intell. Res. **16**, 321–357 (2002)
2. Derviz, A., Podpiera, J.: Predicting bank camels and s&p ratings: the case of the czech republic. Emerg. Mark. Financ. Trade **44**(1), 117–130 (2008)

3. Dima, A.M., Vasilache, S.: Credit risk modeling for companies default prediction using neural networks. Romanian J. Econ. Forecast. **19**(3), 127–143 (2016)
4. Dincer, H., Gencer, G., Orhan, N., Sahinbas, K.: A performance evaluation of the Turkish banking sector after the global crisis via camels ratios. Procedia. Soc. Behav. Sci. **24**, 1530–1545 (2011)
5. Gepp, A., Kumar, K., Bhattacharya, S.: Business failure prediction using decision trees. J. Forecast. **29**(6), 536–555 (2010)
6. Gilbert, R.A., Meyer, A.P., Vaughan, M.D.: Could a camels downgrade model improve off-site surveillance? Can. Parliamentary Rev. **84**, 47–63 (2002)
7. Hardy, M.A.: Regression with dummy variables. no. 93. Sage (1993)
8. Julia, J.F., Server, R.J.: Social economy companies in the Spanish agricultural sector: delimitation and situation in the context of the European union. Ann. Pub. Coop. Econ. **74**(3), 465–488 (2003)
9. Kalak, I.E., Hudson, R.: The effect of size on the failure probabilities of SMEs: an empirical study on the us market using discrete hazard model. International Review of Financial Analysis **43**, 135–145 (2016). https://doi.org/10.1016/j.irfa.2015.11.009
10. Kaur, P.: A financial performance analysis of the Indian banking sector using camel model. IUP J. Bank Manage. **14**(4), 19 (2015)
11. Khermkhan, J., Chancharat, N., Chancharat, S., Theinthong, A.: Differences in financial distress prediction models for small and medium-sized enterprises. Kasetsart J. Soc. Sci. **36**(3), 533–543 (2015)
12. Kim, M.J., Kang, D.K.: Ensemble with neural networks for bankruptcy prediction. Exp. Syst. Appl. **37**, 3373–3379 (2010). https://doi.org/10.1016/j.eswa.2009.10.012
13. Nandi, J.K.: Comparative performance analysis of select public and private sector banks in India: an application of camel model. J. Insti. Pub. Enter. **36**(3/4), 1–28 (2013)
14. Olson, D.L., Delen, D., Meng, Y.: Comparative analysis of data mining methods for bankruptcy prediction. Decis. Sup. Syst. **52**, 464–473 (2012). https://doi.org/10.1016/j.dss.2011.10.007
15. Pavlov, Y.L.: Random forests. Random Forests, pp. 1–122 (2001). https://doi.org/10.1201/9780429469275-8
16. Ptak-Chmielewska, A., Matuszyk, A.: The importance of financial and non-financial ratios in SMEs bankruptcy prediction (2018)
17. Tinoco, M.H., Wilson, N.: Financial distress and bankruptcy prediction among listed companies using accounting, market and macroeconomic variables. In: International Review of Financial Analysis 30, 394–419 (2013). https://doi.org/10.1016/j.irfa.2013.02.013
18. Tobback, E., Bellotti, T., Moeyersoms, J., Stankova, M., Martens, D.: Bankruptcy prediction for smes using relational data. Decis. Sup. Syst. **102**, 69–81 (10 2017). https://doi.org/10.1016/j.dss.2017.07.004
19. Whalen, G.W.: A hazard model of camels downgrades of low-risk community banks (2005)
20. Zoričák, M., Gnip, P., Drotár, P., Gazda, V.: Bankruptcy prediction for small- and medium-sized companies using severely imbalanced datasets. Econ. Model. **84**, 165–176 (2020). https://doi.org/10.1016/j.econmod.2019.04.003

Energy Performance Clustering and Data Visualization for Solar-Wind Hybrid Energy Systems

Harrynson Ramirez-Murillo[1]([✉])([iD]), Fabian Salazar-Caceres[1]([iD]),
Martha P. Camargo-Martinez[1]([iD]), Alvaro A. Patiño-Forero[2]([iD]),
and Francy J. Mendez-Casallas[3]([iD])

[1] Facultad de Ingeniería, Programa de Ingeniería Eléctrica, Universidad De La Salle,
Grupo de Investigación CALPOSALLE, Bogotá D.C., Colombia
{haramirez,jfsalazar,mpcamargo}@unisalle.edu.co
[2] Facultad de Ingeniería, Programa de Ingeniería en Automatización, Universidad De
La Salle, Grupo de Investigación AVARC, Bogotá D.C., Colombia
alapatino@unisalle.edu.co
[3] Facultad de Ingeniería, Programa de Ingeniería Ambiental y Sanitaria, Universidad
De La Salle, Grupo de Investigación Producción Animal Sostenible,
Bogotá D.C., Colombia
fmendez@unisalle.edu.co

Abstract. This research article proposes a methodology based on data analytics, to compute well-known energy performance ratios like Capacity Factor (CF), Performance Yields (Y_r) and Performance Ratio (PR) used for evaluating solar-wind hybrid energy systems. These terms are developed to study performance in renewable energy systems considering an estimation of energy resources. The methodology implemented is divided twofold, first, we deploy a recognized unsupervised machine learning technique as, k-means data clustering algorithm, considering the following feature space: time, solar radiation, wind speed, and temperature, which are renewable energy potentials available in the campus at Universidad de la Salle in Bogotá, Colombia, acquired by a local weather station which is considered as the case study. Second, according to this data-driven model, the performance factors are computed, yielding technological solutions and recommendations considering the data collected, analyzed, and visualized.

Keywords: Clustering algorithm · Machine learning · Solar power generation · Wind power generation · Hybrid power systems

Supported by Vicerrectoría de Investigación y Transferencia (VRIT), at Universidad de la Salle, Bogotá, through the research project under institutional code IELE221-211.

© The Author(s), under exclusive license to Springer Nature Switzerland AG 2022
J. C. Figueroa-García et al. (Eds.): WEA 2022, CCIS 1685, pp. 77–89, 2022.
https://doi.org/10.1007/978-3-031-20610-5_7

1   Introduction

There exists research works to analyze energy potentials of renewable resources which are based on either complex knowledge of geographical regions, both in terms of components and characteristics of the natural environment, or in the interpretation of complex spatial modeling maps [1]. These works established the gap between data analysis tools, information management and evaluation to obtain data-driven mathematical models that represent the energy potential of a given geographical region.

Research works such as [2], energy resource evaluations were performed considering wind, water, photovoltaic (PV) energy, and biomass in Romania using data mining based on clustering techniques, we found that the analysis is expected to be extended considering new algorithms and potential resources. In the study, [3], clustering and Principal Component Analysis (PCA) techniques were applied to estimate photovoltaic energy potential in four cities in Colombia leading a reference work to this research. Finally, in [4] uses a methodology that combines Machine Learning, Image Processing, and Geographic Information Systems for determining large-scale photovoltaic potentials which enabling us to a future extension of the methodology proposed on this paper.

Our main approach is to quantify the feasibility through well-known performance ratios of implementing renewable energy generation systems, based on solar and wind energy, by calculating the annual and seasonal capacity factor (CF), performance yields (Y_r), and performance ratio (PR), considering the effects of available energy resource variability. Three approaches are possible: first, solar and wind power profiles are correlated with power demand; second, residual load curves can be used, where the available renewable energy resource is supplied with a time scale in hours; and finally, by quantifying the penetration level of these technologies, that is, the percentage of total energy supplied by each non-conventional energy generation system considered [5].

Some studies have contemplated solar photovoltaic and wind energy solutions in Bogota, both at urban and rural levels, the main contribution of this research work focuses on depicting a methodology to analyze a particular data set measuring weather variables to study photovoltaic and wind energy potentials available at Universidad de la Salle, in Bogotá, Colombia. For this purpose, the k-means data clustering technique is used, a method that requires prior knowledge of the optimal clusters, which are obtained through the graphical analysis of validation indexes such as Silhouette (S), Partition (SC), Separation (SI) and Xie and Beni (XB). Likewise, the technical feasibility of implementing a solar-wind hybrid system will be estimated, based on the estimation of the corresponding performance ratios CF, Y_r, and PR, according to the available energy resource. Finally, the analysis and conclusions are developed.

2   Methodology

The approach is to identify and discover fundamental patterns of the data set measuring physical quantities obtained of the weather station, referenced as

NOVALYNX 110-WS-18. A k-means-based algorithm is proposed to determine the optimal number of clusters based on similarity metrics between the most representative point of each set. To build this clustering data model different stages are considered, comprising this unsupervised learning process: First, data preprocessing is performed, which includes normalization, cleaning, and data preparation, then a features selection is developed. Subsequently, basic statistical properties are computed, as well as any visualization of connections between the features. Then, the implementation of the unsupervised learning algorithm is considered, to evaluate its performance by employing the validation indexes. Finally, the estimation of the performance ratios is obtained using the clustering model developed to quantify the available energy potential.

2.1 Available Solar Energy

This physical phenomenon represents the emission of energy from the sun in electromagnetic radiation, which is quantified in units of irradiance H_t [Wh/$\left(\text{m}^2\text{day}\right)$] [3]. This form of energy propagates in vacuum space, reaching the surface of the Earth at certain direction and angle, depending on the latitude and longitude for a specific geographic location. Furthermore, solar radiation represents the energy flux that is received on a surface per unit area [Wh/m^2], which can oscillate over the earth's surface around 1000 [Wh/m^2] [6]. The relationship between irradiance and daily radiation is given by Eq. (1):

$$I = \int_{t_1}^{t_2} Rad(t)dt \quad \left[\frac{\text{Wh}}{\text{m}^2\text{day}}\right] \tag{1}$$

This expression is a power definite integral among a period of time t_1 and t_2 resulting in a expression quantifying the total energy provided by the solar resource. On the other hand, the daily solar radiation $Rad(t)$, is fitted through a second grade polynomial equations [7], as shown in the Eq. (2), where t is given in hours [h]. Also, this formulation considers the solar modules dimensions a_{panel} and b_{panel} corresponding to width and length, respectively, the number of solar panels N_{PV}, yielding the daily photovoltaic energy E_{PV} showed in the following Eq. (3):

$$Rad(t) = a_{PV}t^2 + b_{PV}t + c_{PV}t^2 \quad \left[\frac{\text{W}}{\text{m}^2}\right] \tag{2}$$

$$E_{PV} = A_{PV} \cdot I = N_{PV} \cdot a_{panel} \cdot b_{panel} \cdot I \quad \left[\frac{\text{Wh}}{\text{m}^2\text{day}}\right] \tag{3}$$

2.2 Available Wind Energy

An important factor in determining the wind potential of a given location is the air density ρ, which can be obtained directly, i.e., by air mass and volume measurements, or by an indirect method, where it depends on the ambient temperature, atmospheric pressure, and height above sea level [8]. Besides, the instantaneous wind power $P_w(t)$ is proportional to the cube of the wind speed $v(t)$ and the swept area of the wind turbine blades A_w [9], as shown in Eq. (4).

$$P_w(t) = \frac{1}{2} \cdot \rho \cdot A_w \cdot v^3 \cdot C_p \quad [\text{W}] \tag{4}$$

The Wind Power Density (WPD) is a term applied to classifying zones according to their potential, and is obtained by dividing the wind power by the surface area, as shown in the Eq. (5). To obtain the daily available wind power E_W, the Eq. (6) is defined, where r_w and N_w correspond to the turbine blades radius and the number of wind turbines, respectively. Theoretically, there is a limit for the maximum energy that can be harnessed from the wind quantified by the Power Coefficient C_p, where its maximum value corresponds to 0.593 and is defined as the Betz limit [10].

$$WPD(t) = \frac{P_w}{A_w} = \frac{1}{2} \cdot \rho \cdot v^3(t) \cdot C_p \quad \left[\frac{\text{W}}{\text{m}^2}\right] \tag{5}$$

$$E_w = A_w \int_{t_1}^{t_2} WPD(t)dt = N_w \cdot \pi \cdot r_w^2 \cdot \int_{t_1}^{t_2} WPD(t)dt \quad \left[\frac{\text{Wh}}{\text{day}}\right] \tag{6}$$

2.3   Capacity Factor (CF)

The capacity factor (CF) is computed as the ratio between the energy supplied and the rated peak energy in a period of time $E_N = P_N(t_2 - t_1)$ [Wh/day], considering the time interval t_1 and t_2 as independent variable intercepts t. Therefore, any feasible value, depends on either, the energy resource or the technological solution selected. The common feasible value ranges for the CF considering solar and wind energy resources are into CF_{PV} (%) $\in$ [25, 35] % and CF_w (%) $\in$ [25, 45] %, respectively [5]. The terms CF_{PV} (%) y CF_w (%) are shown in Eqs. (7) and (8), where E_{PV} and FE_W are obtained from Eqs. (3) y (6), respectively.

$$CF_{PV}(\%) = \left[\frac{E_{PV}}{E_{NPV}}\right] \times 100[\%] \tag{7}$$

$$CF_w(\%) = \left[\frac{E_W}{E_{Nw}}\right] \times 100[\%] \tag{8}$$

2.4   Performance Yields (Y_r):

This index is defined as the ratio among the total energy density H_t [$Wh/(m^2 day)$], which corresponds to, either, solar energy (1) or wind energy (6), and the reference power density G_0 [$W/(m^2 day)$], according to the energy resource considered, this expression is shown in Eq. (9) [11], where $G_0 = 1000$ [$W/(m^2 day)$] in PV systems, or $G_0 = (1/2) \cdot \rho \cdot v_{nom}^3$ [$W/(m^2 day)$]

in a wind energy system, where v_{nom} consists in the nominal wind turbine speed in $[m/s]$ [12].

$$Y_R = \frac{H_t}{G_0} \; [h] \qquad (9)$$

2.5   Performance Ratio (PR):

This factor shows the real energy system performance referenced before the ideal operation. It is defined as a dimensionless ratio between the real performance Y_f and the reference Y_r, whose units are energy density $[Wh/(m^2 day)]$ given in the Eq. (10) [11]:

$$PR(\%) = \frac{Y_f}{Y_r} \times \; 100[\%] \qquad (10)$$

In this part of the methodology proposed a review on a general framework for studying the formulae and ratios to quantify the energy harnessed by solar and wind resources are depicted. With these expressions, we analyze the potential renewable energy which can be used to deploy the most efficient engineering solutions in the case study selected.

2.6   Data Analysis

Our work focus on developing a strategy to compute the above performance ratios through data science techniques. In order to introduce the estimation approach, we have assumed that an unknown probability density function (PDF) generates the sampled data which are independent and identically distributed. By computing the optimal centroids through validation indexes the underlying PDF is represented as a product of densities, considering the scale and displacement parameters in a maximum likelihood estimation framework. For a further explanation of these propositions, the reader is referred to [13]. To do so the following sections depict the general process to implement the unsupervised machine learning algorithm which implements the data-driven model used to analyze the potential energy harnessed.

Data Normalization. Let $X \in R^n$ correspond to the data obtained from the weather station, it is the input data set with N observations, n corresponds to the number of input features and R is the set of real numbers. From this space, k clusters can be characterized, based on a measure of similarity (dissimilarity) between samples.

In the literature, there are no unique universal rules for either normalization or standardization as a preprocessing method, however, normalization is particularly useful in those algorithms involving neural networks and distance measures such as clustering and classification. For this reason, the $\min - \max$ normalization is adopted in this research work which consists to applying a linear transformation on the sample $x_i \; \forall \; i$, as shown in Eq. (11), which are initially in real-world units, to dimensionless data x_{inorm} in the range $[0,1]$, where 0 value corresponds to $\min(x_i)$ and $\max(x_i)$, respectively.

$$\mathbf{x}_{inorm} = \frac{\mathbf{x}_i - \min(\mathbf{x}_i)}{\max(\mathbf{x}_i) - \min(\mathbf{x}_i)} \tag{11}$$

Fuzzy C-Means Algorithm. The k-means algorithm is a clustering method non hierarchical and unsupervised, therefore is not required a prior knowledge of the data [14]. So, Let a sample set $X = \{x_1, \ldots, x_n\}$, a finite clusters number k, and a centroids set $c_1, \ldots, c_n$. Moreover, it is defined an assignment rule for all the data points in R^n mapping to the set of clusters, considering an euclidean metric as reference in the Eq. (12) in a L_2 space used as a similarity measure.

$$dist(\mathbf{x}_i, \mathbf{c}_j) = ||\mathbf{x}_i - \mathbf{c}_j|| = \sqrt{(\mathbf{x}_i - \mathbf{c}_j)^2} \quad \forall \ i, j \tag{12}$$

The method above is the classical $k-$means algorithm, the fuzzy formulation varies slightly compared to the original technique, such is shown in Eq. (13):

$$J_m = \sum_{i=1}^{N} \sum_{j=1}^{C} u_{ij}^m ||\mathbf{x}_i - \mathbf{c}_j||^2 \quad , \quad 1 \leq m < \infty \tag{13}$$

where m is any value in the real line $[0,1]$, u_{ij} corresponds to the degree of membership of $\mathbf{x}_i$ in the cluster j. The soft partition is carried out through an iterative optimization process of the objective function J_m, and decision variables u_{ij} and $\mathbf{c}_j$, given a closed form solution as shown in Eqs. (14) and (15), respectively.

$$u_{ij} = \frac{1}{\sum_{k=1}^{c} \left(\frac{||\mathbf{x}_i - \mathbf{c}_j||}{||\mathbf{x}_i - \mathbf{c}_k||} \right)^{\frac{2}{m-1}}} \tag{14}$$

$$c_j = \frac{\sum_{i=1}^{N} u_{ij}^m \cdot x_i}{\sum_{i=1}^{N} u_{ij}^m} \tag{15}$$

Principal Component Analysis (PCA): This algorithm explains most variance of the data, considering a low dimensional representation in R^p of the original feature space R^n, with $p < n$, the aim is to find the principal components (eigenvectors) paired with a weight (eigenvalue) comprising a new basis to represent the original data. Hence, a covariance matrix Σ is computed in Eq. (16) as the expected value over the whole data points x_i:

$$\Sigma = \mathbb{E}\left[\boldsymbol{xx}^T\right] \tag{16}$$

Then the optimization problem solved through the computation of covariance matrix eigendecomposition is shown in Eq. (17):

$$\underset{||v||_2 = 1}{\operatorname{argmax}} \boldsymbol{v}^T \boldsymbol{\Sigma} \boldsymbol{v}. \tag{17}$$

Validation Indexes. For the selection of the optimal number of clusters $k = C$, is required to consider the interpretation of validation indexes, since the researcher's decision-making plays an important role in selecting this parameter [15]. For the calculation of these indexes, the sample average distance to the centroid of the same cluster and the nearest one is required, which is equivalent to cohesion and separation, respectively. The indexes considered in this research work, together with their interpretations and criteria for the graphical selection of the optimal clusters, respectively [3], are shown below:

Silhouette Index: is defined as the difference between separation and cohesion, divided by the larger of the two. Graphically, the optimal number of clusters is selected by the first local maximum. The Partition Index, on the other hand, is defined as the quotient of the sum of all cohesions divided by the separations. Graphically, the optimal number of clusters corresponds to the smallest slope of the data. Likewise, considering the Separation Index, the minimum separation distance that allows validating each partition is used for the calculation. The graphical interpretation is similar to that of sc to select the optimal number of centroids. Finally, the Xie and Beni index is calculated as the quotient between the total variance and the minimum separation of the clusters. The optimal number of clusters is selected graphically from the first local minimum.

3 Discussion and Results

In this section, the results analyzed for the Universidad de la Salle at Bogotá, Colombia are shown. The dataset X considered in this research is based on the features: Time t [h], Solar Radiation Rad [W/m^2], Wind Speed Cubed v^3 [m^3/s^3] and Temperature T [°C]. For the sake of clarification, the samples collected in the dataset are dated from 12/13/2018 to 03/09/2020, at times 2:30 and 6:40, respectively. Also, the wind speed cubed v^3 is considered a modified feature, because the daily wind energy available is directly proportional to this quantity, as shown in the Eqs. (4), (5) and (6). Likewise, the actual data are normalized by the Eq. (11) resulting in 56807 normalized registers (observations).

Thereafter, we implement the Fuzzy-C means algorithm in the normalized dataset and subsequently denormalized the centroids obtained, which are shown in Table 1. The optimal number of clusters C corresponds to 3 and is determined by graphical analysis of the validation indexes S, SC, SI and XB, whose interpretation is found in the previous section.

From the coordinates of the true centroids in Table 1, considering the feature Time t [h] as an independent variable for each of the real features $Rad(t)$, $v^3(t)$ and $T(t)$, as shown in the Eqs. (2), (18) and (19), the real polynomial coefficients of Table 2 are obtained by performing a second-degree polynomial fitting.

$$v^3(t) = a_w t^2 + b_w t + c_w \quad \left[\frac{\text{m}^3}{\text{s}^3}\right] \tag{18}$$

$$T(t) = a_T t^2 + b_T t + c_T \quad [°\text{C}] \tag{19}$$

Table 1. Normalized and denormalized centroids coordinates by means of fuzzy C-means

Normalized features	t_{norm} [-]	Rad_{nom} [-]	v_{norm}^3 [-]	T_{norm} [-]
Normalized centroids coordinates	0.1773	0.0145	0.0030	0.3155
	0.5231	0.3289	0.0349	0.6125
	0.8412	0.0156	0.0089	0.4312
Denormalized features	t [h]	Rad [W/m^2]	v^3 [m^3/s^2]	T [°C]
Real centroids coordinates	4.2252	15.3215	1.9429	12.5973
	12.4676	348.4457	22.3315	17.9779
	20.0489	16.5696	5.7057	14.6932

Table 2. Polynomial coefficientes for $Rad(t)$, $v^3(t)$ y T(t)

Features\Coefficients	a	b	c
$Rad(t)$ [W/m^2]	−5.3781	130.4259	−440.4655
$v^3(t)$ [m^3/s^3]	−0.3293	8.3268	−27.8400
T(t) [°C]	−0.0673	1.7666	6.3783

On the other hand, the normalized features in R^3 t_{norm}, v_{norm}^3 y Rad_{norm} are depicted in Fig. 1a, for $C = 3$. The R^2-dimensional planes Rad_{norm} vs. t_{norm}, v_{norm}^3 vs. t_{norm} and T_{norm} vs. t_{norm}, show the level sets which represents the cluster similarity and membership, where the colormap corresponds to a level membership interval between $[0.4, 0.9]$, showed in the Figs. 1b, 1c y 1d, respectively. From the parametric fitted curve based on the features $Rad(t)$, $v^3(t)$ y T(t), is obtained the Fig. 2, for $t \in [0, 24]$ [h].

To compute the total daily available energy in the load E_N [Wh/day], according to the energy resources, at Universidad de la Salle, Bogotá campus, we calculate $E_{NPV} = 116668.5714$ [Wh/day] [16], moreover, potential wind energy is estimated is $E_{Nw} = 2.1504$ [Wh/day], where $P_{Nw} = 100$ [W]. Then, considering the parameterized functions $Rad(t)$ [W/m^2] and $v^3(t)$ [m^3/s^3], they comprise the estimated energy to supply at $t_2 - t_1$ [h]. For this purpose, it is important to clarify that 6 polycrystalline 320 [W] panels are considered, with $a_{panel} = 1.956$ [m] and $b_{panel} = 0.992$ [m], and a wind microturbine model WSC100 of 100 [W], $r_w = 0.26$ [m].

When analyzing the results obtained for CF_{PV} (%) and CF_w (%) in Table 4, the proposed photovoltaic technological solution is technically feasible, while the wind solution does not meet that condition. These results agree with previous studies carried out at Bogotá [3,7,9], with well-known solar and wind energy potentials. However, the latter resource is, mainly, harnessed at the rural level electrification, whereas, at the urban level is recommended to use vertical axis wind turbines with a startup speed for winds below 1.5 [m/s]. Finally, the results obtained for Y_r and PR (%) show the availability in equivalent hours of the

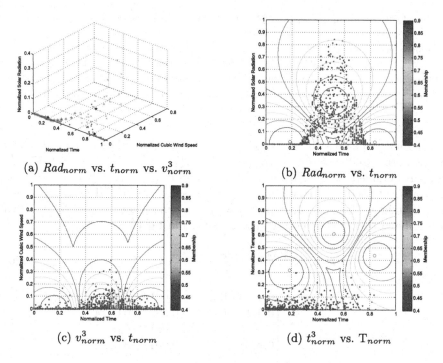

(a) Rad_{norm} vs. t_{norm} vs. v_{norm}^3

(b) Rad_{norm} vs. t_{norm}

(c) v_{norm}^3 vs. t_{norm}

(d) t_{norm}^3 vs. T_{norm}

Fig. 1. Normalized Features in R^3 and R^2

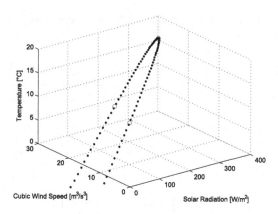

Fig. 2. Parametric curve for $Rad(t)[\text{W/m}^2]$, $v^3(t)[\text{m}^3/\text{s}^3]$ y $T(t)[^\circ\text{C}]$, $t \in [0, 24)[h]$

reference power density G_0 and its approach to an ideal solution for each energy resources considered.

To improve this data visualization applying the PCA analysis, we consider the data covariance matrix Σ of the Eq. (21), which comes from the dataset X. The eigenvalues and eigenvectors of the Table 5 are computed, considering two eigenpairs of greater magnitude, which correspond to λ_3 and λ_4 in the Table 5, with

Table 3. Performance ratios CF (%), Y_r y PR (%) for each energy resource

Available energy resource	t_1 [h]	t_2 [h]	A [m²]	E_N [Wh/DÍA]	CF [%]	Y_r [h]	PR [%]
Photovoltaic	4.0552	20.1962	11.6421	116668.5714	37.6135	3.7693	.62.0857
Wind	3.9652	21.3211	0.2123	1029.2054	2.1504	0.1702	59.3000

a contribution percentage of 93.6521 [%]. Likewise, the relative error obtained for the normalized centroids, corresponds to $E_r(\%) = [0.6772 \ 0.5178 \ 0.4758]^T$, which is obtained by the Eq. (20), where c_j and $c_{jreconstruct}$ correspond to the centroids obtained by Fuzzy C-means and those reconstructed by PCA, which are shown in Tables 1 and 4, respectively. The feature projection on R^2 is shown in Fig. 3 and their coordinates C_{PCA} are shown in Eq. (22).

$$Er(\%) = \frac{\|c_{jreconstruct} - c_j\|}{\|c_j\|} \cdot 100 \ [\%], \forall \ j \tag{20}$$

$$\Sigma = cov(X) = \begin{bmatrix} 0.0844 & 0.0019 & 0.0013 & 0.0151 \\ 0.0019 & 0.0305 & 0.0032 & 0.0174 \\ 0.0013 & 0.0032 & 0.0012 & 0.0017 \\ 0.0151 & 0.0174 & 0.0017 & 0.0226 \end{bmatrix} \tag{21}$$

Table 4. Normalized centroids coordinates and denormalized reconstructed by means of PCA

Normalized features	t_{norm} [-]	Rad_{nom} [-]	v^3_{norm} [-]	T_{norm} [-]
Normalized centroids coordinates reconstructed	0.1770	0.0132	0.0022	0.3174
	0.5234	0.3300	0.0387	0.6104
	0.8406	0.0131	0.0106	0.4344
Denormalized features	t [h]	Rad [W/m²]	v^3 [m³/s²]	T [°C]
Denormalized centroids coordinates reconstructed	4.2175	13.9456	1.4209	12.6315
	12.4751	349.6325	24.7891	17.9406
	20.0348	13.8766	6.8071	14.7519

$$C_{PCA} = \begin{bmatrix} -0.3525 & -0.0726 \\ 0.0890 & 0.2631 \\ 0.3154 & -0.1630 \end{bmatrix} \tag{22}$$

Table 5. Covariance matrix eigenvalues and eigenvectors

Eigenvalues	λ_1	λ_2	λ_3	λ_4
	0.0016	0.0076	0.0421	0.0886
Principal components percentage [%]	1.1303	5.2175	30.1628	63.4893
Eigenvectors	0.0217	0.1393	−0.2331	0.9622
	0.1383	0.5718	0.8013	0.1083
	−0.9888	0.1251	0.0782	0.0232
	−0.0521	−0.7987	0.5453	0.2489

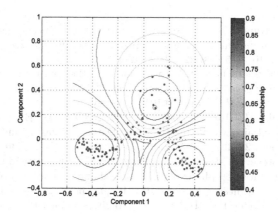

Fig. 3. Eigenvalue projection in R^2, λ_3 y λ_4

4   Conclusions

The main conclusions through the application of this methodology are the following: initially, it is technically feasible to implement a photovoltaic system at Universidad de la Salle, Bogotá, Candelaria campus, whereas a wind energy system does not meet the minimum CF, due to the lack of low speed turbine technologies, the values correspond to 37.6135 (%) and 2.1504 (%), respectively. Then, the $CF_{PV}(\%)$ and $CFw(\%)$ change according to the proposed technological solution, however, the flexibility is closely related to the system autonomy, i.e., as the CF decreases or increases, the design of a hybrid on-grid or off-grid system is required. As long as the CF approaches 1, the required auxiliary storage devices sizing is increased, affecting their economic feasibility. Particularly, a low value of $CF_w(\%)$ shows that commercial wind microturbine models with nominal power ratings below 100 [W] and startup speeds below 1.5 [m/s] are required, which improves the technical feasibility to implement energy solutions for this output power range. Moreover, the reference efficiency Y_R determines the hours of availability of the reference power density G_0, which agrees with the information provided by the interactive atlas of the colombian Institute of Hydrology, Meteorology and Environmental Studies (IDEAM), regarding the distribution of the average daily solar brightness, given in hours of sunshine per day, which corresponds to 3.7693 $[h]$, while for wind resource this information is not available yet. In addition, to indicating the technical feasibility of implementing these technologies using the CF, the PR shows how close to an ideal scenario the proposed energy solutions are. Finally, for a better understanding and visualization the PCA technique leads a different features representation in a reduced dimension, minimizing the loss of information, explaining the variance with certain information and improving the analysis elucidated.

References

1. Farooq, M.K., Kumar, S.: An assessment of renewable energy potential for electricity generation in Pakistan. Renew. Sustain. Energy Rev. **20**, 240–254 (2013). https://doi.org/10.1016/j.rser.2012.09.042
2. Grigoras, G., Scarlatache, F.: An assessment of the renewable energy potential using a clustering-based data mining method. Case study in romania. Energy **81**, 416–429 (2015). https://doi.org/10.1016/j.energy.2014
3. Ramirez-Murillo, H., Torres-Pinzon, C.A., Forero-Garcia, E.F.: Estimación del Potencial Fotovoltaico Mediante Minería de Datos en Cuatro Ciudades de Colombia. TecnoLógicas **22**(46), 65–85 (2019). https://doi.org/10.22430/22565337.1345
4. Walch, A., Castello, R., Mohajeri, N., Scartezzini, J.L.: Big data mining for the estimation of hourly rooftop photovoltaic potential and its uncertainty. Appl. Energy **262**, 114404 (2019). https://doi.org/10.1016/j.apenergy.2019.114404
5. Ershad, A.M., Brecha, R.J., Hallinan, K.: Analysis of solar photovoltaic and wind power potential in Afghanistan. Renew. Energy. **85**, 445–453 (2016). https://doi.org/10.1016/j.renene.2015.06.067
6. Myasnikova, T.V., Kirillova, A.A., Ivanova, S.P., Sveklova, O.V., Nadezhdina, O.A.: Simulation of solar energy photovoltaic conversion. In: 2020 International Youth Conference on Radio Electronics, Electrical and Power Engineering (REEPE), pp. 1–4 (2020). https://doi.org/10.1109/REEPE49198.2020.9059149
7. Romero Pedraza, E.: Estudio de Factibilidad para Implementación de Sistemas Fotovoltaicos y Eólicos, en Parques Metropolitanos de Bogotá", Escuela Colombiana de Ingeniería Julio Garavito, Bogotá D.C. (2018). https://repositorio.escuelaing.edu.co/handle/001/1263
8. Gutiérrez, M.P.B., Ávil, S.A., Patarroyo, D.J.R.: Análisis del Recurso Energético Eólico para la Ciudad de Bogotá DC para los Meses de Diciembre y Enero, vol. 12, no. 1 (2015). https://doi.org/10.1002/pip.2197
9. Loaiza, M.A.: Metodología para la Evaluación del Potencial Energético Solar, Eólico y de Agua Lluvia para Aprovechamiento en Zonas Rurales de Bogotá. Universidad Jorge Tadeo Lozano, Bogotá D.C. (2018). http://hdl.handle.net/20.500.12010/2826
10. Schubel, P.J., Crossley, R.J.: Wind turbine blade design. Energies **5**(9), 3425–3449 (2012). https://doi.org/10.3390/en5093425
11. El Hacen, J.M., Ihaddadene, R., Ihaddadene, N., Elhadji Sidi, C.E.B., EL Bah, M., Logerais, P.: Performance analysis of micro-amorphe silicon PV array under actual climatic conditions in Nouakchott, Mauritania. In: 2019 10th International Renewable Energy Congress (IREC), pp. 1–6 (2019). https://doi.org/10.1109/IREC.2019.8754599

12. Arribas, L., Cano, L., Cruz, I., Mata, M., Llobet, E.: PV-wind hybrid system performance: a new approach and a case study. Renew. Energy **35**(1), 128–137 (2010). https://doi.org/10.1016/j.renene.2009.07.002

13. Sharma, A.: Hierarchical maximum likelihood clustering approach. IEEE Trans. Biomed. Eng. **64**(1), 112–122 (2017). https://doi.org/10.1109/TBME.2016.2542212

14. Looney, E.E., et al.: Representative Identification of Spectra and Environments (RISE) using K-Means. Res. App. **29**(2), 200–211 (2021). https://doi.org/10.1002/pip.3358

15. Sinaga, K.P., Yang, M.S.: Unsupervised k-means clustering algorithm. IEEE access **8**, 80716–80727 (2020). https://doi.org/10.1109/ACCESS.2020.2988796

16. Camacho Caro, B.D., Orjuela Ramírez, A.: Estudio de Eficiencia Energética en la Universidad de La Salle Sede Candelaria, Universidad de La Salle, Bogotá D.C. (2015)

Classification of Fruits Using Machine Vision and Collaborative Robotics

Juan Contreras$^{(\boxtimes)}$ ⓘ and Santiago Florez

Pontificia Universidad Javeriana, Cali, Colombia
{juandavid.contreras,santiagoflorez5628}@javerianacali.edu.co

Abstract. This project presents an automated strategy to classify fruits based on their color and size, by merging a collaborative robot and an Open CV-based computer vision system with a deterministic decision-making algorithm.The project was tested using a UR3 robot which showed improvement in sorting times. It also showed advantages by taking data on fruit characteristics which can be quantified and analyzed.

Keywords: Fruit classification · Computer vision · Collaborative robot

1 Introduction

In the fruit industry, packaging lines are essential to the distribution chains of national and international high-quality fruit markets. Fruits that fail to meet quality standards are donated to food banks for rapid consumption, hoping to avoid food waste. Checking quality-oriented parameters in the fruit sector is relevant for marketing purposes given that approved products are sent to the consumer. The exportation process requires to comply with international standards while guaranteeing end-to-end traceability throughout the value chain. In spite of this requirement, national companies still carry out manual verification processes that are inefficient and subjective, which means that exportation can lack quality-related criteria and, in many cases, fruits can be misplaced and never reach the consumer on time.

According to the Automated Imaging Association (AIA), computer vision encompasses all industrial and non-industrial applications in which the combination of hardware and software provides operational guidance for devices during the execution of functions regarding the capture and processing of pictures [1]. It is a scientific discipline that includes methods for the acquisition, processing, and analysis of real-world images in order to deliver information that can be processed by a machine. Nowadays, vision-based computing capabilities and algorithms can process imagery and video feed with higher efficiency, thus enabling the adoption of machine vision algorithms in the agricultural sector [2]. These algorithms are often used for economic purposes and suitable inspection, measurement and evaluation tasks [3]. The use of machine vision in farms and

© The Author(s), under exclusive license to Springer Nature Switzerland AG 2022
J. C. Figueroa-García et al. (Eds.): WEA 2022, CCIS 1685, pp. 90–100, 2022.
https://doi.org/10.1007/978-3-031-20611-5_8

food processing plants can lead to the acquisition of a wide range of data, such as fruit and vegetable detection, identification, size and weight estimation, leaf area and yield estimation, plant classification and grading [4]. Computer vision algorithms are also used to control actuating mechanisms such as autonomous selective sprayers or weed control applications [5].

Amongst the technological solutions available for computer vision, OpenCV stands out as an open source library designed to solve computer vision problems with multiple functions to obtain, process and edit images [6]. The implementation of OpenCV is based on high-level programming languages such as Python and C++, so it can be easily integrated into applications ranging from artificial intelligence to industrial control [7]. OpenCV will be used in this project to acquire fruit images from a camera system and then process said images to calculate size and maturity index. Maturity is defined by assessing the colours and number of pixels inside the fruit contour.

Collaborative robots (cobots) are robotic systems with built-in security conditions, as well as speed and load-related restrictions which make them safer to work alongside humans without the need to install enclosures. They are designed to perform repetitive and manual tasks, but can also handle jobs that pose risks for operators, such as handling sharp objects or working in hostile temperatures [8]. Unlike traditional industrial robots, cobots are designed to work and interact with people and can be easily programmed. Given their intuitive interfaces, the operator can program new routines into the robot in a matter of minutes. Furthermore, certain features such as a lightweight and compact design, multiple articulated axes and high flexibility, facilitate the integration of these machines in workshops, warehouses and laboratories, even in confined spaces [9].

This research merges the aforementioned technologies (machine vision and collaborative robotics) through an industrial communication network using the open Modbus protocol. This protocol is commonly used in industrial automation given that the Modbus/TCP specification defines a simple interoperable standard suited for any device that supports TCP/IP sockets [10]. The goal of this project is to use machine vision to assess the maturity, shape and size of papaya fruits, so that a cobot can then classify and package them to be sent to different destinations.

2 Fruit Classification Requirements

Firstly, the classification parameters currently used in the manual classification strategy are based on the fruit packaging regulations from production plants located in Valle del Cauca (Colombia). These parameters were inserted in the machine vision algorithm for the classification process. During the linear packaging process, the classification involves a linear conveyor belt that transports fruits while operators review and pack them in different boxes (Fig. 1). The subsequent destinations and qualitative criteria are defined as follows:

1. Exportation: The fruit is completely healthy on the external surface, reaches a maturity degree below 25% and is large in size.

2. National market: The fruit is mostly healthy on the surface, it has minor defects that do not jeopardise the its quality and its size is standard.
3. Donation: The fruit exhibits external damage or has a high level of maturity.

Fig. 1. Manual classification of papaya.

The papaya fruit is usually harvested when its external colour changes from dark green to a lighter shade of green with yellow lines. These are mostly sent to other countries when the yellow hue of the fruit skin is below 25%. Local markets receive fruits with a yellow colour between 50% and 75% depending on its variety. Table 1 encompasses the physiological parameters used for papaya classification. Thus, the fruit status is classified according to the tonality of its skin. A measurement in degrees Brix is also carried out to determine the total sugar content present in the fruit.

3   Classification Software

These are some of the strategies involved in computer vision-based fruit classification:

– Use OpenCV to develop a deterministic program to detect the ripeness level of the fruit.
– Use a machine learning tool such as XGBoost or Random Forests to perform the classification of a given dataset (features and labels).
– Use a deep learning tool such as convolutional neural networks for image classification.

The authors of this project chose the first strategy, involving the Python OpenCV library. The focus consists on capturing an image of the papaya using a conventional camera and then mapping its contour to separate the fruit and the

Table 1. Collection box with papaya characteristics.

Animal	Description	DDS
Grade 0		The pulp has orange tones between the cavity and seed section. It has 8 degrees Brix of sugar content.
Grade 1		The ripening process continues, the fruits show a well-defined yellow area on the shell that covers 25%. The pulp is 90% orange in color and has 10 degrees Brix.
Grade 2		At this point, the fruit has a 50% yellow area on the skin and the pulp is 100% orange at 10 degrees Brix.
Grade 3		The fruit has an 80% yellow area on its skin with a 11 degrees Brix.

rest of the image. Subsequently, the image is processed to calculate the maturity degree based on the number of pixels within certain colour ranges according to Table 1. The main reason for discarding machine learning and deep learning strategies is the lack of a large and properly-labelled dataset required to train the classification algorithms. These stochastic approaches could become an option, in case the deterministic approach is proven to be unsuccessful.

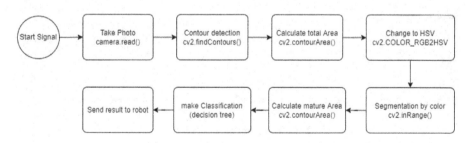

Fig. 2. Flowchart of the classification software.

The proposed classification strategy using OpenCV is detailed in Fig. 2. The diagram shows the different stages and corresponding OpenCV functions, while noting that all details are not included. After the image is captured, the findContours function differentiates the object from the background using a colour-based threshold. The larger contour area is obtained using the contourArea function. The area value is stored to calculate the maturity percentage in subsequent steps.

For an easier colour segmentation, the image is transformed from RGB to HSV colour code. In this scale, the mature section of the fruit can be detected with colour ranges taken from Table 1. The ranges and the HSV image are parsed with the inRange function, which returns a segmented mask. The functions find-Contours and contourArea are used to calculate the mature area of the fruit. Lastly, the maturity percentage is determined as the factor between the mature area and the total area and then passed on to the classification function which sends the result to the robot.

In terms of the software, a decision tree with nested IF clauses performs the classification considering the size of the fruit, its ripeness degree and the estimated damage. As for the international market, a fruit ripening below 30% served as reference, with no more than 8% damage in the entire area and an area larger than 1000 pixels. As for the domestic market, papayas needed to have less than 30% damage on the surface and not meet international market standards. Lastly, fruits that do not meet the above criteria are classified as food bank donations. The classification results are sent to the cobot by writing a register of the UR3 Modbus server.

In order to guarantee the proper operation of the vision system, adequate artificial light conditions need to be maintained. In this sense, the established colour ranges are not affected by environmental conditions.

Figure 3 shows the results obtained during the vision stage. There is a clear detection of colours leading to the calculation of the maturation status of the peel. The mapping of the papaya contour is also visible and used for size estimation.

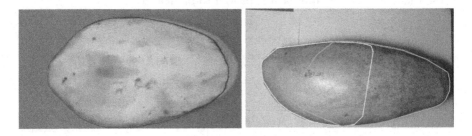

Fig. 3. Vision test results.

4 Robot Station and Integration

A robotic station was implemented in a laboratory environment to test the classification system. As shown in Fig. 4, the UR3 cobot is installed placed on a table and the camera is positioned perpendicularly to the table. Additionally, a LED ring light is added to properly illuminate the fruit. A capacitance sensor is installed in a hole in the table to detect the presence of the fruit. The sensor is connected to the digital input module of the UR3.

Fig. 4. System assembly

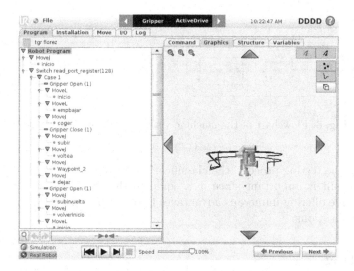

Fig. 5. Robot controller software.

A switch-case statement is used to program the logic of the robot (Fig. 5). In this statement, the internal function read_port_register() reads the internal register value delivered by the vision software and performs a "pick and place" movement according to the value. Case 1 is for moving the papaya to export box, Case 2 is for moving to the national box and Case 3 is for moving to the donation box.

The integration between the robot controller and the computer vision software is performed using the Modbus TCP, following the architecture of Fig. 6. The robot controller has an active Modbus server that can be used to write and read the internal registers of the robot. In this scenario, the server is used to read the digital inputs and to write the general purpose registers. The machine vision software was deployed on a Raspberry Pi 4 connected to the camera and, in the same device, a Modbus client was implemented using the Modbus TCP Python library. The client is connected to the robot server and continuously reads the value of the digital input while waiting for changes in the sensor, thus indicating that the fruit is in position to launch the classification software. After a classification result is obtained, the client writes the result (as an integer) by writing a register of the Modbus Server, indicating to the robot the destination box of the current papaya.

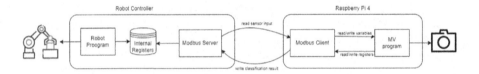

Fig. 6. Flowchart of the machine vision classification software.

During the testing process, the classification process had a resulting time of 6 s. This result is important since it is equal to the time spent in the manual process, while offering numerous advantages to operators and providing data for further applications.

5   Testing

This section discusses the tests and validation of the results obtained throughout the project. Initial lumen saturation tests were carried out in order to improve image capture, given the light cast onto the fruits in the vision system. This ensures a proper classification of the papaya tasked to the robotic agent. It was concluded that the lumen saturation level causes changes in the colour saturation of the fruits, hence the selection of the lighting source is crucial to the success of the application. The luminosity measurement process involved a lux meter that can rapidly measure the actual illuminance of the environment (not the subjective illuminance). The measurement unit is the lux (lx).

The camera was aimed at the papaya in the same direction of light. This softens textures, reduces shadowing and minimizes the influence of the markings, dust and defects of the fruits. The image capture data was simplified by placing white paper on the background.

The tests have three objectives:

- Optimise the contrast of the papaya
- Normalize any variation of the lighting environment
- Simplify subsequent image processing

The photoelectric cell was positioned over the papaya during the lighting measurement, in order to measure the lumens entering directly at the time of the image capture. The next test involved three types of light sources: LED, incandescent light bulb and ring-shaped light (Table 2).

The luminosity tests evidence that the lighting conditions of the system have a direct impact on the image capture of the camera. Therefore, the light must remain between 700 and 2000 lux to ensure clean measures and avoid the presence of false positives and noise in the data.

The overall process performed by the system on the whole lot of fruit according to organoleptic properties is shown. Figure 7 shows a lot evaluated with 17 papayas of which 11 were graded for the international market with an accuracy of 100% with respect to those evaluated with the operators of the grading plant, 4 were graded for the domestic market with an accuracy of 100% and 2 were graded for donations with an accuracy of 100%. Figure 8 shows the degrees of maturity obtained by artificial vision with respect to the state of the papaya. With the help of the program, it can be seen that most of the lot was still in a high state of immaturity and that most of the fruits had low percentages of damage to their skin. Following Fig. 9, it can be seen that the fruits that are smaller in size considering the area in pixels taken by the camera show a more rapid ripening than those with a greater number of pixel area.

These data help to evaluate how the distribution of the lot was with respect to the markets in order to pass on to the analysis and make decisions about the plantation and its process. Data exportation is an essential part of the proposed classification method given that the sample data describes a controlled system delivering charts that can be assessed to propose improvement-oriented initiatives, trace products and give customers high-quality fruits.

Table 2. Luminosity testing

Luminosity level	Environment	HSV-scale image	Observations
785 Lux			Pixels with different textures are captured without light saturation. However, this level of luminosity reveals the loss of certain textures in the maturity scale given their low intensity.
1990 Lux			A large number of pixels is captured with proper resolution without saturation or noise. The capture-related accuracy is higher when measuring the pixels within the maturity transition phase.
42500 Lux			The saturation level hinders the capture of pixels given the strong light intensity and the resulting heat affects the camera operation.

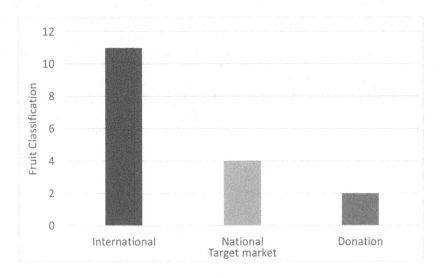

Fig. 7. Market distribution by evaluated lot to computer vision.

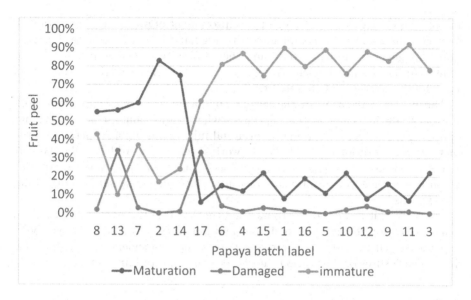

Fig. 8. Distribution of fruit texture states according to computer vision.

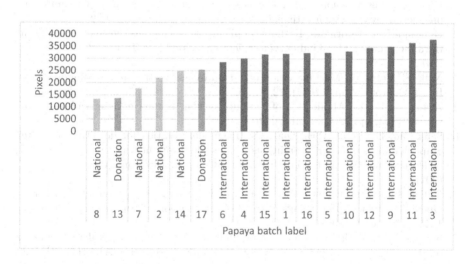

Fig. 9. Papaya lot sizes measured in pixels by computer vision.

6   Conclusions

The fruit classification process based on the combination of computer vision and collaborative robotics is a remarkable growth opportunity for the fruit sector. The integration of automated systems contributes to the overall technification and progress of the sector, through the improvement of production, reduction of delivery time-frames and compliance with regulations and standards. Furthermore, the generation of new data and the possibility to enable product traceability can be used to launch strategic plans, define metrics (KPIs) and carry out other business-oriented activities.

During the validation of the system, operators can experience noticeable drawbacks during classification, specially when they maintain non-ergonomic stances. This can lead to fatigue or eventual injury, causing a reduction of productivity and additional costs linked to work absenteeism. Additionally, the system is certain to measure the parameters according to the programmed criteria, in contrast with the operator whose measurements depend on subjectivity, skills and expertise.

Ultimately, it is noteworthy to mention that putting the system into production requires specific lighting conditions and integration with the conveyor belt. Nonetheless, the use of collaborative robots lowers implementation costs given that no enclosures or adaptations are needed in terms of infrastructure.

References

1. UNIR: ¿qué es la visión artificial? concepto y aplicaciones. https://www.unir.net/ingenieria/revista/vision-artificial/. accedido el 10 de mayo de 2022
2. Gomes, J.F.S., Rodrigues, F.: Leta: applications of computer vision techniques in the agriculture and food industry: a review. Eur. Food Res. Technol. **235**, 989–1000 (2012)
3. Naik, S., Patel, B.: Machine vision based fruit classification and grading-a review. Int. J. Comput. App. **170**(9), 22–34 (2017)
4. Zhang, F., Fu, L.: Application of computer vision technology in agricultural field, vol, 462–463, pp. 72–76, January 2014
5. Sebastián, D., Pérez, F.B., Diaz, C.: Image classification for detection of winter grapevine buds in natural conditions using scale-invariant features transform, bag of features and support vector machines. Comput. Electron. Agric. **135**, 81–95 (2017)
6. Culjak, I., Abram, D., Pribanic, T., Dzapo, H., Cifrek, M.: A brief introduction to OpenCV. In: 2012 proceedings of the 35th International Convention MIPRO, pp. 1725–1730. IEEE (2012)
7. Saxena, M.R., Pathak, A., Singh, A.P., Shukla, I.: Real-time object detection using machine learning and OpenCV. Int. J. Inform. Sci. App. (IJISA) **11**(1), 0974–22 (2019)
8. Fast-Berglund, Å., Palmkvist, F., Nyqvist, P., Ekered, S., Åkerman, M.: Evaluating cobots for final assembly. Proc. CIRP **44**, 175–180 (2016)
9. CADE Cobots. ¿qué es un cobot https://cadecobots.com/que-es-un-cobot/
10. "The Modbus Protocol In-Depth". Engineer ambitiously - ni. Available at: https://www.ni.com/en-us/innovations/white-papers/14/the-modbus-protocol-in-depth.html. [accedido el 1 de abril de 2022]

Artificial Intelligence for Prevention of Breast Cancer

Diana Lancheros-Cuesta[1,2](✉) (iD), Juan Camilo Bustos[1,2], Nicolas Rubiano[1,2],
and Antonio Tumialan[1,2]

[1] Universidad De La Salle, Bogotá, Colombia
{dilancheros,alapatino}@unisalle.edu.co
[2] Ingeniería en Automatización Grupo AVARC, Bogotá, Colombia

Abstract. This paper show a computational tool that allow the analysis of the information obtained from a database that contains features of the fine needle aspiration (FNA) procedure, whose goal is to diagnose breast masses applying artificial intelligence. The methodology include the recollection of data, process of cleaning, neural networks and Bayesian's networks for prediction of the data, evaluation and comparison.

Keywords: Neural networks · Database · Breast cancer · Computational tool

1 Introduction

Breast cancer is a disease in which annually diagnostics approximately a million of women cases around the world, this problematic constitutes a group of diseases with social, economic, and emotional repercussions [5].

Some authors have designed and implemented computational tools and data analysis with artificial intelligence for monitoring different medical diseases [1,2,6,8]. Lugo et al. [3] mentioned that the science and medicine field could be benefited with predictive computational and mathematic models. The automatic learning studies systems able to learn from a set of training data and improve prediction and classification processes. To turn these data into knowledge, these ones need to be processed and analyzed through complex statistic methods, using: artificial neuronal networks, Bayesian classifiers, multivariant logistic regression, among others. This will ease the clinical diagnosis of ailments such as: acute appendicitis, breast cancer, or chronic liver disease.

Reyes et al. [7] identifies opportunity areas on health field which is benefited by the artificial intelligence. Reyes et al. show a model that brings together technological platforms (Hadoop, Mahout, Spark), algorithms (Collaborative filtering, decision trees, clustering), and health fields. This research provides a

Supported by Universidad de La Salle.

© The Author(s), under exclusive license to Springer Nature Switzerland AG 2022
J. C. Figueroa-García et al. (Eds.): WEA 2022, CCIS 1685, pp. 101–108, 2022.
https://doi.org/10.1007/978-3-031-20611-5_9

methodology for a specific example of a patient with different symptoms and show the advantage a technological platform for the monitoring. Jarraya et al. [2] developed the notion of a Bayesian Network (BN) an a new way to build a network of this type is developed, the results of the construction are shown, highlighting the process of how the network is able to communicate better results with this new methodology. Repaca et al. [6] developed a Bayesian Naives for Smart Heart Disease Prediction (SHDP) to predict risk factors related to cardiac disease. The required data is assembled in a standardized way in order to predict the possible cardiac diseases presented on a patient. The result shows that the established diagnosis system helps to predict risk factors related to this type of disease.

This paper show a results about a project it was done a information system where it was collected the information of the FNA procedure of breast cancer patients. This system is a tool for the mastologists who treat this type of cancer and allow to have better management of information. Implementing this computational tool it could make more effective the trace of breast cancer patients.

2 Methodology

In a fine needle aspiration (FNA) biopsy, the doctor uses a very thin hollow needle attached to a syringe to remove a small amount of tissue or fluid from the suspected region. After this the sample is examined to see if it has malignant cells. (American Cancer Society, 2019) The database used was compiled by Dr. Wolberg to diagnose breast masses using (FNA) by his initials translated into Spanish final needle by aspiration method, downloaded from the Wisconsin Breast Cancer Database.

Two methods were used for diagnostic prediction, one using Bayesian learning and the other using the Matlab Neural Network Toolbox.

2.1 Bayesian Learning to the Breast Cancer Diagnosis

Applying the Bayesian Naive theorem, the design, implementation and validation of the algorithm are made; in the Eq. 1 is presented the Bayes theorem [4].

$$P(A_i|B) = \frac{P(B|A_i)P(A_i)}{P(B)} \tag{1}$$

To apply the theorem shown before, it is important to know the conditional probability of all the data, the equation of this probability one is shown below on the Eq. 2 [4].

$$P(B|A_i) = \frac{P(A_i \cap B)}{P(A_i)} \tag{2}$$

Before applying the conditional probability, the characteristics need to be limited on universes of discourse, for example, the data for the radios are 12 and 8, this field can take n values and there are also n quantity of data, reason why the data are dived in two, the ones which are over the average and the ones which are under; for an example of an average value of 10, a value of 12 would belong to the first condition and a value of 8 would belong to the condition 0; according to this, it is calculated the probability that an event A, that is over or under the average, would be benignant or malignant; moreover, having this, the probability of the events can be calculated. It is important to highlight that the complexity increases when there are different events B and more quantity of data. The average value is taken as a determining factor for the selection criteria, where 1 is above the average and 0 below it. Algorithm 1 shows the calculation of the averages of each column, taking into account all the lines of the database. Algorithm 2 shows the separation of the number of malignant and benign cases

---

Algorithm 1. Calculation Average

1: Data Base Read()
2: $j \leftarrow 3$
3: **if** $(j <= 32)$ **then**
4:    average(column j)
5:    $j \leftarrow (j + 1)$

---

in the database. Furthermore, to identify the values that are over and under the

---

Algorithm 2. Separate benignant diagnosis

1: Data Base Read()
2: $i \leftarrow 1$
3: **if** $(i <= row)$ **then**
4:    diagnosis = benign
5:    insert(row)
6:    $i \leftarrow (i + 1)$

---

average, the Algorithm 3 shown

Algorithm 3. Identification of the values that are over and under the average

---
1: Data Base Read()
2: $i \leftarrow 1$
3: $k \leftarrow 3$
4: **if** $(malign(i, k) >= average(k - 2))$ **then**
5:    malign(i,k)=1
6: **else**
7:    malign(i,k) = 0

To calculate the probabilities is necessary to know the number of malignant and benign diagnoses that are over and under the average; this was made with an algorithm of Matlab. Taking this into account, calculate the probabilities of each possibility is required, this was made by means of the following:

- That is malignant and is over the average/number of malignant cases.
- That is malignant and is under the average/number of malignant cases.
- That is benign and is over the average/number of benign cases.
- That is benign and is under the average/number of benign cases.

The database with which the probabilities are found has a total of 499 data, of which the 61.2% (308) are benign and 32.8% (191) are malignant; for the radius, it is known that the average has a value of 14.23 calculated on Matlab, all the data that is over of this average will be 1 and the ones which are under will be 0. It was obtained 163 malignant cases over the average from all the medium radius and 28 under this one. It is obtained that the probability of being malignant and over the average is 0.853. Using the equ. 1 for the other cases, it was evidenced that the probability of being malignant and under the average is 0.1466; for the benign cases that are under the average, it was obtained a probability of 0.873, meanwhile, the benign cases which are over the average had a probability of 0.1266. In this manner, the rest of the columns of the averages table are calculated. Finally, in order to evaluate a data and make a prediction, the Bayes theorem is applied with the Eq. 2. Where: P(Ai B) Represents the probability of being malignant or benign given the 30 characteristics. (B Ai) Represents the multiplication of the whole conditional probabilities obtained. P(Ai) Represents the probability of being malignant or benignant according to the case. P (B) Represents the sum of: P(B Benigno)P(Benigno)+P(B Maligno)P(Maligno).

2.2 Artificial Neural Networks to the Breast Cancer Diagnosis

Once the whole database information is acquired through the information system, it is important to manage that and analyze it, therefore, in this section is developed the idea of using artificial neural networks in order to bring a prediction for the breast cancer diagnosis. the database contains 32 fields, but not all of them are necessary to analyze such as the inputs and outputs; for example, the ID is only a patient's number and in this case, isn't relevant to take it into account as an input of the system, on the other hand, the rest 31 fields, contain all the information of the patient that is relevant to make the final diagnosis; for this database, the second column of it is referred, which reveals if the presented tumor is benign or malignant, in other words, if it has cancer or if it doesn't. To make this transformation is necessary to divide the whole database into the three following groups:

- Train Set: Such as its name shows, these are the selected data to train the neural network to create, which are 314×31 fields, since it's an information matrix.
- Target: These data are the outputs that contain the train set, what means that these are the right data which with the neural network will train.

- Test: Once the neural network is trained, this one is put to be tested by some test data, which are randomly selected from the information base; as a consequence, the results are expected to be the same as the ones concluded by the neural network. It is evidenced a little fragment of the data that will be used to train the neural network. These correspond to the first 372×31 fields of the database (Fig. 1).

id	diagnosis	radius_mear	texture_mer	perimeter_n	area_mean	smoothness	compactnes	concavity_m	concavePoin	symmetry_n	fractal_dime	radius_se	texture_se
842302 M		17,99	10,38	122,8	1001	0,1184	0,2776	0,3001	0,1471	0,2419	0,07871	1.095	905,3
842517 M		20,57	17,77	132,9	1326	0,08474	0,07864	0,0869	0,07017	0,1812	0,05667	0,5435	733,9
84300903 M		19,69	21,25	130	1203	0,1096	0,1599	0,1974	0,1279	0,2069	0,05999	0,7456	786,9
84358402 M		20,29	14,34	135,1	1297	0,1003	0,1328	0,198	0,1043	0,1809	0,05883	0,7572	781,3
843786 M		12,45	15,7	82,57	477,1	0,1278	0,17	0,1578	0,08089	0,2087	0,07613	0,3345	890,2
844359 M		18,25	19,98	119,6	1040	0,09463	0,109	0,1127	0,074	0,1794	0,05742	0,4467	773,2
84458202 M		13,71	20,83	90,2	577,9	0,1189	0,1645	0,09366	0,05985	0,2196	0,07451	0,5835	1377
844981 M		13	21,82	87,5	519,8	0,1273	0,1932	0,1859	0,09353	0,235	0,07389	0,3063	1002
84501001 M		12,46	24,04	83,97	475,9	0,1186	0,2396	0,2273	0,08543	0,203	0,08243	0,2976	1599
845636 M		16,02	23,24	102,7	797,8	0,08206	0,06669	0,03299	0,03323	0,1528	0,05697	0,3795	1187
84610002 M		15,78	17,89	103,6	781	0,0971	0,1292	0,09954	0,06606	0,1842	0,06082	0,5058	984,9
846226 M		19,17	24,8	132,4	1123	0,0974	0,2458	0,2065	0,1118	0,2397	0,078	0,9555	3568
846381 M		15,85	23,95	103,7	782,7	0,08401	0,1002	0,09938	0,05364	0,1847	0,05338	0,4033	1078
84667401 M		13,73	22,61	93,6	578,3	0,1131	0,2293	0,2128	0,08025	0,2069	0,07682	0,2121	1169
84799002 M		14,54	27,54	96,73	658,8	0,1139	0,1595	0,1639	0,07364	0,2303	0,07077	0,37	1033
848406 M		14,68	20,13	94,74	684,5	0,09867	0,072	0,07395	0,05259	0,1586	0,05922	0,4727	1240
84862001 M		16,13	20,68	108,1	798,8	0,117	0,2022	0,1722	0,1028	0,2164	0,07356	0,5692	1073
849014 M		19,81	22,15	130	1260	0,09831	0,1027	0,1479	0,09498	0,1582	0,05395	0,7582	1017
8510426 B		13,54	14,36	87,46	566,3	0,09779	0,08129	0,06664	0,04781	0,1885	0,05766	0,2699	788,6
8510653 B		13,08	15,71	85,63	520	0,1075	0,127	0,04568	0,0311	0,1967	0,06811	0,1852	747,7
8510824 B		9,504	12,44	60,34	273,9	0,1024	0,06492	0,02956	0,02076	0,1815	0,06905	0,2773	576,8
8511133 M		15,34	14,26	102,5	704,4	0,1073	0,2135	0,2077	0,09756	0,2521	0,07032	0,4388	709,6
851509 M		21,16	23,04	137,2	1404	0,09428	0,1022	0,1097	0,08632	0,1769	0,05278	0,6917	1127
852552 M		16,65	21,38	110	904,6	0,1121	0,1457	0,1525	0,0917	0,1995	0,0633	0,8068	901,7

Fig. 1. Database stored

Once the database train set is selected, the next step is to select each one's target, since these data conclude if the tumor is benign or malignant depending on the characteristics already mentioned. To analyze these fields inside the neural network, it was necessary to make them a little transformation, indicating that if a tumor is benign it would take the value of number 2, otherwise, If the tumor is malignant it would take the value of number 4; this is observed in an exported line on Excel from Matlab. After importing the information (Test, Target and Train Set), the next step is to open the Matlab Toolbox. In this case, the 'Feed Forward Backprop' neural network type is used since its information only moves forward, from the input nodes, through the hidden nodes (if any), to the output nodes. There are no loops and cycles on this network. Some of the parameters that must be talked about in this section are the input data, the target data and the adaptative learning function, considering that the last one mentioned is the way how the knowledge is propagated. In this case, two layers and seven neurons are used, taking into account that the said characteristics are enough to allow the network to be correctly trained (Fig. 2).

Figure 3 show the process of iterations and time, likewise the gradient changing and each validation.

On this way, an artificial neural network, that is able to predict if a tumor is carcinogenic or if it's not, is obtained, taking into account the values of a doctor's procedure to give a final diagnosis in a treatment.

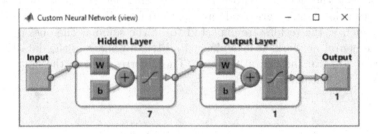

Fig. 2. Architecture neural network

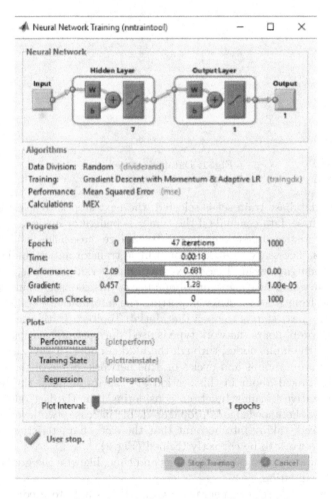

Fig. 3. Neural network learning- Toolbox Matlab

3   Validation and Results

Two validation tests were made in Matlab, since the code was designed to work with a quantity n of data; in the first of them the training was made with 499 data and 39 were left to do tests, where it was obtained a success percentage of 94.74%; when the validation of 538 data was made, it was acquired a success percentage of 93.31%. In the second validation, the training was made with 538 data which obtained a percentage of 94.31%.

4   Conclusions

On the web application a function that allows entering the information (32 fields) was implemented, which are taken to the database on MySQL through a code developed on PHP, where the repository database of the Wisconsin university is hosted; furthermore, to integrate the information, an algorithm that prepares the data was executed giving a format to these; on the same way, a learning Bayesian algorithm was designed which underwent two tests, on the first one, it was made the training with 499 data, and 39 were left to do tests; when these 39 data were validated, a success percentage of 94.74% was obtained, and when 538 data were validated, a success percentage of 93.31% was achieved. On the second test was made a training with the 538 data that had a success percentage of 94.24% when these were validated. Thus, it is concluded that increasing the amount of data to the error range, decreases the prediction considerably. Nevertheless, the same procedure was made with a neural network training using the Matlab Toolbox, giving a 92% of error. Considering this, it is deducted additionally that Bayesian learning is an algorithm that achieves the lowest error ranges when predicting and because of this, it was the one selected to be applied on the website.

References

1. Dalwinder, S., Birmohan, S., Manpreet, K.: Simultaneous feature weighting and parameter determination of neural networks using ant lion optimization for the classification of breast cancer. Biocybern. Biomed. Eng. **40**(1), 337–351 (2020). https://doi.org/10.1016/j.bbe.2019.12.004, https://linkinghub.elsevier.com/retrieve/pii/S0208521619304905
2. Jarraya, A., Leray, P., Masmoudi, A.: Discrete exponential Bayesian networks: an extension of Bayesian networks to discrete natural exponential families. In: 2011 IEEE 23rd International Conference on Tools with Artificial Intelligence, pp. 205–208 (2011). https://doi.org/10.1109/ICTAI.2011.38, ISSN: 2375-0197
3. Lugo-Reyes, S.O., Maldonado-Colín, G., Murata, C.: Inteligencia artificial para asistir el diagnóstico clínico en medicina. Revista Alergia México. **61**(2), 110–120 (2014). https://doi.org/10.29262/ram.v61i2.33, http://revistaalergia.mx/ojs/index.php/ram/article/view/33
4. Puga, J.L., Krzywinski, M., Altman, N.: Bayes' theorem. Nat. Methods. **12**(4), 277–278 (2015). https://doi.org/10.1038/nmeth.3335, https://www.nature.com/articles/nmeth.3335

5. Ramírez, C.M.R.: Plan nacional para el control del cáncer en colombia. Ministerio de Salud, p. 85 (2012)
6. Repaka, A.N., Ravikanti, S.D., Franklin, R.G.: Design and implementing heart disease prediction using naives bayesian. In: 2019 3rd International Conference on Trends in Electronics and Informatics (ICOEI), pp. 292–297 (2019). https://doi.org/10.1109/ICOEI.2019.8862604
7. Reyes, G.V., Thompson, E.B., Vanoye, J.A.R., Penna, A.F.: Modelos De Tecnologias Del Big Data Analytics y su aplicación en Salud. Pistas Educativas. **39**(128), 1174 (2020). http://www.itcelaya.edu.mx/ojs/index.php/pistas/article/view/1174
8. Zemouri, R., et al.: Constructive deep neural network for breast cancer diagnosis. IFAC-PapersOnLine. **51**(27), 98–103 (2018). https://doi.org/10.1016/j.ifacol.2018.11.660, http://www.sciencedirect.com/science/article/pii/S2405896318333767

Predictive Method Proposal for a Manufacturing System with Industry 4.0 Technologies

Santiago Aguirre[1]([⊠]) [ID], Lina Zuñiga[1], and Michael Arias[2] [ID]

[1] Pontificia Universidad Javeriana, Bogotá, Colombia
{saguirre,lmzunigaq}@javeriana.edu.co
[2] Universidad de Costa Rica, San Pedro, Costa Rica
michael.arias_c@ucr.ac.cr

Abstract. Cyber-physical manufacturing systems with industry 4.0 technologies have the ability to generate real-time data on the behavior of the system in each of its components, so predictions can be generated from this data. This article presents a method for the development of a predictive model where process mining techniques and data mining algorithms are combined. Through the discovery techniques of process mining, a descriptive analysis of the system is carried out to subsequently develop a predictive model with predictive data mining algorithms that provide information on the time remaining for a product that is in process to be completed. This prediction allows decision makers to reconfigure the manufacturing system variables and its schedule to optimize its performance. The method was applied in a production system that is currently installed in the Computer Integration Manufacturing Lab at Pontificia Universidad Javeriana.

Keywords: Process mining · Predictive monitoring · Industry 4.0 · Data mining

1 Introduction

The Fourth Industrial Revolution, also known as Industry 4.0, is a concept that seeks to increase the efficiency of production systems by making them more flexible [13] through the incorporation of relevant technologies [20]. A comprehensive definition of this concept [6] makes it possible to recognize four fundamental elements and technologies in the industry: smart factories, cyber-physical systems and internet of things (IoT).

Cyber-physical systems are integrations of computing and physical processes that, through integrated computers and networks, monitor and control processes in real time [9]. The abstractions and models that derive from this integration are often used to monitor and control the performance of these systems, in order to subsequently apply tools, techniques and methodologies that allow them to be optimized.

Among the main characteristics of cyber-physical manufacturing systems is an inherent component of dynamism, which makes the diagnosis of the efficiency of the system a real challenge. However, recent results and developments at the technological level have allowed greater availability and affordability of sensors, data acquisition systems

© The Author(s), under exclusive license to Springer Nature Switzerland AG 2022
J. C. Figueroa-García et al. (Eds.): WEA 2022, CCIS 1685, pp. 109–121, 2022.
https://doi.org/10.1007/978-3-031-20611-5_10

and computer networks, which allow the continuous generation of data. In such an environment, cyber-physical systems can be developed and improved by managing data and leveraging system interconnectivity to achieve intelligent, resilient, and self-adaptive machines [10].

The information that is registered in the monitoring and control nodes of the cyber-physical manufacturing systems can be exploited through process mining, which is made up of techniques and algorithms that allow discovering the real execution model of the processes, monitoring key indicators, analyzing them, and looking for ways to improve them [1]. Process mining techniques have been widely applied for the diagnosis, descriptive analysis, and improvement of all types of processes, including manufacturing systems [5, 8, 12]. However, in the literature review, it was found that limited applications of process mining for the development of predictive models in cyber-physical manufacturing systems [4, 11].

The contribution of this article is based on the combination of process mining techniques, which allow the descriptive analysis of a manufacturing system, with data mining techniques and algorithms such as decision trees, that allow developing predictions of the remaining cycle time of a production order to make decisions that contribute to cycle time and resource use optimization. The proposed method was applied at the Computer Integration Manufacturing Lab located at Pontificia Universidad Javeriana, where there is a cyber-physical manufacturing system with industry 4.0 technologies.

This document is organized as follows: Section 2 describes the background and related work. Section 3 describes the manufacturing system on which the predictive method was developed, and Sects. 4, 5, and 6 describe the developed method and its application. The results are presented in Sect. 7, which ends with the conclusions and future work.

2   Related Work

In recent years, some studies have been conducted for the application of process mining in manufacturing systems that have the capacity to generate data in real time [5, 8, 12]. These case studies enable the identification of opportunities for improvement in various scenarios involving the transformation of inputs into finished products via a manufacturing system. The most relevant case studies are described below.

In the article by Jiménez et al. [8], the simulation of a flexible manufacturing system installed in the laboratory of the Université de Valenciennes in France is described. This system is based on two machine selection rules under normal and non-normal production conditions subject to disturbances. Through process mining, a descriptive analysis of the system was carried out and it was concluded that these techniques can be used to diagnose the behavior of manufacturing systems and to compare the system performance based on different process configurations and product routing.

On the other hand, Schuh et al. [15] proposed a data-based methodology for process performance analysis in the manufacturing industry. The methodology consists of three steps: (1) extracting performance-related event logs; (2) merging and preparing event logs from multiple sources; and (3) process discovery for performance description and analysis. Its main contribution was the incorporation of process mining into all value chain process networks, including sales, manufacturing, and order fulfillment. An application of the methodology was presented in a real case study corresponding to a small metal-mechanic products company, where the real execution model of the fulfillment process was described, starting from the customer need until product delivery.

Process mining is not only useful for process discovery but can also be used to predict process behavior [1]. A relevant case of this application of the discipline is in supply chain analysis, where a scenario consisting of several independent factories was simulated [16]. In this case, customers requested certain products and each factory had until the end of the day to produce those items. Process mining process discovery algorithms, along with decision analysis techniques, were applied to analyze the decisions each factory made and thus predict what decisions it might make in the future.

The remaining production time in a manufacturing process could be predicted through process mining. Choueiri [4] proposed a hybrid predictive model, which starts from the discovery of the process through a process mining algorithm, from which transition systems and statistical regression models were applied to predict the remaining production times. The model was tested on an artificially created log emulating an industrial environment and on a real manufacturing log. The results showed that the approach provided better precision measures compared to the method applied in a previous development by Van der Aalst et al. [2].

Finally, another example of process mining applications for the prediction of their behavior was developed by Lovera et al. [11], who designed a methodology for the introduction of a predictive model in a manufacturing system, allowing the system to make better decisions. The predictive process mining algorithms available in the Apromore software were used as the basis for the development of the proposed methodology and its implementation in the simulated system.

The main limitations of previous predictive developments are based on their applications that are limited to manufacturing environments with a very limited number of configurations regarding the production process (routes) and the number of different products to be produced. The predictive method proposal developed in this article is aimed at a fully automated cyber-physical flexible manufacturing system, where different options for production routes and product configurations are evaluated.

3 Manufacturing System Description

The cyber-physical manufacturing system on which the predictive method was developed is a flexible manufacturing system located at the Engineering Laboratories Building of Pontificia Universidad Javeriana in Bogotá, Colombia. This technology center based on Industry 4.0 technologies seeks the complete digitization of a company's value chains through the integration of data processing technologies, artificial intelligence and IoT sensors. The laboratory has several workstations that include a raw material and finished product warehouse, a conveyor belt for material flow, manipulator robots, and a quality control station by artificial vision.

The manufacturing cell in which the predictive model was applied is made up of five workstations, four made up of a single machine (M2, M3, M4 and M5) and another made up of a storage module (M1). Each module and workstations are configured to perform different manufacturing operations. The workstations are connected through a one-way transport band system. For product movement and assembly, a transport automated guided robot (AGV) is used. This self-propelled resource transports products from station to station and, thanks to a basic behavior system, avoids colliding with other workstations, detects a transfer node (where the production route to follow is decided), and automatically manages speed and stops in front of the workstations.

Sample mobile phones are made in the manufacturing cell, but since the purpose of this manufacturing system is to learn about topics related to industry 4.0, mobile phones are not real. There are 5 types of mobile phones models (A, B, C, D, and E), each one contains a specific type and number of components which are assembled through a sequence of production operations (production routes). Figure 1 shows a representation of the manufacturing system.

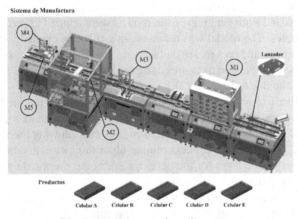

Fig. 1. Flexible manufacturing system

The manufacturing system has four interconnected components that allow modeling and controlling the operations in the system: 1) A manufacturing execution system (MES) allows for the definition and execution of production orders, 2) A database comprised of 65 relational tables that allows for real-time access to information on production orders, products, and system configuration, 3) Physical plant: the physical installation of the manufacturing facility, as well as a 4) Simulator program that allows 3D simulation of the manufacturing system.

4   Method Description

The main objective of this work is the development of a predictive model in the manufacturing system. To carry it out, a work method was designed and implemented based on the steps of the CRISP-DM method (Cross-Industry Standard Process for Data Mining) that has been tested in different industries to guide data mining related projects [7]. Based on the information in this guide, the following work stages were defined and developed: 1) understanding of the manufacturing system, 2) data understanding, 3) data extraction and preparation, 4) descriptive and predictive model development, 5) model evaluation and 6) monitoring and control.

The development of the first stage consisted of making a characterization of the manufacturing system that would allow a contextualization and understanding of how these components work and are integrated. Having this clear, the definition of manufacturing orders was carried out to cover relevant products and production routes. The quantity and product types in each production order were determined in order to obtain execution information with all possible variations. Subsequently, the production orders were simulated to obtain the metadata and relational tables of the execution of each of the events. In total, 36 production orders were executed, resulting in 710 mobile equipment production cases. In stages 2 and 3, an analysis of the data structure was made, it was determined which ones were going to be used and finally the appropriate treatment was made to obtain the final event log to be used in the next stage. An extract from the final database event log can be seen in Table 1.

Table 1. Event log sample.

Case ID	Activity	Resource	Timestamp Start	Timestamp End	Product	OPos
206916001	release a defined part on stopper 1	high_bay_storage	2021/05/29 10:04:01	2021/05/29 10:04:05	Celular Sin PCB	1
206916001	feed back cover from magazine	magazine_application_module	2021/05/29 10:04:50	2021/05/29 10:04:51	Celular Sin PCB	1
206916001	pressing with force regulation	muscle_press_application_module	2021/05/29 10:04:58	2021/05/29 10:05:00	Celular Sin PCB	1
206916001	print label	labeling_application_module	2021/05/29 10:05:04	2021/05/29 10:05:07	Celular Sin PCB	1
206916001	store a part from stopper 1	high_bay_storage	2021/05/29 10:05:23	2021/05/29 10:05:27	Celular Sin PCB	1
206926001	release a defined part on stopper 1	high_bay_storage	2021/05/29 10:04:11	2021/05/29 10:04:16	Celular Sin PCB	2
206926001	feed back cover from magazine	magazine_application_module	2021/05/29 10:04:53	2021/05/29 10:04:54	Celular Sin PCB	2
206926001	pressing with force regulation	muscle_press_application_module	2021/05/29 10:05:02	2021/05/29 10:05:03	Celular Sin PCB	2
206926001	print label	labeling_application_module	2021/05/29 10:05:09	2021/05/29 10:05:11	Celular Sin PCB	2
206926001	store a part from stopper 1	high_bay_storage	2021/05/29 10:05:30	2021/05/29 10:05:34	Celular Sin PCB	2

Stage 4 was the most important stage of the method, since, with the application of process mining techniques, a descriptive analysis and a predictive analysis of the system were obtained. The descriptive analysis sought a deeper characterization than the one carried out in stage 1, since relevant data such as performance metrics of the execution of the processes were obtained and analyzed. For its part, predictive analysis seeks, supported by machine learning techniques, to learn from the behavior of the data and build models that make predictions of the remaining process time to finish manufacturing a product.

The predictive models obtained were evaluated in stage 5, based on performance measures of the predictions when making a comparison with data from the real execution based on the test data set. When making the comparison between several models, the one with the best performance metrics was chosen. Finally, in stage 6, a predictive monitoring control panel was developed that interactively allows those in charge of the process to make use of the predictive model in real time and know the status and predictions of the manufacturing cell. In the following two sections, the modeling stage is explained in more detail.

5   Descriptive Analysis Through Process Mining

The event log obtained at the end of the development of stage 3 of the method were analyzed through process mining. Celonis software was used as a support tool, which allows integrating process mining with machine learning components for process monitoring [19].

5.1 Process Overview

The first part of the descriptive analysis was the analysis of the process cycle time. The review showed that the average manufacturing time for a cell phone is 201 s and that the product that takes the least time to make is cell phone A (it takes around 180 s). Additionally, it was established that the bottleneck is found when the process begins. This is because all launchers stop and cannot continue on the conveyor until the robotic arm of the storage machine picks up or drops off the products as scheduled in the production orders. The next machine that generates an additional delay in the production time of each cell is the robotic assembly cell. It was observed that when the production orders have mobile equipment with plates in consecutive positions, the process time increases considerably.

5.2 Process Discovery

After the general review of the process, we proceeded with the exploration of it in order to analyze and understand it. The first thing that was observed when analyzing the activities and the process sequence in each of the cases is that, due to the configuration of the manufacturing cell, the cases always follow an established sequence according to the initial definition of the process. That is, there are no deviations where one passes from one activity to another without following the established normal production route, as can be seen in the discovery diagram of process mining in Fig. 2.

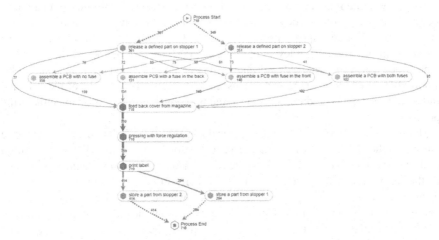

Fig. 2. Real process model

With respect to resource usage and the average processing time, it was found that the robotic assembly workstation (M2) is the one that takes the longest with 26.65 s (see Table 2).

Table 2. Average machine operation time

Work center	Average processing time (seconds)
High bay storage (M1)	5.43
Robot assembly station (M2)	26.62
Magazine application module (M3)	1.15
Muscle press module (M4)	1.07
Labeling module (M5)	2.47

5.3 Variant Comparison

Given the characteristics of the storage module (M1), it is possible to determine in the production order the starting or ending place of each manufactured product, either on rail 1 (R1) or on rail 2 (R2). This variation in the production orders gives flexibility to the manufacturing cell, since depending on where the product starts and ends, the final time of the production order will vary. Each of the four possible variations was analyzed according to average cycle time, standard deviation, longest cycle time, and shortest cycle time. The result of this comparison (see Table 3) determines that the variation in the process that has better execution times is that of the products that start on rail 2 and end up on rail 1, followed by those that leave and end up on rail 2.

Table 3. Product routes variants comparison

Variant	Average cycle time (seconds)	Standard deviation	Longest cycle time (seconds)	Shorter cycle time (seconds)
R1-R1	347.99	202.29	882	53
R1-R2	293.71	180.79	889	63
R2-R1	199.99	136.35	668	45
R2-R1	201.22	124.7	805	53

6 Predictive Analysis

The process flow for the evaluation of the different predictive model based on the data obtained from the 710 cases is shown in Fig. 3. A combination of different modeling techniques were evaluated, which generated several predictive models. Each of them were analyzed and selected based on performance evaluation metrics.

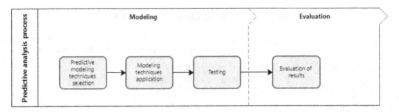

Fig. 3. Predictive analysis process flow

6.1 Predictive Modeling Techniques

To generate the possible models, a combination of three features of the predictive modeling techniques was used: bucketing method, encoding method and learning method.

- Bucketing. The sequences of the different events in the database are divided into several groups and different models are trained for each of these groups [17].
- Encoding: To train a model, all cases and records that are in the same group must be represented as feature vectors of fixed and unified length [17].
- Learning method: Supervised learning methods were used for model training, in this case: decision trees, random forest and gradient boosting. These methods have been using for predictive process monitoring in previous work [2, 11, 17] showing good results in predicting a variable based on a process event log.

The combination and selection of each of these modeling techniques yielded 36 models. Figure 4 shows these combinations schematically.

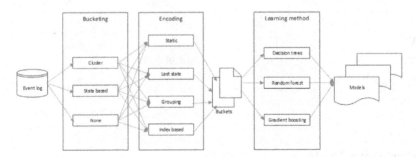

Fig. 4. Predictive model generation

6.2 Model Comparison and Selection

Python development integrated with Nirdizati (2020) was used for the evaluation of the different models that result from the combination of the predictive method, bucketing and encoding options. Phyton was used because of its features not only when training the data but also because of the future possibility of connecting to the manufacturing cell database and making predictions in real time.

To determine the accuracy of the prediction model, a comparison is made between the predicted value and the real value of each model using the test data set (20% of the initial base). Three performance metrics were used: mean absolute error (MAE), root mean square error (RMSE) and coefficient of determination (R2). Table 4 shows the value of these metrics for each model.

Table 4. Prediction model evaluation

Model	Predictive method	Bucketing	Encoding	MAE	RMSE	R2
1	Decision trees	None	Static	26.49	50.64	0.81
2	Decision trees	None	Last state	19.19	28.60	0.67
3	Decision trees	None	Grouping	25.01	53.47	0.80
4	Decision trees	None	Index based	18.30	38.5	0.82
5	Decision trees	Cluster	Static	27.66	55.88	0.83
6	Decision trees	Cluster	Last state	18.92	28.26	0.67
7	Decision trees	Cluster	Grouping	24.45	52.14	0.80
8	Decision trees	Cluster	Index based	18.79	39.57	0.82
9	Decision trees	Last state	Static	15.44	23.09	0.52
10	Decision trees	Last state	Last state	15.44	23.10	0.53
11	Decision trees	Last state	Grouping	15.44	23.11	0.54
12	Decision trees	Last state	Index based	15.44	23.12	0.55
13	Random forest	None	Static	53.59	121.14	0.75
14	Random forest	None	Last state	13.26	20.31	0.45
15	Random forest	None	Grouping	54.89	121.41	0.76
16	Random forest	None	Index based	55.32	121.57	0.76
17	Random forest	Cluster	Static	53.57	121.26	0.75
18	Random forest	Cluster	Last state	13.26	20.31	0.45
19	Random forest	Cluster	Grouping	54.89	121.41	0.76
20	Random forest	Cluster	Index based	55.32	121.57	0.76
21	Random forest	Last state	Static	15.70	23.00	0.52
22	Random forest	Last state	Last state	15.48	23.14	0.53
23	Random forest	Last state	Grouping	15.49	23.15	0.54
24	Random forest	Last state	Index based	15.50	23.16	0.55
25	Gradient boosting	None	Static	16.45	19.96	0.84
26	Gradient boosting	None	Last state	23.59	31.34	0.00
27	Gradient boosting	None	Grouping	28.66	38.18	0.84
28	Gradient boosting	None	Index based	8.64	12.37	0.88
29	Gradient boosting	Cluster	Static	15.16	20.02	0.75
30	Gradient boosting	Cluster	Last state	15.35	20.28	0.76
31	Gradient boosting	Cluster	Grouping	42.27	68.89	0.83
32	Gradient boosting	Cluster	Index based	9.01	14.02	0.87
33	Gradient boosting	Last state	Static	15.41	23.05	0.52
34	Gradient boosting	Last state	Last state	15.42	23.06	0.53
35	Gradient boosting	Last state	Grouping	15.43	23.07	0.54
36	Gradient boosting	Last state	Index based	15.44	23.08	0.55

To facilitate visualization and comparison of performance measures, a scatter plot graph was constructed (see Fig. 5) in which the value of the root mean square error (RMSE) versus the coefficient of determination (R2) for each of the 36 models can be visualized. The labels of each observation on the graph correspond to the identification number assigned to each model (see Table 4). The coefficient of determination was plotted because, unlike the other two performance measures, it reflects how well the model predicts an outcome. Regarding the other two metrics, although both have the analytical advantage of expressing the error in units of time (the unit of measurement of the response variable), the root mean square error (RMSE) was selected because, unlike the mean absolute error (MAE), in its magnitude a relatively high weight is given to large errors, which could be considered significant in the context of the prediction model.

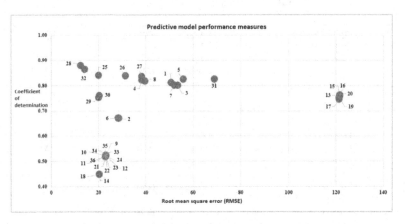

Fig. 5. Comparison of predictive models performance measures

When making an overall comparison of the performance metrics between the 36 models, the models identified with labels 28 and 32 are the ones that present the best results. These two models are characterized by the fact that the learning method used was gradient boosting and the coding of the groups was index-based. Given that between these two models, the one with the best performance metrics is the one with the label 28, this is the one selected to be implemented in the manufacturing cell to make predictions in real time.

When analyzing the graph of the remaining process time predicted value and the real remaining process time value of the results produced by the selected model (see Fig. 6), it can be seen that although there are some outliers, most of the data is aligned into the middle of the graph. This leads to the conclusion that most of the predicted values are very close to the real values.

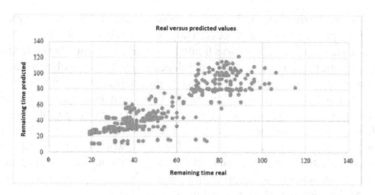

Fig. 6. Comparison of real values vs prediction

7 Results and Discussion

For the development of the methodology, the production of 710 products in the manufacturing cell was simulated. Based on the event log obtained, it was possible to perform a descriptive analysis using process mining tools that allowed mainly to characterize the behavior of the manufacturing process and to determine the resource restrictions. The storage and the robotic assembly workstations are the resources that generate a considerable increase in process times. In the case of the storage workstation, this occurs because all the products must begin and end there, and sometimes there are wait times due to the limited capacity of the robotic arm that moves the product to the conveyor belt.

The predictive model enables determining the best predictive method based on the combination of bucketing and encoding options to predict the remaining process time. Gradient boosting trees predictive methods had the best performance based on root mean square error (RMSE) and the coefficient of determination (R2).

By combining the results obtained by both analyses, it is possible to improve the way in which production orders are scheduled and make timely decisions that improve the efficiency of the system since, on the one hand, the limitations of the system's resources are known, and on the other hand, through predictive monitoring, it will be possible to determine the estimated time of completion of a product or production order. The foregoing will also allow, as long as there is not a high volume of work in process orders, to determine which should be the next one to be produced and in the same sense, to fulfill established commitments or target times.

8 Conclusions and Future Work

Manufacturing environments are being transformed thanks to the fourth industrial revolution called Industry 4.0. Given the flexibility requirements that characterize cyber-physical manufacturing systems, it is essential to develop data analytics methods that leverage the greater availability of data generation and acquisition in order to analyze and improve key performance manufacturing measures. Based on this, through the proposed method developed in this work, a predictive model was obtained for a computer integrated manufacturing system that allows the prediction of the remaining processing time to finish a product that is in process to improve the decision-making.

Although the scope of the work was limited to the development of a single predictive model, through the implementation of the developed method, it is possible to train models to predict other important system metrics such as the production capacity indicators. By predicting the number of mobile equipment that could be manufactured per hour given certain conditions, it would be possible to determine the efficiency of the system and would allow the process leader to make better decisions related to the production order sequencing for optimizing processing times. For future work, it is proposed to use the results of the prediction of the remaining time of the production orders with optimization models for the sequencing of the production orders that allow changes to be made in real time and thus optimize the times and use of resources.

Finally, another promising research perspective is related to the continuous incorporation of real-time data for enhancing the prediction model. The model training could be automated with the variation of certain parameters and its subsequent evaluation through performance metrics. This would allow having better predictors each time, since the predictive model would have more data to learn from.

References

1. Aalst, W.V.D.: Process Mining - Data Science in Action. Springer, Heidelberg (2016). https://doi.org/10.1007/978-3-662-49851-4
2. Aalst, W.V.D., Schonenberg, M.H., Song, M.: Time prediction based on process mining. Inf. Syst. **36**(2), 450–475 (2011)
3. van der Aalst, W., et al.: Process mining manifesto. In: Daniel, F., Barkaoui, K., Dustdar, S. (eds.) BPM 2011. LNBIP, vol. 99, pp. 169–194. Springer, Heidelberg (2012). https://doi.org/10.1007/978-3-642-28108-2_19
4. Choueiri, A.C., Sato, D.M.V., Scalabrin, E.E., Santos, E.A.P.: An extended model for remaining time prediction in manufacturing systems using process mining. J. Manuf. Syst. **56**, 188–201 (2020)
5. Dreher, S., Reimann, P., Gröger, C.: Application fields and research gaps of process mining in manufacturing companies. INFORMATIK **2020** (2021)
6. Hermann, M., Pentek, T., Otto, B.: Design principles for industries 4.0 scenarios. In: 2016 49th Hawaii international conference on system sciences (HICSS), pp. 3928–3937. IEEE (2016)
7. IBM: CRISP-DM help overview (2020). https://www.ibm.com/docs/en/spssmodeler/SaaS?topic=dm-crisp-help-overview. Accessed 2 May 2022
8. Jimenez, J.F., Zambrano-Rey, G., Aguirre, S., Trentesaux, D.: Using process mining for understating the emergence of self-organizing manufacturing systems. IFAC-PapersOnLine **51**(11), 1618–1623 (2018)
9. Lee, E.A.: Cyber physical systems: design challenges. In: 2008 11th IEEE International Symposium on Object and Component-Oriented Real-Time Distributed Computing (ISORC), pp. 363–369. IEEE (2008)
10. Lee, J., Bagheri, B., Kao, H.A.: A cyber-physical systems architecture for industry 4.0-based manufacturing systems. Manuf. Lett. **3**, 18–23 (2015)
11. López Castro, L., Martínez, S., Rodriguez, N., Lovera, L., Santiago Aguirre, H., Jimenez, J.-F.: Development of a predictive process monitoring methodology in a self-organized manufacturing system. In: Trentesaux, D., Borangiu, T., Leitão, P., Jimenez, J.-F., Montoya-Torres,

J.R. (eds.) SOHOMA 2021. SCI, vol. 987, pp. 3–16. Springer, Cham (2021). https://doi.org/10.1007/978-3-030-80906-5_1

12. Lorenz, R., Senoner, J., Sihn, W., Netland, T.: Using process mining to improve productivity in make-to-stock manufacturing. Int. J. Prod. Res. **59**(16), 4869–4880 (2021)

13. Lozano, C.V., Vijayan, K.K.: Literature review on cyber physical systems design. Procedia Manuf. **45**, 295–300 (2020)

14. Nirdizati Org.: Why Nirdizati? (2020). http://nirdizati.org/why-nirdizati/. Accessed 30 April 2022

15. Schuh, G., Gützlaff, A., Schmitz, S., van der Aalst, W.M.: Data-based description of process performance in end-to-end order processing. CIRP Ann. **69**(1), 381–384 (2020)

16. Shmueli, G., Bruce, P.C., Yahav, I., Patel, N.R., Lichtendahl, K.C. Jr.: Data Mining for Business Analytics: Concepts, Techniques, and Applications in R. Wiley (2017)

17. Teinemaa, I., Dumas, M., Rosa, M.L., Maggi, F.M.: Outcome-oriented predictive process monitoring: review and benchmark. ACM Trans. Knowl. Discovery Data (TKDD) **13**(2), 1–57 (2019)

18. Van Dongen, B., van Luin, J., Verbeek, E.: Process mining in a multi-agent auctioning system. In: Proceedings of the 4th International Workshop on Modelling of Objects, Components, and Agents, Turku, pp. 145–160 (2006)

19. Veit, F., Geyer-Klingeberg, J., Madrzak, J., Haug, M., Thomson, J.: The proactive insights engine: process mining meets machine learning and artificial intelligence. In: BPM (Demos) (2017)

20. Yilmaz, S.E.: Overcoming the technology myopia of industry 4.0 (2020). https://eds-b-ebs cohostcom.ezproxy.javeriana.edu.co/eds/pdfviewer/pdfviewervid=5&sid=9b9034fdd93c-405b-866c-a1fe06e1d94a%40sessionmgr101. Accessed 30 April 2022

Artificial Intelligence Methods to Solve Energy Transmission Problems Through Data Analysis from Different Data Sources

Juan Carlos Carreño[1](✉) (iD), Adriana Marcela Vega[2] (iD), and Alvaro Espinel[2] (iD)

[1] Distrital Francisco Jose de Caldas University and Grupo Energia Bogotá, Bogotá, Colombia
jccarrenop@correo.udistrital.edu.co
[2] Distrital Francisco Jose de Caldas University, Bogotá, Colombia

Abstract. This article proposes a discovery methodology of potential artificial intelligence sources that allow problem solving for the industry, specifically electricity transmission. Different data sources used as a reference for academic investigations such as thesis work project and patents were considered to observe the different investigation focus of a particular topic based on a study case.

Keywords: Artificial intelligence · Electric networks · Analysis · Methods · Electrical protection

1 Introduction

The elaboration of most investigation academic projects starts with a relevant-information lookup scheme in which the investigator aims to identify the study lines being followed national or worldwide. However, on most occasions this process is not performed appropriately since they are not following a methodic process and therefore waste time and effort by finding and selecting the most relevant data. To improve this process, is important to start by defining the best references that could be linked, as an example, for the case study referenced in this article, the following should be considered:

- Scientific articles
- Thesis
- Books
- Patents
- Press articles

Then, with the tools and data bases that, in this case, were available and using free-access web pages, each one of the reference sources was linked to the information sources as shown in Table 1.

© The Author(s), under exclusive license to Springer Nature Switzerland AG 2022
J. C. Figueroa-García et al. (Eds.): WEA 2022, CCIS 1685, pp. 122–136, 2022.
https://doi.org/10.1007/978-3-031-20611-5_11

Table 1. Reference sources and their corresponding source of information used.

Reference sources	Information sources
Scientific Articles	Scopus - https://www.scopus.com/ IEEE - https://www.ieee.org/ ScienceDirect - https://www.sciencedirect.com/ ProQuest - https://www.proquest.com/ Google Scholar - https://scholar.google.com/ Oxford Academic - https://academic.oup.com/journals SciELO - https://scielo.org/es/
Thesis	Repository Institucional Universidad Distrital Francisco Jose de Caldas - https://repository.udistrital.edu.co/Repositorio Universidad Tecnológica de Pereira - https://repositorio.utp.edu.co/ Repository Universidad Santo Tomas - https://repository.usta.edu.co/ Repository Institucional de la Universidad Politécnica Salesiana - https://dspace.ups.edu.ec/ Séneca Repositorio Institucional Universidad de los Andes - https://reposi torio.uniandes.edu.co/ Repository Académico Digital Universidad Autónoma De Nuevo León - https://eprints.uanl.mx/ Repository Digital Instituto Politécnico Nacional - https://www.repositor iodigital.ipn.mx/ Repository Institucional Universidad Nacional de Colombia - https://rep ositorio.unal.edu.co/ Repository Institucional CONICET - https://ri.conicet.gov.ar/
Books	Editorial Universidad Nacional de Colombia - http://www.editorial.unal.edu.co/ Editorial Universidad Distrital Francisco Jose de Caldas - https://editorial.udistrital.edu.co/libros.php Amazon - https://www.amazon.com/-/es/ref=nav_logo BuscaLIBRE - https://www.buscalibre.com.co/ Librería Nacional - https://librerianacional.com/ Library Universidad Distrital Francisco Jose de Caldas. - http://sistemade bibliotecas.udistrital.edu.co:8000/index.php/bibliotecas/ingenieria Library Luis Angel Arango - https://www.banrepcultural.org/bogota/biblio teca-luis-angel-arango
Patents	Clarivate - https://www-webofscience-com.bdigital.udistrital.edu.co/wos/woscc/basic-search Google Patents - https://patents.google.com/

2   Study Case

With the continuous development of electric networks and the energetic market, the users have higher requirements each time for the safe and reliability of the energy supply. The electric network is an important character in the transmission and distribution of energy by being the intermediary between the generation plants and the final user [1].

A single fault in the electric system may generate economic losses, security issues, social problems and even cost human lives. Which is why is important to count with an efficient strategy to detect and locate failures to reduce their fixing time and recurrence. Environmental adversities as storms, snow, rain, wind amongst others often cause short circuits. Other natural but problems, Other minor but natural problems such as animals, plants and growing vegetation are also a recurrent cause of short circuits. Thus, these lines are often subject to failures [2]. Despite the security rules and failure prevention techniques, these events occur spontaneously and randomly due to different natural events, equipment failures, human error amongst others [3].

The consequences of these failures require a fast response from the power system event diagnose, so as accuracy in diagnoses regarding the sections where they occur, components and properties of the failure according to analysis and experience of the operative crew based in relevant information generated by multiple protection and electronic devices. Due to the big scale and growing complexity of modern electric networks, traditional methods may lack of capacity to handle big data collected by SCADA systems, for the case of events over the system [4].

Reestablishing the operations of the component or failed part of the system requires to know or determine which was the failed element (for the case of equipment) or where it is located (for the case of a transmission line) [5]. It is necessary to locate the failures in the powerlines to guarantee safety and reliability in the power system [6]. Detection and location remain very important for the continuity of the service. Nowadays, these two activities are still being carried out in a traditional way such as physical teams being sent to locations, and visual identification of a broken circuit which is then isolated from the powerline for its further reparation and reincorporated once the failure is completely isolated [7]. These event-dependent analysis might have longer delayed and uncertainty for decision making in the reestablishment of the circuit [8].

Based on the above, the proposed study case is related to the failure analysis in electricity transmission systems, allowing to process information and make fast operative decisions under the concept denominated 'informed decisions. With the help of artificial intelligence, the identification of failures will be easier due to the register analysis, allowing an event to diagnose in real time, obtaining information such as place of occurrence, possible affectations, potential type of failure and information regarding the perturbation value to reestablish the affected circuits.

3 Analysis Methodology

The key words of the investigation are defined based on the reference sources and their corresponding information sources. This process is done through a top-down analysis to have a visual onto the focus of the investigation worldwide and nationwide to identify the path leading the efforts of the study. This methodology is represented in Fig. 1.

To facilitate this analysis process, the steps described in Fig. 2 were followed which, allow facilitate gathering valuable information that may be applied to the development of any investigation, where multiple tools are used so as data analytics is used to deepen on interest areas and those who allow to generate new knowledge.

Fig. 1. General information analysis methodology.

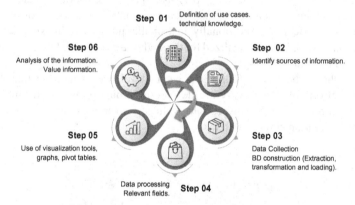

Fig. 2. Steps for the analysis of information.

4   Information Analysis

With this methodology, the analysis is split in two parts, the first one is associated to scientific articles using the tool Elsier (https://www.scopus.com/search/form.uri?display=basic#basic, Jul. 05, 2022), and the second one directed towards patents based on [9], which allows to obtain the investigation focus on an academic level and investigative orientations on an industry level, allowing to know the updated map of the relevant topics in the area of interest and thus support the identification and justification for the study development.

This way, the obtained results are presented in the context of the study case in the investigation area for the scientific articles and patents, the previous with the support of the tools and data bases described previously and compiled according to the exportation of plain archives with different information structures, used to achieve the desired analysis shown in this article.

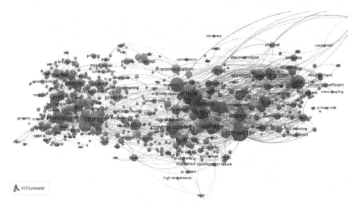

Fig. 3. Research topics around the area of interest of scientific articles.

From Fig. 3, where VOSviewer app is used [10], four marked clusters may be observed highlighting the energy storage sources, control strategies, converters, and wireless power transference. Additionally, in a smaller proportion, but significantly relevant, some interest topics are visualized for the study case which are failures, prediction, decisions, and machine learning.

Figure 4 shows the results found in a patent level, which indicate that the main investigation efforts of the industry are developing around transmission lines, direct current, control modules, robot inspections, voltage converters, energy storage, control systems and oscillation control systems.

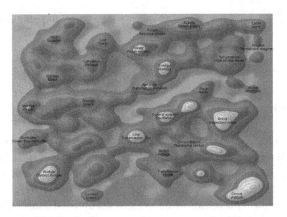

Fig. 4. Surface map of patent research topics.

With these results, the general context of the study area is obtained, and the investigative trends are identified. As part of the analysis exercise, the following key topics are highlighted to continue the search for information and thus find the relevant references that add value to the work that is to be developed. Within what was found both in scientific articles and patents, the topics Transmission Lines, Faults, Decision Making and Machine Learning are extracted, which will later be used to intensify the search in the different sources of information.

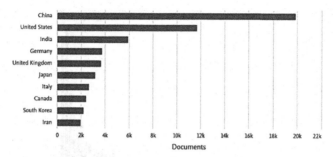

Fig. 5. Geographical location scientific articles.

Continuing, Fig. 5 and Fig. 6 are made to identify the geographic and institutional location of current research around interest, both scientific articles and patents.

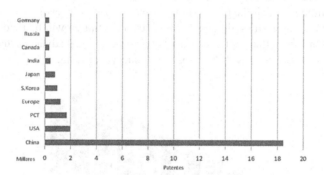

Fig. 6. Geographic location of patents.

From this analysis it is observed that China is a benchmark in the general area of study, highlighting its research effort that revolves around over 20,000 published scientific so as a significant proportion of patents registered, around 19,000. Another benchmark about the study case is the United States, where approximately 12,000 scientific articles have been published and nearly 2,000 patents registered. The marked difference that China imposes on other countries regarding energy and power transmission systems is highlighted. On the other hand, a topic that was identified is that at the level of patents, the leadership is led by two state-owned Chinese companies [11, 12]. The first one was founded in 2002 that acts as an agent in the energy sector that builds and operates electrical networks, serving more than 1.1 billion users. The second one was founded in 2005 and operates electricity networks in five provinces in southern China, with a total service area covering 1 million km^2 and serving over 252 million people.

Another benchmark of the study case is the United States, with approximately 12,000 published scientific articles and nearly 2,000 registered patents. The difference that China has against the US and other countries evidences its advantage in energy and power transmission systems.

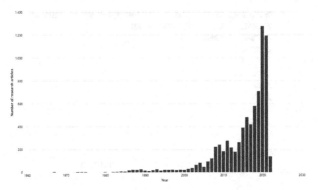

Fig. 7. Behavior of research over time of scientific articles.

Based on the above, Fig. 7 and Fig. 8 show the behavior of scientific articles and patents over time in which the growth trend of energy sector investigations is observed, gaining more and more strength, generating an exponential growth marked since 2010. The studies done about this are the product of the technological advances that have been had in the world associated with the capacity of data processing.

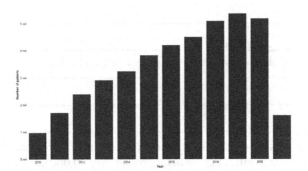

Fig. 8. Behavior of research over time of patents.

From the most general perspective, the search for keywords was carried out in the abstracts and titles of scientific articles and patents with the aim of beginning to guide the relevant concepts that are being worked on around interest, finding the results presented in Fig. 9, in which the word cloud is used to represent it graphically.

This first analysis brings up the concepts of power systems, energy, control systems, storage, methods, monitoring, transmission, data, signals, voltages, current and failures. Within this framework of patents, it is observed that the word 'devices' appear, which somewhat reflect the real application that is developed in the industry.

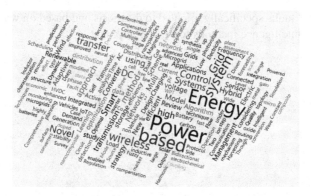

Fig. 9. Key concepts patents and scientific articles.

On the other hand, scientific articles extract the concepts of energy, power systems, control systems, transmission, methods, algorithms, detection, voltage, and loads. Also, different investigation trends such as renewable energies, storage, direct current transmission, wireless technologies, and artificial intelligence implementation methods. Thus, the proposed methodology would imply focusing on the investigation of important topics. It was initially focused on power systems giving an extension to this study line, where the behavior shown in Fig. 10 was identified. The figure shows an important component associated to the technology, artificial intelligence methods, key concepts regarding the diagnose, modelling and failure identification are also mentioned.

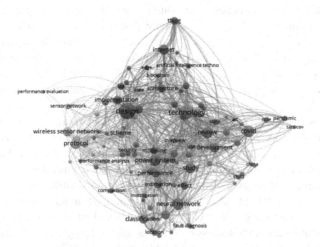

Fig. 10. Extension of the line of study of interest.

From this initial result, the search is focused on electric failures in the transmission line showing the key concept map of Fig. 11. At this point it is observed that the related concepts focus on fault detection, fault location, signals, electrical protections and show some artificial intelligence methods. With this, an interest is generated to deepen into the area of electrical faults specifically oriented to diagnosis and based on what was found, to link artificial intelligence methods for its development.

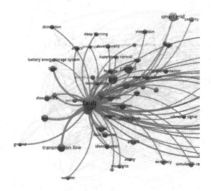

Fig. 11. Search for electrical faults in transmission lines.

Then, we continue with the search for the use of artificial intelligence methods in the energy sector, finding among those used machine learning, predictive methods, optimization algorithms, classifications, deep neural networks, wavelet transformations, clustering, decision trees, neural networks, vector support machines, and some variables used in a bigger proportion such as temperature, energy consumption, costs, energetic demand, solar radiation, time series, amongst others.

The search for patents in energy transmission and the use of analytics and artificial intelligence continues, to observe the behavior that is taking place in this area and its investigative validity. Figure 12 presents the results in which it is identified that the efforts are being oriented to distribution networks, image processing in transmission lines, transmission cables, information modules, information layers, neural networks, and in a large proportion in the online failures with the help of the search platform presented in [9].

Likewise, with the help of the word cloud, the key concepts associated with electrical power systems that link analytics and artificial intelligence are obtained. In the case of patents, a strong component is obtained in transmission lines, of course based on data and methods, which together with some identified variables as current, voltage, load, frequency, distance, monitoring of signals, are used for the identification, evaluation and prediction of aspects related to the transmission of energy. Similarly, in scientific articles related to electrical power systems that link analytics and artificial intelligence, there is an important component in transmission systems, highlighting the concepts of artificial intelligence and learning that use some variables that are identified as voltage, the load, frequency, demand, signal monitoring, efficiency, to take advantage of the data, process it, analyze it and therefore know the state of the observed system to achieve predictions that finally gives greater tools to decision makers.

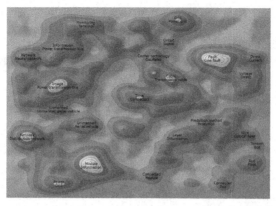

Fig. 12. Search for patents around the area of electrical energy and the use of analytics and artificial intelligence.

5 Results

The main results are shown based on the information analysis, allowing to strengthen the bases of the investigation, and identifying the different aspects that must be deepened for the development of the different stages of the study and the implementation of artificial intelligence in the selected case of use.

Analysis Dashboards

Analysis boards were prepared with the purpose of capturing, in a legible way, the search information of the different databases, which in this case included patents and scientific articles, in which statistical and graphic tools were used to identify the study line of interest and in this way focus efforts to deepen research of value regarding the key input for the development of the degree work. In Fig. 13, with the help of Power BI Microsoft tool, (https://powerbi.microsoft.com/es-es/, Jul. 13, 2022), the investigative control dashboards are displayed to achieve interaction with the information based on the titles, summaries and in general with the information obtained from different sources of information.

The dashboards allow to visualized relevant data of the carried out investigations such as the behavior at the regional and institutional or corporate level in the case of patents, it shows the different developments and studies over time that allows, to a certain extent, to know how current is the topic that is intended to deepen, the word cloud method is also used, which graphically represents the count of words from the search database, which contributes to the identification of keywords for the detailed search of the information that will be used as a reference and that allows efforts to be directed to relevant information for the study area. In the same way, certain basic analytics are carried out graphically, such as the count of investigations, a classification by type and by topic or relevant word. Additionally, custom filters were programmed to understand the information in a simpler way than the flat files that are exported from the different information sources.

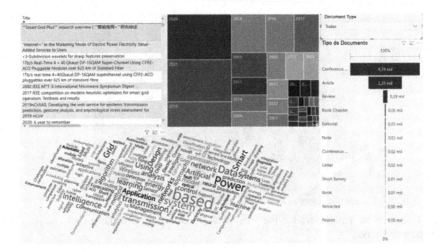

Fig. 13. Dashboard of analysis of patents and scientific articles.

Bibliographic Manager

As part of the methodology for reviewing the different reference documents, the bibliographic manager (Mendeley, 2022) was used (depending on preferences, the bibliographic manager that best suits the needs of the user may be used), in which the different references are created from files exported from information sources or in a personalized way through manual entry. This tool allows users to upload digital files, make annotations and highlight the relevant parts considered by the reader. Additionally, after reading and writing the different notes, it allows to export the citations in standard formats, which can be read by common word processors and in this way control the references of articles, theses and degree works.

Artificial Intelligence Method Matrix

Another important element in the case study is the artificial intelligence methods and, in general, the possible ways that can be used to solve engineering problems and that in the developed exercise seeks to be implemented for the analysis of events that occur in the power transmission systems. Based on this and making the corresponding search in the different sources of information, having the filter results of the data processing mentioned in the previous section as a precedent, the possible techniques that would respond to the proposed activity would be the following:

• Neural Networks	• Information fusion technologies
• Bayesian Networks	• Neural Concurrent Fuzzy
• Petri Nets	• Decision trees
• Optimization Methods	• Genetic algorithms
• Expert Systems	• Clustering Techniques
• Fuzzy Logic	• Lineal regression
• Rough Sets	• Logistic regression
• Fuzzy Sets	• Support-vector Machines
• Multi-agent Systems	• k-nearest neighbors

The results now requires to identify, first of all, which methods in a general way are the most used since they are the ones that have had the most research developments, and secondly, to evaluate the gaps in knowledge that are currently being presented and that in the case of master's and doctoral theses, could be approached, always with the objective of having satisfactory results in the development of the research. For this reason, the following relationship matrix was constructed, which was assembled from the search for information sources and only considering the number of investigations in the determined method and their respective combinations, in any area of study, obtaining the results of Fig. 14.

From these results, it is observed that the methods of greater investigative use in the different areas of knowledge have been optimization methods, followed by logistic regression, linear regression, and genetic algorithms. To a lesser extent but at the same time, neural networks are also considered relevant since even without being the most studied at a general level, presents an important component in terms of the ease of combining with different methods and could be defined as the one with the greatest interoperability, which is why for this reason it is one of the candidate methods to be addressed in the case study.

However, research gaps based on search are manifested in concurrent neuro fuzzy methods, expert systems, information fusion technologies, approximate sets, and Petri nets. Based on these results, the search was focused on the specific research area where the opportunity to delve into the methods of expert systems, rough sets and information fusion technologies was ratified.

Additionally, due to its versatility, there is also the option of combining these methods with neural networks, these being a framework that makes several learning algorithms work together, therefore, processes complex data inputs efficiently. After receiving the input, it changes its internal state and finally produces an output that is based on the input and the activation function [13].

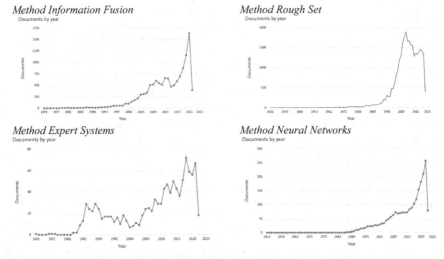

Fig. 14. Method relationship matrix.

Method Information Fusion
Documents by year

Method Rough Set
Documents by year

Method Expert Systems
Documents by year

Method Neural Networks
Documents by year

Fig. 15. Research behavior of the selected methods.

Consequently, from the previous analysis, it can be inferred that these methods are good candidates to be approached, since, on the one hand, they represent a current study that is growing and, on the other hand, they have the opportunity for development since the number of investigations are reduced with respect to the different methods found as a possible solution for the investigation.

As a fundamental idea of what has been observed so far, is to achieve the combination of different methods for the development of the research, for this reason within the searches this component was also covered, obtaining the results presented in Fig. 15 and Fig. 16, where it is observed in general that the investigations oriented to the combination of methods in the particular case of the selection are not continuous and it even can be sporadic in time, which strengthens the concept of generating this interrelation and obtaining an integral model from them.

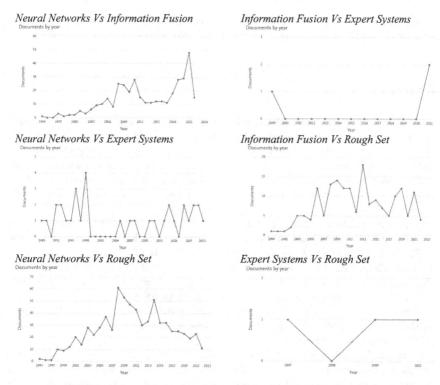

Fig. 16. Research behavior of the combination of selected methods.

6 Conclusions

As stated in the case study, the proposed methodology can achieve more accurate results by linking different sources of information, this with the strategy of targeting the topic through the identification of research trends on an academic level, in the industrial environment. And technological development.

The baseline of study was identified, to develop research oriented to the use of artificial intelligence selecting the methods of neural networks, approximate groups, expert systems, and information fusion, for the case of use oriented to the electrical sector in the specific area of systems power transmission.

As part of the work presented in this article, it is highlighted that data analytics in the initial phase of any research or project is a key part in the new educational and business environments, so it is important that different careers and professions focus it as a transversal knowledge area.

It was established that the combination of different methods for the development of research is convenient because a complement is obtained between the methods that strengthen each other to collectively reduce the weaknesses or limitations of the other, as well as allowing investigative exploration of hybrid models, which, as presented in the article, have been studied and implemented significantly in recent years.

Acknowledgments. Thanks to the Universidad Distrital Francisco José de Caldas - engineering doctorate and to the GESETIC investigation group, for making possible this investigation.

References

1. Xu, J., Yue, H.: Research on fault diagnosis method of power grid based on artificial intelligence. In: 2020 IEEE Conference on Telecommunications, Optics and Computer Science, TOCS 2020, pp. 113–116 (2020). https://doi.org/10.1109/TOCS50858.2020.9339711
2. Mukherjee, A., Kundu, P.K., Das, A.: Transmission line faults in power system and the different algorithms for identification, classification and localization: a brief review of methods. J. Inst. Eng. (India) Ser. B **102**(4), 855–877 (2021). https://doi.org/10.1007/s40031-020-00530-0
3. Doria-García, J., Orozco-Henao, C., Leborgne, R., Montoya, O.D., Gil-González, W.: High impedance fault modeling and location for transmission line☆. Electr. Power Syst. Res. **196**, 107202 (Jul.2021). https://doi.org/10.1016/J.EPSR.2021.107202
4. Chai, E., Zeng, P.P., Ma, S., Xing, H., Zhao, B.: Artificial intelligence approaches to fault diagnosis in power grids: a review. In: Chinese Control Conference, CCC, vol. 2019, pp. 7346–7353, July 2019. https://doi.org/10.23919/ChiCC.2019.8865533
5. Schneider, E.: A1 fundamentals of protection practice network protection & automation guide (2021). Accessed 29 May 2022. https://www.se.com/ww/en/tools/npag-full-online-unlocked-1130re14y/section.html#section1
6. Chakrabarti, S., Chakrabarti, S., Swetapadma, A.: A review on various artificial intelligence techniques used for transmission line fault location. In: Proceedings of the 3rd International Conference on Inventive Computation Technologies, ICICT 2018, pp. 105–109 (2018). https://doi.org/10.1109/ICICT43934.2018.9034333
7. Pouabe Eboule, P.S., Hasan, A.N.: Accurate fault detection and location in power transmission line using concurrent neuro fuzzy technique I (Precyzyjne wykrywanie i lokalizowanie usterek w linii przesyłowej energii przy uzyciu równoległej techniki neuro-rozmytej), Przeglad Elektrotechniczny **97**(1), 37–45 (2021). https://doi.org/10.15199/48.2021.01.07
8. Li, W., Gao, S., Ding, R., Hao, Y., Yang, C.: Fault detection method for energy routing nodes of smart grids oriented to electricity information security. Int. J. Performability Eng. **15**(12), 3304–3311 (2019). https://doi.org/10.23940/ijpe.19.12.p23.33043311
9. Stead, J.: Clarivet. https://clarivate.com/. Accessed 13 July 2022
10. Universiteit Leiden: VOSviewer. https://www.vosviewer.com/. Accessed July 2022
11. State Grid Corp of China: State Grid Corp of China. http://www.sgcc.com.cn/. Accessed 13July 2022
12. Guangdong Power Grid: Guangdong Power Grid. http://eng.csg.cn/h5.html. 13 July 13 2022
13. Garcia, J., Molina, J., Berlanga, A., Patricio, M., Bustamante, A., Padilla, W.: "Ciencia de datos", Técnicas Analíticas y Aprendizaje Estadístico. Publicaciones Altaria, Bogotá (2018)

A Knowledge-Based Expert System for Risk Management in Health Audit Projects

Camilo Alejandro Bustos Téllez[✉] and Eduyn Ramiro López Santana

Universidad Distrital Francisco José de Caldas, Bogotá D.C, Colombia
caabustost@correo.udistrital.edu.co, erlopezs@udistrital.edu.co

Abstract. This paper presents a knowledge-based expert system for risk assessment in health audit projects. The fuzzy group decision making approach (FGDMA) methodology is used to qualify a predetermined list of risks through linguistic terms that are then converted into numerical values. The risks were obtained through a literature review in which 5 risk themes were identified (administrative, legal, workforce, financial, schedule, project, governance, auditor and environment). With these results, a fuzzy canonical model (FCM) is constructed, which is a type of Bayesian network that uses causal diagrams to evaluate the level of risk for each phase of a project: planning, execution and closure. This article represents an approach to the use of this type of methodologies for risk assessment in health audit projects, which can be described as dynamic and complex projects.

Keywords: Fuzzy canonical model · Fuzzy group decision making approach · Project risk management

1 Introduction

Traditional risk identification, assessment and management models have limitations in addressing the complex nature of projects such as health audits. They are usually deterministic models and do not take into account aspects such as causal relationships between risks, or a systematic and repeatable assessment of risk probabilities. Traditional databases are usually not available as sources of information either, so expert opinions become the main source of information. Furthermore, there is little existing literature applied to specific cases of health audit projects.

© The Author(s), under exclusive license to Springer Nature Switzerland AG 2022
J. C. Figueroa-García et al. (Eds.): WEA 2022, CCIS 1685, pp. 137–149, 2022.
https://doi.org/10.1007/978-3-031-20611-5_12

On the other hand, artificial intelligence methods and tools have gained strength due to their ability to provide fairly approximate answers to complex problems, with solution times and low resource consumption compared to other methodologies based on optimization or operations research.

Fuzzy logic is a valuable alternative because it allows collecting the knowledge of experts in such a way that their opinions are not simplified to a single measurement value. In this sense, a methodology based on Fuzzy Group Decision Making Approach (FGDMA) is proposed for the risk collection and assessment, and on Fuzzy Canonical Model (FCM) - a type of Bayesian network (BBN) -, for the evaluation of causal relationships between the planning, execution and closure phases of a project.

This article constitutes an advance in the risk management of health audit projects by combining the fuzzy canonical model (FCM) and fuzzy group decision-making approach (FGDMA) from the perspective of individual project phases. This is because current models lack appropriate methodologies to manage the uncertainty associated with multiple expert opinion, there are few tools to manage risk knowledge expressed in qualitative variables, and the scarcity of inference methods from risk assessment for decision making [1].

This paper is organized as follows: Section 2 presents a literature review on the application of knowledge-based systems for risk management in projects; Sect. 3 describes the FGDMA approach and its methodological development, as well as the basic notions of FCM; Sect. 4 describes the results of the risk assessment and the development of causal diagrams for 3 phases of a health audit project; Sect. 5 presents the results of case study where the FCM was applied; finally concluding remarks are presented in Sect. 6.

2   Systematic Literature Review

In this section, a literature review of the main uses of artificial intelligence tools for project risk management is presented. The search for references was conducted through the Science Direct database, for the time period from 2013 to 2020. Results are summarized in Table 1.

Table 1. Systematic literature review results

Search parameters	Detailed search (overview)	Filters	Final selection
Database **Science direct** **Time horizon** **2013–2020** **Keywords:** **- Expert systems in Project risk management** **- Project management** **- Audit** **- Risk management** **- Artificial intelligence in health audit projects**	**Keywords in abstract** *Expert systems in Project risk management* - Developing countries - Expert decision systems - Mixed qualitative and quantitative risk assessment approach *Project management* - Complexity management strategies - Knowledge management in projects - Public project *Audit* - Expert evaluation - Medical Audit - Universal protocol *Risk management* - Expert knowledge - Project risk management - Uncertainty management *Artificial intelligence in health Audit projects* - Clinical decision support systems - Clinical expertise - Process mining	**Limit to areas** - Risk Management - Project management - Audit - Artificial Intelligence **Language** - English - Spanish **Type of document** - Articles - Conference articles - Review articles	**58 documents** - Relevant: documents with greater affinity to the object of study and relationship with key words were selected - Most cited: the number of citations according to Science Direct results was taken into account as a selection criterion - A second manual selection was made to complement those selected - In some cases it was necessary to consult to databases specialized in health areas Number of documents initially selected: **177**

2.1 Literature Review Results

Parallel to classical risk management approaches, several authors have proposed knowledge-based methodologies to carry out the identification, assessment and control of project risks. Even more so when these have characteristics of complexity and uncertainty. The following is a synthesis of some of the proposals found in the literature review.

Some of these approaches have focused on formalizing the concepts of complexity, its identification and measurement [2–4]. Other approaches have focused on knowledge management, or on the interaction of knowledge management and big data as in the case of [5].

One of these approaches is precisely the Fuzzy Group Decision Making Approach (FGDMA), which gathers the knowledge of experts to estimate the risk level of a project or its phases by assessing the probability and impact [6], the objective is that these serve as decision support [6, 7].

Risk assessment approaches may include a qualitative phase, in which risks are identified through expert interviews, Delphi method [4, 8], literature review, and the quantification phase, where questionnaires, brainstorming, ranked node/paths, risk map and Bayesian truth serum have been used as in [9], mixed methods such as the analytic hierarchy process (AHP) [10], or the analytical network process (ANP) in the case of [11]. Of great importance is the development of causal networks between risks for each phase of the project or its life cycle to understand the dynamic interaction of risks in large-scale project environments or with multiple influencing factors [1, 9].

Another notable advantage of expert systems is that they do not necessarily require quantitative data as input, but rather expert knowledge or very small data sets as in [12], in [13] knowledge-based methods allow dealing with contingency or change management situations in projects, where risks change dynamically over time and require agility for decision making.

In general, risk management goes beyond prevention, but is actually a key success factor for projects, with macroeconomic effects for a country, as well as for cost optimization, schedule and value-added delivery through quality [6, 8].

This paper combines the strategy proposed by [1] combining the FGDMA technique with the Fuzzy Canonical Model (FCM), which is a type of Bayesian network using the Noisy-Or-Gate mechanism that offers less computation time and expert knowledge gathering compared to other types of Bayesian networks. The purpose is to contribute to body of knowledge in risk management in health audit projects in particular, but also knowledge-intensive projects in general.

3   Development of Bayesian Networks

3.1   Fuzzy Group Decision Making Approach (FGDMA)

This article uses the Fuzzy Group Decision Making Approach to evaluate independent risks and determine the degree of causality between risks, as proposed by [1], in each of the diagrams constructed for each project phase: Planning, Execution and Closure. For this purpose, interviews were conducted with experts who rated on a qualitative scale the probability, impact and degree of influence. The step by step can be described as follows:

Fuzzy Triangular Number for Each Linguistic Term (FTN). Table 2 was used as qualitative scale for risk assessment as in [1].

Table 2. Linguistic variable and Fuzzy number equivalence

Level of risk likelihood/consequence	Fuzzy triangular number (FTN)	Defuzzified number range	Description
Extremely high	0.9,1.0,1.0	0.9 to 1.00	The risk event is almost certain to occur and involves and extremely significant risk materialization
Very high	0.7,0.9,1.0	0.7 to < 0.9	The risk event has a very high chance of occurring and involves a most significant risk materialization
High	0.5,0.7,0.9	0.5 to < 0.7	The risk event has a high chance of occurring and involves a significant risk materialization
Medium	0.3,0.5,0.7	0.3 to < 0.5	The risk event is likely to occur and involves a moderately significant risk materialization
Low	0.1,0.3,0.5	0.1 to < 0.3	The risk event has a rare chance of occurring and involves a little significant risk materialization
Very low	0, 0.1, 0.3	0.025 to < 0.1	The risk event has a very rare chance of occurring and involves a very little significant risk materialization
None	0, 0, 0.1	0 to < 0.025	The risk event will never happen

Construct the Fuzzy Decision Matrix (FDM). Using the fuzzy numbers obtained from the surveys, construct a matrix for each probability (RL), Consequence (C) of each individual risk (r) in each particular project phase (p).

$$\left(FDM_{RL/C}^{r} \right)_p = \begin{bmatrix} l_1 & m_1 & u_1 \\ \ldots \ldots \ldots \\ l_n & m_n & u_n \end{bmatrix} \tag{1}$$

Weighting the Experts' Opinion. In order to improve the reliability of the data, the following factors are weighted: Professional Position (PP), Work Experience (EP), Experience acquired in other projects (EO) and Academic Degree (AQ), this is known as weight of professional competence w_i^{Ind}. Assuming that each criterion has equal weight, the overall weight of professional competence of an expert w_i^g is calculated.

$$w_i^{Ind} = (w_{PP} + w_{EP} + w_{EO} + w_{AQ})_i \tag{2}$$

All individual expert weights must sum to unity, to satisfy the condition that the highest fuzzy score is 1 as shown in Table 2.

$$w_i^g = \frac{w_i^{Ind}}{\sum_{i=1}^n w_i^{Ind}}; \sum_{i=1}^n w_i^g \tag{3}$$

Obtain the Weighted Fuzzy Decision Matrix (WFDM). Considering the weighting of each expert, the fuzzy decision matrix is transformed as by multiplying the FDM by the w_i^g

$$\left(WFDM_{RL/C}^r\right)_p = \left(FDM_{RL/C}^r\right)_p * w_i^g = \begin{bmatrix} l_1 w_1^g & m_1 w_1^g & u_1 w_1^g \\ \dots & \dots & \dots \\ l_n w_n^g & m_n w_n^g & u_n w_n^g \end{bmatrix} \tag{4}$$

Calculate the Fuzzy Score (FS). It is obtained as the arithmetic sum of the columns of the WFDM matrix, for each Probability (RL) and Consequence (C)

$$\left(FS_{RL/C}^r\right)_p = \left[\sum_{i=1}^n l_i w_i^g, \sum_{i=1}^n m_i w_i^g, \sum_{i=1}^n u_i w_i^g\right] \tag{5}$$

Obtain the Risk Level. The risk level is obtained by calculating the square root of the multiplication between $\left(FS_{RL}^r\right)_p$ and $\left(FS_C^r\right)_p$

$$(FRS_r)_{L,M,U} = \left(\sqrt{\left(FS_{RL}^r\right)_p * \left(FS_C^r\right)_p}\right)_{L,M,U} \tag{6}$$

Defuzzify the Values. $(FRS_r)_{Deff}$ is computed to define the level of risk on a scale from "Very Low" to "Extreme" (see Table 2).

$$(FRS_r)_{Deff} = \frac{(FRS_r)_L + 4 * (FRS_r)_M + (FRS_r)_U}{6} \tag{7}$$

3.2   Canonical Model

Risk assessment through the canonical model with multi-causal relationships requires the determination of a priori probabilities (independent risks) and conditional probabilities (according to the interaction between risks). This model assumes that the causal influence of a parent risk is independent of that of another parent risk, this is known as the "disjunctive interaction" (i.e. the Noisy Or-gate). Disjunctive interaction occurs when either parent can produce a certain event, and this does not decrease the probability that other parents will simultaneously prevail [1]. The model requires expert evaluation through risk pairs, taking into consideration only these two risks for evaluation. This not only simplifies the computational time to obtain the results, but also facilitates the understanding of what the expert evaluates.

A schematic of the Noisy Or-gate model can be seen in Fig. 1, taken from [14] where disjunctive interactions satisfy two conditions: *accountability*, which requires that if an event E is presumably false *(P(E) = 0)* if all causes of E are false and *exception independence*, holds that if an event E is a typical consequence of one or two causal relations *c1* and *c2*, then the mechanism that inhibits the occurrence of E under *c1* is independent of the mechanism that inhibits E under *c2*. *I* represents an inhibitory mechanism.

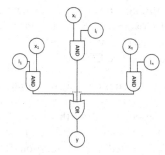

Fig. 1. The noisy OR-gate. A canonical model of disjunctive interactions among multiple causes $X_1...X_n$ predicting the same effect Y.

Finally, the following Bayes equations are used to calculate the probabilities of the dependent risks:

FTN of the Joint Probability and Dependent Risks. That is $(P(y \cap x_i))_{L,M,U}$ and (y), $P(y)_{L,M,U}$ respectively, being:

$$(P(y \cap x_i))_{L,M,U} = (P(x_i))_{L,M,U} \otimes (P_i(y/x_i))_{L,M,U} \qquad (8)$$

FGDMA will serve to find $P(x_i)_{L,M,U}$, i.e. the probability of the identified risks, and $P_i(y/x_i)_{L,M,U}$ through expert judgment, that is the qualification of the causal relationship. Thus, the probabilities of the dependent risks (y) are:

$$(P(y))_{L,M.U} = \left(\sum_{i=1}^{n} (P(y \cap x_i))_{L,M,U} \right) \qquad (9)$$

A Posteriori Probability. Of an independent risk (x_i) given a dependent risk (y):

$$P(xi|y) = \frac{P(y|x_i) \times P(x_i)}{P(y)} \qquad (10)$$

3.3 Expert Elicitation

Opinion elicitation in the context of Bayesian statistics consists of formulating a joint probability based on expert knowledge and beliefs. In order to achieve the expected results, the collection of knowledge must be done in a structured way [6] as follows:

Selecting Experts. A total of 214 experts were invited to answer the surveys, of which a total of 120 responded, the surveys were designed using Google Forms, and in addition to initial invitation, 2 reminders were sent for completion, with the objective of increasing the response rate. The survey was open for 8 weeks, from March 03, 2022 to April 23, 2022.

A total of 8 surveys were designed, of which 5 corresponded to thematic areas that were found to be relevant through the literature review: Administrative risks, Legal, Financial, Workforce, Auditor, Governance, Schedule, Project and Environment [6–9, 13]. The remaining 3 surveys focused on causal relationships for each of the contemplated project phases: Planning, Execution and Closure.

Train the Experts. For this exercise it is not only important that the experts have knowledge on the specific topics but also on how to express that knowledge through qualitative estimates of probability and consequence. For this reason, an explanatory tutorial was pre-recorded before filling out the survey; in the case of the causal relationship evaluations, an illustrative image was inserted in each question. In addition, personal accompaniment was provided in some cases and any doubts that might arise were resolved by e-mail.

Structuring the Questions. For the case of independent risks, the standard questions were "What is the probability of occurrence of risk X in a health audit project?", "What is the level of impact/consequence of risk X in a health audit project?". On the other hand, for the case of causal relationships the questions were structured as "What is the probability that risk Y will materialize if factor X is present?". The structure of the answers was on a qualitative scale (see Table 3), in order to facilitate the collection of knowledge.

Collect and Document Knowledge. The process of knowledge collection can be tedious and time consuming, which is why [15] recommends that sessions should not exceed one hour. For this case, a pilot response was made to determine the estimated time and thus adjust the length of the survey, ranging from 4 to 15 min. The surveys also allowed the expert to save his/her progress automatically, in case he/she wanted to take a break before finishing the survey. Emphasis was also placed on not making the survey too complex and lengthy, because when this happens the response rate decreases [16].

4 Results

4.1 Survey Results

Some basic survey results are shown in the following figures, work experience and educational background. From Fig. 2, 56% of the respondents have 10 or more years

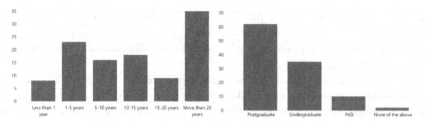

Fig. 2. Survey results: Work experience and academic background

of experience and that 66% of those who responded to the survey have postgraduate studies.

The highest risks rated by the experts are shown in Table 3:

Table 3. Highest risk rated by experts

ID	Risk	Dufuzzified risk score	Level of risk likelihood/consequence
AU2	Insufficient Understanding on Client's Requests	0.759	Very high
G17	Inadequate law and supervision system	0.746	Very high
AU10	Delays in decision making	0.732	Very high
G15	Government corruption	0.731	Very high
AU18	Unreasonable work process (large volumes of data, information to process, information to analyze, poor information and/or tight timelines)	0.729	Very high
P8	Project/Operation changes	0.711	Very high
G2	Contractual risks	0.710	Very high
L5	Failure to purchase or renew insurance or policies	0.709	Very high
AD10	Lack of resources or weak management controls	0.708	Very high
G1	Complex bureaucratic system	0.706	Very high

4.2 Input Data for Bayesian Model

As previously mentioned in Sect. 3.3 Expert elicitation, the causal diagrams for each of the project phases comprising Planning, Execution and Closure were developed based on a literature search of possible project risks. The risks were manually selected and consequently the causal diagrams were also developed. This development was done as a proposal, given the scarce availability of validated causal diagrams or knowledge bases of risks in health audit projects.

The causal diagrams were subjected to constant review to ensure that no risks were duplicated and no nodes or arcs were added that would make the diagram more complex without providing useful information. Planning causal diagram is shown in Fig. 3. This diagram has 24 causal relationships and 25 risks, meanwhile executing and closing diagrams have 39/37 and 25/25 respectively.

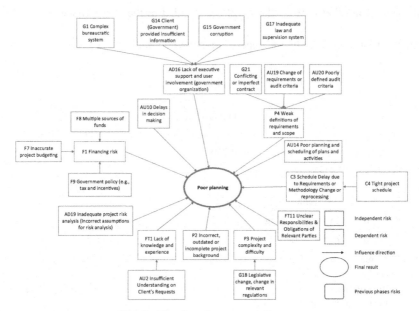

Fig. 3. Planning phase causal diagram.

With the application of the survey (and FGDMA as explained in Sect. 3.1), the score of the independent and dependent risks of the causal diagrams were obtained. With this information, it is possible to construct the conditional probability tables (CPT) through Netica Software as in [1].

Conditional probability tables (CPT) are constructed from independent risks to dependent risks, as suggested by [1, 6] a 20% leaky probability is added to explain the occurrence of the risk or event by a cause not described in the causal diagram.

Finally, the equations are written in Netica program using the following command e.g. $P(F1 \mid F9,F7,F8) = \text{NoisyOrDist}(F1,0.2,F9,0.306,F7,0.411,F8,0.283)$, taking as an example the causal relationships of the financial risk (F1) in the planning diagram Fig. 3, the values 0.306, 0.411, 0.283 represent the weighted values of each risk. That is, taking the conditional probability obtained in the survey through FGDMA, which in this case were 0.633 (F9), 0.852 (F7) and 0.587 (F8) respectively, and dividing each one by the sum of the other risks, i.e. for F9 it is $0.633/(0.633 + 0.852 + 0.587) = 0.306$.

5   Application to a Case Study Project

For the validation of the case study, a health audit project covering administrative, financial and medical components was taken as a reference. This project was contracted by a state entity that provides health services to the teacher's population, it has a duration of 44 months (between 2018 and 2022) and it is geographically dispersed in 13 regions of Colombia.

The leaky probability is modified to 0% since in a sensitivity analysis performed, this obtained the lowest percentage of deviation with respect to the expected output probability [1].

For this case, the causal diagrams previously constructed were taken and risks were updated based on whether they occurred (100% probability) or not (0% probability). This was possible due to the flexibility offered by the model to eliminate, modify or add new nodes to the network, taking into account that in the latter case the causal impacts on the subsequent nodes of the network must also be considered; whether it is desired to update the causal diagrams of a project due to changes, scenario analysis, or if the model is to be used for new projects. The modified risks for the case study are shown in Table 4.

Table 4. Modified nodes to case study

P/Phase	Planning	Execution
0%	G14 Government provided insufficient information, G15 Government corruption, G17 Inadequate law and supervision system, F8 Multiple sources of funds, F7 Inaccurate project budgeting[a], F9 Government policy[a], P2 Incomplete project background, FT11 Unclear Responsibilities & Obligations of Relevant Parties	P18 Completion risk, G9 Government intervention in the project[b], L5 Failure to purchase or renew insurance or policies
100%	G21 Conflicting or imperfect contract, AU19 Change of requirements or audit criteria[a]	AU8 Defective works and reworks, AU19 Change of requirements or audit criteria[a], L2 Filing of a complaint[b], AU6 Delays in the review and/or approval of audit reports[b], FT5 High degree of personal responsibility for the outcome of the project (Only for Closure)

[a]Risk in planning and execution phase.
[b]Risk in execution and closure phase.

As main results of the model, risk (P) had a probability of 37.4%, risk (E) a probability of 36.8% and risk (C) a probability of 49.9%, i.e. at a medium level according to Table 2. The result obtained through these causal diagrams allows cause-effect analysis by introducing variations in independent nodes or in dependent nodes (back-propagation). Analysis can also be focused on the risks considered as critical to prioritize preventive actions and facilitate decision making, acting opportunely to minimize or mitigate such risks. In this sense, the model also contributes to lessons learned for future projects.

6 Conclusions

Comparing the results of the survey with the risks that were not classified as materialized or discarded in the case study, it was found that for the planning phase the risk AU2 Insufficient understanding of customer requirements had the highest level of risk, while in the execution and closure phase the highest level of risk was AU10 Delay in decision making.

On the other hand, for each phase the Planning, Execution and Closure risks obtained a "Medium" level, with the Closure risk being the highest, this is consistent given that it has a greater number of materialized risks of direct impact, unlike the Planning and Execution phases.

As shown in this article, the proposed model allows to systematically manage the knowledge of experts in causal networks to determine the level of risk of a project or of each of its phases. It allows to introduce changes in its parameters to analyze possible scenarios and impacts along the causal networks.

In addition to the above, this model facilitates knowledge gathering compared to other approaches such as fuzzy-BBN or fuzzy-FMEA where this task becomes more tedious as the complexity of the network increases, it also allows analyzing causal networks unlike fuzzy-AHP or fuzzy-TOPSIS models. Compared to models such as fuzzy-AHP or fuzzy-ANP, the proposed model does not require a large number of risk pair evaluations. As a distinguishing feature, this model facilitates dynamic updating of risks as the project progresses, allowing proactive monitoring and control [1].

This knowledge-based expert system can be re-used in similar audit projects by updating causal relationships and probabilities, taking into consideration its simplified knowledge elicitation process and reduced computing time, compared with similar methodologies as mention above.

A systematic approach as the developed in this article can be used as an important tool for project diagnosis and decision making, especially in dynamic and complex projects.

Finally, the development of this knowledge-based expert system for risk management is intended to be an introduction for identification, assessment and control risks in the field of audit projects, especially in environments such as the Colombian and Latin American ones, where the application of this type of methodologies is scarce.

Acknowledgements. We would like to acknowledge to Centro de Investigaciones y Desarrollo Científico at Universidad Distrital Francisco José de Caldas (Colombia) by supporting partially the research project. Last, but not least, the authors would like to thank the comments of the anonymous referees that significantly improved our paper.

References

1. Islam, M.S., Nepal, M.P, Skitmore, M., Kabir, G.: A knowledge-based expert system to assess power plant project cost. Expert Syst. Appl. **136**, 12–32 (2019)

2. Kermanshachi, S., Dao, B., Shane, J., Anderson, S.: An empirical study into identifying project complexity management strategies. Procedia Eng. **145**, 603–610 (2016)
3. Dao, B., Kermanshachi, S., Shane, J., Anderson, S., Hare, E.: Identifying and Measuring Project Complexity. Integrating Data Sci. Constr. Sustain. **145**, 476–482 (2016)
4. Kermanshachi, S., Dao, B., Shane, J., Anderson, A.: Project complexity indicators and management strategies – a Delphi study. Integrating Data Sci. Constr. Sustain. **145**, 587–594 (2016)
5. Ekambaram, A., Sørensen, A.Ø., Berg, H., Olsson, N.O.E.: The role of big data and knowledge management in improving projects and project-based organizations. In: Quintela Varajão, J.E., Cruz-Cunha, M.M., Martinho, R., Rijo, R., Domingos, D., Peres, E. (eds.) CENTERIS 2018, vol. 138, pp. 851–858 (2018)
6. Gingnell, L., Franke, U., Lagerström, R., Ericsson, E., Lilliesköld, J.: Quantifying success factors for IT projects-an expert-based Bayesian model. Inf. Syst. Manag. **31**, 21–36 (2014)
7. Islam, M.S., Madhav, P.N., Skitmore, M.: Modified fuzzy group decision-making approach to cost overrun risk assessment of power plant projects. ASCE Libr. **145** (2019)
8. Xu, Y., Yeung, J.F.Y., Chan, A.P.C., Chan, D.W.M., Wang, S.Q., Ke, Y.: Developing a risk assessment model for PPP projects in China - a fuzzy synthetic evaluation approach. Autom. Constr. **19**, 929–943 (2010)
9. Xia, N., Wang, X., Wang, Y., Yang, Q., Liu, X.: Lifecycle cost risk analysis for infrastructure projects with modified Bayesian networks. J. Eng. Des. Technol. **15**, 79–103 (2017)
10. Zhang, Y., Wang, R., Huang, P., Wang, X., Wang, S.: Risk evaluation of large-scale seawater desalination projects based on an integrated fuzzy comprehensive evaluation and analytic hierarchy process method. Desalination, 1–10 (2020)
11. Cakmak, E., Cakmak, P.I.: An analysis of causes of disputes in the construction industry using analytical network process. Procedia Soc. Behav. Sci. **109**, 183–187 (2014)
12. Oniśko, A., Druzdzel, M.J., Wasyluk, H.: Learning Bayesian network parameters from small data sets: application of Noisy-OR gates. Int. J. Approximate Reasoning **27**, 165–182 (2001)
13. Jung, J.H., Kim, D.Y., Lee, H.K.: The computer-based contingency estimation through analysis cost overrun risk of public construction project. J. Civ. Eng. **20**, 1119–1130 (2016)
14. Pearl, J.: Probabilistic Reasoning in Intelligent Systems: Networks of Plausible Inference. Morgan Kaufman Publishers, Los Angeles (1988)
15. Cooke, R.M.: Experts in Uncertainty: Opinion and Subjective Probability in Science. Oxford University Press, Oxford (1991)
16. Blaxter, L., Hughes, C., Tight, M.: How to Research, 3rd edn. Open University Press, Maidenhead (2006)

Effect of Speckle Filtering
in the Performance of Segmentation
of Ultrasound Images Using CNNs

Caleb D. Romero-Mercado$^{(\boxtimes)}$ ⬤, Sonia H. Contreras-Ortiz ⬤,
and Andres G. Marrugo ⬤

Facultad de Ingeniería, Universidad Tecnologica de Bolivar, Cartagena, Bolivar,
Colombia
`cromero@utb.edu.co`

Abstract. The convolutional neural networks (CNNs) as tools for ultrasound image segmentation often have their performance affected by the low signal-to-noise ratio of the images. This prevents a correct classification and extraction of relevant information and therefore affects clinical diagnosis. We propose a study of the effect of different speckle filtering methods on CNN performance. For the proposed metrics (Jaccard coefficient and BF-Score), it was obtained that the SRAD filter exhibited the best behavior even in the lowest quality data. In addition, the lowest values were obtained for the standard deviation and variance, which translates into lower data dispersion, better repeatability, and, therefore, greater confidence in its accuracy.

Keywords: CNN · Speckle filtering · Segmentation · Ultrasound

1 Introduction

A relevant feature in multimodal systems is that the multiple imaging techniques incorporated allow overcoming limitations and consequently improve visual systems information feedback [10,11]. Several authors have used multimodal ultrasound imaging, including superb microvascular imaging and real-time elastography to improve differentiation and characterization of benign and malignant thyroid imaging [12]. Also, photoacoustic, which is a non-invasive and non-ionizing imaging method, can complement ultrasound (US) imaging methods [7] and achieves high-resolution optical imaging in deep tissues [6]. In that sense, it can be used to evaluate disease activity in rheumatoid arthritis [18].

A particular type of processing image algorithm for medical applications is convolutional neural networks (CNNs) which have become relevant in the science community because they showed a high performance in classification and segmentation tasks. CNN find applications in breast tumors classification [13,14,17] and semantic segmentation [5].

The original version of this chapter was revised: The name of the author Sonia H. Contreras-Ortiz has been corrected. The correction to this chapter is available at https://doi.org/10.1007/978-3-031-20611-5_40

© The Author(s), under exclusive license to Springer Nature Switzerland AG 2022, corrected publication 2022
J. C. Figueroa-García et al. (Eds.): WEA 2022, CCIS 1685, pp. 150–159, 2022.
https://doi.org/10.1007/978-3-031-20611-5_13

However, when CNNs are confronted with data sets where the information of interest is not easily distinguishable, it leads to false positives. This directly impacts reliability in the different fields of application, which in our case translates into a failure as a support tool for diagnostic clinical. It is then that the need arises to create auxiliary tools to improve the performance of the CNN, including external processing devices, filters, and CNN based-filter.

To improve the performance of CNNs, some authors prefer methods that can be encapsulated as preprocessing enhancement techniques, such as morphological operations on images (augmentation, resizing, object removal) [8]. Also, we can find approaches that include the use of FPGA to improve CNN performance, it is used as an accelerator to process increasingly more images per second [9]. Other authors choose more traditional approaches using tools such as the Sobel filter, useful in edge detection tasks [15], or the BM3D filter to reduce image noise [8]. A particularly widely used filter is the Gabor filter [1,4] used in pattern analysis and dimensionality-reducing applications. Moreover, it has been used to design CNN based on it [3].

In the case of ultrasound imaging, a frequently encountered artifact is speckle noise. Due to its nature, it represents an obstacle in segmentation tasks since it causes, together with shadowing, false positives. For this reason, many authors use a speckle filter as a first step in processing this type of image. The purpose of this work is to determine the speckle filter among SRAD, FastNiMeans, Median, and Frost filters, that improves the CNN's performance.

2   Method

2.1   CNN Architecture

The implemented CNN shown in Fig. 1 uses a UNET architecture, where the first stage consists of 3×3 convolutional layers and spatial downsampling via pooling and Re-Lu activation functions. Moreover, a "he normal" kernel initializer was used because that generates tensors with a normal distribution which allows work better with Re-Lu function. In addition, each layer has a padding operation, which adds zero values pixels to maintain the original image size.

There are four max-pooling layers which each reduce the spatial dimensionality of the input by a factor of two, resulting in a total spatial reduction by a factor of 18. The encoder stage has outputs features with spatial dimension $H_c \mathrm{x} W_c$, where $H_c = H/16$ and $W_c = W/16$ for an original image sized $H \mathrm{x} W$.

The next stage consists of the expansive path, which is the opposite of the above layers. It consists of 3×3 convolutional layers and spatial upsampling via pooling and Re-Lu activation functions, which returns the image's original size with the relevant features. *Sigmoid* is the final activation function that allows binary classification for binary image segmentation.

The loss function and optimizer used was *BinaryCrossentropy* and *adam*, respectively. Also, we include a metric based on Jaccard coefficient to visualize during CNN training.

2.2   Dataset

we used a breast phantom *3B-SONOtrain-P125* consisting of three tumors Fig. 2.

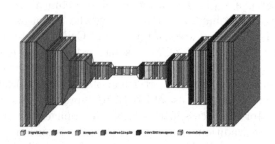

Fig. 1. Architecture of our convolutional neural networks. The input is an ultrasound image with a size of 240 × 320. In the expansive path, we recuperate the spatial information by concatenating the *Conv2DTranspose* output with the sampling corresponding layer in the encoder stage.

Fig. 2. Breast phantom model for ultrasound dataset.

The experimental setup consists mainly of Basler acA1300-200um USB 3.0 camera with 1280 × 1024 pixel resolution and Portable ultrasound BU-907 shown in Fig. 3.

Finally, the ground-truth image was made using the Matlab command *free-hand* which allows drawing tumor boundaries and binarizing the output. The dataset obtained contains 251 US images with an average 321 × 408 resolution shown in Fig. 4.

2.3   Device Computational Features

For the CNN training, we used a virtual machine GPU in Google Colab that provides free computational resources. It has these storage features: GPU memory of 12 GB/16 GB, RAM of 12 GB, and disk space of 358 GB. The processing features are: GPU Memory clock 0.82 GHz/1.59 GHz, performance 4.1 TFLOPS/8.1 TFLOPS, and 2 CPU Cores. All CNN models were trained during 50 epochs with an average training time of 1 h.

3 Performance Metrics

To evaluate the proposed CNN performance, we selected the following statistics:

Fig. 3. Experimental setup for ultrasound dataset acquisition.

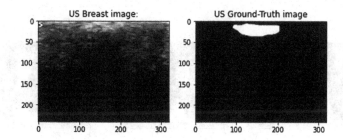

Fig. 4. Samples of Ultrasound breast tumor images.

3.1 BF-Score

It consists in computing the BF (Boundary F1) contour matching score between the predicted segmentation in prediction and the true segmentation in groundTruth. The BF-score is defined as Eq. (1), which is the harmonic mean (F1-measure) of the precision and recall values with a distance error tolerance to decide whether a point on the predicted boundary has a match on the ground truth boundary or not,

$$\text{BF} = \frac{2 * \text{precision} * \text{recall}}{\text{recall} + \text{precision}}, \tag{1}$$

where *precision* is the fraction of detections that are true positives and *recall* is the fraction of true positives that are detected rather than missed.

3.2 Jaccard Index

The Jaccard Index, Eq. (2), also known as the Jaccard similarity coefficient, is a statistic used in understanding the similarities between sample sets. The measurement emphasizes the similarity between finite sample sets and is formally defined as the size of the intersection divided by the size of the union of the sample sets. The mathematical representation of the index is written as

$$J(A, B) = \frac{|A \cap B|}{A \cup B},\tag{2}$$

where A is ground-truth binary images and B the binary image output.

4 Evaluation and Results

Initially, we preprocessed the data set obtained with the breast phantom *3B-SONOtrain-P125* by applying each of the proposed speckle filters. A sample image was chosen where the effect of the filters on the dataset can be evidenced, shown in Fig. 5. In addition, we saved a copy of the original unfiltered dataset to compare the performance with the raw images.

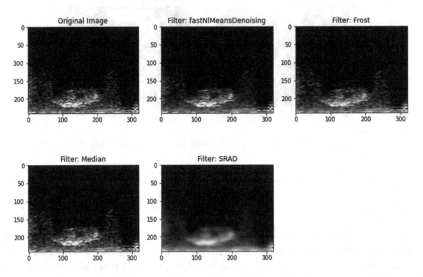

Fig. 5. Filtering using the five methods: (*a*) Original US dataset image, (*b*) speckle filter using Non-local Means denoising algorithm with h = 10, t = 21 and s = 7, (*c*) Based on the local statistics windowing, the frost filter works on preserving the edges while suppressing the noise, (*d*) performs median filtering, where each output pixel contains the median neighborhood pixel value around the corresponding pixel, (*e*) Speckle Reducing AD, based on an anisotropic extension of Frost's and Kuan's LMMSE filters for multiplicative noise.

For each CNN training, we set 50 epochs and used a different filtered dataset. The purpose was behavior evaluation using the Jaccard Index metric and visualization of the loss function. Observing the history training graphics to *Median Filter* shown in Fig. 6, we can see that in all tests, the CNN keeps a general performance of around 70–80%. Also, the loss function graph shows the maximum difference between the train and test around 0.05.

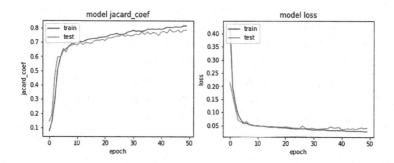

Fig. 6. Jaccard Index and function loss for Median filter training

Once the training has been completed and the models have been generated, the segmentation results can be observed in Fig. 7. The same image in Fig. 5 was selected so that a comparative measure of the effects of the filtering on the final result can be established.

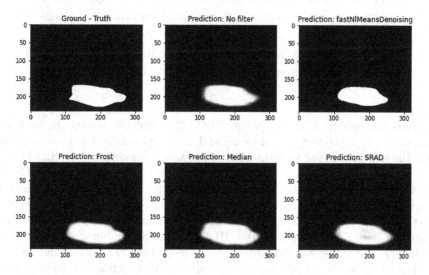

Fig. 7. Predictions of images US dataset, each filtering method was used to dataset preprocessing and then train the CNN to visualize the filter's effect on the network performance.

Finally, to analyze the behavior of the network over the entire test dataset. Central tendency measures were used to get a better notion of its performance. Therefore, for the above performance metrics, the values shown in Table 1 and Table 2 for the Jaccard coefficient and BF-Score were obtained, respectively.

Table 1. Jaccard Index behavior obtained with ground-truth and predictions with each filter

Filters	Statistical Measures						
	Max	*Min*	*Mean*	*Median*	*std*	*var*	*skewness*
No Filter	0.9207	0.1244	0.7969	0.8279	0.1252	0.0157	−3.2629
FastMean	0.9101	0.0000	0.7224	0.7838	0.2025	0.0410	−2.2128
Frost	0.9151	0.0965	0.7881	0.7987	0.1195	0.0143	−3.9076
Median	0.9228	0.0806	0.7807	0.8189	0.1395	0.0195	−2.8827
SRAD	0.9185	0.2951	0.8082	0.8264	0.1020	0.0104	−2.7158

Table 2. BF-score behavior obtained with ground-truth and predictions with each filter

Filters	Statistical Measures						
	Max	*Min*	*Mean*	*Median*	*std*	*var*	*skewness*
No Filter	0.9930	0.3403	0.9390	0.9590	0.0936	0.0088	−5.3947
FastMean	0.9906	0.0000	0.8790	0.9445	0.2001	0.0400	−3.5625
Frost	0.9924	0.2914	0.9347	0.9498	0.0973	0.0095	−5.9367
Median	0.9925	0.2487	0.9280	0.9576	0.1099	0.0121	−4.9793
SRAD	0.9933	0.6531	0.9486	0.9612	0.0531	0.0028	−3.7337

Table 1 shows that, although the SRAD filter did not obtain the best performance, which is 0.9185 (Max value) and was surpassed by the value obtained with the **Median filter** with **0.9228**. In the Min value column, the SRAD filter showed the best performance even at the worst result obtained (0.2951). On the other hand, the values obtained for the mean and median, although showing differences between them, are not very significant. Nevertheless, they serve as a starting point for analysis together with the standard deviation, where we can observe a better behavior with the **SRAD filter** as it allows a segmentation performance of **0.8082 ± 0.1020**. Since the field of study is ultrasound imaging of breast tumors. It is important to consider metrics such as BF-score to evaluate the shape obtained in the segmentation. It was found that for Table 2, the **SRAD filter** shows the best performance in each of the metrics used with a segmentation performance of **0.9486± 0.0028**. This makes it an ideal candidate to improve the proportion of correctly classified pixels and reflect the real shape of the tumor under study as closely as possible.

5   Discussions

A comparative study was proposed in which the effect of different types of speckle filters in the segmentation of ultrasound images could be evidenced, and the best candidate could be determined. In general, during the training of the network, no significant differences were observed in the values of the loss function for the generated models. The results obtained confirm the SRAD filter as the best candidate, analyzing mainly the results of **0.8082±0.1020** and **0.9486±0.0028** for the Jaccard Index and BF-score respectively.

In addition, we found that several studies [2,16] have previously highlighted that the SRAD filter yields the highest value of PSNR, SNR, and the lowest value of MSE, and hence is the most suitable for despeckling of breast ultrasonographic images.

For some metrics obtained in the table, it was evident that the performance of the network even without the filter was sometimes the second best. This may be mainly because the phantom used has only 3 tumors and therefore the acquired dataset represents cross sections of objects that offer relatively little variation in shape. Also, a more exhaustive analysis of the edges of the segmentations obtained is imperative.

6   Conclusion

Image processing algorithms undoubtedly play an important role as supporting tools to improve the performance of CNNs. In particular, in the use of ultrasound imaging, speckle filters allow a clear improvement in the visualization of image details. Given the results obtained, we can conclude that despite the fact that in some metrics, filters such as **FastMean** and **Median** obtained much more favorable results. The **SRAD filter** evidenced a better overall performance in all the metrics used and its implementation offers a clear improvement in the visualization of image details which directly impacts the network performance. Therefore, we can expect greater repeatability in the same results, which translates into greater reliability as a tool. However, it is important to mention that the images used contained shadow artifacts which made it difficult in the first instance to observe the effect of filtering in improving the quality of the images. Therefore, it is recommended that if the network does not have the robustness to generate filters by itself, an additional preprocessing stage can be performed to remove this and other types of artifacts.

7   Future Work

Although the BF-Score gives an approximate idea of the accuracy of the shape with respect to the original, it is considered necessary to use other metrics such as the Hausdorff distance to be able to offer with greater certainty a reliability interval for the segmentation of this type of images. Also, Improve CNN processing time with the implementation of these algorithms in real-time.

Acknowledgments. C. Romero thanks UTB for a post-graduate scholarship.

References

1. Bhatti, U.A., et al.: Local similarity-based spatial-spectral fusion hyperspectral image classification with deep cnn and gabor filtering. IEEE Trans. Geosci. Remote Sens. **60**, 1–15 (2022). https://doi.org/10.1109/TGRS.2021.3090410
2. Byra Reddy, G., Prasanna Kumar, H.: Breast ultrasound image segmentation to detect tumor by using level sets. In: Innovations in Electronics and Communication Engineering, pp. 319–325. Springer (2022). https://doi.org/10.1007/978-981-16-8512-5_35
3. Cesur, E., Yildiz, N., Tavsanoglu, V.: On an improved fpga implementation of cnn-based gabor-type filters. IEEE Trans. Circuits Syst. II Express Briefs **59**(11), 815–819 (2012). https://doi.org/10.1109/TCSII.2012.2218471
4. Chen, M., et al.: Improved faster r-cnn for fabric defect detection based on gabor filter with genetic algorithm optimization. Comput. Ind. **134**, 103551 (2022)
5. Gómez-Flores, W., de Albuquerque Pereira, W.C.: A comparative study of pre-trained convolutional neural networks for semantic segmentation of breast tumors in ultrasound. Comput. Biol. Med. **126**, 104036 (2020)
6. Jeon, M., Kim, C.: Multimodal photoacoustic tomography. IEEE Trans. Multimedia **15**(5), 975–982 (2013). https://doi.org/10.1109/TMM.2013.2244203
7. Kim, J., Lee, D., Jung, U., Kim, C.: Photoacoustic imaging platforms for multimodal imaging. Ultrasonography **34**(2), 88 (2015)
8. Lavreniuk, M., Shelestov, A., Kussul, N., Rubel, O., Lukin, V., Egiazarian, K.: Use of modified bm3d filter and cnn classifier for sar data to improve crop classification accuracy. In: 2019 IEEE 2nd Ukraine Conference on Electrical and Computer Engineering (UKRCON), pp. 1–6 (2019). https://doi.org/10.1109/UKRCON.2019.8879805
9. Lu, L., Liang, Y., Xiao, Q., Yan, S.: Evaluating fast algorithms for convolutional neural networks on fpgas. In: 2017 IEEE 25th Annual International Symposium on Field-Programmable Custom Computing Machines (FCCM), pp. 101–108 (2017). https://doi.org/10.1109/FCCM.2017.64
10. Meza, J., Contreras-Ortiz, S.H., Perez, L.A.R., Marrugo, A.G.: Three-dimensional multimodal medical imaging system based on freehand ultrasound and structured light. Opt. Eng. **60**(5), 054106 (2021)
11. Meza, J., Romero, L.A., Marrugo, A.G.: Markerpose: robust real-time planar target tracking for accurate stereo pose estimation. In: Proceedings of the IEEE/CVF Conference on Computer Vision and Pattern Recognition, pp. 1282–1290 (2021)
12. Pei, S., et al.: Diagnostic value of multimodal ultrasound imaging in differentiating benign and malignant ti-rads category 4 nodules. Int. J. Clin. Oncol. **24**(6), 632–639 (2019)
13. Rouhi, R., Jafari, M.: Classification of benign and malignant breast tumors based on hybrid level set segmentation. Expert Syst. Appl. **46**, 45–59 (2016)
14. Rouhi, R., Jafari, M., Kasaei, S., Keshavarzian, P.: Benign and malignant breast tumors classification based on region growing and cnn segmentation. Expert Syst. Appl. **42**(3), 990–1002 (2015)

15. Sharifrazi, D., et al.: Fusion of convolution neural network, support vector machine and sobel filter for accurate detection of covid-19 patients using x-ray images. Biomed. Signal Process. Contr. **68**, 102622 (2021)
16. Tripathi, P., Dass, R., Sen, J.: A comparative analysis of different despeckling filters using breast ultrasonographic images. In: Marriwala, N., Tripathi, C.C., Jain, S., Mathapathi, S. (eds) Emergent Converging Technologies and Biomedical Systems, pp. 425–430. Springer (2022). https://doi.org/10.1007/978-981-16-8774-7_34
17. Xie, X., Shi, F., Niu, J., Tang, X.: Breast ultrasound image classification and segmentation using convolutional neural networks. In: Hong, R., Cheng, WH., Yamasaki, T., Wang, M., Ngo, CW. (eds) Pacific rim conference on multimedia, pp. 200–211. Springer (2018). https://doi.org/10.1007/978-3-030-00764-5_19
18. Zhao, C., et al.: Multimodal photoacoustic/ultrasonic imaging system: a promising imaging method for the evaluation of disease activity in rheumatoid arthritis. Eur. Radiol. **31**(5), 3542–3552 (2021)

Multivariate Financial Time Series Forecasting with Deep Learning

Sebastián Martelo[1]([✉]), Diego León[1], and German Hernandez[2]

[1] Universidad Externado de Colombia, Bogota, Colombia
sebastian.martelo@est.uexternado.edu.co, diego.leon@uexternado.edu.co
[2] Universidad Nacional de Colombia, Bogota, Colombia
gjhernandezp@unal.edu.co

Abstract. Today, and aware of how unexpected the events that govern the market trend can be, forecasting financial time series has become a priority for everyone, a field in which computational intelligence with networks par excellence, Long-term and short-term neural networks (LSTM) and Gated Recurrent Unit (GRU), has taken the center of the stage. To avoid long-term dependency problems, given their unique storage unit structure, these networks are postulated as the best option when predicting financial time series.

Thus, the motivation of this paper is to compare the transformer model with Long and Short Term Neural Networks (LSTM) and Gated Recurrent Unit (GRU), where the data set of the NASDAQ 100 index will be used, with a time interval "tick by tick" and with a range from January 2020 to July 2020, since those of deep learning (DL) models have presented significantly better results than their traditional counterparts, results with which they will be compared. The results will be categorized according to their performance in a ranking from 1 to 3, where number 1 would be the best option when predicting the behavior of the selected index, demonstrating if the Transformer architecture presents a better performance versus GRU and LSTM.

Keywords: Deep learning · Recurrent neural network · Machine learning · National association of securities dealers automated quotation · Transformer · GRU · LSTM

1 Introduction

Currently, one of the main challenges in the stock market is anticipating market movements and seeking to gain moments of advantage over the other actors involved. The speed of the data to be analyzed is increasing. Consequently, the

Supported by GCP Research Credits Program from Google.

© The Author(s), under exclusive license to Springer Nature Switzerland AG 2022
J. C. Figueroa-García et al. (Eds.): WEA 2022, CCIS 1685, pp. 160–169, 2022.
https://doi.org/10.1007/978-3-031-20611-5_14

volume is limited mainly by the technological capacity that we have available and surpassing the capabilities of human beings.

As stated by Jaime Montantes in his work "Deep Learning in Finance: Is This The Future of the Financial Industry?" today, many people and companies that are promoting the financial sector have had to adapt to mathematics, statistics, and the development of algorithms focused on this industry.

Thus, the motivation of this work is to compare the Transformer model with the Gated Recurrent Unit (GRU) and Long Short Term Memory (LSTM) deep learning models for time series prediction. It is based on a high-frequency data strategy using recurrent neural networks (RNN), where data sets from the NAS-DAQ 100 index will be used, with a "tick by tick" time interval and a defined range from January 2020 to July 2020.

For this, the GRU and LSTM architectures have been taken since the deep learning (DL) models have presented significantly better results than their traditional counterparts, as demonstrated in the work of Vijaysinh Lendave: LSTM Vs. GRU in Recurrent Neural Network: A Comparative Study, results with which they will be compared, categorizing the results according to their performance. In a ranking from 1 to 3, where number 1 would be the best option when predicting the behavior of the selected index, demonstrating and comparing the performance of high-frequency neural networks.

The paper is organized as follows: Sect. 2 presents a description of deep learning for forecasting and architecture that we will be testing, where we talk about the architecture of the LSTM, GRU, and Transformer. Section 3 describes the Experimental setup and methodology of the experiment. Section 4 presents the proposed Workflow. Section 5 presents the data set description and the results with their respective analysis. Finally, Sect. 6 presents conclusions and recommendations for future research.

2 Deep Learning for Forecasting and Architectures

As mentioned above, we are going to compare the Transformer model with the Gated Recurrent Unit (GRU) and Long Short Term Memory (LSTM) deep learning models since the former two are widely recognized for their efficiency and popularity among analysts, as mentioned in the paper "Attention Is All You Need" by Vaswani, Ashish; Shazeer, Noam; Parmar, Niki; Uszkoreit, Jakob; Jones, Lion; Gomez, Aidan N.; Kaiser, Lukasz; Polosukhin, Illia, and the work of dProgrammer Lopez through his article RNN, LSTM and GRU.

The LSTM neural network is a particular version of recurrent neural networks (RNN) with the ability to learn long-term sequences. Designed to avoid dependency problems and, therefore, can remember long sequences over a long period while retaining their effect on the prediction.

There are three gates that LSTM uses: gate-in, gate-forget, and gate-out.

Entrance Gate: Decides what information will be stored in long-term memory, and filters out variable information that is irrelevant.

Data Loss Gate: Decides what information from long-term memory is going to be kept or discarded.

Output Gate: This gate will take the current input, the previous short-term memory, and the newly calculated long-term memory and produce a new short-term memory which will be passed to the cell at the next time step, bringing into consideration the work of Vijaysinh Lendave mentioned above (Fig. 1.

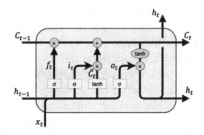

Fig. 1. Long Short Term Memory (LSTM) [19]

On the other side, we have the GRU neural network, which is a version of the RNN networks but the difference is in the operations and the gates, that is, GRU incorporates an update gate and a reset gate, and they are trained to keep information from the past or remove information that is not relevant to the prediction.

Update Gate: Determines the amount of previous information that must be passed to the next state.

Restart Gate: Decides how much past information is not relevant and therefore decides whether the previous state of the cell is important or not, bringing into consideration again the work of Vijaysinh Lendave mentioned above (Fig. 2).

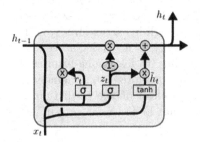

Fig. 2. Gated Recurrent Unit (GRU) [19]

And finally, we have the Transformer architecture, a neural network architecture responsible for manipulating sequential data and used in the field of time series, forecasting, and trading. The architecture of the Transformer network was introduced by Ashish Vaswani, as shown in Fig. 3, and it consists of an encoder-decoder architecture. The encoder is made up of a stack of N = 6 identical layers and is used to analyze a certain context of the input sequence; the decoder is also composed of a stack of N = 6 identical layers and is responsible for generating the output sequence from said context, as mentioned in the paper "Attention Is All You Need."

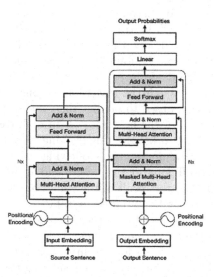

Fig. 3. General architecture of the Transformer [24].

3   Experimental Setup and Methodology

The following describes the steps of the experiment, where we seek to evaluate the thesis of whether the Transformer architecture presents better results than the GRU and LSTM architectures in a data set extracted from the NASDAQ 100 stock market index.

We start with data cleaning, where the first thing that is done is the frequency change of the original data to seconds, to later be able to train a logistic regression model, which will be used for selecting characteristics. During the data cleaning process, the minimum possible data set with null values is eliminated so that all assets remain in the same period.

We continue with the selection of characteristics, in which a logistic regression model is trained. This model is used to obtain a score for each of the assets in the study, and the ten assets with the highest score are selected. This score represents how relevant these assets are to the index. The reason for only selecting ten assets is due to limitations in the hardware used for this study.

Later we move on to data preprocessing, a section in which the logarithmic return of the data is calculated, which will be the target variable to be able to make the predictions. Once the logarithmic return is calculated, the data is rescaled using the mean and standard deviation. The foregoing is relevant in this process since it allows adequate neural network convergence.

Once the data processing is finished, we continue training the artificial intelligence models. For this study, three deep learning models will be trained, an LSTM, a GRU, and a Transformer.

The LSTM is composed of 2 layers, 50 units, ending with a dense layer; For its part, the GRU network will be trained using 2 layers, with 50 neurons each and a final dense layer; and finally, the Transformer network is composed of a MultiHeadAttention layer (can be found on the Keras.io page in the Attention layers code), ending with a dense layer.

The data is resized to match the input dimensions of the neural networks, and a time window of 60 s is used to predict the value of the scaled logarithmic return (normalized return) of the next second. In each case, 200 iterations are used to train the neural networks, and this training uses 3 data sets considering the first three months of training and the following month for testing.

Then, we run the cut-off point for one month and again use the previous three months for the training and the result of the values of the following month; this is done with the three data sets presented in Table 1.

Completing this step, we proceed to the inverse transformation of the data. Once the model infers the logarithmic values, these are rescaled using the mean and standard deviation calculated for the first data set; using the logarithmic return equation, we obtain the price values considering that we already have the price value of the previous second.

Finally, we calculate the MAE and RMSE metrics on the test values, allowing us to determine if we hypothesize that the transformer architecture presents a better result than the GRU and LSTM architectures. Results in Table 2.

4   Workflow

For this experiment we have used Tick History by Refinitiv to extract the data, Python as the programming language, Pandas and Numpy for the description and preprocessing of the data, Keras to train the LSTM and GRU networks, Pytorch to train the Transformers network, Google Cloud Platform (GCP) to host and train the algorithms and finally Hardware GPU T4 to train the algorithms (Fig. 4).

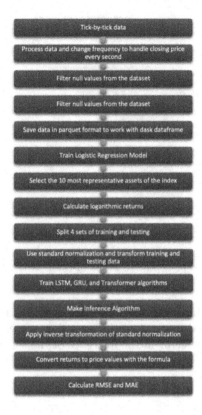

Fig. 4. General architecture of the Workflow

5   Data Set Description and Results

Table 1 below shows the data separation for the training and testing of our experiment:

Table 1. Separation of data for training and test.

Set	Entrenamiento	Test
set1	2020:01-2020:04	2020:05
set2	2020:02-2020:05	2020:06
set3	2020:03-2020:06	2020:07

In addition, in Fig. 5, the ten most representative assets of the NASDAQ index are observed (Data extracted from the results of the logistic regression model), and in Annexes, there is graph A-1 of the NASDAQ index of all the assets that used in the experiment.

In the selection of characteristics, the first 10 assets of the most representative index were taken based on the logistic regression model trained with the

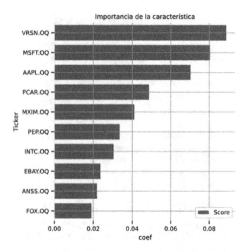

Fig. 5. Most representative assets of the NASDAQ 100 index

historical data of the first 3 months as shown in Fig. 5, the figure presents the score per asset generated by the logistic regression model.

Below in Table 2, the error in the inference of the set data is shown.

Table 2. Error in the inference of the set data.

Ticker	MAE			RMSE		
	GRU	LSTM	TRANSFORMER	GRU	LSTM	TRANSFORMER
AAPL.OQ	3.8964	3.8904	3.9050	0.0633	0.0620	0.0630
ANSS.OQ	15.0159	14.7157	14.4456	0.2473	0.2406	0.2405
EBAY.OQ	1.1799	1.2111	1.3050	0.0270	0.0269	0.0275
FOX.OQ	1.5278	1.5923	1.5838	0.0307	0.0307	0.0302
INTC.OQ	1.2103	1.2164	1.3459	0.0242	0.0244	0.0245
MSFT.OQ	2.4895	2.5116	2.5399	0.0438	0.0435	0.0448
MXIM.OQ	1.7365	1.7467	1.7429	0.0336	0.0339	0.0330
PCAR.OQ	1.9749	1.9568	1.9311	0.0438	0.0434	0.0427
PEP.OQ	2.2958	2.3066	2.2565	0.0477	0.0481	0.0475
VRSN.OQ	8.9012	8.8316	8.4838	0.1742	0.1710	0.1691

Based on the table of metrics presented in Table 2, it is seen that there is no significant difference between the evaluated models. However, regarding the MAE metric, the GRU model presents better results in most assets; on the other hand, the RMSE presents better results with the Transformer model.

This makes it impossible to determine which model prevails over the others, considering that there is no significant difference in the results obtained by the regression on the errors

The models were trained under the same conditions, taking care to avoid overfitting using a dropout strategy of 0.1. In the case of LSTM and GRU, each model took about half an hour per training (200 iterations), and the Transformer model took 1 h. Per training (200 iterations), using a virtual machine with a T4 GPU with 30 GB of RAM, training 90 models, ten assets, 3 data sets, and three models taught independently.

Finally and to perform a statistical check, the Friedman test is performed with the scipy.stats library, the null and alternative hypotheses are (H0): The mean of each population is equal, alternative hypothesis (Ha) at least one population mean is different from the rest; as a result, the statistic is 0.27, and the p-value is 0.875, being greater than 0.05, with which we accept the null hypothesis, and the means of the values are not statistically different Figs. 6, 7 and 8.

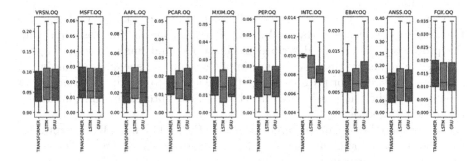

Fig. 6. Model error in Data Set 1

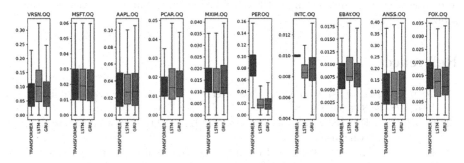

Fig. 7. Model error in Data Set 2

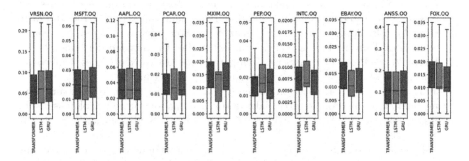

Fig. 8. Model error in Data Set 3

6   Conclusion and Recommendations

As a conclusion of the experiment, graphs 5–1, 5–2, and 5–3 present the boxplot graphs of the test results for each model. For data sets 1 and 2, we can see in the INTC and PEP tickers how the performance of the Transformer model is significantly lower than the other two models; this may be due to the behavior of the time series during those specific periods. Similarly, we can find these differences by comparing all the data sets and without predominating a specific model, concluding that at the index level and considering the errors, the best architecture cannot be determined, and selecting which model is better than the other unanimously.

Considering the previous results and based on Occam's knife (Models, Mental: How to Use Occam's Razor Without Getting Cut), in this case, and with the processing limitations described in this work, and finally considering the technical complexity that the models imply, specifically speaking of hardware, software, and skills. For programming, it is suggested to use the GRU model for time series prediction, considering that it requires less processing time, hardware, and technical knowledge.

It is proposed to use deeper architectures in the LSTM and GRU networks for the following developments. Likewise, for the Transformer model, it is suggested to optimize hyperparameters, moving the number of service heads and verifying by asset, using different data sets in different periods, with different frequencies and time windows, and testing with combinations of the architectures previously seen.

References

1. Deep Learning with Python. Apress, Berkeley, CA (2021). https://doi.org/10.1007/978-1-4842-5364-9_8
2. Copeland, B: artificial intelligence (2022). http://www.britannica.com/technology/artificial-intelligence.
3. Roberts, D.A., Boris, H.: The Principles of Deep Learning Theory. Cambridge: Cambridge University (2021)
4. Durán, J.: Todo lo que Necesitas Saber sobre el Descenso del Gradiente Aplicado a Redes Neuronales. http://medium.com/metadatos/todo-lo-que-necesitas-saber-sobre-el-descenso del-gradiente-aplicado-a-redes-neuronales-19bdbb706a78 (2019)
5. Caicedo, E.F., Jesus's Alfonso L.: Una aproximación práctica a las redes neuronales artificiales. Universidad del Valle, Cali, Colombia : Universidad del Valle (2017)
6. Fierro, A.A.: Predicción de Series Temporales con Redes Neuronales. Universidad Nacional de La Plata, Tesis de Especialización, Argentina (2020)
7. Julio Ignacio, V.P.: Predección de series financieras del mercado latinoamericano mediante redes neuronales artificiales, a través de un algoritmo de colonias de abejas. Valparaíso, Chile, Universidad Técnica Federico Santa María, Tesis de Pregrado (2017)
8. Polo, D.M., Caballero, L.P., Gómez, E.M.: Comparación de Redes Neuronales aplicadas a la predicción de Series de Tiempo. En: Prospect Vol 13 (2015), Nr. 2

9. Francesco, R., Francesca, T., di Stallo, A.L., Sebastiano, B.: Machine Learning for Quantitative Finance Applications: a Survey. En: Applied Sciences 9 (2019), Nr. 24. - ISSN 2076–3417

10. Andrés, A., Jaime, N., Diego, L., German, H., Javier, S.: Deep Learning and Wavelets for High-Frequency Price Forecasting (2018)

11. Arnold, L., Rebecchi, S., Chevallier, S., Paugam-Moisy, H.: An Introduction to Deep Learning. ESANN, https://www.elen.ucl.ac.be/Proceedings/esann/esannpdf/es2011-4.pdf (2011)

12. Ding, X., Zhang, Y., Liu, T., Duan, J.: Deep learning for event-driven stock prediction. In: Proceedings of the Twenty-Fourth International Joint Conference on Artificial Intelligence (ICJAI) (2015).http://ijcai.org/papers15/Papers/IJCAI15-329.

13. De Goijer, J., Hyndman, R.: 25 Years of Time Series Forecasting. J. Forecast. **22**, 443–473 (2006)

Optimization

The Notion of the Quasicentral Path in Linear Programming

Miguel Argáez[1]([⊠]) ⓘ, Osvaldo Mendez[1], and Leticia Velázquez[2] ⓘ

[1] The University of Texas at El Paso, El Paso, TX 79902, USA
margaez@utep.edu
[2] Rice University, Houston, TX 77005, USA

Abstract. The notion of the central path plays an important role in the development of most primal-dual interior-point algorithms. In this work we prove that a related notion called the quasicentral path, introduced by Argáez in nonlinear programming, while being a less restrictive notion it is sufficiently strong to guide the iterates towards a solution to the problem. We use a new merit function for advancing to the quasicentral path, and weighted neighborhoods as proximity measures of this central region. We present some numerical results that demonstrate the effectiveness of the algorithm.

Keywords: Interior-point methods · Second primal-dual methods · Linear programming

1 Introduction

The area of linear programming has been extensively studied in the last decades obtaining several well-known theoretical and numerical results. A book by Wright [11] presents most of the theoretical advances in linear programming, and a paper by Bixby [4] gives a brief summary of the computational developments for solving real-world linear programs. In particular, the work of Karmarkar [7] is noted for its role in promoting primal-dual interior-point algorithms (See, for example Kojima, Mizuno, and Yoshise [8], Lustig, Marsten, and Shanno [9], El-Bakry, Tapia, Tsuchiya, and Zhang [6], and Zhang [12]). Such approaches are based on using a central region, called the central path, as a guide for obtaining approximate solutions. Here, we introduce a new methodology that is based on a different central region

In this work, we carry over a globalization strategy, presented by Argáez and Tapia [2], from nonlinear programming to linear programming. This strategy consists of following a related notion of the central path, called quasicentral path, as a central region for guiding the iterates towards a solution of the problem. An important result is that the dual variable y is not needed, at least explicitly, to find a solution to the problem. Specifically, we prove that if the initial point is chosen so that the norm of the dual conditions is less than or equal to the norm of the primal conditions, then the convergence behavior to zero of the dual conditions depends on the convergence behavior of the primal conditions.

© The Author(s), under exclusive license to Springer Nature Switzerland AG 2022
J. C. Figueroa-García et al. (Eds.): WEA 2022, CCIS 1685, pp. 173–184, 2022.
https://doi.org/10.1007/978-3-031-20611-5_15

Therefore we can exclude the dual conditions of the central path, obtaining the notion of quasicentral path as a central region suitable for guiding the iterates to a solution of the problem.

This leads us to present a path-following algorithm that is set in the framework of the Kojima et al. [8] algorithm. The path-following algorithm that we are proposing begins with a linesearch Newton's method applied to the perturbed KKT conditions for a fixed value $\mu > 0$ until an iterate belongs to a specific weighted neighborhood of the quasicentral path. If a solution of the problem is not found, then the perturbation parameter μ is reduced, a new weighted neighborhood is defined, and the Newton linesearch procedure is repeated. In order to monitor progress to the quasicentral path we present a new merit function and as proximity measures to this region we use specific weighted neighborhoods. Some important global properties of the merit function are presented, including a brief comparative discussion between weighted and non-weighted neighborhoods.

Finally, numerical experimentation is presented. We emphasize that the numerical experimentation shows only that the proposed technique works as well as current techniques on small to medium size problems. Further research is needed to demonstrate its competitiveness for a class of large-scale problems.

2   Problem Formulation

We consider the linear programming problem in the standard form

$$
\begin{aligned}
\text{minimize} \quad & c^T x \\
\text{subject to } & Ax = b \\
& x \geq 0,
\end{aligned}
\tag{1}
$$

where $c, x \in^n$, $b \in^m$, $A \in^{m \times n}$ ($m < n$), and A is full rank. This problem is called the primal problem. The dual problem associated with problem (1) can be written

$$
\begin{aligned}
\text{maximize} \quad & b^T y \\
\text{subject to } & A^T y + z = c \\
& z \geq 0,
\end{aligned}
\tag{2}
$$

where $y \in^m$ and $z \in^n$.

A point (x, z) is said to be a positive point if $x > 0$ and $z > 0$. A point (x, y, z) is said to be an interior point for the primal and dual problems if (x, z) is a positive point.

The optimality conditions, known as the Karush-Kuhn-Tucker (KKT) conditions, for the primal and dual problems are

$$
F(x, y, z) = \begin{pmatrix} Ax - b \\ A^T y + z - c \\ XZe \end{pmatrix} = 0,
\tag{3}
$$
$$
(x, z) \geq 0.
$$

where $X = \mathrm{diag}(x)$, $Z = \mathrm{diag}(z)$, and $e = (1, \ldots, 1)^T \in^n$.

For problems (1) and (2), we define the feasible set as

$$\mathcal{F} = \Big\{(x, y, z) \in^{n+m+n}: Ax = b, A^T y + z = c, (x, z) \geq 0\Big\},$$

and the strictly feasible set as

$$\mathcal{F}^o = \Big\{(x, y, z) \in \mathcal{F} : (x, z) > 0\Big\}.$$

The solution set is

$$\mathcal{S} = \Big\{(x^*, y^*, z^*) \in \mathcal{F} : X^* Z^* e = 0\Big\}.$$

This set is one of the faces of the polyhedral $\mathcal{F}$.

If $\mathcal{F}^o$ is not empty, then S is also not empty and bounded. All the points in the relative interior, $ri(S)$, are strictly complementarity solutions, i.e., $x_i^* + z_i^* > 0$ for $i = 1, ..., n$. And the zero-nonzero pattern of the points in $ri(S)$ is invariant. Therefore, for any $(x^*, y^*, z^*) \in ri(S)$ the following index sets $\mathcal{B} = \{i : x_i^* > 0,$ for $i = 1, 2, ..., n\}$ and $\mathcal{N} = \{i : z_i^* > 0,$ for $i = 1, 2, ..., n\}$ are independent of the choice of a solution in $ri(S)$. Moreover, by strict complementarity $\mathcal{B} \cup \mathcal{N} = \{1, 2, ..., n\}$ and $\mathcal{B} \cap \mathcal{N} = \emptyset$.

In particular, among the set of solutions in $ri(S)$ there is one solution, called the analytic center, and denoted by (x_c^*, y_c^*, z_c^*), such that

$$(x_c^*, y_c^*, z_c^*) = \arg \max \prod_{i \in \mathcal{B}} x_i \prod_{j \in \mathcal{N}} z_j.$$

In some linear programming applications, the primary objective is to compute the analytic center; however, the primary objective of this work is to promote the notion of the quasicentral path for solving linear programming problems.

The analytic center is associated with the notion of central path. For $\mu > 0$, the central path is defined as the set of points (x, y, z) satisfying the following perturbed KKT conditions

$$F_\mu(x, y, z) = \begin{pmatrix} Ax - b \\ A^T y + z - c \\ XZe - \mu e \end{pmatrix} = 0, \qquad (4)$$
$$(x, z) \geq 0.$$

This system has a unique solution $(x(\mu), y(\mu), z(\mu))$ for each fixed μ. Therefore the set $\{(x(\mu), y(\mu), z(\mu)), \mu > 0\}$ defines a smooth curve called the central path. As μ converges to zero the central path runs through the strictly feasible set $\mathcal{F}^o$, keeping an adequate distance from the non-optimal faces of $\mathcal{F}$, and ending at the analytic center, i.e.,

$$(x(\mu), y(\mu), z(\mu)) \rightarrow (x_c^*, y_c^*, z_c^*) \text{ as } \mu \rightarrow 0.$$

This classical result is applied in linear programming for obtaining an optimal solution of the primal and dual problems simultaneously.

Even though the notion of the central path plays an important role in the primal-dual interior-point methodology, a related notion of this region called the quasicentral path can be considered also as a central region for calculating a solution of the primal-dual problem. Then, the principal objective in this paper is to promote the notion of the quasicentral path.

In the work by Argáez and Tapia [2], a related notion of the central path was considered in nonlinear programming. In the arena of linear programming this notion is defined as follows: The quasicentral path is defined as the set of points (x, z) satisfying the following relaxation of the perturbed KKT conditions

$$\hat{F}_\mu(x, z) = \begin{pmatrix} Ax - b \\ XZe - \mu e \end{pmatrix} = 0, \qquad (5)$$
$$(x, z) > 0,$$

parameterized by $\mu > 0$.

Remark 1. It is worth noticing that the quasicentral path defines a variety instead of a path.[1]

The next property shows that the quasicentral path is equivalent to the region of strictly feasible points for the primal problem. Therefore following this region as a central region is equivalent to being strictly feasible with respect to the primal problem.

Property 1. For $\mu > 0$, the projection of the quasicentral path defined by (5) on the x-space, coincides with the set of strictly feasible points.

Let x be a strictly feasible point. Define the vector

$$z = \mu x^{-1}.$$

Then it is easily checked that (x, z) is on the quasicentral path. Conversely, x is a strictly feasible point if (x, z) is on the quasicentral path. The following discussion in Property 2 provides the motivation for the use of the quasicentral path as a central region.

Property 2. If the initial point is not a feasible point and by applying a damped Newton's method, then the dual residual, e_d^k, converges to zero if and only if the primal residual, e_p^k, converges to zero.

---

[1] Argaez and Tapia chose the name of quasicentral path due to the fact that one of the conditions of the central path is omitted. The authors are fully aware of the fact that they use the term "quasicentral path" to denote mathematically would be known as a variety. However, we choose to retain the already established terminology originally introduced by Argaez and Tapia [1,2].

By applying a damped Newton's method to primal and dual residuals at an infeasible starting point, then

$$e_p^1 = b - Ax_1 = (1 - \alpha_1)e_p^o, \text{ and}$$
$$e_d^1 = c - A^T y_1 - z_1 = (1 - \alpha_1)e_d^o.$$

Iteratively, we obtain

$$e_p^k = b - Ax_k = (1 - \alpha_k)e_p^{k-1} = \prod_{j=1}^{k}(1 - \alpha_j)e_p^o, \text{ and}$$

$$e_d^k = c - A^T y_k - z_k = (1 - \alpha_k)e_d^{k-1} = \prod_{j=1}^{k}(1 - \alpha_j)e_d^o.$$

The proof follows from the last two equations. This property shows that e_p^k and e_d^k converge to zero at the same rate, but not necessarily in the same number of Newton iterations. Nevertheless, if the initial point is chosen so that $\|e_d^o\| \leq \|e_p^o\|$, then the above property shows that the convergence to zero of the dual conditions depends on the convergence to zero of the primal conditions. In other words, e_d^k is zero if e_p^k is zero. In this situation, then we can remove the dual conditions from the central path, and consider the quasicentral path as a central region to be followed for obtaining a solution of the primal and dual problems simultaneously.

3 A Path-Following Algorithm

We present a path-following algorithm that uses the quasicentral path as a central region to guide the iterates toward a solution to the problem. To make progress in this region we use a new merit function, and specific weighted neighborhoods (see Definition 1) as measures of proximity to the quasicentral path. We start with an initial positive point (x, z) such that the error of the dual conditions e_d^o be less than or equal to the error of the primal conditions e_p^o, i.e. $\|e_d^o\| \leq \|e_p^o\|$.

The algorithm being proposed is a path-following version of the Kojima-Mizuno-Yoshise algorithm. We follow the same globalization philosophy as in Argáez-Tapia [2], which consists of excluding the dual variable y and the dual condition e_d for effects of global convergence.

Algorithm 1

Step 1. Consider an initial positive point (x, z) and $\mu > 0$. Set $e_d = c - z$, $e_p = b - Ax$, $e_c = \mu e - XZe$, such that $\|e_d\| \leq \|e_p\|$.
Step 2. Newton step. Solve the linear system for $(\Delta x, \Delta y, \Delta z)$

$$\begin{pmatrix} A & 0 & 0 \\ 0 & A^T & I \\ Z & 0 & X \end{pmatrix} \begin{pmatrix} \Delta x \\ \Delta y \\ \Delta z \end{pmatrix} = \begin{pmatrix} e_p \\ e_d \\ e_c \end{pmatrix} \tag{6}$$

Step 3. Maintain x and z positive. Choose $\tau \in (0,1)$ and calculate $\tilde{\alpha} = \min(1, \tau\hat{\alpha})$ where

$$\hat{\alpha} = \frac{-1}{\min(X^{-1}\Delta x, Z^{-1}\Delta z)}.$$

Step 4. Sufficient decrease. Find $\alpha = (\frac{1}{2})^t \tilde{\alpha}$ where t is the smallest positive integer such that

$$\Phi_\mu(x + \alpha\Delta x, z + \alpha\Delta z) \leq \Phi_\mu(x, z) + 10^{-4}\alpha\nabla\Phi_\mu(x, z)^T(\Delta x, \Delta z).$$

Update $(x, z) = (x, z) + \alpha(\Delta x, \Delta z)$, $e_p = (1 - \alpha)e_p$, and $e_d = (1 - \alpha)e_d$.

Step 5. Proximity to the quasicentral path. Choose an $\gamma \in (0,1)$.

If $\left(\|e_p\|^2 + \|(XZ)^{-1/2}(XZe - \mu e)\|^2 \right) \leq \gamma\mu$, then go to Step 6.

else, set $e_c = \mu e - XZe$, and go to step 2.

Step 6. Stopping criteria.

If $\left(2\|e_p\| + x^T z)/(1 + \|b\| \right) < \epsilon$, then stop

else update μ, set $e_c = \mu e - XZe$, and go to Step 2.

Remark 2. In Step 4, the updates e_p and e_d are explained by Property 2, and the merit function Φ_μ is presented in Definition 1.

Remark 3. Observe that for fixed $\mu > 0$, the Algorithm 1 applies a linesearch Newton's method to the perturbed KKT conditions until an iterate (x, z) satisfies the inequality given in Step 5. This part of the algorithm is called the inner loop. If the iterate is not a solution of the problem, then the parameter μ is reduced and the procedure is repeated. The sequence consisting of the iterates that satisfy the inequality in Step 5 is called the outer loop of the algorithm.

4   Merit Function and Global Properties

In the Algorithm 1 only the variables x and z are taken into account. The variable y is considered only implicitly. We use the notation $\tilde{v} = (x, z)$ as opposed to the standard notation $v = (x, y, z)$, in which the three variables are displayed.

Now for $\mu > 0$, the Newton step at the positive point $\tilde{v} = (x, z)$ is defined by $\Delta\tilde{v} = (\Delta x, \Delta z)$ where Δx and Δz are obtained from (6).

The purpose in this section is to present a new merit function that it forces the Newton iterates to advance towards the quasicentral path.

Definition 1. *For $\mu > 0$, we define the function*

$$\Phi_\mu : {}^{n+n}_{++} \rightarrow {}^n$$

$$\Phi_\mu(x, z) = \frac{1}{2}\|Ax - b\|^2 + \sum_{i=1}^n \left(x_i z_i - \mu \ln(x_i z_i) \right). \tag{7}$$

It is apparent from the way the problem is formulated, that the variables x and z are positive and therefore the function Φ_μ is well defined.

Property 3. For fixed $\mu > 0$, $n\mu(1 - ln(\mu))$ is the global minimum of the function Φ_μ and is attained at each point on the quasicentral path. In other words,

$$\min \Phi_\mu(x, z) = n\mu(1 - \ln(\mu)) = \Phi_\mu(x_\mu^*, z_\mu^*)$$

for each (x_μ^*, z_μ^*) on the quasicentral path.

It is easy to verify that $\Phi_\mu(w) = w - u\ln w$, $w > 0$ attains its global minimum at $w = \mu$. Therefore $\sum_{i=1}^n (x_i z_i - \mu \ln(x_i z_i))$ attains its global minimum, $n\mu(1 - \ln\mu)$, at every point (x, z) on the quasicentral path. It follows that

$$\Phi_\mu(x, z) \geq n\mu(1 - \ln(\mu)).$$

The conclusion follows since we have $\Phi_\mu(x_\mu^*, z_\mu^*) = n\mu(1 - \ln(\mu))$ at each point (x_μ^*, z_μ^*) on the quasicentral path.

Property 4. For fixed $\mu > 0$, the Newton direction $\Delta\tilde{v} = (\Delta x, \Delta z)$ is a descent direction for Φ_μ at each positive point $\tilde{v} = (x, z)$ not on the quasicentral path, i.e.,

$$\nabla\Phi_\mu(\tilde{v})^T \Delta\tilde{v} < 0.$$

The components of the gradient of Φ_μ with respect to x and z are

$$\nabla_x \Phi_\mu(x, z) = A^T(Ax - b) + z - \mu x^{-1} \quad \text{and} \quad \nabla_z \Phi_\mu(x, z) = x - \mu z^{-1}.$$

The directional derivative of Φ_μ in the direction $\Delta\tilde{v} = (\Delta x, \Delta z)$ at $\tilde{v} = (x, z)$ is given by

$$\nabla\Phi_\mu(x, z)^T \begin{pmatrix} \Delta x \\ \Delta z \end{pmatrix} = \nabla_x \Phi_\mu(x, z)^T \Delta x + \nabla_z \Phi_\mu(x, z)^T \Delta z.$$

$$= (Ax - b)^T A\Delta x + (z - \mu x^{-1})^T \Delta x + (z - \mu z^{-1})^T \Delta z.$$

If we set $W = (XZ)^{-1/2}$, and by using the first and third block of equations of (6), we obtain

$$\nabla\Phi_\mu(x, z)^T \begin{pmatrix} \Delta x \\ \Delta z \end{pmatrix} = -\left(\|Ax - b\|^2 + \|W(XZe - \mu e)\|^2 \right) < 0. \tag{8}$$

This inequality establishes the theorem. **Sufficient Decrease.** Since Φ_μ is a continuously differentiable function by Proposition 4.2 bounded from below, and by Proposition 4.3 since the Newton direction $\Delta\tilde{v} = (\Delta x, \Delta z)$ is a descent direction for Φ_μ, then it is known from [5] that for any fraction $\beta \in (0, 1)$, there exists an $\alpha^* > 0$ such that the following rate of decrease

$$\Phi_\mu(\tilde{v} + \alpha\Delta\tilde{v}) \leq \Phi_\mu(\tilde{v}) + \beta\alpha\nabla\Phi_\mu(\tilde{v})^T \Delta\tilde{v} \tag{9}$$

holds for any $\alpha \in (0, \alpha^*]$.

A continuation, we prove that the merit function Φ_μ plays a key role in preventing that the sequence $\{X^k Z^k e, k \in \mathbb{N}\}$, generated by the Algorithm 1, goes to zero or infinity for any fixed $\mu > 0$.

Property 5. For fixed $\mu > 0$, the sequence $\{X^k Z^k e, k \in \mathbb{N}\}$ is bounded and bounded away from zero.

From inequality (9), we know that the sequence $\{\Phi_\mu(x^k, z^k), k \in \mathbb{N}\}$ is non-increasing, and since $\Phi_\mu(x^k, z^k)$ is bounded below by $n\mu(1 - \ln \mu)$, then

$$n\mu(1 - \ln \mu) \leq \Phi_\mu(x^k, z^k) \leq \Phi_\mu(x^o, z^o).$$

If $x_j^k z_j^k \to 0$ or ∞ then $x_j^k z_j^k - \mu \ln(x_j^k z_j^k) \to \infty$. This contradicts the above inequality. Thus, there exists a positive constant C such that for every $k = 1, 2, \ldots,$

$$\frac{1}{C} \leq x^k z^k \leq C. \tag{10}$$

This concludes the proof.

5   Proximity to the Quasicentral Path

It is important to observe that the absolute value of the directional derivative of Φ_μ in any Newton direction $\Delta \tilde{v}$ can be interpreted as a weighted deviation from the quasicentral path. Therefore we use this value as a measure of proximity to the quasicentral path. We formalize this idea with the following definition.

Definition 2. *We say that a positive point (x, z) is sufficiently close to the quasicentral path if*

$$\mathcal{N}_W(\gamma\mu) = \left\{ (x, z) \in^{n+n} : \|Ax - b\|^2 + \|W(XZe - \mu e)\|^2 \leq \gamma\mu \right\}$$

where $W = (XZ)^{-1/2}$, and $\gamma \in (0, 1)$.

In particular if $W = I$, the set defined above becomes

$$\mathcal{N}_2(\gamma\mu) = \left\{ (x, z) \in^{n+n} : \|Ax - b\|^2 + \|(XZe - \mu e)\|^2 \leq \gamma\mu \right\},$$

and this set can be interpreted as a deviation from the quasicentral path measured in the 2-norm.

In order to facilitate the comparison between $\mathcal{N}_W(\gamma\mu)$ and $\mathcal{N}_2(\gamma\mu)$, we introduce the following definitions.

Definition 3. *We say that a positive point (x, z) is far away from the solution set if $x_i z_i > 1$, for $i = 1, \ldots, n$.*

Definition 4. *We say that a positive point (x, z) is close enough to the solution set if $x_i z_i < 1$, for $i = 1, \ldots, n$.*

Now we express the relationship between $\mathcal{N}_W(\gamma\mu)$ and $\mathcal{N}_2(\gamma\mu)$.

Property 6. For $\mu > 0$, if $0 < x_i z_i \leq 1$, $i = 1, \ldots, n$, then $\mathcal{N}_W(\gamma\mu) \subseteq \mathcal{N}_2(\gamma\mu)$.

Since $0 < x_i z_i \le 1$, then $0 < (x_i z_i - \mu)2 \le (x_i z_i - \mu)2/(x_i z_i)$. Therefore

$$0 < \|XZe - \mu e\| \le \|W(XZe - \mu e)\|.$$

The proof follows directly from the above inequality.

Property 7. For $\mu > 0$, if $x_i z_i > 1$, $i = 1, \ldots, n$, then $\mathcal{N}_2(\gamma \mu) \subseteq \mathcal{N}_W(\gamma \mu)$.

Since $x_i z_i > 1$, then $(x_i z_i - \mu)2/(x_i z_i) \le (x_i z_i - \mu)2$. Therefore

$$0 < \|W(XZe - \mu e)\| \le \|XZe - \mu e\|.$$

The proof follows as that of Property 5.

From Properties 4 it is readily concluded that far away from the solution set, weighted neighborhoods are contained in the 2-norm neighborhoods, whereas near the solution set, the 2-norm neighborhoods are contained in the weighted neighborhoods. Therefore, near to a solution, the use of weighted neighborhoods may allow larger step lengths. This is the reason that we are proposing weighted neighborhoods as a measure of closeness to the quasicentral path.

6 Numerical Experimentation

In this section, we show how Algorithm 1 presented in Sect. 3 performs numerically in obtaining a solution for a set of test problems. It is important to state that our current goal is not to compare the numerical behavior with other algorithms, but to show that using the quasicentral path as a central region it is enough for guiding the iterates toward a solution to the problem. Now, Algorithm 1 was written in MATLAB version 6a, and the implementation was done on a Sun Ultra 10 machine running the Solaris system. The numerical experiments were performed on the set of NETLIB test problems. In Tables 1–2, we summarized the numerical results obtained by Algorithm 1 where the first four columns contain the problem number, problem name, and dimensions of the problem, respectively. The next two columns state the number of linear systems solved by Algorithm 1 and its corresponding CPU time in seconds. Finally, the last three columns denote the primal objective and the norms of the primal and dual conditions at the initial point. The primal conditions are denoted by $e_p^0 = \|Ax_0 - b\|$ and the dual conditions are given by $e_d^0 = \|z - c\|$ where the initial value of the variable y_0 is set to zero.

Now, this implementation of the algorithm entails the selection of an initial interior point (x_0, y_0, z_0) satisfying the inequality

$$\|z_0 - c\| \le \|Ax_0 - b\|. \tag{11}$$

The initial point is chosen by following a procedure widely used in the literature: we take $y_0 = 0$, then pick x_0 and z_0. If the point $(x_0, 0, z_0)$ satisfies the condition (11), we let this be our initial point.

Otherwise, we solve for ξ the following inequality

$$\|z_0 - c\| \le \|A(\xi x_0) - b\|, \tag{12}$$

Table 1. Numerical results

Problem Name	m	n	Iterations	CPU time	Residual	$\|e_d^0\|$	$\|e_p^0\|$
25fv47	798	1854	24	5.18	5.94e−13	2.78e+03	2.74e+04
80bau3b	2235	11516	40	21.91	8.10e−09	8.72e+04	6.07e+05
agg3	516	758	18	2.39	4.25e−11	9.45e+03	7.42e+06
bandm	269	436	18	0.90	.57e−09	2.37e+02	2.56e+03
bnl2	2268	4430	32	14.85	1.12e−11	3.13e+03	7.54e+04
boeing1	347	722	22	1.85	4.31e−09	4.47e+01	2.18e+04
capri	267	476	20	1.38	9.23e−12	2.61e+01	1.69e+04
cycle	1801	3305	29	15.91	3.61e−09	6.96e+01	2.24e+04
czprob	737	3141	36	4.95	5.56e−11	5.66e+04	1.29e+06
d2q06c	2171	5831	31	32.93	1.83e−12	1.63e+04	1.97e+05
d6cube	404	6184	31	16.28	8.38e−11	2.63e+03	3.91e+06
degen3	1503	2604	27	25.31	7.48e−09	2.40e+03	4.75e+04
dfl001	6071	12230	48	1900.29	1.71e−08	1.11e+05	1.18e+05
e226	220	469	21	0.94	1.43e−12	3.71e+02	3.47e+03
etamacro	357	692	27	2.11	7.40e−10	2.93e+03	3.93e+03
fffff	800	501	24	3.04	1.79e−09	3.81e+01	3.16e+07
finnis	492	1014	30	1.93	1.51e−09	3.13e+04	2.96e+05
fit2d	25	10524	43	53.88	5.79e−10	3.20e+03	1.34e+05
fit2p	3000	13525	14	178.19	1.08e−10	3.26e+03	6.54e+05
ganges	1137	1534	19	3.24	2.10e−11	7.48e+01	2.89e+06
giffpin	600	1144	19	1.57	3.14e−10	2.98e+04	1.13e+09
greenbeb	2317	5415	37	18.73	1.26e−09	4.05e+04	7.16e+05
grow22	440	946	16	2.86	1.15e−09	1.30e+02	1.67e+03
maros-r7	3136	9408	14	181.33	1.08e−10	3.26e+03	6.54e+05
modszk1	686	1622	24	2.15	1.19e−09	4.03e+04	5.24e+06
perold	625	1530	57	7.93	4.30e−12	1.30e+00	2.84e+05
pilot	1441	4657	32	52.85	2.51e−09	5.16e+00	6.24e+04
pilot87	2030	6460	36*	170.58	5.31e−08	7.20e+02	4.23e+05
scagr25	471	671	15	0.93	3.26e−09	2.76e+04	1.89e+05
scfxm2	644	1184	20	1.87	3.16e−11	7.20e+02	7.19e+04
scfxm3	966	1776	20	2.55	1.16e−11	1.08e+03	8.81e+04
scorpion	375	453	15	0.75	1.49e−10	7.43e+03	1.49e+04
scrs8	485	1270	26	2.03	4.04e−11	3.56e+04	3.83e+06
scsd8	397	2750	11	2.50	7.59e−12	0.00e+00	1.28e+01
sctap3	1480	3340	19	3.40	1.12e−11	2.32e+04	1.53e+05
seba	515	1036	23	6.49	2.81e−10	1.20e+04	2.58e+05
share1b	112	248	21	0.74	1.53e−11	6.79e+02	7.70e+05
shell	496	1487	20	1.70	2.01e−12	3.70e+04	8.16e+06
ship08l	688	4339	15	3.86	4.12e−12	6.59e+04	7.42e+04
ship12l	838	5329	16	4.00	3.62e−12	7.30e+04	7.36e+04
siera	1222	2715	19	5.21	1.28e−11	2.64e+04	3.83e+05
standmps	467	1258	26	1.62	3.64e−12	2.50e+03	2.48e+06
stocfor2	2157	3045	21	4.66	2.21e−10	4.32e+03	2.38e+06
stocfor3	16675	23541	34	46.55	2.35e−09	6.52e+03	6.63e+06
truss	1000	8806	20	9.07	5.90e−10	6.83e+04	1.37e+05
wood1p	244	2595	21	14.41	329e−10	2.16e+01	7.65e+04
woodw	1098	8418	28	13.68	1.74e−11	7.80e+01	1.23e+05

which is equivalent to

$$\xi 2\|Ax_0\|^2 - 2\xi\langle Ax_0, b\rangle + \|b\|^2 - \|z_0 - c\|^2 \geq 0. \tag{13}$$

It is easy to verify that in the present situation, the equation

$$\xi 2\|Ax_0\|^2 - 2\xi\langle Ax_0, b\rangle + \|b\|^2 - \|z_0 - c\|^2 = 0 \tag{14}$$

has two real distinct roots $\xi_1 < 1 < \xi_2$.

If $\xi_1 \leq 0$, the inequality (13) holds as long as $\xi \leq \xi_2$, then we set $\xi = \xi_2$. Else, we might take

$$\xi \in (0, \xi_1] \cup [\xi_2, \infty)$$

and set $(\xi x_0, 0, z_0)$ as our initial point where $\xi = 10 * \max\{\xi_1, \xi_2\}$. In the previous conclusions, we assume that $A * x_0 \neq 0$. The parameters τ and γ are set to 0.99995 and .5, respectively.

7 Conclusions

In this work, we have presented an infeasible primal-dual interior-point method for solving linear programs, a global convergence theory, and a numerical experimentation of the strategy. We show that the use of the quasicentral path, while being a less restrictive notion than the central path, it is sufficiently strong to guide the iterates toward a solution to the problem. Moreover, our methodology includes a new merit function and weighted proximity measures. The numerical results support the proposed globalization strategy for solving linear programming problems. Future works include more numerical experimentation and comparisons with other strategies for solving large-scale linear programs.

Acknowledgement. Drs. Argáez and Mendez would like to acknowledge the support of the Department of Mathematical Sciences and Dr. Velázquez the Richard Tapia Center of Excellence and Equity in Education at Rice University. The authors thank Dr. Richard A. Tapia for his reviews and helpful comments on this paper.

References

1. Argáez, M.: Exact and inexact Newton linesearch interior-point methods for nonlinear programming. Ph.D thesis, Department of Computational and Applied Mathematics, Rice University (1997)
2. Argáez, M., Tapia, R.A.: On the global convergence of a modified augmented Lagrangian linesearch interior-point Newton method for nonlinear programming. J. Optimi. Theory Appl. **114**(1), 1–25 (2002)
3. Argáez, M., Tapia, R.A., Velázquez, L.: Numerical comparisons of path-following strategies for a primal-dual interior-point method for nonlinear programming. J. of Optimi. Theory Appl. **114**(2), 255–272 (2002)
4. Bixby, R.: Solving real-world linear programs: a decade and more of progress. Oper. Res. **50**(1), 3–15 (2002)

5. Dennis, J.E., Jr., Schnabel, R.B.: Numerical Methods for Unconstrained Optimization and Nonlinear Equations. SIAM, Philadelphia (1996)
6. EL-Bakry, A.S., Tapia, R.A., Tsuchiya, T., Zhang, Y.: On the formulation of the primal-dual interior point method for nonlinear programming. J. Optimi. Theory Appl. **89**, 507–541 (1996)
7. Karmarkar, N.: A new polynomial-time algorithm for linear programming. Combinatorica **4**, 373–395 (1994)
8. Kojima, M., Mizuno, S., and Yoshise, A. 1989. A primal-dual interior point method for linear programming. In: Megiddo, N. (ed.) Progress in Mathematical Programming: Interior-Point and Related Methods, pp. 29–47. Springer, New York (1989). https://doi.org/10.1007/978-1-4613-9617-8_2
9. Lustig, I.J., Marsten, R., Shanno, D.F.: interior point methods for linear programming: computational state of the art. ORSA J. Comput. **6**(1), 1–14 (1994)
10. Ortega, J.M., Rheinboldt, W.C.: Iterative Solution of Nonlinear Equations in Several Variables. Academic Press, New York (1970)
11. Wright, S.J.: Primal-Dual Interior-Point Methods. SIAM, Philadelphia (1997)
12. Zhang, Y.: User's guide to LIPSOL. Technical report TR95-19, Department of Mathematics and Statistics, University of Maryland Baltimore County, Baltimore, MD 21228 (1995)

P-Median Equivalence and Partitioning in Logistics Problems

María Beatriz Bernábe Loranca[1]([✉]), Rogelio González Velázquez[1],
Erika Granillo Martínez[2], Carmen Cerón Garnica[1], and Alberto Carrillo Canán[3]

[1] Facultad de Ciencias de la Computación, Benemérita Universidad Autónoma de Puebla,
Puebla Pue Puebla, México
beatriz.bernabe@gmail.com
[2] Facultad de Administración, Benemérita Universidad Autónoma de Puebla, Puebla Pue
Puebla, México
[3] Facultad de Filosofía y Letras, Benemérita Universidad Autónoma de Puebla, Puebla, México

Abstract. This work consists of pointing out the algorithmic equivalence of the
PAM algorithm (Partitioning Around Medoids) and the P-Median when their properties are contrasted to establish if there is an algorithmic similarity. So, under the
conjecture that both algorithms are equivalent in terms of the objective function
and the configuration of the groups they generate. The objective of this work
focuses on comparing the optima and centroids (medoids and medians) for both
proposals.

The experiment that supports the assumption of equivalence between PAM
and the P-Median is based on the Toluca Valley Metropolitan Zone instance. Once
the data for different sizes in the groups were processed, the time, the quality of
the solutions and the structure of the groups were recorded. It was concluded that
PAM and the P-Median provide consistent results to the proposed hypothesis.

Keywords: Branch and bound · LINGO · PAM · P-Median · Optimal

1 Introduction

It is important to highlight the computational complexity involved in solving the partitioning problem [1]. This problem is considered as a NP-hard combinatorial problem
that requires its solution to be generated from the use of non-exact optimization methods. In general terms, the methodologies for solving this problem can be divided into
exact and approximate methods [2]. Since PAM and P-median can be solved under
exact procedures, this work focuses on analyzing their performance in three directions:
1) equivalence in the value of the objective function, 2) comparison of centroids and 3)
computational cost [3].

Once the equivalence between PAM and the P-Median has been demonstrated with
Lingo and considering that commercial software offers local optima of the criteria that
are optimized, it is possible to choose a Medoid Partitioning PAM algorithm to solve the
P-median problem when software like Lingo is not enough to solve very large instances.

© The Author(s), under exclusive license to Springer Nature Switzerland AG 2022
J. C. Figueroa-García et al. (Eds.): WEA 2022, CCIS 1685, pp. 185–197, 2022.
https://doi.org/10.1007/978-3-031-20611-5_16

On the other hand, because it is an NP-hard problem, different search atrategies are proposed. The model specifically in Lingo is binary integer, using the brach and bound method and in the case of PAM, it is implemented in the combinatorial optimization version. The comparison of both methods serves to establish a relationship that points to a more diversified search.

The empirical evidence provided is based on the BGSAs (Basic Geostatistical Areas) of the Toluca Valley Metropolitan Area ZMVT and Mexico Valley Metropolitan ZMVM.

The work is structured as follows: introduction as Sect. 1. Section 2 deals with the preliminaries of this manuscript. Section 3 focuses on the general aspects related to partitioning and k-medoids. Section 4 presents the P-Median and PAM model. Section 5 deals with the computational experience and finally the conclusions are presented.indented.

2 Preliminaries

Broadly speaking, clustering is divided into two types: Partitioning methods and Hierarchical methods.

The algorithm that is tested in this manuscript belongs to the first section and is considered as a computational tool to solve or to support the solution of logistics and zone design problems. On the other hand, although the P-Median cannot and should not be labeled as a partitioning algorithm, many authors have implemented the P-Median using partitioning when the branch-and-bound algorithm used by commercial optimizers is limited in solving the P -Median. Even a geographic partitioning problem can be modeled as a P-Median problem.

The present document is concerned with obtaining exemplary and exact partitions since metaheuristic approximations are not included in this discussion due to their random nature. In this regard, it is appropriate to comment on the computational complexity of partitioning. The partitioning problem consists of finding the partition $P \in P_k$ that maximizes the inter-class inertia $B(P)$, that is, maximizing the intensity of the separation between the centers of the groups. The computational complexity of this problem is of the NP-hard type [2]. The combinatorial size of this problem can be seen with the following example. If we denote by $S(n, k)$ and B_n the number of partitions of Ω in k non-empty classes and the total number of partitions of Ω respectively, then for example $S(60, 2) \approx 0.58 \times 10^{18}$, $S(60, 5) \approx 0.72 \times 10^{40}$, $S(100, 5) \approx 0.66 \times 10^{68}$, while $B_{10} = 115975$, $B_{15} \approx 0.14 \times 10^{10}$ $yB_{40} \approx 0.16 \times 10^{36}$. In a partitioning problem where Ω has 100 objects and the number of classes is $k = 5$, if there were a computer on earth so fast that it was capable of calculating $B(P)$ for each of the partitions P of Ω in a time of 10^{-10} seconds in search of a global maximum, it would take the computer a little more than 2×10^{48} centuries to complete the analysis of all the partitions of the problem [2].

2.1 K-Means Partitioning: Beginnings and Generalities

Although k-means is not compared or discussed in this article, to put the situation in reasonably broad terms, k-means is briefly described given its popularity, relevance, and basic characteristics that other algorithms have respected and taken but at the same time they have improved to overcome their weaknesses. That is, similar proposals have been put forward under different forms and hypotheses, even improving their theoretical and algorithmic aspects, as well as modifications of the method for example: partitioning on medoids.

With the publication of Sokal 1963, cluster analysis emerges as an important area of study [4]. With Lerman 1970, the publication of a compendium of books and articles that laid the foundations of this area of study begins, exposed chronologically that also delve into the mathematical nature of the grouping problem [5–7]. On the other hand, the publication of Hartigan 1975 impacts the academic world for his study on computational aspects of algorithms, which implied that the basic problems and methods of clustering became widely known by the scientific community [8].

The k-means algorithm tries to minimize the classic criterion of distance of each of the sample observations from the mean of its squared group. This algorithm presents a series of extensions and generalizations, among which the fuzzy case, the maximum likelihood case, and those criteria based on convexity, among others. One of the main approaches to clustering techniques is based on the criterion of the sum of the squares of the variance known as k-means. Among the disadvantages of K averages are: 1) Finding the K value is a difficult task, 2) Not effective when used with global clustering, 3) If different initial partitions are selected, the result of the clusters may vary, 4) The algorithm does not handle clusters of different sizes and density.

3   Partitioning (k-Medoids)

Partitioning algorithms have long been very popular clustering, sorting, or partitioning algorithms before the advent of data mining. Informally, partitioning is understood as follows: Given a set D of n objects in a d-dimensional space and an input parameter k, a partitioning algorithm organizes the objects into k clusters such that the total deviation of each of them relative to their cluster center or cluster distribution is minimized. The deviation of a point can be calculated differently in different algorithms and is more commonly called a similarity function.

Among partitioning algorithms, partitioning by medoids stands out. Unlike the k-means algorithm, the k-medoids method uses the most central object (medoids) in a cluster to be the center of the cluster instead of taking the mean value of the objects in a cluster. Therefore, the k-medoids method is less sensitive to noise and outliers. However, this implies a higher computational cost. The following algorithm describes the general aspects of k-medoid algorithms:

3.1   Iterative Relocation Algorithm (IR)

The generalized iterative relocation algorithm is composed of 2 steps:

1) Input: The cluster number k, and a database containing n objects, 2) Output: A set of k clusters that minimizes a criterion function E.

The initialization state k-medoids and variants is equal to IR in the sense that the random selection of the k objects are the center of the clusters (groups). From the k-means properties, k-medoids clustering takes the procedure of assigning an object to its nearest center, which is solved in step 4 of the IR algorithm making step 3 redundant, so K-medoids it is far from both IR and k-means in that at most one center will be changed in step 4 for each iteration. This change of center should give rise to a decrease in the criterion function, which is usually the squared error function in the minimization of distances between objects and centroids and implicitly uses a distance measure [9].

To develop step 4, a k-medoid algorithm like PAM is considered [3]. It then iterates through all k cluster centers and tries to replace each one with one of the other $(n - k)$ objects. For each of these replacements, if the squared error function E decreases, the replacement will take place causing the next iteration of the IR algorithm to occur. However, if no such replacement is found after going through all k clusters, there will be no change in E, so the algorithm ends with a local optimum. Since PAM attempts to replace each of the k centers of the cluster with one of the $(n - k)$ objects and each of these attempts results in $(n - k)$ operations to compute E, the total complexity of PAM in one iteration is $O(k(n - k)^2)$. For large values of n, this calculation becomes very expensive [9].

Due to its complexity, PAM works well for small data sets, but is not well suited to large data sets. This statement justifies the choice of small size tests for the analysis pursued in this paper. On the other hand, to deal with larger data sets, other strategies must be developed and will be addressed in future work. For example, the problem of large amounts of data in medoid partitioning was exposed by Kaufman and Rousseeuw and they developed a method based on sampling, called CLARA (Clustering LARge Applications) [3].

3.2 PAM: General Aspects and Algorithm

An evaluation of the PAM algorithm can be approached in different ways, however, experience dictates that not knowing the algorithmic details nor being directly involved with the implementation will probably lead to dubious results. Thus, the Java code programmed years ago was evaluated, in addition to reviewing the classical literature on K-medoids to be described as a summary in this section.

3.2.1 K-Medoid Scopes

The K-medoids algorithm is used to find medoids in a cluster that is the center point of a cluster. K-Medoids is more robust compared to K-Means, since in K-Medoids it finds k as a representative object to minimize the sum of the dissimilarities of the data objects, while K-Means uses the sum of the Euclidean distances to the square for data objects.

Starting from the benefits of K-Medoids based on object representation techniques to reduce the drawbacks of the K-Means algorithm, the first was used in this manuscript for the stated objectives [10].

Medoids are the most centered data object in the cluster and are sometimes known in a broad sense as centroids. The medoids are randomly selected from the K_y data objects to form the K_y cluster, and the other data objects are placed near the medoids in a cluster. All data objects in the cluster are then processed to repeatedly find new Medoids to represent the new cluster. After finding the new medoids all data objects are linked to the cluster. The location of the medoids changes accordingly with each iteration. Thus k_y

clusters representing n data objects are formed (the heading, k_y is the respected notation of authors Mark and Katherine [10]).

3.2.2 K-Medoid Algorithm

Input: K_y: the number of clusters,: a data set containing n objects.
Output: A set of k_y: clusters.
   Algorithm:

- Randomly select k_y as Medoids for n data points.
- Find the closest Medoids by calculating the distance between n data points and k Medoids and assign the data objects.

  - For each Medoids m and each data point o associated with m do
  - Exchange m and calculate the total cost of the configuration
  - Select the Medoids with the lowest cost of the configuration.

- If there are no changes to the assignments, repeat steps 2 and 3 alternately.

4 P-Median

The P-Median is that given a set of points (location of consumers) and a matrix of distances (costs) from each and every one of the points, choose p points (location of facilities) in order to minimize the sum of the distances of all points to the nearest chosen point.

   The development of the P-Median problem (PMP) statement took place in the 1960s, attributed to Hakimi in the discrete case [11]. In 1970 ReValle and Swain presented the first integer programming formulation for the P-Median problem [12]. In general, the P-Median problem can be expressed mathematically as a discrete optimization problem. A wide coverage of the methods to address the P-Median problem can be found in Reese [13] where a set of articles on the P-Median classified as one of the main problems of the LAP type (Location-Allocation Problem) is also analyzed [13]. This problem determines the location of facilities and assigns demand points to a facility. The P-Median model can be stated in terms of graphs as: Let $G = (V, E)$ be an undirected graph where V is the set of n vertices and E is the set of edges with an associated weight that can be the distance between the vertices $d_{ij} = d(v_i, v_j)$ for all $i, j = 1, \ldots, n$ according to a certain metric, with the distances a symmetric matrix is formed, find $V_p \subseteq V$ such that $|V_p| = p$, where p can be either variable or fixed, and that the sum of the shortest distances from the vertices in $\{V - V_p\}$ to their nearest vertex in V_p is minimized. Said in this way, the PMP is a combinatorial and belongs to the NP-Hard class proven by Kariv and Hakimi in 1979 [14].

4.1 P-Median Model

The P-Median problem considers the following situation: it is required to partition a finite set of objects into exactly p groups. Each of these groups will be characterized by one of the objects, which is selected as the median of the group, and the subset of objects assigned to said median. For each pair of objects a distance is specified and it is required to minimize the sum of distances between the objects and the medians to which they are assigned.

Let $N = \{1, \ldots, n\}$ be the set of objects. For each pair (i, j), $i \in N$, $j \in N$, d_{ij} denotes the distance (similarity) between objects i and j. Given the number p, which denotes the number of groups, we need to partition the set N into p disjoint subsets, that is, $N = \bigcup_{k=1}^{p} N_k$ y $N_r \cap N_s = \varnothing$, for all $r, s \in \{1, \ldots, p\}$, $r \neq s$.

Next, the mathematical programming model for the problem is shown and the following decision variables are defined:

$$y_i = \begin{cases} 1, & \textit{if object i is selected as median,} \\ 0, & \textit{in other case.} \end{cases}$$

and

$$x_{ij} = \begin{cases} 1, & \textit{if object j is assigned to the mediana, i,} \\ 0, & \textit{in other case.} \end{cases}$$

The problem can be modeled as follows:

$$\min \sum_{i \in N} \sum_{j \in N} d_{ij} x_{ij} \tag{1}$$

$$bound\ to \sum_{i \in N} x_{ij} = 1\, j \in N \tag{2}$$

$$\sum_{i \in N} y_i = p \tag{3}$$

$$x_{ij} \leq y_i\, i \in N, j \in N \tag{4}$$

$$x_{ij} \leq \{0, 1\}\, i \in N, j \in N \tag{5}$$

$$y_i \leq \{0, 1\}\, i \in N \tag{6}$$

Constraints (2) ensure that each object is assigned to one of the medians. Constraint (3) ensures that p objects are selected as medians. Finally, constraints (4) to (6) ensure that objects can only be assigned to selected medians [13].

4.2 PAM Objetive Function

PAM is a non-hierarchical method where the dataset is partitioned into a previously specified number of k clusters (groups), then observations are iteratively assigned to the clusters until some stopping criterion (function to be optimized) is satisfied, for instance, that the sum of squares within the clusters is minimal [3].

The PAM function is based on the search for k representative objects called medoids (medoides) among the objects of the data set. These medoids are calculated in such a way that the total dissimilarity of all objects towards their nearest medoid is minimal, that is, the goal is to find a subset $\{m_1 \ldots m_k\} \subset \{1 \ldots n\}$ that minimizes the objective function: $\sum_{i=1}^{n} min_{t=1,\ldots,k} d(i, m_t)$.

Each object is assigned to the cluster corresponding to the closest centroid. That is, the object i is placed in the cluster v_i when the medoid m_{vi} is closer to i than any other medoid $m_w, o: d(i, m_{vi}) \leq d(i, m_w)$ para to do $w = 1, \ldots, k$ [3].

5 Computational Experience

The purpose of this work is to reveal that under the same conditions, PAM and P-Median are equivalent models. This assumption can be verified if the results are compared in two aspects: cost of the objective function and configuration of the resulting partition.

It is convenient to mention that the idea to determine the equivalence between PAM and the P-Median took place when a trivial reflection surrounded a problem of location and territory design that could be addressed with the P-Median, but in the same way with the partitioning. Classic. So, the most used methodologies in territorial partitioning were evoked, where the location-allocation models and those of set partitioning stand out.

In the particular case of territorial design, territorial partitioning is modeled as a P-Median problem. However, in broad terms, partitioning can be solved as a P-Median problem or PAM uses partitioning for its solution, even when exact methods are not an alternative. At this point, it is argued that if there are two equivalent algorithms, the decision to choose one of them lies in knowing which algorithm generates better quality solutions in better computation time. Then, from this perspective and with the purpose of examining the behavior of PAM and the P-Median to determine their equivalence, a basic experiment was designed that contrasts three fundamental aspects and that guarantee, in some way, the proposed similarity: 1) function of cost, 2) centroids 3) computational cost and configuration of the groups. Informally, this situation can be expressed by considering that because PAM creates partitions, that is, each group in the partition has a "center" called the medoid, which attracts objects that minimize their distance from the medoid through the function of cost, the challenge is to test PAM against another algorithm whose algorithmic semantics are similar. In this scenario, the P-Median model was chosen, which has an equivalent method if the following situation is considered: It is required to partition a finite set of objects into exactly p groups. Each of these groups will be characterized by one of the objects that is selected as the median of the group and the subset of objects assigned to said median. For each pair of objects a distance is specified and it is required to minimize the sum of distances between the objects and the medians to which they are assigned.

According to the above, it is emphasized that the purpose of this work is to evaluate 2 algorithms widely cited in the literature to measure similar characteristics. These algorithms are also formulated as methods and are known in broad terms as location-assignment and partition classification (PAM and P-Median respectively).

The experiment was designed so that the cost of computation was reasonable and in the same way that the software chosen to program the P-Median could provide solutions without exceeding the limitations of Lingo.

Lingo solves the P-Median with Branch and Bound and returns an exact value in the result of the objective function and implicitly produces a partition. On the other hand, PAM provides a partition under an exhaustive-combinatorial scheme and assumes that under these conditions PAM and P-Median are equivalent methods in at least 3 points: 1) they use a distance matrix in the data input, 2) they generate a partition, 2) they use the same cost function, 3) each center of the groups that make up the partition has the same goal (basically the equivalence is centered on point 2, the other points are tacit).

5.1 Experiment

This subsection describes the computational experience to determine the equivalence between PAM and P-Median.

Tables 1, 2, 3 and 4, concentrate the results of the tests made to the P-Median with Lingo, and PAM with a combinatorial partition classification algorithm. As can be seen, the results are not identical, except to $k = 5$ (whose cost can be seen in Table 2).

It is insisted that the difference in the objective function is an "epsilon", which is justified in the numerical calculation by the approximation or truncation.

Table 1. Performance tests with the centers of each group

K	P-Median with Branch and Bound (Lingo)			PAM		
	Cost	Time (Seconds)	Medians	Cost	Time (Seconds)	Medoids
4	11.16330	1383.21	72, 95, 132, 283	11.16329	0	252, 72, 132, 283
8	5.995200	1941.34	1, 21, 29, 46, 70, 90, 113, 314	5.9951	3	21, 196, 1, 314, 307, 46, 113, 90
12	3.934600	2547.67	27, 46, 63, 82, 91, 111, 128, 142, 155, 257, 267, 322	3.9392	60	296, 123, 149, 129, 27, 63, 181, 91, 267, 257, 108, 142
24	1.721400	2165.05	7, 36, 47, 50, 51, 54, 63, 75, 87, 90, 102, 111, 114, 116, 119, 135, 159, 186, 195, 210, 264, 272, 307, 311	1.7219	75	116, 186, 132, 329, 20, 142, 63, 50, 215, 210, 250, 119, 135, 307, 36, 159, 53, 264, 272, 7, 311, 114, 102, 111

The medians and medoids are identified for the P-Median and PAM, respectively. For example, for k = 4, the median = 95 and the medoid = 252, it can be seen that they are the only centroids that do not coincide. Similarly, for k = 24, the medians 47, 51, 54, 75, 87, 90 are different from the medoids 20, 53, 132, 142, 215, 250, 329; the rest of the objects are the same. Figure 1 shows that the computational cost of PAM is better up to $k = 66$ groups with respect to Branching and Bounding for the P-Median in Lingo.

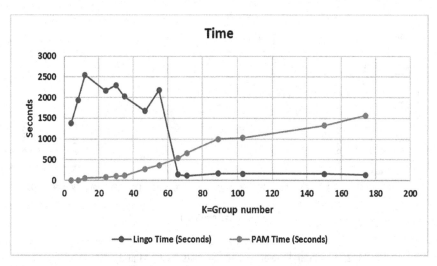

Fig. 1. Computational cost comparison

In Tables 1 and 2 the cases were obtained from the tests performed. It is observed that for the instance of $k = 4$ and $k = 8$, PAM produces an optimal value lower than the P-Median of Lingo with a difference of -0.00001 and -0.00010 respectively. As can be seen for $k = 12$ and $k = 24$, Lingo minimizes the target better than PAM (the difference is still one epsilon). On the other hand, Table 2 shows that both the PAM and the P-Median have the same target cost.

Table 2. Comparison between the two identical solution costs for $k = 5$

PAM	Lingo	PAM = Lingo	Outcome
6.88E-02 (0.06879999)	6.88E-02 (0.0688)	0. 068 = 0.068	Same

In Fig. 2, the scale has been enlarged so that the minuscule difference in objective costs for the algorithms in question is evident. Despite this, the equivalence conjecture for PAM and P-Median is maintained.

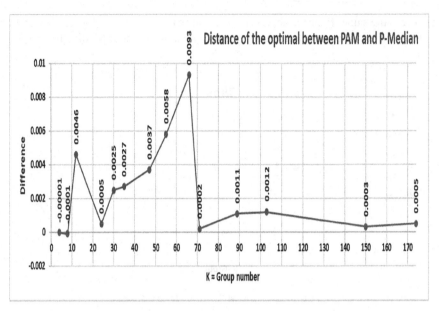

Fig. 2. Upper and lower bounds on costs for PAM and P-Median.

The following Table 3 reveals the test record that reached exactly the same optimum and even the same groups with their respective centers for both algorithms.

Table 3. Groups with their respective centers for ZMVT

		PAM		P-Median	
K	Cluster	Medoid	Group's elements	Median	Group's elements
5	1	3	1, 2, 4	3	1, 2, 4, 5
2	28	15, 19, 22, 23, 26, 27	14	16, 17, 20, 21, 24	
3	14	16, 17, 20, 21, 24	18	11, 13	
4	18	11, 13	25	6, 7, 8, 9, 10, 12, 29, 30	
5	25	5, 6, 7, 8, 9, 10, 12, 29, 30	28	6, 7, 8, 9, 10, 12, 29, 30	

After analyzing different partitions of the P-Median in Lingo and PAM, conclusions are reached that perhaps many researchers have experienced, for example: the inability of Lingo to generate solutions due to the large number of variables generated by the implicit Branching and bounding In this work, the instance of the ZMVT is 469 objects and in order for Lingo to be able to compete fairly with PAM, it was observed that it only supports up to 369 objects.

Considering the ZMVM of Mexico City made up of 5023 geographic objects of which only 369 were taken due to Lingo limitations. As can be seen in Table 4, the optimal values are almost the same and the difference that is minimal responds to the same relationship for the ZMVT.

Table 4. Groups with their respective centers to ZMVT

K	P-Median with Branch and Bound (Lingo)			PAM		
	Cost	Time seconds	Medians	Cost	Time seconds	Medoids
3	29.2452	1268	50, 130, 327	29.2452	0	327, 50, 130
9	13.6455	1805	50, 55, 127, 180, 227, 282, 297, 339, 357	13.6455	5	50, 227, 282, 357, 297, 55, 127, 180, 339
15	9.8517	2307	2, 17, 39, 48, 89, 101, 164, 172, 188, 232, 259, 271, 305, 342, 357	9.873702	20	232, 88, 127, 164, 39, 101, 42, 200, 159, 50, 227, 308, 358, 259, 342
27	6.101	2694	1, 2, 8, 11, 17, 31, 39, 50, 53, 98, 116, 123, 146, 154, 159, 200, 203, 240, 264, 275, 283, 293, 303, 313, 325, 348, 362	6.135596	91	116, 17, 50, 11, 136, 39, 53, 342, 46, 283, 31, 213, 127, 179, 146, 203, 123, 232, 369, 313, 275, 264, 8, 1, 2, 305, 159

6 Conclusions

It is known that a problem is of combinatorial optimization (CO) if in them the decision variables formed by vectors X, only admit integer values and its space of feasible solutions Ω is formed by permutations or subsets of natural numbers. PAM belongs to this combinatorial category.

On the other hand, the P-Median can be solved with some optimization software such as Lingo, whose implementation responds to the Branch and Bound algorithm, which produces an exact solution. However, the constraints of the optimizers to solve the P-Median are faced with the number of variables that are generated by the programmed algorithm of the model, which in this case is binary-integer.

A dilemma that researchers have in problems of this magnitude is to put aside the optimization software and program the P-Median model with some general purpose software. The P-Median is commonly implemented with the characteristics of classical partitioning, as long as it is not necessary to incorporate heuristic methods to achieve an approximate solution.

In the literature there are different ways to express both partitioning and the P-Median, even with different notation, but all the descriptions have the same intention: to create groups with a centroid in such a way that the distance to any other object in the set of data is minimal.

It has been insisted that the centroids in the P-Median are the medians, such a concept should not be confused with the statistical median, since the P-Median is the generalization of the median commonly known as a descriptive statistical measure, that is, the median geometry of a discrete set of sample points or data in a Euclidean space, the point (center) that minimizes the sum of the distances to the sample points, which generalizes the concept of the statistical median. The meaning of this median focuses on the property of minimizing the sum of distances for one-dimensional data, as well as providing a measure of central tendency in higher dimensions.

It is possible to affirm that the geometric median is a location estimator in statistics, it is even a standard indicator in the resolution of the facility location problem, where it models the problem of locating a facility to minimize the cost of transportation [15].

Formally for a given set of m points $x_1, x_2, \ldots x_m$ with each $\in R^n$ the geometric median is defined as $Argmin \sum_{i=1}^{n} \|x_i - y\|_2$, where argmin means the value of the $y \in R^n$ argument and which minimizes the sum. In this case, it is the point y from where the sum of all Euclidean distances to x_i is minimum.

This statement justifies that the geometric median is the core part of the P-Median model and is also incorporated as the medoid in the partitioning added to the restrictions; that is, a partition of a set A is formed by the subsets $A_1, A_2, \ldots A_n$ which must satisfy: The union of all subsets is equal to the given set $A_1 \cup A_2 \cup \cdots \cup A_n = A$ and all the subsets are disjoint among themselves and that no subset is empty.

The partitioning for a data set is mathematically stated as the P-Median and vice versa. This implies that both models share the objective function, except that the centers of the groups are medoids for the PAM partitioning. The medoids are centers of groups and the researcher chooses at his discretion the best way to place the medoids in the center of the clusters, and according to the definition of geometric median, that center agrees with the concept of median.

Reviewing the costs of the methods presented, the values are equal with a very poor discrepancy due to the precision of the arithmetic significant figures in the truncation and approximation. This situation can be solved in PAM with some numerical method such as Newton-Fourier, Bisection or Fixed Point, the opposite case would be in Lingo, because we do not know how they approximate or truncate the decimals in the cost function and that is where lies the epsilon difference between the values of the PAM and P-Median objective functions in Lingo. However, the IEEE standards in the 754 standard dictate that commercial software define 3 floating point formats (32, 64, and 128 bits), therefore, the approximation problem can be fixed in PAM and thus achieve objective values that are exactly the same [16].

Regarding the difference of the centers of the groups, it is easier to explain the situation, because PAM in this article offers only one solution, which does not mean that it is the only one, it is possible to generate more optimal ones, or in other words, in an algorithm combinatorial like PAM, when solutions are compared in the code and they are equal, the algorithm chooses any of them because all the optimal solutions generated are "equally good", then one of these will totally coincide with the one produced by Lingo.

References

1. Díaz, J., Bernábe, M., Luna, D., Olivares, E., Martínez, J.: Relajación lagrangeana para el problema de particionamiento de áreas geográficas. Revista de Matemática: Teoría y Aplicaciones **19**(2), 169–181 (2012)
2. Piza, E., Murillo, A., Trejos, J.: Nuevas técnicas de particionamiento en clasificación automática. Revista de Matemática Teoría y Aplicaciones **6**(1), 51–66 (1999)
3. Kaufman, L., Rousseeuw, P.: Clustering by means of medoids. In: Y. Dodge, pp. 405–416 (1987)
4. Sokal, R., Sneath, P.: Principles of numerical taxonomy. Freeman and Company 60 s. San Francisco-London (1963)
5. Lerman. I.: Les bases de la classification automatique. Publications de l'Institut de Programmation de la Faculté des Sciences de Paris. Paris (1970)
6. Jardine, N., Sibson, R.: Mathematical taxonomy. John Wiley & Sons (1971)
7. Anderberg, M.: Cluster Analysis for Applications, 1st edn. Academic Press, New York (1973)
8. Hartigan, J.: Cluster algorithms. John Wiley & Sons (1975)
9. Han, J., Kamber, M., Tung, A.: Spatial clustering methods in data mining: a survey. In: Geographic Data Mining and Knowledge Discovery, pp. 188–217 (2001)
10. Mark, J.V., Katherine, S.P., Jennifer, B.: A new partitioning around medoids algorithm. J. Stat. Comput. Simul. **73**(8), 575–584 (2003)
11. Hakimi, S.: Optimum location of switching centers and the absolute centers and medians of a graph. Oper. Res. **12**(3), 450–459 (1964)
12. Church, R.: Cobra: A New Formulation of the Classic P-Median Location Problem. In: Annals of Operation Research, pp. 103–120 (2003)
13. Reese, J.: Solution methods for the P-Median problem: An annotated bibliography. Netw. Int. J. **48**(3) 125–142 (2006)
14. Jiang, H., Zhang, X., Li, M.: Backbone of the P-Median Problem. In: Orgun, M.A., Thornton, J. (eds.) AI 2007. LNCS (LNAI), vol. 4830, pp. 699–704. Springer, Heidelberg (2007). https://doi.org/10.1007/978-3-540-76928-6_78
15. Wolf, G.: Foundations of location analysis. In: Horst, A.E, Vladimir, M. (eds.) Series: International Series in Operations Research & Management Science, vol. 155, pp. 577–578. Journal of Geographical Information Science, London (2012)
16. IEEE Standard for Floating-Point Arithmetic. In: IEEE Std 754–2019 (Revision of IEEE 754–2008), pp. 1–84 (2019)

A Hybrid Algorithm Based on Ant Colony System for Flexible Job Shop

William Torres-Tapia[✉][iD], Jairo R. Montoya-Torres[iD], and José Ruiz-Meza[iD]

Research Group on Logistics Systems, Universidad de La Sabana, km 7 autopista norte de Bogotá, D.C. Chia, Colombia
{williamtorta,jairo.montoya,joserume}@unisabana.edu.co

Abstract. Today's competitive marketplace leads customers to demand a higher level of customer satisfaction, by expecting their orders to be delivered quickly. This forces organizations to implement strategies that decrease order delivery time. Typically, to meet this objective, companies schedule production as much efficiently as possible. The success of production scheduling depends on decisions, leading to determining the sequence of activities and the allocation of machines or resources to optimize an objective function. A well-known machine configuration is the Job Shop and its variants, including the Flexible Job Shop (FJS). To solve the FJS, numerous algorithms have been designed, with the most common and computationally efficient being Tabu Search and Genetic Algorithms and their hybridizations. This paper aims to develop a hybrid algorithm with non-common metaheuristics to solve the Flexible Job Shop with makespan minimization. A hybrid algorithm composed of two interacting phases is developed: the first phase is the diversification, which is based on the Ant Colony Optimization algorithm, while the second phase is the improvement which is based on the Iterated Local Search. Instances from the literature are solved to test the algorithm. The results are compared with the best solutions from the literature, showing the power of the proposed algorithm.

Keywords: Production scheduling · Flexible job shop · Metaheuristic · Iterated local search · Ant colony optimization

1 Introduction

Production scheduling is concerned with the allocation of tasks (e.g., jobs, parts and operations) to resources (e.g., machines, workers) to be processed and/or manufactured in an optimal way [1]. The success of production activities for operations management depends on scheduling decisions [10]. These decisions lead to determining the sequence of activities and the allocation of resources to optimize an objective function [27].

One of the most famous production scheduling problems is the Job Shop (JS). JS is a well-known NP-hard problem [11]. Important operational decisions include scheduling decisions in which various types of flexibility have been considered, which refers to the ability of an operation to be performed in different ways [9]. The Flexible Job Shop

Supported by School of Engineering Universidad de La Sabana.

© The Author(s), under exclusive license to Springer Nature Switzerland AG 2022
J. C. Figueroa-García et al. (Eds.): WEA 2022, CCIS 1685, pp. 198–209, 2022.
https://doi.org/10.1007/978-3-031-20611-5_17

(FJS) is an extension of the JS where each operation can be performed on a set of machines, which increases the flexibility and computational tractability of the problem [27]. FJS is more realistic for modeling a wide range of real-life applications as it can capture key features of modern service and manufacturing systems [9].

The computational complexity of FJS suggests the adoption of heuristic and meta-heuristic methods that produce reasonably good schedules in a reasonable time [19]. Papers that provide high-quality solutions to the problem are found in the literature. Most of these papers focus on solving this problem using Tabu Search (TS) and Genetic Algorithms (GA) [26]. In the proposed paper, the aim is to present a hybrid algorithm where Ant Colony Optimization (ACO) and Iterated Local Search (ILS) interact to solve the FJS. The makespan is chosen as optimization objective, i.e., the time required to complete all the jobs. It is the most common indicator to evaluate the performance in production scheduling problems [19].

This paper is organized as follows. Section 2 reviews academic literature related to the problem under study. The problem itself is formally described in Sect. 3. The proposed solution approach is detailed in Sect. 4, while the results of computational experiments are presented in Sect. 5. The paper concludes in Sect. 6 and outlines some opportunities for future research.

2   Related Literature

The JS is a type of machine scheduling problem. The first paper that names the JS is [21]. Since then, numerous papers have been published addressing different solution approaches and many variants of JS have emerged in the literature (see [28]). One of the most studied variants in the literature is the Flexible Job Shop (FJS). Focusing on the FJS, one of the first studies addressing the problem proposed a bottleneck heuristic. Another pioneering paper is [3] where a polynomial algorithm is developed for the case of two jobs.

In the literature, the solution methods can be classified into two categories: the hierarchical approach and the integrated approach [19]. In the former approach, some papers (e.g., [3], [18]) use dispatching rules to make the assignment of machines to operations and a Tabu Search algorithm is used to solve the problem. The integrated approach includes [4, 13, 16], which proposed Tabu Search in which reassignment and rescheduling are considered as two different types of movements. In [4], a neighborhood structure for the problem is defined where there is no difference between reassigning and re-sequencing an operation. In [16], the TS techniques presented in [4] are improved and two neighborhood functions are formulated. Other algorithms to solve the FJS are found in the literature such as Genetic Algorithms [17, 19], Simulated Annealing (SA) [14], Particle Swarm Optimization (PSO) [6] and ACO [25]. Hybrid Algorithms (HA) have taken force in recent years and have found very good solutions. The works in [12, 15] combines variants of the genetic algorithm with the Tabu Search algorithm. Analyzing the literature, most of the algorithms used to solve the FJS are based on TS, GA and their hybridizations [26].

In such a context, the novelty of the current paper is that a hybridization of two different algorithms such as ILS and ACO is used to efficiently solve the FJS. As our experimental analysis using benchmark data sets will show, this hybridization achieves several of the best solutions known in the state of the art.

3   Problem Description

In the classical Job Shop (JS), there is a set of n jobs $J = \{J_1, ..., J_n\}$. The set of operations required to process each J_i is represented as $S_i = \{O_{i,1}, ..., O_{i,s}\}$. Each operation $O_{i,s}$ has to be processed on a set M of m machines that are always available for processing. Each machine can only process one operation at a given time. Each J_i has a fixed processing route, which may be different from the others. In the FJS, the machine required to execute operation $O_{i,s}$ is not provided in advance, instead, it must be selected from a subset $R_{O_{i,s}} \subseteq M$ of eligible machines. Therefore, the processing time $P_{O_{i,s}}$ of operation $O_{i,s}$ depends on the selected machine from $R_{O_{i,s}}$. Each $i \in J$ has a completion time C_i. The makespan is defined as $\max C_i \; \forall i \in J$. A mathematical for the FJS can be found in [20]. The assumptions considered in this document are:

1. Jobs are independent, with no preference and arrive at instant zero.
2. Each machine can only handle one job at a time.
3. The different operations of a job cannot be processed simultaneously and the processing of a job cannot be interrupted once started (i.e., preemption is not allowed).
4. The setup time for machine operations and the transport time between machines are incorporated into the processing time.

To better explain the FJS, the example in Table 1 will be used. This example consists of four jobs and three machines available on the workshop at the start of production. Each job J_i is composed of four operations $O_{i,j}$. The first operation of job 3 is flexible because it can be performed on either machine 1 or 2.

Table 1. An illustrative example of the FJS

Eligible machines and processing times for operations			
Job 1	2	3	4
J_1 $M_3(180)$	$M_2(240)$	$M_1(60)/M_3(305)$	$M_2(180)/M_3(300)$
J_2 $M_1(60)/M_2(223)$	$M_2(120)$	$M_1(240)/M_3(160)$	$M_3(320)$
J_3 $M_1(240)/M_2(180)$	$M_1(80)$	$M_2(241)$	$M_3(250)$
J_4 $M_3(140)$	$M_1(221)/M_2(322)$	$M_1(125)/M_2(220)$	$M_2(120)$

The optimal solution with minimum makespan is shown in the Gantt chart of Fig. 1. The routes are: M_3 ($O_{11} \to O_{41} \to O_{23} \to O_{24} \to O_{34}$), M_2 ($O_{22} \to O_{12} \to O_{33} \to O_{14} \to O_{44}$), and M_1 ($O_{21} \to O_{31} \to O_{32} \to O_{42} \to O_{13} \to O_{43}$). Note that the completion times for jobs are 841, 800, 1050 and 961 min for batches 1, 2, 3 and 4 respectively.

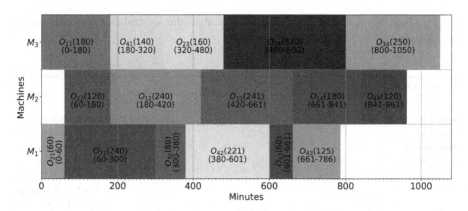

Fig. 1. Gantt diagram when minimizing Makespan in instance TRM00.

4 Proposed Solution Approach

To solve the problem, we propose a hybrid algorithm that consists of two phases: diversification and improvement. The diversification phase is based on ACO. We have used the variation of the ACO algorithm called MMMAX and proposed by [8,22] to prevent the ant colony from falling into local optimum. This strategy looks for the pheromone level in the whole algorithm run to be between the range $[\tau_{xy_i}^{LB}, \tau_{xy_i}^{UB}]$. In this algorithm, each ant $k \in K$ constructs a feasible solution in parallel. Each ant k finds each machine production route by tracking the artificial pheromones; to this end, k must solve the disjunctive arcs of each machine by using Eq. (1), which represents the probability of selecting an arc $x \rightarrow y_i$ that belongs to the set of possible feasible solutions Y, where τ_{xy_i} represents the pheromones of the arc, v the visibility of the path, i is the set index of possible connections to the operation x, V is defined as $\frac{1}{w}$, where w is the starting time of operation y_i.

$$P_{xy_i}^k = \frac{(\tau_{xy_i})^{\alpha}(v_{xy_i})^{\beta}}{\sum_{\forall i \in Y}(\tau_{xy_i})^{\alpha}(v_{xy_i})^{\beta}} \forall i \in I \tag{1}$$

$$\tau_{xy} = (1-\rho)\tau_{xy} + \Delta\tau_{xy}^S \tag{2}$$

$$\Delta\tau_{xy}^S = \begin{cases} \frac{1}{M_S}, & \text{if the arc } (x,y) \in S \\ 0, & \text{otherwise} \end{cases} \tag{3}$$

Once all k ants finish constructing their respective solution, the ant with the best makespan K_{best} is selected. The algorithm then enters the improvement phase. From the improvement phase, the local optimum S is obtained. Then, it is evaluated if S is the best solution found S^*. After that, the pheromones of all arcs xy are updated using Eq. (2), where ρ represents the evaporation percentage, and $\Delta\tau_{xy}^S$ is defined as the operation that adds pheromones to the arcs belonging to S after having gone through the improvement phase (see Eq. (3)) . The number of pheromones added to the arcs of S is calculated as $\frac{1}{M_S}$, where M_S is the Makespan of S. This algorithm is explained in detail in the pseudocode 1.

Algorithm 1. Diversification phase

Require: τ_{xy}	▷ Pheromones of all feasible $(x - y)$ arcs
Require: ρ	▷ Pheromone evaporation factor
Require: T_R	▷ Total running time
Require: T_C	▷ Current running time
Require: K	▷ Colony ants

1: **repeat**
2:     $S \leftarrow 0$ ▷ Local Solution
3:     $S^* \leftarrow 0$ ▷ Best Solution
4:     $k_{Best} \leftarrow \emptyset$ ▷ Best repeat ant
5:     **for each** $k \in K$ **do**
6:         $k \leftarrow$ build a feasible solution (k) ▷ execute Eq. 1
7:         **if** $k < k_{Best}$ **then**
8:             $k_{Best} \leftarrow k$
9:         **end if**
10:     **end for**
11:     $S \leftarrow$ Improvement phase (K_{Best}) ▷ go to the improvement phase
12:     **if** S<S* **then**
13:         $S^* \leftarrow S$
14:     **end if**
15:     **for each** $x - y \in$ feasible arcs **do**
16:         $\tau_{xy} \leftarrow (1 - \rho)\tau_{xy}$ ▷ Pheromone evaporation
17:         **if** $x - y \in \Delta\tau_{xy}^S$ **then**
18:             $\tau_{xy} \leftarrow \tau_{xy} + \frac{1}{M_S}$ ▷ execute Eq. 3
19:         **end if**
20:     **end for**
21: **until** $T_R \geq T_C$ ▷ Time control

The improvement phase is composed of an ILS procedure hybridized with a Variable Neighborhood Descent (VND) algorithm that is executed ε number of times. In the literature, VND is well known for its strong ability to explore distant neighbors [7]. The proposed VND starts by executing the neighborhood based on the motion called operation insertion. For this purpose, the estimation functions formulated by [16] Head, Tail and Arc (HTA) motion feasibility test developed by [9] were used. The algorithm continues its execution of the arc inversion neighborhood once it finds the local optimum. To carry out the arc inversion, the estimation functions proposed in [23] were used. After the VND algorithm execution is completed, a series of ξ perturbations are performed to escape from local optima. These perturbations are random and are based on feasible insertions of operations. When the algorithm finishes, it returns to the diversification phase. Intending to reduce the computational time, the literature has shown that moving the operations by blocks for the JS and its derivations decreases the size of the neighborhoods [5]. Thus, our algorithm focuses on moving the operations belonging to the critical route of the batches that affect the value of the criterion to be optimized (i.e., makespan). This phase is explained in depth in the Algorithm 2.

Algorithm 2. Improvement phase

Require: k_{Best}
Require: ξ ▷ Number of perturbations
Require: ε
  1: $S \leftarrow k_{Best}$ ▷ Initial solution
  2: $S \leftarrow$ VND(S)
  3: $S* \leftarrow k_{Best}$ ▷ Local solution
  4: $i \leftarrow 0$
  5: **repeat**
  6:     $j \leftarrow 0$
  7:     **repeat**
  8:         $S \leftarrow$ perturbation(S)
  9:         $j + +$
10:     **until** $j \geq \xi$
11:     **if** S<S* **then**
12:         $S* \leftarrow$ S
13:     **end if**
14:     $S \leftarrow$ VND(S)
15:     $i \leftarrow i + 1$
16: **until** $i \geq \varepsilon$
17: Diversification phase(S)

---

5 Computational Experiments and Results

The proposed solution approach was run on a PC with 4.1 GHz, 4 cores and 20 GB RAM. The experiments were carried out with the *e-data* set of the instances published by [13] for the FJS. The hybrid algorithm was coded in Java language. The associated experiments for the calibration of the parameters associated with the hybrid algorithm are presented in Sect. 5.1 while computational results and algorithm performance are shown in Sect. 5.2.

5.1 Parameter Calibration

Taking into account that the difficulty of each instance according to [15] is proportional to the flexibility f of the problem and considering that the instances *la26*, *la27*, *la28*, *la29* and *la30* are the instances with the highest degree of f within the instances to be evaluated [12]. Figure 2 presents the convergence curve of the algorithm in each of the above-mentioned instances for an execution of 25 min with the parameter settings proposed by [24]. From these results, the stopping time of the algorithm was set at 17.5 min due to the majority of the tested instances converged within that time, as shown in Fig. 2.

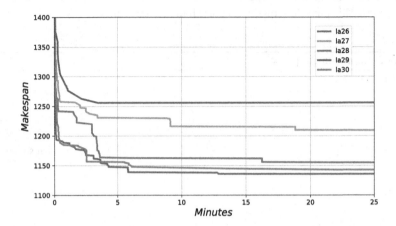

Fig. 2. Hybrid algorithm convergence

In order to set the parameters of the ACO algorithm, we used the values defined by [25] as follows: $k = 39$, $\rho = 0.1$, $\tau_{xy_i}^{Initial} = 0.1$, $\beta = 0.3$, $\alpha = 0.8$, $\tau_{xy_i}^{LB} = 0.01$, $\tau_{xy_i}^{UB} = 10. = 0.8$. In addition, to evaluate the impact of some critical parameters of the ACO algorithm, we followed the experiment proposed in [24] for $k = 4$, $\rho = 0.06$, $\tau_{xy_i}^{Initial} = 0.35$, and $\beta = 1$. The number of permutations $\xi = 4$ was configured based on [9]. We tested with two values of ε which are as follows: 25 and 10000. Taking into account that a two-replication factorial experiment will be performed on an instance with a high f value, we have performed 64 replications on the TRM25 instance.

An Analysis of Variance (ANOVA) test was performed with 97% confidence to test which of the factors affects the model. The result was that the significant parameters are k and ε. To verify the normality and homoscedasticity of the sample, a confidence level of 97% was proposed. The normal behavior of the model residuals was verified by two tests: Shapiro-Wilk and Kolmogorov-Smirnov with Lilliefors correction. Next, we checked that the sample met the homoscedasticity criteria using Bartlett's test. Finally, the Durbin-Watson test was used to verify that the sample data were independent.

To select the parameter level that minimizes the makespan, we relied on Tukey's test and the box plot shown in Fig. 3. The result was that the ε should have a value of 10000 and k a value of 39. Considering that the other parameters studied do not influence the algorithm, we decided to continue with the levels proposed by [24].

5.2   Computational Results and Algorithm Performance

For each instance evaluated in this computational experiment, Table 2 shows the number of available machines m and the number of jobs J. This table contains the best makespan obtained for each of the instances by the algorithm proposed in this paper (called ACOILS). In order to evaluate its performance, the computational results of state-of-the-art algorithms are given in Table 2: TSN1, TSN2 [13], IATS [4], TS [16],

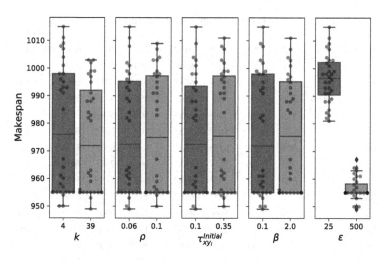

Fig. 3. Box plot comparing the means of the levels for each factor

HA [15] and HASSPR [12]. Note that the best-known results are reported in this table with an asterisk and the results in bold reach the lower bound (LB) proposed by [16]. In order to evaluate the performance of the algorithms, the relative percentage deviation (RPD) was calculated for each of the 43 instances. RPD is computed using Eq. (4), where *BK* is the best solution reported by the algorithm. Computational times cannot be fairly compared because these are not reported in published works.

$$RPD = \frac{BK - LB}{LB} * 100 \qquad (4)$$

Analyzing the efficiency of the algorithms, ACOILS obtains 28 of the 43 best solutions found, while TSN1 10, TSN2 9, IATS 19, TS 31, HA 33 and HASSPR achive 43. However, this is not a good measure to evaluate the performance of each algorithm, considering that the differences between the makespan reported for each instance by the algorithms are very short. Therefore, a Kruskall-Wallis test was performed with a confidence level of 95% to compare the RPD obtained by each algorithm, considering that the data residuals did not behave normally and were not homoscedastic. The test showed that there are significant differences between the means of the RPD of each algorithm. To identify if the algorithm proposed in this paper had better or worse performance compared to the other published algorithms, the Mann-Whitney test with Bonferroni correction was used. The results indicate that our algorithm has an average RPD equal to that of HA, TS and HASSPR algorithms and differs from the TS1 TS2, IATS algorithms.

Complementing the previous analysis, Fig. 4 shows that the algorithms TSN1, TSN2 and IATS have the worst performances, this affirms that there is a difference with our algorithm. Concluding, the results obtained by ACOILS perform as well as the best results published in the literature [12, 15, 16] and are better than the metaheuristics published in [2, 4].

Table 2. Computational results

Instance	JXM	TSN1	TSN2	IATS	ACOILS	TS	HA	HASSPR	LB
la01		611	618	609*	**609***	609*	609*	609*	609
la02		655*	656	655*	**655***	655*	655*	655*	655
la03	10×5	573	566	554	**550***	550*	550*	550*	550
la04		578	578	568*	**568***	568*	568*	568*	568
la05		503*	503*	503*	**503***	503*	503*	503*	503
la06		833*	833*	833*	**833***	833*	833*	833*	833
la07		765	778	765	**762***	762*	762*	762*	762
la08	15×5	845*	845*	845*	**845***	845*	845*	845*	845
la09		878*	878*	878*	**878***	878*	878*	878*	878
la10		866*	866*	866*	**866***	866*	866*	866*	866
la11		1106	1106	1103*	**1103***	1103*	1103*	1103*	1087
la12		960*	960*	960*	**960***	960*	960*	960*	960
la13	20×5	1053*	1053*	1053*	**1053***	1053*	1053*	1053*	1053
la14		1151	1123*	1123*	**1123***	1123*	1123*	1123*	1123
la15		1111*	1121	1111*	**1111***	1111*	1111*	1111*	1111
la16		924	961	915	**892***	892*	892*	892*	892
la17		757	757	707*	**707***	707*	707*	707*	707
la18	10×10	864	864	843	**842***	842*	842*	842*	842
la19		850	813	796*	**796***	796*	796*	796*	796
la20		919	919	864	**857***	857*	857*	857*	857
la21		1066	1085	1046	1017	1017	1014	1010*	895
la22		919	905	890	887	882	880*	880*	832
la23	15×10	980	980	953	**950***	950*	950*	950*	950
la24		952	952	918	909	909	909	908*	881
la25		970	969	955	943	941	941	939*	894
la26		1169	1149	1138	1125	1125	1123	1109*	1089
la27		1230	1236	1215	1186	1186	1184	1181*	1181
la28	20×10	1204	1197	1169	1149	1149	1147	1144*	1116
la29		1210	1205	1157	1126	1118	1115	1111*	1058
la30		1253	1286	1225	1212	1204*	1204*	1204*	1147
la31		1596	1593	1556	1542	1539	1541	1533*	1523
la32		1769	1757	1698*	1698*	1698*	1698*	1698*	1698
la33	30×10	1575	1575	1547*	1547*	1547*	1547*	1547*	1547
la34		1627	1636	1623	1599*	1599*	1599*	1599*	1592
la35		1736*	1736*	1736*	**1736***	1736*	1736*	1736*	1736
la36		1247	1235	1171	1162	1162	1160*	1160*	1006
la37		1453	1456	1418	1397*	1397*	1397*	1397*	1355
la38	15×15	1185	1185	1172	1143	1144	1143	1141*	1019
la39		1226	1226	1207	1186	1184*	1184*	1184*	1151
la40		1214	1236	1150	1146	1150	1146	1144*	1034
mt06	6×6	57	57	55*	**55***	55*	55*	55*	55
mt10	10×10	917	899	878	**871***	871*	871*	871*	871
mt20	20×5	1109	1135	1106	1091	1088*	1088*	1088*	1088

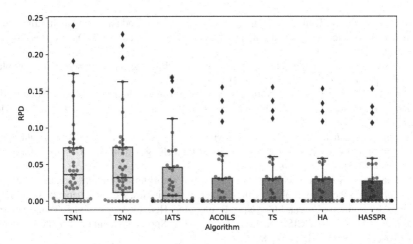

Fig. 4. Box plot of the RPD of each algorithm

6 Conclusions

In this paper, we propose an approach to solve the flexible job shop scheduling problem. Based on the analysis of the current academic literature, most of the solution approaches are based on TS and GA algorithms. For this reason, this paper proposes a hybrid metaheuristic combining ACO and ILS. Computational experiments were performed using benchmark instances from the literature. The selected objective function was the makespan. The results showed that the proposed solution approach obtains results that can be compared with the best results reported in the literature.

Following the findings of this work, several opportunities for further research are identified. For example, it would be interesting to formulate a multi-objective algorithm. Moreover, it would be interesting to solve the problem using new objective functions, such as the carbon emissions of the machines. In addition, other constraints could be added to the problem, such as machine failures, setup and transportation times, preventive and corrective maintenance, multiple resources per operation, among others.

Acknowledgements. The work presented in this paper was supported by a postgraduate scholarship from the School of Engineering Universidad de La Sabana, Colombia, awarded to the first author.

References

1. Amjad, M.K., et al.: Recent Research Trends in Genetic Algorithm Based Flexible Job Shop Scheduling Problems. Math. Probl. Eng. **2018**, 9270802 (2018)
2. Brandimarte, P.: Routing and scheduling in a flexible job shop by tabu search. Ann. Oper. Res. **41**(3), 157–183 (1993)
3. Brucker, P., Schlie, R.: Job-shop scheduling with multi-purpose machines. Computing **45**(4), 369–375 (1990)

4. Dauzère-Pérès, S., Paulli, J.: An integrated approach for modeling and solving the general multiprocessor job-shop scheduling problem using tabu search. Anna. Operat. Res. **70**, 281–306 (1997)
5. Dell'Amico, M., Trubian, M.: Applying tabu search to the job-shop scheduling problem. Ann. Oper. Res. **41**(3), 231–252 (1993)
6. Ding, H., Gu, X.: Improved particle swarm optimization algorithm based novel encoding and decoding schemes for flexible job shop scheduling problem. Comput. Operat. Res. **121**, 104951 (2020)
7. Duarte, A., Sánchez-Oro, J., Mladenović, N., Todosijević, R.: Variable neighborhood descent, pp. 341–367. Springer International Publishing, Cham (2018). https://doi.org/10.1007/978-3-319-07153-4_9-1
8. García-León, A.A., Torres Tapia, W.F.: A hybrid algorithm to minimize regular criteria in the job-shop scheduling problem with maintenance activities, sequence dependent and set-up times. In: Figueroa-García, J.C., Garay-Rairán, F.S., Hernández-Pérez, G.J., Díaz-Gutierrez, Y. (eds.) WEA 2020. CCIS, vol. 1274, pp. 208–221. Springer, Cham (2020). https://doi.org/10.1007/978-3-030-61834-6_18
9. García-León, A.A., Dauzère-Pérès, S., Mati, Y.: An efficient Pareto approach for solving the multi-objective flexible job-shop scheduling problem with regular criteria. Comput. Oper. Res. **108**, 187–200 (2019)
10. García-León, A.A., Torres Tapia, W.F.: A general local search pareto approach with regular criteria for solving the job-shop scheduling problem multi-resource resource flexibility with linear routes. In: Figueroa-García, J.C., Duarte-González, M., Jaramillo-Isaza, S., Orjuela-Cañon, A.D., Díaz-Gutierrez, Y. (eds.) Applied Computer Sciences in Engineering, pp. 764–775. Springer International Publishing, Cham (2019). https://doi.org/10.1007/978-3-030-31019-6_64
11. Garey, M.R., Johnson, D.S., Sethi, R.: The complexity of flowshop and jobshop scheduling. Math. Oper. Res. **1**(2), 117–129 (1976)
12. González, M., Vela, C., Varela, R.: Scatter search with path relinking for the flexible job shop scheduling problem. Eur. J. Oper. Res. **245**(1), 35–45 (2015)
13. Hurink, J., Jurisch, B., Thole, M.: Tabu search for the job-shop scheduling problem with multi-purpose machines. OR Spektrum **15**(4), 205–215 (1994)
14. Kaplanoğlu, V.: An object-oriented approach for multi-objective flexible job-shop scheduling problem. Expert Syst. Appl. **45**, 71–84 (2016)
15. Li, X., Gao, L.: An effective hybrid genetic algorithm and tabu search for flexible job shop scheduling problem. Int. J. Prod. Econ. **174**, 93–110 (2016)
16. Mastrolilli, M., Gambardella, L.M.: Effective neighbourhood functions for the flexible job shop problem. J. Sched. **3**(1), 3–20 (2000)
17. Nayak, S., Sood, A.K., Pandey, A.: Integrated approach for flexible job shop scheduling using multi-objective genetic algorithm. In: Govindan, K., Kumar, H., Yadav, S. (eds.) Advances in Mechanical and Materials Technology, pp. 387–395. Springer, Singapore (2022). https://doi.org/10.1007/978-981-16-2794-1_35
18. Paulli, J.: A hierarchical approach for the fms scheduling problem. Eur. J. Oper. Res. **86**(1), 32–42 (1995)
19. Pezzella, F., Morganti, G., Ciaschetti, G.: A genetic algorithm for the flexible job-shop scheduling problem. Comput. Operat. Res. **35**(10), 3202–3212 (2008)
20. Roshanaei, V., Azab, A., ElMaraghy, H.: Mathematical modelling and a meta-heuristic for flexible job shop scheduling. Int. J. Prod. Res. **51**(20), 6247–6274 (2013)
21. Sisson, R.L.: Methods of sequencing in job shops-a review. Oper. Res. **7**(1), 10–29 (1959)
22. Stützle, T., Hoos, H.: Improvements on the ant-system: Introducing the max-min ant system. In: Artificial Neural Nets and Genetic Algorithms, pp. 245–249. Springer, Vienna (1998). https://doi.org/10.1007/978-3-7091-6492-1_54

23. Taillard, D.: Parallel taboo search techniques for the job shop scheduling problem. ORSA J. Comput. **6**(2), 108–117 (1994)
24. Torres-Tapia, W., Montoya-Torres, J.R., Ruiz-Meza, J., Belmokhtar-Berraf, S.: A Matheuristic based on ant colony system for the combined flexible jobshop scheduling and vehicle routing problem. In: 10th IFAC Conference on Manufacturing Modelling, Management and Control. Elsevier, Nantes, France (2022)
25. Wang, L., Cai, J., Li, M., Liu, Z.: Flexible job shop scheduling problem using an improved ant colony optimization. Sci. Program. **2017**, 9016303 (2017)
26. Xia, W., Wu, Z.: An effective hybrid optimization approach for multi-objective flexible job-shop scheduling problems. Comput. Ind. Eng. **48**(2), 409–425 (2005)
27. Xie, J., Gao, L., Peng, K., Li, X., Li, H.: Review on flexible job shop scheduling. IET Collaborative Intell. Manuf. **1**(3), 67–77 (2019)
28. Xiong, H., Shi, S., Ren, D., Hu, J.: A survey of job shop scheduling problem: The types and models. Comput. Oper. Res. **142**, 105731 (2022)

Cost Optimization of an Assembly Sequence of an Electric Propulsion Module of an Electro-Solar Boat

Manuela Montoya-Rivera(✉) [ID], Gilberto Osorio-Gómez [ID],
and Juan Carlos Rivera Agudelo [ID]

Research Group on Design Engineering (GRID), EAFIT University,
Carrera 49 No 7 Sur–50, Medellín, Colombia
{mmontoyar2,gosoriog,jrivera6}@eafit.edu.co

Abstract. Cost optimization of the assembly sequence of an electric propulsion module of an electro-solar boat is carried out with a genetic algorithm and compared with the results of a constructive method, identifying that the most influential variable of the whole model is time.

Keywords: Modularity · Assembly sequencing · Optimization · Cost minimization · Heuristic methods · RCPSP (*Reconstrain Planning Scheduling Problem*)

1 Introduction

Due to the number of parts and assembly requirements, the more complex a system is, the assembly sequence empirically or based on the engineer's experience can be complicated and not necessarily lead to the best solution. However, there is a need to define the best assembly sequence based on project requirements, component constraints, or characteristics for which Assembly Sequence Planning (ASP) approaches exist. In some cases, the assembly sequence of the system is already defined. Still, the resources available to perform each process activity may be variable and directly affect the cost of the complete process. Then, it is possible to implement an optimization algorithm, which according to some restrictions defined by the engineer, allows for reducing the cost of the assembly process. For the optimization of the assembly sequences, there are different methods. The heuristics are the most used because they allow finding the best solution within a set of feasible solutions without investing large computational capacity or time, in contrast to the development of an exact method.

This paper analyzes a case study on assembling an electro-propulsion system for an electro-solar boat by implementing a genetic algorithm. Optimizing the

Supported by ENERGÉTICA 2030 and EAFIT University.

© The Author(s), under exclusive license to Springer Nature Switzerland AG 2022
J. C. Figueroa-García et al. (Eds.): WEA 2022, CCIS 1685, pp. 210–221, 2022.
https://doi.org/10.1007/978-3-031-20611-5_18

cost of the assembly sequence defined with the genetic algorithm is compared with a constructive method corresponding to the solution's first approximation. In this way, the performance of a heuristic method is analyzed in this type of assembly problem.

Section 2 justifies the development of the genetic algorithm according to state-of-the-art related to the research on optimization strategies for assembly analysis and definition. Section 3 describes the characteristics of the case study selected for implementing the proposed approach. Then, Sect. 4 presents the genetic algorithm proposed for the cost optimization of the assembly sequence, followed by the results in Sect. 5. Finally, conclusions are stated in Sect. 6.

2 State of the Art

According to Rashid et al. [9], assembly is considered one of the most critical processes in manufacturing since it consumes 50% of the total production time and 20% of the manufacturing costs. Moreover, these scheduling problems are considered NP-hard, where the complexity of the solution increases as a function of the number of components, so computational approaches are used to solve them.

Deepak et al. [4] pointed out that the assembly scheduling problem can be approached from three points: Assembly sequence planning (ASP), Assembly line balancing, or Planning of the assembly route. The one of interest for the proposed situation is the ASP for cost minimization, considering that the different assembly stages are already defined, and the available resources for each activity are optimized. Genetic algorithms, Ant colony optimization, Particle swarm optimization, hybrid algorithms, or other approximation of heuristic methods are commonly used to solve this optimization problem.

Rashid et al. [9], from a review of multiple articles, showed that typically the objectives sought to be achieved in assembly sequence planning are (1) Minimal assembly direction change, (2) Minimal tool change, and (3) Minimal assembly type change. Melckenbeeck et al. [6] proposed a methodology to calculate the feasibility of an assembly step and calculate the optimal assembly sequence by initially obtaining the geometry of an assembly from a CAD tool, then generating a connection graph and evaluating Design for Assembly (DFA) rules to generate the assembly sequences finally.

Sinanog and Börklü [10] considered subassembly, stability, and geometry constraints and considered all assembly stages to optimize the assembly of a set of mechanical parts using neural networks. Habibi et al. [5] stated that the realization of projects plays a fundamental role in underdeveloped countries since they allow the development and growth of the economy. Therefore, correctly planning these projects is essential, looking for the reduction of costs.

The Reconstrain Planning Scheduling Problem (RCPSP) is a general planning problem with multiple applications in manufacturing, production planning, project management, etc. It has been studied since 1960 as a NP-hard problem, where the primary solutions are obtained from heuristics. In recent years, its solutions have also migrated to metaheuristic, and hybrid methods [7]. Initially, they seek to determine the time required to execute the activities to achieve an objective. Still, by including the precedence list, the time of the activity, and the available resources, it is possible to optimize not only time but also costs and resources or have a multi-objective problem.

Balouka and Cohen [1] presented the minimization of the duration time of a project using the Benders approximation, deciding how the activity is executed, the resources, and the precedencies. Habibi et al. [5] used Particle swarm optimization to optimize a RCPSP with multiple resource levels. Bhaskar et al. [2] used a heuristic method to optimize a RCPSP with fuzzy activity times, showing that it is possible to add different features to the RCPSP depending on the resources, execution modes, activities, times, and other parameters of the problem.

Regarding research related to assembly problems of boats, Qu et al. [8] planned an assembly sequence for a ship hull by integrating constraints with a genetic algorithm, considering that this is manufactured in blocks. Hence, there are multiple possible assembly sequences. Taraska et al. [11] reviewed existing assembly methods for ship structures, concluding that all methods require significant expert involvement and that, in recent years, artificial intelligence algorithms have become more involved.

Thus, RCPSP becomes useful to mathematize the boat propulsion module assembly problem, where the assembly sequence is already defined by the precedence in the contact relationship between the components. Still, different resources are available, with which the sequence that minimizes the assembly costs must be determined, solving it from a genetic algorithm that is part of the heuristic methods.

3   Case Study: Electro-propulsion System

An electro-propulsion system is considered a complex product involving the interaction of multiple components to fulfill its primary function. Figure 1 shows the propulsion system of the electro-solar vessel, which consists of the electrification of a Yamaha outboard unit with a Wolong electric motor. This electrification is made from the transmission shown in Fig. 2, which includes the belt assembly (Fig. 3) and the cooling system sub-assembly (Fig. 4).

The proposed approach seeks to minimize the costs of implementing the assembly sequence of the electric propulsion module of the vessel. Each activity has three possible modes of execution, the number of available resources varies, and the metadata directly involved in the assembly is included, such as the sequence defined from the component relationships, the available space, the required personnel, the tools, and the cost of all of the above. All this information should be used to define an optimal assembly sequence according to the time, cost, and resources.

The assembly sequence of the electric propulsion module is as follows, and the different parts are in Fig. 2, Fig. 3, and Fig. 4:

Fig. 1. Electro propulsion system of an electro-solar vessel

- Preparation:
  1. Disassemble the main propeller.
  2. Disassemble the lubrication system.
- Assembly (Tasks 7 and 14 can be performed in parallel):
  1. Assemble the bottom plate to the lower frame.
  2. Assemble the horns.
  3. Assemble the lower horns.
  4. Subassemble shafts and pulleys.
  5. Assemble the belt.
  6. The shafts are taken on bearings of the lower frame to the butt.
  7. Subassemble the tensioner.
  8. The bushings and spacers are assembled on the output side shaft and motor side shaft.
  9. Mount of the upper horns on the upper frame.
  10. Screw the front and rear turrets on the frames.
  11. Make the axles concentric and screw them to the turrets.
  12. Mount the electric motor on the upper frame.
  13. Mount the rear turret on the upper frame.
  14. Sub assemble the exchanger.
  15. Install the exchanger.
  16. Position the gearbox over the outboard intermediate unit and tighten it with six main screws.
  17. Mount the controller bracket on the upper frame plate.

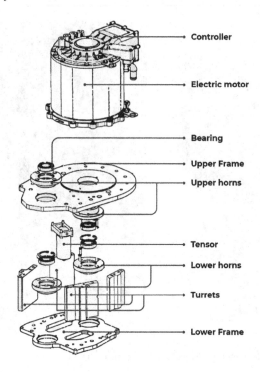

Fig. 2. Gearbox assembly of electro-propulsion system

18. Mount the nylon bushings and anti-vibration mount to the upper frame plate.
19. Mount the controller on the bracket.
20. Make the connection of the 3 phases: U, V, and W.

4   Cost Optimization Approach

4.1   Generalities

Genetic Algorithms (GA) are search and optimization methods based on natural selection and genetics principles. The chromosomes correspond to the coding of the decision variables, and each of its digits or letters is a gene. Finding reasonable solutions and implementing natural selection requires an objective function to determine which solutions are close to the expected (optimal).

Within the genetic algorithms, the concept of population is also essential, which corresponds to the candidate solutions, and its size is generally parameterized. The steps of this algorithm are:

1. Initialization: The initial population is generated, usually randomly.

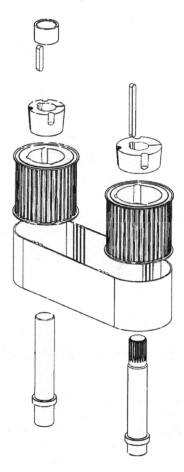

Fig. 3. Belts assembly of an electro-propulsion system

2. Evaluation: Once the solution is initialized, the function values of each candidate are evaluated.
3. Selection: The best solutions are selected over the worst ones.
4. Recombination: Parts of two or more parent solutions are combined, which creates possible new best solutions.
5. Mutation: A solution is modified locally and randomly.
6. Replacement: The new population, created from selection, recombination, and mutation, replaces the initial population.

Finally, steps 2-6 are repeated until the stopping criterion is reached, which, depending on the size of the problem, will be to find the most optimal possible solution [3].

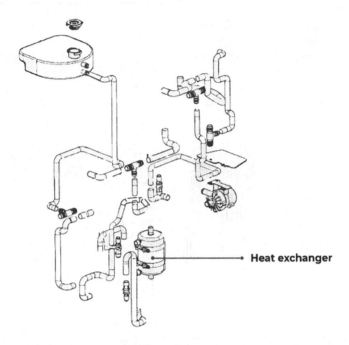

Fig. 4. Cooling system assembly of an electro-propulsion system

There are multiple ways to perform selection, recombination, and mutation, which correspond to intensification methods, which allow exploiting a good solution to improve it (selection), and diversification methods, which would enable exploring other solutions in the feasible region (recombination and mutation).

To improve the efficiency of genetic algorithms, hybrid algorithms are often performed where evolutionary algorithms are combined with any other type of algorithm to find better solutions or decrease the computation time [3].

Assembly problems are usually solved from evolutionary algorithms, as already pointed out in the state of the art. For this case study, a genetic algorithm will be initially implemented and refined with a random key, thus proposing a hybrid method.

4.2 Mathematical Model

The presented optimization problem is possible to pose as follows:

Parameters:

- List of activities with precedence.
- R_K: Resources (Tools and staff).
- R_k^0: Initial resource.
- t: Time.
- T: Limit time to assemble.

Variables:

$$\varepsilon_m^{it} = \begin{cases} 1 & \text{if the activity I starts in the period t, in the mode m} \\ 0 & \text{otherwise} \end{cases} \quad (1)$$

Objective function:

$$\sum C_K(R_K - R_K^0) \quad (2)$$

s.t

$$\sum_m \sum_{t=esn}^{lsn} t\varepsilon_m^{it} \leq T \quad (3)$$

$$\sum_m \sum_{t=esn}^{lsn} \varepsilon_m^{it} = 1 \quad (4)$$

$$\sum_m \sum_{t=esn}^{lsn} t\varepsilon_m^{jt} - \sum_m \sum_{t=esn}^{lsn} t\varepsilon_m^{jt} \geq d_i^{m'} - M(\sum_m \sum_{t=esn}^{lsn} \varepsilon_m^{it}) \quad \forall \quad m', (i,j) \in H \quad (5)$$

$$\sum_j \sum_m \sum_{\tau=tj}^{t} r_m^{jk}\varepsilon_m^{it} \leq R_K \quad \tau = max\{0, t - d_j^m + 1\} \quad (6)$$

$$R_K \geq r_m^{jk} \quad (7)$$

$$R_K \geq R_k^0 \quad (8)$$

This approach ensures the execution of all activities within the time limit, respecting precedence and using the available resources, considering that there is a base or initial resource.

4.3   Implementation

Costs of tools and human resources are presented in Table 1, in addition to the fact that the space has a cost of $350,081 per day.

Then, three possible modes (random) of execution of the activities are proposed, taking into account that:

– Each activity can be carried out with a maximum of 5 people.
– The execution time of each activity must be between 0.5 and 5 d.

Table 1. Tools and human resource

Tools	1. Crane	2. Allen wrench set	3. Socket set	4. Piston wrench set	5. Sling set
Cost/day	$ 182,509	$ 6,844	$ 27,376	$ 9,125	$ 22,813
Tools	6. Open-end wrench set	7. Screwdrivers set	8. Torque wrench	9. Tweezers	10. Mallet
Cost/day	$ 182,500	$ 13,688	$ 91,254	$ 18,251	$ 6,844
Tools	11.Press	12. Hammer	13. Hexagonal wrenches		
Cost/day	$ 68,440	$ 13,688	$ 4,563		
Staff	Technician	Engineer			
Cost/day	$ 68,920	$ 115,900			

The execution modes can be seen below, where the tools required in each activity are detailed according to the number of people (Table 2).

The Preliminary constructive method provides information on each mode's total costs through a matrix, in which, using the Python function, the smallest value is searched in each row. In this way, it is selected in which mode each task will be executed to minimize the costs.

A simple genetic algorithm is proposed where a random population of 100 solutions is initially generated. From this, a selection of the best 50 solutions is made to intensify the solution, and to these, the diversification methods are applied: recombination and mutation.

Table 2. Modes of execution

Task	MODE 1			MODE 2			MODE 3		
	Tools	Staff	Days	Tools	Staff	Days	Tools	Staff	Days
1	1, 5, 8, 2 ->(2, 3, 4, 6, 7)	2	3.6	1, 5, 8, 3 ->(2, 3, 4, 6, 7)	3	3.3	1, 5, 8, 2 ->(2, 3, 4, 6, 7)	2	2.1
2	9, 4 ->(2, 3, 6, 7)	4	4.7	9, 2, 3, 6, 7	1	3.5	9, 5 ->(2, 3, 6, 7)	5	0.6
3	5 ->(1, 8, 10)	5	2.4	5 ->(1, 8, 10)	5	3.1	2 ->(1, 8, 10)	2	0.6
4	9, 11, 5 ->(8, 10, 12, 13)	5	0.9	9, 11, 5 ->(8, 10, 12, 13)	5	1.3	9, 11, 2 ->(8, 10, 12, 13)	2	1.7
5	3 ->12	3	1.7	12	1	3.1	3 ->12	3	2.9
6	9, 11, 3 ->(8, 10, 12, 13)	3	2.8	9, 11, 8, 10, 12, 13	1	2.3	9, 11, 2 ->(8, 10, 12, 13)	2	2.6
7		3	2.1		3	4		5	3.6
8	11, 3 ->(10, 12)	3	2.4	11, 2 ->(10, 12)	2	0.7	11, 5 ->(10, 12)	5	1.6
9	11, 3 ->(9, 12, 13)	3	3.3	11, 5 ->(9, 12, 13)	5	0.8	11, 9, 12, 13	1	1.4
10	4 ->(10, 12)	4	4.8	5 ->(10, 12)	5	2.6	3 ->(10, 12)	3	0.6
11	2 ->12	2	3.3	2 ->12	2	4.8	2 ->12	2	1.7
12	10, 12	1	0.5	2 ->(10, 12)	2	4	10, 12	1	3.1
13	2 ->(10, 12)	2	3.1	5 ->(10, 12)	5	1.5	4 ->(10, 12)	4	0.8
14	1, 3 ->13	3	3.2	1, 3 ->13	3	1.7	1, 4 ->13	4	0.5
15	10, 13	1	4.8	4 ->(10, 13)	4	5	10, 13	1	3.9
16	4 ->(3, 7, 9, 10)	4	4.6	5 ->(3, 7, 9, 10)	5	2	2 ->(3, 7, 9, 10)	2	1.1
17	3, 7	1	2.2	3, 7	1	4.8	4 ->(3, 7)	4	1
18	1, 2 ->(8, 10, 13)	2	2.5	1, 3 ->(8, 10, 13)	3	5	1, 3 ->(8, 10, 13)	3	2.9
19	2 ->(6, 8, 13)	2	3.9	3 ->(6, 8, 13)	3	4.9	5 ->(6, 8, 13)	5	2.4
20	6	1	1.4	6	1	4.2	3 ->6	3	1.8
21	2 ->(6, 13)	2	1.8	5 ->(6, 13)	5	0.8	4 ->(6, 13)	4	3.7
22	3	1	3.7	3	1	1.8	2 ->3	2	1.3

Recombination consists of randomly selecting a task and exchanging its execution mode with the mode of the next solution in the same task. In contrast, mutation consists of randomly selecting a task and then randomly generating the execution modes for each of the following tasks.

5 Cost Optimization Results

The algorithm (GA) generates how each task is executed. It is worth highlighting that having implemented a single generation, each iteration offers different results, and not consistently applying recombination and mutation improves the solution. The solution generated for the algorithm is presented in Table 3, compared with the results of the constructive method. It is highlighted that mutation and recombination are found within a *while* cycle and the results presented correspond to the execution of this cycle 10,993 times.

Table 3. Genetic Algorithm and Constructive method Implementation Results: Execution Mode for Each Task

Task	GA	CM
1	3	3
2	3	3
3	3	3
4	1	1
5	3	1
6	2	2
7	2	1
8	2	2
9	2	2
10	3	3
11	3	3
12	1	1
13	2	3
14	3	3
15	3	3
16	3	3
17	1	3
18	1	1
19	1	1
20	1	1
21	2	2
22	2	3
Minimum total cost	$ 28,605,090	$ 24,968,658.00

Figure 5 shows how the cost decreases as a function of the GA iterations, indicating that the algorithm tends to converge.

6   Conclusions

The RCPSP allows modeling the problem with excellent fidelity since it facilitates the establishment of the restrictions to each of the activities and having the precedence established; the algorithm should only seek to optimize the minimum cost of the entire assembly sequence.

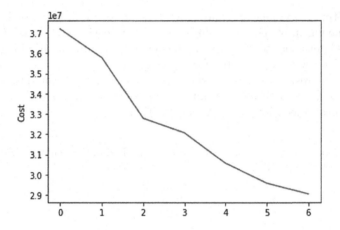

Fig. 5. Iteration number vs. Objective cost

The results show that the problem's most influential variable is time since the cost of the resources depends on it. Therefore, the solution will tend to select the mode where it is necessary to invest less time when minimizing costs. This also shows that the time invested will be optimized by relating costs to time if the cost is minimized.

The cost found in the constructive method is lower than in the genetic algorithm since the constructive method proposes an exact way to solve the problem, and the genetic algorithm requires many more iterations to reach this solution (10,993).

For future work, it is essential to relate the information on resources and time for all the modules' assembly activities. In addition, deepening the implementation of the genetic algorithm, identifying variations in the intensification, and diversifying strategies would be helpful to increase the academic value of the algorithm and improve the solution. This way, the most optimal solution can be found in the shortest time and with the least possible computational expense.

Acknowledgement. This research has been developed in the framework of the "ENERGÉTICA 2030" Research Program, with code 58667 in the "Colombia Científica" initiative, funded by The World Bank, through the call "778-2017 Scientific Ecosystems", is managed by the Colombian Ministry of Science, Technology, and Innovation (Minciencias), with contract No. FP44842-210-2018.

References

1. Balouka, N., Cohen, I.: A robust optimization approach for the multi-mode resource-constrained project scheduling problem. Euro. J. Oper. Res. **291**, 457–470 (2021). https://doi.org/10.1016/j.ejor.2019.09.052
2. Bhaskar, T., Pal, M.N., Pal, A.K.: Discrete Optimization A heuristic method for RCPSP with fuzzy activity times (2010). https://doi.org/10.1016/j.ejor.2010.07.021
3. Deb, K.: Multi-objective optimization. In: Search Methodologies, pp. 419–421 (2014)
4. Deepak, B.B.V.L., Gunji, B., Bahubalendruni, R., Bhusan Biswal, B.: Assembly sequence planning using soft computing methods: A review. Article in ARCHIVE Proceedings of the Institution of Mechanical Engineers Part E Journal of Process Mechanical Engineering (1989). https://doi.org/10.1177/0954408918764459, https://www.researchgate.net/publication/324081167
5. Habibi, F., Barzinpour, F., Sadjadi, S.J.: Resource-constrained project scheduling problem: review of past and recent developments. J. Project Manag. **3**, 55–88 (2018). https://doi.org/10.5267/j.jpm.2018.1.005, www.GrowingScience.com
6. Melckenbeeck, I., Burggraeve, S., Doninck, B.V., Vancraen, J., Rosich, A.: Optimal assembly sequence based on design for assembly (DFA) rules. Procedia CIRP **91**, 646–652 (2020). https://doi.org/10.1016/j.procir.2020.02.223
7. Pellerin, R., Perrier, N., Berthaut, F.: A survey of hybrid metaheuristics for the resource-constrained project scheduling problem. Euro. J. Oper. Res. **280**, 395–416 (2020). https://doi.org/10.1016/j.ejor.2019.01.063
8. Qu, S., Jiang, Z., Tao, N.: An integrated method for block assembly sequence planning in shipbuilding. Int. J. Adv. Manuf. Technol. **69**(5), 1123–1135 (2013)
9. Rashid, M.F.F., Hutabarat, W., Tiwari, A.: A review on assembly sequence planning and assembly line balancing optimisation using soft computing approaches, Mar 2012. https://doi.org/10.1007/s00170-011-3499-8
10. Sinanog, C., Rıza Börklü, H.: An assembly sequence-planning system for mechanical parts using neural network. In: Assembly Automation (2005). https://doi.org/10.1108/01445150510578996, www.emeraldinsight.com/researchregister
11. Taraska, M., Iwankowicz, R., Urbanski, T., Graczyk, T.: Review of Assembly Sequence Planning Methods in Terms of Their Applicability in Shipbuilding Processes. Polish maritime research (2018)

Hybrid ILS-VND Algorithm for the Vehicle Routing Problem with Release Times

William Torres-Tapia(✉)[iD], Jairo Montoya-Torres[iD], and José Ruiz-Meza[iD]

Research Group on Logistics Systems, Universidad de La Sabana, km 7 autopista norte de Bogotá, D.C., Chia, Colombia
{williamtorta,jairo.montoya,joserume}@unisabana.edu.co

Abstract. Modern market behavior and globalization have increased the complexity of supply chains, dealing logistics managers to implement strategies to fulfill customers' needs. Hence, product transportation activities are highly dependent on production outputs. In the literature, the product distribution in supply chains has traditionally been approached as a vehicle routing problem, for which several variants have been studied. However, traditional approaches consider that the set of delivery orders are available at the initial time of route design. So, inspired by the complexity of production-distribution problems, this paper addresses the case in which delivery orders have different availability at the time of designing the distribution routes (i.e., each order has its own release time). The problem is modeled as a mathematical program and solved using an Iterated Local Search algorithm hybridized with Variable Neighborhood Descent (ILS-VND). Experiments are run using adapted benchmark instances and results show the efficiency and effectiveness of the proposed algorithm.

Keywords: Metaheuristic · Vehicle routing problem · Variable neighborhood descent · Iterated local search

1 Introduction and Motivation

A supply chain is a network of actors (companies and organizations) directly or indirectly involved in fulfilling a customer request. When dealing with goods manufacturing, the supply chain not only includes manufacturers and suppliers, but also transporters, warehouses, retailers, and customers themselves [16]. From the view of the focal enterprise, the operational functions in the supply chain can be defined as procurement, production, and distribution. These three main activities are highly interconnected, and decisions at each stage do impact the other stages. Indeed, at the operational level, for example, decisions regarding the frequency of raw material arrival from the supplier determines the earliest time a production order can start at the manufacturing floor, while the completion times of production orders at the manufacturer defines the order availability for delivery by the transporter. The opposite is also valid: production planning is influenced by the planning of transportation of finished products.

Supported by School of Engineering Universidad de La Sabana and research grant INGPHD-10-2019 from Universidad de La Sabana.

ⓒ The Author(s), under exclusive license to Springer Nature Switzerland AG 2022
J. C. Figueroa-García et al. (Eds.): WEA 2022, CCIS 1685, pp. 222–233, 2022.
https://doi.org/10.1007/978-3-031-20611-5_19

However, because of the complexity of such integrated problem, decisions regarding production and transportation are most frequently made separately so that efficiencies at each stage can be reached [4]. On another hand, in order to supply these requests, companies are forced to increase inventory levels without taking into account that they impact the logistics costs of the product [11]. According to the literature (e.g., [12,19], the logistics costs can constitute up to 30% of the product's final cost. At the same time, transportation and inventory holding are the logistics activities that mainly absorb costs. Empirical studies have shown that each of them represents between 50% and 66% of the total logistics costs [2].

In the search of alternatives that allow obtaining a balance between customer satisfaction and logistics costs, several approaches have been studied in the literature to optimize the design of distribution routes. By doing so, it is possible to achieve a reduction in total operating costs of between 3% and 20% [17]. The problem of designing distribution routes is generally approached in the literature as the Vehicle Routing Problem, which is known to be NP-hard, since it generalizes the Travelling Salesman Problem (TSP) and the Bin Packing Problem (BPP) which are both well-known NP-hard problems [6]. This intractability means that optimal solutions are difficult to obtain in reasonable computational time. Hence, researchers and practitioners alike prefer the use of approximate algorithms to solve these problems.

A huge variety of versions of the VRP has been studied in the literature, as witnessed by several recent literature review papers (i.e., [1,3,5,7–9,13–15]). Among the different variants, the vehicle routing problem with order ready times has been rarely studied. In such a context, the aim of this paper is to propose both a mathematical formulation and a solution procedure for the VRP with order release times (VRP-RT). This variant of the problem is inspired from industrial applications arising in the combined production scheduling and vehicle routing problem [10,20].

This paper is organized as follows. Section 2 describes the problem under study and its mathematical formulation. The proposed solution procedure based on the hybridization of Iterated Local Search and Variable Neighborhood Descent (ILS-VND) is presented in Sect. 3. Computational experiments and the analysis of results are presented in Sect. 4. This paper ends in Sect. 5 by presenting some conclusions and drawing opportunities for future research.

2 Problem Description and Mathematical Model

Starting from a set of production orders manufactured at the production stage of a supply chain, they are then delivered to a set of geographically dispersed customers. The completion times of each production order once manufacturing has finished become a release or ready time for delivery start. This delivery of finished products is modeled as a vehicle routing problem with release times (VRP-RT), which is computationally difficult to solve since it belongs to the class of NP-hard problems.

Formally speaking, a set of n production orders are to be manufactured and then shipped to customers once completed. The delivery is carry out using an infinite fleet of vehicles (e.g., trucks) with unlimited capacity Vehicles leave the factory every h hours. Each production order B_i consists of a set j of products $B_i = \{J_{i,1}...J_{i,n}\}$ to be delivered to a customer with a known location. In addition, each delivery order B_i has a release time C_i defined by the completion time of manufacturing. We consider that vehicles must return to the factory after the delivery route is completed. Therefore, the vehicle routing problem is modeled as a VRP with order release times. In addition, each route r includes a start travel time H_r, a total travel time D_r, and the delivery time of the last order CR_r. The longest delivery time CR_{Max} is defined as $\max\{CRr\}\forall r \in R$. The routing problem is modeled in a complete undirected graph $G' = (V', A')$, where $V' = (1...n)$ is the set of nodes (clients), and A' is the set of arcs connecting each pair of nodes (clients). Each arc has a non-negative integer value $T_{l,h}$ representing the time a vehicle travels from node l to node h.

Since the objective of the problem is to minimize the maximum delivery date of the orders CR_{Max}, a mathematical program can be proposed as follows:

Sets:

I : Order sets ($i \in I = \{0, 1....n\}$)
R Set of routes ($r \in R = \{1....R_n\}$)
Alias: $j = i$

Parameters:

C_i : Release time of the order i.
$T_{i,j}$: Distance between points i, j.
M : Very large number.
N : Total number of orders.
R : Total number of routes.
Mk : Makespan.
C_{min} : Completion time of first order in production.

Decision variables:

H_r: Route start time r.
D_r: Route total travel time r.
$BN_{i,r} = 1$ if order i is shipped on route r, 0 otherwise
CR_{MAX}: Delivery time of last order.
$XR_{r,i,j} = 1$ if order j is delivered after order i on route r, 0 otherwise
$U_{r,i}$: Number of arcs of node j on route r

Objective function:

$$Min : CR_{MAX} \tag{1}$$

S.A

$$H_r = C_{min} + h \,\forall r = 1 \tag{2}$$

$$H_r = H_{r-1} + h \,\forall r > 1 \tag{3}$$

$$H_r + M * (1 - BN_{i,r}) \geq C_i \,\forall i \,\forall r \tag{4}$$

$$\sum_{\forall r} BN_{i,r} = 1 \forall i \tag{5}$$

$$\sum_{\forall j \neq i \neq 0} XR_{r,i,j} = BN_{i,r} \forall i > 0 \ \forall r \tag{6}$$

$$\sum_{\forall i \neq j \neq 0} XR_{r,i,j} = BN_{j,r} \forall j > 0 \ \forall r \tag{7}$$

$$\sum_{\forall j} XR_{r,0,j} = 1 \ \forall r \tag{8}$$

$$\sum_{\forall i} XR_{r,i,0} = 1 \ \forall r \tag{9}$$

$$U_{r,i} + 1 \leq N * (1 - XR_{r,i,j}) + U_{r,j}) \ \forall i > 0, j > 0 \ \forall j \neq i \ \forall r \tag{10}$$

$$D_r = \sum_{\forall i} \sum_{\forall j} T_{i,j} * XR_{r,i,j} \ \forall r \tag{11}$$

$$CR_{MAX} \geq D_r + H_r \ \forall r \tag{12}$$

$$H_r, D_r \in Z \ \forall r \tag{13}$$

$$BN_{i,r} \in \{0,1\} \ \forall r \ \forall i \tag{14}$$

$$XR_{r,i,j} \in \{0,1\} \ \forall r \ \forall i \ \forall j \tag{15}$$

$$CR_{MAX} \in Z \tag{16}$$

In this mathematical formulation, constraints (2) ensure that the first vehicle undertakes the trip h time units after the production system finishes processing the first order. Constraints (3) declare that subsequent trips start at intervals of h time units. Constraints (4) guarantee that orders start after the production completion time. Constraints (5), (6) and (7) make sure that all orders are assigned to a vehicle. Constraints (8) and (9) guarantee that the vehicle on each route starts and ends the route at the factory. Equations (10) correspond to subtour elimination. The total travel time for each r is calculated using Constraints (11). Constraints (12) compute the longest delivery time in the system. Finally, Constraints (13), (14), (15) and (16) ensure values of decision variables.

3   Proposed Solution Procedure

This paper proposes the solution approach shown in Fig. 1. This solution approach is divided into five steps. In the first step, the start times of each vehicle are determined and the orders to be delivered are assigned to the vehicle. For the allocation, the vehicle loads all orders that have a release time lower than the route start time and that have not been allocated yet. Next, the Nearest Neighbor (NN) heuristic is used to obtain an initial solution for each route. To improve these solutions, the Iterative Local Search (ILS) metaheuristic hybridized with the Variable Neighborhood Descent (VND) heuristic. Finally, the maximum delivery time is calculated.

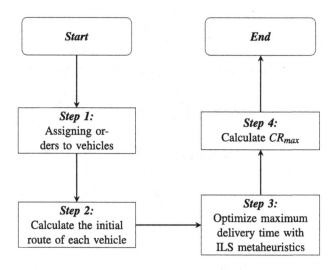

Fig. 1. Solution approach

Algorithm 1. ILS

Require: S_0
1: $S \leftarrow VND(S_0)$
2: $BS \leftarrow S$
3: **repeat**
4:      $S \leftarrow Perturbation(S)$
5:      $S \leftarrow VND(S)$
6:      **if** $S < BS$ **then**
7:          $BS \leftarrow S$
8:      **end if**
9: **until** The stop criterion was achieved

The ILS metaheuristic is described in Algorithm 1, where S_0 is the initial solution obtained with the NN heuristic. The current solution is defined as S while the best solution is defined as *BS*. In line 1, the algorithm improves the initial solution using the VND heuristic. In line 2, the best solution of the problem is updated. The loop between line 4 and line 8 is executed until the running time of the algorithm has elapsed. In line 4, a perturbation is applied to the current solution in order to avoid staying in a local optimum solution. This paper uses the 2-OPT movement. Line 5 refreshes the current solution using the VND heuristic. Line 6 evaluates if the current solution is the best available solution. If so, the best solution of the algorithm is updated in line 7.

The VND algorithm is described in Algorithm 2, where S_0 is defined as the initial solution, S as the current solution and $S*$ as the local solution of the algorithm. N is the set of neighborhoods, while K is the index of N and T as the total number of neighborhoods. N is composed of the "Relocate" and "Swap" moves and are explained next. The algorithm starts by converting the initial solution into the current solution and into the best solution (see lines 1 and 2). In line 3, the first neighborhood of N is selected. Until the local search has been applied to the last neighborhood, the algorithm is executed cyclically from line 5 to line 11. In line 5, S is updated by applying the local search on the N_k neighborhood. In local search algorithm, best move that improves the assignment is selected. An evaluation is made to see if the current solution is better than the local solution in line 6. If so, the local solution is updated and the search is directed to neighborhood 1 (see lines 7 and 8). Otherwise, the algorithm moves to the next neighborhood (see line 10). Finally in line 12, the best local solution is returned.

Algorithm 2. VND

Require: S_0
Require: $N = \{N_1, ..., N_T\}$
 1: $S \leftarrow S_0$
 2: $S^* \leftarrow S_0$
 3: $K \leftarrow 1$
 4: **while** $K \leq T$ **do**
 5:     $S \leftarrow LS(S, N_k)$
 6:     **if** $S < S^*$ **then**
 7:         $S^* \leftarrow S$
 8:         $K \leftarrow 1$
 9:     **else**
10:         $K \leftarrow K + 1$
11:     **end if**
12: **end while**
13: **Return:** S^*

Neighborhoods. The neighborhoods used to solve this problem were Relocate and Swap. Relocate is performed between the same route and on other routes. In order to apply Relocate on other routes, we evaluate if the vehicle start time is greater than the order release time. When this occurs, Δ_A and Δ_B are determined as shown in Eqs. (17) and (18). In Fig. 2, node x, which belongs to route B and is located between nodes i and j (see graph 1), is relocated on route A between nodes k and l (see graph 2). To compute the new CR_{Max}, Eq. (19) is used. If the movement is applied on the same route to update the CR_{max}, we use Eq. (20).

$$\Delta_A = T_{i,j} - T_{i,x} - T_{x,j} \tag{17}$$

$$\Delta_B = T_{k,x} + T_{x,l} - T_{k,l} \tag{18}$$

$$CR_{MAX} = \max\{CR_A + \Delta_A, CR_B + \Delta_B, \max\{CR_r\} \forall r \in R - \{A,B\}\} \tag{19}$$

$$CR_A = CR_A + \Delta_A + \Delta_B \tag{20}$$

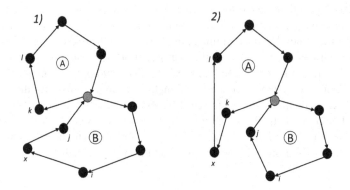

Fig. 2. Relocate

4   Computational Experiments and Results

The proposed solution approach was run on a PC with 4.1 GHz, 4 cores and 20 GB RAM. Since there are not benchmark instances available in the literature for the problem under study, experiments were carried out by adapting the VRP datasets from [18]. The mathematical model was coded in Python programming language and solved using Gurobi 9.12 and the solver CPLEX 20.10, while the algorithm was coded in Java language. To divide the routes, we established that each vehicle starts its delivery every 2 h from the factory.

4.1   Algorithm Calibration

In order to calibrate the parameters of the algorithm, a preliminary experiment was carried out using a sample of five (out of 30) instances. These instances were selected based on their size. The instances selected allowed to define the running time of the algorithm. Each of these instances was run for one hour and convergence curves were drawn (see Fig. 3). Most of the instances converge in less than one minute. However, instance TRM30 converges in around 2 min. Therefore, the running time for the other instances was set to 5 min to prevent losing good results.

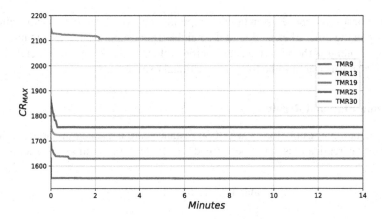

Fig. 3. Algorithm convergence

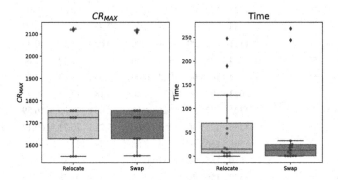

Fig. 4. Box-plot factorial experiment

A factorial experiment was also designed to define the order of execution of the two neighborhoods in the VND algorithm. This experiment is composed of two factors. The first factor evaluates which of the two neighborhoods should be executed first, while the second factor is the set of five instances previously selected. Each experiment was run for 5 min as defined above, and run using three replications to obtain statistical results. The best solution and the time required to reach it are both registered. Figure 4 contains the box plot for the CR_{MAX} and running time. In addition, we verified that output variable CR_{MAX} meets the assumptions of normality, stochasticity and independence. For this, we used Kolmogorov-Smirnov, Bartlett and Durbin-Watson tests. The sample gave us that the residuals do not behave normally, therefore a parametric test cannot be applied. Therefore, nonparametric Wilcoxon signed-rank test for related data was selected with 95% confidence level. It was obtained that the order of execution of the neighborhoods does not significantly influence CR_{MAX}, as illustrated in Fig. 4. Also, to identify if there is a significant difference around the running time of the algorithm, normality assumptions were tested. As a result, the sample errors with respect to time do not behave normally. Considering that the data are not related, the Wilcox test was hence performed, giving as a result that there is a significant difference in the time to obtain the best solutions. To sum up, this experiment showed that there is no significant difference in the order of execution of the neighborhoods, but results are obtained faster if the swap neighborhood is executed before relocate. Therefore, this neighborhood configuration was used for the full computational experiment.

4.2   Computational Results

The computational results for the set of 30 instances are presented in Table 1. For each instance, five replications were performed. In Table 1 the number of clients of the

Table 1. Computations results

Instance	Total customers	CR_{MAX}				Time (seconds)			
		Min	Avg	Max	σ	Min	Avg	Max	σ
TRM0	20	1326	1326.00	1326	0.00	0.00	0.01	0.03	0.01
TRM1	50	938	938.00	938	0.00	12.32	68.20	173.95	63.36
TRM2	50	1111	1111.00	1111	0.00	0.02	0.14	0.39	0.15
TRM3	50	984	984.00	984	0.00	0.37	1.49	2.60	0.93
TRM4	50	1034	1034.00	1034	0.00	0.04	1.13	2.47	0.95
TRM5	50	1023	1023.00	1023	0.00	0.18	17.73	36.40	16.96
TRM6	75	1323	1324.20	1325	1.10	2.00	64.20	216.59	87.62
TRM7	75	1255	1255.00	1255	0.00	25.21	70.71	160.14	53.75
TRM8	75	1566	1568.40	1574	3.58	43.71	157.92	288.12	115.95
TRM9	75	1550	1551.60	1552	0.89	0.24	10.89	53.13	23.61
TRM10	75	1599	1599.40	1601	0.89	23.80	107.38	224.08	86.87
TRM11	100	1978	1992.80	2000	8.56	58.18	128.12	224.24	69.89
TRM12	100	1684	1687.60	1690	2.19	28.30	114.51	236.12	84.82
TRM13	100	1724	1724.00	1724	0.00	0.70	5.97	18.67	7.71
TRM14	100	2023	2025.80	2029	2.68	9.73	161.48	236.92	97.39
TRM15	100	1623	1625.80	1627	1.79	11.16	85.75	165.53	62.44
TRM16	50	1484	1484.00	1484	0.00	0.09	0.43	0.91	0.30
TRM17	50	1162	1163.60	1164	0.89	5.22	74.81	133.92	60.04
TRM18	50	1473	1473.00	1473	0.00	0.00	0.57	1.05	0.40
TRM19	50	1629	1629.00	1629	0.00	2.71	24.97	82.08	32.78
TRM20	50	1429	1429.00	1429	0.00	4.59	42.45	109.15	41.28
TRM21	75	2012	2016.40	2018	2.61	59.30	169.61	282.07	90.45
TRM22	75	1877	1882.20	1887	5.02	49.19	112.37	204.75	63.99
TRM23	75	1664	1664.00	1664	0.00	1.48	2.85	5.45	1.54
TRM24	75	1767	1767.00	1767	0.00	0.54	32.95	74.97	27.07
TRM25	75	1755	1755.00	1755	0.00	0.60	14.98	32.92	14.05
TRM26	100	1967	1970.20	1979	5.22	1.26	79.98	241.66	96.55
TRM27	100	1910	1914.40	1918	2.97	6.76	124.61	246.18	101.51
TRM28	100	1926	1930.00	1934	3.74	29.43	167.35	270.54	103.31
TRM29	100	1806	1809.60	1814	3.58	111.66	159.44	281.26	69.12
TRM30	100	2108	2112.00	2116	4.00	80.56	195.04	252.83	70.92

Table 2. ILS and CPLEX comparison

Instance	Best bound	Time	CPLEX Solution		ILS-VND	
			CR_{MAX}	GAP	CR_{MAX}	GAP
TRM0	1296	10080.3072	1326	2.26%	1326	2.26%
TRM1	830	10080.1479	944	12.08%	938	11.51%
TRM2	942	10080.4242	1111	15.21%	1111	15.21%
TRM3	860	10080.2357	984	12.60%	984	12.60%
TRM4	907	10080.1708	1034	12.28%	1034	12.28%
TRM5	891	10080.2108	1025	13.07%	1023	12.90%
TRM6	1153	10080.2576	1341	14.02%	1323	12.85%
TRM7	1117	10080.3813	1255	11.00%	1255	11.00%
TRM8	1404	10080.2377	1608	12.69%	1566	10.34%
TRM9	1369	10080.494	1560	12.24%	1550	11.68%
TRM10	1542	10080.1304	1599	3.56%	1599	3.56%
TRM11	1891	10080.7479	–	–	1978	4.40%
TRM12	1635	10080.3015	1686	3.02%	1684	2.91%
TRM13	1534	10080.2128	1748	12.24%	1724	11.02%
TRM14	1891	10080.3009	–	–	2023	6.52%
TRM15	1547	10080.3097	1739	11.04%	1623	4.68%
TRM16	1440	10080.1349	1484	2.96%	1484	2.96%
TRM17	1092	10080.168	1172	6.83%	1162	6.02%
TRM18	1473*	1242.91237	1473	0.00%	1473	0.00%
TRM19	1629*	133.738267	1629	0.00%	1629	0.00%
TRM20	1412	10080.113	1429	1.19%	1429	1.19%
TRM21	1993	10080.2151	–	–	2012	0.94%
TRM22	1871	10080.96	–	–	1877	0.32%
TRM23	1664*	694.355682	1664	0.00%	1664	0.00%
TRM24	1767*	1265.75726	1767	0.00%	1767	0.00%
TRM25	1738	10080.2264	1755	0.97%	1755	0.97%
TRM26	1937	10080.1774	1967	1.53%	1967	1.53%
TRM27	1819	10080.1982	1912	4.86%	1910	4.76%
TRM28	1855	10080.1998	2016	7.99%	1926	3.69%
TRM29	1712	10080.2067	1868	8.35%	1806	5.20%
TRM30	2078	10081.0267	–	–	2108	1.42%

instance is shown. The best solution of the algorithm, the average of the five replications, the worst solution found and the standard deviation for each instance are reported. Also, the table reports the lowest, the average and the highest response time for each instance. The first conclusion from these results is that the proposed algorithm has a low variance. In addition, a comparison with the solution obtained with the mathematical model is presented (see Table 2). The execution time of the mathematical model was limited to three hours per instance. From the results returned by the solver, the table reports the relaxed lower bound, the integer feasible solution (if found), the GAP between them, and the running time. From these results, four optimal solutions were found (TRM18, TRM19, TRM23 and TRM24), while the solver could not find feasible solutions for instances TRM11, TRM14, TRM21, TRM22 and TRM30. For the solutions that are feasible, the most complex instances are TRM0, TRM1, TRM2, TRM3, TRM4, TRM5, TRM6, TRM7, TRM8 and TRM9.

Comparing the feasible results returned by the ILS-VND algorithm with the solver, it is observed that the algorithm in a short period of time yields to better solutions. In addition, we observe that the algorithm is able to find optimal solutions as it finds the optimum of the solutions TRM18, TRM19, TRM23 and TRM24. Moreover, for serveral instances (TRM0, TRM12, TRM16, TRM20, TRM21, TRM22, TRM25, TRM26 and TRM27) the gap is even lower than 3%, which is very good performance. Although for the most complex instances outlined above, the gap with respect to the relaxed lower bound is very high, and in most cases it outperforms the solutions found by the solver.

5 Conclusions and Perspectives

This paper proposed a mathematical model and a hybrid algorithm to solve the vehicle routing problem with order release times. This problem, inspired by practical real-life situations of production-distribution systems, has been rarely studied in the literature, making this paper one of the first contributions. The proposed algorithm consists on an Iterated Local Search and a Variable Neighborhood Descent. Computational experiments were carried out using adapted benchmark instances from the literature. Experimental results are promising and motivate further studies about this problem.

Following the findings of this work, several opportunities for further research are identified. For example, several parameter sets of the metaheuristic can be tested, followed by the design of a solution procedure that addresses the joint production and routing problem. It would also be interesting to formulate a multi-objective algorithm, to address also environmental or social performance indicators, in addition to routing costs or times. In addition, other constraints could be added to the problem, such as time windows, service times, vehicle capacity, etc.

Acknowledgements. The work presented in this paper was supported by Universidad de La Sabana, Colombia, under a postgraduate scholarship from the School of Engineering awarded to the first author, and by internal research funds under project INGPHD-10-2019.

References

1. Archetti, C., Feillet, D., Gendreau, M., Grazia Speranza, M.: Complexity of the VRP and SDVRP. Transp. Res. Part C: Emerg. Technol. **19**(5), 741–750 (2011)
2. Ballou, R.: Logística. Administración de la cadena de suministro, Pearson Educación (2004)
3. Cordeau, J.F., Laporte, G.: The dial-a-ride problem: models and algorithms. Ann. Oper. Res. **153**(1), 29–46 (2007)

4. Díaz-Madroñero, M., Mula, J., Peidro, D.: A mathematical programming model for integrating production and procurement transport decisions. Appl. Math. Model. **52**, 527–543 (2017)
5. Eksioglu, B., Vural, A.V., Reisman, A.: The vehicle routing problem: a taxonomic review. Comput. Ind. Eng. **57**(4), 1472–1483 (2009)
6. Garey, M., Johnson, D.: Computers and Intractability: A Guide to the Theory of NP-completeness. W. H. Freeman, Mathematical Sciences Series (1979)
7. Gendreau, M., Laporte, G., Potvin, J.Y.: Metaheuristics for the capacitated vrp. Discrete Mathematics and Applications, pp. 129–154 (2002)
8. Irnich, S., Toth, P., Vigo, D.: Chapter 1: The family of vehicle routing problems. Vehicle Routing, pp. 1–33
9. Laporte, G.: The vehicle routing problem: an overview of exact and approximate algorithms. Eur. J. Oper. Res. **59**(3), 345–358 (1992)
10. Martins, L.d.C., Gonzalez-Neira, E.M., Hatami, S., Juan, A.A., Montoya-Torres, J.R.: Combining production and distribution in supply chains: The hybrid flow-shop vehicle routing problem. Comput. Ind. Eng. **159**, 107486 (2021)
11. Mentzer, J.T., Flint, D.J., Hult, G.T.M.: Logistics service quality as a segment-customized process. J. Mark. **65**(4), 82–104 (2001)
12. Min, H., Zhou, G.: Supply chain modeling: past, present and future. Comput. Ind. Eng. **43**(1), 231–249 (2002)
13. Montoya-Torres, J.R., López Franco, J., Nieto Isaza, S., Felizzola Jiménez, H., Herazo-Padilla, N.: A literature review on the vehicle routing problem with multiple depots. Comput. Ind. Eng. **79**, 115–129 (2015)
14. Mourgaya, M., Vanderbeck, F.: The periodic vehicle routing problem: classification and heuristic. RAIRO - Oper. Res. **40**(2), 169–194 (2006)
15. Psaraftis, H.N.: Dynamic vehicle routing: status and prospects. Ann. Oper. Res. **61**(1), 143–164 (1995)
16. Shapiro, L.: The embodied cognition research programme. Philos Compass **2**(2), 338–346 (2007)
17. Solina, V., Mirabelli, G.: Integrated production-distribution scheduling with energy considerations for efficient food supply chains. Procedia Comput. Sci. **180**, 797–806 (2021)
18. Solomon, M.M.: Algorithms for the vehicle routing and scheduling problems with time window constraints. Oper. Res. **35**(2), 254–265 (1987)
19. Thomas, D.J., Griffin, P.M.: Coordinated supply chain management. Eur. J. Oper. Res. **94**(1), 1–15 (1996)
20. Torres-Tapia, W., Montoya-Torres, J.R., Ruiz-Meza, J., Belmokhtar-Berraf, S.: A matheuristic based on ant colony system for the combined flexible jobshop scheduling and vehicle routing problem. In: 10th IFAC Conference on Manufacturing Modelling, Management and Control. Elsevier, Nantes, France (2022)

The Organization of Fruit Collection Transport in Conditions of Extreme Rurality: A Rural CVRP Case

Helmer Paz-Orozco[1]([✉]), Osman Meléndez-Bermúdez[1], Jesús Gonzalez-Feliu[2],
Daniel Morillo[3], Carlos Rey[4], and Gustavo Gatica[5]

[1] Engineering Faculty, Corporación Universitaria Comfacauca, Popayán, Colombia
hpaz@unicomfacauca.edu.co
[2] Excelia Business School, Centre de Recherche en Innovation et Intelligence Managériales,
La Rochelle, France
[3] Pontifica Universidad Javeriana, Cali, Colombia
[4] Data Science Unit, Universidad de Concepcion, Concepcion, Chile
[5] Engineering Faculty, Universidad Andrés Bello, Santiago, Chile

Abstract. Routing under rural conditions is a technical and logistical challenge. In classic vehicle routing, the objective is to minimize traveled distances that reduces transportation costs, mainly approximated as Euclidean. However, the type and performance of the vehicle, and the condition of the roads, must be correlated to generate realistic models. A mathematical model, based on mixed-integer programming, is proposed to determine the cost of transportation in rural conditions. The novelty of the research arises on introducing different types of roads and then circulation conditions and a global cost structure function. The study area is a rural Municipality, from Cauca-Colombia. A real intervention-research case study is defined, modelled and optimized using a commercial solver. After a fourteen-month intervention, a computational experiment is generated, which establishes only five routes. Thus, a total transportation cost of $ USD 1,546.98 is obtained with the proposed model, which supposes a reduction of 29% with respect to the transport system before the intervention.

Keywords: Perishable food · Mixed integer programming (MIP) · Vehicle routing · Rural area · Food supply chains

1 Introduction

Colombia is an important avocado producer, the world's fourth-largest [1]. In 2019, it exported 45,139 tons of Hass avocado. Those exports increase by 48.5% and 41.7% in tons and value, respectively, between January to November 2019 [2].

The production of Hass avocado in Colombia, increased by 89% in the last five years [1]. The main producing Departments are Eje Cafetero, Tolima, Cauca, Antioquia, Huila, and Valle del Cauca [3].

All perishable products need the deployment of logistical activities for their distribution, which can present drawbacks [4, 5]. The most relevant ones are the scheduling

© The Author(s), under exclusive license to Springer Nature Switzerland AG 2022
J. C. Figueroa-García et al. (Eds.): WEA 2022, CCIS 1685, pp. 234–242, 2022.
https://doi.org/10.1007/978-3-031-20611-5_20

of transport routes to reduce costs [6, 7]. Logistics costs impact 12.8% on the sale price. However, in the Department of Cauca, they reach 23.8% [8].

This research focuses on optimizing the transportation costs of Hass avocado for export, with farmers from the Municipality of Timbío-Cauca. Vehicle load capacity and costs are considered, from the production units to the collection center. In a Municipality that has a geographical extension of 205 Km2 and 74% of arable areas [9].

The main issues in fruit collection transport are related to the organization of routes, so less-than-truckload transport (LTL) in a mainly rural environment [10, 11]. LTL optimization is mainly made via the Vehicle Routing Problem [12, 13] (VRP), which is a classic of combinatorial optimization with various applications and generalities [14, 15]. However, the literature generally minimizes costs by decreasing the distance traveled, considering Euclidean, Manhattan or empirical travel distances [16, 17], mainly based on an urban basis [18]. However, there are other factors that impact costs, such as type of roads, calculation of non-Euclidean distances, inertia, aerodynamic drag [19, 20].

According to [21], the fixed and variable costs of transporting a vehicle depend on factors not directly related to the trip. They stand out, type of load, speed, road conditions, performance, fuel price, depreciation, maintenance, and wages. Some authors consider factors that impact costs, as well as environmental impact [22, 23].

The literature shows few studies related to the impact of fuel consumption in rural conditions (tertiary and secondary roads) [24, 25]. In Colombia, of the total of tertiary roads, 96% are in poor condition and only 6% are considered in proper condition [26].

For Colombia, the sum of costs for storage, transportation, administrative and customer services are established as logistics cost [27]. Transportation costs are reported to reach 35.2% [8]. Therefore, minimizing costs, and in particular for small agricultural producers, contributes to the economic sectors.

This paper, via a real case study, proposes an optimization model is presented that assigns a cost per kilometer traveled in rural conditions. The contribution of the article is the objective function (FO), which integrates the vehicle operation costs already established [28]. In addition, the state of the road, type of vehicle, speed by sections, fuel consumption, and topography (flat, undulating, mountainous) are incorporated. Next section presents the methodology used to generate the optimization model. Then, the third section presents the characterization of the problem, parameters, variables, and the developed model. Subsequently, the compared results are presented comparing the use of the model with a business-as-usual scenario, i.e. without using the proposed model.

2   Methodology

2.1   General Methodology

The methodology considers three phases, presented in Fig. 1. The first phase includes fourteen-month fieldwork to identify the operational costs of moving the load to the market of interest. As a tool to capture the data, a mixed questionnaire is used. In addition, the georeferencing of productive units and the identification of roads (primary, secondary, and tertiary) are included. The second phase corresponds to a review of the

Vehicle Routing Problem (VRP), to identify which generalization of the VRP to adapt to the identified conditions. The third phase considers designing and adjusting the mixed-integer programming model to program the model in GAMS. The model considers the variables and parameters of the problem, as well as the objective function, to estimate total costs in rural conditions. Then a computational experiment is designed and executed to finish with the analysis of the results and conclusions of the investigation.

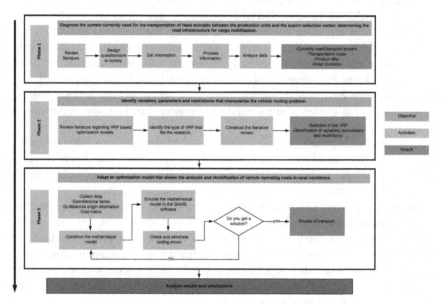

Fig. 1. Methodological design [Source: own elaboration]

2.2 Formulation of the Proposed Mathematical Model

For the Hass avocado harvest in the Municipality of Timbío, the formulation, the three-index vehicle flow [29] is used. Where, X_{ijk} indicates whether a vehicle k travels from client i to client j; Y_{ik} determines if customer i is served by vehicle k.

A depot and a fleet of vehicles with homogeneous capacity, search for a set of routes at minimum cost that start and end at the central depot [14]. The sets used, parameters, variables, and the developed model are presented below.

Sets
N = {0, 1, 2, ... m} Set of all nodes (collection center and farmers). Set of all nodes (collection center and farmers).

K = {1, 2, ... n} Set of all vehicles.
A = {(i, j); i, j ∈ N, i ≠ j} Set of all bows.
Parameters and Indices

$k = 1, \ldots n$ index representing the vehicle

$i = 1, \ldots m$ index representing farmers

$i = 0$ represents the collection center

O_i Farmer's offer i, $i = 1, \ldots m$ [Kg]

Q_k Vehicle capacity k, $k = 1, \ldots n$ [Kg]

T_{kij} Estimated time of a vehicle to travel from i to j; $i, j = 0, \ldots m$ [h]

VTP_{kij} Average vehicle speed on flat ground [Km/h]

$\%TP_{ij}$ Route percentage on flat terrain

VTO_{kij} Average vehicle speed on rolling terrain [Km/h]

$\%TO_{ij}$ Route percentage in rolling terrain

VTM_{kij} Average vehicle speed in mountainous terrain [Km/h]

$\%TM_{ij}$ Percentage of the route in mountainous terrain

f_{ij} Factor for road condition between the arches i, j

ICC_{kij} Fuel consumption indicator according to the type of terrain between $i\,a\,j$; $i, j = 0, \ldots m$ [USD/km]

CV Variable cost per kilometer traveled

CF Fixed vehicle cost

Decision Variables

X_{ijk}: Binary variable equal to 1, when using arc (i, j) for vehicle k; 0 otherwise.

y_{jk}: Binary variable equal to 1 if node j is visited by vehicle k, 0 otherwise.

Objective Function

$$MinC = \sum_{i,j,k}[\{(VTP_{kij} * \%TP_{ij} * f_{ij}) + (VTO_{kij} * \%TO_{ij} * f_{ij})$$
$$+ (VTM_{kij} * \%TM_{ij} * f_{ij})\} * ICC_{kij} * T_{kij}] * X_{ijk}$$
$$+ \sum_{i,j,k}\left\{\frac{1.05 * (CV + CF)}{(1 - 0.133)}\right\} * X_{ijk}$$

The objective function is made up of two components. The first cost associated with speed and fuel consumption. In addition, the time to travel the arc (i, j) and a factor associated with the state of the road. Second, the total variable cost of vehicle operation and the fixed cost for the use of vehicles [28, 30].

Constraints

$$\sum_{i}^{N} X_{ijk} \leq 1 \quad \forall j \in N, k \in K \tag{1}$$

$$\sum_{j}^{N} X_{ijk} \leq 1 \quad \forall i \in N, k \in K \tag{2}$$

$$\sum_{i}^{N}\sum_{j}^{N} X_{0jk} = \sum_{i}^{N}\sum_{j}^{N} X_{ijk} \quad \forall k \in K \tag{3}$$

$$\sum_{i}^{N} X_{ijk} - \sum_{j}^{N} X_{ijk} = 0 \quad \forall i \in N, k \in K \tag{4}$$

$$\sum_{k}^{K} \sum_{i}^{N} X_{ijk} \leq K \tag{5}$$

$$\sum_{i}^{N} X_{ijk} \geq y_{jk} \quad \forall i = 1, \dots n; k \in K \tag{6}$$

$$\sum_{k}^{K} y_{jk} = 1 \quad \forall i = 1, \dots n \in N \tag{7}$$

$$\sum_{j}^{N} O_i * y_{jk} \leq Q_k \quad \forall k \in K \tag{8}$$

$$U_i - U_j + \left(N * X_{ijk} \right) \leq (N - 1) \quad \forall i, j \in N \tag{9}$$

Restriction group (1) and (2) limit one route per vehicle. The first corresponds to the number of times that a vehicle leaves node i. The second, the number of times it reaches node j. Restriction (3) ensures that all vehicles start and end their journey in the collection center. Constraint (4) ensures the continuity of the model. The restriction (5) allows not to exceed the available vehicle fleet. Constraint (6) assigns node j to vehicle k passing through that node. Restriction (7) ensures that each farmer is assigned exactly one single vehicle. Restriction (8) ensures that the sum of the quantity of avocado collected on a route does not exceed the capacity of the vehicle. Finally, restriction (9) allows us to eliminate sub-tours.

3   Results

The research considers a computational experiment for choosing declared preferences. Thus, firms are prepared to estimate travel demand for transport. From a driver survey, which contains 22 records, the value of travel time and charging costs are calculated.

3.1   Producer Characterization

The definitions and parameters necessary to formulate the model are established. First, the results of the application of a questionnaire are presented. Then, the characterization of the rural road network according to [31].

73% of farmers sell the fruit to a marketer. Only 9% of the vehicles are from wholesalers, while 18% correspond to intermediaries. 73% of farmers hire a C2 type vehicle [31]. The vehicle's capacity varies from 5 to 8 tons, which is underutilized. The cost per trip that the farmer assumes individually, fluctuates between $ USD 146.4 and $ USD 349.22.

Timbío has 52% of tertiary roads with 115.63 km of non-linear coverage and corresponds to the connection between the Municipality and its farmhouses (Municipal Municipality of Timbío Cauca, 2019). The deficit status can be seen in Fig. 2, which corresponds to the Municipality of Timbío. Furthermore, depending on the type of terrain, it is considered whether it is flat, undulating, or mountainous, determined by the percentage of longitudinal inclination [31].

Fig. 2. Tertiary route Municipality of Timbío [Source: own elaboration]

The proposed model considers speed and fuel consumption, according to the type of terrain and condition of the roads, as presented in Table 1. In addition, the Google Earth © program was used to establish the road slopes of each arch *(i,j)* that connect the productive units. The state of the network that connects each productive unit, are in the regular state (Secretariat of Infrastructure of the Department of Cauca, 2019). In addition, the type of vehicle you access is not greater than two axles.

Table 1. Type of land according to the percentage of slopes (Source: [31])

Terrain type	% longitudinal slope	State of the road
Plan	Slope less than 3%	Good, fair or poor condition
Wavy	Pending between 3% & 6%	
Mountainous	Pending between 6% & 8%	

3.2 Solution of the Mathematical Model

The proposed model is programmed in GAMS and CPLEX v.12.6.2.0, Intel Core i5, 2.5 GHz, 4 GB of RAM, and a 64-bit Windows operating system. The model suggests making 5 routes with a total transportation cost of $ USD 1,546.98. Table 2 presents the capacity of the vehicle, kilograms of avocado harvested, the sequence of the farmers visited, and the efficiency of the carrying capacity.

Table 2. Routes generated by GAMS (Source: own elaboration)

Route	Vehicle capacity (Kg)	Kg collected	Producers visited	% occupation
1	9000	7550	C_0-C_1-C_3-C_4-C_0	83,9
2	9000	8600	C_0-C_5-C_{10}-C_0	95,6
3	9000	5700	C_0-C_8-C_9-C_0	63,3
4	9000	8500	C_0-C_2-C_7-C_0	94,4
5	9000	7450	C_0-C_6-C_{11}-C_0	82,8

Table 2 shows that the route with the most producers visited is route number 1. The highest percentage of load capacity utilization is obtained on routes 2 and 4 and the lowest on route 3. For routes 1 and 2 an efficiency of 83.9% and 82.8%, respectively, is obtained. Hass avocado production per harvest period is 127.5 tons located in 4 areas, where the crops of 11 producers are currently located.

The results of the transportation system show a decrease in costs, which reach 29% ($ USD 1,546.98), compared to the total costs of $ USD 2,182.42 reported in November 2019. The model indicates that only 3.2% of the value sold to the wholesaler (USD 1.22 / Kg) is to pay for the mobilization of the fruit. In addition, to increase profitability by 27% if the farmer is associated.

The impact of tertiary roads in rural areas is determined. Figure 3a presents the reduction of the Average Speed Route (ASR F_{ij}). This is reduced by 50% compared to that considered by the Ministry of transport since the condition of the roads makes it difficult to maintain a constant speed. Figure 3b shows the cost of fuel with respect to speed according to the type of terrain.

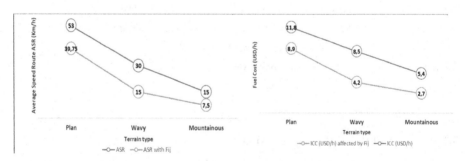

Fig. 3. ASR effect and fuel consumption vs. land type [Source: own elaboration]

4 Conclusion

After 14-month fieldwork, an optimization model is validated, to establish a set of optimal routes and minimize costs. The impact of rural roads on the cost of transportation is determined. The contribution of the article is to quantify the cost of transportation, considering roads in rural areas and in poor condition. The topography is different from paved roads, fuel costs are reduced by 38% and speed decreases on average by 50%.

Transportation costs are reduced by 29%, the level of efficiency in cargo capacity, and the number of vehicles used is optimized. From using eleven vehicles, it was reduced to five, that is, an average of 85% efficiency in occupying the load capacity on each route. A competitive advantage is obtained by associating producers to transport and generate collaborative logistics that minimizes costs and increases profitability. For the analyzed scenario, the model can generate a saving of 28% ($ USD 9,280.85), only with six trips and five vehicles. With the above logistics, each producer assumes an individual cost and an annual transport cost that reaches $ USD 13,086.4.

References

1. Ministerio de Agricultura y Desarrollo Rural. (diciembre de 2019). Cadena aguacate: indicadores e instrumentos. Bogota: Sistema de información de gestión y desempeño de organizaciones de cadenas. Obtenido de https://sioc.minagricultura.gov.co/Aguacate/Documentos/2019-12-30%20Cifras%20Sectoriales.pdf
2. Ministerio de Agricultura y Desarrollo Rural. (31 de enero de 2020). https://www.minagricultura.gov.co. Obtenido de https://www.minagricultura.gov.co/noticias/Paginas/El-aguacate-hass-colombiano-a-ota-en-el-Super-Bowl-2020.aspx
3. Instituto Colombiano Agropecuario. (31 de agosto de 2019). El ICA, principal jalonador de las exportaciones de aguacate Hass colombiano al mundo
4. Rossi, T., Pozzi, R., Pirovano, G., Cigolini, R., Pero, M.: A new logistic model for increasing economic sustainability of perishable food supply chains through intermodal transportation. Int. J. Logist. Res. Appl. **23**(3), 311–327 (2020). https://doi.org/10.1080/13675567.2020.1758047
5. Winarno, H., Perdana, T., Handayati, Y., Purnomo, D.: Regional food hubs for distribution of regional food logistics (case study on the establishment of a food distribution center in Banten Province, Indonesia). In: IOP Conference Series: Materials Science and Engineering, 771 (2020). https://doi.org/10.1088/1757-899X/771/1/012068
6. Theeraviriya, C., Pitakaso, R., Sethanan, K., Kaewman, S., Kosacka-Olejnik, M.: A new optimization technique for the location and routing management in agricultural logistic. J. Open Innov. Technol. Market Complexity **6**(1), 11 (2020). https://doi.org/10.3390/joitmc6010011
7. Zulvia, F.E., Kuo, R.J., Nugroho, D.Y.: A many-objective gradient evolution algorithm for solving a green vehicle routing problem with time windows and time dependency for perishable products. J. Clean. Prod., 118428 (2019). https://doi.org/10.1016/j.jclepro.2019.118428
8. Departamento Nacional de Planeación DNP. (2018). Encuesta Nacional de Logística
9. Alcaldía Municipal de Timbío Cauca. (2016–2019). Plan de desarrollo 2016–2019. Timbío, Cauca
10. Batero Manso, D.F., Orjuela Castro, J.A.: Inventory routing problem in perishable supply chains: a literature review. Ingeniería **23**(2), 117–143 (2018)
11. Orjuela-Castro, J.A., Orejuela-Cabrera, J.P., Adarme-Jaimes, W.: Perishable food distribution in the last mile: a multi-objective VRP model. Int. J. Inf. Decision Sci. **13**(4), 322–334 (2021)
12. Gonzalez-Feliu, J.: Multi-stage LTL transport systems in supply chain management. In Cheung, J., Song, H. (eds.) Logistics: Perspectives, Approaches and Challenges, pp. 65–86. Nova Science Publishing, New York (2013)

13. Orjuela-Castro, J.A., Sanabria-Coronado, L.A., Peralta-Lozano, A.M.: Coupling facility location models in the supply chain of perishable fruits. Res. Transp. Bus. Manage. **24**, 73–80 (2017)
14. Toth, P., Vigo, D. (eds.): Vehicle routing: problems, methods, and applications. Society for Industrial and Applied Mathematics (2014)
15. Gatica, G., Contreras-Bolton, C., Venegas, N., Opazo, O., Linfati, R., Escobar, J.W.: A web application for location and vehicle routing in disaster. Iteckne **14**(1), 62–69 (2017)
16. Laporte, G.: Fifty years of vehicle routing. Transp. Sci. **43**(4), 408–416 (2009)
17. Gonçalves, D.N.S., Gonçalves, C. de M., Assis, T.F., Silva, M.A.:Analysis of the difference between the euclidean distance and the actual road distance in Brazil. Transp. Res. Procedia **3**, 876–885 (2014). https://doi.org/10.1016/j.trpro.2014.10.066
18. Cattaruzza, D., Absi, N., Feillet, D., González-Feliu, J.: Vehicle routing problems for city logistics. EURO J. Transp. Log. **6**(1), 51–79 (2017)
19. Chilma, V.F., Sarache, W.A., Costa, Y.J.: Una Solución al enrutamiento de vehículos en ciudades montañosas considerando aspectos ambientales y económicos. Scielo **29**(3), 3–14 (2018). https://doi.org/10.4067/S0718-07642018000300003
20. Turkensteen, M.: The accuracy of carbon emission and fuel consumption computations in green vehicle routing. Eur. J. Oper. Res. **262**(2), 647–659 (2017). https://doi.org/10.1016/j.ejor.2017.04.005
21. Xiao, Y., Zhao, Q., Kaku, I., Xu, Y.: Development of a fuel consumption optimization model for the capacitated vehicle routing problem. Comput. Oper. Res. **39**(7), 1419–1431 (2012). https://doi.org/10.1016/j.cor.2011.08.013
22. Çimen, M., Soysal, M.: Time-dependent green vehicle routing problem with stochastic vehicle speeds: an approximate dynamic programming algorithm. Transp. Res. Part D: Transp. Environ. **54**, 82–98 (2017). https://doi.org/10.1016/j.trd.2017.04.016
23. Zhang, J., Zhao, Y., Xue, W., Li, J.: Vehicle routing problem with fuel consumption and carbon emission. Int. J. Prod. Econ. **170**, 234–242 (2015). https://doi.org/10.1016/j.ijpe.2015.09.031
24. Qiang, X., Appiah, M.Y., Boateng, K., Appiah, F.V.: Route optimization cold chain logistic distribution using greedy search method. Opsearch **57**(4), 1115–1130 (2020). https://doi.org/10.1007/s12597-020-00459-4
25. Padilla, M.P., Canabal, P.A., Pereira, J.M., Riaño, H.E.: Vehicle routing problem for the minimization of perishable food damage considering road conditions. Logist. Res. **11**(2), 1–18 (2018). https://doi.org/10.23773/2018_2
26. Instituto Nacional de Vías. Colombia Rural, Estrategia del gobierno Nacional para la intervención de la red terciaria. Bogotá, D.C (2019)
27. De la Hoz Hernandez, J., et al.: Management model for the logistics and competitiveness of SMEs in the city of Barranquilla. In: Rocha, Á., Reis, J., Peter, M., Bogdanovic, Z. (eds.) Marketing and Smart Technologies. Smart Innovation, Systems and Technologies, vol. 167, Springer, Singapore (2020)
28. Ministerio de transporte: Modelo para la determinación de costos de referencia. Bogotá, D.C (2016)
29. Toth, P., Vigo, D. (eds.): The vehicle routing problem. Society for Industrial and Applied Mathematics (2002)
30. Asociación Nacional de Empresarios de Colombia – ANDI: Manual básico de gestión de transporte de carga por carretera. Bogotá, D.C (2018)
31. Instituto Nacional de Vías: Manual de diseño geométrico de carreteras. Bogotá, D.C (2008)
32. Ministerio de transporte: Resolución 004100 del 28 de diciembre de 2004. Bogotá D, C (2004)

Design of Electric Vessels Test Routes Using Image Processing and Optimization Techniques

Alejandro Uribe$^{(\boxtimes)}$ ⓘ, Miguel Calvache ⓘ, Camilo Álvarez ⓘ,
and Alejandro Montoya ⓘ

School of Applied Sciences and Engineering, Universidad EAFIT, Carrera 49 N 7 Sur-50,
05001 Medellín, Antioquia, Colombia
{auribev1,macalvachg,acalvarezv,jmonto36}@eafit.edu.co

Abstract. Vessels are one of the transportation modes with high contribution to global warming and air pollution since their operation depends mostly on the use of fossil fuels. Given a large number of navigable rivers and the need for rural transportation in small and intermediate cities in Latin America, these vehicles are widely used, thus the need to propose sustainable alternatives arises. The ENERGETICA 2030 program is developing an electric vessel for passenger transportation between the municipalities of Magangué and Pinillos in Colombia; however, tests must be designed to replicate the operating conditions in a controlled environment. In this paper, we propose a method for route design based on image processing and optimization algorithms. Through the *OpenStreetMap* API, we extracted information from water bodies in images, then using the skeletonization method, we created graph structures and by means of the Dijkstra and Backtracking algorithms, the minimum distance feasible routes were selected. The Puerto Berrío (PB) - Puerto Nare (PN), Puerto Nare - Puerto Triunfo (PT) and Guatapé dam routes were chosen for the case study. It was found that to represent the exact distance of the Magangué – Pinillos route, the tests must be performed at the Guatapé dam. In case of giving priority to the similarity between segments, the PB - PN route must be selected. In future work we will consider obtaining real-time water level information and to strengthen the optimization algorithms to repeat nodes visited in the route evaluation.

Keywords: Image processing · Skeletonization · Shortest path algorithm · Backtracking · Water bodies

1 Introduction

As with all means of transportation, vessels contribute to air pollution and climate change [1]. This is due to the fact that they are fundamental in the development of the global economy and that their operation depends on the use of fossil fuels [2, 3]. However, oil reserves will tend to run out and fossil fuel prices to increase [4]. Therefore, conventional energy systems with internal combustion engines must be replaced by cleaner alternative solutions as mentioned by Hemdana *et al.* [5]. They also propose the electrification of ships with batteries and the design of new propulsion modes to address these solutions and

© The Author(s), under exclusive license to Springer Nature Switzerland AG 2022
J. C. Figueroa-García et al. (Eds.): WEA 2022, CCIS 1685, pp. 243–253, 2022.
https://doi.org/10.1007/978-3-031-20611-5_21

meet sustainable development objectives, public expectations and regulatory challenges. Mira *et al.* states that intermediate and small cities in Latin America and the Caribbean use fluvial transport more than ground transport [6]. They mention that this mode has gained relevance in the transport of people and goods, with a specific increase in countries with larger water resources and a greater number of navigable rivers. This inland waterway potential and the need for sustainable mobility solutions have driven the development of electric vessels. Given the limited energy supply of these vehicles and the fact that the energy demand on the water is higher compared to land vehicles, efficiency becomes an important factor to consider in the design of electric vessels [7]. From data it is possible to simulate energy models to predict the behavior of the vessel and efficiently manage its energy. Information on location, orientation and altitude becomes useful for active control of the vessel to achieve such efficiency [8].

ENERGETICA 2030 is an alliance currently developing an electro-solar vessel for river transport operations [9]. The route selected for the electric fluvial mobility case study corresponds to approximately 60 km between Magangué and the municipality of Pinillos. Since this is a relatively new technology in the local context, it is necessary to validate the performance of the vessel in a controlled environment and feed the energy control models with the collected data. It is for this reason that in this paper we propose a tool for the design of electric vessel tests in fluvial areas based on image processing and the use of optimization techniques. As a case study, we present the analysis between Magangué – Pinillos and the auxiliary test routes Puerto Berrío (PB) - Puerto Nare (PN) and Puerto Nare (PN) - Puerto Triunfo (PT). In addition, we show the method usability in large bodies of water such as the Guatapé dam, Antioquia. The paper is organized as follows: Sect. 2 mentions similar approaches found in the literature review. Section 3 defines important concepts to be considered and the approach. Section 4 shows the results and its discussion. Finally, Sect. 5 contains the conclusions and future work.

2 Literature Review

The literature review is divided into two sections, the first corresponding to the image processing and feature extraction of water bodies and the second to the algorithms for route design.

2.1 Image Processing and Feature Extraction of Water Bodies

These techniques are used in different fields of work including cartography, surface contouring as well as for environmental purposes such as diagnosing of ecosystems conditions [10]. Some approaches are mentioned below. Tambe *et al.* Implemented a multi-feature based convolutional neural network (CNN) architecture called W-net to perform segmentation of water body images extracted automatically by satellites [11]. The W-Net achieved high performance by training the system with a smaller number of images, extracting water pixels with high accuracy considering the pixel continuity inspection at the boundaries and mitigating blurring effects. Other satellite approaches are observed as the work by Liao *et al.* Where a process of urban water extraction in SAR (synthetic aperture radar) images was performed by integrating surface morpho-logical features to control the multiple radar bounces that resulted in complicated water backscattering patterns near urban elements such as buildings [12]. Remote sensing techniques were used by Xu *et al.* to monitor changes in lakes using Landsat 8 Operational Land Imager (OLI) images of five lakes in Central Asia [13]. Using K-means clustering algorithms and the flood filling method (KCFFM), they sought to improve the accuracy and stability of complex background extraction results by including the influence of ice and snow as noise parameters in lakes. Other authors as Jin *et al.* Proposed the delineation of fluvial networks from Sentinel-2A/B MSI images by means of adaptive multiscale regional growth methods (AMRGM) [14]. By implementing a bias-corrected fuzzy C-means method (BCFCM) they corrected some landscape effects to subsequently use an algorithm based on the Hessian matrix to improve river morphology features and size manipulation. We also found sensor approaches for environmental applications. Cobby *et al.* Used a LiDAR as a data source to map the topographic height and size of objects on the surface to determine the distributed floodplain on 2D maps [15]. Feature extraction from fluid-based images is not new, for example, by machine learning algorithms and image processing, Rajpurohit *et al.* Managed to do identification of acute lymphoblastic leukemia in microscopic images of blood [16].

2.2 Algorithms for Route Design

Given the need to take advantage of the information of river images to plan routes, algorithms must be implemented to find the shortest feasible distance between two points and that given certain initial conditions allow the design of electric vessel itineraries. Rosita *et al.* Stated that the Dijkstra algorithm is an efficient method for problems where the optimal route is desired based on the definition of inter-route weights [17]. The following are some of the approximations that have been made with this algorithm. Due to the massification of domiciliary services in China and to meet delivery times, Liu *et al.* Implemented the Dijkstra algorithm to evaluate road parameters and find the optimal route [18]. Another application is the optimization of routes under toxic gas dispersion in real time. For this case Wang *et al.* Proposed to combine the computational fluid dynamics (CFD) code and Dijkstra to calculate the optimal pathway with the minimum total inhaled dose [19]. A second type of methods that allow the design of feasible routes for testing vessels are backtracking algorithms that use brute force to find a desired solution given certain initial conditions. This technique was used in the reconfiguration of ethernet data flow when affected by permanent node failures [20]. In this work, Li *et al.* Proposed a solution based on a reconfiguration method with backtracking ensemble pruning to solve tree search models built with network topology and idle link slots. Another approach involves the routing of waste collection vehicles. In this case Akhtar *et al.* Used a backtracking algorithm to find routes that minimize the sum of distances traveled by waste management qualified vehicles [21].

Following the literature review, we did not find any research using image processing for the design of electric vessel routes in fluvial bodies by implementing optimization techniques. In this article, we propose a method in which, through open data API queries, images with information of water bodies are obtained and then, by means of processing techniques and optimization algorithms, routes can be designed for testing and navigation. In the following, the approach is described.

3 Approach

The following describes the method and its components, which are essentially divided into a preprocessing stage and a route design stage. Figure 1 shows the pseudocode that summarizes the entire process.

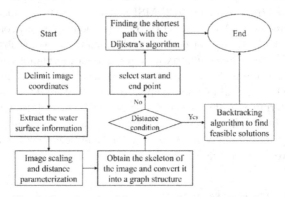

Fig. 1. Pseudocode of the process for test route design.

3.1 Preprocessing

In order to design routes in fluvial areas, the first step was to obtain the information corresponding to water bodies and to differentiate it from land bodies. There are certain open projects such as *OpenStreetMap* that facilitate this task [22].This project distributes geographic information under open license and allows obtaining vectorized images of water bodies like dams, lakes or rivers through its Python library *OSMnx*. Although projects such as *Osmapi* are used for nautical visualization, it was decided to use the *OSMnx*

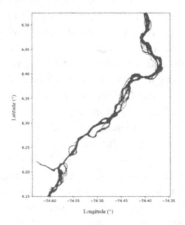

Fig. 2. Water body extraction for PB – PN river route, Colombia.

library because of its extensive documentation and user-friendly interface. The *geometries_from_bbox* function allow selecting a water body and extracting the information of its entire course from the head to the mouth. By means of the corner's coordinates, we were able to delimit a segment of interest and through the labels corresponding to whether it is water or land body, we identified and separated the useful information. Figure 2 shows the image where the water body was extracted from the river section between PB and PN, Colombia. The image is plotted differentiating any body of water labeled with blue and any other label with the default color white.

After extracting the area of interest, some noise components may remain in the image. We remove them manually by changing the pixel value in the selected sections, however it can be done using tools that remove blobs of pixels with densities below a defined threshold. A commonly used library is *OpenCV* where filters and transformations can be used to remove elements that do not correspond to the river or water body. The distance traveled on the river is an important input for estimating the vessel's consumption. The image provides information for each of the pixels that compose it, however, only related to the presence of water. To calculate the distance, it is necessary to know the size of each pixel. This was achieved by knowing the bounding coordinates and estimating the length between corners and then interpolating. We computed this measure with the *Geopy* function *distance.geodesic* that finds the geodesic distance from an ellipsoidal model for two coordinates [23].

Depending on the image used and its pixel count, finding the optimal path can be a computationally demanding process, therefore, reducing the path information to one pixel simplifies the subsequent calculations. For this reason, the image is binarized with *OpenCV* and skeletonized. *Skeletonize* is a method from the library *Scikit-image* that consists of reducing binary objects to one-pixel wide representations [24]. This can be useful for feature extraction, for the representation of an object's topology and, for the practical case, it allows to find the mean route in a water body. The method works by making successive runs over the image; the edge is identified and removed for each set of pixels with the condition of not interrupting the object connectivity. We selected a section of this image to proceed with the analysis and to illustrate the techniques used. Figure 3 shows: a) the skeletonized body and b) the skeletonization in green color overlayed with the original image.

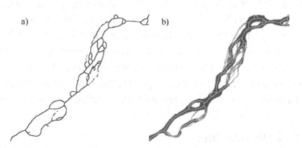

Fig. 3. a) Skeletonized body of route segment, b) Skeletonization overlaying the original image. (Color figure online)

3.2 Route Design

We propose two approaches for test design using the information obtained in previous steps. The first consist of estimating the minimum distance between two pixels. This tool can be used to plan electric vessel trips providing route information by knowing both starting and ending points. The distance and optimal path estimation were performed with the pixel measurement obtained in previous steps. For this, it was necessary to convert the skeleton into a graph. A graph is a set of nodes connected by arcs that allow representing binary relationships between elements of a set. Therefore, from a given node, the path to a neighbor can be followed by an arc with a weight corresponding to the distance between them. To find the shortest path between two points, Dijkstra's algorithm was used. This method is based on graph structures, and it is commonly used in routing protocols such as Open Shortest Path First because of its low computational cost. From this approach it is possible to obtain the route and the distance traveled. This distance depends on the skeleton resulting from the preprocessing, which in turn varies according to the initial image. Figure 4 shows the skeletonization in blue and the shortest path in red.

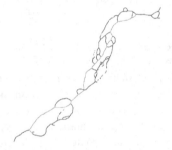

Fig. 4. Shortest path for an initial and final pixel in the skeletonized body. (Color figure online)

The second approach is used when the distances are predefined, and it is desired to evaluate how far from a starting point the electric vessel could go. This solution can be used when routes must be identified for testing electric motors at constant revolutions for a certain period of time or for charging and discharging the battery to complete a predefined number of cycles. This requires evaluating the possible routes and if the conditions are met, selecting the path as the solution. For this reason, this proposal uses a backtracking algorithm where the routes that do not meet the requirements are discarded until there is a feasible route. The only restriction considered is to reach the distance provided in the parameters. Using the graph structure of the previous approach, this algorithm was implemented to obtain feasible routes within water bodies.

4 Results and Discussions

As mentioned above, the route selected for the ENERGETICA 2030 case study is the Magdalena River between Magangué and Pinillos, Colombia. The electric vessel development is being carried out in Medellín, Colombia. Therefore, for practical purposes, nearby rivers and dams were selected to conduct the tests. Specifically, we considered the routes PB – PN, PN – PT and the Guatapé dam in the department of Antioquia. The purpose was to compare which of the routes can resemble the conditions of Magangué – Pinillos to develop the tests. Figure 5 shows the water body information extracted for each of these locations. In addition, Table 1 shows the detailed coordinates that delimit the data.

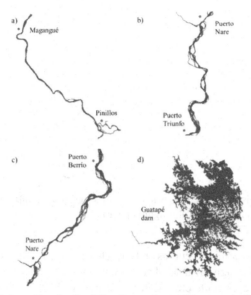

Fig. 5. Water body information for the following routes: a) Magangué – Pinillos, b) PN – PT, c) PB – PN, d) Guatapé dam.

Table 1. Coordinates of water bodies for the study case.

Location	North-East (Lat, Lon)	North-West (Lat, Lon)	South-East (Lat, Lon)	South-West (Lat, Lon)
Magangué - Pinillos	9.295, -74.392	9.295, -74.787	8.862, -74.392	8.862, -74.787
PN - PT	6.248, -74.674	6.248, -74.528	5.883, -74.674	5.883, -74.528
PB - PN	6.523, -74.347	6.523, -74.636	6.149, -74.347	6.149, -74.636
Guatapé dam	6.334, -75.128	6.334, -75.262	6.186, -75.128	6.186, -75.262

Two approaches were used to compare the trips. The first consisted of identifying the visual similarity between routes based on an initial comparison image and the shortest route obtained with Dijkstra algorithm from the skeletonization of a river body. Since the largest linear distance at the Guatapé dam corresponds to 16 km being only 26% of the distance to be traveled between Magangué and Pinillos, it was not considered for this analysis. Then, we used the images of the PN – PT and PB – PN routes processed with the mentioned methods for the comparison with Magangué – Pinillos. For this purpose, it was necessary to scale the two images so that each pixel represents the same dimensions and rotate the images in such a way that the routes partially coincide. Figure 6 shows the Magangué – Pinillos route in blue, the skeletonization of the route in comparison in green and the shortest path for this route in red.

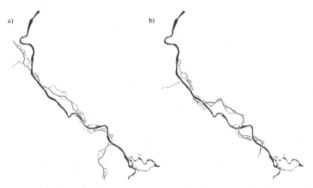

Fig. 6. Scaled comparison between the water body of Magangué - Pinillos and the skeletonized route of a) PB – PN, b) PN – PT. (Color figure online)

Despite some similarities in curves and straight distances, it was necessary to extract more information to design the tests. The second approach consisted of calculating the linear distances that each route covers. To determine the length, we characterized each pixel in such a way that after finding the optimal route between two points with the Dijkstra algorithm, the distance between each pair of nodes could be added up. The results are summarized in Table 2. The distance in Guatapé dam is variable depending on the start and end points considered so it is not presented.

Table 2. Shortest distance estimated with the Dijkstra algorithm for each route.

Starting point	End point	Distance (m)
Magangué	Pinillos	66,184.73
PN	PT	42,269.49
PB	PN	49,645.28

In order to design the tests in the Guatapé dam, its image was skeletonized to establish a route. Since this water body is an artificial lake and there are small islands within it, after applying the skeletonization algorithm, we obtained closed shapes allowing the possibility of different routes. If Dijkstra's algorithm is used on the dam, the shortest distances and routes between the selected ports can be calculated allowing to estimate parameters that feed the electric vessel control system for other types of tests to be performed. In this case, we wanted to represent the Magangué - Pinillos conditions. For this we used the Backtracking algorithm to test by brute force the possible routes that cover the distance obtained in the previous step given a fixed starting point. Figure 7 shows the skeletonization of the dam in dark blue and the representation of the distance from Magangué Pinillos across it in red color. The route obtained from the skeleton of the dam seeks to take advantage of all possible routes, therefore, when it is desired to represent long distances, circuits and sharp curves will be found. It is important to note that the distance displayed is half of the real distance, since the test considered the round trip to return to the origin port. Obtaining these results, it was determined that to represent the exact distance, the tests must be performed at the Guatapé dam. In case the fluvial conditions must be recreated, considering the distance and similarity without repeating routes, the PB - PN route may be selected.

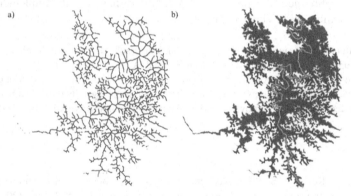

Fig. 7. a) Skeletonized Guatapé dam, b) Magangué - Pinillos route within the dam. (Color figure online)

The proposed method only considers Euclidean distances to find feasible solutions, therefore changes in altitude between coordinates, water flow, weather and vessel autonomy are parameters that are not taken into account and therefore cause inaccurate estimations. However, this approach serves as a starting point for the design and sizing of routes in controlled environments for the vessel developed within the framework of the ENERGETICA 2030 program.

5 Conclusions

With the proposed method for the development of tests and planning of electric vessel routes in fluvial water bodies, we obtained results that allow to replicate the operating conditions in a controlled environment keeping in mind some considerations. The images obtained from *OpenStreetMap* allowed the intended analysis, however, since the water level depends on the time of the year and the data of this project does not capture this behavior, estimation errors may occur. Depending on whether there is a greater or lesser water surface in the image, the skeleton obtained, and the optimal route calculated will vary. If the route design method intends to be used during the vessel's operation, it is necessary to obtain the information of the water bodies in real time. For this purpose, we will consider other technologies such as satellite images or radars in further research. This would allow the proposed method to be replicable at any time of the year and even under dry or freezing river conditions.

For the route design algorithm based on graphs, skeletonization was an effective method to reduce computation time of the optimization methods used. Simplifying a route to the size of one pixel reduces the number of nodes to be evaluated proportionally to the number of pixels removed. In addition, this easy-to-implement method allowed obtaining clean images that capture the relevant information of the water bodies for the design of tests and navigation routes. On the other hand, the implemented Backtracking algorithm did not allow repeating nodes already visited. This did not represent a problem during the development of the research since the distances to be evaluated were not large enough to require the evaluation of these conditions, however, the implementation of this functionality will be considered as future work.

Acknowledgements. Authors would like to thank Universidad EAFIT and the alliance "ENER-GETICA 2030" for funding this research. ENERGETICA 2030 is a Research Program with code 58667 from the "Colombia Científica" initiative, funded by The World Bank through the call "778-2017 Scientific Ecosystems". The research program is managed by the Colombian Ministry of Science, Technology, and Innovation (Minciencias) with contract No. FP44842-210-2018.

References

1. Howitt, O., Revol, V., Smith, I., Rodger, C.: Carbon emissions from international cruise ship passengers' travel to and from New Zealand. Energy Policy **38**, 2552–2560 (2010). https://doi.org/10.1016/j.enpol.2009.12.050
2. Çeven, S., Albayrak, A., Bayır, R.: Real-time range estimation in electric vehicles using fuzzy logic classifier. Comput. Electr. Eng. **83** (2020). https://doi.org/10.1016/j.compeleceng.2020.106577
3. Perčić, M., Frković, L., Pukšec, T., Ćosić, B., Li, O.L., Vladimir, N.: Life-cycle assessment and life-cycle cost assessment of power batteries for all-electric vessels for short-sea navigation. Energy **251**, 123895 (2022). https://doi.org/10.1016/j.energy.2022.123895
4. Nuchturee, C., Li, T., Xia, H.: Energy efficiency of integrated electric propulsion for ships – a review. Renew. Sustain. Energy Rev. **134**, 110145 (2020). https://doi.org/10.1016/j.rser.2020.110145
5. Hemdana, I., Dallagi, H., Bouaicha, H., Zaoui, C., Nejim, S.: Hybrid electrical power supply for an electric propelled boat. In: 2018 International Conference on Advanced Systems and Electric Technologies IC_ASET 2018, pp. 319–326 (2018). https://doi.org/10.1109/ASET.2018.8379876
6. Mira, J., Mendoza, F., Betancur, E., Manrique, T., Mejía-gutiérrez, R.: A propulsion system design methodology based on overall efficiency optimization for electrically powered vessels. IEEE Trans. Transp. Electrif. **8**(1), 239–250 (2022). https://doi.org/10.1109/TTE.2021.3104763
7. Gomez-Oviedo, S., Mejia-Gutierrez, R.: An interactive tool for propeller selection according to electric motor exploration: an electric boat design case study. In: 2020 EEE Transportation Electrification Conference & Expo, ITEC 2020, pp. 147–151 (2020). https://doi.org/10.1109/ITEC48692.2020.9161467

8. Mendoza, F., Vélez, C., Echavarría, S., Montoya, A., Manrique, T., Mejía-Gutiérrez, R.: Variable-Prioritizing and Instrumentation for monitoring of an electrically-powered fluvial vessel through a FDM approach. In: Applied Computer Sciences in Engineering, pp. 480–492 (2021). https://doi.org/10.1007/978-3-030-86702-7_41
9. Energetica2030, "P3. Movilidad electrica," (2019). https://www.energetica2030.co/p3-mov ilidad-electrica/. Accessed 01 Mar 2022
10. He, Y., et al.: Water clarity mapping of global lakes using a novel hybrid deep-learning-based recurrent model with Landsat OLI images. Water Res. **215**, 118241 (2022). https://doi.org/ 10.1016/j.watres.2022.118241
11. Tambe, R.G., Talbar, S.N., Chavan, S.S.: Deep multi-feature learning architecture for water body segmentation from satellite images. J. Vis. Commun. Image Represent. **77**, 103141 (2021). https://doi.org/10.1016/j.jvcir.2021.103141
12. Liao, H.Y., Wen, T.H.: Extracting urban water bodies from high-resolution radar images: measuring the urban surface morphology to control for radar's double-bounce effect. Int. J. Appl. Earth Obs. Geoinf. **85**, 102003 (2019). https://doi.org/10.1016/j.jag.2019.102003
13. Xu, Y., Lin, J., Zhao, J., Zhu, X.: New method improves extraction accuracy of lake water bodies in Central Asia. J. Hydrol. **603**(PD), 127180 (2021). https://doi.org/10.1016/j.jhydrol. 2021.127180
14. Jin, S., et al.: River body extraction from sentinel-2A/B MSI images based on an adaptive multi-scale region growth method. Remote Sens. Environ. **255** (2021). https://doi.org/10. 1016/j.rse.2021.112297
15. Cobby, D.M., Mason, D.C., Davenport, I.J.: Image processing of airborne scanning laser altimetry data for improved river flood modelling. ISPRS J. Photogramm. Remote Sens. **56**(2), 121–138 (2001). https://doi.org/10.1016/S0924-2716(01)00039-9
16. Rajpurohit, S., Patil, S., Choudhary, N., Gavasane, S., Kosamkar, P.: Identification of acute lymphoblastic leukemia in microscopic blood image using image processing and machine learning algorithms. In: 2018 International Conference on Advances in Computing, Communications and Informatics , ICACCI 2018, no. Cll, pp. 2359–2363 (2018). https://doi.org/10. 1109/ICACCI.2018.8554576
17. Rosita, Y.D., Rosyida, E.E., Rudiyanto, M.A.: Implementation of dijkstra algorithm and multi-criteria decision-making for optimal route distribution. Procedia Comput. Sci. **161**, 378–385 (2019). https://doi.org/10.1016/j.procs.2019.11.136
18. Liu, S., Jiang, H., Chen, S., Ye, J., He, R., Sun, Z.: Integrating Dijkstra's algorithm into deep inverse reinforcement learning for food delivery route planning. Transp. Res. Part E Logist. Transp. Rev. **142**, 102070 (2020). https://doi.org/10.1016/j.tre.2020.102070
19. Wang, J., Yu, X., Zong, R., Lu, S.: Evacuation route optimization under real-time toxic gas dispersion through CFD simulation and Dijkstra algorithm. J. Loss Prev. Process Ind. **76**, 104733 (2022). https://doi.org/10.1016/j.jlp.2022.104733
20. Li, J., Li, Q., Xiong, H.: A backtracking ensemble pruning based reconfiguration method for time-triggered flows in TTEthernet. IEEE Access **9**, 156868–156879 (2021). https://doi.org/ 10.1109/ACCESS.2021.3129252
21. Akhtar, M., Hannan, M.A., Begum, R.A., Basri, H., Scavino, E.: Backtracking search algorithm in CVRP models for efficient solid waste collection and route optimization. Waste Manag. **61**, 117–128 (2017). https://doi.org/10.1016/j.wasman.2017.01.022
22. OSM partners, "OpenStreetMap." https://www.openstreetmap.org/about. Accessed 07 June 2022
23. GeoPy Contributors, "GeoPy's documentation." https://geopy.readthedocs.io/en/stable/. Acc essed 08 June 2022
24. skimage development team, "Skeletonize." https://scikit-image.org/docs/stable/auto_exam ples/edges/plot_skeleton.html. Accessed 07 June 2022

Optimization of Routes for Covered Walkways at University Campus by Kruskal Algorithm

Juan Manuel Zambrano-Restrepo[1]([✉]), Nelson Javier Tovar-Perilla[1] [iD],
Luz Adriana Sanchez-Echeverri[2] [iD], and Laura Patricia Carranza-Murillo[3] [iD]

[1] Departamento Nacional de Planeación, Ibagué, Colombia
jmzares@gmail.com, nelson.tovar@unibague.edu.co.uz
[2] Facultad de Ciencias Naturales y Matemáticas, Universidad de Ibagué, Ibagué, Colombia
luz.sanchez@unibague.edu.co
[3] Escuela de Ciencia Básica Tecnología e Ingeniería, Universidad Nacional Abierta y a
Distancia – CEAD Ibagué, Ibagué, Colombia
laura.carranza@uunad.edu.co

Abstract. The adverse weather conditions affect the mobility in the open spaces at university campus due the difficulty to walk in sunny or runny days. This paper describes the process to define the routes to be covered at university campus, the selection of the routes is based on the necessity of those could connect all the dependencies with minimum total distance. Kruskal algorithm was used to obtain the routes that ensure minimum total distance to be covered and the intercommunication directly or indirectly between the 22 nodes around the campus which represents all campus dependencies. Finally, a mathematical model of binary integer linear programming was formulated basis on the solution obtained by Kruskal algorithm. The solution shows as result 271.38 m of walkways to be covered that was obtained after 12 interactions of Kruskal algorithm.

Keywords: Kruskal algorithm · Minimum spanning tree · Covered routes

1 Introduction

Currently in organizations it is common to establish parameters under which workers must carry out their work, given an environment and the conditions that it can offer, which within the framework of safety and health at work is known as work organization [1]. Under this premise, it can be specified that for a worker to function efficiently or to increase their productivity, their work environment must be adequate based on predetermined needs and emphasizing various factors that can intervene and affect or benefit to the worker.

When workers are expose to adverse and changed climate conditions such as runny o sunny days, people can be subjected to contracting pulmonary diseases. These changes "make the body's defense mechanisms fall and diseases are activated, because the bacteria and viruses associated with the respiratory tract move in environments cold and wet [2]. Exposure to these adverse weather conditions; they represent a risk to people's

© The Author(s), under exclusive license to Springer Nature Switzerland AG 2022
J. C. Figueroa-García et al. (Eds.): WEA 2022, CCIS 1685, pp. 254–264, 2022.
https://doi.org/10.1007/978-3-031-20611-5_22

health, which manifests itself more aggressively in people with respiratory problems. Due to the disease's risks and, thinking about the well-being of the workers, it is necessary to differentiate the environments where this risk occurs in order to make the required adjustments and thus mitigate its impact on the people exposed to it [3].

The depletion of stratospheric ozone leaves humans too exposed to ultraviolet radiation and its effects, making environments conducive to proliferation of diseases [4, 5].

Due to the increase in rainfall and radiation as part of an acceleration in climate change, it has been seen that there is an explicit need to generate covered corridors inside organizations that have open spaces to reduce the effect that atmospheric conditions can exert about community members.

Since the associate cost to construct covered walkways are high is necessary that organization optimize the routes ensure a minimum total distance that has a direct impact in less implementation costs. In engineering, there are a study related with route optimization; the study of routing problems starts from a classic operations research problem: The Traveling Salesman Problem (TSP). The objective of the TSP is to calculate the shortest distance route for a delivery driver to visit all his customers (in different cities) and then return to the starting point [6]. During the last decades, the development of computer tools for the resolution of real route design problems has increased. These tools are based on conceptual models inspired by aspects such as biological systems, artificial intelligence, or mathematical theories, and incorporate algorithms and functions, depending on the problem to be solved [7]. Currently, classical routing problems incorporate new constraints or modify the nature of the parameters to solve more complex problems that can be replicated in real contexts [8–11].

Many distribution route planning problems have found alternative solutions in graph theory [7, 12]. This is because graph theory facilitates the modeling of the problem due to the conceptual similarity of the structures. As shown in Fig. 1, the objective of routing problems is to minimize the cost, distance, or time required by a set of source nodes to satisfy the demands of a set of destination nodes [13].

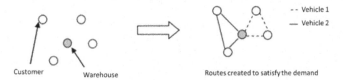

Fig. 1. Schematization of a routing problem. Source: Adapted from Rangel Valdez, 2015.

To define the optimum routes, there exist different methods one of the most common methods used is the algorithm of minimum spanning tree developed by Kruskal [14]. The Minimum Spanning Tree (MST) stands out as one of the seminal approaches to routing problems. The MST is characterized by allowing easy and fast calculation of the edges that keep the graph connected in a single component, identifying clusters in sets of nodes, and giving approximate solutions to hard problems such as the Steiner tree and the TSP [12, 16]. MST provides efficient solutions which make it practical to solve when dealing with large graphs and polynomial-time algorithms (Pop 2020). Proof of this is the algorithms developed by Dijkstra (1959), Prim (1957), and Kruskal (1956). MST algorithm can link the nodes of a network, directly or indirectly, with the minimum length of the connecting branches.

This paper presents the applications of Kruskal algorithm to obtain the routes that ensure minimum total distance to be covered and the intercommunication directly or indirectly between the 22 nodes around the campus. Moreover, a mathematical model was developed based on the Kruskal algorithm solution.

2 Methodology

A. Localization
The work was developed in a Regional Colombian University with around 5000 students; its main source of income come from enrolled students. It is located in the central region of the country on the central mountain range. The city average high temperatures of about 28 °C and average low temperatures of about 18 °C and on average 1,700 mm (66.9 in) of rain annually. However, due the climate changes the climate conditions have been intensified.

B. Problem conceptualization
The Fig. 2 shows the steps carried out to the developed this work.

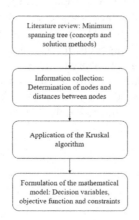

Fig. 2. Steps for work development.

Literature review: Minimum spanning tree (concepts and solution methods): A literature review was carried out on the concept, solution methods and application of the Kruskal algorithm for the solution of the minimum spanning tree problem.

Information collection: Determination of nodes and distances between nodes: For the collection of information, different meetings were held with people from the University to learn about the physical space, the accesses and the dependencies that are part of the university campus; Likewise, the network of connections and distances between the different nodes were defined.

Application of the Kruskal algorithm: The first step in applying Kruskal's algorithm is the identification of nodes (dependencies) that ensure the interconnection around the campus. Then nodes must be classified of external and internal nodes. The external nodes are those which there is only one possible connection to reach and therefore must be in the optimal route, on the other hand, the internal nodes correspond to the dependencies that have more than one path to reach them.

Although there was identified internal and external nodes Kruskal's algorithm was developed only with internal nodes; and the algorithm's solution the connections to the external nodes are added to obtain the network and the total distance to be covered.

The next step was to create the graph G (N, E, w) containing all the nodes (N), the axes connecting the nodes (E), and the distances (w) from each axis.

From this point, the different iterations of the algorithm are created, for which the sets N and E(u, v) are created, which represents the connections between node u and node v. An (empty) set T containing the least spanning tree is initialized. As long as the number of axes is less than the number of nodes minus 1 (E < n−1), then the edge with the shortest distance must be selected and must be included in the set T, taking into account that between E(u,v) and E(v,u) must be selected only one to avoid cycles.

Formulation of the mathematical model: Decision variables, objective function, and constraints: The mathematical model created was a binary linear programming model [7]. In the first instance, the decision variables of the model that correspond to the assignment of the route that goes from the i-th node to the j-th node were determined; these decision variables are binary in nature (0 if the path is in the optimal solution; 1 if the path is not in the optimal solution). Subsequently, the objective function was proposed that corresponded to the minimization of the sum of the distance from the i-th node to the j-th node and vice versa. Finally, the restrictions that correspond to a restriction for each node were proposed, given that each node must be connected to the network, the sum of the output connections of each node must be equal to 1.

The model was raised and solved in the Guzek software.

3   Results

A. Internal and external nodes – Influence Zone
22 dependencies around the university were defined (Table 1). These dependences ensure directly and indirectly communication of the campus; there were identified 13 internal nodes and 9 external nodes. Figure 3 shows the University's campus map with the identification of the dependences, the red line encloses the influence zone which is the cluster of all internal nodes.

Fig. 3. University campus map with 22 identified dependences

Table 1. Internal and external nodes of university

Label	Dependence (Node)	Node type
1	Main entrance	Internal
2	Event room	Internal
3	Engineering laboratory	Internal
4	Library	Internal
5	Student entrance	Internal
6	Chapel	Internal
7	Postgraduate building	Internal
8	Special project office	Internal
9	Administration building	Internal
10	Administration school	Internal
11	Central square	Internal
12	Engineering school	Internal
13	Humanities school	Internal
14	Academic office	External
15	Welfare office	External
16	Student parking	External

(continued)

Table 1. (*continued*)

Label	Dependence (Node)	Node type
17	Chemistry lab	External
18	Legal office	External
19	Professor parking	External
20	Gym	External
21	President building	External
22	Administrative entrance	External

B. Distance Between Nodes

Once identified the existing connections between dependences in the campus, the distances are obtained. Since COVID restrictions were present during the work developed, distances were obtained from scale map. Table 2 shows the distance matrix.

Table 2. Distance matrix between nodes in meters

	1	2	3	4	5	6	7	8	9	10	11	12	13	14	15	16	17	18	19	20	21	22
1		48,4	46,1	46,1	67,1	73,1	63,8	71,3	71,3	75,0	71,3											
2			24,8	30,8	51,8	57,8	48,4	55,9	55,9	59,6	55,9								27,8			
3				24,0	45,0	51,0	41,6	49,1	49,1	52,9	49,1	11,63										
4					27,0	33,0	25,1	30,4	30,4	34,9	31,1	33	26,3									
5						12,0	0,0	43,1	43,1	41,6	43,1											
6							6,8	49,1	49,1	52,9	49,1											
7								27,0	27,0	30,8	27,8											
8									1,5	16,9	24,0											
9										16,9	24,0											
10											11,3											
11																						
12													3				3,8					
13																					9,8	11,6
14																6						
15																	25,5		11,3			
16																						
17																						
18																						
19																						
20																						
21																						
22																						

Some distances between the identified nodes share part of the path as can be seen in Fig. 4 (blue square) where the path between 4 and 3 shares part of the path between 2 and 3.

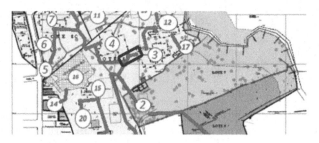

Fig. 4. Path shares between different nodes.(Color figure online)

To solve the problem with path shares could be possible include another intermediate node that does not represent any dependence; however, it was decided to subtract the distance share paths between connections in the Kruskal solution. This share paths distance is 33.75 m it was calculated from university map.

C. Kruskal algorithm application
The Kruskal algorithm was applied with the aim to define the network that solves minimum spanning tree problem between internal nodes. According to the existing connection between internal nodes, the first iteration of Kruskal algorithm were carried out for nodes, axes and T = { } that represents the connections of optimal route.

Nodes = {1,2,3,4,5,6,7,8,9,10,11,12,13}.

Axes = {1–2, 1–3, 1–4, 1–5, 1–6, 1–7, 1–8, 1–9, 1–10, 1–11, 2–1, 2–3, 2–4, 2–5, 2–6, 2–7, 2–8, 2–9, 2–10, 2–11, 3–1, 3–2, 3–4, 3–5, 3–6, 3–7, 3–8, 3–9, 3–10, 3–11, 4–1, 4–2, 4–3, 4–5, 4–6, 4–7, 4–8, 4–9, 4–10, 4–11, 4–12, 4–13, 5–1, 5–2, 5–3, 5–4, 5–6, 5–8, 5–9, 5–10, 5–11, 6–1, 6–2, 6–3, 6–4, 6–5, 6–7, 6–8, 6–9, 6–10, 6–11, 7–1, 7–2, 7–3, 7–4, 7–5, 7–6, 7–8, 7–9, 7–10, 7–11, 8–1, 8–2, 8–3, 8–4, 8–5, 8–6, 8–7, 8–9, 8–10, 8–11, 9–1, 9–2, 9–3, 9–4, 9–5, 9–6, 9–7, 9–8, 9–10, 9–11, 10–1, 10–2, 10–3, 10–4, 10–5, 10–6, 10–7, 10–8, 10–9, 10–11, 11–1, 11–2, 11–3, 11–4, 11–5, 11–6, 11–7, 11–8, 11–9, 11–10, 12–3, 12–4, 12–13}.

T = { }.

Iterations were carried out looking for the axis with the minimum weight in each one, while the number of axes is less than the number of nodes minus one, when this condition is not met, that is, the number of axes selected for the generation of the tree is equal to or greater than the number of nodes minus 1, the iterations must stop. Table 3 shows the iterations of Kruskal algorithm.

Table 3. Kruskal algorithm iterations

Iteration	MV (m)	Accumulated (m)	T	Stop Condition
1	1,5	1,5	{8-9}	E < n-1 = 1<13-1 = 1 < 12
2	3	4	{8-9, 12-13}	E < n-1 = 2<13-1 = 2 < 12
3	6,8	11,3	{8-9, 12-13, 6-7}	E < n-1 = 3<13-1 = 3 < 12
4	11,3	22,6	{8-9, 12-13, 6-7, 10-11}	E < n-1 = 4<13-1 = 4 < 12
5	11,63	34,23	{8-9, 12-13, 6-7, 10-11, 3-12}	E < n-1 = 5<13-1 = 5 < 12
6	12	46,23	{8-9, 12-13, 6-7, 10-11, 3-12, 5-6}	E < n-1 = 6<13-1 = 6 < 12
7	16,9	63,13	{8-9, 12-13, 6-7, 10-11, 3-12, 5-6, 9-10}	E < n-1 = 7<13-1 = 7 < 12
8	24	87,13	{8-9, 12-13, 6-7, 10-11, 3-12, 5-6, 9-10, 3-4}	E < n-1 = 8<13-1 = 8 < 12
9	24,8	111,93	{8-9, 12-13, 6-7, 10-11, 3-12, 5-6, 9-10, 3-4, 2-3}	E < n-1 = 9<13-1 = 9 < 12
10	25,1	137	{8-9, 12-13, 6-7, 10-11, 3-12, 5-6, 9-10, 3-4, 2-3, 4-7}	E < n-1 = 10<13-1=10 < 12
11	27	164	{8-9, 12-13, 6-7, 10-11, 3-12, 5-6, 9-10, 3-4, 2-3, 4-7, 7-8}	E < n-1 =11<13-1 =11 < 12
12	46,1	208,5	{8-9, 12-13, 6-7, 10-11, 3-12, 5-6, 9-10, 3-4, 2-3, 4-7, 7-8, 1-3}	E < n-1 =12<13-1=12 < 12

MV= minimum value
T= Connections of optimal route

As is possible to observe in Kruskal solution, the total distance to cover was 208.5 m; however, to this solution need to subtract the share paths (33.75 m) it means that optimal distance to cover in the internal nodes is 174.75 m. To complete the interconnection into university campus it is necessary to add the external nodes to Kruskal optimal solution; the total distance to cover between external nodes and influence zone was 96.63 m. Figure 5 shows the campus map with the walkways to be covered obtained with Kruskal algorithm and its connection with external nodes. The total distance to be covered to guarantee the connection of all University dependences was 271.38 m.

D Mathematical model
Based on the Kruskal algorithm solution, a mathematical model was proposed using binary integer linear programming. Table 4 shows the notation used to formulate the model.

Fig. 5. University campus map with 22 identified dependences

Table 4. Parameters and decision variables of proposed model

Decision variable	
X_{ij}	Assignment of the path that goes from the i-th node to the j-th node. i,j indicated nodes (dependences) around the university campus
Objective function	
The objective function is given by minimizing the sum of the distance from the i-th node to the j-th (d_{ij}) node and vice versa. $$Min\ Z = \sum_i \sum_j d_{ij} * X_{ij}$$	
Constrain	
Assuming that all nodes must be connected at least once, restrictions are set in the form of equalities based on the possibilities of direct connection for each node and the minimum value that these equalities can take is 1. **Scope of the Constrain** It guarantees that each node is connected, and that the connection based on the optimization criterion will be the one with the lowest weight. $$\sum_j X_{ij} = 1 \quad \forall i$$	

The optimal solutions obtained from the mathematical model was $X_{8,9}$; $X_{13,12}$; $X_{6,7}$; $X_{10,11}$; $X_{3,12}$; $X_{5,6}$; $X_{4,7}$; $X_{3,4}$; $X_{2,3}$; $X_{7,8}$; $X_{1,3}$; $X_{9,10}$; $X_{2,19}$; $X_{15,18}$; $X_{15,20}$; $X_{21,13}$; $X_{22,13}$; $X_{14,16}$; $X_{12,17}$

It should be remembered that the result obtained refers to the minimum travel distance in the case of internal nodes, that the result is contemplating the passage through a section within a route on more than one occasion, so by taking away from the chosen route it is possible to find the minimum distance to cover. To calculate the minimum distance to cover, the path of the minimum spanning tree obtained from the proposed model is taken and a cascade measurement is performed, taking a random axis node in the first phase, and subtracting the previous distance in the following phases. Considering aforementioned facts total distance between internal nodes is shown in Table 5.

Table 5. Total distance to cover obtained by mathematical model

Phase	Total distance to cover (m)
1	1,5
2	17,625
3	28,875
4	51,375
5	58,125
6	70,125

Adding the total distance of connections with external nodes (96.63 m), the minimum total distance to be covered is 271.38 m which agree with the solution obtained by Kruskal algorithm.

4 Conclusions

From the application of the Kruskal algorithm, it was possible to formulate the mathematical model. The application of this algorithm facilitated the distinction of the nodes to be selected, which made it possible to see more clearly the restrictions to be proposed in the model.

Kruskal's algorithm is a sequential algorithm that dynamically allows finding a route without going into complex analyses. It is an effective algorithm in terms of generating minimum expansion trees and based on research in most cases it allows efficient results to be obtained, which was verified by means of the proposed mathematical model.

References

1. Nilsen, M., Kongsvik, T., Almklov, P.G.: Splintered structures and workers without a work-place: how should safety science address the fragmentation of organizations? Saf. Sci. **148**, 105644 (2022)
2. Liang, L., Gong, P.: Climate change and human infectious diseases: a synthesis of research findings from global and spatio-temporal perspectives. Env. Int. **103**, 99–108 (2017)

3. Organización Internacional del Trabajo: Seguridad y salud en el trabajo (2020). https://www.ilo.org/global/standards/subjects-covered-by-international-labour-standards/occupational-safety-and-health/lang--es/index.htm
4. Figueroa-Lopez, F.: Climate change and the thinning of the ozone layer: implications for dermatology. Actas Dermosifiliogr. **102**, 311–315 (2011)
5. Roca-Villanueva, B., Beltrán-Salvador, M., Gómez-Huelgas, R.: Change climate and health. Rev. Clin. Esp. **219**(5), 260–265 (2019)
6. Medina, L.B.R., Rotta, E.C.G., La, Castro, J.A.O.: Una revisión al estado del arte del problema de ruteo de vehículos: evolución histó-rica y métodos de solución. Ingeniería, **16**(2), 35–55 (2011). https://doi.org/10.14483/23448393.3832
7. Espinal, C., Alberto, A., Flórez, C., Miguel, J., López, S., Carlos, J.: Aplicación de la teoría de grafos en la solución de problemas con impacto ambiental. Producción + Limpia, **6**(1), 9–20. http://www.scielo.org.co/scielo.php?script=sci_arttext&pid=S1909-04552011000100002&lng=en&tlng=es. Acécesed 1 Sept 2022
8. Dutta, J., et al.: Multi-objective green mixed vehicle routing problem under rough environment. Transport **37**(1), 51–63 (2021). https://doi.org/10.3846/transport.2021.14464
9. Rezaei Kallaj, M., Abolghasemian, M., Moradi Pirbalouti, S., Sabk Ara, M., Pourghader Chobar, A.: Vehicle routing problem in relief supply under a crisis condition considering blood types. Math. Probl. Eng. 1-10 (2021). https://doi.org/10.1155/2021/7217182
10. Sánchez, D.G., Tabares, A., Faria, L.T., Rivera, J.C., Franco, J.F.: A clustering approach for the optimal siting of recharging stations in the electric vehicle routing problem with time windows. Energies **15**(7), 2372 (2022). https://doi.org/10.3390/en15072372
11. Zheng, W., Wang, Z., Sun, L.: Collaborative vehicle routing problem in the urban ring logistics network under the COVID-19 epidemic. Math. Probl. Eng. **2021**, 1–13 (2021). https://doi.org/10.1155/2021/5539762
12. Romero Riaño, E., Martínez Toro, G.M., Rico-Bautista, D.: Árbol de caminos mínimos: enrutamiento, algoritmos aproximados y complejidad. Revista colombiana de tecnologias de avanzada (RCTA) **1**(31) (2018). https://doi.org/10.24054/16927257.v31.n31.2018.2780
13. Rangel Valdez, N.: Capítulo 2. Tecnológico Nacional de México (2015)
14. Kruskal, J.B.: On the shortest spanning subtree of a graph and the traveling salesman problem. Proc. Am. Math. Soc. **7**, 48–50 (1956)
15. Schrijver, A.: Theory and Linear and Integer Programming, Wiley, West Susex (1986)
16. Pop, P.C.: The generalized minimum spanning tree problem: an overview of formulations, solution procedures and latest advances. Eur. J. Oper. Res. **283**(1), 1–15 (2020). https://doi.org/10.1016/j.ejor.2019.05.017L. A. Mora, Gestión Logística integral, Bogotá: Ecoediciones (2008)

Stating on the Use of Operations Research for Historical Analysis: A Hierarchic-Transport Model Clio-Combinatorics Approach and Its Applications in Current Problem Solving

Jesús Gonzalez-Feliu[1]([✉]) and Gustavo Gatica[2]

[1] Excelia Business School, La Rochelle, France
gonzalezfeliuj@excelia-group.com
[2] Engineering Faculty, Universidad Andres Bello, Santiago, Chile
ggatica@unab.cl

Abstract. This paper aims to identify whether any underlying relevant optimization logic prevailed in the distribution of French troops in the Plan XVII of World War I. After explaining the context and the assumptions of our analysis, we propose a combinatorial optimization problem based on travel time minimization, as well as four possible solving methods. The solutions of those methods are compared among them and with the actual Plan Joffre XVII to conclude on the most suitable logic for troop allocation. Moreover, a discussion on the pertinence of the logic found as well as main implications of the proposed framework.

Keywords: Clio-combinatorics · World War I · MIP model · Hierarchical transportation problem · Retrospective analysis

1 Introduction

Logistics is an important field in research and practice, since it has many applications and contributes to the economic development of regions and countries [1]. To support logistics and supply chain management, many tools and methods can be used, among them the methods of operational research seem to have a certain diffusion and unification, mainly in research and sometimes in practice. This is the case of combinatorial optimization [2–4], today applied in both current and probably future situations.

However, in logistics but also in other fields, alternative uses of those methods and techniques can be envisaged. Since macroeconomics, microeconomics, econometrics and applied statistics have already applied to explain economic history facts and situations [7] and a relatively new field seeks to apply system dynamics and other applied mathematics methods to explain historical facts [6], operational research can play a role in the field of quantitative history, not only to explain decision logics, but also to show how those decisions would be taken differently to support future decisions [7, 8]. Indeed, operational research has many applications and visions, among then the contextual perspective [9] aims to develop methods not disconnected from the reality that aims to be represented, but related to and validated with respect to that reality.

© The Author(s), under exclusive license to Springer Nature Switzerland AG 2022
J. C. Figueroa-García et al. (Eds.): WEA 2022, CCIS 1685, pp. 265–276, 2022.
https://doi.org/10.1007/978-3-031-20611-5_23

The use of mathematical methods to solve real, practical problems is not new: we can find many mathematical frameworks, some of them now being basic notions taught at school, which were developed for practical reasons. Although the term "operations research" is associated to war with a first official mention in 1942, with the creation of military research groups on the subject, their bases and mathematical methods are more ancient, and many theories and mathematical problems of operations management derive from works developed from the 16th century [10].

Moreover, since operations research was formalized in a military context and many countries developed military universities and colleges giving military engineers a solid mathematical basis, it seems relevant to think that military strategy followed operations management and combinatorial optimization principles, and that before World War II [10].

Concerning World War I, various unanswered questions have been raised in 2014 (date of the first century of the war's beginning). One of those questions, very controversial in France, is that of troop assignment, since different regions claim being punished in the assignment of troops. Moreover, several authors state on the importance of troop allocation to the issue of the war and more precisely to the number of deaths and its geographical distribution [11]. In this context, and extending previous works [5–8], it seems interesting to explore if the troop assignment of Plan XVII followed an optimization logic, and if yes which one. This work goes beyond previous ones by a new modelling approach to troop assignment and transport, not seeing it as a classical transportation problem [12–14] either using Euclidean distances or travel times, but on the basis of a hierarchical transport problem, i.e. presenting a graph with three levels of nodes (origins, destinations and intermediary hubs).

Therefore this paper aims to question whether the French troop allocation follows any optimization logic. To do this, we define a suitable combinatorial optimization problem then solve it with a heuristic method of operational research able to be reproduced in the time of Joffre, in order to accurately reproduce the optimization logic of Plan XVII. The novelty of the proposed research is that the combinatorial optimization problem does not lead with a total optimization (i.e. finding a theoretical optimum) but on finding, from a set of possible optimization methods and procedure able to be applied in 1913, which would obtain as a solution the final Plan XVII validated by the High French Command. The paper is organized as follows: First, we present the background and context of our operation research analysis, focusing on the main assumptions made to make a quantitative representation of the troop assignment problem of Joffre. Second, we introduce the proposed methodology and explain in detail how it is articulated. Third, we propose the results of the troop allocation logic assessments and compare them. Moreover, those results are discussed on a contextual viewpoint, focusing on the pertinence of the chosen methods as well as on the possible bias that would exist when defining the French troop allocation plan. We also discuss the main implications of our results and the possible causes of divergence between the combinatorial logic of troop allocation and that of Plan XVII. Finally, the proposed methodology is generalized into an abductive path for operations research and potential applications for current and future engineering decision support are introduced.

2 Background and Context

The French Troop Allocation, called also Plan XVII or Plan Joffre (directed by Marshal Joseph Joffre) belongs to a larger defensive tactical plan resulting from seventeen other plans (two of them having respectively numbers 15 and 15 bis), which were elaborated successively between the end of the 19th century and 1913. Those plans include different tactical elements, as the choice of war fronts, the division of the French territory in military regions (mainly for soldier supply questions), troop location and allocation (infantry, both main corpses and reserve, cavalry and other specialized corpses), movement chaining, communication issues and military tactics, among others. In this paper, we focus on main infantry corpses, which constitute the basis of the French Army and, since neither having a particular specialization nor territorial specificities), can be considered as homogeneous in terms of characteristics among all the French territory.

The details of Plan XVII can be found in [16, 17], where extended summaries are provided. This plan is defensive in nature [18], and was created to contain probable German attacks on their common frontier. In 1913, the forecast of military intelligence expected those attacks only on the Franco-German border, excluding any other confrontation line [19]. The main military destinations of French troops would then be divided into five armies and located according to Table 1.

Table 1. Composition of regular infantry armies' assignment in Plan XVII, adapted from [5].

	# Army Corpses	Final destination	Stations of concentration
1st army (Dole)	5	Mulhouse and Sarrebourg	Remiremont to Charmes
2nd army (Dijon)	5	Morhange	Pont-Saint-Vincent to Neufchâteau
3th army (Châlons)	3	Metz	Saint-Mihiel to Verdun
4th army (Fontainebleau)	2	Argonne (mobile army)	Saint-Dizier to Bar-le-Duc
5th army (Paris)	5	Belgian border, Ardennes	Hirson to Dun-sur-Meuse

According to [17], the problem of troop allocation was strongly related to the transport network. Moreover, Marshall Joffre states that the troop allocation plan was mainly a question of military logistics [16]. Taking into account the geography of transport in France in 1914 [20], the only possible transport mode to deploy troops efficiently was the railway (road transport was only used to reach railway stations from origins and destinations from corresponding railway arrival stations). More details about the railway characteristics and the transportation issues are found in [5].

From the assumptions of troop transport exposed above, we can define the optimization problem for troop allocation that meets the requirements stated previously, within the constraints imposed by the railway network. It is important to begin by clarifying the decision variables. The main goal is to assign troops on a given front. The decision variable refers to the troops of each region. In this study, the selected variables are the army corps: each army corps will be assigned in its entirety to a single front, without the ability to split in order to cover several destinations.

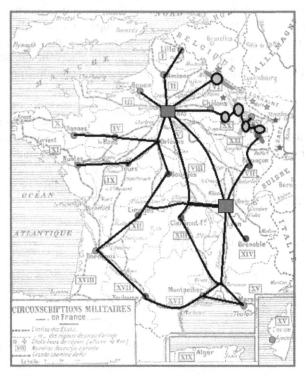

Fig. 1. Simplified railway transport network for troop deployment in 1914

Regarding optimization, to be able to make a model, it is important to first define the objective function. In this context, it seems then to be to minimize the total travel time of all troops from their origin to their destination at the front line [5, 8]. After that, it is important to set the constraints. The first and main constraint is that the assignment of troops needs to be respected. We assume that the troops' needs for each front are fully used as input. More precisely, the front is divided into 5 main areas: Belgium-Ardennes, Argonne, Mulhouse-Sarrebourg, Morhange and Metz. This choice reflects the decision of the staff to strengthen the border with Germany and therefore to concentrate troops in this area. For each of the 5 fronts identified, troops from the staff requirements are as follows: 5 corps in Belgium-Ardennes, 2 in Argonne, 5 in Mulhouse-Sarrebourg, 5 in Morhange area, and 3 in Metz, making a total of 20 corps (the region 19, Algeria, because of its remoteness, is not taken into account in this assignment of the troops). In Fig. 1 we present a simplified representation of the network that includes three types of nodes:

origins (the 20th military regions' concentration points, colored dots), intermediary hubs (grey squares), mainly at Paris and Lyon, and destinations, represented by grey circles.

To find them the best allocation of French troops, different methods can be used. We recall that the aim of this research is not to obtain the theoretical optimum but to find a possible optimization logic that would be used in 1913, among the methods either already existing or simple heuristic logics able to be applied at that time (i.e. simple moves like the nearest neighbor, which seem logic and which can be implemented without computational tools). For that reason, we will focus only on methods able to be implemented at the time of Plan XVII's construction. After a review of mathematics and OR history books, as well of several papers concerning OR and combinatorial optimization timelines, we identified the following methods and foundations. The first theoretical foundation is that of the assignment problem, which derives from the Transportation problem. This problem was already studied by Monge [12], founder of the military education patterns of French troops. Transportation problems can take different forms and be solved with different methods [13, 21–23]. However, since the most efficient methods for assignment and transportation problems were developed in the 1940's or later [10, 13], we will concentrate on possible methods (not all related directly to those problems) that were known or intuitive in 1913. Linear modelling and programming is often related to Gauss [24] and his works to solve linear equations, but known exact methods started being developed after the end of World War I [10]. This led us to two main categories of heuristic methods to be used:

- Geographic methods, issued from the works of Euler [25] and Monge [12], were at the beginning applied to continuous problems. However, set partitioning on the basis of geographic data and assignment using geographic properties seems a suitable alternative at the beginning of the 20th century.
- Greedy or nearest neighbor approaches, although formalized in the 1950's, the logic seems very intuitive: and the principle of the nearest neighbor was already known in 1913, as well as other Graph Theory principles and path construction algorithms [25].

3 Methodology

As defined in [8], we apply clio-combinatorics to the issue of troop allocation. Indeed, when dealing with military economics and management history, operations research plays an important role in the transportation of troops. More precisely, combinatorial optimization is useful to identify and analyze several military choices that have been taken from a large set of alternatives. In a way, the principle is the same as that of current combinatorial optimization (for present problems or forecasting issues), but the objectives are different. Indeed, the main aim of clio-combinatorics is not to fully optimize an organization (here, a military scheme) but to find the most suitable choice taken into account in a given historical context.

The goal of the proposed framework is to reproduce the reasoning behind a historical choice. This will be done with simple algorithms that could be actually deployed in 1913 during the preparation of war. This framework supposes that the choice and its consequences are known, i.e. we know the troop allocation plan and can reproduce it in any mathematical representation. To complete this framework, we propose here to model the location decisions via a mixed integer program (MIP), which would have been deployed in 1913 with the tools and methods available at the time and represents suitably the troop allocation problem. To do this, we report to graph theory modelling. Let us consider a set of zones representing the French territory. Each zone can be characterized by its main city (which will be the departure point of each army corps). This main city can be represented as a graph node, noted i; those nodes will take a value from 1 to 21 (identically to the number of each military region defined in Plan XVII. As said above, region 19 is not included since not being considered in the Plan XVII infantry assignment main plan. Origin nodes are then belonging to set V_O, which counts 20 nodes. The destinations are represented by the five battle-front lines, noted j (which values will be an integer number from 1 to 5). Destinations are belonging to set V_D, which contains 5 nodes. At origin, each region provides one army corps. At destination, each front line must receive a number of army corps already defined by the High French Command, noted b_j. Taking into account the railway configuration, two main concentration points, noted as hubs, are defined (one at Lyon and the other at Paris), they belong to set V_H. We note x_{ij} the binary variable that identifies if army corpse i travels from its origin to front line j directly, y_{ij} the one that states if army corpse i travels from its origin to Hub j and 0 z_{ij} the one that states if an army corpse at hub i travels from it to destination j and. In order to assign each army corps i to front line j, we need to define an optimization criterion, or objective function.

The resulting MIP formulation can be defined as follows:

$$MinZ = \sum_{i \in V_O; j \in V_D} x_{ij} + \sum_{i \in V_O; j \in V_H} y_{ij} + \sum_{i \in V_H; j \in V_D} z_{ij} \qquad (1)$$

$$\sum_{j \in V_D} x_{ij} + \sum_{j \in V_H} y_{ij} = 1; \forall i \in V_O \qquad (2)$$

$$\sum_{i \in V_O} x_{ij} + \sum_{i \in V_O} y_{ij} = b_j; \forall j \in V_D \qquad (3)$$

$$\sum_{i \in V_O} y_{ik} = \sum_{j \in V_D} z_{kj}; \forall k \in V_H \qquad (4)$$

$$x_{ij}, x_{ij}, x_{ij} \text{ binary } \forall i, j, k \qquad (5)$$

The objective function (1) is the minimization of the total transport cost. This cost can be defined in terms of distance and time. In the present case, both could be used since the travel time between two given points of the network, taken into account the railways at the time, can be set as proportional to the distance.

Constraints (2) ensure that each army corpse is assigned once and only once. Constraints (3), that each front line is supplied with the required number of corpses. Constraints (4) ensure that each army corpse passing through a hub is assigned to a front line. Equations (5) define the Boolean nature of all decision variables.

This problem is a hierarchical, derivation of the well-known transportation problem, and can be solved with the simplex method. However, in a clio-combinatorics viewpoint, the aim of the optimization here is not to find the real optimum but a near-optimal solution using a method available at the time this optimization was made, and compare the solution with the real troop allocation plan. If we solve this problem with a simplex method, we observe strong differences with the real plan, but this is due to the technological gap, which proves that in 1913 optimization tools were not ready to obtain an optimum of this problem. In [8], a first solution to this clio-combinatorics issue is proposed, but using Euclidean distances and a single-stage network. The proposed algorithm is a derivation of the well-known greedy procedure, also known as the nearest neighbour algorithm, but with an ad-hoc iterative procedure which is not intuitive, although giving satisfactory results.

Consequently, a similar approach is made here, but with a slight differences. Since two different ways to move the troops are possible (direct or using a hub) but not all the assignments allow both, the set of origins is divided in three subsets:

• The first will include the origins that need to pass through Paris, without any other possibility.
• The second contains those for which a direct transport to one of the destinations. In this case, the assignment is obvious since other possibilities suppose physically going backward to then return forward.
• The third is composed of those origins for which different possibilities are seen, without an obvious issue in terms of optimization.

Concerning destinations, previous works show that army 4 (the mobile army) presents incoherences in assignments, leading to the that this army has been assigned on another logic. However, we will not assume on a pre-assignment but on the assignment of the two army corpses for which it is more difficult or costly to be assigned to the other fronts.

Then, to start the assignment, we pre-assign set 2 (since only one assignment per origin seems logic). Then, starting by set 1 in increasing order of original numbering, a greedy procedure is applied: each origin is assigned to the closest army that is still missing troops to have a complete army). After that, we apply the same principle to set 3 but comparing assignments by Paris and assignments by Lyon (the two main possibilities) and choosing the least cost path. Finally, the two remaining armies are assigned to army 4 (the mobile one).

4   Results

We present in Table 2 the results of three French Troop allocation plans: the first is the application of the greedy algorithm presented above to the problem defined in [8], i.e. on a direct assignment based only on Euclidean distances. The second is the result of this algorithm on the problem defined above, i.e. based on an hierarchical transport network. Finally, the third corresponds to the real Plan XVII.

We observe that the direct assignment has a good correspondence (80%) with the real Plan Joffre but presents some differences, mainly Because Tours being processed before Nantes, those two assignments are exchanged. Same reasoning for Limoges and

Bordeaux. The proposed approach 90% of ocrrespondance, the only exchange being that of Tours and Nantes (only processing Nantes before Tours would lead to the same result as on Plan XVII), but not for the mobile army. Indeed, if we consider real distances and the hierarchic network, the two regions that are the most difficult to be allocated are Limoges and Toulouse. With the assumption of assigning the two remaining army corpses (not assigned because the further ones) to the mobile army, we obtain exactly the same assignment for this destination. Therefore, we found an optimization logic for the Plan XVII, the only difference could be explained by a question of time or distance estimation that would make the two assignments (Nantes and Tours) almost equivalent, but this would need further investigation.

Table 2. Main results of clio-combinatorics assessment.

Region	Main city	Direct assignment	Hirerarchical network	Real assignment
1	Lille	5	5	5
2	Amiens	5	5	5
3	Rouen	5	5	5
4	Le Mans	3	3	3
5	Orléans	3	3	3
6	Châlons	3	3	3
7	Besançon	1	1	1
8	Bourges	1	1	1
9	Tours	5	5	2
10	Rennes	5	5	5
11	Nantes	2	2	5
12	Limoges	2	4	4
13	Clermont-Ferrand	1	1	1
14	Lyon	1	1	1
15	Marseille	2	2	2
16	Montpellier	2	2	2
17	Toulouse	4	4	4
18	Bordeaux	4	2	2
20	Nancy	2	2	2
21	Épinal	1	1	1
	Gap to Plan XVII	16 (80%)	18 (90%)	-

5 Generalization of the Proposed Methodology and Its Use in Current and Future Applications

The proposed methodology and results are applied to identify and understand historical questions, and need, for a wide application on the history field, the collaboration of history experts [5]. This primary use of the methodology has a scientific and academic interest, but the proposed viewpoint and methodological path of operations research presented here has also a particular interest on current and future engineering problems and applications. This section presents a generalization of the proposed methodology on an "abductive operations research" path and its main applications.

Before presenting the proposed methodology, it is important to briefly examine the two main visions of operations research (OR). The main, dominant vision of operations research, based on mathematical modelling and problem solving via mathematical or algorithmic methods is known as "hard OR"; However, as appointed by [26, 27], those methods need to address structured, quantifiable problems. They rely mainly on the reproduction of past models (or their adaptation) and in many cases the application field is adapted to the nature and capabilities of the chosen model. That approach remains deductive in essence, so we will call those methods as *deductive OR*. In deductive OR, a mathematical model, with a mono or multli-objective function and a set of constraints is defined, then solved via various techniques of mathematical or algorithmic nature, aiming to find an optimal (solution) or near-optimal (heuristic methods) solution. However, in corporate realities, problems are not always structured, cost-oriented and quantifiable, but are more related to *"what is messy, qualitative, value loaded, and unstructured"* [26]. In those situations, other types of methods need to be deployed. That need led to the development of a set of methods that follow the same principles of operations research but which are not optimization-based, at least not on a pure mathematical optimization viewpoint. They are often grouped on the banner of Problem Structuring Methods [27, 28] since they aim at structuring the decision needs and process and propose solutions that satisfy those needs but which are not issued from an optimum search. They remain mainly qualitative (in the sense they do not use mathematical formalisms and in general not quantitative data) but follow the OR logic. Often called "soft OR", those methods are inductive by nature, so we will call them *inductive OR*. However, as appointed by [28] they are seen as opposing the deductive OR methods, and two different communities have been developed. But, as already stated by [9], in the decision analysis process and when dealing with a decision problem, both phases are important: that of understanding the problem and that of finding a solution to the problem. Deductive methods are strong to propose quantitative support to justify a solution whereas inductive ones are crucial to understand the decision problem and address it in the most suitable way. They are then not to be seen as opposing btu as complementary.

For that reason, the methodology proposed here, which addressed a known problem (since it is a historical decision situation) allowed us to think following the third path, that of abdusction, intended as the combination of induction to understand and define the problem, reducing the formalization of possibilities to a subset for which deduction becomes not arbitrary but a logic consequence, then deduction to formalize the problem and propose a first solution, and finally an iterative process of comparing the solution to the reality (needs, means, resources, methods) and eventually modifying the model and solving method to reach the most suitable solution to the problem [29]. The historical situation is a good example of how abductive OR can be applied and tested, and allows to validate the path since the final decision is known (we are dealing with a past decision and trying to reproduce its reasoning). But the methodology can be used to real decision problems (and in a preliminary way it has already started to be deployed in some situations).

If we aim to generalize the proposed method for a use in current and future situations, we can propose a general methodological canvas which can be organized in 7 stages:

1. Context definition [30], mainly built via observation, exchange with the involved stakeholders and eventually a previous documentation of the context and past decisions that have been taken in the same company or field.
2. Definition of stakeholders' goals, means and resources [30], via an enquiry in the application field (company) using both quantitative and qualitative data and information retrieval methods.
3. Problem definition, via inductive methods like problem structuring or interactive planning [26–28].
4. Transformation of the problem on a decision model, which can be quantitative (i.e. with a mathematical formalization) or qualitative (with a graphical and logical formalization of causes-effects but not a mathematical formulation).
5. Problem solving phase, which can be of two natures:

   a. If the model is quantitative, model formalization in relation with the context, then search of a solving method related to the stakeholders goals, means and resources and identification of a first solution or set of solutions via deductive methods.
   b. If the model is not qualitative (PSM), search of a satisfactory solution (i.e. an alternative) or a set of alternatives. They would be assessed via multi-criteria analysis or other deductive methods to add objectiveness to the solution choice.

6. Solution Probleming phase: Once a solution is found, it is shown to the stakeholders and analyzed by its capabilities to respond to the goals with the given means and resources. If the solution's capabilities are satisfactory, the problem can be considered as solved, if not, it is needed to go to steps 5 or 6 to review the solution or the solving method.

With this method, we avoid questioning about the suitability of the decision problem since it is assessed in seps 2 and 3. Then, the decision model (4) is by its obtention validated by the stakeholders, so considered as representing the reality and then being an opt in (with respect to the opt out phenomenon), so relevant.

Main applications are numerous, but we will remain here around transport and logistics problems. One of the first type of applications is on decentralized, multi-stakeholder, small producer supply chains, where the main supply chain management paragdigms (which imply strong degrees of integration) cannot be used. Indeed, in those supply chains, a plethora of stakeholders, sometimes who do not have an adequate mathematical background, need to collaborate and agree on solutions. The proposed approach allow to construct a common goal for those stakeholders, manage collaboration and consensus issues and propose a common decision problem. Moreover, since it will propose quantitative results, a cost-benefit reflection can be carried out, giving a standard way of justifying and validating solutions. The solutions probleming phase will then allow to ensure the acceptation of the chosen final solution.

A second group of applications deal with multi-criteria analysis (both for mono and multi-stakeholder decision support). The main limits of multi-criteria analysis are the definition of the solutions, the choice of the criteria and ensuring the coherence and relevance of the choices made to build and feed the multi-criteria choice model. Adding to that a previous problem structuring phase would reinforce the validity and the justification of the chosen criteria, the solution probleming phase made after finding a set of solution priorizations will support the acceptability and operationality of the chosen solution.

Although those are only two examples, they show the potential and the topicality of the proposed methodological path.

6 Conclusion

This paper helps to fill in part a lack of knowledge concerning the logic behind the French troop allocation at the onset of World War I. We gave evidence, in a new way, that sending troops on the front before the shock was partly guided by considerations of combinatorial optimization strategy corresponding to a mixed procedure that combines a Minimum Spanning Tree approach completed by a Nearest Neighbor assignment. Results show that the logic of assigning the most costly regions (in terms of transport) to the mobile army seems to be coherent with the final troop allocation of Plan XVII. Thus, the present work raises several practical implications. The first is the use of contextual OR in logistics management, to reproduce possible optimization logics related to military historical facts. That use of the proposed framework is applicable to historical event but its capability to explain some unanswered questions needs to be then related to the work of historians, with whom a consolidated collaboration is needed. Other military questions can be examined, like troop food supply, troop camp location or resource supply to assess whether these logistics questions had an influence on the issues of conflicts and of which nature. Another use of the proposed framework is that of reproducing transport flows in historical events, not necessarily related to military logistics. Transportation problems or vehicle routing algorithms, if contextualized, can be useful to reproduce logistics flows of ancient cities, for which partial logistics information is available. A final practical implication is the use of the proposed method, in an interactive way, for present logistics problems, like group decision in terms of urban logistics, for which the reproduction of the different choice logics of each stakeholder can be a support for communication and consensus searching.

References

1. Lambert, D.M., Stock, J.R., Ellram, L.M.: Fundamentals of logistics management, McGraw-Hill/Irwin (1998)
2. Nemhauser, G.L., Wolsey, L.A.: Integer Programming and Combinatorial Optimization. Wiley, Chichester, GL (1988)
3. Grötschel, M., Lovász, L., Schrijver, A.: Geometric Algorithms and Combinatorial Optimization, vol. 2. Springer Science & Business Media (2012)
4. Hillier, F.S.: Introduction to Operations Research. Tata McGraw-Hill Education (2012)

5. Gonzalez-Feliu, J., Ovtracht, N., Parent, A.: Gare et Front: la logique de répartition des troupes dans le plan XVII de Joffre. Revue d'histoire des chemins de fer, 50–51, 23–50 (2018)
6. Turchin, P.: Arise 'cliodynamics.' Nature **454**(7200), 34–35 (2008)
7. Kirby, M., Capey, R.: The area bombing of Germany in World War II: an operational research perspective. J. Oper. Res. Soc. 661–677 (1997). https://doi.org/10.1057/palgrave.jors.260 0420
8. Gonzalez-Feliu, J., Parent, A.: Clio-combinatorics: a novel framework to analyze military logistics choices using operations research techniques. In: Ochoa, A., Cedillo, G., Sánchez, J., Margain, L. (eds.) Handbook of Research on Military, Aeronautical, and Maritime Logistics and Operations, IGI Global, Hershey, February, p. 587 (2016)
9. Ackoff, R.L.: Optimization + objectivity = optout. Eur. J. Oper. Res. **1**(1), 1–7 (1977)
10. Gass, S.I., Assad, A.A.: An Annotated Timeline of Operations Research: An Informal History. Kluwer, Boston (2005)
11. Guironnet, J.P., Parent, A.: Morts pour la France: demographic or economic factors? Defence Peace Econom. **30**(2), 197–212 (2019)
12. Monge, G.: Mémoire sur la théorie des déblais et des remblais. Imprimerie Royale (1781)
13. Hitchcock, F.L.: The distribution of a product from several sources to numerous localities. J. Math. Phys. **20**(2), 224–230 (1941)
14. Samueli, J.J., Boudenot, J.C.: Garpard Monge et la géométrie descriptive. In 30 ouvrages de mathématiques qui ont changé le monde, ch. 17, Ellipses, Paris, pp. 231–243 (2006)
15. Gonzalez-Feliu, J.: Multi-stage LTL transport systems in supply chain management. In: Cheung, J., Song H. (eds.) Logistics: Perspectives, Approaches and Challenges, Nova Science, New York, pp. 65–86 (2013)
16. Joffre, J.: Mémoires du Maréchal Joffre (1910–1917). Tome premier, Paris : Plon (1932)
17. Le Hénaff, J.H.F.: La préparation et l'exécution d'un plan de transport de concentration (août-octobre 1914). Revue militaire française, no **10**, 62–84 (1922)
18. Bourget, P., Anthoine, P.: La «déposition» du général anthoine sur la guerre de 1914–1918. Guerres mondiales et conflits contemporains, no **156**, 105–108 (1989)
19. Audoin-Rouzeau, S., Becker, J.J. (eds.): Encyclopédie de la Grande Guerre, 1914–1918: histoire et culture. Bayard Centurion, Paris (2004)
20. Maurette, F.: Géographie de la France. Editions Hachette, Paris (1927)
21. Arnold, P., Peeters, D., Thomas, I.: Modelling a rail/road intermodal transportation system. Transp. Res. Part E **40**(3), 255–270 (2004)
22. Barnhart, C., Laporte, G. (eds.): Transportation. Elsevier. Handbooks in operations research and management science, 14, Amsterdam (2007)
23. Gelareh, S., Nickel, S.: Hub location problems in transportation networks. Transp. Res. Part E: Logist. Transp. Rev. **47**(6), 1092–1111 (2011)
24. Gauss, C.F.: Theoria Combinationis Observationum ErroribusMinimis Obnoxiae. Werke, 4, Göttingen (1826)
25. Biggs, N.L., Lloyd, E.K., Wilson, R.J.: Graph Theory 1736–1936, Oxford University Press, Oxford (1976)
26. Ackoff, R.L.: On the use of models in corporate planning. Strateg. Manag. J. **2**(4), 353–359 (1981)
27. Rosenhead, J., Mingers, J.: A new paradigm of analysis. In: Rosenhead, J., Mingers, J. (eds.) Rational Analysis for a Problematic World, 2nd edn., pp. 1–20. Wiley, Chichester (2001)
28. Mingers, J., Rosenhead, J.: Problem structuring methods in action. Eur. J. Oper. Res. **152**(3), 530–554 (2004)
29. Gonzalez-Feliu, J.: Considerations on Set Partitioning and Set Covering Models for Solving the 2E-CVRP in City Logistics: Column Generation and Solution Probleming Analysis.Logistics and Transport Modeling in Urban Goods Movement. IGI Global (2019)
30. Ackoff, R.L.: A Concept of Corporate Planning. John Wiley & Sons (1970)

Simulation

Methodology for Selecting Scenarios in Improvement Process with Multiple Performance Measures

Germán Méndez-Giraldo$^{(\boxtimes)}$ (iD)

Universidad Distrital F. J. C, Bogotá, Colombia
gmendez@udistrital.edu.co

Abstract. The Research group in Acquisition and representation of knowledge through expert systems and simulation "ARCOSES" (for its acronym in Spanish) developed a hybrid methodology composed of several techniques of Industrial Engineering to select the best scenario in a simulation process when there are multiple performance measures. This situation is typically presented in case of business improvement processes, where is necessary to balance different performance measures and in some cases, these are possibly in conflict. When these cases of multiple performance measures occur, it is possible to use different techniques such as design of experiments (DOE), simulation optimization (SO), meta models (MM) or the response surface methodology (MSR). These consist of a set of mathematical and statistical tools; their goal is to select the best solution. However, it has been found that these techniques can be difficult to implement because the analyst or decision-maker does not always have the mathematical bases or enough time for their execution. Therefore, a methodological proposal was developed, presented an implemented in a case of processes of improvement where the best solution is calculated through a standardized homogeneous rating based on the different goals to be achieved.

Keywords: Simulation experimentation · Multicriteria optimization · Response surface · Taguchi method · Output analysis

1 Introduction

When simulation is used, specifically the discrete digital simulation (DDS), it is desired to increase the understanding not only on how the real system works, but how to improve them too. It is important knowing why simulation, as a mathematical technique, has been widely used in the processes improvement; the use of simulation can move from improving a chemical process in which different batch sizes are proposed [1] to improving an emergency department to reduce the times on different stages of service by increasing more servers [2] or to improve aircraft reconditioning processes in the naval forces [3]. Nearly a million articles (993,191) are about process improvement, and most of them have been written in the last two decades. Specifically, in the last decade more than 650 thousand articles on this subject have been written and published. Not negligible is the

© The Author(s), under exclusive license to Springer Nature Switzerland AG 2022
J. C. Figueroa-García et al. (Eds.): WEA 2022, CCIS 1685, pp. 279–293, 2022.
https://doi.org/10.1007/978-3-031-20611-5_24

use of simulation to compare process improvements, since in this same period more than 10,200 articles use DDS tool in one way or another; only in the manufacturing area there are 143,732 articles in the last decade, in which the discrete digital simulation is used in 3,507 cases.

Business process improvement (BPI) can be understood as the use of different methodologies including simulation to analyze the processes and procedures that are carried out in organizations in order to identify areas in which they can improve aspects such as current accuracy, effectiveness, and efficiency; and later redesign them aiming for their improvement. Specifically, BPI tries to find ways to reduce the time it takes to complete processes, eliminate waste, improve quality of products or services, comply with rules and regulations, satisfy sales agreements, improve customer satisfaction, among many others [4, 5]. For all this, it is possible to use different methodologies using not only soft but also strong tools to support BPI's activities within a company, some of these are: Six Sigma, Lean Management, Agile Management, Total Quality Management (TQM) and Kaizen mainly. The most important thing is to indicate that, regardless of the methodology used, the BPI requires describing and documenting of the current process, analyzing it in detail, later redesigning it and finally implementing the changes [6].

Using simulation technique implies following a specific methodology, although it may vary from author to author, such as in [7–11]. When analyzing these proposed methodologies, is verified that the same steps are generally followed: 1) Define simulation goal, 2) Define and understand system, 3) Gather information and transform it into knowledge, 4) Develop a mathematical model that represents the real system 5) Translate it to a programming language, 6) Validate the model, 7) Propose solutions and improvement alternatives, 8) Document, and 9) Implement best proposal. Hence, it is very important to indicate that once a simulation goal is defined, the analyst tries to find how the system runs and fits the mathematical and computing model with the real-life system. As stated in [12], one of the first steps in any simulation study is to choose one performance measure or multiples measures to evaluate the improvement. In other words, define what measures will be used to assess how "good" the system will be. In [13] some techniques used for the validation of models of both an objective and subjective nature, where the model outputs (including its animation) compare with statistical data, and both confirm through to interviews with system experts. In the objective techniques, in addition to those already mentioned, it is possible to implement the sensitivity analysis to see how much the model reacts to parametric changes, for this is suggested implementing Turning tests and analysis of traces.

On the other hand, in [14] it is indicated that there are two types of experimentation according to its objective: 1) For comparing scenarios, that uses formal analysis based on statistics tests; or the analyst can use informal techniques based on visual analysis, comparing graphic outputs after model is executed. 2) Those of experimentation to search the best alternatives using formal techniques as experimental design (DOE), meta-modeling or optimization searches through heuristics and metaheuristics. According with [14], the search experimentation is possibly one of the most important and active areas of research within DDS, especially during the last decade, where the goal is to find the best solutions to practical problems. It is also concluded that a significant number of simulation users do not consider that search experimentation is possible since both the DOE and the use of metamodels are complex and confusing, dis du to them having a lack of knowledge of these techniques. The use of search experimentation also seems more likely to be applicable in traditional industrial simulation domains since they require, in any case, to implement the best improvement.

In general, all these statistical techniques include tools to select the best scenario. For this case, parametric values of different independent variables have the best performance of the simulated system to be implemented later in the real system. But these tools can be expensive or difficult to implement for analysts with less knowledge, as well as in case they want to improve different performance measures, or also when these have different criteria of optimization. In these cases, and in others, where the mathematics become even more complex, because they require a multi-variated function of any order, it is necessary to use partial derivatives to find a "pseudo-optimal" resolution. In any case, the random factor of these process cannot be ignored and could change the results of this techniques. All this means researchers must develop different alternatives that, although they are not considered in theoretical optimization field, do provide good approximations to these challenges.

2 Material and Methods

In [15] research from 2011 to 2015 referred, this work studied the experimentation techniques in DDS, those of search for optimal simulation, experimental design and one based on metamodels were analyzed. 348 surveys were collected with experts from both the academic and productive environments exclusively, and a third group that alternated their activities both in the academic and productive environments; it should be noted that the most used technique was optimization, closely followed by experimental design, and metamodels were used rarely; However, the use of these techniques did not reach a frequency close to half, in any case. It is also indicated that academic users utilized experimentation based on optimization in almost the same proportion as experimental design, but in the case of industry users or mixed environments users, they worked with experimental design in a greater proportion compared to optimization, and they very rarely used metamodels. Finally, when carried out with optimization techniques, most of the time, specific purpose application tools such as Arena and Simul 8 were used as opposed to general purpose languages.

To confirm the previous study, papers sampling was made in order to know what kind of experimentation is carried out in the process improvement processes; a sample of a size equal to 50 articles selected at random and whose only condition was that they use DDS for process improvement, was selected. For the analysis of the documents, they reviewed if the analyst used an experimental design methodology which answer could be (Y/N), how many performance measures and how many scenarios it performed; these last two variables were numeric variables of the kind of non-negative and integer. The results of this analysis are presented in Table 1.

Table 1. Review of the experimental design.

DOE is used?	Yes		No	
	N° Papers	%	N° Papers	%
Use of DOE	19	38	31	62
One performance measure	8	16	8	16
Two performance measure	4	8	12	24
Three performance measure	4	8	5	10
4 or more	3	6	6	12
Between 1 to 10 scenarios	4	8	29	58
Between 11 to 100 scenarios	9	18	2	4
Between 100 to 500 scenarios	4	8	0	0
More than 500 scenarios	2	4	0	0

From this sample, it can be indicated that 3 out of 5 papers (references) reviewed did not use an experiment design process (62%). Likewise, only 32% of references used a single performance measure and 32% used two performance measures, between 3 to 5 measures were 28% of the articles, and more than 5 measures only 8% of the papers. On the other hand, the use of less than 10 scenarios represented 66% of the cases, between 10 and 100 scenarios in nearly 22% of cases, 8% of papers between 100 and 500 scenarios and more than 500 scenarios only in 4% of the cases. It is important to indicate that the number of scenarios were positively correlated with the use of DOE. In contrast, the number of scenarios is highly correlated, but in an inverse way with the performance measures, this means when it used more scenarios, the analysts decided to use fewer performance measures.

Although it has been indicated that both the optimization techniques or the DOE mainly focus on the work of a single objective function and that due to the difficulty in the implementation, a generalized technique is not used when you want to work with multiple objectives, it is worth mentioning that some of the works have been proposed try to solve this gap. In [16] a variant of simulation optimization is proposed, where the authors indicate that these techniques allow finding the best values of the input variables, that is, those that most influence the response of the system and that provide the optimal conditions for the operation of the same. In other words, it allows obtaining the best combination of resources to optimize a measure of effectiveness, analyzing variation in quantity of resources while considering restrictions. Then they use multicriteria techniques to generate multiple alternatives for solving the problem and their evaluation is carried out through an AHP approach. This is validated both in [17] where a model is proposed to improve processes using the six-sigma methodology together with simulation; for all the reasons given for the little use of the DOE and the multiple difficulties in evaluating different performance measures, a methodology shown in Fig. 1 is proposed. This proposal facilitates the selection of the best alternative when multiple performance measures are presented, a situation frequently presented when approaching an improvement project in companies. To explain this methodology, each of its stages is exposed in detail.

1. *Selection of Performance Measures:* In this case, it begins with the choice of one or more performance measures by a committee of experts or by the manager of the improvement project. This must be established according to the first step of the simulation methodology, specifically when the objective of the simulation is defined. From these options, the importance values can be calculated according to the methodology proposed by Saaty in his AHP methodology, where it defines the weights for the multiple performance measures selected. It is also possible to simplify this process by defining the weight of the performance measures among the stakeholders of the improvement project, so that these can be equiprobable values or weighted to each of the performance measures defined previously. It is important to stablish the direction of the performance measure, because functions have a specific criterion that can be either maximization or minimization and that is understood here as: more-better or less-better.

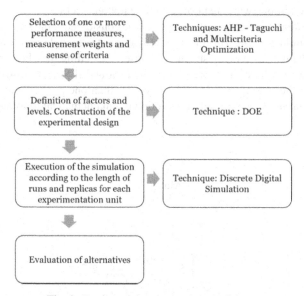

Fig. 1. Design of the proposed methodology.

2. *Analysis of the Experimental Design:* The exogenous variables that modify each one of the performance measures agreed must be selected. In this case, these factors can also be selected in the first place, based on the analyst's knowledge, and secondly on the preliminary validation tests made both in the input and output analysis. At the same time, it is necessary to define for each factor the levels or values that it

can take. Subsequently, the experimental design is carried out where it is considered that, if there are (k) factors and if the number of levels of factor (j) is denoted by $\left(n^j\right)$; the experimental unit (E_u) would then be equal to that expressed in (1) and the total experimental unit (E_t) would be that presented by (2) where the number of replicas r is necessary to considered.

$$E_u = \prod_{j=1}^{k} n^j \tag{1}$$

$$E_t = r \prod_{j=1}^{k} n^j \tag{2}$$

3. **Execute Simulation:** This is common in whatever simulation methodology but first, it must be validated with an output analysis process to determine the correlation between the model against the normal operating conditions of the real system; for this, is necessary to determine the nature of the system, if it is terminal or not; this means if there is an event called k that is repeated periodically and that marks a condition of vacuum and inactivity to the system, if this occurs it is a terminal system, otherwise it is not. Depending on the nature of the system the initial conditions (C_i), the length of each run (L) and the number of replications (r) to run, are all selected. All these conditions were mentioned in the previous section.

4. **Evaluate Alternatives:** To do that, it should be considered if the simulation is mono-criteria or multi-criteria. This means if only evaluates a single performance measure or not, in the first case the best value is chosen depending on whether the objective is to maximize where the largest value is taken and if you want to minimize, the smallest; in the second case, when it has more than one performance measure, the mathematical model described in the following mathematical relationships must be met:

$$\underset{j}{\text{Max}}\left\{TR_j\right\} \tag{3}$$

$$TR_j = \sum_{i=1}^{n} w_i Sn_i^j \tag{4}$$

$$Sn_i^j = \begin{cases} 5 - \dfrac{4 \times \left(s_i^{maxj} - s_i^j\right)}{\left(s_i^{maxj} - s_i^{minj}\right)} ifd_i^+ \\[3mm] 5 - \dfrac{4 \times \left(s_i^{minj} - s_i^j\right)}{\left(s_i^{minj} - s_i^{maxj}\right)} ifd_i^- \end{cases} \tag{5}$$

Where:

TR_j: It is the set of the totals responses or set of global ratings of all of scenarios j.

w_i: It is the weight assigned to performance measure i, with n different performance measures considered.

Sn_i^j: It is the normalized response of the performance measure i evaluated by running the scenario j with simulation parameters given by: C_i, L and r.

$s_i^{\max j}$: It is the maximum response found in the performance measure i obtained when running all the j scenarios, with simulation parameters given by: C_i, L and r.

$s_i^{\min j}$: It is the minimum response found in the performance measure i obtained when running all the j scenarios, with simulation parameters given by: C_i, L and r.

s_i^j: It is the response found of the performance measure i obtained when running the scenario j with simulation parameters given by: C_i, L and r.

d_i^+: It is the direction of the response of the performance measure i and that indicates that the more value has the response, it is better.

d_i^-: It is the direction of the response of the performance measure i and that indicates that the less valor has the response, it is better.

The last equation Eq. (5) reflects the linear interpolation that qualifies the performance measure as a function of all the responses of DOE; if the performance measure shows a positive direction, a rating of 5 is assigned and the lowest value is assigned the value of 1, while the others are calculated using this Eq. (5). In the case that the performance average has a negative direction, the lowest value is assigned a rating of 5 and the highest value a rating of 1 and the others calculated using Eq. (5). To calculate the best scenario, the ratings obtained for each performance measure in each scenario are weighted with the weights assigned to these performance measures according to Eq. (4), and from all this sum of weighted ratings the maximum value is taken.

3 Experimentation

This methodology has been successfully applied in multiple systems; as an example of the proposed methodology, a case of business process improvement is shown, thus, firstly, the most relevant aspects of the simulation methodology and secondly the proposal methodology for selecting the best scenario are showed.

1. *Description of the system:* The simulation model was applied to a pharmaceutical company, which is dedicated to conducting quality control analyzes at a microbiological, physicochemical, biological, toxicological and ecotoxicological level. It provides its services of toxicological tests to industries that manufacture products for use in the veterinary, human and agricultural fields. About 100 different tests are carried out, requiring 15 types of solutions based on two types of purified, deionized water, as well as with different pH levels. These supplies become "bottlenecks" for testing. In this paper they are denoted as type I and II solutions that are required for multiple tests, as well as for the maintenance of the vivarium or "animal houses" and non-destructive testing with different species. Every time a requirement for type I or II solutions is generated, the supply warehouse, according with the inventory level, either dispatch it or put a manufacturing order. The improvement process was to establish the best inventory policy to adjust, on the one hand, the increased demand for solutions due to the growth of the company's operations and, on the other, to reduce not only inventory costs but also the number of tests waiting for its supply.

2. *Define the objective of the simulation:* In this case it is an inventory model where you want to evaluate the best policy (Q, r) to determine the quantity to be manufactured of the two types of solutions according to the reorder point to reduce costs while

maximizing the number of work orders that fully satisfy their solutions, requirement type I or II.

3. **Get information:** In this case, the official records of consumption and supply of solutions supplied by the company's administration were taken, however, there were no statistics on how many tests and how many liters of type I or II solutions were not supplied on time. To solve this problem, the simulation model was used to determine these values and its results were validated with the expert users. Information was collected for variables and parameters according to the operation of the system such as: arrival of requirements, type of test, type of solution to be supplied, quantity required and delivered time; as well as other information associated with the inventory model as amount of solution to be produced by type, supply frequency and delivery times, costs associated with the maintenance, manufacturing, and shortages. All these costs are shown in dollars.

4. **Develop the mathematical model:** This is a hybrid system of queuing theory and stock management. The flow chart that describes the operation model is presented in Fig. 2. There is an arrival process where, according to the type of proof (PT), the solution requirement is calculated according to the p.d.f. defined in the input analysis process. Depending on the type of solution, it is analyzed whether there are stocks, and in this case the quantity of solution required is dispatched. Once the solution is fully or partially supplied, inventory levels are adjusted according to the type of mix, if the stock level is less or equal to the reorder value, a manufacturing order is issued which has a waiting time according with its lead time. Once the solution batch arrives, stock level is updated according to its type. At the end of each day of the run, the values of the different inventory costs are updated. All these parameters are given by the laboratory management and are taken into consideration.

5. **Translate the mathematical model into a programming language:** Due to the final user requirements, the simulation model was developed in the Excel application and the computer program is made using VBA macros.

6. **Validate the model:** The system is non-terminal because it operates 7×24, that is every day of the week, every hour of the day. To carry out the validation process, 90-day statistics were taken, and having the storage tanks with half capacity were considered as initial conditions. The average monthly consumption of type I and type II solutions corresponding to the company's demand were taken as performance measures; these values are in liters, and they are presented in Table 2.

It is concluded that the simulation model is valid because there is not a statistically significant difference between average results of the consumption of type I solution and type II solution in liters per month between the real and simulated scenarios.

Table 2. Simulation results.

Solution	Real		Simulated		C. I.	C. I.
	$\overline{X}$	S	$\overline{X}$	S	U. I.	U. I.
Type I	87,119.2	40,727.8	72,073.6	39,057.8	100,011.9	44,135.3
Type II	50,629.3	26,247.5	47,393.4	26,422.5	66,293.6	28,493.2

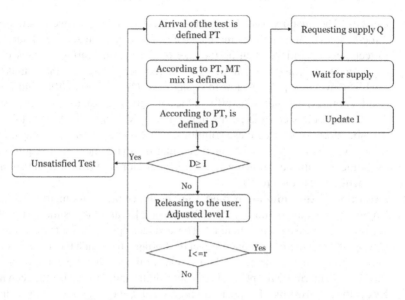

Fig. 2. Process followed in the simulation model.

7. ***Propose solutions and improvement alternatives:*** In this case that is the entire methodological process proposed, which is the objective of this document, for that reason the methodology deployment is shown step by step.

   a. **Selection of performance measures:** In this case, 3 measures were used to improve the customer service function, to reduce unsatisfied work orders, since it is a quality measure, as the laboratory does not want to have shortages in the services of supply from solutions to tests and animals' care. They were on average shortage 1065 for type I solution and 205 L for type II each month. The other two performance measures used are the total costs of the policy of inventory management and the profits generated that are affected by delays when having to make solutions at last time. The direction of each of these three performance measures is shown in Table 3.

   b. **Construction of DOE:** The description of the design of experiments is shown in Table 4. Currently there are two tanks of 5000 and 3000 L for type I and type II respectively, but these tanks could be expanded into two others of the same

Table 3. Direction of performance measures.

Performance measure	Description	Direction
1	Unsatisfied orders	(−) the less value is better
2	Inventory policy total cost	(−) the less value is better
3	Utility	(+) the more value is better

capacity. The quantity to order and the reorder points (Q, r) were determined through analytical models to find the best levels to achieve zero stockouts. Due to technical conditions such as the size of the manufacturing batches or the capacity of the equipment, it was considered percentages of these tanks for establish inventory policies. For the quantities (Q) were 30 to 40% and for the reorder point (r) between 40 to 60% of the capacity of the tanks were considered. The reorder points considered the delay in supply, that is, the time it takes for the laboratory to produce these solutions, which varies from 1 to 3 days. From these levels and factors, it is concluded that the experimentation requires 216 experiments, with the following parameters: duration (L) 90 days of 24 h, number of repetitions (r) equal to 10.

c. **Execution of the simulation model for each scenario:** As mentioned, a run length of 3 months is run, that is, 90 days of 24 h and the results of the three performance measures are obtained. These values appear in Table 5, where it is highlighted that there is a reduced level of shortage, for which the main objective of the improvement is achieved. Only a part of the results of the simulation are showed considering at the beginning, in the middle and at the end of the scenarios.

d. **Evaluation of results:** To illustrate these results, the calculation to obtain the qualification is shown indicating, for example, that since there is no shortage, all of these obtain the maximum score and the other two performance measures are evaluated according to the methodology proposed above, where the maximum and minimum values are considered. In addition, for getting the qualification for each performance measure in intermediate values, is obtained by linear inter-polation. In Table 6 this evaluation is showed specifically, the normalized total response (NTR), which correspond to the values of the same scenarios presented in Table 5.

8. Table 7 shows the 10 best scenarios according to the normalized total response. The case of using the alternative selection methodology with the proposed methodology is considered, where the first weighting is equal for each of the three performance

Table 4. Direction of performance measures.

Factor	Levels	Values
Tank capacity (in liters)	One or two tanks and their combinations	(5,000–3,000); (5,000–6,000); (10,000–3,000): (10,000–6,000)
Quantity to order Q	Based on tank size in 100-L batch multiples. 30%, 35%, 40%, for type I and 30% y 35% for type II	(30%–30%); (30%–35%); (35%–30%); (35%–35%); (40%–30%); (40%–35%)
Reorder point r	According to tank size in multiples of 100-L batch. 40%, 50%, 60%	(20%–20%); (20%–40%); (20%–60%); (40%–20%); (40%–40%); (40%–60%); (60%–20%); (60%–40%); (60%–60%)

measures (PM1 = PM2 = PM3). The second weighting is where PM1 = 2PM2 and PM2 = 2PM3, which is the point of view of the production and quality department, then it is better to choose the scenario where there are fewer shortages of solutions type I or II, since in these cases, solutions must be manufactured by the analyst with probably less standard in quality and more waiting time. The third weighting is the point of view of the finance department where PM2 = 2PM1 and PM3 = 2PM2, which means that profit and costs are more important than shortages quantities. Table 8 shows the 10 best scenarios when is used the traditional methodology only one performance measure is evaluated at a time.

Table 5. Sample of the results of the experimentation.

S	PM-1	PM-2	PM-3
1	3,128.0	17,509.8	102,521.6
2	1,165.0	31,527.5	302,840.8
3	1,136.0	39,241.2	513,402.0
4	1,843.0	47,563.2	723,885.2
5	0.5	53,340.7	938,166.8
6	0.0	54,097.3	1,161,217.6
7	1,728	58,350.6	1,380,890.3
104	0.0	471,336.0	22,492,022.9
105	0.0	472,738.0	22,678,126.2
106	2.9	471,172.0	22,929,501.9
107	0.0	472,709.0	23,160,248.2
108	0.0	474,144.0	23,362,325.1
109	1,809.0	473,694.0	23,502,603.8
110	0.8	479,407.0	23,802,697.1
210	0.0	647,174.0	46,002,079.9
211	1.0	646,761.0	46,237,125.6
212	0.0	648,355.0	46,301,754.7
213	0.0	649,731.0	46,521,640.1
214	0.3	649,620.0	46,795,712.0
215	0.0	651,100.0	47,259,980.0
216	0.0	652,441.0	47,406,447.0

Table 6. Sample of the qualification of the experimentation.

S	PM-1	PM-2	PM-3	NTR
1	1.30	5.00	1.00	2.43
2	3.60	4.91	1.02	3.18
3	3.70	4.86	1.03	3.18
4	2.80	4.81	1.05	2.89
5	5.00	4.77	1.07	3.61
6	5.00	4.77	1.09	3.62
7	3.00	4.74	1.11	2.93
104	5.00	2.14	2.89	3.34
105	5.00	2.13	2.91	3.35
106	5.00	2.14	2.93	3.36
107	5.00	2.13	2.95	3.36
108	5.00	2.12	2.97	3.36
109	2.90	2.13	2.98	2.65
110	5.00	2.09	3.00	3.36
210	5.00	1.03	4.88	3.64
211	5.00	1.04	4.90	3.65
212	5.00	1.03	4.91	3.65
213	5.00	1.02	4.93	3.65
214	5.00	1.02	4.95	3.66
215	5.00	1.01	4.99	3.67
216	5.00	1.01	5.00	3.67

Table 7. Comparison of selected scenarios with the proposal methodology.

Selection of scenarios with proposed methodology					
Weighting 1		Weighting 2		Weighting 3	
S	NTR1	S	NTR2	S	NTR3
215	3.67	215	4.43	216	3.86
216	3.67	216	4.43	215	3.85
214	3.66	214	4.42	214	3.83
211	3.65	211	4.41	213	3.82

(*continued*)

Table 7. (*continued*)

| Selection of scenarios with proposed methodology | | | | | |
| Weighting 1 | | Weighting 2 | | Weighting 3 | |
S	NTR1	S	NTR2	S	NTR3
212	3.65	212	4.41	211	3.81
213	3.65	213	4.41	212	3.81
210	3.64	210	4.40	210	3.80
208	3.63	208	4.39	209	3.78
209	3.63	209	4.39	208	3.77
6	3.62	206	4.38	206	3.75

Table 8. Comparison of selected scenarios in traditional way.

| Selection of scenarios with traditional methodology | | | | | |
| Only PM-1 | | Only PM-2 | | Only PM-3 | |
S	MD1	S	MD2	S	MD3
5	5.00	1	5.00	216	5.00
6	5.00	2	4.90	215	4.99
8	5.00	3	4.90	214	4.95
9	5.00	4	4.80	213	4.93
14	5.00	5	4.80	212	4.91
15	5.00	6	4.80	211	4.90
17	5.00	7	4.70	210	4.88
18	5.00	8	4.70	209	4.85
23	5.00	9	4.70	208	4.83
24	5.00	10	4.70	207	4.82

4 Conclusions

This hybrid methodology makes it possible to work with different performance measures, a typical situation in the improvement of business processes; in a conventional way with a single performance measurement this is "optimized" myopically. On the other hand, the methodology presented is more flexible because it can be combined with other techniques such as AHP so that preferences between performance measures can be established; Whether it is assigned in different ways such as the average or weighted values or any other form in such a way that it is respected that the sum of weights is always 1. In the applied exercise, different ways of evaluating scenarios are shown with different modalities, all of them used easily for assigning weights to performance measures. This is important for stakeholders because it allows them to reflect on different points of view of multiples decision-makers according to their objectives, which are finally reconciled according to the organization's mission or their strategic objectives.

The best options are given with the expansion of the storage capacities of type I and II solutions where, in addition to clearly improving quality aspects due to the reduction of shortages, they also allow improving storage costs, taking higher reorder points, but also with the largest production quantities. Then it is possible to get the lower total costs and improving profits because of economies of scale, as well as allowing work orders to be processed more quickly, since when the analyst require solutions of type I or II and it is not available the same analyst has to manufacture his requirement, delaying the delivery of laboratory results or delay supplies of the different species in the vivarium. It is also convenient to mention that the complete improvement exercise contemplated two other macro scenarios where the conditions of increasing demand by 10% and the second by 20% were simulated, with this the experimental design went from 216 scenarios to 648 possibilities, where the possibilities of selecting scenarios for the future were confirmed. This methodology is very easy to apply and well accepted by users who finally use it and decide with it.

References

1. Sharda, B., Bury, S.J.: Evaluating production improvement opportunities in a chemical plant: a case study using discrete event simulation. J. Simul. **6**(2), 81–91 (2012)
2. Choon, O.H., Dali, Z., Beng, P.T., Magdalene, C.P.Y.: Uncovering effective process improvement strategies in an emergency department using discrete event simulation. In: Operational Research for Emergency Planning in Healthcare, vol. 1, pp. 139–163. Palgrave Macmillan, London (2016)
3. Heath, S., Yoho, K.D.: Using simulation to illuminate process improvement opportunities in a US naval aircraft overhaul facility. Prod. Plann. Control **28**(14), 1152–1164 (2017)
4. Harrington, H.J.: Business process improvement. Association for Quality and Participation (1994)
5. Andersen, B.: Business Process Improvement Toolbox. Quality Press (2007)
6. Rashid, O.A., Ahmad, M.N.: Business process improvement methodologies: an overview. J. Inf. Syst. Res. Innov. **5**, 45–53 (2013)
7. Law, A.M., Kelton, W.D., Kelton, W.D.: Simulation Modeling and Analysis, vol. 3. McGraw-Hill, New York (2000)
8. Banks, J. (ed.): Handbook of Simulation: Principles, Methodology, Advances, Applications, and Practice. John Wiley & Sons, Hoboken (1998)
9. Fishman, G.S.: Discrete-Event Simulation: Modeling, Programming, and Analysis. Springer Science & Business Media (2013). https://doi.org/10.1007/978-1-4757-3552-9
10. Ríos, D., Ríos, S., Martín, J.: Simulación. Métodos y aplicaciones. Bogotá: Alfaomega (2000)
11. Centeno, M., Méndez, G., Baesler, F., Álvarez, L.: Introducción a la Simulación Discreta (1.ª ed., pp. 29–34). Bogotá: Universidad Distrital F. J. C. Bogotá: Universidad Distrital F. J. C (2015)
12. Nakayama, M.K.: Output analysis for simulations. In: 2006 Winter Simulation Conference, pp. 36–46. IEEE Computer Society, December 2006
13. Sargent, R.G.: Verification and Validation of Simulation Models. In: Proceedings of the 2010 Winter Simulation Conference, pp. 166–183. IEEE, December 2010

14. Hoad, K., Monks, T., O'brien, F.: The use of search experimentation in discrete-event simulation practice. J. Oper. Res. Soc. **66**(7), 1155–1168 (2015)
15. González Sánchez, C., Garza Ríos, R., Pérez Malo, E.: Enfoque híbrido simulación-proceso analítico jerárquico: Caso de estudio del rediseño de un restaurante. Revista de Métodos Cuantitativos para la Economía y la Empresa **17**, 23–41 (2014)
16. Garza Ríos, R.C., González Sánchez, C.N., Rodríguez González, E.L., Hernández Asco, C.M.: Aplicación de la metodología DMAIC de Seis Sigma con simulación discreta y técnicas multicriterio. Revista de Métodos Cuantitativos para la Economía y la Empresa **22**, 19–35 (2016)
17. Garza Ríos, R., Martínez Delgado, E.: Evaluación y selección del layout de una instalación con el empleo de un enfoque híbrido simulación multiatributo (2019)

Agent-Based Simulation Model for the Validation of an Organizational Structure Aiming at Self-organization and Increasing Agility

Paula Sofía Castro Acevedo(✉) and Luz Esperanza Bohórquez Arévalo

Universidad Distrital Francisco José de Caldas, Bogotá, Colombia
sofiacastroa090@gmail.com
https://www.udistrital.edu.co

Abstract. There are several investigations that show the incidence of the structure in the agility of the system to adapt to the changing conditions of the environment.

In the business context, hierarchical control structures predominate, which although they manage to reduce the risks derived from limited rationality, reduce the agility of the system. To date there are several investigations that show that self-organized structures increase levels of agility. However, research on self-organizing structures in the business context is in its early stages.

This research proposes a model of organizational structure that promotes self-organization. The proposed model is validated through a simulation model based on agents in which the agility to take advantage of the opportunities and threats of the environment of two organizations is compared in which the hierarchical structure predominates in one and the other favors self-organization.

The results of the simulation made it is possible to show that in environments characterized by high levels of change, the self-organized structure presents higher levels of agility.

Keywords: Agent-based simulation · Agility · Organizational structure and self-organization

1 Introduction

Agility in organizations is achieved by organizational structure as a key enabler [35, 38, 42] describes among others as organizational and structural enablers of agility, strategic orientation, business model selection, centralized or decentralized decision making and environmental scanning and control to make high-level decisions. Hierarchical control structures are those defined from organizational theory, where rules, routines, hierarchy, use of authority, span of control and roles are fully defined and restricted [14, 16]. The hierarchical structure is very efficient for performing a defined and specific task at high volume, but presents inefficiencies when the environment is changing and therefore the task must change. Several researches have shown that hierarchical structures in

© The Author(s), under exclusive license to Springer Nature Switzerland AG 2022
J. C. Figueroa-García et al. (Eds.): WEA 2022, CCIS 1685, pp. 294–309, 2022.
https://doi.org/10.1007/978-3-031-20611-5_25

highly dynamic environments such as the current ones fail to detect in a timely manner the stimuli from the environment [32] and are precarious for processing information from the environment [9]. Self-organization refers to "the spontaneous creation of a globally coherent pattern from local interactions, which has a distributed character, this organization tends to be robust and resilient to disturbances." [24]. For reference [5], self-organization occurs when the structures of a system emerge at a global and emergent level from interactions between its components.

2 Theoretical Model of Structure Self-organice

Figure 1 shows a representation of the interrelationship between these factors in a self-organized structure, with the structural factors shown in red, the dynamic factors in green and the characteristics of each of them in white.

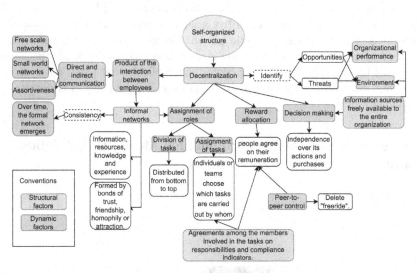

Fig. 1. Theoretical model of business structure for the promotion of self-organization [4].

2.1 Structural Features

Decentralization is a characteristic of self-organizing systems [11, 14, 22, 25, 30, 39, 44]. It is incorporated within the model as a structural feature as without this characteristic self-organization cannot develop as an emergent behavior in organizations. The interaction of its collaborators. Informal networks are the starting point in self-organizing systems for the shaping of the [19]. Informal networks are considered a structural feature because if their legitimacy and support is not guaranteed to carry out the organization's tasks, the emergence of emerging behaviors would be restricted as a necessary result to guarantee the structure's flexibility and adaptability. In the organizational context, as mentioned by the references [5, 19, 29] information is the most important input for proper decision making and knowledge development. Self-organized systems in contrast to hierarchical systems do not have one or more central controllers who coordinate, control and reward the performance of an organization's collaborators.

2.2 Dynamic Behaviors that Emerge from Structural Features

Decentralization as a structural feature allows the emergence of dynamic behaviors that empower the members of the organization to make the most appropriate decisions based on informal patterns of interaction for the assignment of roles, the allocation of rewards, decision making, and the identification and action in the face of internal and environmental threats and opportunities.

Decision-making is considered a dynamic factor in the structure model since the collaborators are empowered to make decisions about their actions autonomously but respecting the agreements among their peers. Informal networks are presented as a structural factor that models dynamic behaviors such as direct and indirect communication and formal networks. The existence of free-scale networks, small-world networks and assortiveness gives the system an agile information processing. Formal networks are considered in this model as an emerging element and therefore dynamic, because as documented by the reference [25] the conformation of roles must start from informal relationships but over time the existence of stability in these patterns is necessary to maintain performance [20].

3   Design of the Agent-Based Simulation Model for Validation of the Proposed Theoretical Model

3.1   Purpose

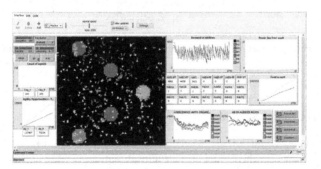

Fig. 2. Interface of netologo

For the description of the simulation model, the ODD (Overview, Design concepts, and Details) metodology proposed by [22] is used. The purpose of the simulation model is to validate the proposed theoretical model through agent-based simulation. Three theoretical proposals of agent-based simulation are taken as a basis for the design of the simulation: the one proposed by the reference [38] where two business organizations are simulated, one hierarchical and the other tending to self-organization; This proposal is taken as a basis because it covers many of the characteristics of self-organized systems, among which are decentralization in decision-making to determine whether or not to undertake joint action to take advantage of or face threats from the environment.

3.2   Objective of the Model

The objective of the simulation model in this research is to provide an experimentation tool to evaluate the proposed theoretical model to verify if its structural features increase agility in business organizations as presumed in the theory.

3.3   Main Hypothesis H0

The structure that promotes self-organization presents higher levels of agility to take advantage of the opportunities and mitigate the threats of the environment compared to hierarchical structures.

3.4   Secondary Hypotheses

H1: The structural factor dynamic roles increases agility in business organizations (Implicit in the configuration of the organization with a tendency to self-organization "Y").

H1: The structural factor decentralization increases agility in business organizations (decentralization?).

H2: The structural factor informal networks increase agility in business organizations (free-scale?).

H3: The structural factor of free and available information sources increases agility in business organizations (creation-ideas?).

H4: The structural factor agreements among the members of the organization increase agility in business organizations (retribution: constant o comission).

The simulation model starts from five main entities. Two breeds of agents in netlogo syntax, the agents of breed "r" and the agents of breed "y", a third entity corresponding to the opportunities, a fourth corresponding to the threats, a fifth to the environment or the "patch" in netlogo syntax and finally the links or "links|". The structure of the |configuration of the entities is based on the simulation model proposed by the reference [37].

3.5   Agents of the "R" Breed

The agents of breed "r" correspond to the set of collaborators of the hierarchical organization. This breed of agents is organized in groups of 10 agents where one of them is the leader and authorizes or disallows the actions of the other agents in the group. The agents of this breed have Netlogo's own state variables such as identification (who), color (color), heading (heading), among others. Others from Posada's (2018) model are included, such as the binary variable (is-carring?) that indicates whether the agent is bringing an opportunity to its organization, the energy level (energy) that indicates the amount of resources the agent has to stay alive, the binary variable (is-approaching?) that allows establishing whether the agent is in the direction of attending to an opportunity or a threat, the binary variable (is-confronted? which allows to establish whether the agent is involved in confronting a threat at that moment, the altruism level variable (altruism) which is an intrinsic characteristic of the agent related to the tendency towards the benefit of the organization, the identification or (who) of the leader of his group (leader-id), the (confidence-table) which is a table where the identification of the agents that make up his group and the level of confidence associated with each one of them is stored.

3.6   Agents of the "Y" Breed

The agents of breed "y" correspond to the set of collaborators of the organization for the promotion of self-organization. In terms of attributes it has the same Netlogo's own as those described for breed "r". From the reference [37] model, the same attributes of the "r" breed are included, including (altruism), which is a characteristic of the agents that indicates the tendency to be guided by common interests for the organization or by their own interests, the attribute (is-approaching) that indicates whether the agent is heading to attend the request for help from another member of its organization, the attributes (xsrc and xsrc) that store the location of a food source to communicate it to other agents of its organization. Also included is the list of attributes (lh-y) that indicate the level of development of the agent's skills and identifies it and the list of attributes (lhc-y) which indicates the level of resources that have been reached by the agents involved in a joint action to send the information to other agents that may join.

3.7   Opportunities

Opportunities are a variety of agent that remain static in the simulation environment. They represent large sources of resources that require the joint action of several agents in order to be taken and exploited within the organization. The opportunities are configured differently depending on the level of resources they can offer to the organization and the level of requirements they have to be exploited. This entity has the level of skill required for each of the skills considered (S-ability) and the auxiliary variables (S-ability-T, S-ability-R and S-ability-Y) are included to make comparisons between the skill levels required and those provided by the agents of the business organizations.

3.8   Threats

The threats are agents that can move through the environment and have the purpose of attacking or taking energy away from the members of the organizations, any of them. A threat can be countered by the intervention of several agents from any of the organizations. To achieve this purpose, the agents must all meet the ability requirement of the threat. This entity has as state variables Netlogo's own variables. From the reference [37] proposal they have the energy level variable (energy) that indicates the amount of resources that the threat has to stay alive, the binary variable (is-confronted?) that allows to establish if the threat is involved in confrontation with an agent at that moment.

3.9   Spatial Units or "PATCHES"

For this particular case, the spatial unites fulfill three main purposes: they indicate the location of the facilities of each of the organizations or nests, they also determine the location of small food sources that can be used individually by the agents of the organizations and they keep relevant information about the interactions of the agents and other agents of the simulation. From the above, the state variables associated with the patches are netlogo's own such as (pcolor) which indicates the color of the patch, this variable allows identifying if the patch belongs to a nest, to a food pile or is a common patch (black) according to its color. The reference [37] adds for patches state variables such as (food) which indicates the amount of individual resources in that patch, (food-source-number) which is an identifier for each of the food piles, the variables (r-nest? and y-nest?) which are two binary variables that determine whether or not that patch belongs to each of the organizations, the variables (r-nest-scent) and (y-nest-scent) are pheromone indicators or information sent by the nest so that agents belonging to an organization can locate it, (spiders-attack) is a variable that allows calculating the attack of the threats and (ants-counterattack) that calculates the attack level of the group of ants.

3.10   Links

The link are a type of agent that allows to link or indicate a relationship and in this particular case that there is a trust relationship between two agents of the "and-ant" type, this type of agents are included to model the free scale network that is the configuration of the agents of the organization with a tendency to self-organization. The links have for this case only Netlogo's own state variables such as color (color), whether or not it is visible (hidden?), shape (shape), among others. In this particular case, the most interesting variables are (end1 and end2) that besides identifying the link, store the information of the two "and-ant" type agents that are connected. The mechanism is repeated in the same way for all agents until the whole population is completed. The scale-free law used for this model is presented in Fig. 3

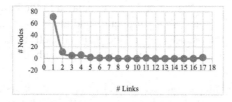

Fig. 3. Informal network power law

3.11   Variables Input Variables for the Evaluation of the Theoretical Model

Taking into account that the purpose of this simulation is the evaluation of each of the structural features of the proposed theoretical model in stable and dynamic environments.

Binary buttons were configured to enable or disable each of these behaviors, which in turn are associated with different methods that configure the simulation differently. The "free-scale?" button is related to the informal networks structural feature and has the methods "if-alone-find-partner", "find-partner", "create-link-setup", "setup-confidence-table-links-and-ants" and "create-link-join-action" The "decentralization?" button is associated with the decentralization feature and modifies the decision functions in the "help-contacts" and "help-request" methods. The "creation-ideas?" button is related to the feature free and available sources, and is associated with the methods "create-forage" and "setup-leader-id-y-ants". The "retribution" button is related to the feature agreements between members of the organization and has the "sum-forces" method associated with it. Finally, the "environment-dynamic?" button configures whether the environment is static or dynamic and is associated with the "environment-power-law" method.

Output Performance Variables

Finally, the model has as performance variables variables (wtd-scs-opp-r), (wtd-scs-opp-y) (wtd-scs-thr-r) and (wtd-scs-thr-y) calculate the number of opportunities and threats for each organization weighted by the required skill levels. The variables (wtd -opp-total) and (wtd -thr-total) calculate the total opportunities and threats weighted by the skill levels that occurred during a simulation run.

$$AgilOrgY = \frac{(wtd - scs - thr - y) + (wtd - scs - opp - y)}{(wtd - opp - total) + (wtd - thr - total)} \tag{1}$$

$$AgilOrgR = \frac{(wtd - scs - thr - r) + (wtd - scs - opp - r)}{(wtd - opp - total) + (wtd - thr - total)} \tag{2}$$

3.12 Process Scheduling

This section initially describes the main simulation methods of initialization and execution called "SETUP" and "GO" in the syntaxis of netlogo.

Method of Initialization

The method of initialization "To setup" was associated to the bottom "Setup" and has the purpose of initializing the initial parameters and methods of the simulation model. This section describes the pseudocode of the method itself, in the *ANNEX A*, a list is presented with the description and pseudo-code of the methods associated with it.

1. It initializes the global variables as internal variables and calls the method "sentido" which initializes the global variables "H-ACTIVE" and "H-quantity".
2. Then, if the parameter "free-scale? "is active, through the "born-y-ants" methods, two agents of this organization are created and a link is created between them and through a "while" command a number of "population"-2 agents is created iteratively, where each time a new agent is created, a new link is created with the "create-link-setup" methods and when all the agents are created, their contact list is built and the leaders are assigned through the "setup-confidence-table-links-y-ants" and "setup-leader-id-y-ants" methods.

3. The opportunities are generated by calling the regenerate-forage method with parameters "frg_cant" of 10 and "setuporgo" of 0. Variables that are identified as evaluation are initialized with a value of 0.
4. The variables identified as evaluation variables are initialized with a value of 0.
5. The "regenerate-spiders" method is called to initialize the threats.
6. The "setup-patches" method is called to configure the patches.
7. Initialize the time or "Ticks" by means of the netlogo command "reset-ticks".

Method of Execution or Associated with the "GO" Button
The method associated to the execution o "To go" method in the sintaxis of netlogo aims at programming the commands to be executed each time a discrete unit of time or tick occurs. This section describes the pseudocode of the method itself, in the ANNEXES B to G a list is presented with the description and pseudo-code of the methods associated with it.

1. If the number of agents in organization "Y" is 2, if there are no agents in organization "R" or if the ticks are greater than 15000, the time or "ticks" stops.
2. If the number of agents of both organizations divided by the number of threats plus one unit is greater than 100, the "regenerate-spiders" method is activated.
3. If the "free-scale?" option is active, the number of agents of the "Y" organization is less than the "population" population and if the number of food quantity of the "Y" organization is greater than zero, a new Y agent is created by means of the "born-y-ants" method. After that, a link is randomly created with another existing agent by means of "create-link-setup", its contact list is updated and a contact is assigned as in the "setup" method.
4. If the sum of the "food" variable of all the patches is less than 1, the "setup-food" and "recolor-patch" methods are called which remake the depleted food stacks.
5. If the number of opportunities is less than 15, the "regenerate-forage" method is activated with parameters "frg_cant" equal to 5 and "setuporgo" equal to 1.
6. Agents in the "R" organization are called "ask r-ants" command. If the agent ID "who" minus the population "population" is greater than or equal to the current tick and less than half the population, the agent must stop, this part of the code allows the agents in the first ticks to leave one by one. If the agent parameter "is-confronted?" is active, it identifies if the agent is a leader and calls the other agents in its group for help via the "help-contacts-r threat" method, if it is another agent, the "help-boss" method is used.
7. Agents in the "Y" organization are called by the "ask y-ants" command. If the agent ID "who" minus the population "population" is greater than or equal to the current tick and less than the population, the agent must stop, this part of the code allows the agents in the first ticks to exit one by one. If the agent parameter "is-confronted?" is active, the other agents in its group are called for help via the "help-contacts threat" method, if it is another agent it uses the "help-boss" method. In case it is not in a confrontation, if the "is-carrying?" variable is active the "carriyng-y-ants" method is activated and in case it does not have this parameter active, the amount of "LH-Y" skill is decreased

8. Threats are called by means of the "ask spiders" command. After that, the "catch-r-ant" and "catch-y-ant" methods are called. If the threat has the "is-confronted?" parameter active, the "confronted-spiders" method is called. In case this parameter is not active, the "move" method is called, its energy level is decreased through "set energy energy − 1" and if the energy level becomes negative, it dies.
9. If the "creation-ideas?" parameter is active and the number of ticks is greater than 200. If the "free-scale?" parameter is also active, the "identify_creator_fs" method is called and in case "free-scale?" is not active, the "identify_creator_nfs" method is called.

4   Validation of the Simulation Model

Therefore, a shorter fractional factorial experiment (Type V) of 128 combinations was chosen and 30 replicates were made of each combination. According to the analysis of variance provided by the statistical software minitab, it could be established that the significant variables to explain the agility of organization Y are: "Population" "environment-dynamic?", "free-scale?", "creation-deas?" and "unlearning" for having "p-values" lower than 0.05 with a significance level of 95%, and that the model as a whole explains 89.9% of the variance. These results, where it can be concluded that most of the internal variables are not significant, an effect that is coherent with the proposed design since these variables were used within the simulation model as auxiliary variables that are necessary to represent the methods and/or behaviors, but do not seek to generate effects on the Agile org Y (1) response variable.

Table 1. Variables and levels factorial design of experiments (full) 6 variables debugged. Own elaboration

Variable	Min	Max
enviroment-dynamic?	0	1
Population	50	200
free-scale?	0	1
descentralization?	0	1
Creation-ideas?	0	1
unlearning	0.23	1

However, since most of the main factors are not significant, it was decided to conduct a new experiment with the purification of the previous one, taking the significant variables, together with the decentralization variable, since it is of interest to the research, with the same minimum and maximum levels of the previous experiment (Table 1). The trait retribution is not considered in the analysis because it is much farther away from the F value of significance and therefore it is concluded that the way in which the retribution is carried out from the design that was proposed has no effect on the behavior of agility.

In this case, since there are only six variables, it was decided to perform a full factorial analysis of 64 configurations with all possible combinations between factors, and 10 replications were made for each of them. As for the non-significant variables, constant values were assigned. At this point it is important to note that when either of the two populations was extinct, the agility variable was taken as zero in both organizations, since the comparison is not beneficial if there is no competition.

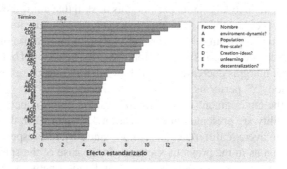

Fig. 1. Pareto diagram of effects factorial experiment (complete) 6 variables

The Fig. 5 shows the p-values of the analysis of variance obtained in minitab for the refined experiment of 6 variables, in this experiment interactions between factors of up to 4 combinations were reviewed. According to the results, it was possible to establish that in this case all the main variables to be studied (blue and green in) were significant because they have values less than 0.05 with a significance level of 95% and therefore have an impact on the response variable.

Regarding the residuals (Fig. 2), it is evident that they are random with a histogram of central tendency and that they fit closely to a normal behavior, which indicates that the runs do not follow patterns in their results.

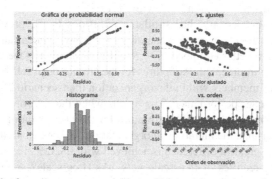

Fig. 2. Residual plot for agile response variable org Y factorial experiment (complete) 6 variables

5 Evaluation of Simulation Scenarios

The third scenario is the one configured for a population of 200 individuals with a level of unlearning of 0.23. According to the information gathered, it was possible to establish that when the population level is increased (100% compared to scenario 2) the probability of the organizations becoming extinct is still very low (2 out of 160, 1.25%), which indicates that in this case (as in scenario 2) the existence of more individuals in the organizations allows the existence in general terms of the minimum skill levels for them to find within their collaborators the amounts of skill that allow the consumption of resources to be lower compared to those that they manage to capture for the organization. The conclusions obtained from this scenario are very similar to those of scenario 2: the same patterns are repeated in terms of the difference in the behavior of both organizations, but in this case the margins decrease, which shows that the structure for the promotion of self-organization "Y" performs better in this scenario.

Thus, when the environment is configured as static (environment-dynamic? = 0, lower levels of agility are presented in organization "Y" than when the environment is dynamized with an average difference of 444.369 and 464.132 respectively, obtaining the same conclusion as in the previous scenario. In the case of the static environment, when the structural features free-scale and decentralization networks are active (free-scale? = 1, decentralization? = 1) the hierarchical organization performs better than the structure for fostering self-organization by a low margin of 6%, indicating that in this scenario the mentioned structural factors still largely limit the performance of the structure for fostering self-organization (configuration 6) as in scenario 2. In this case, agility starts to increase for the structure for fostering self-organization to the extent that the other structural features are active within the organization. Thus, the largest difference in agility is obtained when all structural features are active with a difference of 53.45%, in second place the combination of features idea generation (creation-ideas? = 1) and free-scale networks (free-scale? = 1) with 52.23%, in third place is idea creation (Creation-ideas? = 1) with 20.26%, the fourth place, with 18.87%, occurs when the traits creation-ideas and decentralization are active in combination; followed by the fifth place, with 15.13%, when all the traits are inactive or only the dynamic roles are active; finally in the sixth place, decentralization? = 1 with 15.11%.

Consequently, this scenario has similar conclusions to the previous one where, despite the fact that no changes are generated in the environment and that hierarchical organizations are better equipped in terms of skill inputs to face the opportunities and threats of the environment, the structures for the promotion of self-organization, with a greater number of members within the organization than scenario 2, manage to adapt better and have a better performance. The results when the environment is configured as dynamic, show that in all cases the structure for the promotion of self-organization "Y" performs better than the hierarchical organization "R". When all the structural features are active, the greatest difference is achieved with 68.32%, in second place is the combination of the features of free-scale networks (free-scale? = 1) and creation of ideas (Creation-ideas? = 1) with 67.11%, followed in third place by the combination of creation of ideas (Creation-ideas? = 1) and decentralization (decentralization? = 1) with 34.93%. This was followed in fourth place by creation-ideas? = 1 with 30.52%; in fifth place by dynamic roles with 30.42%; in sixth place by decentralization? = 1 with 26.69%; in seventh place by free-scale networks (free-scale? = 1) with 19.58%; and finally, the combination of free-scale networks (free-scale? = 1) and decentralization (decentralization? = 1) with 17.25%. According to these results it can be established that to a greater or lesser extent all structural traits improve agility in business organizations and that if they are applied in combination the best performance is achieved with greater impacts in dynamic environments. In scenarios 4 to 9 the probability of extinction is very high and therefore they are not considered for the analysis.

The Table 2 shows a summary of the results of the agility variables, resource appropriation and the difference for each of the organizations in the evaluation runs shown in this chapter. In addition, a percentage comparison of the results with respect to the maximum value of each variable is shown. The table shows a heat map showing the configurations with the best results for the variables analyzed (green), those with intermediate values (yellow), and the configurations with the lowest results (red). It can be seen, for example, that the variations in the hierarchical structure "R", being a standard organization, change very little if they share the same environment, whether static or dynamic. On the contrary, in the self-organized structure "Y", which is influenced by the factors studied, these percentages are more variable.

Table 2. Results and percentage comparison of agility and resource appropriation for the relevant scenario configurations. Own elaboration

	AGILITY		RESOURCES		% of Difference from the maximum result			
	Agil R	Agil Y	Re-sources Y	Resources R	Dif Agil (Y-R)	% Dif agil	% Rec Y	%Rec R
C1	389.823	611.111	125.100	6.124.783	221.288	18%	31%	92%
C2	402.829	465.962	5.625.703	6.657.527	63.133	5%	19%	100%
C3	386.276	691.991	10.082.369	6.020.637	305.715	25%	34%	90%
C4	398.054	644.491	8.573.562	6.245.979	246.437	20%	29%	94%
C5	384.286	1.591.145	29.284.282	6.069.100	1.206.859	100%	100%	91%
C6	402.841	488.708	5.786.941	6.315.238	85.867	7%	20%	95%
C7	389.988	644.039	9.970.906	5.841.647	254.051	21%	34%	88%
C8	386.418	1.558.018	28.936.346	5.982.822	1.171.600	97%	99%	90%
MAX	402.841	1.591.145	29.284.282	6.657.527	1.206.859			
C9	196.119	498.398	5.872.134	715.602	302.279	28%	23%	39%
C10	188.587	393.908	3.919.583	846.872	205.321	19%	16%	46%
C11	186.812	509.543	6.368.829	844.908	322.731	29%	25%	46%
C12	218.108	494.610	6.332.839	1.198.303	276.502	25%	25%	65%
C13	224.154	1.266.269	23.405.641	1.581.923	1.042.115	95%	94%	86%
C14	248.502	462.597	4.772.895	1.702.889	214.095	20%	19%	92%
C15	190.132	538.943	7.191.506	846.713	348.811	32%	29%	46%
C16	250.699	1.345.016	25.024.391	1.848.887	1.094.317	100%	100%	100%
MAX	250.699	1.345.016	25.024.391	1.848.887	1.094.317			

In the review of the levels of agility of the organization with a tendency to self-organization "Y", it is identified first of all that the configurations from 1 to 8 that correspond to a static environment in global terms had lower results than the configurations from 9 to 16 that correspond to the dynamic environment. Regarding the static scenario, it is observed that in all configurations the organization with a tendency to self-organization "Y" had a higher level of agility than the hierarchical organization "R", this result contradicts the theoretical assumption that in static environments hierarchical organizations have a higher performance, Similarly, it is observed that the structural feature that provides lower levels of agility is the one corresponding to configuration 2 when only free scale networks are active, which is consistent with the theoretical review where it is evident that this type of networks delay the actions of the organization unnecessarily because the environment does not change. As for the configuration with the best results with respect to agility, it is evident that it corresponds to number 5 when the traits creation of ideas are active, which is the one with the best individual results together with free scale networks, which shows that the trait free scale networks individually is not relevant, but that it strengthens the creation of ideas. In the analysis of the dynamic environment, it is evident that the lowest result as in the static environment configurations is when only scale-free networks are present, but when the other structural traits are applied together, the results are the highest possible.

6 Discussion and Conclusions

The experimentation through the agent-based simulation environment reveals that organizations for the promotion of self-organization are by a wide margin of difference more agile than traditional hierarchical structures, since as evidenced by the results of the experimentation, they manage in dynamic environments on average to act against 80% of the opportunities and threats of the environment which is 68% higher than the results obtained by the hierarchical organization. Similarly to the dynamic environment and contrary to the results of the reference [38] and the reference [32], among other authors, who state that in static environments hierarchical organizations are more agile; the organization with a tendency to self-organization presents higher results than the hierarchical one facing on average 78.3% of the opportunities and threats of the environment, which is 53% higher than the level of agility of the hierarchical organization. The above results show that according to this research in static environments the organization with a tendency to self-organization manages to adapt and maintain itself through innovation and the creation of new projects since it is the trait that most impacts agility with a difference of 52% in the levels of agility but informal networks and decentralization limit its behavior reaching in this case to have better results the hierarchical organizations.

Thus, it was found that all the proposed traits, with the exception of retribution, contribute positively to the improvement of agility in business organizations. From the literature review, it is interpreted that the pay factor has no effect on agility because variables related to the motivation of the individual as a dynamic variable that shapes the decisions of the members of an organization are not considered. As for the other factors, it is established that the creation of ideas adjusted to the changing conditions of the environment have the greatest impact on agility, and that free-scale networks together with decentralization enhance this impact, with free-scale networks being more relevant. As for decentralization, bearing in mind that this parameter changes the decision function for the agents with respect to the weight they give to the opinion of the leader, in the context of this simulation, when the feature free-scale networks is active, the agents with more connections and therefore greater possibilities of convening are assigned as leaders. Thus, this assignment is changeable and decentralized, which may indirectly affect the feature free-scale networks despite the fact that the radio button is only limited to the decision function in terms of leader weight.

In this way, it was verified that all the proposed traits, with the exception of retribution, contribute positively to the improvement of agility in business organizations. From the review of the literature, it is interpreted that the compensation factor has no effect on agility since variables related to the motivation of the individual are not considered as a dynamic variable that shapes the decisions of the members of an organization. As for the other factors, it is established that the creation of ideas adjusted to the changing conditions of the environments are the ones that have the greatest impact on agility, and that free-scale networks together with decentralization enhance this impact, being more relevant that of scale-free networks. Regarding decentralization, bearing in mind that this parameter changes the decision function for the agents regarding the weight they give to the opinion of the leader, in the context of this simulation when the scale-free networks trait is active they are assigned as leaders the agents who have more connections and therefore greater chances of being called. In this way, this assignment is changeable and decentralized, which can indirectly affect the free-scaling networks trait even though the option button is only limited to the decision function regarding the weight of the leader.

It is also highlighted that the best result in terms of agility is achieved when all the features studied are jointly incorporated, including that of dynamic roles that are implicit in the configuration of the structure tending to self-organization. This result validates the hypothesis that the model for promoting self-organization is more agile in dynamic environments. Regarding the working hypotheses that were built for the simulation model, all are validated in the same way with the exception of hypothesis 4 related to remuneration. Regarding static environments, it is surprising in this research that companies with a tendency to self-organization present higher levels of agility than hierarchical organizations, which contradicts the findings in the literature consulted. Thus, it is necessary to further investigate the implications of this result. However, this finding can be interpreted from two perspectives, the first is that the structure with a tendency to self-organization in this simulation also manages to adapt to constant conditions and the second, that the statement that hierarchical organizations are more agile that those tending to self-organization in static environments is based on empirical evidence on the study of only this type of organization, since the structures tending to self-organization did not exist in this context.

Thus, it stands out as the most relevant emerging element, the reconfiguration of the organizational structure under the application of informal networks, where it is evident that the constant interaction of the agents reduces the scale of the network in such a way that the Agents that are initially more connected end up reducing their level of connectivity. On the contrary, the agents that had a few connections at the beginning due to acting in joint actions to take advantage of the opportunities and threats of the environment, in the end manage to connect with a greater number of agents, changing the topology of the network to a stable form. Which indicates the formalization as a result of interactivity and not as an external decision, as occurs in hierarchical structures.

References

1. Aghina, W., De Smet, A., Weerda, K.: Agility: It Rhymes with Stability. McKinsey on Organization: Agility and Organization Design, McKinsey & Company May 2016
2. Barabasi, A.-L., Albert, R.: Emergence of scaling in random networks. Science **286**, 509–512 (1999). https://doi.org/10.1126/science.286.5439.509
3. Bianconi, G., Mulet, R.: On the flexibility of complex systems. arXiv preprint cond-mat/0606237 (2006)
4. Bohorquez-Arévalo, L.E., Castro-Acevedo, P.S.: Structure and fostering entrepreneurial self-organization: an approach from the concept of agility. In: Innovation and the Digital World.

Influence of Agile Structures and Intellectual Capital. Barranquilla, Editorial Uniautónoma (2020). http://hdl.handle.net/11619/3985

5. Bonabeau, E., Dorigo, M., Théraulaz, G.: Swarm Intelligence: From Natural to Artificial Systems. Oxford University Press, New York (1999)

6. Bonabeau, E., Meyer, C.: Swarm intelligence a whole new way to think about business. Harvard Bus. Rev. 106–114 (2001)

7. Broekstra, G.: Complexity is a consequence of living in a Sandpile world. In: Building High-Performance, High-trust Organizations Decentralization 2.0, pp. 1–23. Palgrave Macmillan UK, London (2014). https://doi.org/10.1057/9781137414724_1

8. Casciaro, T., Lobo, M.S.: When competence is irrelevant: the role of interpersonal affect in task-related ties. Adm. Sci. Q, 53(4), 655–684 (2008). https://doi.org/10.2189/asqu.53.4.655. https://doi.org/10.2189/asqu.53.4.655

9. Castro Acevedo, P.S., Bohórquez Arévalo, L.E.: Self-organized structures, control hierarchy and information processing agility. Entrepr. Dim., 16(1), 117–134 (2018). https://doi.org/10. 15665/dem.v16i1.1483

10. Charbonnier-Voirin, A.: The development and partial testing of the psychometric properties of an organizational agility measurement scale. Management 14(2), 119–156 (2011). https:// management-aims.com/index.php/mgmt/article/view/4058

11. Cosh, A.; Fu, X., Hughes, A.: Organizational structure and innovation performance in different environments. Small Bus. Econ. 39 (2012). https://doi.org/10.1007/s11187-010-9304-5

12. Christensen, C.M.: The Innovator's Dilemma: When New Technologies Cause Great Firms to Fail. Harvard Business School Press, Boston (1997)

13. Davis, G.F.: Do theories of organizations progress. Organ. Res. Methods 13(4), 690–709 (2010)

14. Di Marzo Serugendo, G., Gleizes, M.-P., Anthony, K.: Self-organization in multi-agent systems. Knowl. Eng. Rev. 20 (2005). https://doi.org/10.1017/S0269888905000494.

15. Eisenhardt, K.M., Furr, N.R., Bingham, C.B.: ENCRUCIJADA-Microfoundations of performance: Balancing efficiency and flexibility in dynamic environments. Organ. Sci. 21(6), 1263–1273 (2010)

16. Feld, S.L.: The focused organization of social ties. Am. J. Sociol. 86, 1015–1035 (1981)

17. World Economic Forum: The future of jobs (2016). https://es.weforum.org/reports/the-fut ure-of-jobs

18. Gentile-Lüdecke, S., Torres de Oliveira, R., Paul, J.: Does organizational structure facilitate incoming and outgoing open innovation in SMEs? Small Bus. Econ. 55(4), 1091–1112 (2020)

19. Gulati, R., Nohria, N., Zaheer, A.: Strategic networks. Strat. Manag. J. 21, 203–215 (2000)

20. Gulati, R., Puranam, P., Tushman, M., Soda, G., Zaheer, A.: A network perspective on organizational architecture: performance effects of the interplay of formal and informal organization. Strateg. Manag. J. 33 (2012). https://doi.org/10.1002/smj.1966

21. Grimm, V., Berger, U., DeAngelis, D.L., Polhill, J.G., Giske, J., Railsback, S.F.: The ODD protocol: a review and first update. Ecol. Model. 221(23), 2760–2768 (2010)

22. Hamel, G.: General management: first, let's fire all the managers. Harvard Bus. Rev. 89. 48-+(2011)

23. Heylighen, F.: The growth of structural and functional complexity during evolution. Evol. Complex. 8, 17–44 (1999)

24. Holbeche, L.: Organizational effectiveness and agility, J. Organ. Effect. People Perform. 5 (2018). https://doi.org/10.1108/JOEPP-07-2018-0044

25. Jobidon, M.-E., Turcotte, I., Aubé, C., Labrecque, A., Kelsey, S., Tremblay, S.: Role variability in self-organizing teams working in crisis management. Small Group Res. 48 (2016) https:// doi.org/10.1177/1046496416676892

26. Kilduff, M., Tsai, W.: Social Networks and Organizations. Sage, London (2003)

27. Kilduff, M., Krackhardt, D.: Interpersonal Networks in Organizations: Cognition, Personality, Dynamics, and Culture (Vol. 30). Cambridge University Press (2008)
28. Kolb, D.A.: Experiential Learning: Experience as the Source of Learning and Development. Prentice Hall, New York (1984)
29. Maldonado, C.E., Gómez-Cruz, N.A.: The world of complexity sciences. An investigation on what they are, their development and possibilities. Research papers, Universidad del Rosario (2010). www.urosario.edu.co/Administracion/ur/Investigacion/Centro-de-Estudios-Empresariales-para-la-Perdurabi/LMyS/Documentos/El-Mundo-de-las-Ciencias-de-la-Com plejidad.pdf
30. Martela, F.: What makes self-managing organizations novel? Comparing how Weberian bureaucracy, Mintzberg's adhocracy, and self-organizing solve six fundamental problems of organizing. J. Organ. Des. **8**(1), 1–23 (2019). https://doi.org/10.1186/s41469-019-0062-9
31. Marhraoui, M.A., Manouar, A.E.: IT-enabled organizational agility –proposition of a new framework. J. Theor. Appl. Inf. Technol. **95**, 5431–5442 (2017)
32. Mintzberg, H.: An emerging strategy of "direct" research. Adm. Sci. Q. **24**(4), 582–589 (1979)
33. Newman, M.: Assortative mixing in networks. Phys. Rev. Lett. **89**, 208701 (2002). https://doi.org/10.1103/PhysRevLett.89.208701
34. North, M.J., Macal, C.M.: Managing Business Complexity: Discovering Strategic Solutions with Agent-Based Modeling and Simulation. Oxford University Press, Oxford (2007)
35. Overby, E., Bharadwaj, A., Sambamurthy, V.: Enterprise agility and the enabling role of information technology. Eur. J. Inf. Syst. **15**(2), 120–131 (2006)
36. Patri, R., Suresh, M.: Modelling the enablers of agile performance in healthcare organization: a TISM approach. Glob. J. Flex. Syst. Manag. **18**(3), 251–272 (2017)
37. Posada, J.: Design of an agent-based simulation for enterprise self-organization. Master's thesis. Universidad Distrital Francisco José de Caldas. Bogotá, Colombia (2018)
38. Sherehiy, B., Karwowski, W., Layer, J.K.: A review of enterprise agility: concepts, frameworks, and attributes. Int. J. Ind. Ergon. **37**(5), 445–460 (2007). https://doi.org/10.1016/j.ergon.2007.01.007
39. Tallon, P.P., Queiroz, M., Coltman, T., Sharma, R.: Information technology and the search for organizational agility: a systematic review with future research possibilities. J. Strat. Inf. Syst. **28**(2), 218–237 (2019). https://doi.org/10.1016/j.jsis.2018.12.002
40. Teece, D., Peteraf, M., Leih, S.: Dynamic capabilities and organizational agility: risk, uncertainty, and strategy in the innovation economy. Calif. Manag. Rev. **58**(4), 13–35 (2016). It has been published in final form at https://doi.org/10.1525/cmr.2016.58.4.13
41. Turnbull, S.: A new way to govern: organizations and society after Enron. SSRN Electron. J. **14**(1), 1–33 (2002). https://doi.org/10.2139/ssrn.319867
42. Vargas M.P.: Evaluating the effect of different configurations of the collective intelligence genome on organizational agility using multi-agent simulation (2021)
43. Vedel, J.B., Kokshagina, O.: How firms undertake organizational changes to move to more exploratory strategies: a process perspective. Res. Policy **50**(1), 104118 (2021). https://doi.org/10.1016/j.respol.2020.104118
44. Watts, D.: Six Degrees of Separation. The Science of re-des in the Age of Access. Paidós, Barcelona (2006)
45. Wilensky, U.: NetLogo preferential attachment model. Center for Connected Learning and Computer-Based Modeling, Northwestern University, Evanston, Illinois (2005). http://ccl.nor thwestern.edu/netlogo/models/PreferentialAttachment
46. Worley, C.G., Williams, T.D., Lawler III, E.E.: The Agility Factor: Creating Adaptive Organizations for Superior Performance. John Wiley & Sons (2014)

Replicator Dynamics of the Hawk-Dove Game with Agent-based Simulation

Leila Nayibe Ramírez Castañeda[✉][iD]

Corporación Unificada Nacional de Educación Superior, Bogotá D.C., Colombia
leilanayibe@yahoo.com

Abstract. This paper shows the dynamic system of Haw-Dove Game with Agent-based simulation considers how a fraction of agents in a game with symmetrical payoff of 2 X 2, and pure strategies (Hawk-Dove). In this research introduce the replicator dynamics equations of the Hawk-Dove game for the two-player. Also, these was compared with 2 experiments where the data, for 20 periods of time. The fraction of birds playing under the strategy was iterative and its asexual reproduction improves the performance of the strategy, generating its multiplication within the population. The dynamic replicator describes the behavior of strategies during the evolution of the species in any period of time. The results of Agent-based simulation using software Mathematica for the different experiments demonstrate the behavior of a strategy winner or loser. The strategy Hawk considers like aggressive that decrease while that strategy dove increase.

Keywords: Replicator dynamics · Game theory · Nash equilibrium

1 Introduction

There are many interesting applications in game theory in which biology stands out, and above all it allows to understand evolutionary biology, although species such as insects cannot reason, their behavior is instinctive, but what can be said is that a part is encoded in the genes of the organism. The same goes for computer viruses that are stored on your hardware and can migrate from one computer to another. Replicator dynamics behaviors can be distinguished through two contexts:

- The strategy copies itself.
- A strategic behavior is chosen in a game that is repeated in a new scenario after a period of time (Evolution).

These criteria are known as replicators. Evolution games offer a dynamic perspective that is complemented by classical equilibrium notation in conflict situations. The vast majority of jobs that use replicator dynamics consider games with 2

Supported by organization CUN.

© The Author(s), under exclusive license to Springer Nature Switzerland AG 2022
J. C. Figueroa-García et al. (Eds.): WEA 2022, CCIS 1685, pp. 310–319, 2022.
https://doi.org/10.1007/978-3-031-20611-5_26

players. The structure of the population is divided into two groups, (Binmore 1994) (Taylor and Jonker 1978) the effects of paying for interactions between players before and after reproduction are analyzed, where what is implicitly known as the dynamics of the replicator is evaluated (van Veelen 2011). In fact, game theory allow to analyze the outcome of the interaction between strategies for a player or n-players. Any applications are education process, environmental management, energy systems, wireless communications, economic decisions, etc. The objective of this research is to understand the concepts basic of game theory for to identify the best strategy with output maximize profit in different experiments. This proposed methodological approach is a initial scenario for to understand the behavior of players when choose strategies with results either conciliation or conflict. This concepts could be implemented in a futures researches through agent-based simulation for to understand the coordination and strategies between different types of roles (producers, distributors and consumers) in a supply chain management.

2   Basic Concepts of Evolutionary Game Theory

In this section, presents a summary of the main concepts that define evolutionary game theory. These concepts allow to understand the results presented in this paper.

2.1   Game Theory

Game theory is a set of mathematical tools that allow to understand the strategies that could be used by "rational humans", which are represented by agents that aim to maximize the resulting utility in a given process and that is affected by the strategies of all the participating agents, taking into account the conditions of the environment (Cura 2006).

The simplest games only has two players. Player i is endowed with a finite number of strategies and payoff occur when the player makes use of a strategy, in interaction with the other player. The game theory has an economic interpretation, (von Neumann and Morgenstern 1947) where payoff are understood as profits, but Maynard Smith has given another interpretation in terms of success in reproducing a species. The main step to solve the game was presented by Jhon Nash, when introducing the concept of balance (Maynard 1982; Nash 1950).

In the development of this article we will work on the game of Hawk - Dove, which is taken to the context of understanding how a species of birds, can play the pure strategies of Hawk - Dove, and that to allow its survival in a period of time will depend on the selected strategy, the success of the strategy is known as the fitness of the strategy in time that will allow the species to stay or disappear, the payoff matrix, shows the number of births, which will depend on the replicator used either as a Dove or Hawk.

Nash Equilibrium. In 2 X 2 games, with a couple of strategies in a Nash equilibrium there is no single change of strategy that allows the player to improve their profitability. When limited to a symmetrical game, it can be said simply, that if both players are playing with the same strategy neither of them has any incentive. The Nash equilibrium allows to analyze the behavior of the agents in a game to identify the strategies that allow to optimize the results. When there is a Nash equilibrium, the strategy is considered evolutionary stable (Hofbauer and Sigmund 2003; Maynard 1982), which means that it will remain indefinitely over time (Roca et al. 2009). In detail the Nash equilibrium can be defined with the following payoff matrix, for strategies A and B (Nowak 2006). The strategies A y B receive a payoff of a, b, c, d. We have the following criteria:

- A is a strict Nash equilibrium if $a > c$
- A is a Nash equilibrium if $a \geq c$
- B is a strict equilibrium if $d > b$
- B is a Nash equilibrium if $d \geq b$

In the game theory, Nash equilibrium allow to define a solution a non cooperative game for two o more players.

2.2 Replicator Dynamics

The dynamic equation of the replicator, thanks to Taylor and Jonker, who proposed it for the first time with great success for an evolving (Taylor and Jonker 1978) and dynamic game. The replicator equation provides the evolutionary mechanism through which players can reach a Nash equilibrium. The hypotheses that try to explain the replication equation are shown below (Defender 2000) (Hofbauer and Sigmund 2003; Maynard 1982):

- The population is infinitely large
- Individuals meet randomly or play each other against each other, in such a way that the profitability of the strategy is proportional to the average profitability of the current state of the population.
- No mutations are found, that is, the increase in strategies or the decrease in their frequency is due only to reproduction.
- The variation of the population is linear in the difference of the payoff.

From these hypotheses that are established for the equation it can be said that the dynamics of the replicator is a set of differential equations that reflect the idea that strategies that are performed relatively well become more abundant in the population. The dynamics of the replicator (Taylor and Jonker 1978) denoted in Eq. (1) for the Hawk and Dove game studied in this work is given by: (Binmore 1994).

$$\frac{\delta_p}{\delta_\tau} = p \left(f_H (p) - f \overline{(p)} \right) \tag{1}$$

where
p : Fraction of birds playing under the Strategy of hawks,
1-p: Fraction of birds playing under the strategy of dove,
$f_H(p)$: Number of births for a bird that played as a hawks in period t,
$f(p)$: Average aptitude of the population as a whole,
τ: Fraction of a period of time t.

The average aptitude of the population as a whole can be obtained from Eq. (2).

$$f(p) = (1 - p)(f_D(p) + pf_H(p)) \tag{2}$$

Other important functions within this article, define the expected number of birds that assume the dove strategy understood in Eq. (3), which expects a mother with the replicator P (Replicator Dove) is

$$\tau f_D(p) = \tau U + \tau(1 - p) \tag{3}$$

The number of birds hosting the replicator H (Replicator Hawk) is

$$\tau f_H(p) = \tau U + 2\tau(1 - p) - \tau p \tag{4}$$

Substituting Eq. (3) and (4) in the replicator Eq. (1). The result of the differential Eq. (5)

$$\frac{d_p}{d_\tau} = p(1 - p)(1 - 2p) \tag{5}$$

This differential equation governs the evolution of birds, and by solving it you can know the number of birds that play as hawks at any time t.

3   Methodology

For the study of this article, the agent-based simulation tool developed in the mathematica software that contains the following criteria to carry out the game is used. The initial population of birds in the game is constant and equal to 100. The probability of playing with the dove strategy is equal to 1 - p, playing as a hawk is p.

3.1   Payoff Matrix and Strategies

Opponents in the game are selected at random. The interaction in the search for nesting sites is given by the payment matrix defined in Table 1. The payoff for each strategy was adapted of Roca et al. (2009) Outlined below

  (i) If Dove vs. Dove strategies are found, each U+1 agent will receive a payment.
 (ii) If the interaction is of Dove with Hawk, dove receives a payment of U and Hawk of U+2.

(iii) Since the conditions of the game are symmetrical Hawk vs Dove receive the same benefit.
(iv) If the interaction occurs between Hawk vs. Hawk a benefit of U-1 is received.
 (v) When the games are given by the interaction of Hawk Vs. Dove and Dove Vs. Hawk. The Dove player is totally excluded from the game.

Table 1. Payoff matrix for hawk - Dove game

Strategy	Dove	Hawk
Dove	**U+1**	U+2
	U+1	U
Hawk	**U**	U-1
	U+2	U-1

The probability of selecting a strategy to survive is the same. The births sand increase, if the strategy used is Hawk since it is considered that this type of strategy is more aggressive, when competing for the same territory for the reproduction of the species, the payment received for the game strategy, considers the opportunity to reach, more births of birds that is identified with the parameter U, therefore if observed in Table 1, it can be observed that the interaction between Hawk - Dove, the bird that plays under the Hawk strategy will have the highest number of births in the next generation of birds (Binmore 1994).

In the second iteration of the game, the bird population is equal to the birds that remained in the first iteration plus their descendants who are equal to U and who will play the same strategy as their parents. Algorithm 1 implemented in mathematica is shown below:

```
1  Initial population
2  Evaluate each agent of the initial population
3  repeat
4  Select two agents randomly
5  Get the behavior of each agent
6  Establish fitness according to payoff matrix
7  until n agents
8  Replace the agent population with the agents obtained
9  repeat
10 Select two agents randomly
11 Get the behavior of each agent
12 Establish fitness according to payoff matrix
13 until n agents are obtained
14 end
15 end
```

To understand the dynamics of the replicator in this evolved game, reproduction is asexual and the parameters in which the experiments are carried out are shown in Table 2.

4   Results

In the first experiment carried out it can be observed that with a probability equal to zero the number of birds that play as a hawk disappears and the population increases if the selected strategy is dove as shown in Fig. 1.

Table 2. Parameters for the analysis of the Hawk-Dove Game

Parameters	Experiment 1	Experiment 2
Initial population size	100	100
U (births)	2	−1
P(probability of playing as a hawk)	0,0.2,0.5,0.7	0,0.2,0.5,0.7
T time periods	20	20

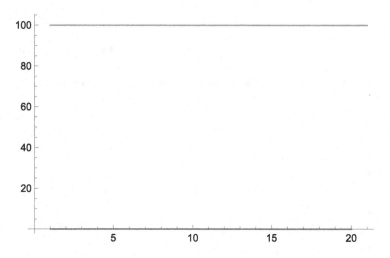

Fig. 1. Fitness of the game Hawk- Dove with P = 0.0 U = 2, mathematica 2022.

When the strategy of playing as a Hawk is 0.2 the results indicate that playing as a pigeon increases the population of birds, this result is evidenced as shown in Fig. 2.

To validate that the probability of playing as a Hawk notoriously affects the selection strategy, the experiment with the P = 0.5 is observed, the results can be seen in Fig. 3.

Although the initial population plays with the same probability in the selection of the strategies it can be said that playing as a dove allows to increase the population, despite the conditions that the game has where this strategy is the weakest in the interaction with hawk. Finally, as the population playing as a hawk increases, it is determined that this strategy is maintained after the asexual reproduction of the individuals in the game, as shown in Fig. 4.

For the second experiment, a birth rate of U = −1 and a probability of playing as a Hawk of 0.5 will be analyzed where the following can be observed.

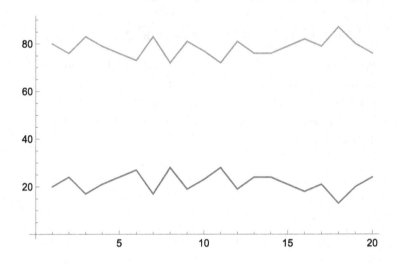

Fig. 2. Fitness game Hawk- Dove with P=0.2 U=2, mathematica, 2022.

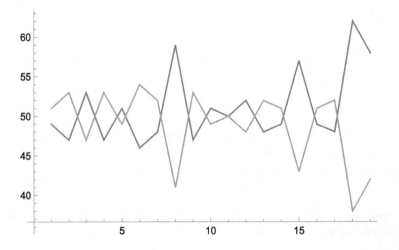

Fig. 3. Fitness game Hawk- Dove with P = 0.5 U = 2, mathematica 2022.

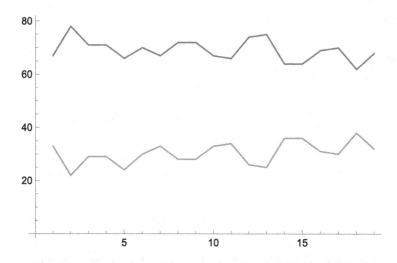

Fig. 4. Fitness game Hawk- Dove with P = 0.7 U = 2, mathematics, 2022.

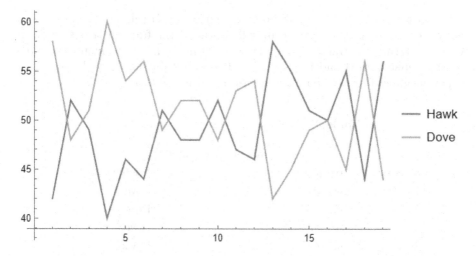

Fig. 5. Fitness game Hawk - Dove with P = 0.5 U = −1, mathematica, 2022.

Although the payout function decreases the number of births of any of the pure strategies, the dove strategy is still the most successful in the time period of evolution as shown in Fig. 5. Where the population of birds playing as a dove continues to increase in different periods of time. The Eq. (5) of the replicator, which explains the behavior of the game is plotted to understand the behavior defined above and the following result is obtained: (Binmore 1994)

The stationary points for the replicator function are given by, and represented graphically by 5,1 and 4 respectively, which is interpreted if $p < 1/2$ the function is strictly increasing, if $p > 1/2$ the strictly decreasing function. If the function

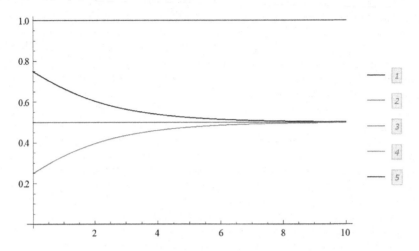

Fig. 6. Dynamic Replicator Function for the Game Hawk-Dove, mathematica 2022

takes the value of p = 1 there will only be replicators H (players like hawk) and no replicators P (players like Dove) will appear. If the fraction of replicators P were small, then the fraction would grow over time to reach the number of birds hosting replicators H and P. $\tilde{p} = 0$, $\tilde{p} = 1$, $\tilde{p} = 1/2$. In summary the results of experiments with parameter changes are shown in Table 3:

Table 3. Results obtained from experiments

Scenarios	U	p	Average birds playing strategy		Winning strategy
			Hawk	Dove	
1	2	0	0	100	Dove
2	2	0,2	21	79	Dove
3	2	0,5	49	51	Dove
4	2	0,7	69	31	Hawk
5	−1	0	0	100	Dove
6	−1	0,2	21	79	Dove
7	−1	0,5	49	51	Dove
8	−1	0,7	71	29	Hawk

In Table 3 it can be concluded that the payoff matrix does not have a major impact on the selection of the strategy given by the agents, and the strategy with greater fitness is to play as a dove, the probability that favors the growth of the hawk replicator is the p > 0.5 that confirms the behavior of the replicator equation for the game from Fig. 6.

5   Conclusions

The average fitness of the strategies in the experiments developed is 65% for the dove strategy and 35% for the hawk strategy. Confirming that the replicator P, has greater success during the evolution of a period T = 20. The payoff for each of the strategies do not significantly interfere with the selected strategies. The number of births with the dove strategy increases the bird population over time. The reproduction rate for each agent is proportional to the population rate with which the game was started. It can be concluded that there is a Nash equilibrium given that the fraction of players who play each pure strategy is the same probability of the corresponding strategy. To give more realism to the game, external variables that were not simulated in the game must be considered, such as the amount of food available for the bird species and additionally improve the real conditions of reproduction since the simulation of this work is based on asexual reproduction that is not very common in natural biological environments. Applications of evolved games are used in the context of biology to study responsiveness from a strategy of how an animal species can be maintained in a hostile environment, such as the social behavior of male-female strategies in a cultural setting. The dynamics of the replicator are also used in the economic context to study the responsiveness of a selected market strategy, where the players are two firms, and understand the performance of the utility generated by the strategy in a period of time, establishing success in the medium term. The dynamics of the replicator also allow us to study behaviors such as fashion multiplies in a given social context.

References

Binmore, K.: Game Theory. Mc Graw Hill, Madrid (1994)

Cure V.L.: Juego ficticio para resolver un juego de demanda dinámica en una cadena de abastecimiento de dos niveles con toma de decisión en un nivel. Universidad del Norte, Barranquilla (2006)

Gintis, H.: Game Theory Evolving. Princeton University Press, Princeton (2000)

Hofbauer, J., Sigmund, K.: Evolutionary Games and Population Dynamics. Cambridge University Press, Cambridge (1998)

Hofbauer, J., Sigmund, K.: Evolutionary game dynamics. Bull. Am. Math. Soc. **40**(4), 479–519 (2003)

Maynard, S. J.: Evolution and the Theory of Games. Cambridge University Press, Cambridge (1982)

Nash, J.: Equilibrium points in n-person games. Proc. Natl. Acad. Sci. **36**(1), 48–49 (1950)

Nowak, M.: Evolutionary Dynamics. The Belknap Press, Cambridge (2006)

Roca, C., Cuesta, J.A., Sánchez, A.: Evolutionary game theory: temporal and spatial effects beyond. Phys. Life Rev. **6**(4), 208–249 (2009)

Taylor, P., Jonker, L.: Evolutionary stable strategies and game dynamics. Math. Biosci. **40**, 145–156 (1978)

Van Veelen, M.: The replicator dynamics with n players and population structure. J. Theor. Biol. **276**(1), 78–85 (2011)

von Neumann, J., Morgenstern, O.: The Theory of Games and Economic Behavior. Princeton University Press, Princeton (1947)

Food Availability Dynamic Model for Colombia

Germán Méndez-Giraldo$^{(\boxtimes)}$ (iD), Paula Peña-Martínez, and Felipe Farfán-Reyes

Universidad Distrital F. J. C., Bogotá, Colombia
gmendez@udistrital.edu.co

Abstract. In the last few decades, rapid socioeconomic transformations have been observed throughout the world, these have aimed the increase of per capita income, to reduce poverty, and the improvement of food security. Despite these positive achievements, close to 1 billion people continue to live in extreme poverty, of whom around 80% suffer from chronic hunger. The region of Latin America and the Caribbean is not immune to these problems; on the contrary, it has been one of the main regions that suffers from the malnutrition of its population. In the Colombian case, the number of people in this situation corresponds to around 8% of its population; however, the FAO indicated that Colombia, together with Peru and Suriname, are the only three countries in the region that can meet the minimum requirements for fruits and vegetables per capita. These apparent contradictions aided the design of a model that allowed the evaluating of both food availability and access to it. The methodology proposed by the ARCOSES Research Group was implemented, where the variables and indicators were raised in aspects such as food security, nutritional requirements, Colombian population size, national agricultural production, imports, exports, and logistical losses in the supply chain. This made it possible to identify that, although Colombia has food availability at the country level, it is unequal and asymmetric per food group. To guarantee full access, prompt and assertive intervention by the Colombian government is required.

Keywords: Dynamic simulation · Food security · Food access · Nutritional requirements

1 Introduction

In the report carried out by the FAO in 2021, on the level of food and nutritional security in the world, they mention among many aspects, the increase in the number of people with inadequate access to food is close to 2,370 million people, and 3,000 million live with unhealthy food diets. Almost 150 million children under the age of 5 worldwide were affected by stunting, while 38 million were overweight; and more than 672 million adults were obese. All this indicates how malnutrition, overweightness and obesity coexist in many countries [1]. The term Food Security appears for the first time at the World Food Conference held in 1974, in which the world declaration on the eradication of hunger and malnutrition is approved, where it is recognized "establishment of a world food security system that ensure sufficient availability of food at reasonable prices regardless

© The Author(s), under exclusive license to Springer Nature Switzerland AG 2022
J. C. Figueroa-García et al. (Eds.): WEA 2022, CCIS 1685, pp. 320–336, 2022.
https://doi.org/10.1007/978-3-031-20611-5_27

of fluctuations or vagaries of weather." In the 1970s, the concept of Food Security emerged based on the adequate supply or availability of food worldwide, in the 1980s both economic and physical access to food were incorporated; in the 1990s, security and cultural preferences were considered, reaffirming Food Security as a human right [2]. The concept of Food Safety has been in constant evolution and will continue to evolve given the dynamics of the environment and as new requirements about concept of human well-being. The famine that occurred in Africa in 1984–1985, the economical structural changes and its effects and a new development paradigm focused on human well-being were some of the triggers for changes in the concept [3]. Initially, there was an interest in guaranteeing the availability of food at global and national levels, later food security at the local and family level were given more importance; many topics were developed as the concept o "food anthropology" presented in [4]. Many authors, summarized in [5], indicate that food security depends on natural, physical and, of course, human resources. Some relevant aspects such as rainfall, soil quality, agronomic and climatic stability and access to forest resources, access to agricultural infrastructure, ownership of livestock and land, and finally the ethnographic conditions should be considered.

The growth of the world population, the crisis of the economic model that has been implemented, the negative environmental impact due to the overexploitation of natural resources, are amongst the main causes of world food insecurity. Consequences of an unsustainable form of production, wasted food throughout the production chain, as well as large levels of inequality among the population, have caused the appearance of malnutrition problems. "In Latin America and the Caribbean, hunger affects 39.3 million people, 6.1% of the regional population. Between 2015 and 2016, the number of undernourished people grew by 200,000 people [6]. "Economic growth and demographic dynamics are key factors in the transformations that are currently taking place [7]. The constant population increase generated a growth in the demand for food throughout the world, and an aggressive exploitation of natural resources was the way of supplying the new demand, negatively impacting the environment which has led those responsible for sustainability planning to think of different alternatives to meet the food needs of the world population. A change of course is vital: continuing with the same scenario is no longer an option, if agricultural and food systems continue their current path, food insecurity and unsustainable economic growth will be the expecting results [8]. In Colombia, both national and international laws establish the right of every person to access accessible and stable sources of nutritious food [9]; however, close to 50% of population are living in food insecurity. Although nutrition involves many facets, it is important to point out that it must be understood as the process through which people reach their potential for physical and mental growth; it is a characteristic of the quality of a person's diet in relation to their nutritional needs; and it is a benchmark or metric against which the efficiency of numerous development goals is evaluated, [10].

To deal with food security problems, Colombia proposed the National Plan for Food and Nutritional Security (PNSAN) 2012–2019, which is a set of objectives, goals, strategies and actions proposed by the Colombian State, in a framework of co-responsibility with civil society [11], which are intended to protect the population from undesirable and socially inadmissible situations such as hunger and inadequate nutrition; and to ensure the population access to food in a timely, adequate and quality manner. This plan considered three specific topics; the first one was of course availability and access to food; secondly, was regarding the quality of life and well-being, and the last one was related to the quality and safety of food, and for them a series of indicators in each of the divisions of the topics were developed in order of controlling its advances. From all this, it was intended to design a dynamic simulation model of food security that allows the identifying the country's capacity to satisfy the nutritional requirement of its population. To achieve this, the state of the art in terms of food sustainability, nutritional requirements by age group, productive capacity of the agricultural sector in the country, behavior of imports and exports and the impact of logistics loss was reviewed. All these aspects are evaluated to satisfy nutritional requirements, which will be explained in the next section, and which allowed the components of the dynamic simulation model to be determined and thus facilitate the formulation of policies and scenarios that allow the evaluation of food security in the country.

2   Material and Methods

Given the complexity of the system under study, the model uses the methodology described in [12]. The structure is showed in Fig. 1, it is composed of three major stages of knowledge acquisition, knowledge representation and decision making. These are described below.

2.1   Knowledge Acquisition Stage

In the first phase, the phenomenon of food security for Colombia with emphasis on the physical availability of food to address the problems of food insecurity and poor nutrition of the country's population is defined as the problem of interest. Given this, it is necessary to develop a simulation model that allows formulate strategies to guarantee total coverage throughout the nation. So, 109 documents were revised as direct source, of which 74 were documents of 5 years or less, and 25 between 5 to 10 years. 51 sources were referred to the Colombian context, 21 from the Latin American environment and the remaining from the European or North American context. Finally, 53 documents were from official sources such as governmental or multilateral organizations.

The problem, in an abbreviated way, is that although Colombia has achieved a very significant reduction in undernourished people during the last decade, (9.7% of total population in 2006 to 4.8% in 2018), chronic malnutrition continues to affect mainly rural areas, with a prevalence of 15.4% compared to 9% in urban areas. Considering that it is necessary to identify key factors that influence the nutrition of Colombians, information of the World Health Organization (WHO), the Food and Agriculture Organization of the United Nations FAO, Colombian Institute of Family Welfare - ICBF (by its acronym in Spanish), the National Planning Department - DNP (by its acronym in Spanish), the Security Observatory Food and Nutritional Security - OSAN (by its acronym in Spanish) was revised. Food security considers 4 basic components incorporated in its definition: availability, stability, access and control, consumption, and biological use [13]. The first is related to production, imports, storage, among others. The second attempts to supply agricultural activities (cyclical or seasonal) through contingency measures for food deficit periods. The third one includes the production resources such as, water, land, technology, among others. Finally, consumption refers to food stocks meeting nutritional needs, while biological utilization is related to the individual use of food in activities as intake, absorption, and transformation of food.

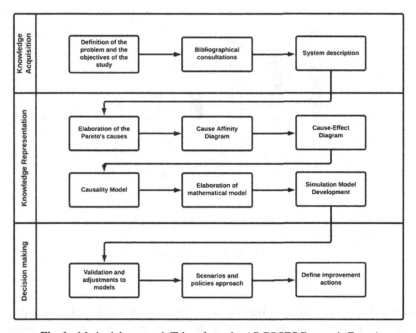

Fig. 1. Methodology used (Taken from the ARCOSES Research Group)

The lack of institutionalism is evident in a developing country such as Colombia, because regardless of having natural and biological resources, there is not a strategic importance of agriculture at the economic development, neither is national food security considered. Food imports generate a decrease in the income of farmers and an increase in poverty levels, affecting economical and internal sustainability of the agricultural sector, on which many families depend. Consequently, access to food is invalidated, which is one of the most important components to guarantee food security. Therefore, it is necessary to carry out a reform in the agrarian and food system of the country to allow the offering of solutions for the reduction of hunger and poverty.

2.2 Knowledge Representation Stage

The main causes of malnutrition which leads to poor food availability are the poor definition of nutritional requirements in each of the different age groups with 30.2%; inadequate food production both regionally and nationally in 22.7% of cases; as well as sociodemographic variables that involve the different contexts of the population in 18.6%, food imports with 9.9% and with 8.1% for exports, both define the food balancing, food losses and wastes with 6.4%, and finally with 4.1% other causes, see Figure 2. These causes are briefly described below.

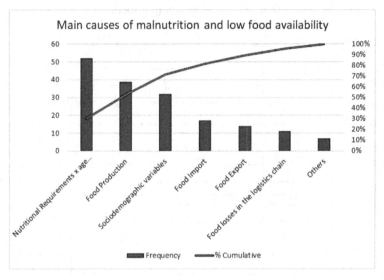

Fig. 2. Pareto of causes

- Sociodemographic variables: It is necessary to discriminate the national population by each of the age groups, because nutritional requirement varies according to the age group and gender. When gender does not have influence, this group will be mixed, in the other case the group will be differentiated by men or women. The age-gender population groups under study are 0 to 2, 3 to 5, 6 to 9, 10 to 13, 14 to 17 (men and women), 18 to 59 (men and women) and over 60 years old (mixed).
- Nutritional Requirements per age group: The ICBF establishes an official diet for the Colombian population depending on the age group each person belongs to. It also divides food into six large groups according to its nutritional characteristics, these are: Group I made up of cereals, roots, tubers and bananas; group II for fruits and vegetables; group III which consists of milk and dairy products; group IV for meat, eggs and legumes; group V made up of sugars and fats (this group was not considered in this work because given the low relative frequency); and finally group VI of nuts and seeds.
- Exchanges by nutritional group: For the design of feeding schemes, it is necessary and fundamental to be clear about the difference between two concepts: portion and exchange. The "portion" refers to the amount of food that must be consumed per mealtime; while "exchange" is the specific amount of food that has a similar supply of energy or nutrients with another food from the same group, which can be replaced or exchanged with each other [14] (ICBF; FAO, 2015).
- The National Food Production: According to the latest official data provided by the National Agricultural Survey (NAS) for 2017, 78.2% of the available productive area

was dedicated to livestock activity, 7.3% to agricultural activity, 11.9% to forests and 2.5% of the land area was dedicated to other uses. The total reported production of agro-industrial crops was 32,592,356 T., of which 68.2% were sugarcane, 24.3% oil palm; for the group of tubers, where potato has the highest production with 3,706,563 T., while regarding fruit trees, banana is the most representative with a production of 2,020,915 T. Concerning cereals, rice stands out with 3,292,983 T., yellow corn with 939,677 T., and white corn with 390,179 T. Finally, in the group of vegetables, onion registered the greatest participation 20% equivalent to vegetables at 510,312 T., followed by the cultivation of tomato 18.6% with 473,772 T., [15].

- National Food Imports: For 2019, international purchases or imports of agricultural products, food and beverages were 6,908.0 million CIF dollars, equivalent to a 13.5% share compared to the total of the other economic sectors of the country, presenting an increase of 10.5% compared to 2017. Imports in Colombia originated mainly from the United States with 25.3% of the total registered in 2018, followed by China 20.6%, Mexico 7.6%, Brazil 5.5%, Germany 4.2%, Japan 2.5%, India 2.3%, and other countries 31.8% [16].

- National Food Exports: According to data reported by DANE, for the year 2019 exports of agricultural products, food and beverages represented 7,301.3 million dollars FOB, equivalent to a 17.5% share compared to the total exports, presenting a decrease of 0.7% compared to 2017. As for the destination countries of Colombian exports, the United States continues to be the main buyer, representing 25.4% of the total value exported, followed by China 9.7%, Panama 7.3%, Ecuador 4.4%, Turkey 4.0%, Mexico 3.9%, Brazil 3.7%, and other countries 41.5%, [17].

- Food losses in the logistics chain: According to a study carried out by the FAO, there are five sources of food losses and waste (FLW) in food supply chains: a) agricultural production, b) post-harvest handling and storage, c) processing, d) distribution and e) consumption of vegetables and animal products [18]. In a recent study carried out by the DPN in Colombia, of 28.5 million tons of potential food to consume per year, including dairy products, fruits, vegetables, roots, tubers, grains, fish, and cereals; The FLW are equivalent to approximately 9.76 million tons per year (34%), of which 6.22 million tons are lost (22%) and 3.54 million tons are wasted (12%) [19].

It is important to indicate two aspects to consider in the scope of this model; the first is that it does not consider all aspects of food safety, as others could be developed considering aspects such as the biological use of food or its quality [20].; secondly, the aspects of the perishability of foods treated in a very interesting way in [21, 22]. Are not considered. From the Pareto diagram, a cause-effect diagram was constructed which allowed the creation of the causality model that later gave the basis for the continuous simulation model. This causal model, see Fig. 3, shows that it is possible to identify the input and output factors of the system, that is, the causes that increase the availability of food and those that decrease it. These factors include production, logistical losses, nutritional tables, among others.

In this context, and recognizing the interrelation of demographic, economic, social, and environmental variables for sustainable development, the population is considered firstly as subject and object of the actions of progress and secondly as demanding resources. The positive signs indicate that the condition is reinforced, in this case, the

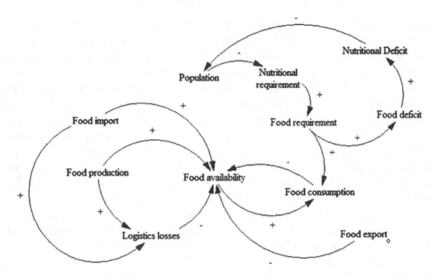

Fig. 3. Causal diagram

greater the food production, the greater its availability, although this greater production also results in an increase in logistical losses because these occur in the agricultural processes. The same happens with the negative sign, where it is indicated that a greater increase in one of the cause variables will cause decreases in the effect variable; for example, a greater the consumption of food causes its availability to be lower. From this causal diagram the simulation model of the system is developed, designing policies as independent systems that directly affect the food security of the Colombian population. The model was made in the program iThink by "isee Systems" company tool. Following, are important parameters in the simulation model: The time unit is defined in years and horizon of the simulation runs was between 2008 to 2025. The simulation step selected was 1 year and the integration method used was first order Euler. Finally, assumptions and parameters in the model were based on information for the Colombian case.

It is necessary to delimit and focus the model objectives, firstly to determine compliance with the nutritional requirement seen mainly from food availability. Second, the base unit of measurement is food exchanges, used to determine the nutritional requirement, national agricultural production and imports and exports. Third, the productive capacity of each department (territorial unit) was considered in relation to the nutritional requirements of its population. Fourth, the most representative products or groups of products are defined by the ICBF. Fifth, imports and exports are seen from a global point of view at the country level and sixth the time base unit of measurement of the model is 1 year because is the same unit for official statistics and agricultural production cycles. The initial information for the development of the model shows evolution of the Colombian population, this was extracted from the 2005 DANE national census, and its projection for 1985 and 2020; its estimation it is given by Eq. 1. Once the population function is defined, it is also necessary to discriminate the national population by each one of the age groups, for each one of the 32 departments of Colombia. This is necessary because the nutritional requirement varies according to age group and gender. These values are calculated with fuzzy numbers obtained from the same census.

$$F(t) = 152, 18(t - 1.984)^3 - 11.059(t - 1.984)^2 + 786.556(t - 1.984) + 30\,'000.000 \tag{1}$$

The nutritional requirement in Colombia is given by the ICBF, in the official diet for the Colombian population depending on the age group, it also divides food into four large groups according to the nutritional characteristics of each of the foods and their substitutes. This also defines a special unit called "exchange", from this moment on all in-formation must be handled in these units. This can be seen in Eq. 2.

$$RNxDep_{klj} = RNxGrupoAlim_{kl} * PobNalxDep_{kj} \tag{2}$$

where: k represents the age group and gender; l represents the food group and j refers to the Department analyzed. The variable $RNxDep$ is the accumulated nutritional requirement for each food group in each department and for each age and gender group. While $RNxGrupoAlim$; refers to the same nutritional requirements by food group in each age group and gender. Finally, the variable $PobNalxDep$ represent to the population corresponding to each age and gender group; in the case of the model, these variables are integrated so that they meet the annual requirements.

To determine the national agricultural production, it was necessary to relate information from different official sources such as the Ministry of Agriculture, FAO, and some associations of food producers and other entities from which information was related to the 40 products or groups of products that are within the food groups specified by the ICBF is taken; the model used for this purpose is given in Eq. 3.

$$National\ Production\ (t)_m = National\ Production\ (t - 1)_m + Production\ growth\ (t) \tag{3}$$

These values are classified by each food group according to their nutritional characteristics, the exchanges of the nutritional requirement are calculated through the conversion factors of each of the foods. Another component of the model is the production share by department for each type of food, and is added in the national level represented in exchange levels of them. To determine the agricultural exports and imports they are grouped in 13 main groups of products were traded in the country's foreign trade. The food subgroups defined by the ICBF are used to calculate the nutritional requirement and the national agricultural production to homogenize and integrate at the level of exchanges per year for each food group.

Due to their nature, logistical losses are applied to the national production of each food subgroup defined in national production, calculated by $Plogistica_{qr}$, and Int_{nqj}; these variables define the production with their respective logistical impact, where the indices q refer to the subgroups of foods produced and the subindex r indicates the logistical stage; this is presented in Eq. 4.

$$ProducionPLogist_{nqj} = Int_{n\ nj} * \sum_{r=1}^{r} PLogistica_{qr}; \forall q \tag{4}$$

2.3 Decision Making Stage

To define compliance with the nutritional requirement, six analysis scenarios were established in order to identify the impact generated by logistics losses, exports, and imports of food. It was necessary to find the compliance of nutritional requirement in each of the six cases, not only at the departmental but also and the national level. All these scenarios were based on food availability.

1. No logistics impact, without imports or exports, at a disaggregated level.
2. With logistics impact, without imports or exports. at a disaggregated level.
3. No logistics impact, with imports and exports, at the aggregate level.
4. With logistics impact, without imports or exports, at the aggregate level.
5. No logistics impact, with imports or exports, at the aggregate level.
6. With logistics impact, with imports and exports, at the aggregate level.

When the simulation model was executed and in order to verify its validity, a set of 10 runs were simulated to obtain the desired level of precision based a t-student statistician with 95% of confidence and a relative sampling error of 1%. The results of the number of runs necessary are showed in Table 1.

Table 1. Number of replicas required.

Variable of interest	Number of runs
Nutritional requirement G1	9
Nutritional requirement G2	10
Nutritional requirement G3	27
Nutritional requirement G4	1
National production G1	25
National production G2	1
National production G3	17
National production G4	9
Nutritional requirement G1	9

For purposes of improving the level of precision of the simulation, the model was executed with 50 replicates. For the validation process, nine years of history were used to compare the real values against the simulated ones. The variables compared were General population (GP); Population variation by age group (GPA); Population variation by department (PD); National Production of food group G1 (NP1); National Production of food group G2 (NP2); National Production of food group G3 (NP3); National production of food group G4 (NP4), see Table 2.

Table 2. Percentage of the mean relative error between the real data and the simulated data for the period 2010–2018.

Year	GP	GPA	PD	NP1	NP2	NP3	NP4
1	0,36	5,70	2,42	3,06	3,17	1,92	2,01
2	0,34	4,67	2,70	2,81	3,48	2,59	3,28
3	0,31	3,63	3,04	2,64	2,37	1,42	5,86
4	0,27	2,52	3,30	4,81	3,05	2,02	3,07
5	0,24	1,60	3,66	3,12	1,90	0,77	2,35
6	0,21	0,65	3,91	2,53	1,75	2,21	3,40
7	0,19	0,46	4,17	4,32	1,57	5,98	2,87
8	0,18	1,15	4,34	2,38	1,43	0,74	4,30
9	0,17	1,96	4,54	4,13	2,06	0,77	1,17

There is a very low weighted average error in the main variables of the model for which the validity of the results is accepted, and then it is possible to estimate the compliance with the nutritional requirement projected for 2025. Table 3 shows both the national production exchanges (NPE) and the nutritional requirement exchanges (NRE). These values are in millions, and it is considered as scenario 1. Table 4 shows the CR compliance rates for both the national production as well as the nutritional requirement rate (IC1); the national production adding imports and exports against the nutritional requirement (CI2); the national production and logistic losses against the nutritional requirements (CI3) and finally the compliance index for the national productions adding imports, exports, and the logistic losses against the nutritional requirements (CI4). To facilitate results visualization only the 2009, 2013, and 2017 periods are showed which were based on historical data, and periods 2021 and 2025 which are projected by the simulation model.

Table 3. Results – Compliance with the nutritional requirement by food group Scenario 1.

Group	Variable	2009	2013	2017	2021	2025
1	NPE	162.794	169.401	195.542	213.178	231.455
	NRE	99.627	104.279	109.017	114.099	119.567
2	NPE	79.485	92.242	91.847	97.610	103.182
	NRE	63.647	66.621	69.646	72.894	76.388
3	NPE	32.991	34.082	35.373	35.525	35.614
	NRE	57.985	60.705	63.444	66.423	69.603
4	NPE	57.072	65.935	75.095	80.963	87.076
	NRE	103.730	108.562	113.506	118.788	124.480

Table 4. Results – Fulfillment of the nutritional requirement by food group Scenario 2 to 5.

Group	Variable	2009	2013	2017	2021	2025
1	CI1	1,634	1,625	1,794	1,868	1,956
	CI2	2,225	2,294	2,576	2,655	2,720
	CI3	1,014	0,991	1,099	1,137	1,176
	CI4	1,620	1,672	1,897	1,940	1,977
2	CI1	1,249	1,385	1,319	1,389	1,351
	CI2	0,910	1,095	0,998	1,015	1,028
	CI3	0,949	1,053	1,002	1,020	1,029
	CI4	0,697	0,840	0,764	0,780	0,791
3	CI1	0,569	0,561	0,558	0,535	0,512
	CI2	0,566	0,561	0,562	0,539	0,517
	CI3	0,443	0,438	0,434	0,417	0,398
	CI4	0,441	0,438	0,438	0,421	0,404
4	CI1	0,560	0,607	0,662	0,682	0,700
	CI2	0,560	0,640	0,704	0,729	0,752
	CI3	0,434	0,480	0,523	0,540	0,554
	CI4	0,447	0,515	0,567	0,588	0,607

These results highlight that the availability of cereals, roots, tubers, and bananas could satisfy the food requirements in the country. Regarding fruits and vegetables, although there is no evidence of food exchange shortages, this could happen when logistical losses or export aspects are considered. It is indicated that only 80% of the population complies whit this food requirement. A reason for that is due to the fact that around 35% of national production is exported, especially fruit, and only 2% of national production is imported. For group 3, (milk and its derivatives), it is evident that there is no complete availability and that, if the effects of logistical losses are added it further decreases the availability of this group, it is estimated that by 2025 only 40% will be able to access these food group. Finally, the group of meats and legumes, is not enough to satisfy the requirements; and if logistical losses are considered, by the year 2025 it is estimated only 60% of the national population will not have difficulties accessing products of this food group.

3   Results

Food security has political, economic, and social implications that have to be considered in order to provide well-being to the country's population and avoiding the appearance of problems derived such as malnutrition, low availability, and poor food accessibility. This is why the government must allocate resources for the implementation of policies that focus on the production of food that is necessary to satisfy the nutritional and food needs of all national population, mainly in the poorest regions. In the case of this research, the following scenarios and policies were established:

1) Scenarios (S):

   a. National population according to census
   b. +5% in the national population
   c. −5% in the national population

2) Policies (P):

   a. Logistics losses according to FAO
   b. + 5% logistics losses
   c. −5% logistics losses
   d. +10% logistics losses
   e. and. −10% logistics losses

Tables 5, 6, 7 reflect and evaluate the main results of these scenarios and policies. Results are for national production and nutritional requirements (in millions of exchanges), and these are presented for the four compliance indices in each of the four food groups.

Table 5. Results of Scenario 1 for the 5 different policies.

Group	Variable	S = a; P = a	S = a; P = b	S = a; P = c	S = a; P = d	S = a; P = e
1	NPE	231.455	232.459	231.334	232.908	228.922
	NRE	119.567	119.559	119.517	119.532	119.619
	CI1	1,936	1,944	1,936	1,949	1,914
	CI2	2,72	2,719	2,699	2,708	2,688
	CI3	1,176	1,218	1,141	1,268	1,078
	CI4	1,977	2,01	1,922	2,043	1,872
2	NPE	103.172	103.812	102.575	103.308	103.640
	NRE	76.388	76.379	76.355	76.365	76.426
	CI1	1,351	1,359	1,343	1,353	1,356
	CI2	1,028	1,049	1,029	1,04	1,034
	CI3	1,029	1,046	1,009	1,056	0,988
	CI4	0,791	0,815	0,781	0,819	0,762
3	NPE	35.614	35.412	35.694	35.583	35.456

(*continued*)

Table 5. (*continued*)

Group	Variable	S = a; P = a	S = a; P = b	S = a; P = c	S = a; P = d	S = a; P = e
	NRE	69.603	69.627	69.554	69.601	69.657
	CI1	0,512	0,509	0,513	0,511	0,509
	CI2	0,517	0,514	0,518	0,517	0,514
	CI3	0,398	0,403	0,395	0,41	0,387
	CI4	0,404	0,408	0,4	0,415	0,392
4	NPE	87.076	86.724	87.203	86.788	87.001
	NRE	124.480	124.475	124.435	124.450	124.509
	CI1	0,7	0,697	0,701	0,697	0,699
	CI2	0,752	0,75	0,754	0,75	0,751
	CI3	0,554	0,559	0,549	0,566	0,541
	CI4	0,607	0,613	0,603	0,619	0,595

Table 6. Results of Scenario 2 for the 5 different policies.

Group	Variable	S = b; P = a	S = b; P = b	S = b; P = c	S = b; P = d	S = b; P = e
1	NPE	232.408	232.628	231.422	229.184	229.914
	NRE	125.251	125.769	125.644	125.799	125.593
	CI1	1,856	1,85	1,842	1,822	1,831
	CI2	2,605	2,568	2,573	2,559	2,583
	CI3	1,134	1,154	1,083	1,178	1,029
	CI4	1,898	1,888	1,831	1,929	1,799
2	NPE	102.416	102.704	102.292	101.282	102.930
	NRE	80.019	80.351	80.267	80.367	80.240
	CI1	1,28	1,278	1,275	1,26	1,283
	CI2	0,992	0,996	0,99	0,988	1,004
	CI3	0,966	0,994	0,951	0,984	0,948
	CI4	0,757	0,781	0,746	0,779	0,75
3	NPE	35.594	35.621	35.678	35.608	35.986
	NRE	72.856	73.235	73.110	73.238	73.100
	CI1	0,489	0,486	0,488	0,486	0,492

(*continued*)

Table 6. (*continued*)

Group	Variable	S = b; P = a	S = b; P = b	S = b; P = c	S = b; P = d	S = b; P = e
	CI2	0,494	0,492	0,493	0,492	0,497
	CI3	0,381	0,385	0,374	0,391	0,374
	CI4	0,386	0,39	0,379	0,396	0,379
4	NPE	86.309	87.225	87.441	86.360	87.007
	NRE	130.402	130.912	130.832	130.973	130.748
	CI1	0,662	0,666	0,668	0,659	0,665
	CI2	0,713	0,716	0,718	0,709	0,715
	CI3	0,524	0,535	0,523	0,535	0,512
	CI4	0,575	0,585	0,573	0,586	0,563

Table 7. Results of Scenario 3 for the 5 different policies.

Group	Variable	S = c; P = a	S = c; P = b	S = c; P = c	S = c; P = d	S = c; P = e
1	NPE	230.536	229.937	230.841	231.093	232.809
	NRE	113.592	114.154	113.856	113.793	113.912
	CI1	2.030	2.014	2.027	2.031	2.044
	CI2	2.856	2.822	2.837	2.851	2.864
	CI3	1.224	1.264	1.193	1.315	1.159
	CI4	2.071	2.090	2.023	2.153	2.000
2	NPE	100.799	103.423	101.234	102.250	102.112
	NRE	72.570	72.932	72.738	72.699	72.776
	CI1	1,389	1,418	1,392	1,406	1,403
	CI2	1,034	1,065	1,031	1,053	1,07
	CI3	1,06	1,096	1,039	1,104	1,032
	CI4	0,797	0,83	0,778	0,834	0,796
3	NPE	35.487	35.579	35.350	36.071	35.634
	NRE	66.077	66.417	66.279	66.263	66.282
	CI1	0,537	0,536	0,533	0,544	0,538
	CI2	0,542	0,542	0,54	0,55	0,543
	CI3	0,421	0,424	0,41	0,434	0,406
	CI4	0,426	0,429	0,416	0,44	0,411

(*continued*)

Table 7. (*continued*)

Group	Variable	S = c; P = a	S = c; P = b	S = c; P = c	S = c; P = d	S = c; P = e
4	NPE	86.038	87.251	86.793	87.351	87.437
	NRE	118.259	118.844	118.536	118.462	118.600
	CI1	0,728	0,734	0,732	0,737	0,737
	CI2	0,783	0,789	0,789	0,792	0,792
	CI3	0,576	0,589	0,572	0,599	0,57
	CI4	0,633	0,645	0,629	0,655	0,625

4 Discussion

The results show that the best combination, as expected, is the scenario of national population decrease and the -10% logistical loss to satisfy the nutritional requirement, which implies that there will be less waste during production. However, there is evidence of a lack of compliance in the different indices for both the dairy group and the meat and legumes group, which is aggravated when considering the effects of exports that reduce compliance with these Nutritional indices for the Colombian population. These results clearly show that Colombia, despite having the competitive advantage of being in a geographical area that allows the potential development of the food industry, which allows it to adequately satisfy the nutritional requirements of its population, mainly in the food groups 1 (Cereals, roots, tubers, and bananas) and 2 (Fruits and Vegetables), the country cannot do the same with the dairy and meat groups mainly. On the other hand, this availability of food is not equal in all the regions, especially in those that are far from the large productive areas and that also present more malnutrition situations.

The participation of the State is required for Colombia to develop and strengthen an industry with great potential, which can generate economic benefits for many the country's inhabitants and help diversify the economy. Given the deficit in food group 3, in terms of milk, although imports are greater than exports, these figures are very low compared to the level of national production. However, a logistical losses impact of around 20% of national production is estimated, which further reduces the availability of this product throughout the national territory, due to this, is estimated that by 2025 only 40% of the population will not have difficulties to access this product. As for food group 4, that of the protein contribution in the diet of the national population, it has a positive impact of the exchange of the commercial balance around 7% of the production, however, a loss from logistical impact is estimated close to 20% of the country's production. In year 2025 it is estimated that 40% of the national population could have difficulties accessing the products that make up this group alimentary. These two groups have to reduce these losses with a better integration of its logistics chain that goes from the producer to the final distribution.

References

1. FAO: El estado de la seguridad alimentaria y la nutrición en el mundo: Transformación de los sistemas alimentarios en aras de la seguridad alimentaria, una nutrición mejorada y dietas asequibles y saludables para todos (2021)
2. Ramirez, R.F., Vargas, P.L., Cardenas, O.S.: La seguridad alimentaria: una revisión sistemática con análisis no convencional. Revista Espacios. **41**(45), 319–328 (2020)
3. Chammem, N., Issaoui, M., De Almeida, A.I.D., Delgado, A.M.: Food crises and food safety incidents in European union, united states, and Maghreb area: current risk communication strategies and new approaches. J. AOAC Int. **101**(4), 923–938 (2018)
4. Aguirre, P.: Alternativas a la crisis global de la alimentación. Nueva sociedad **262**, 1–11 (2016)
5. Ngachan, S.V., Das, A.: Climate proofing of agriculture for food security. conservation agriculture for advancing food security in changing climate. In: Das, A., et al. (eds.) Today & Tomorrow's Printers and Publishers, vol. 2, pp. 37–57, New Delhi-110 (2018)
6. Ortale, M.S., Santos, J.A.: Pobreza, seguridad alimentaria y políticas sociales en Argentina (2014–2018). In: V Seminario Internacional Desigualdad y Movilidad Social en América Latina (Santiago de Chile, 6 a 8 de mayo de 2019) (2020)
7. FAO: El estado de la seguridad alimentaria y la nutrición en el mundo: Transformación de los sistemas alimentarios en aras de la seguridad alimentaria, una nutrición mejorada y dietas asequibles y saludables para todos (2020)
8. Le Coq, J.F., Grisa, C., Sabourin, E., Sotomayor, O.: Políticas públicas y desarrollo rural en América Latina: Balance y perspectivas. Memorias del Seminario de la Red de Políticas Públicas y Desarrollo Rural en América Latina (PP-AL). Red PP-AL (2019)
9. Eichmann, M.: ¿Cómo se encuentra regulado el derecho a la alimentación de niños, niñas y adolescentes en Colombia?: análisis a partir de los casos de muerte por desnutrición en niños menores de 5 años en el periodo 2018–2020 (2020)
10. Bhadra, P., Deb, A.: A review on nutritional anaemia. Indian J. Nat. Sci. **10**(59), 18466–18474 (2020)
11. Méndez Cotrino, P.A.: Seguridad alimentaria en Colombia. Una propuesta para la sostenibilidad de la Política de Seguridad Alimentaria y Nutricional PSAN (2019)
12. Méndez, G.A., Fajardo, R., Peña, S.C., Carantón, M.F.: Asignación de recursos del Sistema General de Regalías, un análisis desde la perspectiva de la Dinámica de Sistemas. I+ D Revista de Investigaciones. **9**(1), 93–106 (2017)
13. Torres, F.T., Martínez, A.R.: La situación regional y las escalas de la seguridad alimentaria en México. Revista legislativa de estudios sociales y de opinión pública **12**(25), 51–93 (2019)
14. ICBF: Guías Alimentarias Basadas en Alimentos para la población Colombiana mayor de 2 años (2020)
15. DANE: Boletín Técnico Encuesta. Encuesta Nacional Agropecuaria, pp. 1–31 (2017a). https://www.dane.gov.co/files/investigaciones/agropecuario/enda/ena/2017/boletin_ena_2017.pdf
16. DANE: Boletín Técnico, Importaciones 2018, pp. 1–44 (2019). https://www.dane.gov.co/files/investigaciones/boletines/importaciones/bol_impo_dic18.pdf
17. DANE: Boletín Técnico Exportaciones (EXPO) Diciembre 2018 (2019). https://www.dane.gov.co/files/investigaciones/boletines/exportaciones/bol_exp_dic18.pdf
18. FAO: Pérdidas y desperdicio de alimentos en el mundo - Alcance, causas y prevención. In: Roma (2012). https://doi.org/10.3738/1982.2278.562
19. DPN: Estudio pérdida y desperdicio de alimentos en Colombia (2016). https://mrv.dnp.gov.co/Documentos%20de%20Interes/Perdida_y_Desperdicio_de_Alimentos_en_colombia.pdf
20. DNP: Documento CONPES 113 Política Nacional de seguridad alimentaria y nutricional (PSAN) (2008)

21. Orjuela Castro, J.A.: Incidencia del diseño de la cadena de suministro alimentaria en el equilibrio de flujos logísticos. Sede Bogotá (2018)

22. Orjuela-Castro, J.A., Caicedo-Otavo, A.L., Ruiz-Moreno, A.F., Adarme-Jaimes, W.: Efecto de los mecanismos de integración externa en el desempeño logístico de cadenas Frutícolas. Un enfoque bajo dinámica de sistemas. Revista Colombiana de Ciencias Hortícolas. **10**(2), 311–322 (2016)

A Low-Cost 3D Mapping System for Indoor Scenes Based on a 2D LiDAR On-Board an UGV

Harold Murcia[1]([✉]), Julián Cháux[2], and Yeison Aldana[1]

[1] Facultad de Ingeniería, Universidad de Ibagué, Ibagué 730001, Colombia
harold.murcia@unibague.edu.co
[2] Centro de la Industria, la Empresa y los Servicios, SENA, Huila 410001, Colombia

Abstract. Point clouds are a popular solution for developing applications that require three dimensions, which can be generated from different methods, among which 3D LiDAR devices stand out. However, this technology can be difficult to access in some cases due to its high costs. The simplest LiDAR sensors have a short range and are two-dimensional laser scanners, but together with rotations, moving platforms, RGB cameras, position sensors, and fusion algorithms, it is possible to develop a platform that achieves colored point clouds for indoor mapping. In this paper, we propose a framework to build a 3D model for an indoor scene based on a Turtlebot vehicle, a 2D Hokuyo LiDAR from design to implementation. Furthermore, according to the possible application variants, we propose two acquisition schemes for the point cloud generation. The performance of our system is verified on different indoor datasets. Our code implementation is available online.

Keywords: Laser applications · Robot vision systems ·
Reconstruction algorithms · Signal processing · Machine vision

1 Introduction

Autonomous vehicles are used to support humans in performing repetitive, dirty, and dangerous tasks. In this case, where a mobile system, such as a robot, is required, there are a lot of applications where 2D and 3D measurement systems take an important role in position, movement, obstacle avoidance, and trajectory tracking. Their use is gaining popularity in different application fields among which stand out: service, inspection and critical missions, driving solutions for tasks such as logistics, transportation, telemedicine care, and disinfection among others. One of the most important challenges for the implementation of intelligent solutions with mobile robotics is the ability of robots to navigate

Supported by Universidad de Ibagué 19-489-INT.

© The Author(s), under exclusive license to Springer Nature Switzerland AG 2022
J. C. Figueroa-García et al. (Eds.): WEA 2022, CCIS 1685, pp. 337–352, 2022.
https://doi.org/10.1007/978-3-031-20611-5_28

in unfamiliar environments. Problems arise when the robot does not know its environment or its exact location, which implies a stage of perception of the environment. Having a map and an exact location makes it possible to navigate in the environment, avoid obstacles, choose the best navigation route, and extract important information from the environment.

3D reconstruction is part of mapping and localization to obtain true morphological information about the surroundings. LiDAR mapping can provide high-frequency range measurements where errors are relatively constant, regardless of the distances measured. Other advanced methods include position estimates from the same perception sensors, such as visual odometry [5], LiDAR odometry [12], or iterative nearest point ICP [3]. Here we consider a simple case of map generation with low-cost components, using the simplest 2D Hokuyo rangefinder, wheel encoder odometry estimates, an IMU inertial measurement unit, and a normal camera to obtain color information from the environment. The method proposes two isolated algorithms, one that estimates a trajectory from the navigation elements and another that together with a kinematic model accumulates the laser measurements, conditioned to generate a point cloud in offline mapping applications. Ground reconstruction systems are usually called Terrestrial Laser Systems TLS and are generally fixed scanners. Mobile alternatives have some advantages concerning fixed scanners, however, the implementation of calibration algorithms and 3D reconstruction of environments requires, in addition to the necessary perception hardware, a mobile platform that can be related to the additional parts of the system, e.g.: power sources, navigation sensors, communications elements, and computing units [8]. LiDAR 3D point clouds can be generated with different sensors, the most employed commercial 3D rangefinders in mobile robotics are the Velodyne family devices, but these sensors are not easily accessible given their high costs, which range from 4000 USD.

2   Related Work

Various research projects have tackled the problem of 3D reconstruction based on 2D LiDAR sensors as in [6], where the development of a 3D reconstruction system based on a two-dimensional HOKUYO URG-04LX-UG01 laser scanner and a simple stepper motor was proposed. The system used a transformation model to generate LAS files with an experimental acquisition algorithm implemented with ROS in Python language. Similar work is shown in [4], which proposes a compact 3D laser scanner, based on pitching a commercial 2D rangefinder with a commercial version called UNOlaser.

Some mobile versions have been reported as a variant to fixed systems, however, don't include UGV's to move the perception elements into the operating environment. [10] proposes a multi-sensor fusion method to build an accurate 3D map about an unknown indoor scene and outdoor by optimizing a 2D map and accomplishing a calibration between 2D LiDAR and a panoramic camera. In [9] authors propose an efficient 3D mapping system with a multi-sensor calibration method to provide colored mapping for GPS-/global navigation satellite system-denied environments. The mobile options were tested with both backpacked and car-mounted systems on indoor and outdoor scenes.

3D mapping using mobile robots is a different problem because this configuration also includes actions to define the movements and accurate motion estimation by involving methods such as: extended Kalman filter EKF and visual-odometry based on laser sensors and cameras. Because unlike outdoor robots which in normal navigation conditions base their positioning on GNSS systems, indoor operating robots must use other alternatives, e.g.: pseudo-GNSS/INS module integrated framework which utilizes probabilistic Simultaneous Localization and Mapping (SLAM) techniques to estimate the platform pose and heading from 3D laser scanner data. Conventional 3D mappings with mobile platforms use 3D depth sensors or a combination of several 2D devices [1], however, although these configurations exhibit some advantages such as speed and ease, they have greater access restrictions due to their high costs. In [7], the implementation of an indoor MMS (Mobile Mapping Systems) using an unmanned ground vehicle (UGV) and a 3D laser scanner for the task of generating high-density maps of indoor areas denied by GNSS (Global Navigation Satellite System) is presented. To mitigate the absence of GNSS data, this work proposes an integrated pseudo-GNSS/INS module framework that uses simultaneous location and mapping techniques to estimate the position and heading of the platform from the 3D laser scanner data. With a correct pose estimation, the depth information obtained from LiDARs can be transformed into the world frame and simultaneously built a map by gathering multiple point clouds. In [13] authors use the laser to provide the initial value of pose optimization for the tracking thread of ORB-SLAM2 [5]. Similarly, some authors propose dense reconstructions of 3D indoor scenes from the combined use of multiple types of sensors. Besides, the loop-closure optimization process can be carried out by training classifiers according to those features extracted from heterogeneous sensors and the registration progress [11]. In [2] a solution to 3D mapping using a 2D laser in a fixed position of 90° with respect to the floor and pose estimation from an IMU-aided visual SLAM system is proposed. The proposed approach and its performance are demonstrated and evaluated by our indoor experiments using a Turtlebot mounted with a Kinect camera, an IMU and a 2D laser scanner.

Although no research project was found with our exact proposed scheme which consists of a 2D laser sensor on a rotating element on-board a terrestrial vehicle to generate 3D point clouds with its implementation variants, the Table 1 summarizes the principal work of different authors that reported contributions around the 3D mapping with LiDAR sensors in indoor scenes.

3 Materials and Methods

The present work contemplated four stages determined as follows: 1) adjustment of the robot movements and readings, 2) obtaining an estimation of the robot position and trajectory, 3) development of an algorithm for the calibration and

Table 1. Descriptive table of related works

Application	Type of mapping	Used LiDAR	Ref.
IMU-aided visual SLAM mapping	Without color, on-board UGV	Hokuyo UTM-30LX	[2]
Visual and LiDAR-based mapping	With color, multiple 2D LiDAR, mobile platform	2X Hokuyo UTM-30LX	[10]
Backpacked and car-mounted mapping	Indoor/outdoor, with color, multiple 3D LiDAR	2x Velodyne VLP-16	[9]
Pose estimation with multi-modal sensors	On-board UGV, 2D LiDAR	SICK TiM561	[11]
Mobile mapping with multiple pose estimation	Large scale, without color, on-board UGV, 3D LiDAR	Velodyne VLP-16	[7]
Fusion information for 3D mapping	On-board UGV, with color, 2D LiDAR + MS Kinect V2	Rplidar A2	[13]

generation of three-dimensional reconstructions of the navigation environment and 4) experimental validation of the implemented methods. During the first stage, the robot's movement and sensor reading parameters were tuned by developing software nodes on Robotic Operating System - ROS in its Kinetic version. After the conditioning, we proceeded with the implementation of algorithms to estimate the robot position by processing signals from the wheel encoders and the IMU, so that it is possible to generate an $P_{(X,Y,\alpha,\beta,\gamma)}$ path of the robot's travel in an indoor scenario with the assumption of a planar surface $Z = 0$. Then, we proceeded with the study and proposal of a kinematic model that includes the information coming from the 2D LiDAR with the servomotor angle and the robot path to generate a 3D reconstruction of the space travelled. In the same way, before validation experiments, the second stage of calibration and parameter estimation was carried out with the purpose of adding a color dimension to the information obtained, by assigning R, G, B values in each voxel of the point cloud. Finally in the validation stage, since accessing 3D reconstruction platforms by way of mapping is a difficult task, because of the cost or type of platform used commercially, the validation of the built 3D map was carried out with a comparison of the reconstruction of reference objects using geometric error indicators with respect to manual measurements in regular objects.

3.1 Acquisition System

The measurement errors of a LiDAR sensor have different origins. Therefore, is important to characterize the sensor to be used in order to establish its behaviour under different situations and thus be able to discriminate its response for the benefit of the applications. Our system is composed of the HOKUYO URG-04LX-UG01 LiDAR sensor, which has a measuring area from 20 to 5600 mm mm in 240° field of view, with an angular resolution of approximately 0.36°, accuracy of ±30 mm and a sampling period of 100 ms; a RGB camera LOGITECH C920 with 78° field of view and resolution options 1080p/30 fps - 720p/30 fps 640 × 480 px; and a motion control device with one degree of freedom Dynamixel AX-12A with 15.3 kg· cm/212 oz· in stall torque, 0.169 s/60° no-load speed & 59 RPM and 0.29°/0.0051 resolution.

The mobile platform used was a Turtlebot 2, a low-cost robot widely used in education and development projects. A Dynamixel servomotor was installed on the robotic platform, which supports the LiDAR sensor and the RGB camera. This modification offers an additional degree of freedom over the scanning position of the laser sensor. Furthermore, this modification was made to avoid possible angular deviations between the RGB camera and the laser sensor, between the laser sensor and the servomotor and also between the servomotor and the robotic platform, with the intention of avoiding possible distortions in the final reconstruction after simplifying the kinematic model. The angular correspondences were physically calibrated at the laboratory of metrology of SENA-NEIVA Colombia with a machine for three-dimensional scanning by contact reference NIKON LK V 8.7.6.

Position Estimation Test. The mobile robot used is equipped with a Kobuki robot base, a dual-core netbook, the gyroscope is compatible with ROS. All components have been integrated into a development platform, which combines the information received from the direct odometry of the robot through the encoders with the information thrown by the IMU. This integration makes that the errors in the robot movement produced by external conditions like the surface where the robot moves, and that are reflected in the data thrown by the encoders, are compensated by the information thrown by the IMU and estimate a more accurate position.

The robot was placed inside a room in order to estimate the accuracy of the robot's movements. or this test, a rectangle route of 7m × 8.8 m was defined and drawn on the ground, the robot followed it in a manual mode from a joystick handled by a pilot. Multiple laps were made, performing in each one experimental modification in the parameters of the Kalman Extended Filter (EKF) in the "*robot_localization*" algorithm. The estimated path were compared with respect to the ideal route until a satisfactory tuning. Figure 1 summarizes the progress in the results obtained by the modifications made to the filter parameters for three laps until an acceptable response is obtained for the estimation of the robot position. Once the position estimation algorithm was tuned, verification of its performance was carried out. Given the absence of a reference instrument to compare the trajectory with ground truth, an ideal square path $f_{(x,y)}$ fragmented into four parts was defined from the route traced on the floor and the distance between the estimated position from the robot at each sample and the ideal path defined as a straight line was calculated. An error indicator was determined in each of the four segments using RMSE, the values obtained were: 0.2048 m, 0.1213 m, 0.3084 m and 0.1696 m with an average value of 0.2010 m in the test with 31.6 m of travel and 360° of counterclockwise rotation.

3.2   Kinematics Model

The purpose of the system is to transform and accumulate the acquired LiDAR detection from a point reference called P_i, to a reference coordinate frame centered on a point called P_0, where P_0 is the reference point of the robot, which corresponds with the initial position of the robot $P_{(x,y,z,\gamma)} = [0,0,0,0]$ for our case. The final point cloud consists in a XYZ space as a function of the horizontal scan angle of the LiDAR θ, the radial distance r, some constant parameters that represent the distances between the points and possible angular deviations, the vertical angle of the servomotor ϑ and the transitional pose estimation generated by the Kalman Extended Filter expressed in its 2D XY axis, as well as the rotation angle of the robot γ. Figure 2 illustrates the position of transformation points with respect to the illuminated object, the laser sensor, the servomotor, the Turtlebot and the scene.

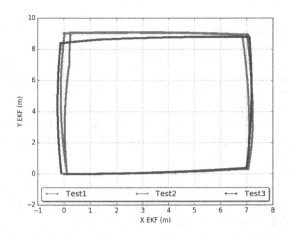

Fig. 1. Position estimation responses for parameter tuning on EKF. Green corresponds to an initial set of parameters, red is a first modification and blue path correspond to the last tuning. (Color figure online)

Mapping consists in the accumulation of transformed point clouds taken in account the robot movements, and at the same time including color to each sweep made of the point cloud by assigning the RGB values of a pixel or set of pixels to each voxel in the point cloud. In this way, each point in the cloud can be defined as $P_{(x,y,z,R,G,B)}$. Some of the transformation matrices of this sequence are fixed, because they represent constant displacement parameters, on the other, hand some of them are variable because they include the displacement of the robot or the angular rotation of the servomotor. Two mapping variants are proposed in this work: the first one called "Scan and Go" with a fixed angle in the inclination of the servomotor, in this mode, the robot moves continuously in a trajectory; and a second variant called "Stop and Scan" in which the robot occasionally stops during its journey to scan the environment by turning the servomotor from above to the floor. Assuming that there are no angular deviations between the transformation frames, the general transformation equation used for the 3D reconstruction is as follows:

$$P_0 = T_{p0} \cdot R_{z\gamma} \cdot T_{p2} \cdot R_{x\vartheta} \cdot T_{p1} \cdot P_i \tag{1}$$

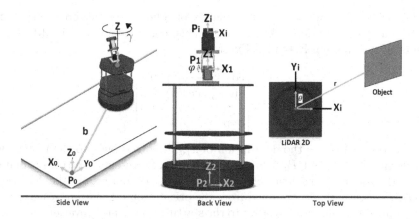

Side View   Back View   Top View

Fig. 2. Schematic diagram and notations for the reconstruction system based on rigid transformations from LiDAR raw data to an initial reference point

where P_i corresponds to the initial axis, T_{p1} and T_{p1}, T_{p2}, T_{p0} represents translations between the reference points and frames, and $R_{x\vartheta}$, $R_{z\gamma}$ are the rotation matrices for the servomotor and yaw orientation respectively.

The general Eq. (1) shows the transformation in four steps from an initial $Pi_{(x,y,z)}$ obtained as a follows:

$$P_i = \begin{bmatrix} r \cdot \sin(\theta) \\ r \cdot \cos(\theta) \\ 0...0 \\ 1...1 \end{bmatrix} \tag{2}$$

T_{p1} corresponds to the transformation to point P_1 and is given by Eq. (3):

$$T_{p1} = \begin{bmatrix} 1 & 0 & 0 & t_{x1} \\ 0 & 1 & 0 & t_{y1} \\ 0 & 0 & 1 & t_{z1} \\ 0 & 0 & 0 & 1 \end{bmatrix} \tag{3}$$

where t_{x1}, t_{y1}, t_{z1} are constant measurement parameters on the platform. On the one hand, for the "scan and Go" mode, ϑ is a constant parameter equal to 45°, and in turn, the matrix $R_{x\vartheta}$ becomes a constant parameter matrix. On the other hand, for the "Scan and Stop" mode ϑ is a variable parameter which can have values between −45° and +45° and in turn the matrix $R_{x\vartheta}$ becomes a variable parameter matrix. T_{p2} corresponds to the transformation to point P_2 and is given by Eq. (4):

$$T_{p2} = \begin{bmatrix} 1 & 0 & 0 & t_{x2} \\ 0 & 1 & 0 & t_{y2} \\ 0 & 0 & 1 & t_{z2} \\ 0 & 0 & 0 & 1 \end{bmatrix} \tag{4}$$

Equation (5) shows $R_{z\gamma}$, it is a matrix of robot rotation about the Z axis and the angle of rotation is known as γ. This angle value is obtained from the output of the Kalman Extended Filter.

$$R_{z\gamma} = \begin{bmatrix} \cos(\gamma) & -\sin(\gamma) & 0 & 0 \\ \sin(\gamma) & \cos(\gamma) & 0 & 0 \\ 0 & 0 & 1 & 0 \\ 0 & 0 & 0 & 1 \end{bmatrix} \tag{5}$$

Equation (6) shows the description of T_{p0}, it corresponds to the translation transformation to point P_0. This variable matrix represents the transformation due to the robot's movement. The components of this matrix are the XY increments in meters Δ_x, Δ_y obtained from the orientation estimation, which generates a pose estimation with respect to the starting point. The elevation variations Z are ignored by assuming an environment with a flat surface.

$$T_{p0} = \begin{bmatrix} 1 & 0 & 0 & \Delta_x \\ 0 & 1 & 0 & \Delta_y \\ 0 & 0 & 1 & 0 \\ 0 & 0 & 0 & 1 \end{bmatrix} \tag{6}$$

The scan mode: "Scan and Go", is a continuous mode, i.e. the robot doesn't need to slow down during its trajectory. The servomotor on which the LiDAR sensor is supported operates with a fixed tilt angle, e.g. with a 45° of incidence in the central beam with respect to the floor. This reconstruction method has been used to generate 3D models by using a 2D LiDAR. The scanning mode: "Stop and Scan", stops the robot from moving at some points where the pilot considers it, to perform scans with the servo motor in a range of inclinations from +45° to −45°, a common practice in fixed scanners [6]. This method has an effect on the point clouds that allows more information to be obtained, especially towards a higher view, however, the scanning times will be longer than in "Scan and Go" mode. Basically, the differences in the kinematic models of the scanning modes mentioned above differ in the rotation matrix that defines the angle inclination of the LiDAR.

3.3   Colour Conditioning and Integration

The integration of color to a point cloud generated by a LiDAR is the addition of information for the representation of environments through reconstructions made by robots in order to have the most features of that environment for decision making. This integration must be done in a synchronized way, where for each point X, Y, Z of the point cloud the information R, G, B, of the pixel corresponding to that point in the photograph taken of the sensed object, is added. The proposed method consists of the following steps:

Position Robot: The dynamixel servomotor was positioned at $0°$ to the horizon. The robot was positioned in front of a white flat wall at a distance of approximately one meter from the HOKUYO. This distance was checked by reading the information on the HOKUYO in its central beam.

Locate Reference Object: A reference object with known dimensions was placed in front of the wall, with a color totally different from the wall color, making sure that this reference object is within the field of vision of the camera.

RGB Horizontal Calibration: An algorithm was implemented to establish the best horizontal alignment of the reference object with respect to the beam of the HOKUYO and the RGB camera, developed in Python version 3.6 and OpenCV version 4.0, which makes the user manually arrange the box in such a way that the mentioned conditions are met. The step-by-step is presented as follows: 1. Detection of image edges using the Canny algorithm, 2. Determine the coordinates of the external contour boundary rectangle with minimum area, 3. Clockwise coordinate arrangement for defining the lower-left and lower-right points required for the box orientation check, 4. Analysis of the coordinates (Y) of the points defined in the previous point to establish a possible rotation of the box, 5. Manually align, 6. Once aligned: Output of the coordinates in pixels of the upper-left point of the box and dimensions in pixels of the width and height of the box.

XYZ Horizontal Calibration: In this step, the servomotor was positioned in such a way that the infrared beam of the HOKUYO hits the housing. The objective of this step is to establish the number of ranges that occupy certain reference object without concerning the distance where it is. To obtain this data, an algorithm was implemented to extract the number of ranges of the HOKUYO that affect the reference object and its position or angle within the 726 values of the horizontal sweep. Figure 3 shows the variables considered for the mathematical formulation useful in this step to describe horizontal tuning, which is: U is the measured distance between the HOKUYO and the wall, V is the measured distance between the HOKUYO and the reference object, R is the range measured by the HOKUYO. The HOKUYO creates a matrix with 726 range values and n is the index of the range matrix currently measured by the HOKUYO, which has 726 values.

Equation (7) shows the resulting matrix of the algorithm.

$$m = \begin{bmatrix} R_n & R_{n+1} & ... & R_{n+l} \\ n & n+1 & ... & n+l \end{bmatrix}_{2xl} \tag{7}$$

where R_n is the current range in the n index of the range array measured by the HOKUYO. And where l is the number of beams hitting the reference object and that meet the condition $R_n \approx V$.

Horizontal Synchronization: In this step, the data of the previous steps are integrated, to relate the ranges measured by the LiDAR and its corresponding color pixel in a horizontal way. Equation $Q = \frac{W}{l}$ relates the width of the box in pixels to the width of the box in a number of incident infrared ranges. Where Q indicates the resolution measured in pixels for each range of the HOKUYO horizontally, W the width of the reference object (box) in pixels and Eq. (7), l, is the width of the box measured by the horizontal sweep.

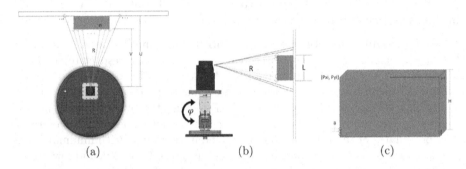

(a)   (b)   (c)

Fig. 3. Description of the horizontal and vertical calibration: a) Top view of a horizontal scan used in the XYZ tuning: R is the range measured by the HOKUYO, n is the index of the range matrix currently measured by the HOKUYO, U and V are the distances measured between the HOKUYO, the wall and the reference object, respectively; b) Description of the calibration in the vertical scan used in the vertical tuning; and c) Description of vertical synchronization, B represents the resolution, measured in pixels, for each range of the HOKUYO vertically.

Vertical Tuning: An algorithm was implemented to moves the servomotor from a minimum angle to a maximum angle and to extract for each angle the value of the central beam measured by the LiDAR. The obtained data include the number of ranges, values, positions and angles of the infrared rays affecting the reference object. The variables considered for the mathematical formulation useful in this step are described below:

- L is the height of the reference object.
- R is the range measured by the HOKUYO.
- R_ϑ is the range of the center beam measured by the HOKUYO, that is when $\theta = 0$.
- j is the servo's rotational feed rate.
- δ is the minimum feed resolution of the servo motor.

Equation (8) shows the resulting matrix of the algorithm.

$$k = \begin{bmatrix} R_\vartheta & R_{\vartheta+\delta} & \cdots & R_{\vartheta+j*\delta} \\ \vartheta & \vartheta+\delta & \cdots & \vartheta+j*\delta \end{bmatrix}_{2xj} \tag{8}$$

where R_ϑ is the current range of the center beam, when $\theta = 0$, in the j index of the servo drive feed. And where j is the number of ranges measured by the HOKUYO that meet the condition $R_\vartheta \approx V$.

Equation (9) shows the servo drive angle:

$$\vartheta = \vartheta_{min} \pm j * \delta \tag{9}$$

Vertical Synchronization: The algorithm takes a picture for each j advance of the dynamixel servo motor. This means that the number of pictures taken depends on the number of vertical advances. Equation (10) shows the mathematical definition for the number of photographs f:

$$f = \frac{\vartheta_{max} - \vartheta_{min}}{\delta} \tag{10}$$

The problem of vertical calibration consists of relating the beam of the HOKUYO with its corresponding row of pixels in the photograph taken by each advance. To solve this problem, a fixed condition was established, which is that the camera is mechanically anchored to the HOKUYO, therefore, the infrared beam will always point to the same row or rows of pixels in the photograph. Figure 3c shows the graphic description of vertical colour calibration. Where H represents the height of the reference object, j is the number of beams incident on the reference object and B represents the resolution, measured in pixels, for each range of the HOKUYO vertically and is defined in Equation $B = \frac{H}{j}$. With the assignment of rows of pixels to each range of infrared beams of the HOKUYO, the vertical position in the photo from where the color information will be extracted was found. In horizontal synchronization step of the proposed method, it was ensured that the infrared beam of the HOKUYO, with a dynamixel angle in 2.62 radians, would hit the box. Therefore, the position of the row of pixels in that photo must be related to the beam of the HOKUYO.

4   Results and Discussion

4.1   Point Cloud Generation

The proposed system was implemented and tested at indoor environments in which in addition to the objects belonging to a house, other objects were placed within reach of the LiDAR scan, in order to observe its reconstruction in the resulting point cloud. Figures 5 shows the obtained results of the reconstruction in this test for both, "scan and go" and "stop and scan" methods were tested with color information.

The method used in this project to establish the kinematics of the reconstruction makes that the error by this one is reduced since all the mathematical and mechanical elements are taken into account to take the information of the point

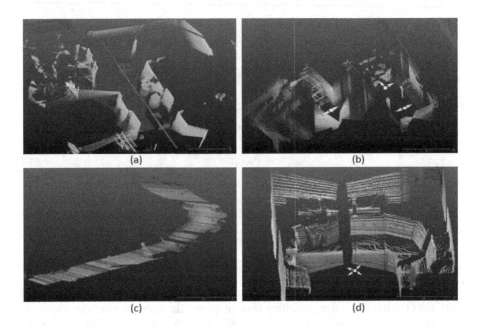

Fig. 4. Generated scene reconstructions by using the proposed system: **a)** "scan and go" into a regular flat, red line represents the trajectory and color depends of the altitude, **b)** "scan and stop" into a regular flat, grey points represent the scanning way points, color depends of altitude, **c)** "scan and go" with scene color, and **d)** "scan and stop" with scene color (Color figure online)

cloud from the axis of the LiDAR to the base of the robot, point in which all the kinematics information of the robot converges to integrate the position of this one with the 3D point cloud. In both scan modes, it is the pilot who remotely manipulates the robot and its trajectory. In the second mode, it is the pilot who defines from control the places to make the scans, as well as the maximum and minimum angles of inclination. This stops in the point cloud that so high or low is reconstructed the scene. At the end of the trajectory, in any case, the pilot sends the combination from the control to finish with the data collection and start the reconstruction phase. The addition of color in the point cloud is an optional feature that is added from the manipulation functions if the pilot decides to do so. Since the opening of the laser sensor is much larger than that of the RGB camera, there are points in the LiDAR that do not receive a color pixel assignment. Therefore they are eliminated from the point cloud leaving only the voxels that are synchronized with the RGB camera (Fig. 4).

Operation and processing time are considerable variables that differentiate the two methods. The reconstruction time for "scan and go" mode is affected by: Time for the extraction of the color information dynamically, time for the LiDAR scan, which is approximately 100 ms per scan and time for the calculation of the position. The reconstruction time for "scan and stop" mode is affected by: Time for the extraction of the color information dynamically, time for the LiDAR scan, which is approximately 100 ms per scan, time for the calculation of the position and additional, this mode is affected in the operation time by the speed of movement of the servomotor, because in this mode a vertical scan is made to perform the scan. Second operating mode the reconstruction time is considerably longer compared to the first method, due to the vertical scan at each point in the environment. The scanning time at each point is approximately 94.14 s for a 90-degree scan angle: from $+45°$ to $-45°$.

In this way, according to the characteristics of each mode, it is possible to identify possible applications in each case, e.g.: "scan and go" option could be useful for applications such as: Applications where information is required from objects or items below a specific height, such as in agricultural applications where information needs to be extracted from plants, land, furrows, etc.; airborne robotics applications, where the scan is done by directing the LiDAR laser to a specific point, to perform reconstructions below that point and applications where depth or color information must be dynamically or in real time, for immediate decision making. On the other hand "stop and scan" option could be useful for applications such as: Applications where it is required to have three-dimensional information of complete spaces regardless of the height of the space. To change the minimum and maximum scanning height, the mechanical limits of the servo motor must be changed, as this is the element that limits vertical scanning and applications that require to have complete information regardless of the time of reconstruction.

4.2   System Evaluation

To evaluate the correspondence with the real scene of the generated point cloud, two reference scenes were defined to extract longitudinal measurements and compare with reference values. Reference values were obtained from manual measurements and represent both, horizontal and vertical segments. For ease of reference, a wall and an open door were chosen as reference objects for a total of six measurements to be compared. Figure 5 shows the real and reconstructed scenes with the description of evaluation segments.

Table 2. Comparison between real values and obtained measurement

Item	Manual [cm]	Obtained [cm]	Error [%]
A	608	628.55	3.380
B	252	259.15	2.837
C	490	475.13	3.035
D	65	67	3.077
E	200	198.56	0.720
F	249	251.2	0.884

Table 2 presents the comparison between the six reference measurements, the six obtained measurements from the point cloud and their experimental errors which are between 0.72% and 3.38%.

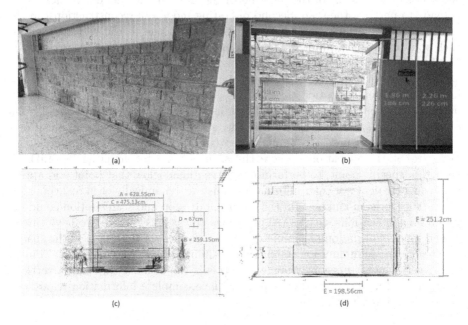

Fig. 5. Validation scenes wall at 1774 lux and open door at 254 lux: **a**) graphic description of the wall scene, **b**) graphic description of the open door scene, **c**) wall segmentation from 3D reconstruction, and **d**) open door segmentation from the 3D reconstruction.

The scheme with the greatest similarity to the configuration proposed in this study is the one presented in [2], given that it makes use of only one 2D element on-board a TurtleBot platform to perform the complete reconstruction. The results show a point cloud of a reconstruction of an indoor scene without RGB colour information corresponding to the photograph of the environment of the experiment presented, but with some gaps of information such as the floor. Similarly, all other indoor scanning systems report the use of 3D elements by nature with accuracies between 3.07 and 3.66 cm [9]; device measurement accuracies around 3.0 cm [7] and aided by GPS or visual odometry methods [13].

Despite the difficulty of making accurate quantitative assessments on these real-world scans, it can be seen from each result that indoor mobile 3D mapping systems report longitudinal errors in the order of centimetres, this reconstruction error has a relationship with the accuracy of each laser sensor as well as the performance of the positioning system. However, the cost of the perception elements used is much higher in most of the reviewed works; leaving aside the costs related to structures and positioning sensors. We compare our system with state-of-the-art publicly available mobile point cloud generation systems. Table 3 shows a quantitative comparison of the quality of the point clouds generated from the determination of the root mean square error RMSE of the averages obtained from each reviewed work and data from Table 2, as well as the estimated cost of the reconstruction sensors involved in each platform.

5 Conclusions

This paper describes the development of a low-cost 3D color mapping system for indoor scenes based on a 2D LiDAR on-board an UGV with a total price around 2500 USD. From the obtained data during the characterization tests, it is concluded that the dispersion in the measurement grows proportionally with the distance, the objects with pronounced edges and the light of the measurement environment and therefore, in turn, the areas of the point clouds that represent parts of the scene with greater illumination or distance, tend to have a lower accuracy. In the same way, two scanning modes were presented: "scan and go" and "stop and scan". The first method is a continuous scanning with a fixed inclined angle in the laser sensor. The second method although it takes longer, it scans taller objects in scenes better and it usually generates point clouds with a higher number of samples is useful when the application requires 360-degree scans, as it requires only two scans with a half-turn difference from the z-axis.

Table 3. Comparison of the quality of the generated point clouds with the determined RMSE and the estimated perception cost.

RMSE [m]	Used sensors	Cost	Ref.
Not reported	Hokuyo UTM-30LX	≈4500 USD	[2]
0.0187	2X Hokuyo UTM-30LX; Flir ladybug5	>25000 USD	[10]
Not reported	2x Velodyne VLP-16	>8000 USD	[9]
0.0452	SICK TiM561; Asus Xtion Pro Live	>3600 USD	[11]
Not reported	Velodyne VLP-16	>4000 USD	[7]
Not reported	Rplidar A2; Kinect V2	>700 USD	[13]
0.1084	URG-04LX-UG01; Logitech C920	≈970 USD	Ours

A camera calibration method to add RGB data to each obtained voxel was proposed and validated. The method requires a cubic target and uses depth gradient from borders and image processing to synchronize the camera and the LiDAR. The reconstructed 3D scenes presented deviation errors between 0.72% and 3.38%. Our system obtained a RMSE equal to 10.84 cm on longitudinal vertical and horizontal measurements, higher than other works which report errors around 1.8–4.5 cm but with a significant difference in the cost of the used vision sensors.

Future work includes the study of using LiDAR SLAM methods to improve the trajectory estimation and thus in turn improve the quality of the generated point clouds. Similarly exploring new methods of fusion between the point cloud and the camera that achieve integration more easily.

References

1. Chen, J., Cho, Y.K.: Real-time 3D mobile mapping for the built environment. In: ISARC 2016–33rd International Symposium on Automation and Robotics in Construction (2016)
2. Chen, M., Yang, S., Yi, X., Wu, D.: Real-time 3D mapping using a 2D laser scanner and IMU-aided visual SLAM. In: 2017 IEEE International Conference on Real-Time Computing and Robotics, RCAR 2017, vol. 2017-July, pp. 297–302. Institute of Electrical and Electronics Engineers Inc., March 2018
3. Mendes, E., Koch, P., Lacroix, S.: ICP-based pose-graph SLAM. In: SSRR 2016 - International Symposium on Safety, Security and Rescue Robotics (2016)
4. Morales, J., Martinez, J.L., Mandow, A., Pequeno-Boter, A., Garcia-Cerezo, A.: Design and development of a fast and precise low-cost 3D laser rangefinder. In: 2011 IEEE International Conference on Mechatronics, ICM 2011 - Proceedings (2011)
5. Mur-Artal, R., Tardos, J.D.: ORB-SLAM2: an open-source SLAM system for monocular, stereo, and RGB-D cameras. IEEE Trans. Rob. **33**, 1255–1262 (2017)
6. Murcia, H.F., Monroy, M.F., Mora, L.F.: 3D scene reconstruction based on a 2D moving LiDAR. In: Florez, H., Diaz, C., Chavarriaga, J. (eds.) ICAI 2018. CCIS, vol. 942, pp. 295–308. Springer, Cham (2018). https://doi.org/10.1007/978-3-030-01535-0_22
7. Shamseldin, T., Manerikar, A., Elbahnasawy, M., Habib, A.: SLAM-based Pseudo-GNSS/INS localization system for indoor LiDAR mobile mapping systems. In: 2018 IEEE/ION Position, Location and Navigation Symposium, PLANS 2018 - Proceedings, pp. 197–208. Institute of Electrical and Electronics Engineers Inc., June 2018
8. Wan, J., Tang, S., Yan, H., Li, D., Wang, S., Vasilakos, A.V.: Cloud robotics: current status and open issues. IEEE Access **4**, 2797–2807 (2016)
9. Wen, C., et al.: Toward efficient 3-D colored mapping in GPS-/GNSS-denied environments. IEEE Geosci. Remote Sens. Lett. **17**(1), 147–151 (2020)
10. Wu, Q., Sun, K., Zhang, W., Huang, C., Wu, X.: Visual and LiDAR-based for the mobile 3D mapping. In: 2016 IEEE International Conference on Robotics and Biomimetics, ROBIO 2016, pp. 1522–1527. Institute of Electrical and Electronics Engineers Inc. (2016)
11. Yang, S., Li, B., Liu, M., Lai, Y.K., Kobbelt, L., Hu, S.M.: HeteroFusion: dense scene reconstruction integrating multi-sensors. IEEE Trans. Visual Comput. Graphics **26**, 3217–3230 (2019)
12. Zhang, J., Singh, S.: LOAM: Lidar Odometry and Mapping in Real-time
13. Zhang, Y., Zhang, H., Xiong, Z., Sheng, X.: A visual SLAM System with Laser assisted optimization. In: IEEE/ASME International Conference on Advanced Intelligent Mechatronics, AIM, vol. 2019-July, pp. 187–192. Institute of Electrical and Electronics Engineers Inc., July 2019

Power Simulation Process Through the Analysis of Geometry, Irradiance and Interconnection Impact in Photovoltaic Roof Tiles

Juan Acosta$^{(\boxtimes)}$ (ID) and Ricardo Mejía-Gutiérrez (ID)

Design Engineering Research Group (GRID), Universidad EAFIT,
Carrera 49 No 7 Sur–50, Medellín, Colombia
{jcacostas,rmejiag}@eafit.edu.co

Abstract. Renewable energies have been consolidated as one of the most important alternatives to achieve a successful energy transition and thus mitigate environmental concerns. Although, they represent a challenge in terms of production costs, it is important to highlight that the implementation of renewable energies contributes to address climate change. In Latin American countries, such as Colombia, there is a great potential for the production of renewable energy since its main sources are hydraulic, wind, thermal and photovoltaic. Consequently, this article will focus on the Building Integrated Photovoltaics (BIPV) concept, which allows to increase renewable energy collection, while merging PV cells with constructive elements; being a complimentary support for the energy transition. In this study, the BIPV concept will be specifically oriented to the application of solar roofs. These approach triggers some opportunities, as planar solar surfaces will not comply the morphological properties of regular roof tiles. A proposed geometry for a BIPV application will be analyzed, in terms of energy collection capabilities, according to geometric properties. The impact of shadows and electrical reconfiguration, will be considered in a simulation. Then, a process to evaluate the power generation potential will be studied to analyze feasibility of integrating photovoltaic modules on household roofs.

Keywords: Solar energy · Photovoltaic · Roof tiles · Irradiance simulation · Electrical reconfiguration

1 Introduction

The high global demand for energy and its consequent pollution of the planet has become into an environmental problematic with considerable effects [1]. It is for this reason that renewable energies have been taking an important position in the international framework [2]. Locally, Colombia has a great potential in terms of energy from sources such as hydro, wind, thermal and photovoltaic

© The Author(s), under exclusive license to Springer Nature Switzerland AG 2022
J. C. Figueroa-García et al. (Eds.): WEA 2022, CCIS 1685, pp. 353–365, 2022.
https://doi.org/10.1007/978-3-031-20611-5_29

[3]. It is certainly valid to mention that renewable energies represent a challenge compared to the affordability of conventional energies, however, they also represent a cost-benefit alternative that is continuously evolving and is becoming one of the best strategies to face climate change and others related adverse problems [4].

One initiative that have been developed even at a commercial level to support the energy transition consists in the use of photovoltaic modules in buildings; this is known as Building Integrated Photovoltaics ("BIPV"). In this concept, the photovoltaic (PV) modules are not fixed to the building, but are part of it, offering good electrical-thermal supply potential [5]. This article will analyze the concept of BIPV specifically oriented to roofs and the use of this area commonly irradiated by solar rays. Additionally, given the tropical zone in which Colombia is located and the high presence of rainfall, tile roofs have important advantages thermoacoustics, aesthetics, impermeability, flame retardant, and resistance [6].

Next, a state of the art review of solar roof tiles, photovoltaic energy, interconnection of PV modules and reconfiguration algorithms will be given. Then, the simulation process will be explained to obtain the results that will allow the analysis to be carried out. The case study of this article consists of evaluating the technical feasibility of integrating photovoltaic modules in tile-type roofs, and for this purpose the irradiance phenomena will be simulated, then these will be the input for a Matlab-Simulink® model that, given the irradiance data, returns the effective power of the array, comparing with a completely flat roof and a tile roof with and without a reconfiguration algorithm.

2   State of the Art

2.1   Solar Roof Tiles Context

A solar roof tile is an application of BIPV technology, and in contrast to Building Applied Photovoltaics technology ("BAPV") it is a roof with integrated photovoltaic modules. These roofs contains arrays of solar cells that can be made of materials such as gallium arsenide (GaAs), indium phosphide (InP), synthesized polymers, compounds of copper, indium, gallium and selenium or better known as multijunction and, most commonly used, silicon (monocrystalline and polycrystalline) [7]. In terms of geometries (tiles), in the literature there are applications of BIPV technology, in the work of Heinstein et al. [8] applications ranging from urban, rural and even cultural sectors are shown. In addition to this, mirrors and reflective elements are also used in PV modules [9].

Commercially, the energy conversion efficiencies of a photovoltaic cell are in the order of 24.7% for monocrystalline silicon. However, it has been determined that multijunction cells, due to the combination of materials, reach efficiencies of up to 39.3% [7], although these ones are not yet commercially feasible.

2.2   Photovoltaic Theoretical Framework

The performance of a photovoltaic module can be analyzed in several ways, one of which is through power. This, in turn, is defined by the scalar product of current and voltage, variables that are consolidated in the characteristic curve VI of each PV module. Table 1 shows the variables that will be used to define the behavior of the PV module.

Table 1. Model variables.

Symbol	Variable	Symbol	Variable
E_{GO}	Bandgap energy (GAP) of the semiconductor	K_I	Short-circuit current temperature coefficient under standard conditions
G	Solar irradiation	η	Diode ideality factor
G_n	Nominal solar irradiance (STC conditions)	N_S	Number of cells connected in series
I	Output current	q	Electron charge
I_D	Diode current	R_{SE}	Series resistance
I_{PH}	Photovoltaic current	R_{SH}	Shunt resistance
I_{RS}	Reverse saturation current	T	Operating temperature
I_S	Saturation current	T_n	Nominal temperature (STC conditions)
I_{SC}	Short circuit current	V	Output voltage
I_{SH}	Derivación de corriente	V_{OC}	Open circuit voltage
k	Boltzman's constant	V_T	Seal thermal voltage PN

The following equations [10] allow estimating the values of the VI curve for a PV module based on a radiation G and a temperature of operation T:

- **Photovoltaic current:** total output current generated by the PV module.

$$I = I_{PH} - I_D - I_{SH} \tag{1}$$

- **Photocurrent:** current generated by exposure to radiant energy.

$$I_{PH} = [I_{SC} + K_i * (T - T_n)] * (G/G_n) \tag{2}$$

- **Diode current:** current that flows through the diode.

$$I_D = I_S * \left(exp \left(\frac{V + I * R_{SE}}{\eta * N_S * V_T} \right) - 1 \right] \tag{3}$$

- **Junction thermal voltage PN:** voltage produced within the P-N junction due to the action of temperature.

$$V_T = (k * T) / q \tag{4}$$

- **Shunt current:** current losses typically due to manufacturing defects.

$$I_{SH} = \frac{V + I * R_{SE}}{R_{SH}} \tag{5}$$

- **Saturation current:** current that flows through the P-N junction.

$$I_S = I_{RS} * \left(\frac{T}{T_n}\right)^3 * exp\left[\frac{q * E_{GO}}{\eta * k} * \left(\frac{1}{T_n} - \frac{1}{T_n}\right)\right] \tag{6}$$

- **Reverse saturation current:** current flowing through the P-N junction diode when it is reversed biased.

$$I_{RS} = \frac{I_{SC}}{exp\left(\frac{V_{OC}}{N_S * \eta * V_T}\right) - 1} \tag{7}$$

2.3 Photovoltaic Modules Interconnection Topologies

A photovoltaic modules array can be interconnected in different ways, each of them constituting a different topology and a unique behavior. Reviewing the literature, it is found that within the most commonly used interconnection strategies as a benchmark are Series-Parallel (SP), Bridge-link (BL), Honeycomb (HC), and Total Cross Tied (TCT) [11]. TCT and BL has a better performance, and the practical implementation of TCT and BL schemes should not escalate the cost [12]. Figure 1 shows these classical interconnection topologies in PV modules.

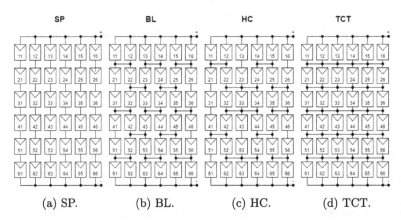

(a) SP.　　　　(b) BL.　　　　(c) HC.　　　　(d) TCT.

Fig. 1. Classical interconnection topologies in PV modules.

2.4 Algorithms for Electrical Reconfiguration by Switches

A set of photovoltaic modules can have a base topology as described above, additionally, it can also be dynamically reconfigured according to the irradiance conditions received by each of the modules at any given time. This is achieved by algorithms that compare the behavior of the modules and connect them through switches seeking to obtain the highest power. These switches grows quadratically with the number of modules [13], therefore, and for this application, it is convenient to try to reduce the number of modules by increasing their unit size. In the literature there are some algorithms to reconfigure photovoltaic modules. Nguyen and Lehman [14] define 2 control algorithms, these differ mostly in that one of them performs the control mainly by voltages and the other one does it by currents. Babu et al. [15] propose an algorithm for the extraction of maximum power under partial shading conditions for a PV array based on particle swarm optimization. Deshkar et al. [16] and Fathy [17] look for the same goal but using a genetic algorithm and a modified artificial bee colony algorithm, respectively. Romano et al. [18] use a reconfigurable switching matrix controlled by an iterative algorithm that seeks to obtain the best configuration by comparing a equalization index defined as the differences between the operating currents in the PV array.

In this paper, the algorithm proposed by Calcabrini et al. [13] is applied to our simulations, this algorithm works based on the ordering and comparison of the currents of the PV modules. Since in a series array, the current limits performance as it decreases along the string, and this ultimately results in significant power losses [19]. Therefore, parallel connection (for similar voltages) is the best option in terms of power since current drops in one PV module will not affect the others. However, parallel connection leads to higher currents, so the transport and conversion of power downstream is more inefficient [20].

3   Simulation Process to Analyze the Photovoltaic Roof Behavior

This section presents the development of the procedure to simulate the behavior of the PV roof. Figure 2 shows a block diagram illustrating the methodology of the simulation process. Initially, geometry will be defined by obtaining the CAD model, then the ray tracing for this geometry will be simulated in TracePro® software. Finally, the power behavior for the PV array will be obtained applying Eqs. 1 to 7 in Matlab-Simulink®.

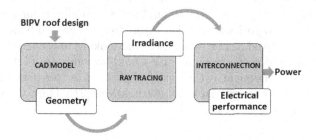

Fig. 2. Block diagram corresponding to the simulation process.

3.1   Geometrical Set-Up for Energetic Analysis

Between possible three-dimensional geometries that photovoltaic panels can adopt, a design commonly used in non-photovoltaic roofs was selected due to its good functional performance, it is shown in Fig. 3a.

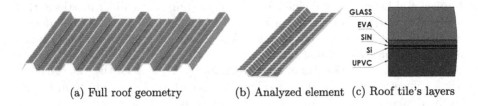

(a) Full roof geometry   (b) Analyzed element   (c) Roof tile's layers

Fig. 3. CAD model of the roof morphology.

To obtain more accurate results the element is modeled by parts, since the solar roof would be made up of glass, EVA, silicon nitrate, silicon, and UPVC (see Fig. 3c). The commercial thicknesses used for the CAD modeling for the materials are shown below in the Table 2. The simulation software has built-in optical coefficients of refraction, absorption and transmittance for each material at predetermined wavelengths.

Table 2. Thicknesses.

Layer	Material	Thickness
1	UPVC	2.5 mm
2	Silicon	0.2 mm
3	Silicon Nitrate	0.1 mm
4	EVA	0.5 mm
5	Glass	3 mm

As can be seen, for each section of the roof (see Fig. 3b), PV rows are located in 6 different kind of positions, as shown in Fig. 4a. A similar behavior is expected for rows 1 and 4. Also positions 2 and 6 might have an inverted behavior, and the same for positions 3 and 5. For this reason and looking to reduce the number of switches, it was decided that each module would be composed of 2 rows of equal type of position. Consequently, this helps to obtain a better performance when operating under dynamic partial shading conditions [21]. Thus, the modules are defined as shown in the Fig. 4b.

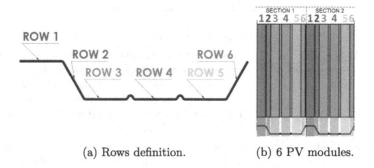

(a) Rows definition.   (b) 6 PV modules.

Fig. 4. Modules definition.

3.2 Radiation Simulation Through Ray Tracing

Taking geometry as input, TracePro® simulates the path of rays from a source (the sun), and how they behave with respect to geometry, i.e. how reflection and absorption phenomena occur and, finally, how they are translated into energy or power flow. Figure 5 shows the setup and a view of the ray tracing in the simulation.

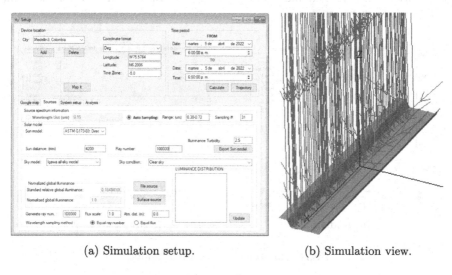

(a) Simulation setup.   (b) Simulation view.

Fig. 5. TracePro® simulation.

Models and Conditions: The following table summarizes the implications of the main models and conditions specified in the simulation setup (Table 3).

Additionally, it is important to remark that the TracePro® simulation does not consider thermal phenomena that may affect the behavior of the rays. It is

Table 3. Models and conditions

Model	Implication
ASTM G173-03: Direct+circumsolar - sun model	This model is an standards defined for terrestrial use, it has a defined spectrum for solar concentrator work, including the direct beam of the sun plus the circumsolar component in a 2.5° disk around the sun. It has an integrated power density of 900 W/m² [22].
Igawa all - sky model	It is a model that allows to estimate the absolute values of the sky luminance and its distribution at any location for which the global iluminance is available [23].
Clear sky	It is a sky condition that assumes that the sky is free from dullness or clouds [24].

also assumed that all incident photons succeed in breaking the electron valence bond regardless of the fact that, physically, they might do not have the necessary energy to do so. Finally, by means of the ray tracing simulation, it is obtained for each row how much radiation and irradiance it receives during the day; this information was compiled and is shown in Fig. 6 below for each row, for the total, and for planar roof.

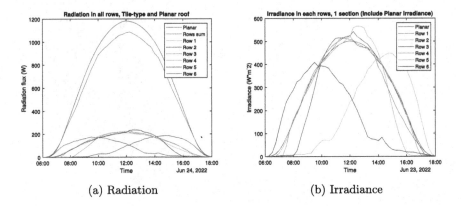

(a) Radiation   (b) Irradiance

Fig. 6. Ray tracing simulation results.

3.3 Energy Improvement Through Dynamic Electrical Reconfiguration

In this section, there is presented a Matlab-Simulink® implementation to extract voltage and current from obtained data. Also, the algorithm for dynamic reconfiguration is explained.

Power Obtained: Equations 1 to 7 are implemented in Matlab-Simulink® to estimate the power generated during a day based on the geometry and irradiance defined in previous sections for each module, as is shown in Fig. 7.

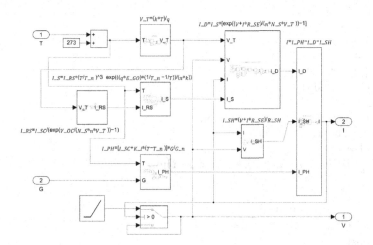

Fig. 7. Simulink® model.

First, it is necessary to establish the values of the parameters that the model needs to work properly, these are shown in Table 4.

Table 4. Variables definition [10].

Variable	Value	Variable	Value
I_{SC}	8,21	E_{GO}	1,1
V_{OC}	32,9	G_n	1000
N_S	54	T_n	298
n	1,3	K_i	0,0032
R_{SH}	415,405	k	1,38E−23
R_{SE}	0,221	q	1,60E−19

Reconfiguration Algorithm: The dynamic interconnection between the PV modules is performed by Algorithm 1. The decision constants K_1, K_2 and K_3 are parameters that define the sensitivity of the algorithm to changes in current. In this study, K_1 was used as 1.0, K_2 as 1.8 and K_3 as 3.0.

Data: $I_A, I_B, I_C, I_D, I_E, I_F$ // Measure modules current
Result: $I_1, I_2, I_3, I_4, I_5, I_6$ // Sort currents
$d_{1-6} \leftarrow I_1 - I_6;$
$d_{1-3} \leftarrow I_1 - I_3;$
$d_{4-6} \leftarrow I_4 - I_6;$
$d_{1-2} \leftarrow I_1 - I_2;$
$d_{3-4} \leftarrow I_3 - I_4;$
$d_{5-6} \leftarrow I_5 - I_6;$
if $d_{1-6} < T_1$ **then**
| Choose s6p1
else
| **if** $max(d_{1-3}, d_{4-6}) < T_2$ **then**
| | Choose best s3p2
| **else**
| | **if** $max(d_{1-2}, d_{3-4}, d_{5-6}) < T_3$ **then**
| | | Choose best s2p3
| | **else**
| | | Choose s1p6
| | **end**
| **end**
end

Algorithm 1: Reconfiguration algorithm [13].

Figure 8 shows a graph with the power results obtained by implementing the electrical reconfiguration algorithm and by not. Additionally, all-serie and all-parallel topologies results are also shown.

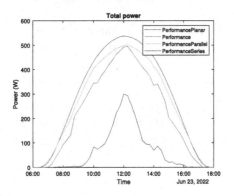

Fig. 8. Power calculated.

4   Analysis and Conclusions

In this work, flat arrays of photovoltaic modules were compared with tile arrays. The first ones belong to BAPV group and the latter to the BIPV group. In practice, BAPV requires a larger number of elements, since PV modules are placed on top of a conventional flat roof. While PV solar roof exposed here is part of the roof itself, wich at the same time has all the thermoacoustic, aesthetic, waterproofing, fireproofing and mechanical resistance advantages of regular roof tiles. In addition, in this work it has been found that the difference at maximum power points between tile and planar roof is less 10%. So it is valid to admit that a solar tile roof with the proposed geometry has an acceptable technical feasibility.

Additionally, the reconfiguration algorithm used allows obtaining a relatively similar performance to the parallel reconfiguration. Although it does so obtaining lower currents by not always opting for parallel reconfiguration, and generating more power than the series configuration. So that the reconfiguration algorithm does have the functionality to reconfigure the PV module array according to each position of the sun. Because the way in which the rows of cells receive irradiance is changing during all the time lapse. It is also concluded that as the sun moves, the modules that are leaned have a behavior that favors at the beginning or end of the day. Furthermore, at that periods of time they receive even better irradiance than a horizontal roof. During all day the horizontal modules behave as in the case of the totally flat roof. Aditionally, these also receive rays reflected by the leaned surfaces at the same time, which favors the irradiation.

Future Work: In future work related to the subject in question, it is proposed to vary the angles and distances of the geometry. Changing the decision constants may also result in a better behavior. It is also suggested to make the reconfiguration algorithm more versatile and effective by expanding the number of possible reconfigurations. As well as changing the leaned surfaces to reflective elements such as mirrors that may also be a good idea. All of the above is proposed with the objective of maximizing power and obtaining better results, and in that optimal point, finally evaluating the cost-financial implications about that geometrically good roof type with an efficiently and dynamically reconfigurable topology.

Acknowledgements. This research has been developed in the framework of the "ENERGETICA 2030" Research Program, with code 58667 in the "Colombia Científica" initiative, funded by The World Bank through the call "778-2017 Scientific Ecosystems", managed by the Colombian Ministry of Science, Technology and Innovation (Minciencias), with contract No. FP44842-210-2018.

References

1. Algarin, C.R., Rodríguez Álvarez, O.: Un panorama de las energías renovables en el mundo, latinoamérica y colombia. Espacios **39**(10) (2018)
2. Mohtasham, J.: Renewable energies. Energy Procedia **74**, 1289–1297 (2015)
3. Ramirez, E.R.: Transición energética en colombia, oportunidad para las energías renovables. Ingenio Magno **10**(1), 6–10 (2019)
4. Giraldo, M., Ramírez, R.V., Quintanilla, A.U.: Las energías alternativas¿ una oportunidad para Colombia? Punto de vista **9**(13), 5 (2018)
5. Biyik, E., et al.: A key review of building integrated photovoltaic (BIPV) systems. Eng. Sci. Technol. Int. J. **20**(3):833–858 (2017)
6. Subashi De Silva, G.H.M.J., Surangi, M.L.C.: Effect of waste rice husk ash on structural, thermal and run-off properties of clay roof tiles. Constr. Build. Mater. **154**, 251–257 (2017)
7. Oyola, J.S., Gordillo, G.: Estado del arte de los materiales fotovoltaicos y de la tecnología solar fotovoltaica. Prospectiva **5**(2), 11–15 (2007)
8. Heinstein, P., Ballif, C., Perret-Aebi, L.-E.: Building integrated photovoltaics (BIPV): review, potentials, barriers and myths. Green **3**(2), 125–156 (2013)
9. Torres-Madroñero, J.L., et al.: Formulation and simulation of a hybrid solar PV-wind generation system with photovoltaic concentration for non-interconnected areas to the energy grid. In: E3S Web of Conferences, vol. 181, p. 02002. EDP Sciences (2020)
10. Sumathi, S., Ashok Kumar, L., Surekha, P.: Solar PV and Wind Energy Conversion Systems: An Introduction to Theory, Modeling with MATLAB/SIMULINK, and the Role of Soft Computing Techniques, vol. 1. Springer, Cham (2015). https://doi.org/10.1007/978-3-319-14941-7
11. Belhachat, F., Larbes, C.: PV array reconfiguration techniques for maximum power optimization under partial shading conditions: a review. Sol. Energy **230**, 558–582 (2021)
12. Kaushika, N.D., Gautam, N.K.: Energy yield simulations of interconnected solar PV arrays. IEEE Trans. Energy Convers. **18**(1), 127–134 (2003)
13. Calcabrini, A., Muttillo, M., Weegink, R., Manganiello, P., Zeman, M., Isabella, O.: A fully reconfigurable series-parallel photovoltaic module for higher energy yields in urban environments. Renew. Energy **179**, 1–11 (2021)
14. Nguyen, D., Lehman, B.: A reconfigurable solar photovoltaic array under shadow conditions. In: 2008 Twenty-Third Annual IEEE Applied Power Electronics Conference and Exposition, pp. 980–986. IEEE (2008)
15. Babu, T.S., Ram, J.P., Dragičević, T., Miyatake, M., Blaabjerg, F., Rajasekar, N.: Particle swarm optimization based solar PV array reconfiguration of the maximum power extraction under partial shading conditions. IEEE Trans. Sustain. Energy **9**(1), 74–85 (2017)
16. Deshkar, S.N., Dhale, S.B., Mukherjee, J.S., Babu, T.S., Rajasekar, N.: Solar PV array reconfiguration under partial shading conditions for maximum power extraction using genetic algorithm. Renew. Sustain. Energy Rev. **43**, 102–110 (2015)
17. Fathy, A.: Reliable and efficient approach for mitigating the shading effect on photovoltaic module based on modified artificial bee colony algorithm. Renew. Energy **81**, 78–88 (2015)
18. Romano, P., Candela, R., Cardinale, M., Vigni, V.L., Musso, D., Sanseverino, E.R.: Optimization of photovoltaic energy production through an efficient switching matrix. J. Sustain. Dev. Energy Water Env. Syst. **1**(3), 227–236 (2013)

19. Nguyen, D., Lehman, B.: An adaptive solar photovoltaic array using model-based reconfiguration algorithm. IEEE Trans. Industr. Electron. **55**(7), 2644–2654 (2008)
20. La Manna, D., Vigni, V.L., Sanseverino, E.R., Di Dio, V., Romano, P.: Reconfigurable electrical interconnection strategies for photovoltaic arrays: a review. Renew. Sustain. Energy Rev. **33**, 412–426 (2014)
21. Tatabhatla, V.M.R., Agarwal, A., Kanumuri, T.: Performance enhancement by shade dispersion of solar photo-voltaic array under continuous dynamic partial shading conditions. J. Clean. Prod. **213**, 462–479 (2019)
22. Gueymard, C.A.: Parameterized transmittance model for direct beam and circumsolar spectral irradiance. Sol. Energy **71**(5), 325–346 (2001)
23. Igawa, N., Nakamura, H.: All sky model as a standard sky for the simulation of daylit environment. Build. Environ. **36**(6), 763–770 (2001)
24. Oh, S.J., Dutton, S., Selkowitz, S., Han, H.J.: Application of a coelostat daylighting system for energy savings and enhancement of indoor illumination: a case study under clear-sky conditions. Energy Build. **156**, 173–186 (2017)

Temperature Performance Simulation in a Solar-Electric Vessel Battery Design

Samuel Bustamante-Castaño$^{(\boxtimes)}$ and Ricardo Mejía-Gutiérrez

Design Engineering Research Group (GRID), Universidad EAFIT,
Carrera 49 No 7 Sur–50, Medellín, Colombia
{sbusta14,rmejiag}@eafit.edu.co

Abstract. Public health and environmental protection are some of the most important matters that drive the decarbonization process all around the globe, making the transition to greener or electric transport a priority. For Colombia, and several countries with sailable rivers, electric transportation can take different shapes made to suit the needs of particular geography and demography outside the main cities. Solar-powered electric vessels pose an alternative for these regions and a challenge for the design, as some typical issues of electrical transportation take even more relevance. Finding a good proportion of weight and energy capacity is as essential as the management given to energy storage. One of the aspects that make electric vehicle transportation feasible is battery advancements, yet battery product lifetime depends on the management between use cycles. Keeping certain temperature margins in operation allow batteries to age slower and avoid unbalancing problems and safety hazards. This paper aims to compare battery montages and caging in order to select the one that presents a thermal behavior that can be adequately implemented on the vessel.

Keywords: Electric vessel · Battery · Temperature · River

1 Introduction

Globally, road transport is responsible for 30% of NO_2 emissions, 10% of total PM, and 54% of CO_2; urban mobility accounts for 40% of all CO_2 emissions of road transport. To curb this trend, policies have been adapted all around the world, recognizing the urge to accelerate the transition towards decarbonized mobility, with a gradual replacement of fossil fuel powered vehicles as a solution to ensure environmental sustainability [1]. Although land transport predominates, maritime, and river mobility, has gained popularity for people and goods transport, in nations with a greater amount of water bodies, such as those located in Latin America and the Caribbean [2], which account for the largest number of navigable rivers in the world. Energy requirements are much more demanding

© The Author(s), under exclusive license to Springer Nature Switzerland AG 2022
J. C. Figueroa-García et al. (Eds.): WEA 2022, CCIS 1685, pp. 366–378, 2022.
https://doi.org/10.1007/978-3-031-20611-5_30

in water than in land transport, mainly due to the difference in density and viscosity of the surrounding fluids[1]. However, the waterway potential and the need for sustainable mobility solutions, triggered the development of electric boats, which exhibited exponential growth since 1995 due to the development of power electronics and batteries increased autonomy [3,4].

1.1 Colombian Water Freight

The inland waterway is one of the most important transport alternatives in Colombia. Every year, the The Caribbean watershed moves around 3 million people [5], being the Magdalena river the most used. Regarding freight transport, the river moves almost 7 million tons per year. However, high operation costs, related to fuel prices have caused a diminish in the frequency of inland waterway transport in the last years [6]. Magangué is one of the most important river ports in the Magdalena due to its role as a central city for many towns in the basin. There, passenger transportation is mainly conducted using "Chalupas", which can carry up to 26 people and use a 200 hp outboard internal combustion engine obtaining speeds up to 60 km/h. However, these engines generate both environmental pollution and high fuel consumption increasing the cost of the trips. Therefore, a solar-powered electric boat arises as an alternative to improve water transportation for the communities in the basin [6] (Fig. 1).

Fig. 1. Proyect interest routes

1.2 Case Study

A passenger transport vessel designed to operate on Colombian fluvial routes, such as Magdalena river over the area of Magangué serves as our study case. The energy storage system was selected based on certain operation conditions, contemplating a maximum weight, number of passengers, and working routes.

---

[1] https://candelaspeedboat.com/company/.

Various battery packs are distributed along the vessel, guaranteeing overall stability and optimal weight distribution. Although becoming more accessible, batteries are a resource worth keeping safe, especially in the large quantities that are required for such vehicles. Therefore, proper management is sought in order to ensure their maximum lifetime. Lithium-ion batteries must operate within a safe operation area, which is restricted by temperature and voltage windows. Exceeding the restrictions of these windows can and will cause quick mitigation of the battery performance and even result in a security hazard. Pesaran et al. [7] showed that the optimal temperature range for LIBs is 15 °C–35 °C. Once the temperature is out of these comfortable regions, LIBs will degrade faster with an increased risk of facing safety problems that include fire and explosion. Thermal management takes importance and becomes one of the challenges for battery storage, as it requires consensus between the battery distribution and fixing within the vessel and the cooling strategies available to implement on the previously designed battery space.

2   State of the Art

A literature review is made for both, cooling methods and battery casing on electric-powered vessels. Battery thermal management is controlled with active or passive cooling or a mix of both. Passive cooling is rarely implemented on its own and is executed by elements such as heatsinks, and phase change materials, which aid in natural convection or absorb heat up to a certain degree. Active cooling is conducted through forced fluid circulation, with more robust systems. Thermal management efficiency varies with the implemented method and the way how it is displayed. Direct liquid cooling is, thermally speaking, the best solution, yet its implementation is harder and overall weight increases. Air cooling stands as a cheaper and relatively simpler option. However, battery and fan disposition is crucial to allow appropriate cooling and to avoid large temperature gradients between cells. Deng [8] and Guodon [9] conducted several experiments for battery cooling, showing some pros and cons of different cooling methods, construction of hybrid models, and less common methods, such as thermoelectric cooling (TEC).

Commercial battery packs for vessels are mostly found for naval use on larger ships. Lechlanché[2] shows a modular battery rack, where modules contain few batteries arranged for an specific voltage and current output; the modules can be stacked to increase the overall energy output. As they seem to be designed for larger vessels, their refrigeration system is throght liquid cooling. The containers are metal racks and insulated with plastic casing. Other solution, which allows modularity and includes liquid cooling system with a metal closed casing and more robust BMS, is proposed by Kokam[3]. Details of the battery shape and distribution within the stackable modules seems unavailable for both modules.

---

[2] https://www.leclanche.com/wp-content/uploads/2021/02/Leclanche-Marine-Battery-Systems.pdf.

[3] https://kokam.com/en/product/module/marine.

The state of the art offers mostly alternatives for bigger vessels with higher load capacity. Additionally, the predefined battery topology makes it hard to adapt any conventional or premade battery module. Air cooling is also implemented for ease, yet further iterations can allow a hybrid cooling system to be added.

3   Model Design

The target is to dive further within the energy storage subsystem. A battery topology was selected based on the power demanded, weight distribution, and stability of the vessel. Battery caging and assembly are to be selected based on thermal performance for a previously chosen cooling system. The battery's thermal behavior is modeled so it can be implemented on further simulations.

3.1   Battery Model

Battery topology consists of 17 series of 4 cells each. The selected battery is a lithium Niquel-Manganesum-Chrome (NMC) prismatic cell under the reference SEPNi8688190P-5P1S, commercialized by Soundon New Energy Technology. Table 1 shows some of the technical characteristics of the battery:

Table 1. Battery technical characteristics

Reference	SEPNi8688190P-5P1S	
Capacity	87,5 [Ah]	
Nominal Voltage	3,65 [V]	
Internal Resistance	0, 25-0, 34 mΩ(*Exp*)	≤ 3, 5 mΩ(*Manufacturer*)

The main goal of the simulation is to identify a component distribution that allows better cooling of the battery pack. Following that logic, it is important to establish the battery's behaviour, to introduce it properly into the simulation. A model for the battery heat generation is sought; one that can be built with the data from a former experiment, conducted to measure some of the cell's parameters under different discharge rates. The cell was placed inside a ceramic casing, and discharged at different rates (0.5C, 1C and 2C). Data of voltage, capacity and temperature was taken during the discharge process until cut-off voltage was reached. The first approach to determine the battery heat generation is through Bernardi's equation, which is commonly used and performs well when the battery discharge rate is kept constant.

$$q = I^2R - I(T\frac{dU}{dT}) \tag{1}$$

Heat generation can be represented through Joule effect (heating by the internal resistance of the battery $q = I^2 * R$) with a negligible error due to entropic heating $I(T\frac{dU}{dT})$. However, experiments in this regard show that for the used battery chemistry (NMC), the main factor in heat generation at temperatures higher than 5 °C is polarization on the electrochemical interface of the battery [10].

Preliminary simulations confirm that the heat generated by the estimated range of internal resistances isn't enough to reach the same final temperature as in the experiment during the sampled time. As not enough information is available to calculate the entropy coefficient $\frac{dU}{dT}$, an alternate way of approximating the heat generation is implemented. The experimental setup can be considered a closed system. Therefore, the heat generation of the battery is balanced by other heat transfer phenomena [11,12].

$$q = mC_p\frac{dT(t)}{dt} + \frac{h}{d}V(T(t) - T_{env}(t)) \tag{2}$$

Equation (2) doesn't contemplate heat transfer via radiation or conduction towards the ceramic insulator, as the contact between insulator and battery was minimal, and wall temperature wasn't measured to evaluate the impact of those phenomena. The first parameter represents the sensible heat, caused by the temperature change within the battery. The second term represents the heat exchange by convection inside the experiment caging. m is the mass of the battery kg, C_p is specific heat of the battery $Jkg^{-1}C^{-1}$, h is the convection coefficient $Wm^{-2}C^{-1}$, V the volume m^3 and d the battery thickness m. Equation (2) can be manipulated into Eq. (3) to get a constant value for heat generation.

$$q = mC_p\frac{T_f - T_o}{t} + \frac{h}{d}V\Sigma(T - T_{env}) \tag{3}$$

3.2   Battery Casing

The battery packs are to be contained on a glass fiber bulkhead that protrudes from the vessel's floor. The cooling air inlet is beneath the batteries on the bottom of the vessel's bulkhead. On the longitudinal ends of the bulkhead, wide openings work as openings for power wiring to pass and hot air to exit. The vessel contains a total of 4 battery packs along its length. Two configurations for the battery packing are designed:

a) **Steel Sheet Box.** The first design, as shown in Fig. 2, consists of an assembly where the principal structural member is a 3 mm thin steel-sheet case covered with dielectric paint. The case fits tightly inside the bulkhead. On top of it, a lid crafted of the same sheet is placed and secured with bolts to prevent the access of fluid or other materials. Only one end of the case (opposite to the air inlet) has air vents, yet air might be able to exit through holes where metal shafts cross to secure the battery. This robust model had little consideration for total weight but was conceived to give additional protection to the batteries in very critical cases, such as the bulkhead flooding. It was initially designed to hold 17s6p, so the internal space is over-dimensioned for the current battery

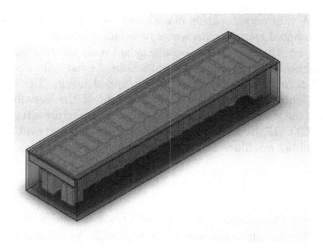

Fig. 2. Battery pack on the Steel Sheet Cage

topology. The batteries are cornered to one side except for the ends, where copper conductors were modified to allow easier manipulation of external wiring. The cost to manufacture a single box with its lid is roughly 932.020 COP, by laser cutting the steel shet, bending it and welding its edges.

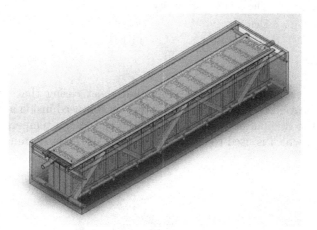

Fig. 3. Battery pack on the Truss-Frame structure

b) Truss-Frame Structure. The second design, shown in Fig. 3, is a truss made out of an aluminum angle profile. The frame-like truss performs as the structural support for the batteries, keeping them tight and steady. The lower profiles are screwed to the bottom of the bulkhead to keep the structure fixed to the floor. A thin acrylic cap is placed and secured on top of the batteries to prevent unwanted contact with water or a falling object, shall the bulkhead be uncovered. For this proposal, the battery is evenly distributed and centered inside the bulkhead. The aluminum profiles hold the batteries about 7 mm over the bulkhead floor in case any liquid gets trapped inside. The truss allow an even distribution of loads, and the overall weight of the assembly is lower in comparison to the steel sheet casing. The cost to manufacture a truss structure is roughly 277.800 COP, by having a machine operator cut and drill the aluminum profile on a milling machine.

4   Simulation SetUp

The simulations are developed with SolidWorks's add-on, Flow Simulation, a CFD that allows working with heat transfer as well. A cad model from is made to simulate a single battery thermal behavior under 1C discharge. The model, seen on Fig. 4 is composed of two prismatic solids that resemble the dimensions of the battery. The first one takes parameters found in the literature for the battery chemistry as shown in the Table 2. Properties taken from [13]

Table 2. NMC Properties

Property	Value	Unit
Thermal Conductivity	2, 9–4, 3	W/mC
Density	~4530	kg/m^3
Specific Heat	1,04	KJ/KgC

The outer solid resembles the aluminum sheet casing that surrounds the battery. Both solids representing the battery are encased inside a ceramic insulator as in the original experiment. The CFD can take a temperature curve as a parameter, which is used to estimate the value of the heat transfer coefficient

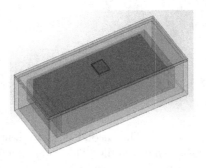

Fig. 4. Battery cad model

(averaged to 7 W/m^2C). A constant value for heat generation is calculated using the experimental data and Eq. (3)

With the estimated constant value for heat generation, a volumetric heat source is configured as a boundary condition. The model is set to run the same time as the physical experiment: a total of 3420 s; this is to allow a comparison between simulation and experimental data in a time-dependent study. The result is a linearized approximation of the temperature curve of the battery with a calculated R^2 of 0.9947. Figure 5 shows the experimental temperature curve and the simulated temperature behavior from the constant heat generation rate. Once the battery model is validated, it gets prepared for the simulation.

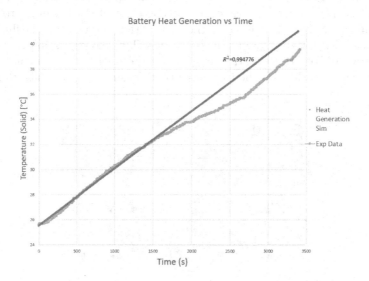

Fig. 5. Experimental data vs simulated temperature

The assemblies are simplified by removing bolts, screws, and other unnecessary elements (simulation-wise) to focus computational resources on the interest components. Both CFD studies are crafted under the same parameters: Time-dependent study, for a maximum of 3420 s, with a time-step of 10 s. No heat exchange from the bulkhead wall to the environment. Initial ambient temperature is 23 °C and the solids temperature is 25.3 °C. The fan is represented as a flow inlet located under the bulkhead, working at maximum capacity all the time (0.061 m^3/s). The flow outlets from the system are configured on the longitudinal openings of the bulkhead. Heat can be transferred via conduction and convection, radiation is neglected. The solver estimates the convection coefficient based on the flow conditions during the simulation. The CFD square meshes the volume, and refines around the batteries and their proximity.

5   Results

To evaluate the performance of each configuration, the comparative scopes will be flow inside the bulkhead, average bulk temperature of the fluid, maximum cell temperature, and maximum temperature difference between cells.

5.1   Fluid Conditions

The CFD results allow to inspect the flow trayectories inside the bulkhead. Figure 6 shows a top view of both configuration's air flow.

On both cases, the main problem is that air speed is drasticly reduced, as the inlet is right bellow the batteries, causing most of the blown air to scatter randomly; a vortex is also caused on the bottom right corner. Average fluid speed is the same for both cases, rounding 0.04 m/s. Truss configuration allows some air to flow underneath the batteries, while for the steel casing configuration, air circulates mainly through the free space that doesn't contains cells. Regarding

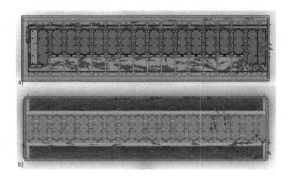

Fig. 6. A) Metal case flow distribution - B) Truss flow distribution

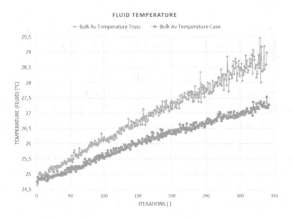

Fig. 7. Bulk fluid avg temperature

fluid temperature, Fig. 7 shows a plot of the average bulk temperature of the air, indicating that the air for the truss is hotter than that of the case. This means that more heat is taken from the batteries to the air. The average temperature on the outlet matches the average bulk temperature value, taking away the possibility that hot air is getting trapped on the bulkhead. However, as the truss doesn't block any air outlets, the difference between the air that exits the system is about 2–3 °C on each outlet.

5.2   Battery Conditions

On both studies, 5 batteries where choosen to compare their thermal behaviour. Figure 9 shows the numeration of said batteries and color scheme of temperatures from a top plane cut, while Fig. 8 display the temperature curve of the selected cells on each configuration.

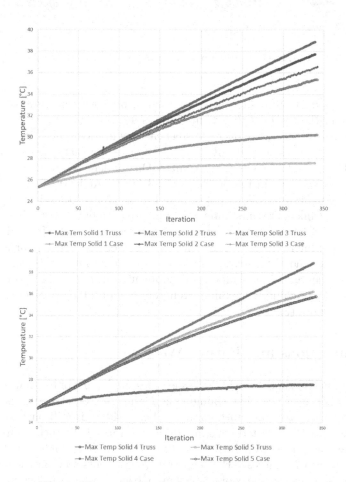

Fig. 8. Thermal behavior for the selected batteries

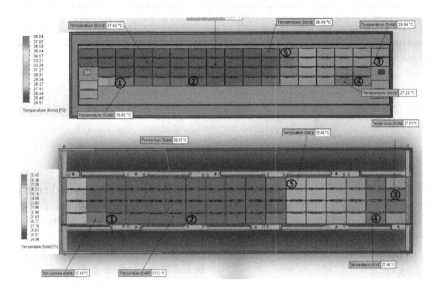

Fig. 9. Battery temperature - A) Steel case B) Truss

From Fig. 9, it is possible to see a pattern on both configurations. On the inmediacy of the fan inlet, low temperatures are keept, up to 27 °C. The truss structure has an advantage over the steel case, as it allows air to escape directly on the bulkhead end close to cell 3 and 4. Appart from that, the thermal behavior of both configurations is fairly similar. On the left side, temperature grows until reaching maximum temperature of 38–39 °C. At least 10 rows have cells with temperatures over 35 °C. Solids 1 and 2, which are located on the opposite side of the air inlet, presents lower temperature of about 1 °C on the steel case. Solids 4 and 3 have a lower temperature on the truss, and for solid 5, there is barely any difference. The defficency on air inlet provoques poor air circulation, and subsequently generates similar cooling issues for both configurations. Althought, the maximum temperature gradient is of almost 12 °C on the truss configuration, reaching a maximum temperature of 39.37 °C, one grade above the case configuration.

6   Conclusions and Future Work

Both configurations present similar issues. Despite having only a few advantages (Thermically), over the next configuration, the choosen structure is the truss frame. According to some authors, a cell below 40 °C is still on it's safe operating zone. For the selected constant discharge rate (1 C), such temperature is not surpassed, yet real operating conditions might have higher, not constant discharge rates that increase the temperature gradients seen on the simulation. Therefore, actions over the cooling system, particularly the air-flow inlet must be assessed. The truss architecture is more "flexible" and takes less volume, making it easier to iterate over other fan configurations inside the bulkead. Further analysis shall be made to find a better disposition of air inlets, as it is clear that the current location creates poor flow conditions between batteries. Changing the spot, and adding other inlet or outlet fans can aid in controling better the internal flow to avoid vortex and looses, as well as maintaining the temperature uniform. The reduction of weight on the structure allows the exploration of other, cooling aids, such as fins or phase change materials, althought space on the vessel and weight distribution might limit the alternatives. To gain a better parametrisation of the heat generation curve, more sohisticated experiments should be conducted to measure its changes over time.

Acknowledgements. Authors would like to thank Universidad EAFIT to support this research through the Research Assistantship grant from project 952-000029. This research has been also developed in the framework of the "ENERGETICA 2030" Research Program, with code 58667 in the "Colombia Científica" initiative, funded by The World Bank through the call "778-2017 Scientific Ecosystems", managed by the Colombian Ministry of Science, Technology and Innovation (Minciencias), with contract No. FP44842-210-2018.

References

1. European Environment Agency. Air quality in europe-2017 report. Technical Report 13 (2017). https://www.eea.europa.eu/publications/air-quality-in-europe-2017
2. Azhar Jaimurzina and Gordon Wilmsmeier. La movilidad fluvial en américa del sur: avances y tareas pendientes en materia de políticas públicas. 2017
3. Pestana, H.: Future trends of electrical propulsion and implications to ship design. Proc, Martech (2014)
4. Lapko, A.: Is it time for motorboat e-mobility? Transp. Res. Procedia **39**, 280–289 (2019)
5. ARCADIS Nederland BV and SAS JESYCA. Plan maestro fluvial de colombia 2015 (2015)
6. Mira, J.-D., et al.: Preliminary design tools applied to a solar powered vessel design: a South American river analysis. pp. 1–9, September 2020
7. Pesaran, A., Santhanagopalan, S., Kim, G.-H.: Addressing the impact of temperature extremes on large format li-ion batteries for vehicle applications (presentation), nrel (national renewable energy laboratory) (2013)
8. Deng, Y., et al.: Effects of different coolants and cooling strategies on the cooling performance of the power lithium ion battery system: a review. Appl. Thermal Eng. **142**, 10–29 (2018)
9. Xia, G., Cao, L., Bi, G.: A review on battery thermal management in electric vehicle application. J. Power Sources (2017)
10. Lyu, P., Huo, Y., Qu, Z., Rao, Z.: Investigation on the thermal behavior of ni-rich nmc lithium ion battery for energy storage. Appl. Thermal Eng. **166**, 114749 (2020)
11. Lin, C., et al.: Comparative study on the heat generation behavior of lithium-ion batteries with different cathode materials using accelerating rate calorimetry. vol. 142, pp. 3369–3374. Elsevier Ltd. (2017)

12. Kulranut, J., Depaiwa, N., Yenwichai, T., Intano, W., Masomtob, M.: Improvement of estimation method for battery cell heat generation. J. Res. Appl. Mech. Eng. **9**, 2229–2252 (2021)
13. Cheng, E.J., Hong, K., Taylor, N.J., Choe, H., Wolfenstine, J., Sakamoto, J.: Mechanical and physical properties of lini0.33mn0.33co0.33o2 (nmc). J. Eur. Ceramic Soc. **37**, 3213–3217 (2017)

Simulation and Prototype of Flexible Sensor Devices Using Graphite on Paper Substrate

Luiz Antonio Rasia[1]([⊠]) [ID], Lucas Schwertner[1] [ID], Patrícia Carolina Pedrali[1] [ID], and Julia Rasia[2] [ID]

[1] Regional University of the Northwest of the State of Rio Grande do Sul, Ijuí, Brazil
{rasia,patricia.pedrali}@unijui.edu.br
[2] Center for Rural Sciences - CCR, UFSM – Federal University of Santa Maria, Santa Maria, Brazil

Abstract. In this article, a brief review is made on the development of sensor devices based on the cantilevered beam principle made of thin-film paper obtained from pencil graphite, deposited by mechanical exfoliation. The main equations are described, the electromechanical parameters are surveyed, the computational simulation is performed, the sensors under tension and compression are characterized, an interface is set up using a microcontroller and the main characteristic curves are shown. Sensor devices can be applied in IoT, animal and human care and monitoring, agriculture, pharmaceutical devices, medicine, bioengineering, and other areas.

Keywords: Wearable sensor · Strain sensor · Sensors devices

1 Introduction

In this work, a mechanical stress sensor device with a cantilever structure is proposed, manufactured with semi-metallic graphite film obtained by the mechanical exfoliation technique or Graphite on Paper - GoP, without the use of chemical and ecologically biodegradable products [1–6].

Cantilever structures can be very small and therefore sensitive enough to detect small mechanical stresses or even other physical magnitudes according to their proposed structural arrangement [7].

Sensor devices with a paper substrate are highly flexible, biocompatible, biodegradable and can be used, for example, in Point-of-Care - PoC diagnostic tests, pharmaceutical, agricultural, environmental, food, safety, monitoring, and other areas of the science and engineering [1, 8–10].

The force devices or tactile sensors can be reproduced through micro cantilevers whose functional principle is described in this work and widely discussed in [2, 5, 11, 12], as illustrated in Fig. 1.

Many of these sensing devices use smartphones to provide information or data about motion recognition, health monitoring, smart clothing, electronic skin as they are sensitive, accurate, wearable, and low in manufacturing cost when compared to silicon [2, 11, 12].

© The Author(s), under exclusive license to Springer Nature Switzerland AG 2022
J. C. Figueroa-García et al. (Eds.): WEA 2022, CCIS 1685, pp. 379–385, 2022.
https://doi.org/10.1007/978-3-031-20611-5_31

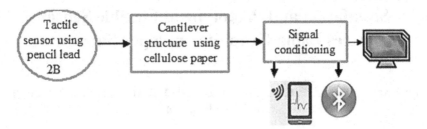

Fig. 1. Technical diagram illustrating the force sensor, materials, working principle and possible interfaces.

Table 1 presents a brief review of the main characteristics of the materials used in the processing of the various sensor devices described. In this work, a brief review is made, and a possible application is suggested. The open and filled balls show the intensity, advantages, and disadvantages when the materials are compared [12].

Table 1. A mini overview of different materials for adapted disposable sensor design [12].

Material	Cost	Flex-ibil-ity	Recycla-ble	Transpar-ency	Biodegrada-ble	Stretchabil-ity
Silicon	000	0	●●	000	0	000
Glass	0	000	●●	●●●	000	000
Ceramics	000	000	●●	0	●	000
Paper	●●●	●●●	●●●	0	●●●	0
Nanocellu-lose	●	●●●	●●●	●●	●●●	000
Cellophane	●●●	●●	●●●	●●●	●●●	●
Nitrocellu-lose	●	●	●●●	0	●	000

1.1 Material, Physical Principle and Structure of a GoP Sensor Device

A cantilever beam can be approximated for a spring-mass system, when it is a dynamic system, that is, oscillating in a physical medium of constant, b. If the system is not damped $b = 0$, the frequency natural of motion is given by,

$$\omega_{nat} = \sqrt{\frac{k}{m}} \qquad (1)$$

where, m, is the mass of the beam. Figure 2 illustrates the system, as a function of the oscillation frequency, $\omega = 2\pi f$. In this work, air at room temperature is considered, whose semi-metallic films are deposited on an A4 paper substrate through 2B pencil-trace, a technique known as GoP – Graphite on Paper or PoP – Pencil on Paper [1, 5] of according to Ohm's Law,

$$R = \rho \frac{l}{wt_g} \tag{2}$$

where, R, is the electrical resistance, w, is the width of the resistor, l, is the length, and t_g, is the thickness graphite film.

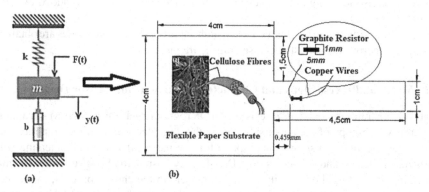

Fig. 2. (a) Mass-Spring-Damper System and (b) equivalent cantilevered beam. Inset shows photograph of cellulose structure and fiber illustration.

When there is no damping, the cantilever responds to the equation of motion at the natural frequency of oscillation given by,

$$m\frac{d^2y}{dt^2} + b\frac{dy}{dt} + ky = F(t) \tag{3}$$

where, m, is the mass, b, is the damping constant, k, is the spring constant and, y, is the displacement of the mass. The generalized force that excites the spring-mass system is $F(t)$.

The deflection of the beam is given by the equation,

$$y = \frac{FL^3}{3EI} \tag{4}$$

where, L, is the length, $E = T/\varepsilon$, the modulus of elasticity, ε, is the mechanical strain, and, I, the moment of inertia of the beam.

If the damping effect is present, use the natural frequency to rewrite Eq. (3) assuming the excitation force is $F(t) = 0$,

$$\frac{d^2y}{dt^2} + 2\xi\omega_{nat}\frac{dy}{dt} + \omega^2_{nat}y = F(t) \tag{5}$$

where, ξ, is the damping factor of the system given by the equation,

$$\xi = \frac{b}{2\omega_{nat}m} = \frac{b}{2\sqrt{km}} \tag{6}$$

The resonant frequency due to mass change is called the sensitivity, S, of a cantilever sensor. This parameter is very important for this type of sensors based on beam deflection since it is possible to detect minimal mass variations.

The sensitivity of a mass on this oscillating system is given by the differential equation [7],

$$S_{massa} = \frac{\partial \omega_0}{\partial m_{eff}} = \frac{\omega_0}{2m_{eff}} \approx \frac{\Delta \omega_0}{\Delta m} \tag{7}$$

where, $\Delta \omega_0$, is the change in frequency and resonance due to the mass added over the cantilever, i.e., Δm.

A high sensitivity can be obtained when high values of vibrational modes are obtained since the effective mass must decrease at these frequencies.

1.2   Material, Process Steps and Characterization of a GoP Sensor Device

Figure 3 illustrates in (a) the piezoresistor, (b) micrograph made through SEM - Scanning Electron Microscopy of the paper substrate without the deposition of the graphite, with 430x magnification, (c) shows the graphite film on paper after thermal annealing with 180x magnification and (d) shows the EDS - Energy Dispersion Spectrum after thermal annealing, indicating the intensity of carbon present in the chosen process, to produce sensing elements and electromechanical devices, using graphite of pencil 2B and in (e) process steps with a photograph of the manufactured piezoresistor.

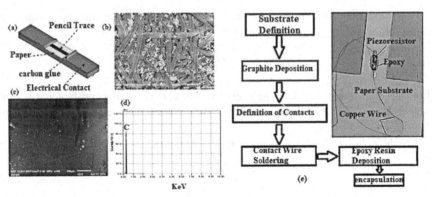

Fig. 3. 2B pencil graphite on paper, deposition steps and photograph of a piezoresistor on a paper beam.

2   Results and Discussions

Using experimental data, from mathematical simulation, executed in the MATLAB software, it was possible to determine some of the parameters for the design of a strain gauge force sensing element through the models proposed in this work, according to Table 2.

Table 2. Parameters found for flexible GoP device development.

Physical quantity	Measured value	Method used
L (m)	0.0450	Vernier calipers
R (Ω)	79087	Ohmmeter
t_g(m) graphite film	$7.36 \times 10^{-9} \approx 73.6$ nm	Calculated
ρ (Ωm) graphite film	1.14×10–5	Calculated
E (N/m^2) celulose paper	2.6×10^9	Experimental
t (m) cellulose paper	0.000088	Micrometer
m (kg)	0.00123	Analytical balance
y(m)	0.0249	Calculated/Experimental
b (N.s/m)	0.038	Calculated
ξ_{damp}	0.7293	Calculated
k (N/m)	0.55	Experimental
f(Hz)	3.37	Calculated
ω_{nat}(rad/s)	21.17	Calculated
ω_{damp} (rad/s)	14.49	Calculated

In this specific case, a maximum amplitude was considered as a function of the added mass from which the beam is set to oscillate at room temperature and constant air flow. The response of the damped oscillating system is shown in Fig. 4. Internally Fig. 4 is illustrating the maximum stress and mechanical compression peaks, given an ambient temperature of 25 °C and constant airflow, in accordance with [14].

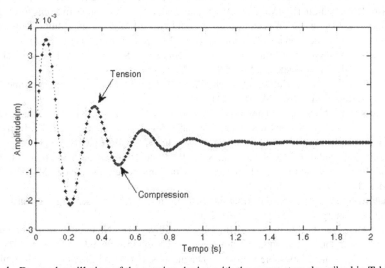

Fig. 4. Damped oscillation of the sensing device with the parameters described in Table 2.

The answer shown in Fig. 4 is the solution of the differential Eq. (4) in the presence of a viscous medium indicated by the parameters b and ξ_{damp} shown in Table 2.

These results are used, mathematically, for programming the microcontroller and conditioning the signals of the manufactured sensor device and possible applications in future interfaces in accordance with the [15].

3 Conclusion

The application areas of sensors that use the cantilever principle are very broad, but low-cost systems, such as the one proposed, are more difficult to calibrate due to the manual procedures employed. In this work, a cantilever was built using the GoP technique and the system was tested using a microcontroller system presenting a coherent response with the computer simulations.

The characterized sensor device presented a maximum oscillation frequency of 3.37 Hz and a damping factor of 0.7293 indicating its functionality as expected. Using these procedures, it is possible to make flexible graphite and paper sensor devices with low cost compared to traditional sensors.

References

1. Rasia, L.A., Andrades, C.E., Heck, T.G., Rasia, J.: Aproach pencil-on-paper to flexible piezoresistive respiration sensor. In: Applied Computer Sciences in Engineering. 8th Workshop on Engineering Applications, WEA 2021 Proceedings, pp. 290–298 (2021)
2. Vu, C.C., Kim, J.: Waterproof, thin, high-performance pressure sensors-hand drawing for underwater wearable applications. Sci. Technol. Adv. Mater. 22, 718–728 (2021)
3. Hua, Q., et al.: Bioinspired electronic whisker arrays by pencil-drawn paper for adaptive tactile sensing. Adv. Electron. Mater., 1–5 (2016)
4. Xu, Y., et al.: Paper-based wearable electronics. iScience, pp. 1–24 (2021)
5. Rasia, L.A., Pedrali, P.C., Valdiero, A.C.: characterization of piezoresistive sensors of graphite on paper substrate. In: Proceedings of the 16th LACCEI International Multi-Conference for Engineering, Education and Technology, LACCEI, pp. 1–6, Lima, Peru (2018)
6. Huber, T., Muössig, J., Curnow, O., Pang, S., Bickerton, S., Staiger, M. P.: A critical review of all-cellulose composites. J. Mater Sci., 1171–1186 (2012)
7. Boisen, A., Dohn, S., Keller, S.S., Schmid, S., Tenje, M.: Cantilever-like micromechanical sensors. Rep. Prog. Phys. 74, 30 (2011)
8. Alshaal, S.E., Michael, S., Pamboris, A., Herodotou, H., Samaras, G., Andreou, P.: Enhancing virtual reality systems with smart wearable devices. In: 2016 17th IEEE International Conference on Mobile Data Management, pp. 346–348. IEEE (20016)
9. Verma, R.P., Sahu, P.S., Dabhade, A., Saha, B.: Reduced graphene oxide-based stretchable strain sensor for monitoring of physical activities and minute movement. Materials Today: Proceedings, pp. 1–7 (2021)
10. Shafiee, H., et al.: Paper and flexible substrates as materials for biosensing platforms to detect multiple biotargets. Sci. Rep. 5, 8719 (2015)
11. Bhattacharjeea, M., Nemadea, H.B., Bandyopadhyay, D.: Nano-enabled paper humidity sensor for mobile based point-of-care lung function monitoring. 94, 544–551 (2017)
12. Dincer, C., et al.: Disposable Sensors in Diagnostics, Food, and Environmental Monitoring. Adv. Mater., 1–28 (2019)

13. Sayegh, M. A., Daraghma, H., Mekid, S., Bashmal, S.: Review of Recent Bio-Inspired Design and Manufacturing of Whisker Tactile Sensors. Sensors, pp. 1–22 (2022)
14. Takei, K., Yu, Z., Zheng, M., Ota, H., Takahashi, T., Javey, A.: Highly sensitive electronic whiskers based on patterned carbon nanotube and silver nanoparticle composite films. PNAS 111(5), 1703–1707 (2014)
15. Cheng, G., Ehrlich, S.K., Lebedev, M., Nicolelis, M.A.L.: Neuroengineering challenges of fusing robotics and neuroscience. Sci. Robot. 5, 1–4 (2020)

A Software for Simulating Robot Swarm Aggregation

Oscar Acevedo[1](✉) [ID], Y. Yuliana Rios[1] [ID], Jorge Duque[1] [ID],
Eduardo Gomez[1] [ID], and Luis García[2]

[1] Universidad Tecnológica de Bolívar, Cartagena, Bolívar, Colombia
{oacevedo,yrios,jduque,egomez,lgarciag}@utb.edu.co
[2] Universidad Simón Bolívar-Audacia, Barranquilla, Colombia
luis.garciag@unisimon.edu.co

Abstract. Swarm robotics is a topic that focuses on studying a system composed of many homogeneous robots that collaborate to achieve a common goal. Swarm robotics presents several exciting challenges for engineers, with the development of controllers being one of the most critical. For this purpose, models and simulators have been developed to allow designers to test their designs. This paper presents a swarm robot simulator, made in Matlab, whose objective is to study robot aggregation, which is considered an essential swarm behavior. Simulations and results of a classical algorithm for environment-guided aggregation are presented to determine its ability to aggregate robots and how its efficiency is affected by environmental variations.

Keywords: Beeclust · Aggregation · Swarm robotics

1 Introduction

Robot swarm is based on the concept of achieving a complex task through the collaborative work of many simple robots. To achieve this, many scientists have relied on studies of animals exhibiting this behavior, such as ants, birds, and fishes. These studies propose different concepts, techniques, and methodologies to bring these behaviors to robots [6].

It is assumed that the members of a swarm are homogeneous robots with similar hardware and software specifications, so they cannot perform the task alone. These disadvantages are compensated by cooperative work, i.e., somehow getting the robots to join their efforts to accomplish the task [6].

From animal studies, specific characteristics of a swarm have been determined: local interaction between robots and between robots and their environment, local communication or no communication at all, and decentralized control. Based on these characteristics, the swarm has two essential properties: robustness and scalability. Robustness relates to the ability of the swarm to complete its task regardless of the loss of robots. Scalability refers to the swarm's ability to maintain or improve efficiency by increasing the number of robots. It is important to note that practical factors limit the efficiency achievable by increasing the number of robots [11].

© The Author(s), under exclusive license to Springer Nature Switzerland AG 2022
J. C. Figueroa-García et al. (Eds.): WEA 2022, CCIS 1685, pp. 386–399, 2022.
https://doi.org/10.1007/978-3-031-20611-5_32

One of the challenges in robot swarm design is the control system. This system is designed focused on a single robot, keeping in mind achieving the task assigned to the whole swarm [9]. In other words, a design is made at a local or microscopic level to reach a global or macroscopic behavior. A swarm design methodology proposes dividing the swarm behavior into a combination of basic behaviors [8]. Thus, this methodology is divided into two levels, the first level implements the basic behaviors individually, generating a "behavioral library", and the second level combines them through a high-level methodology, such as finite state machines.

Examples of basic behaviors identified in robot swarms are aggregation, dispersion, pattern formation, flocking, and object clustering [6]. Some of these basic behaviors require other behaviors to be executed beforehand to improve their efficiency. For example, monitoring requires robots to aggregate ahead at a given point in the location to be explored to ensure good coverage. In the context of a robot swarm, aggregation refers to the collection of robots. Some environment features may guide this collection, or the swarm itself decides where to gather. This is called self-organization [9].

This paper explores the behavior of an algorithm designed for environment-guided aggregation, called Beeclust [10]. This paper presents the behavior of the algorithm under an environment where the reference signal changes over time, exploring the ability of the algorithm to adapt to the changes. The interaction of two swarms in the same arena is also explored, to determine how the interference of second swarm affects the aggregation.

The paper is organized as follows: Sect. 2 presents a review about robot swarm aggregation. Section 3 presents the Bleeclust algorithm. Section 4 presents the simulator and its configuration. Section 5 presents results and finally, Sect. 6 concludes.

2   Review

The literature on swarm robotics is extensive and diverse, so this section presents a brief review of works based on the Beeclust algorithm for environment-guided robot aggregation.

Research on robot swarms started several years ago; however, it was after year 2005 that many papers were published in this area. For example, in that year, authors in [11] published what are considered the main properties of robot swarms.

In 2009, paper [10] was published, which presents one of the most representative algorithms for environment-guided robot aggregation. This algorithm, called Beeclust, originated from observing and modeling newborn bees, which collaboratively search for the hive's hottest spot. The resulting algorithm is robust and straightforward, which is demonstrated by the various research carried out to date, both at the level of simulation and its implementation in a laboratory environment. Because of this, the algorithm has become a reference for works in the same area. [12] has focused on studying the algorithm in the face of changes in the environment where the swarm is located.

Some works focused on changes to the basic algorithm to improve its efficiency. These changes are organized into three groups: non-random decisions in some states of the algorithm, hardware changes that enhance decision making, and additional capabilities such as pheromones and landmarks detection to help the robot find the optimal aggregation point. As specific examples, the Work [2] includes modifications to two stages of the algorithm to improve its efficiency. Further work included a fuzzy controller in computing rotation angle [3]. Work expands the algorithm to include "pheromones" [4], and work [1] includes landmarks in the environment to help robots to locate the aggregation point.

From these papers, the importance of the Beeclust algorithm for robot aggregation is appreciated. These works analyze the algorithm in various scenarios and study the different parts of the algorithm, proposing changes that increase its complexity to improve its efficiency. Apart from the referenced works, there are additional works that model the algorithm at a macroscopic level, and other works develop further experiments in more complex environments.

3   The Beeclust Algorithm

The Beeclust algorithm was presented in 2009 by [10]. This algorithm models the behavior of newborn bees, which instinctively seek the hive's warmest point to live. The publication showed that bees use a collaborative method to find the hive's warmest area under a specific situation. The results presented by [10] demonstrate that the algorithm effectively predicts bee behavior and can be implemented as a source-based aggregation algorithm for a robot swarm. In addition, the algorithm includes typical characteristics of robot swarms, i.e., collaborative work, non-communication, scalability, and decentralized control. The Beeclust algorithm is shown in 1.

Algorithm 1. Beeclust algorithm

1: Move forward
2: **if** obstacle detected **then**
3:     stop motion
4:     **if** obstacle is wall **then**
5:         go to step 15
6:     **end if**
7:     **if** obstacle is robot **then**
8:         go to step 12
9:     **end if**
10: **end if**
11: go to 1
12: Read sensor
13: Compute delay
14: Wait until timeout
15: Rotate randomly
16: Go to step 1

The Beeclust algorithm leaves the decision for the rotation angle to a random function. This strategy makes the algorithm low complexity, allowing it to implement a robot with reduced hardware and software capabilities successfully. It is also the main algorithm drawback because it may miss the warmest point even when the robot is located next to it.

The algorithm analysis shows its effectiveness depends on two factors: the collision between robots and the waiting time. This waiting time is a function of the source value at the collision point. The following function is frequently used to calculate the waiting time [10],

$$time = t_{max} \cdot \frac{s^2(t)}{s^2(t) + \theta},\tag{1}$$

where t_{max} is the maximum waiting time, $s(t)$ is the source sensor value and θ defines the slope of the curve. The range of values for the source sensor is usually taken directly from the AD converter in the robot hardware. Values for other parameters are chosen from preliminary experiments.

Using this function, a robot outside the source area will have a very short waiting time. Conversely, when the robot is inside the source area, its waiting time will be very long, allowing the group's lifetime under the source to be longer, increasing the probability that other robots will join the group. This situation also implies that groups far away from the source will be dissolved quickly.

4   Simulator

The Beeclust algorithm evaluation uses a simulator implemented in Matlab. The simulator has a high-level object called *arena*, which describes the environment in which the robot swarm lives and also contains general simulation parameters. The arena holds two objects: a *source* and a *robot* (see Fig. 1).

The *source* object describes environment features (also called the cue) that guide robot aggregation. Referring to work [10], the environment feature guiding robot aggregation was illumination, so the *source* object for this case returns a lux value as a function of arena coordinates.

If the area occupied by the *source* is assumed circular, a simple relationship can be determined between the area of the robot, which is also circular, and the area of the source [5]. This relationship allows to calculate how many robots are "covered" by the source and to estimate the swarm behavior at different source area sizes. Equation 2 presents the relationship.

$$R_{source} = \sqrt{K \cdot n} \cdot R_{sensor},\tag{2}$$

where R_{source} is the radius for a circular source area, R_{sensor} is the robot sensor disk radius, n is the swarm robot size and K is a source to swarm area ratio, with $K \geq 1$.

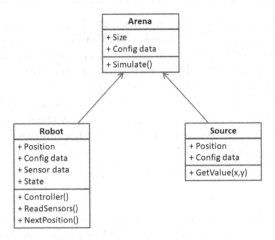

Fig. 1. Class association diagram

The K parameter is needed because the area shape of all robots aggregated under the source is irregular and random, so there is no guarantee that the entire swarm can be grouped under the source. Then, the size of the source area is defined as a scale ratio to the swarm area, expressed by the parameter K.

The *robot* object describes the functionality of a robot from the unicycle model and a circular body, where the control law is Algorithm 1, which was implemented as a finite state machine. An essential issue in the robot model is the definition of the obstacle sensing area. The robot uses an ideal sensing disk model for obstacle sensing, so detection in the simulator uses the circle intersection function between each pair of robots.

For the execution of the simulation, a discrete event simulation methodology was used, where each *tick* event calls each robot object to update its state according to the information it collects from the environment. The *source* object may be called by this event in case of defining dynamic parameters for its behavior. Figure 2 shows a screenshot of simulation execution.

5   Experiments and Results

The experiments focus on exploring the behavior of the Beeclust algorithm with a set of complex source patterns, like the environments described in articles [12] and [7]. Preliminary experiments were conducted to determine the algorithm's behavior under a single source with constant environment characteristics to adjust some simulation parameters. The size of the arena is 1×1.5 m for all experiments. Robot parameters were kept constant for all experiments.

The first experiment explores the algorithm's behavior in the presence of a complex source, which consists of a combination of two normal functions centered at two user-specified points. Each normal function has constant parameters,

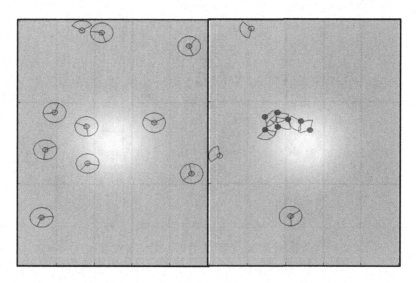

Fig. 2. Preliminary simulation screenshots

however, the amplitude is modulated by a external factor whose value ranges between 0 and 1, as shown in Eq.3.

$$S(x, y) = \alpha \cdot P_1(x, y) + \beta \cdot P_2(x, y) \tag{3}$$

where $P_i(x, y)$ is a normal function, α and β are the modulating factors. Thanks to factors α and β, several scenarios can be modeled, such as a source with one or two maximum, a global maximum and a local maximum, among others. The experiment was set to automatically adjusts the factors value every 200 s, so the resulting source function $S(x, y)$ has a dynamic behavior. Table 1 shows the order for factor values used.

Table 1. Simulated scenario

α	β	t	Scenario
0.5	0.5	$t \leq 200$	(a) two local maximum
1.0	0.5	$t \leq 400$	(b) one global maximum and one local maximum (attenuated)
0.0	1.0	$t \leq 600$	(c) one global maximum
0.5	0.0	$t \leq 800$	(d) one global maximum (attenuated)
0.5	1.0	$t \leq 1000$	(e) one local maximum (attenuated) and one global maximum

The data to be collected from the experiment is the number of robots aggregated under each point over time. Figure 5 presented simulation screenshots and Fig. 4 presents the simulation results.

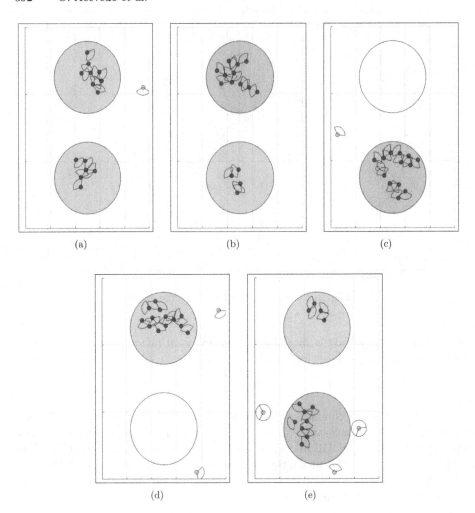

Fig. 3. Simulation screenshots for first experiment

Figure 5 presents a screenshot of the simulation for the first experiment, where an image is presented for each of the combinations of factors presented in Table 1. The area of each point (normal function) is delimited by a circle whose intensity of filling is a function of the factor for that area. A circle without filling means a factor of 0, so that point does not contribute to the final value of the source.

Figure 4 presents a plot of the number of robots around each point over time. Figure 4(a) represents the first point, located at the top of the arena and Fig. 4(b) the second point, located at the bottom of the arena. Each graph is divided into 5 parts, corresponding to the values assigned to each factor. As an aid, an icon at the top of the graph expresses the value of the factor for the respective normal

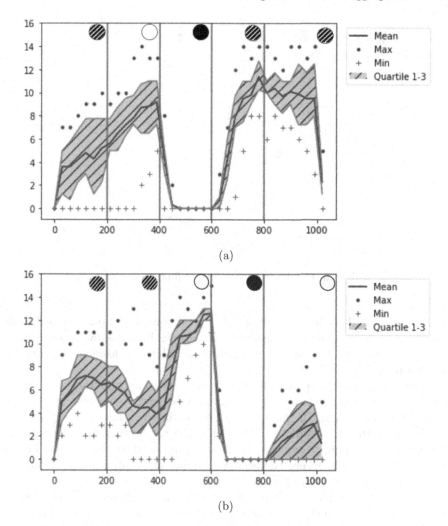

Fig. 4. Simulation results for the first experiment

function, where a white circle means a value of 1, a circle with a line pattern means a value of 0.5 and a black circle represents a value of 0.

As can be seen, for the time interval from 0 to 200 s, both points are affected by the same factor value, so, from the swarm point of view, this is equivalent to two maximum points, therefore, a similar distribution of robots at each point is expected, which is evidenced in the graph by the average value obtained, being around 4 robots at the upper point and 6 robots at the lower point.

During the time interval from 200 to 400 s, the upper point has a factor of 1, so this point becomes a global maximum. It is expected that most robots will tend to aggregate around this point and that a small group of robots will be aggregated at the lower point. It is not expected that by the designated time

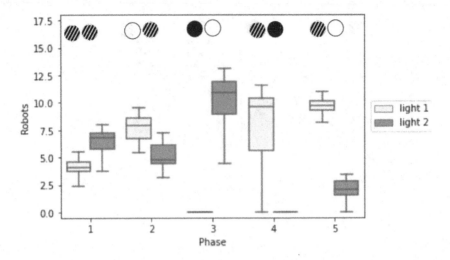

Fig. 5. Combined results for the first experiment

the cluster around the lower point will disappear completely, but a considerable reduction in its population is expected. The graphs indeed show this behavior, where the upper point contains about 8 robots while the lower point contains about 4 robots.

During the time interval from 400 to 600 s, the factor of the upper point becomes 0, nullifying it completely, so that only the lower point remains, becoming a global maximum. In this case, the robots in the swarm are expected to cluster under the only available point, while the robots that were clustered at the upper point begin to separate from the group as their timer ends. This is evident in the graph, where the average number of robots reaches 12 for the lower point and 0 for the upper point.

During the time interval from 600 to 800 s, the lower point is canceled by assigning it a factor of 0 and the upper point reappears by assigning it a factor of 0.5, becoming the new maximum of the arena. In essence, a similar behavior to the previous case is expected, where robots will now cluster at the upper point and no robots will cluster at the lower point. Since the factor for the upper point is 0.5, the number of clustered robots is expected to be less than the previous case, as in essence the waiting time for each robot is halved, and robots may seek to leave the cluster more frequently than in the previous case. The graph confirms in general the described behavior, however, the number of robots aggregated under the upper point is higher than expected, being around 10 robots, close to the previous case.

Finally, for the 800 to 1000 s interval, a factor of 1 is assigned to the lower point, becoming the new global maximum of the arena. In this case, a similar result to that obtained in the 200 to 400 s interval is expected, but with most of the robots gathered in the lower point. The graph does not show the expected behavior, but a growth of robots at the lower point and a tendency to reduce the number of robots at the upper point. One reason for this is the time allocated for this combination of factors. If more time were allocated to the simulation, one would indeed have a similar result to that expected. However, it is believed that the main reason for the difference in the results lies in the combination of factors prior to the current combination. For the interval from 200 to 400 s, the previous combination was 2 local maxima, so the distribution of robots in the arena was somewhat similar at both points and the waiting times for each robot were similar, so that, at the end of this interval, the robots were in similar conditions for both points. In contrast, for the current combination, the previous combination was a single maximum at the upper point, so many robots were at the upper point and none at the lower point. This favors that the group at the upper point is still maintained under the current combination, although its size is slowly reduced as time passes. From this, although the result was not exactly as expected, it can be explained by considering the previous case.

Figure 5 presents a box plot for both points for each factor combination considered in the experiment.

The second experiment consists of two different sources and two robot swarms in the same arena. The objective, in this case, is to explore how the interaction between swarms affects the aggregation time. For this, one swarm is considered as a reference swarm and the other swarm as a perturbation. Each swarm size is changed in each scenario to evaluate its effect on the aggregation time for the reference swarm. Figure 6 presents simulation screenshots.

The target source for the reference swarm is the upper circle. The target source for the disturbance swarm is the lower circle. The robots in the reference swarm are colored yellow and the robots in the disturbance swarm are green. All robots take the color red when they are in the $WAIT$ state.

The data collected from each scenario consists of the aggregation time for the reference swarm. The aggregation time is determined when 75% of the robots are gathered under the source. For the case of 20 robots, which arguable do not fit under the source, the condition was adjusted to define the aggregation time when ten robots are under the source, which is the maximum number of robots "covered" for the specified source size. Each scenario lasted 200 s and was repeated ten times to calculate statistical data. An important point to note is that a default value of 200 s was assigned to the aggregation time when an experiment ends, and not enough robots are successfully aggregated under the target source. Figure 7 presents the simulation results.

Each image in Fig. 7 presents the results for aggregation time for three reference robot swarm sizes (4, 10 and 20). The x-axis (group B) presents the size of the perturbation swarm. As can be seen, the first value is zero. This means that there are only robots from the reference swarm in the arena, so the values presented in this scenario serve as a reference to determine the effect of the perturbation swarm.

In the case of a reference swarm of size 4 (image (a) in Fig. 7), it is difficult for the robots to aggregate in the source by themselves, because few contact events are generated, resulting in very few groups, usually of short duration. When

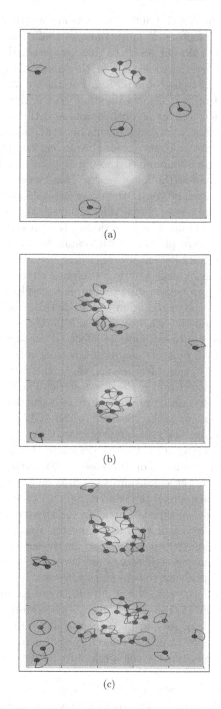

(a)

(b)

(c)

Fig. 6. Simulation screenshots for second experiment

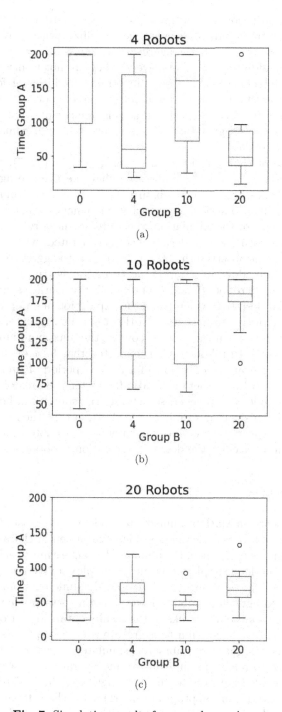

Fig. 7. Simulation results for second experiment

robots from perturbation swarm (group B) appear (4, 10 and 20), it is observed that the average time tends to decrease and stabilizes with 20 robots. From the algorithm, it is expected that the aggregation time will be reduced as shown in the graph, since adding more robots, even if they are not from the same swarm, increases the contacts between robots and the possibilities of forming groups. However, the most stable behavior was not expected to occur with 20 robots in perturbation swarm, as it is expected that this number of robots would to some extent prevent swarm aggregation because contacts now become very frequent, slowing down aggregation.

For the case of the 10-robot swarm (image (b) in Fig. 7), the behavior is within the expected results. It is observed that the average aggregation time increases as robots from group B (disturbance) are added. Unlike the previous case, a swarm of 10 robots without perturbation manages to aggregate on average 100 s after the start of the simulation, therefore, as more robots from the other swarm appear, eventually a hindering effect is generated, which may slow down the aggregation. It is observed that the average time to aggregate almost doubles when 20 robots are added in group B (perturbation swarm).

For the case of 20 robots (image (c) in Fig. 7), the average aggregation time is somewhat similar despite the increase in the population of group B (perturbation swarm). It is important to note that, in this test, the aggregation measure was adjusted to the time when the source "covers" the maximum number of robots, which in this case is 10 robots, so it is expected that 50% of the robots in the swarm cannot aggregate or only do so for a short period of time. Another note is that according to Eq. 2, there is a ratio factor for the area of the source and the number of robots it can cover, so actually the source can hold more robots than calculated. This can be seen in Fig. 7(c). From this, the results obtained in this case are as expected, as well as it is interesting to note that despite having many robots, in most cases the desired aggregation is obtained.

6   Conclusions

This paper presented a Matlab simulator to model the Beeclust algorithm, which aims to aggregate robots based on specific environmental characteristics. From the two experiments performed, the ability of the algorithm to achieve the aggregation of robots under a simple source and a complex source was verified, demonstrating the algorithm's ability to adapt to a dynamic environment. The algorithm's ability to aggregate robots despite another swarm that may affect its performance was analyzed. Thanks to the results obtained, not only can we verify the qualities of the algorithm to aggregate robots despite its simplicity, but we also validated the software's ability to simulate the swarms of robots. Future work is expected to refine the simulator to incorporate other ways of describing sources with complex patterns to guide the aggregation, the presence of immobile obstacles, and a more appropriate interface for the software configuration. It is also expected to incorporate other algorithms for aggregation. With respect to the Beeclust algorithm, the simulator will evaluate the algorithm's improvements and the implementation of variants that will improve its efficiency and robustness.

References

1. Amjadi, A.S., Raoufi, M., Turgut, A.E.: A self-adaptive landmark-based aggregation method for robot swarms. Adapt. Behav. (2021). https://doi.org/10.1177/1059712320985543
2. Arvin, F., Samsudin, K., Ramli, A.R., Bekravi, M.: Imitation of honeybee aggregation with collective behavior of swarm robots. Int. J. Comput. Intell. Syst. 4, 739–748 (2012). https://doi.org/10.1080/18756891.2011.9727825. New pub: Atlantis Press
3. Arvin, F., Turgut, A.E., Bazyari, F., Arikan, K.B., Bellotto, N., Yue, S.: Cue-based aggregation with a mobile robot swarm: a novel fuzzy-based method. Adapt. Behav. 22, 189–206 (2014). https://doi.org/10.1177/1059712314528009
4. Arvin, F., et al.: Phi$ Clust: pheromone-based aggregation for robotic swarms. In: IEEE International Conference on Intelligent Robots and Systems, pp. 4288–4294 (2018). https://doi.org/10.1109/IROS.2018.8593961
5. Arvin, F., Turgut, A.E., Krajník, T., Yue, S.: Investigation of cue-based aggregation in static and dynamic environments with a mobile robot swarm. Adapt. Behav. 24, 102–118 (2016). https://doi.org/10.1177/1059712316632851
6. Bayindir, L.: A review of swarm robotics tasks. Neurocomputing 172, 292–321 (2016). https://doi.org/10.1016/j.neucom.2015.05.116
7. Bodi, M., Thenius, R., Szopek, M., Schmickl, T., Crailsheim, K.: Interaction of robot swarms using the honeybee-inspired control algorithm BEECLUST. Math. Comput. Modell. Dynam. Syst. 18, 87–100 (2012). https://doi.org/10.1080/13873954.2011.601420
8. Duarte, M., et al.: Evolution of collective behaviors for a real swarm of aquatic surface robots. PLoS ONE 11(3), e0151834 (2016)
9. Hamann, H.: Swarm robotics: a formal approach (2018). https://doi.org/10.1007/978-3-319-74528-2
10. Kernbach, S., Thenius, R., Kernbach, O., Schmickl, T.: Re-embodiment of honeybee aggregation behavior in an artificial micro-robotic system. Adapt. Behav. 17, 237–259 (2009). https://doi.org/10.1177/1059712309104966
11. Şahin, E.: Swarm robotics: from sources of inspiration to domains of application. In: Şahin, E., Spears, W.M. (eds.) SR 2004. LNCS, vol. 3342, pp. 10–20. Springer, Heidelberg (2005). https://doi.org/10.1007/978-3-540-30552-1_2
12. Schmickl, T., et al.: Get in touch: cooperative decision making based on robot-to-robot collisions. Autonom. Agents Multi-Agent Syst. 18(1), 133–155 (2009)

Full State Feedback of DC-Motor Position and Speed Control Using LQR and Kalman Filter

Duván A. Marrugo, Angie L. Vitola, Juan C. Peña, J. Duque[iD],
and J. L. Villa[✉][iD]

Universidad Tecnológica de Bolívar, Cartagena de Indias, Colombia
{marrugod,vitolaa,penaj,jduque,jvilla}@utb.edu.co

Abstract. DC motors are used in various industrial, robotic and motion control applications, and generally angular position and speed are used as the main control variables. This paper presents the design of an LQR controller with a Kalman Filter (KF) for state estimation during position and speed control of a DC motor. The proposed controller is evaluated for low and high speed reference profiles to demonstrate its efficiency in different types of applications. This approach is compared with the classical control method using a PID controller. From the results, it is observed that the settling time of the LQR-KF method is less, being 30% more efficient than the PID. In addition, the use of LQR provides an optimal state feedback control that minimizes the quadratic state error and control effort. The experimental results demonstrate the feasibility of the controller design for high precision applications.

Keywords: Optimal control · DC motor · Angular position · Speed · LQR · Kalman Filter

1 Introduction

The most common type of actuator that converts electrical energy into mechanical motion is the electric motor [17]. Direct Current (DC) motors provide an attractive alternative to AC motors in high-performance motion control applications. DC motors are in particular popular in low-power and high precise servo applications due to their reasonable cost and ease of control [9]. DC motors are used in various industrial, robotics and motion control applications. Generally, speed and position are the two parameters essential for control in a DC motor [13]. Traditionally motor controls in industrial applications employ a cascade control structure. The outer speed and inner current control loops are designed as PD, PI or PID controllers. However, the cascaded control structure assumes that the inner loop dynamics are substantially faster than the outer one [2,9].

In recent years several publications propose alternative approaches to identify and control DC motors. [17] describes a generalized PID speed control design technique of DC using LQR approach. In addition, [2] presents a switched LQR

© The Author(s), under exclusive license to Springer Nature Switzerland AG 2022
J. C. Figueroa-García et al. (Eds.): WEA 2022, CCIS 1685, pp. 400–411, 2022.
https://doi.org/10.1007/978-3-031-20611-5_33

speed controller, designed from the linear model of the DC motor, and compare its performance with a cascade control design in terms of accuracy, robustness and complexity. Also, in [17] is presented an LQR approach to determine the optimal PID speed control of the DC motor. When we talk about optimal control, we refer to the control system that is able to bring a process to stabilization around a given working point while minimizing the cost involved in the dynamic operation of the controlled plant; this is precisely the LQR control, adjusting a proportional controller using mathematical algorithms to minimize the cost function, i.e. the adjustments that mitigate unwanted deviations are found, since the cost function is defined by the sum of the deviations of the output measurements of the process with respect to the desired values, [14]. Optimal control is also a part of strategies developed to give much better performance than the conventional methods [15]. Linear Quadratic Regulator (LQR) belongs to this family of optimal control [8]. LQR is used for linear plants with quadratic performance which provides a feedback path to ensure that the trajectory is computed again in case any disturbance affects the plant [3].

On the other hand, due to the requirement of real time processing, the structure needs to be handled in an online way. Kalman filter (KF), due to its recursive nature, is one of the most widely adopted tools for achieving this purpose. In doing so, the time series models are converted into state space models, including a state transition equation and an observation equation for the hidden state process and the observation process, respectively [5].

This paper presents the design of a LQR controller with a KF for angular position and speed control for a DC motor system. The proposed controller is evaluated for high and low speed reference profiles to demonstrate its efficiency for high-performance motor applications. The paper has been divided in five sections: the introduction is presented in Sect. 1. Section 2, describes the related works focus on solving the control problem. Section 3, describes the methodology used: mathematical modeling of DC-Motor, hardware setup and LQR controller design. The results are presented in Sect. 4. Finally, Sect. 5 summarizes the major conclusions of the paper.

2   Related Work

In addition, to achieve optimal control, an objective function is set, and an attempt is made to minimize it. To achieve these objectives, it is necessary to study the behavior of the system under several types of controllers and optimization algorithms, considering parameters such as steady state error, rise and settling time, percentage of overshoot, etc. Therefore, nowadays a lot of research has been done to perform angular position or speed control of a DC motor.

In [1], the optimal speed control of a DC motor is performed by applying Grey Wolf Optimization (GWO) in tuning the PID controller parameters. The results, in terms of settling and rise times, are lower than those presented by other methods previous to this research. It can be observed that, once the PID controller is tuned by GWO, its performance does not depend on the variations in the DC motor parameters, obtaining a good system response for different operating points. However, the objective function used provides considerable overshoot.

In [4] the performance of the model reference adaptive control (MRAC) with PID compensator and the fuzzy PID self-tuning controller is compared for different required values of speed and time, in spite of the load disturbance and parameter variations. The results indicate that with the MRAC without PID a high overshooting and steady state error is obtained, but when combined with the PID compensator, the performance increases considerably. Finally, it is concluded that both controllers are robust, but the MRAC and PID approach is clearly superior, especially for systems that are subject to sudden disturbances.

In [7] an Atom Search Optimization (ASO) algorithm and its chaotic version (ChASO) are presented for the speed control of a DC motor, determining the optimal parameters of a FOPID controller. The methodology is applied on 6 optimization problems and a comparison of results for different algorithms is presented. The ChASO approach has higher stability indices than other algorithms and has no overshoot, optimizing the dynamic response of the control system. The comparison results show that the ChASO-FOPID approach has the best transient response in the problems posed and a good response in terms of overshoot, settling time, settling and rise time. In addition, it is more robust to model uncertainties, managing to suppress abrupt changes in the response due to perturbations.

In [12] an optimization algorithm is presented to find the optimal values of a PID controller for speed control of a DC motor under different disturbances. The approach of the algorithm (CVOA) is based on the coronavirus dispersion model (COVID-19), so it avoids setting arbitrary initial values, since these are already tuned according to the disease statistics. In this work, an objective function is used to obtain the desired results, in terms of rise time, overshoot, settling time, and steady-state error. The results are compared with those obtained by methods such as Genetic Algorithm and Harmony Search, and it is obtained that the CVOA-based PID approach can improve the performance of the motor system, obtaining a minimum rise time and settling time and an acceptable overshoot, being the best option in the comparison.

In [6], angular position control of a DC motor using a PID controller and the Linear Quadratic Regulation (LQR) approach for optimal control is performed. This methodology is compared with the tuning of the same controller using the Root Locus Method. The results indicate that optimal control using LQR exhibits low settling time and overshoot, unlike the other method. However, both methods still produce a steady state error. In this work, it is determined that PID control with LQR is the best approach because it attempts to minimize the energy used to reach the reference by minimizing overshoot. In addition, the PID-Root Locus method has a longer settling time because the integral control continues to sum the errors received by the sensor.

3   Methodology

In the following section it will be explained how the dynamic model of the motor was obtained and the necessary steps for the design and implementation of the controller.

3.1   DC Motor Mathematical Model

12 V brushed DC gearmotor with a 50:1 metal gearbox and an integrated quadrature encoder that provides a resolution of 64 counts per revolution of the motor shaft, which corresponds to 3200 counts per revolution of the gearbox output shaft, is used in this work. The gearbox is mainly composed of spur gears, but has helical gears for the first stage to reduce noise and improve efficiency. This type of motor has a D-shaped output shaft 16 mm long and 6 mm in diameter.

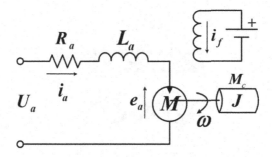

Fig. 1. DC motor physical setup.

For the analysis it will be assumed that the input of the system is the voltage source (V) applied to the armature of the motor, while the output is the rotational speed of the shaft $\dot{\theta}$ [16]. The armature-controlled dc motor system is shown in Fig. 1. The linear model of a simple dc motor as a function of speed consists of an electrical equation and a mechanical equation. Applying Kirchhoff's Voltage Law (KVL) and Newton's second law, Eq. 1 and 2 are obtained.

$$J\ddot{\theta} + b\dot{\theta} = Ki \tag{1}$$

$$L\frac{di}{dt} + Ri = V - K\dot{\theta} \tag{2}$$

In state space form, the above governing equations can be expressed by choosing rotational speed and electric current as state variables. Again, armature voltage is treated as the input and rotational speed is chosen as the output. As shown in the Eq. 3.

$$\frac{d}{dt}\begin{bmatrix}\dot{\theta}\\i\end{bmatrix} = \begin{bmatrix}-\frac{b}{J} & \frac{K}{J}\\-\frac{K}{L} & -\frac{R}{L}\end{bmatrix}\begin{bmatrix}\dot{\theta}\\i\end{bmatrix} + \begin{bmatrix}0\\\frac{1}{L}\end{bmatrix}V \tag{3}$$

$$y = \begin{bmatrix}1 & 0\end{bmatrix}\begin{bmatrix}\dot{\theta}\\i\end{bmatrix}$$

where b, K, J, R and L correspond to the motor viscous friction constant, motor torque constant, rotor moment of inertia, electrical resistance and electrical inductance respectively.

3.2   Methodological Design

The general procedure for obtaining the model parameters and control design es depicted in Fig. 2.

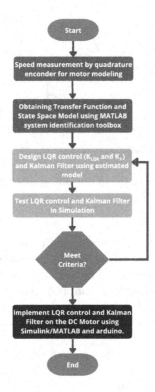

Fig. 2. Methodology used for the implementation of angular position and speed control.

Table 1. DC motor specifications

Parameters	Value
Voltage	12 V
No-load performance	200 RPM, 200 mA
Stall extrapolation	21 kg · cm, 5.5 A

3.3 Hardware Setup

Figure 3 shows the block diagram of the system used in this research. The specifications of the dc motor with built-in encoder are summarized in Table 1.

The motor driver is the TB6612FNG. An Arduino Uno controls and communicates with the PC to send the data through serial communication communication.

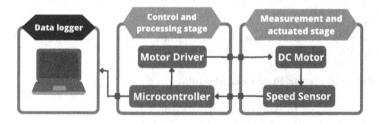

Fig. 3. Block diagram of system implementation

3.4 Motor Modeling

Even though the variable to be controlled is the angular position of the motor, initially the characterization of the motor is performed with the speed variable. Both the input signal to the system, which is the voltage, and the output signal, which is the speed, are collected with a sampling time of 0.01 s. These data are used to find the system model using MATLAB's System Identification Toolbox.

The Toolbox allows to select the estimation method. In order to improve the set up time of our system, the method of obtaining by means of a transfer function model is selected, this allows to select the number of zeros and poles of our system. In our case, zeros are not desired in our plant. In the Eq. 4 the continuous time transfer function can be observed, which allows to approximate the behavior of the system. This approximation was obtained with a mean square error of 87.5% and a data fit of 94.88%.

$$TF(s) = \frac{y}{u} = \frac{47.04}{s^2 + 22.16\,s + 45.82} \tag{4}$$

From Eq. 4, Eq. 5 is obtained, which represents the state space model of the system in second order form. This model is fully controllable and observable. Prior to implementation on the real system real hardware system, the control algorithm is tested in MATLAB/Simulink, as observed in the following subsection.

$$\begin{bmatrix} \dot{x}_1 \\ \dot{x}_2 \end{bmatrix} = \begin{bmatrix} 0.6597 & 0.62 \\ 0.5 & 0 \end{bmatrix} x + \begin{bmatrix} 0.25 \\ 0 \end{bmatrix} u \tag{5}$$

$$y = \begin{bmatrix} 0.0822 & 0.07725 \end{bmatrix} x + \begin{bmatrix} 0.03115 \end{bmatrix} u$$

In the Algorithm 1 the procedure for obtaining the estimated model of the plant for the design of the control is indicated.

Algorithm 1: DC motor characterization using the System Identification Toolbox.

Input: $u(k)$, $y(k)$
Output: A, B, C, D
1 Create model of linear dynamic systems from measured input-output data.
2 Import time domain data $\leftarrow u(k), y(k)$
3 **while** $A, B, C, D \leftarrow \emptyset$ **do**
4 | **Solve Transfer Function Models**
5 | *Transfer Fuctions($N.Poles = 2 \cup N.Zeros = 0 \cup Ts = 0.01$)*
6 | Import Model to Workspace $Tf \leftarrow Eq.4$;
7 | $[A \quad B \quad C \quad D] = Space State(Tf) \leftarrow Eq.5$;
8 **return** A, B, C, D

3.5   Controller Design

LQG control is a type of optimal control. It is the combination between LQR and Kalman filter [10]. LQG solves the weakness of LQR control that requires the number of sensors as the number of states and replaces them with an observer, the Kalman filter [11]. This is very useful since not all states of the system can be measured.

The state estimation is performed using a feedback form of the predicted error, where the model is obtained from the characterization indicated in the Algorithm 1. Optimal control and optimal estimation are dualities, like control and observation, so the Kalman filter has the same shape equation as LQR. In Fig. 4, the block diagram associated with the integral state feedback controller can be seen.

Equations 6, 7 and 8 represent the extended matrices associated with the closed-loop analysis of the system for speed control.

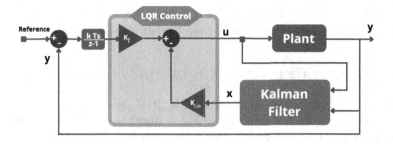

Fig. 4. Block diagram of full-state feedback LQG speed control.

$$A_{extended} = \begin{bmatrix} A & zeros(2,1) \\ -C & 1 \end{bmatrix} \tag{6}$$

$$B_{extended} = \begin{bmatrix} B \\ 0 \end{bmatrix} \tag{7}$$

$$C_{extended} = \begin{bmatrix} C \\ 0 \end{bmatrix} \tag{8}$$

For the tuning of the controller, it is necessary to estimate the gains K_{LQR} and K_f which represent the LQR gain and the integral gain, respectively. In Algorithm 2, the process for estimation using preset functions in MATLAB is observed.

Algorithm 2: Estimation of controller gains for Integral LQR control

---

Input: $u(k)$, $y(k)$
Output: K_{LQR}, K_f
1 Obtain system space state $SS \leftarrow Eq.5$
2 Obtain eigenvalues $\leftarrow Eig(SS)$
3 Find extended matrices from feedback system $\leftarrow Eq.6, 7$ and 8
4 **Estimate Gain**
5 $K = dlqr(A_{extended} \cup B_{extended} \cup Q_{extended} \cup R \cup zeros(1,3))$
6 **LQR gain:** $K_{LQR} = K[1:2]$
7 **Integral gain:** $K_J = -K[3]$
8 **return** K_{LQR}, K_f

Where $Q = \begin{bmatrix} 1 & 0 \\ 0 & 1 \end{bmatrix}$ and $R = \begin{bmatrix} 0.01 \end{bmatrix}$ are the state weight and the weight for the control input, respectively. $Q_{extended}$ is the weight matrix for the state feedback system, it can be seen in Eq. 9.

$$Q_{extended} = \begin{bmatrix} Q & zeros(2,1) \\ zeros(1,2) & 1000 \end{bmatrix} \tag{9}$$

In addition to the feedback gain of K states, *dlqr* returns the infinite horizon solution S of the associated discrete-time Riccati equation.

$$A^T SA - S - (A^T SB + N)(B^T SB + R)^{-1}(B^T SA + N^T) + Q = 0 \qquad (10)$$

Finally, for angular position estimation, it is necessary to include in the analysis a tuning gain K_P, as shown in Fig. 5, from the closed-loop speed control by means of a LQR control with state estimation by Kalman filter.

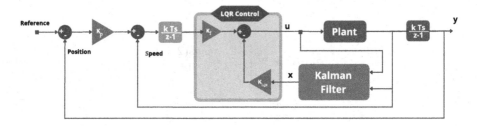

Fig. 5. Block diagram of full-state feedback LQG position control.

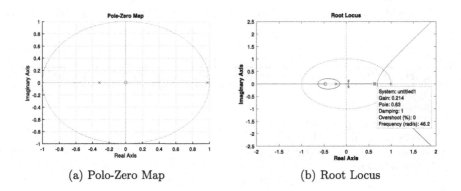

(a) Polo-Zero Map   (b) Root Locus

Fig. 6. System stability test.

4   Experimental Results

The determination of the gain associated with the proportional constant for the determination of the position was performed from the analysis of the root locus of the closed-loop system, as shown in Fig. 6(b).

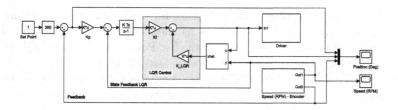

Fig. 7. Block diagram of full-state feedback LQG angular position Control.

For the implementation, the system proposed in Sect. 3.5 was used. Using Arduino/Simulink communication, and implementing the block diagram proposed in Fig. 7, we performed the test for 3 angles, 90°, 180° and 200°. Where the estimated values for $K_P = 0.214$, $K_f = 37.87$ and $K_{LQR} = [\,7.2 \;\; 5.40\,]$.

As a comparison method a classical PID control is implemented, which allows a comparison between the result from it and the proposed integral state feedback control. The control tolerance for the test is ±3.5%.

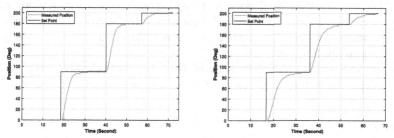

(a) DC motor angular position control test using LQR estimation and Kalman filter.

(b) DC motor angular position control test using PID.

Fig. 8. DC motor position control controls implementation.

Table 2. Descriptive data statistics.

	LQR and Kalman Filter	PID
Count	7182.0	7421.0
Mean	102.7	107.835
Std	77.4	81.27
Max	202	202

The Fig. 8 shows the comparison between the two implemented controls. The same angular position set points were used. In Fig. 8(a), the response of the state estimation controller is observed, on average for each position, the settling time was 8.4 s. In comparison with the PID, as shown in Fig. 8(b), which is slower, since it takes 12.1 s on average to reach the Set Point. Notably, the LQR control and the Kalman filter reaches the Set point faster than the PID controller. As shown in Table 2, the PID controller shows a greater data dispersion around the set point. Based on this, the LQR controller shows a better performance in terms of being able to reach the desired target value.

5   Conclusions

This paper demonstrates a design of an optimal controller using an Kalman Filter for speed control of a DC motor. A LQR based angular position control system is designed with Kalman filter as the estimator. The results show that LQR with Kalman filter, which uses only one state as feedback and predicts the other states as well as the system parameters, is seen to be a controller for optimal position and speed control of a DC motor. The LQR design provides an optimal state feedback control minimizes the quadratic state error and control effort. The auxiliary integral error state and feedforward compensation of the nonlinear friction reduce the residual error across the entire range of reference. The experimental results demonstrate the feasibility of the controller design for high precision applications.

In future work, we propose to make the design of adaptive controllers to handle variations of load and the identification of periodical disturbances.

References

1. Ahmed, A., Gupta, R., Parmar, G.: GWO/PID approach for optimal control of DC motor. In: 2018 5th International Conference on Signal Processing and Integrated Networks, SPIN 2018, pp. 181–186 (2018). https://doi.org/10.1109/SPIN.2018.8474105
2. Chevrel, P., Sicot, L., Siala, S.: Switched LQ controllers for DC motor speed and current control: a comparison with cascade control. In: PESC Record. 27th Annual IEEE Power Electronics Specialists Conference, vol. 1, pp. 906–912 (1996). https://doi.org/10.1109/PESC.1996.548689
3. Dani, S., Sonawane, D., Ingole, D., Patil, S.: Performance evaluation OF PID, LQR and MPC for DC motor speed control. In: 2017 2nd International Conference for Convergence in Technology (I2CT), pp. 348–354 (2017). https://doi.org/10.1109/I2CT.2017.8226149
4. El-samahy, A.A., Shamseldin, M.A.: Brushless DC motor tracking control using self-tuning fuzzy PID control and model reference adaptive control. Ain Shams Eng. J. 9, 341–352 (9 2018). https://doi.org/10.1016/J.ASEJ.2016.02.004
5. Guo, J., Huang, W., Williams, B.M.: Adaptive Kalman filter approach for stochastic short-term traffic flow rate prediction and uncertainty quantification. Transp. Res. Part C Emerging Technol. 43, 50–64 (2014). https://doi.org/10.1016/j.trc.2014.02.006. https://www.sciencedirect.com/science/article/pii/S0968090X14000382. Special Issue on Short-term Traffic Flow Forecasting

 6. Handaya, D., Fauziah, R.: Proportional-integral-derivative and linear quadratic regulator control of direct current motor position using multi-turn based on Lab-View. J. Rob. Control (JRC) **2**, 332–336 (2021). https://doi.org/10.18196/JRC. 24102D
 7. Hekimoglu, B.: Optimal tuning of fractional order PID controller for DC motor speed control via chaotic atom search optimization algorithm. IEEE Access **7**, 38100–38114 (2019). https://doi.org/10.1109/ACCESS.2019.2905961
 8. Khatoon, S., Gupta, D., Das, L.K.: PID & LQR control for a quadrotor: modeling and simulation. In: 2014 International Conference on Advances in Computing, Communications and Informatics (ICACCI), pp. 796–802 (2014). https://doi.org/ 10.1109/ICACCI.2014.6968232
 9. Ruderman, M., Krettek, J., Hoffmann, F., Bertram, T.: Optimal state space control of DC motor (2008)
10. Madhukar, P., Mishra, P.K.: Linear quadratic gaussian control design with extended Kalman filter. Int. Res. J. Adv. Sci. Hub **2**, 31–42 (2020). https://doi. org/10.47392/irjash.2020.34
11. Maghfiroh, H., Nizam, M., Praptodiyono, S.: PID optimal control to reduce energy consumption in DC-drive system. Int. J. Power Electron. Drive Syst. **11**, 2164–2172 (2020). https://doi.org/10.11591/ijpeds.v11.i4.pp2164-2172
12. Shamseldin, M.A., Barbosa, R., Jesus, I.: Optimal coronavirus optimization algorithm based PID controller for high performance brushless DC motor. Algorithms **14**, 193 (2021). https://doi.org/10.3390/A14070193. https://www.mdpi. com/1999-4893/14/7/193/htm
13. Dani, S., Sonawane, D., Ingole, D., Patil, S.: Performance evaluation of PID, LQR and MPC for DC motor speed control (2017)
14. de Velasco, J.M., Galvis, L.T.P.: Diseño e implementación de un control òptimo lqr con la tarjeta raspberry pi (2016)
15. Vishal, V., Kumar, V., Rana, K., Mishra, P.: Comparative study of some optimization techniques applied to DC motor control. In: 2014 IEEE International Advance Computing Conference (IACC), pp. 1342–1347 (2014). https://doi.org/ 10.1109/IAdCC.2014.6779522
16. Xiang, Z., Wei, W.: Design of DC motor position tracking system based on LQR. J. Phys. Conf. Ser. **1887**(1), 012052 (2021). https://doi.org/10.1088/1742-6596/ 1887/1/012052
17. Yu, G.R., Hwang, R.C.: Optimal PID speed control of brush less DC motors using LQR approach. In: 2004 IEEE International Conference on Systems, Man and Cybernetics (IEEE Cat. No. 04CH37583), vol. 1, pp. 473–478 (2004). https://doi. org/10.1109/ICSMC.2004.1398343

Applications

Experimental Data-Driven Insertion Force Analyses of Hypodermic Needles in a Soft Tissue with an In-House Test Bench

Erick D. Chávez Pereda[1] , Julián D. Loaiza Duque[1] ,
María A. Cerón Hurtado[1,2] , Hernán A. González Rojas[1] ,
and Antonio J. Sánchez Egea[1(✉)]

[1] Universitat Politècnica de Catalunya, Av. de Víctor Balaguer, 1,
08800 Vilanova i la Geltrú, Barcelona, Spain
`antonio.egea@upc.edu`
[2] Universidad Autónoma de Occidente, Calle 25# 115-85 Km 2 Vía Cali - Jamundi,
760030 Cali, Colombia

Abstract. Hypodermic needles are used in a wide range of medical procedures. In these procedures, an insertion force is applied to the needle to insert it through the soft tissue. In that way, when the tip of the needle encounters the surface of the tissue, several opposing forces are generated, such as stiffness, friction, and cutting forces, because of the tissue surface tension and viscoelastic properties. In addition, insertion force can influence tissue tearing and needle deflection. Thus, it is crucial to understand and analyze these forces and their effect on the tissue. We experimentally tested several commercial hypodermic needles at different diameters and bevel angles of the needle tips using an in-house test bench at different insertion velocities. In addition, chicken breasts were used as biological tissue to test the needles. As a result, the experimental cutting force increases linearly concerning the diameter of the needle and the insertion velocity. Also, the shear stress remains constant concerning insertion velocity and increases linearly with needle diameter and length. In conclusion, the results let us understand that the insertion mechanism is not trivial due to the influence of the geometry and relative velocity of the needle while penetrating the tissue and the mechanical properties of the soft tissue. All these combined parameters present challenging research to optimize medical procedures with needles.

Keywords: Hypodermic needle · Insertion force · Cutting force · Shear stress · Insertion velocity

1 Introduction

Needles are one of the most widely used tools in medical procedures today. These are minimally invasive tools, from the most routine to the most complex surgical

© The Author(s), under exclusive license to Springer Nature Switzerland AG 2022
J. C. Figueroa-García et al. (Eds.): WEA 2022, CCIS 1685, pp. 415–422, 2022.
https://doi.org/10.1007/978-3-031-20611-5_34

procedures [3]. Although they are widely and effectively used, there has been a growing interest in studying the behavior of the needle during the puncture of a tissue. It seeks to establish how it is possible to minimize the impact on the patient and how to improve the performance of the needle. Some forces occur as a tissue response to needle insertion, and it is believed that reducing these forces would directly impact tissue tearing and puncture accuracy. In addition, tissues may recover more quickly after insertion by reducing tearing. Although this may not be critical in blood tests or local anesthetic insertion, it is crucial in brain insertion [1].

Using of hypodermic needles is a widespread practice to overcome the skin barrier physically. Several features determine the insertion force of these needles. In particular, the geometry and specific bevel features of the needle directly impact the insertion force, which can cause the needles to deflect and change their trajectory [11]. The trajectory estimation when inserting the needle is of particular importance in delicate operations such as biopsies, in which tissue samples are removed from the body. In the case of a biopsy, improving the accuracy of each puncture can result in the extraction of the desired samples in optimal conditions for analysis. This trajectory estimation also allows for delicate procedures without affecting the nearest organs. For example, in the case of epidural anesthesia, puncture precision could reduce the risk of dural puncture. The above occurs when the needle or catheter punctures the dural and the arachnoid, causing prolonged headaches over time [7]. In the mechanics of needle insertion, several counter-insertion forces depend on the surface tension of the tissue and its viscoelastic properties.

During needle insertion, three forces can be found: stiffness, friction, and cutting force [9]. The stiffness force is denoted when the needle tip first interacts with the tissue surface, and the latter starts to deform until the needle successfully overcomes the elastic limit of the surface. Immediately after that, the needle tip begins to penetrate the inner layers of the tissue, causing the needle walls to insert into the tissue. Here, two new forces appear, cutting and frictional forces, which increase according to the contact area between the tissue and the inserted needle [8]. The magnitude of these forces is also directly correlated with the insertion velocity [4,6] and the needle geometrical features [10], such as the bevel angles and the length. Equation 1 combines all the forces mentioned during the insertion tests. The mathematical approach to the contribution of each component has been extensively studied by Jiang et al. [4].

$$F_{in} = -F_{stiff} - (F_{cut} - F_{fric}) \tag{1}$$

These needle insertion forces are experimentally studied using an in-house mechanical bench with a linear actuator to provide relative movements to the needle and a load cell to record the insertion forces. It is similar to the one developed by Giovannini et al. [2]. This project evaluates needle insertion in soft tissues with different relative movements. In particular, it focuses on the characterization of the insertion forces and shear stress produced by this mechanical bench with different hypodermic needle gauges and insertion velocities. To this end, we aim to determine the relationship between these two parameters, needle diameter and insertion velocities, and the insertion forces to penetrate soft tissue, specifically ex vivo chicken breast.

2 Methodology

2.1 Biological Tissue

The biological tissue used in the first experimental phase corresponds to fresh chicken breasts, bought the same day the tests were conducted. Likewise, the breasts were stored in a transparent container in a refrigerator at 8°C to preserve their properties efficiently. The container used had a flat, straight base and walls to avoid exerting compression on the samples, thus not changing their viscoelastic properties.

2.2 Insertion Force

A linear actuator was used to clamp the needles and induce different axial displacements with the needles. Specifically, four different insertion speeds were evaluated: 3.95, 7.8, 11.6, and 15.5 mm/s. A load cell with a 1000 g capacity, and a sensitivity of 0.4 g, was used to record the insertion forces. Three forces were recorded during the insertion cycle. One of these forces is the stiffness force, which is recorded upon overcoming the surface tension of the soft tissue. Then, once penetration of the needle into the soft tissue has been initiated, the coupled cutting and needle friction forces were recorded. During the cut produced by the needle tip through the tissue layers, the perimeter of the inserted needle area is subjected to the friction of the already cut tissue. Figure 1 shows a schematic of the needle penetration and the forces involved in the insertion process.

2.3 Needle Geometry

The measurement of the needle diameter was performed with a micrometer. Specifically, three measurements per parameter were performed. Then, an optical microscope (model: BC Mricolance) was used to measure the characteristics of the bevel angles and length of the four needle's gauges: $18G^{1/2''}$, $21G^{1''}$, $23Gx^{1''}$, and $27G^{1/2''}$. Table 1 shows the usual bevel hypodermic needle parameters. An optical microscope was used to determine the main features of the needle bevel: angles and length. The image post-processing to determine the pixel-wise measurements was performed with Gimp 2. Figure 2 shows the average value and the standard deviation of the bevel angles and the bevel length of the different hypodermic needles tested.

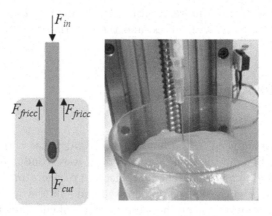

Fig. 1. Outline of needle penetration and involved cutting forces

Table 1. Needle geometric specifications.

Needle gauge	Diameter (mm)	Leng. level (mm)	α_1 (°)	α_2 (°)	α_3 (°)
$18G^{1/2''}$	1.2 ± 0.01	8.03 ± 0.03	12.2 ± 1	19 ± 0.5	24 ± 0.5
$21G^{1''}$	0.8 ± 0.03	7.5 ± 0.04	13 ± 1	20 ± 0.5	24.4 ± 0.5
$23Gx^{1''}$	0.6 ± 0.03	6.2 ± 0.04	12 ± 1	17 ± 1	23 ± 0.5
$27G^{1/2''}$	0.4 ± 0.05	3.5 ± 0.05	12.8 ± 1	15.6 ± 1	25 ± 0.5

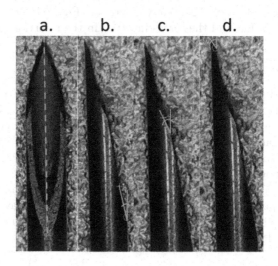

Fig. 2. Main bevel features of the needle: length bevel, 1st bevel angle (α_1), 2nd bevel angle (α_2) and 3rd bevel angle (α_3)

3 Results

Experimental results have captured the influence of needle geometry and insertion velocity on needle insertion forces. Sixteen insertion tests, four insertion velocities for each of the four needle gauges, have been performed to determine the insertion forces. First, Fig. 3a shows the characteristic curves of the insertion forces for the $27G^{1/2''}$ needle at the four insertion velocities established. During the needle insertion cycle, three different phases can be identified. In phase A, the stiffness cutting and friction forces increase linearly until the maximum penetration is reached. In phase B, there is a change of direction in the direction of the needle, and a viscoelastic settling of the soft tissue on the needle occurs. Finally, during phase C, the extraction of the needle is observed, and, therefore, it is recorded exclusively as the friction force. On the other hand, Fig. 3b shows the stiffness, cutting, and friction forces of the hypodermic needle at the four insertion velocities. The linear trends show the experienced behavior of the coupled forces, where the higher the penetration velocity, the higher the cutting forces recorded.

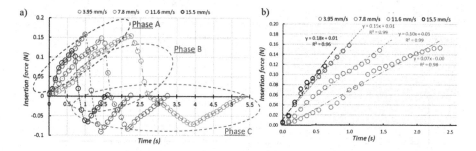

Fig. 3. a) Insertion forces of the $27G^{1/2''}$ gauge hypodermic needle for the studied insertion velocities. b) Cutting forces during the needle insertion velocities.

Insertion velocity and needle diameter directly influence insertion forces, increasing the forces to penetrate soft tissue when higher insertion velocities and needle diameters are used. In addition, it should be noted that as the velocity of insertion increases, the slope between samples of cutting forces tends to decrease. Consequently, a stationary point will be reached where the insertion velocity does not influence the cutting forces in this soft tissue. Furthermore, the needle friction forces can be recorded independently when the needle is withdrawn from the soft tissue. It is observed that this frictional force increases up to a certain point, at which point its trend changes. The slope of this force also depends linearly on the needle diameter, being higher for a larger diameter. This trend change is attributed to creep and relaxation of the tissue for a constant deformation over time. Tests for larger needle diameters take more time than smaller ones, and consequently, the relaxation of the tissue is more visible at larger diameters. The same phenomenon is denoted at smaller insertion velocities, where the relaxation takes more time than at faster velocities.

Furthermore, Fig. 4 shows the influence of insertion velocities from 3.95 to 15.5 mm/s on the tested needle geometries. The cutting forces behave similarly for the different needle geometries, except for the largest diameter needle, $18G^{1/2''}$, with a diameter of 1.2 mm. The cutting force is significantly higher than the other samples studied insertion velocities. Moreover, the most significant increase in slope is found for low insertion velocities. Note that the slope of the cutting force becomes steeper when lower insertion velocities are established, which seems to indicate that it is more difficult for the needle to overcome the surface tension of this soft tissue at low velocities.

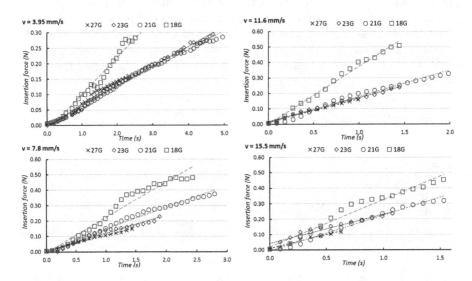

Fig. 4. Cutting forces based on the geometry of the hypodermic needle and insertion velocity.

The instantaneous shear stress (τ_f) associated with the friction force is defined as the quotient of the needle friction force and the contact section, see equation (2). This shear stress is calculated in one insertion cycle to determine the needle friction force associated with the contact area of the needle with the soft tissue. In addition, it is determined how this parameter behaves with needle diameter and insertion velocity. Figure 5 shows the instantaneous needle shear stress for the four hypodermic needles at four insertion velocities.

$$\tau_f = \frac{F_{fric}}{\pi D_n L} \qquad (2)$$

where τ_f is the shear stress associated with the frictional force, F_{fric} is the friction force recorded during the extraction needle, D_n is the diameter of the needle, and L is the inserted needle length.

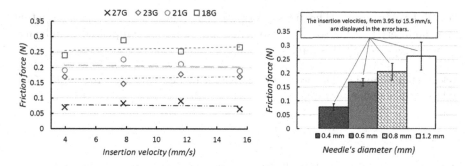

Fig. 5. Shear stress associated to the friction force for the different insertion velocities and needle's diameter.

The results indicate that the insertion velocities do not affect the shear stress of the needle. However, a difference in needle shear stress is observed when comparing different needle dimensions, attributed to the larger contact surface between the needle and the soft tissue. It should be noted that the contact surface of the needle depends not only on the diameter but also on the length of the inserted bevel, which differs according to the type of needle. As the characteristics of the bevel angles are equivalent in all the needles, we cannot analyze the influence of these bevel features with the change in friction, as already reported by other authors [5].

4   Conclusion

The main contributions of this experimental work can be summarized in the followings bullets:

- The in-house developed test bench for needle insertion and the selected load cell accurately recorded the insertion forces in a soft tissue.
- The influence of needle diameter and insertion velocities has been adequately addressed for cutting and needle friction force. As expected, larger diameter and faster velocities induce higher insertion forces.
- The shear stress associated with the friction force has shown that the creep behavior of the soft tissue over the needle is independent of insertion velocity and increases linearly with needle diameter due to the larger contact area.

In future work, we will analyze the relationship of all needle geometrical parameters with the three associated forces in a soft tissue insertion cycle. Also, it is considered the implementation of other needle-related movements, such as rotary or vibratory movements, and, consequently, modifying the mechanical testing conditions. In addition, further research tests with polyvinyl alcohol dummies mimicking tissue samples are planned.

Conflict of Interest. The authors declare that they have no known competing financial interests or personal relationships that could have appeared to influence the work reported in this paper.

Acknowledgements. This work was supported by Serra Húnter Programme (Generalitat de Catalunya).

References

1. Casanova, F., Carney, P.R., Sarntinoranont, M.: Effect of needle insertion speed on tissue injury, stress, and backflow distribution for convection-enhanced delivery in the rat brain. PLoS ONE **9**, e94919 (2014)
2. Giovannini, M., Ren, H., Cao, J., Ehmann, K.: Study on design and cutting parameters of rotating needles for core biopsy. J. Mech. Behav. Biomed. Mater. **86**, 43–54 (2018)
3. Gupta, J., Denson, D.D., Felner, E.I., Prausnitz, M.R.: Rapid local anesthesia in humans using minimally invasive microneedles. Clin. J. Pain **28**, 129–135 (2012)
4. Jiang, S., Li, P., Yu, Y., Liu, J., Yang, Z.: Experimental study of needle-tissue interaction forces: effect of needle geometries, insertion methods and tissue characteristics. J. Biomech. **47**, 3344–3353 (2014)
5. Konh, B., Hutapea, P.: Finite element studies of needle-tissue interactions for percutaneous procedures1. J. Med. Dev. **9**(3) (2015). https://doi.org/10.1115/1.4030573, 030941
6. Mahvash, M., Dupont, P.: Mechanics of dynamic needle insertion into a biological material. IEEE Trans. Biomed. Eng. **57**, 934–943 (2010)
7. Meiklejohn, B.H.: The effect of rotation of an epidural needle. an in vitro study. Anaesthesia **42**, 1180–2 (1987). https://doi.org/10.1111/j.1365-2044.1987.tb05224.x, www.ncbi.nlm.nih.gov/pubmed/3434738
8. Okamura, A., Simone, C., O'Leary, M.: Force modeling for needle insertion into soft tissue. IEEE Trans. Biomed. Eng. **51**, 1707–1716 (2004)
9. Scali, M., Breedveld, P., Dodou, D.: Experimental evaluation of a self-propelling bio-inspired needle in single- and multi-layered phantoms. Sci. Rep. **9**, 19988 (2019)
10. Webster, R., Memisevic, J., Okamura, A.: Design considerations for robotic needle steering, vol. 2005, pp. 3588–3594. IEEE (2005). https://doi.org/10.1109/ROBOT.2005.1570666,ieeexplore.ieee.org/document/1570666/
11. Zhao, S., Gao, D., Zhao, M., Fu, J.: Trajectory estimation of flexible needle using PVA tissue material. IOP Conf. Ser. Mater. Sci. Eng. **646** (2019)

Simulation Based GNU Radio Tool
for DSP Significant Learning

German Augusto Ramírez[1]([✉]), Yaneth Patricia Caviativa[2],
Fabian C. Castro[1,2], Fredy Alberto Sanz Ramirez[1,2],
and Valentino Jaramillo Guzmán[1,2]

[1] Universidad Nacional, Bogotá, Colombia
germanramirez@unal.edu.co
[2] Universidad Manuela Beltran - Vicerrectoria de investigación, Bogotá, Colombia
{janeth.caviativa,fabian.castro,fredy.sanz}@umb.edu.co,
valentinojaramillog@yahoo.es

Abstract. This contribution presents an approach to strengthen the internalization of theoretical concepts related to digital signal processing - DSP and communications systems by means of active learning using the GNUradio framework, highlighting the experimental work in the strengthening of learning

Results show that user implemented blocks have capabilities comparable to the ones included in GNU radio library and the student's requested feeling of "real life" deployments, with the advantage of being flexible, software dependent, multipurpose hardware, which can be used in the laboratory for teaching and further research. On the other hand, significantly learned materials can be retained for a relatively long period of time, months, even years

Keywords: Active learning · Significant and autonomous learning · Software defined radio · FM digital receiver · GNU radio

1 Introduction

In engineering education, it is of essential value the involvement of the participant in its own learning process, conditioned by the increasing degree of autonomy that allows him the strategic use of educational resources made available by the instructors, forming the student for the autonomous management of learning, through an intended action. Autonomy in learning allows the student to make decisions that lead him to regulate his own learning according to a specific goal and a specific context or learning conditions [5]. Therefore an autonomous person is "one whose system of self-regulation works in a way that allows him to successfully satisfy both the internal and external demands that arise" [2].

At the basis of the definition of autonomy is the student's ability to learn to learn, which results from being increasingly aware of his process of cognition, that is, of metacognition. Metacognition is a process that refers to the person's knowledge or awareness of their own mental processes (on how they learn) and

© The Author(s), under exclusive license to Springer Nature Switzerland AG 2022
J. C. Figueroa-García et al. (Eds.): WEA 2022, CCIS 1685, pp. 423–436, 2022.
https://doi.org/10.1007/978-3-031-20611-5_35

the control of the cognitive domain (on the way they learn). Both are oriented
to the service of an improvement of the personal study that leads to satisfactory
results of learning [3]

Autonomy in learning process of topics such as Digital Signal Processing and
Communication Systems could be hard to achieve because this topics involves
a number of mathematical concepts that can be cumbersome for the beginner
student, an a proven way to deal with the effective learning of those concepts
is the experimental, hands-on, work. However, expensive and single purpose
equipment, subject to obsolescence, are everywhere collecting dust in universities' laboratories, as constant hardware updates can not be afforded by most of
them. On the other hand, software simulation is a great aid for presenting these
topics, although oftentimes students complain about the lack of "real life" feeling
with "plain simulations", and the objective of long term compromise with the
autonomous learning process can not fully be achieved. In this regard Software
Defined Radio - SDR is foreseen as a bridge to fill the gap between software computations and real life, hardware based, signal processing in a flexible, scalable
and affordable way.

The negative point with some SDR frameworks available is that those are "too
complex" for the sophomore to theses topics, hence the student ends with frus-
tration and restraining to the basic front end functionalities without digging
further on alternate paths to achieve same results or new ways to go deep in
creating new functions. Hence this works intends to show a simple implementation, aimed at the significant learning of concepts in communications systems
that can be easily replicated.

1.1   Background

Software defined radio - SDR is a communications system paradigm in which
many of the traditional functions of the radio transceiver are carried out by
software commands rather than by hardware realizations. SDR is considered to
be born in the 1995 seminal work by Mitola [4], in which alternative architectures
are defined for the development of SDR and the further step of Cognitive Radio
- CR. Other aspects of SDR and CR like regulatory issues, service provision, and
convergence, usually overlooked in technical literature, are early explored in [5].

Likewise, an historical perspective. Including current challenges of SDR/CR
can be found in [7] where the topicality of the issue is exposed.

From the days when dedicated processors and specific mission software where
the only practical alternative to the realization of SDR, computational power
has increased and costs have shrunken according to the expectations [9], this
factors combined have allowed recent developments of SDR and CR on general
purpose and low cost hardware and soft- ware platforms as for example [6], as
well as the emergence of professional grade flexible SDR radio front ends as
the Universal Software Radio Peripheral - USRP [6] which has enabled several
research projects.

Software based reception of FM signals can be achieved in several ways, and
as a problem of practical interest in the transition from analog to digital radio

receivers, many approaches for detection have been previously presented and are vastly reported in the literature, for example using digital signal processors - DSPs, or field programmable gate arrays - FPGAs as in [6,8], or directly with a personal computer with a proper radio receiver as in [10] where a RTL-SDR dongle is used as radio front end and a PC is used for the signal processing stage using signal manipulations directly implemented in Python. GNU Radio software [1], is a very popular tool for research and education [3,6], in communications and digital signal processing, as well as for practitioners and hobbyists projects. It allows prototyping and experimentation independently of the hardware platform supporting simulation mode and real time signal processing when paired with appropriate transceivers. However, either by lack of experience/confidence or availability of documentation, many of the novice GNUradio users restrain to the basic library top level built-in detection blocks, which oftentimes become black boxes for students using them, ignoring the building capabilities of low level blocks (adders, multipliers, delayers and so on), and even worse, few users delve into the 'deep' capabilities for building custom blocks either based on Python or C++, and for creating non-linear flow-graphs using Python, which are basic steps towards a research focused education.

That is why this work presents the use of GNUradio as a simulation and testing tool for real time signal processing education, with the well known practical case of FM detection, based on custom blocks realizations. The simplicity of the process is shown, and it is emphasized that this results are easily reproducible and extensible in the classroom or teaching laboratory, encouraging students and instructors to develop their own signal processing blocks for testing the mathematical concepts behind SDR.

2   Design and Previous Setup

This project is based on common and widely available tools for signal processing prototyping, on the software side two PCs running GNU radio are used, whereas a pair of USRP N210 are used as external hardware for transmission and reception. The following subsections, describe the hardware and software components.

2.1   Hardware Setting

The hardware setting for this experiment is quite simple, in the transmitter side it consists of a PC, which performs all the calculations, running GNU radio on Linux connected via Ethernet to a USRP N210 using a CBX daughter-board tuned at 2450 MHz, similarly, the receiving side is composed of a PC connected to a USRP N210 with a CBX daughter-board also tuned at 2450 MHz.

The choose of USRP, although its cost might seem ex- pensive at a first glance, is well justified compared to the specific mission educational hardware because of its flexibility, compact size and better resilience to obsolescence, as any signal type, coding and modulation, can be supported in a wide frequency band, making it suitable for teaching in courses of signal processing, basic and advanced communications, RF and microwave transmission, as well as for a variety of research projects. This does not mean or imply that other multipurpose SDR hardware available is not equally well suited for similar applications.

According to the manufacturer, the Universal Software Radio Peripheral - USRP [9], is a general purpose transceiver that can be combined with a series of daughter boards that extend/complement its capabilities to transmit/receive signals from DC to 6 GHz. The USRP N210, see Fig. 1, includes a Xilinx R Spartan R 3A-DSP 3400 FPGA, 100 MS/s dual ADC, 400 MS/s dual DAC and Gigabit Ethernet connectivity through which the USRP N210 can stream up to 50 MS/s to and from host applications. Likewise, the CBX daughter-board is a full-duplex, transceiver that covers a frequency band from 1.2 GHz to 6 GHz with a instantaneous bandwidth of 40 MHz.

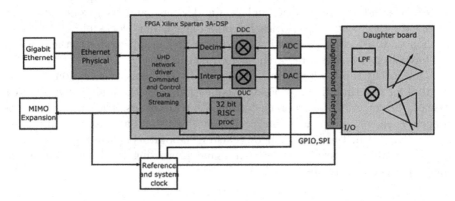

Fig. 1. Schematic USRP architecture (from N210 datasheet)

2.2   Software Setting

On the software side, GNU radio is used both in the transmitter and in the receiver, in a first approach the graphic, low level blocks, construction capabilities of GNU radio companion - GRC are used to straightforwardly implement the selected detectors. Afterwards, each of the detectors are implemented by Python code using the block construction and encapsulation capabilities of GNU radio. The choose of GNUradio over better known, licensed, possibly better documented, programming platforms, is made because of its free use for research and teaching purposes. Likewise, in comparison with other free alternatives, such as programming directly in Python or C++, GNUradio environment is chosen considering the average student for whom the easiness of relating math concepts to block diagrams in GRC proven to be better than dealing with the programming issues in a first approach.

3   Mathematical Framework

There is a variety of FM detectors available, from the old days analog detectors to their digital counterparts, that in most cases are simply a reinterpretation of the analog ones. In this work, five of them are chosen for implementation, namely:

- Delay detector.
- IQ quadrature delay detector.
- IQ 'asin' detector.
- Mixed detector
- Differential detector

The mathematical models and their differences and equivalences should be stated in the classroom previous to any hardware or software contact. A brief description of the signal models and detectors used is provided in the next paragraphs.

Digital FM signal: It is well known that any base-band discrete time signal can be expressed either by its in-phase and quadrature parts or in the magnitude and angle format 1:

$$x_r[n] = x_r[n] + J_{X_i}[n] = r_x[n]e^{j\vartheta x[n]}$$
$$r_r[n] = x_r^2[n] + x_i^2[n]$$
$$\vartheta[x] = atan\left(\frac{x_i[n]}{x_r[n]}\right) \tag{1}$$

$$X[n] = X_i[n]e^{jw_c n}$$
$$X[n] = x_r[n]cos(w_c n) - x_i[n]sin(W_c n) \tag{2}$$

In the case of the discrete time FM signal, it can be modeled as as:

$$X_r[n] = Re\left\{A_c e^{jw_c n}e^{j\varphi[n]}\right\}$$
$$\varphi[n] = K_m \sum_{\lambda=-\infty}^{m} m[\lambda] \tag{3}$$

where $T = 1/fs$ is the sampling time, m[n] is the modulating or information signal, and kf is the frequency deviation.

It is assumed, from the architecture of the receiver and the UHD driver documentation, that in GNU radio the signal provided by the USRP source block corresponds to a base-band magnitude and angle representation, hence the demodulation of the digital FM signal only needs to take care of the detection part, after proper filtering and down-sampling. Therefore, all the expressions presented apply for the base-band FM signal.

Delay detector: The delay detector, shown in Fig. 2, is one of the most simple digital FM detectors that takes the signal in its magnitude and angle format and

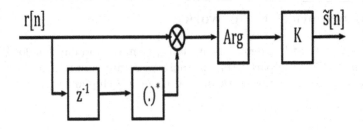

Fig. 2. Delay detector

the estimated signal is obtained by means of the manipulations shown in Eq. 4. Hence K = fs/kf, where $fs = 1/T$ is the sampling rate.

$$r[n] = \alpha e^{j\varphi[n]}$$
$$\tilde{s}[n] = Karg(r[n]r * [n-1]) \qquad (4)$$
$$\tilde{s}[n] = Karg(r[n]r * [n-1])$$

$$\tilde{s}[n] = K(\varphi[n] - \varphi[n-1])$$
$$\tilde{s}[n] = Km[n] \qquad (5)$$

IQ quadrature delay detector: In case that I and Q signals are readily available, the delay detector can be trans- formed to the diagram of Fig. 3, the signal manipulations to estimate the information signal are shown in Eq. 6.

$$p[n] = atan(\frac{r_i[n]}{r_r[n]}) \qquad (6)$$

$$\tilde{s}[n] = K(\varphi[n] - \varphi[n-1]) \qquad (7)$$

IQ 'asin' detector: Also in case that I and Q signals are readily available another kind of detector based on transcendental functions is presented in Fig. 4, the signal manipulations to estimate the information signal are show in Eq. 8

$$s_s[n] = r_r[n-1]r_i[n] - r_i[n-1]r_r[n]$$
$$s_s[n] = cos(\varphi[n-1])sin(\varphi[n]) - sin(\varphi[n-1])cos(\varphi[n]) \qquad (8)$$

$$s_s[n] = sin(\varphi[n] - \varphi[n-1])r_r[n] = x_r^2[n] + x_i^2[n]$$
$$\tilde{s}[n] = Km[n] \qquad (9)$$

Hence $K = fs/kf$.

Mixed detector: Another kind of FM detector based on IQ signals, shown in Fig. 5 is the called mixed detector, whose description is given in Eq. 10.

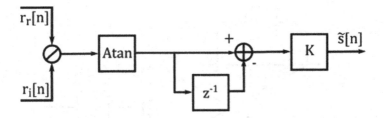

Fig. 3. IQ quadrature delay detector

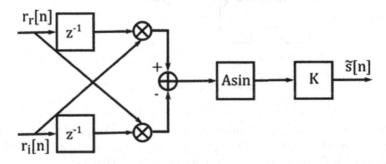

Fig. 4. I and Q delay *asin* detector

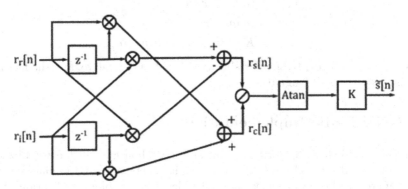

Fig. 5. Mixed detector

$$r_s[n] = R_i[n]r_r[n-1] - r_r[n]r_i[n-1]$$
$$r_s[n] = R_i[n]r_r[n-1] + r_r[n]r_i[n-1]$$
$$r_s[n] = sin(\varphi[n])cos(\varphi[n-1]) - cos(\varphi[n])sin(\varphi[n-1])$$
$$r_s[n] = sin(\varphi[n] - \varphi[n-1]) \tag{10}$$
$$r_c[n] = cos(\varphi[n])cos(\varphi[n-1]) - sin(\varphi[n])sin(\varphi[n-1])$$
$$r_c[n] = cos(\varphi[n] - \varphi[n-1])$$

Also $K = fs/kf$.

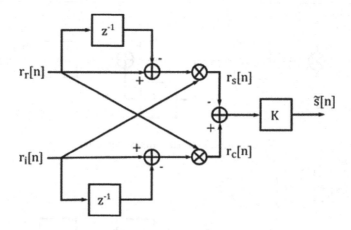

Fig. 6. Differential detector

Differential detector: The final tested realization corresponds to the so called differential detector, shown in Fig. 6, whose main advantage relies in the absence of transcendental functions, its equations are summarized in 11.

$$r_s[n] = (r_r[n] - r_r[n])r_i[n]$$
$$r_c[n] = (r_i[n] - r_i[n])r_r[n] \tag{11}$$
$$\tilde{s}[n] = K(r_r[n]r_i{}'[n] - r_r{}'[n]r_i[n])$$

Comparing the expression for $\tilde{s}[n]$ with the atan derivative, and the fact that for the base-band FM signal.

4   GNU Radio Implementation

As mentioned before, a block diagram and a Python custom block realization were performed for each detector, in Fig. 7 it is shown the GRC diagram used to compare the low-level block and embedded Python block realization of the differential detector. A channel model is used to account for different signal to noise scenarios, what can be very useful in the simulation mode.

Likewise, Fig. 8 shows the code of the custom block that performs exactly the same function as the diagram. Note that the input and output to this block are actually vectors whose length are determined by the page-size, by default 4096 bytes. GNUradio allows a similar implementation with custom blocks in C++ once the algorithms are tested to behave correctly in Python, this approach was discarded in this work due to the low computational cost of the signal processing tasks performed and the exploratory scope.

Also, two set-ups where tested, a simulation only mode in which no transmission/reception hardware was used, and the real time signal processing where the USRP were attached to the processing PCs. The first case allows to reinforce the mathematical concepts and test different scenarios, whereas the second case is more related to the kind of real life experience students demand from laboratory work.

5 Result

5.1 Simulation Mode

This mode makes allusion to the basic use of GNU radio or GRC in a standalone format, i.e. without any external hardware for transmission or reception of incoming signals. In this case the building blocks of transmitter and receiver are emulated in a single GRC session see for example Fig. 7 and 8, this mode is very useful for testing blocks and algorithms.

In the "transmitter" side a simple VCO was used to create a sinusoidal FM digital signal, relevant parameters of the signal and the simulation are set as: frequency deviation $k_f = 75\,\mathrm{kHz/V}$, bandwidth of the modulating signal $B_m = 15\,\mathrm{kHz}$, maximum amplitude of the modulating signal Am = 1 V, modulation index = 5, Carson's bandwidth $B_c = 180\,\mathrm{kHz}$, channel noise deviation $n = 10\,\mathrm{mV}$, and sampling frequency $f_s = 600\,\mathrm{kHz}$.

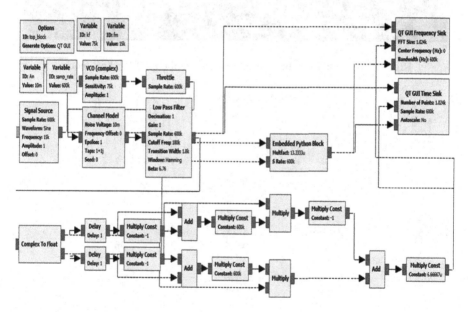

Fig. 7. Differential detector individual block and embedded Python block Code used for differential detector embedded Python block

In Fig. 9 the simulation comparison of the previously described differential detector is presented, both in discrete block construction and embedded Python code block, there can be appreciated a very good agreement between both implementations and the original signal.

```
8
9   import numpy as np
10  from gnuradio import gr
11
12
13  class blk(gr.sync_block):   # other base classes are basic_block, decim_block, interp_block
14      """Embedded Python Block example - a simple multiply const"""
15
16      def __init__(self, multFact=1.0, s_rate=32e3):   # only default arguments here
17          """arguments to this function show up as parameters in GRC"""
18          gr.sync_block.__init__(
19              self,
20              name='Embedded Python Block',   # will show up in GRC
21              in_sig=[np.float32, np.float32],
22              out_sig=[np.float32]
23          )
24          # if an attribute with the same name as a parameter is found,
25          # a callback is registered (properties work, too).
26          self.multFact = multFact
27          self.s_rate = s_rate
28
29      def work(self, input_items, output_items):
30          """example: multiply with constant"""
31          for i in range(0, len(input_items[0])-1):
32              pre_sample_re = input_items[0][i]
33              cur_sample_re = input_items[0][i+1]
34              pre_sample_im = input_items[1][i]
35              cur_sample_im = input_items[1][i+1]
36              r_s = self.s_rate*(cur_sample_re-pre_sample_re)*cur_sample_im/(cur_sample_re**2+cur_sample_im**2)
37              r_c = self.s_rate*(cur_sample_im-pre_sample_im)*cur_sample_re/(cur_sample_re**2+cur_sample_im**2)
38              output_items[0][i] = (r_c-r_s) * self.multFact
39          return len(output_items[0])
```

Fig. 8. Code used for differential detector embedded Python block

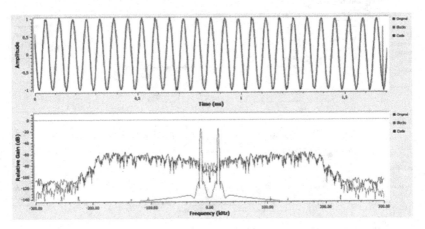

Fig. 9. Differential detector in simulation mode

Also, in Fig. 10 the simulation mode comparison of all the proposed detectors, constructed with discrete blocks in GRC, is presented. There can be appreciated a very good agreement among all the methods used related to the original signal retrieval. From the point of view of the newcomer student this reinforces the fact

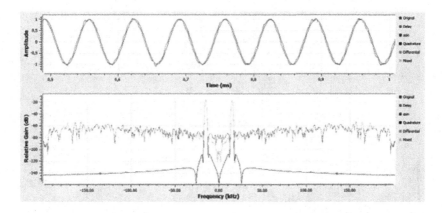

Fig. 10. Comparison of the detectors in simulation mode

that there is not only a way to perform a signal processing function, but many alternatives from which to choose the most suited to the task at hand validations, for this purpose the use of external hardware is included for transmitting and receiving the FM signals. The set-up is as described previously in the hardware section.

In addition to the aforementioned parameters for the creation of the FM signals, it should be mentioned that on the transmitter side the signal is interpolated before transmission to better accommodate the characteristics of the USRP, this is accomplished increasing the sampling rate by means of a 25× upsampling to get a data rate of 15 MS/s. Accordingly, on the receiving side the incoming signal is down-sampled by this same factor, presenting to the detector a signal with 600 kS/s data rate as previously tested in simulation

Also, the channel model is taken away as real noise and attenuation are added to the signals in the wireless link, moreover, the GNUradio wide band FM - WBFM receiver block is included for comparison purposes. The signal processing blocks and code mentioned in previous sections remains unaltered.

In Fig. 10 there can be appreciated the spectrum of the transmitted, and received signals. Also, there is shown the comparison of spectrum for the detected signals with the diverse algorithms under test, as can be appreciated, other than amplitude variations the spectrum shows a similar behavior among the custom realizations and the GNU radio WBFM block (Fig. 11).

Further exploration and practical results, such as comparisons of total harmonic distortion - THD of the receivers, reception of FM radio stereo audio signals, using the proper receiver, can be simply a RTL-SDR that can tune the frequency bands from 88 to 108 MHz, transmission and reception of Binary Frequency/Phase Shif Keying B(F/P)SK Signals, among others can be left for students as coursework.

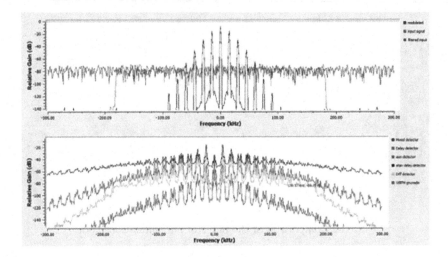

Fig. 11. Mixed detector

6   Conclusions

An easy and straightforward implementation, using low level GNUradio blocks and Python coded embedded blocks, of five digital detectors for angular modulated signals have been presented. The comparison of results shows that the performance of the realized blocks is consistent and similar between them and compared to predefined high level blocks. With this implementation, the use of GNU radio has proven very useful in the rapid prototyping of well known communication signals, hence its use in academy is encouraged for teaching and self-learning digital signal processing for communication systems. Likewise, the USRP N210 has proven suitable for real time signal transmission and reception, giving the students' requested feeling of "real life" deployments, with the advantage of being flexible, software dependent, multipurpose hardware, which can be used in the laboratory for teaching and further research. On the other hand, significantly learned materials can be retained for a relatively long period of time, months, even years, whereas retention of knowledge after rote learning by rote is a short time interval, measured in hours or days [11]. Therefore the strategy of GNURadio in digital signal processing through the implementation of digital FM receiver architectures internalizes the theoretical work through the practice with the construction of block diagrams and programming in Python, resulting in significant learning and autonomous learning with engineering students to perform digital signal processing in telecommunications. Information and communication technologies - ICTs have opened new possibilities for teaching and learning, its great potential is evident in the possibility of interaction. These technologies integrated to a learning environment with different degrees of internalization, prioritizing the experimental, makes available to the instructor information and communication channels to promote different forms of teaching at the time that develops autonomous learning for the student, which raises the teacher the challenge of taking advantage of this strategy in digital signal processing and communications courses. As [12] points out, the development of autonomy will not only depend on the student's interaction with the content through the use of ICTs in a learning environment; but also of the tutorial actions that motivate and help the student in the acquisition of increasing autonomy in learning; in addition to interaction with the tutor, there are interactions between participants, which can exert an educational influence on their peers, promoting the exchange or confrontation between points of view.

Acknowledgements. To the people of "Grupo de Investigación en Electrónica de Altas Frecuencias y Telecomunicaciones" - CMUN, and communications laboratory for the constant discussion and their collaboration during the experimental validation of the proposed experiments.

References

1. Grabner, M.J., Li, X., Fu, S.: An adaptive blast successive interference cancellation method for high data rate perfect space-time coded mimo systems. IEEE Trans. Veh. Technol. **69**(2), 1542–1553 (2019)
2. Hatai, I., Chakrabarti, I.: FPGA implementation of a digital FM modem. In: 2009 International Conference on Information and Multimedia Technology, pp. 475–479. IEEE (2009)
3. Katz, S., Flynn, J.: Using software defined radio (SDR) to demonstrate concepts in communications and signal processing courses. In: 2009 39th IEEE Frontiers in Education Conference, pp. 1–6. IEEE (2009)
4. Mack, C.A.: Fifty years of moore's law. IEEE Trans. Semicond. Manuf. **24**(2), 202–207 (2011)
5. Monereo, C., Castelló, M.: Las estrategias de aprendizaje: cómo incorporarlas a la práctica educativa [learning strategies: how to incorporate them into educational practice]. barcelona: Edebé. nelson, t. & narens, l. (1990). metamemory: A theoretical framework and new findings. The psychology of learning and motivation 26, 125–141 (1997)
6. Nagurney, L.S.: Software defined radio in the electrical and computer engineering curriculum. In: 2009 39th IEEE Frontiers in Education Conference, pp. 1–6. IEEE (2009)
7. Ramírez, M.G.S.: Autonomía moral: Una posibilidad para el desarrollo humano desde la ética de la responsabilidad solidaria. Revista de psicología **12**(1), 27–35 (2003)
8. Rico, S.G., Sánchez, J.M.R.: "competencias" del maestro de niños superdotados. RIFOP: Revista interuniversitaria de formación del profesorado: continuación de la antigua Revista de Escuelas Normales **16**, 97–110 (1993)
9. Uengtrakul, B., Bunnjaweht, D.: A cost-efficient software defined radio receiver for demonstrating concepts in communication and signal processing using python and RTL-SDR. In: 2014 Fourth International Conference on Digital Information and Communication Technology and its Applications (DICTAP), pp. 394–399. IEEE (2014)
10. Vachhani, K., Mallari, R.A.: Experimental study on wide band FM receiver using gnuradio and RTL-SDR. In: 2015 International Conference on Advances in Computing, Communications and Informatics (ICACCI), pp. 1810–1814. IEEE (2015)

11. Radio, G.N.U.: GNU radio (2012). http://gnuradio.org
12. O'shea, T.J., West, N.: Radio machine learning dataset generation with gnu radio. In: Proceedings of the GNU Radio Conference, vol. 1, no. 1 (2016)

Design of a Self-adjusting Reactive Power Compensation Prototype for Residential Application

Fabian Unibio$^{(\boxtimes)}$, Luis D. Pabon Fernandez, Edison A. Caicedo, Jorge L. Diaz Rodriguez, and Aldo Pardo Garcia

Universidad de Pamplona, Pamplona, Colombia
unibio15@hotmail.es

Abstract. This work deals with the development of a self-adjusting reactive compensator prototype for residential applications and its simulation in Matlab. A reactive power compensation technique is established, with a simple topology and a control strategy that keeps the system compensated for load fluctuations. Finally, the adequate functioning of the prototype in the different load scenarios is verified and for which the behavior of the power factor is optimized.

Keywords: Power factor correction · Reactive power compensation · Residential users · Simulation

1 Introduction

Nowadays, electrical power systems have been expanding and improving mainly due to customer requirements. Also, power quality has been a topic that has gained great relevance among researchers. Essentially, for the management of reactive power in electrical power systems. On the other hand, devices have been created to provide a solution to reactive power that have focused on three-wire systems.

The electricity companies are not currently charging customers for residential voltage levels (voltage level 1) for reagents. Metering equipment has begun to be changed and replaced by smart meters that calibrate four quadrants and that can estimate this energy [1]. For this reason, there will be an increase in the bill and although in residential use the reactive power is very low, it is considerable. The initiative mitivates the design of a prototype that fulfill the residential characteristics.

The usual techniques in three-phase power systems are identified, taking the shunt technique as a reference. This allows the parallel connection of the equipment for the manipulation of currents that are injected into the system. Making a synthesis of the typologies such as the use of a single-phase full H-bridge from a three-wire full-bridge analysis that uses the D-STATCOM. A control system based on the rotation of magnetic fields of synchronous machines is established, using the Clarke and Park transformations to find a current that allows us to improve the power factor. In addition, modeling PWM pulses on the basis of current that allow creating a closed loop system for the

© The Author(s), under exclusive license to Springer Nature Switzerland AG 2022
J. C. Figueroa-García et al. (Eds.): WEA 2022, CCIS 1685, pp. 437–449, 2022.
https://doi.org/10.1007/978-3-031-20611-5_36

self-adjustment of the compensator when experiencing variations in the load. With the simulation of a single-phase compensator prototype in Matlab software, it is possible to analyze the different scenarios in which the prototype operate [2–4].

2 Compensation Technique

The bypass capacitor supplies reactive power and boosts local voltages. They are used throughout the system and are applied in a wide range of sizes. Bypass capacitors were first used in the mid-1910s for power factor correction. Due to their large size and cheaper dielectric materials, and other improvements in capacitor construction, they bring significant reductions in price and size.

Nowadays, they are a very economical means of supplying reactive power [5, 6]. The main advantages of bypass capacitors are their economic cost and their adaptability of installation and operation. The main drawback of shunt capacitors is that their reactive power output is adjusted to the square of the voltage. Consequently, the reactive power output is reduced at low voltages when it is most likely to be needed [7–9].

The flowchart of the compensation algorithm, whose parts will be described in the following sections, is shown below (Fig. 1):

3 Compensator Topology

3.1 Full Bridge Topology

The Distribution Static Compensator or D-STATCOM can be classified on the basis of different topologies, number of switching devices, and on the basis of neutral current compensation, etc. D-STATCOMs are developed to meet the requirements of different applications in the distribution system, based on the various D-STATCOM VSI (*Voltage Source Inverter*) topologies.

Three-phase three-wire D-STATCOMs used to offset consumer load as it improves power quality in the three-phase distribution system. The three-phase full-bridge topology shown in Fig. 2. In which, the sum of the current (I) across its three branches must be zero. Compensation for the zero sequence current that might follow in the load will not be possible, nor will it be able to remove any DC current flowing into the source from the load. This will result in distortion in the source current [10, 11].

A D-STATCOM converter is controlled using pulse width modulation (PWM) or other voltage/current modeling techniques [8]. D-STATCOMs are used more frequently than STATCOM controllers. Compared to STATCOMs, D-STATCOMs have a considerably lower power rating and consequently faster power electronics switches. The PWM carrier frequency used in a distribution controller can be much higher than in a FACTS (Flexible AC Transmission System) controller [12, 16].

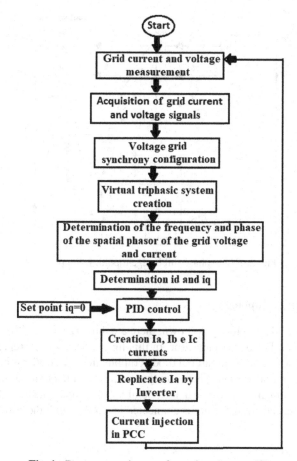

Fig. 1. Bypass capacitor configuration. Source: [8].

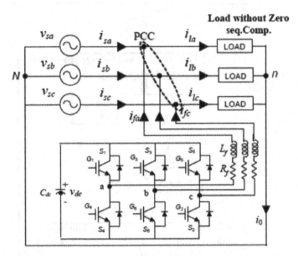

Fig. 2. Three phase full bridge topology. Source: [10].

3.2 VSI H-bridge Topology

In Fig. 3, the H-bridge topology is shown, there are three H-bridge VSIs that are assembled to a common DC buffer capacitor. In this figure, each switch represents a power semiconductor device and antiparallel diode combination. Each VSI is connected to the network through a transformer. The six output terminals of the transformer are star connected. These terminals can also be delta assembled to compensate for a delta connected load. In this case, each transformer is connected in parallel with the corresponding load [18].

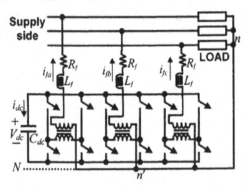

Fig. 3. H-bridge topology with common DC power capacitor. Source: [10].

The purpose of including the transformer is to provide isolation between the legs of the inverter. Which prevents the DC storage capacitor from being short-circuited through switches in different inverters. The inductor Lf represents the leakage inductance of each transformer and the additional external inductance. The copper loss of the connection

transformer is represented by a resistance Rf. Due to the presence of isolation transformers this topology is not suitable for compensation of load currents containing DC
components. For this reason, isolation transformers are excluded in the compensation
system approach, in the same way it is necessary to use an RL filter in the location of
the Rf resistance [10, 13, 16].

4 Network Synchrony Configuration

As a first phase of the control modeling, synchronization with the network must be maintained, this is achieved through a phase-locked loop algorithm (PLL), whose function is
to synchronize a three-phase virtual system with the single-phase electrical system, by
obtaining the frequency and angle of the system voltage wave. [14, 17].

In Fig. 4, the PLL block is evidenced, which establishes a model of the phase control
system where the phase and frequency of the sinusoidal single-phase signal are tracked,
this process is carried out from an internal frequency oscillator [10].

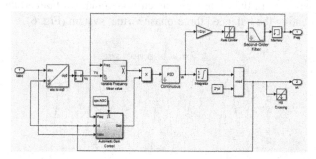

Fig. 4. Phase-locked loop block, PLL from the Simulink library.

A virtual three-phase system was modeled using the Clarke and Park transformations
that allows to decouple variables and solve equations involving quantities that vary over
time, by referring all the variables to a common reference frame. A PLL block was used
for network synchronization. To obtain the b and c phases voltages was carried out with
two PLL blocks from the Simulink library.

The first block describes the function in which the required phase shift is entered
mathematically, in this case the phase shift performed was 120° electrical (three-phase
system). Similarly, the second block applies a delay to the first input signal. The voltage
signal and the function named above are taken. In order to obtain the offset in the block,
the function $y = u(t-t_o(t))$ is implemented.

The three-phase system obtained is shown in Fig. 5.

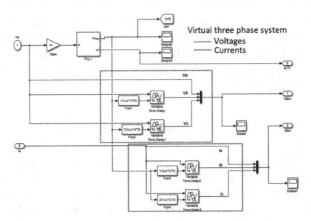

Fig. 5. Virtual three-phase system (FFF). Source: Authors.

From the 180 V peak-to-peak voltage single-phase system, we obtain two out-of-phase voltage signals. In the same way, the current signal is obtained and then phase-shifted, thus creating the balanced three-phase virtual system (Fig. 6).

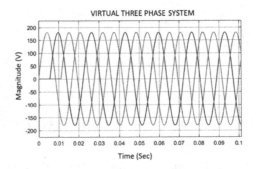

Fig. 6. Virtual three-phase voltage signals.

Once the system was synchronized and the wave signals created, the same tools of the unified theory of electrical machines were used. Among them, the Clarke and Park transforms that will facilitate the control of the reactive power, and that will be injected or consumed by the prototype. In this way, if the inverse process is carried out, we obtain the current to be modulated in Pulse Width Modulation (PWM).

5   Closed Loop Control

The purpose of closed loop control is for the system to have a defined behavior in terms of supplying reactive power from the network. That is, from the values calculated by the Clarke and Park transformations, the value of iq must tend to zero. Therefore, the control maintains the zero value of said current based on the difference between the setpoint block (constant) and the measured current Iq. The PID control configuration is done according to the Tune function that is defined in the Simulink library. The current Id is responsible for the active power, the objective is to compensate reactive power, discarding the id values [19, 20].

The system requires active power for the operation of the capacitor and the RL filter. The inverse transformations of Clarke and Park are performed on the power supplied by the network, thus modulating the main carrier signal.

6   Single-Phase Complete Bridge

Previously, the different types of D-STATCOM topologies that fit three-phase systems were mentioned. Each one of the typologies has different relevance before the multiple electrical phenomena that must be reduced [10]. The best fitting topology is the three phase full bridge topology. Which is effectively used for power factor correction of electrical systems, voltage regulation and load balancing. This work focuses on single-phase residential networks, for which the chosen topology is adjusted for a single-wire application [10].

In Fig. 7, the single-phase full bridge topology is indicated. This block is made up of an H bridge using power electronics built from IGBTs with antiparallel diodes. The purpose of the capacitor shown is to provide the reactive currents that will be injected into the network for power factor compensation [15]. Similarly, Fig. 9 shows the RL filter that is connected in line with the inverter that has the purpose of minimizing the harmonic distortion in the intensity injected into the system [10, 8].

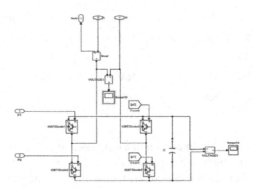

Fig. 7. Block single-phase full-bridge topology.

7   Simulation

7.1   Simulation Scheme

Figure 8 shows the complete scheme of the model. It can be seen each one of the blocks that make up the prototype of the single-phase system which is the aim of this work.

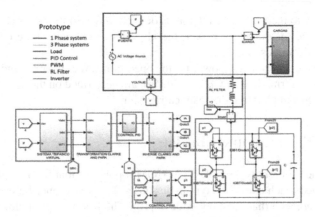

Fig. 8. Simulation scheme of the complete prototype in Simulink.

The virtual three-phase system, the control system, the pulse generator (PWM) and the inverter responsible for the reactive compensation. Finally, the load block is displayed.

The load scenarios that are established are four and go according to the operating modes of a D-STATCOM, these are: resistive mode, inductive mode and capacitive mode. Table 1 shows the different loads with their specific values.

Table 1. Loads values.

Loads	Resistance (Ω)	Inductance (H)	Capacitance (μF)
Load 1: R	25	NA	NA
Load 2: RL	25	0.3	NA
Load 2: RC	37	NA	106.7
Load 3: L	NA	0.3	NA

The system performs the simulation in a time interval of 2 s that will be divided into 4 periods of 0.5 s. For which switches were used that allow the input and output of each of the loads. In this way, the behavior of the load without connection of the compensator can be observed, appreciating voltage and current. This would be typical in measurement processes in residential load scenarios, especially single-phase loads. Figure 11 shows the block with the respective load scenarios named above.

7.2 Simulation Results

The whole system simulation took a total time of 2 s, in which the values of reactive and active power, power factor and network voltage profile were analyzed.

Two simulations are carried out. The first corresponds to the single-phase system without the prototype. The second one corresponds to the prototype connected to the network. These two scenarios are proposed in order to observe the performance given by the designed system.

In Fig. 9, the active power during the four load scenarios is shown at first. This is reflected in the change it makes during the pre-established times of switching by the switches where small transient processes are observed. Each loads are consuming active power due to the characteristics of the load.

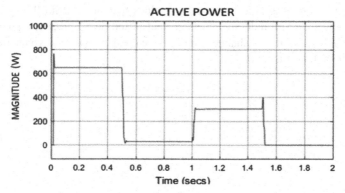

Fig. 9. Load Active power.

In Fig. 10, the reactive power during the four load scenarios is shown. This is reflected in the change that is made during the pre-established switching times by the switches and where small transients are seen.

Each of the loads is consuming a value of reactive power, due to the nature of the load. Likewise, as the purpose of the work focused on the compensation of reactive power, it can be seen that: in the first cycle of 0.5 s where a purely resistive load is connected, no reactive power is required.

On the other hand, in the following cycles a variation of the reactive power is observed. In power, it selects positive values indicating the consumption of reactive power. Likewise, it took negative values, which indicates that reactive power is being injected into the network.

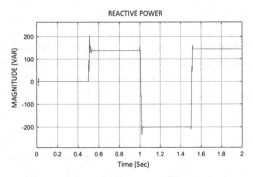

Fig. 10. Load reactive power.

Figure 11 shows variable power factor values that range from 0 to 1 due to the resistive, capacitive and inductive loads present in the proposed single-phase system. The oscillations at each load change are due to the breaker switches, which are activated to establish another load.

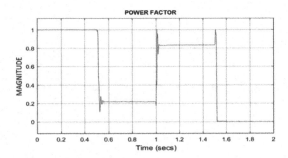

Fig. 11. Power factor.

Figure 12 shows the comparison between the reactive power of the load and the reactive power observed by the network. The power in the system changes with respect to that of the load, because the control is programmed with the option of taking the reactive power to zero, regardless of whether it is inductive or capacitive that generates the load.

When the load is changed, a transient is observed which depends on the type of load and the current that circulates through it, at each instant of time, causing the network to supply these small transients of reactive power.

Figure 13 compares the power factor for 2 s between the load before and after the common coupling point of the prototype. Transients continue to occur due to the change in position of the switch that controls the input of each load. In addition, the correction of the power factor in each load is evidenced. In which it is possible to observe the transitory process referring to the correction provided by the compensator.

When the load is purely resistive at 0 s of simulation, the compensator does not generate any current that modifies the displacement of the wave for reactive power, giving the power factor of the resistive load (1 pu).

Making the change at 0.5 and 1 s shows the natural response of an RL and RC circuit, respectively. Regardless of the value of the power factor of each load, it is seen as the PID controller. Which takes about 1 s in a given time.

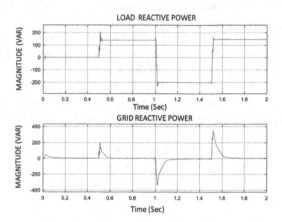

Fig. 12. Load and network reactive power.

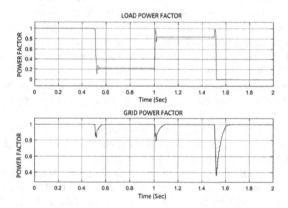

Fig. 13. Load power factor and corrected power factor.

The pure inductive load has a slightly longer synchronization time than the previous loads. Likewise, its power factor is lower and it is due to the fact that the current in an inductance changes gradually or cannot change abruptly. Unlike loads that have active power dissipation that prevent overcurrent peaks, which would generally act as filters. As can be seen in Figs. 12 and 13, the responses of the regulation in the compensation of reactive energy and the power factor, present a slow behavior, this is due to the adjustment made in the PID controllers. In the same way, this behavior can be improved by optimizing the controllers, so the optimization of the controllers is proposed for a future job.

8 Conclusions

The proposed prototype has a very good behavior in terms of reactive power compensation, it is capable of responding quickly to changes in demand and is projected as low-cost solution for residential compensation.

It is recommended to implement a current control of I_d through the Clarke and Park transformations, to mitigate the active power consumed by the low-pass filter and the one required by the prototype capacitor so that it maintains a constant voltage state.

The topology for the single phase PLL implemented showed an adequate performance in the evaluated conditions, observing the synchronization of the virtual phases, verifying that from the virtual three-phase system a single-phase reactive power control can be created.

Research on a real single-phase residential compensation system is still under development and this work intends to review the subject.

References

1. Wath, M.G., Ballal, M.S.: reactive power management in roof -top solar net metering - case study thereof. In: 2018 International Conference on Smart Electric Drives and Power System (ICSEDPS), pp. 64–68 (2018). https://doi.org/10.1109/ICSEDPS.2018.8536036
2. Gómez, E.: Compensación De Potencia Reactiva. Tesis de pregrado para optar por el título de Ingeniero Electricista, Instituto Politécnico Nacional, México (2009)
3. Chapman, S.J.: Máquinas Eléctricas, 5th edn. McGraw-Hill, New York (2012)
4. Li, E., Sheng, W., Wang, X., Wang, B.: Combined compensation strategies based on instantaneous reactive power theory for reactive power compensation and load balancing. In: 2011 International Conference on Electrical and Control Engineering, pp. 5788–5791 (2011). https://doi.org/10.1109/ICECENG.2011.6057765
5. Jambukar, A.A., Satarkar, M.F.A.R.: Simulation analysis of switching of shunt capacitor bank in 220/22 kV substation. In: 2018 Second International Conference on Intelligent Computing and Control Systems (ICICCS), pp. 1554–1559 (2018)
6. Chen, S.X., Foo, Y.S.E., Gooi, H.B., Wang, M.Q., Lu, S.F.: A centralized reactive power compensation system for LV distribution networks. In: 2015 IEEE Power & Energy Society General Meeting, p. 1 (2015). https://doi.org/10.1109/PESGM.2015.7285675
7. Jianguo, Z., Qiuye, S., Huaguang, Z., Yan, Z.: Load balancing and reactive power compensation based on capacitor banks shunt compensation in low voltage distribution networks. In: Proceedings of the 31st Chinese Control Conference, pp. 6681–6686 (2012)
8. Kumar, N., Buwa, O.: A review on reactive power compensation of distributed energy system. In: 2020 7th International Conference on Smart Structure System, ICSSS 2020, pp. 16–21 (2020)
9. Prabha, K., Malik, O.: Power System Stability and Control, 2nd edn, p. 1176. Mc Graw Hill, New York (1994)
10. Negi, P., Pal, Y., Leena, G.: A review of various topologies & control schemes of DSTATCOM implemented on distribution systems. Majlesi J. Electr. Eng. 11(1), 25–34 (2017)

11. Mendoza-Niebles, J.C., Pabon-Fernandez, L.D., Caicedo-Peñaranda, E.A., Pardo-García, A., Díaz-Rodríguez, J.L.: Control síncrono de potencia de un D-STATCOM de bajo costo. Revista Aibi (2020)

12. Liang, K., Huang, S., Shen, H., Li, F., Liu, L.: Switch-linear hybrid analysis and application in reactive power compensation of single-phase SVG. In: Proceedings - 2017 32nd Youth Academy Annual Conference on Chinese Association and Automation, YAC 2017, pp. 715–719 (2017)

13. Ghiţă, C., Crăciunescu, A., Năvrăpescu, V., Deaconu, I.D., Chirilă, A.I., Ilina, I.D.: Optimal reactive power compensation using synchronous generators. Renew. Energy Power Qual. J. 1(8), 747–750 (2010)

14. Shan, R., Yin, Z., Xiao, X.: A novel low harmonic dynamic static var compensator research. In: 2009 4th IEEE Conference on Industrial Electronics and Applications, pp. 1395–1398 (2009). https://doi.org/10.1109/ICIEA.2009.5138431

15. Moreno-Muñoz, A.: Power Quality Mitigation Technologies in a Distributed Environment, Cordoba (2007)

16. Ye, K.Z.: Compensación de potencia reactiva trifásica usando un convertidor CA/CA monofásico. In: Actas de APEC 97 - Conferencia sobre electrónica de potencia aplicada, vol. 1, pp. 213–219 (1997)

17. Kullan, M., Muthu, R., Mervin, J.B., Subramanian, V.: Design of DSTATCOM controller for compensating unbalances. Circ. Syst. 07(09), 2362–2372 (2016)

18. Okeke, T.U., Zaher, R.G.: Flexible AC transmission systems (FACTS). In: 2013 International Conference on New Concepts in Smart Cities: Fostering Public and Private Alliances (SmartMILE), pp. 1–4 (2013)

19. Almánzar, I.B., Aybar Mejía, M.E., Blanco, M., Vicini H.R.A.:. Compensación de reactivos en instalaciones de sistemas solares fotovoltaicos penalizadas por bajo factor de potencia (2020)

20. Deshpande, S., Bhasme, N.R.: A review of topologies of inverter for grid connected PV systems. In: 2017 Innovations in Power and Advanced Computing Technologies (i-PACT), pp. 1–6 (2017)

A Machine Learning Based Command Voice Recognition Interface

Daniel-S. Arias-Otalora, Andrés Florez, Gerson Mellizo,
C. H. Rodríguez-Garavito(✉)📷, E. Romero, and J. A. Tumialan

Universidad de La Salle, Cra 2 No 10-70, Bogotá, Colombia
{darias82,rflorez62,gmellizo27,cerodriguez,
eromero09,jtumialan}@unisalle.edu.co

Abstract. As a trend in the tech industry, human-machine interaction has increasingly become friendly and intuitive. In this context, our work presents the implementation of a voice command recognition system based on Machine Learning composed of an audio capture system, phoneme segmentation, description of voice commands from standardized power density histograms, classifier training, and functional tests on a graphical interface. The results showed that the best classification algorithm when implementing different classifiers was Support Vector Machine (SVM), with an efficiency of 95.4%, as expected, given its optimal structure.

Keywords: Voice recognition · Spectral density · Machine learning

1 Introduction

Thanks to the evolution of technology along with the advent of the fourth and fifth industrial revolutions in the last two decades, the human-machine interaction has been led to be continuously more user-friendly [1]. In this sense, the capacity of transmitting information through the human voice offers multiple possibilities for controlling hardware in both domestic services and production systems. For instance, voice assistants that understand human language, as Alexa or Siri [10], are now available at home. They can be connected through the internet of things with almost any electrical device that performs a specific task and control it. There are lots of services in hardware and software level for speech recognition, some of them such as Kaldi (DNN-HMM) and Mozilla's DeepSpeech (end-to-end), or APIs like IBM Watson, Microsoft Azure and Google Speech which are evaluated in [9].

Similarly, there have been great achievements in robot interactions for medical care purposes, such as the assisted surgery case reported in [6] where voice commands are used to manipulate an endoscope as the end-effector of a robotic

---

Supported by Universidad de La Salle Bogotá.

© The Author(s), under exclusive license to Springer Nature Switzerland AG 2022
J. C. Figueroa-García et al. (Eds.): WEA 2022, CCIS 1685, pp. 450–460, 2022.
https://doi.org/10.1007/978-3-031-20611-5_37

support, or the voice control system implemented for wheelchairs and robotic rehabilitation [5] as well as assistive robotic devices like proposed in [4].

Moreover, voice detection opens up new possible use-cases such as the diagnosis of diseases indirectly reflected in the voice. Among these applications, there is a COVID19 screening with very good results regarding specificity, sensitivity and accuracy, all above 90% [2]. This approach has been used to address some other pathologies, such as the Parkinson's disease for diagnosis and monitoring [3].

Regarding the algorithms and techniques that are used for recognizing voice commands we present an simple and efficient approach, taking as a core to voice recognition several machine learning classifiers, such as K-nearest neighbor (KNN), artificial neural networks (ANN), and support vector machines (SVM). Here our work implements a pipeline of the process for command recognition, such as preprocessing data with voice filtering, eliminating non-relevant information by statistical analysis in sliding windows, and feature extraction with voice transformation domain to density frequency by standardized histograms. Finally, classifier training is developed base on the training set just extracted. Additionally, as a test strategy for the voice command recognition system, we use a graphical interface for interaction with a user.

2 Methodology

The proposed solution is based on the application of machine learning theory to characterize voice commands and to identify them by means of a classification system. The proposal has the following parts according to the Fig. 1: Firstly, the voice signal is processed to obtain an appropriate descriptor, invariant to the user's voice tone and color. Afterwards, a database is built to train the patterns on the chosen classifier. And finally, a voice command system is implemented to allow user interactions with a graphical interface.

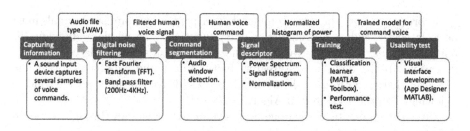

Fig. 1. Diagram of the descriptor acquisition process.

2.1   Voice Commands Description

Regarding the development of the voice command descriptor the following process was taken into account. The audios are recorded with a microphone and stored as audio (.WAV) files.

Then, the signal is filtered using a band-pass filter to avoid undesired noise and retain the human voice in the range from 200 Hz to 4 KHz, as described in Algorithm 1, obtaining results as it is shown in Fig. 2.

Algorithm 1. Human voice filter

$Freqs \leftarrow FrecuenyDomain(wave_t)$
$wave_f \leftarrow FFT(wave_t)$
$filter \leftarrow thr_{lowFreq} < absValue(Freqs) < thr_{highFreq}$
$wave_{filtered} \leftarrow filter \times wave_f$
$wave_{voice} \leftarrow FFT^{-1}(wave_{Filtered})$

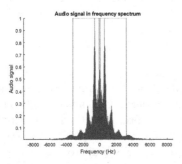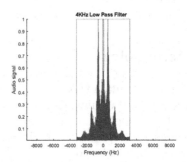

Fig. 2. FFT graph comparison of the signal before (left) and after (right) the low-pass filter.

In order to create the voice command descriptor every command signals must be isolated through a rectangular window function. The whole audio signal is normalized and segmented by time windows by means of calculated standard deviations. If the deviation is greater than 0.3 an audio window is found and wherever there is a group of them, then it is possible to determine a time window following the process stated in Algorithm 2.

After the segmentation is done over several time windows through the standard deviation criteria, the results can be seen in Fig 3.

When the windows are defined, its power spectrum is determined using the Fast Fourier Transform (FFT) where its histogram and normalization are obtained from to build the used descriptors for the different clasifiers trainnig as it is described in Algorithm 3 and shown in Fig 4.

The performance of the audio classifiers used during the experimentation is evaluated via the Classification Learner app from MATLAB, based on the

Algorithm 2. Sliding windows

$Time \leftarrow TimeDomain(wave_t)$
$wane_n \leftarrow Normalise(wave_t)$
$wave_{std} \leftarrow STD(wave_n)$
$window_{size} \leftarrow 200ms \times fs$
$windows = length(wave_t)/window_{size}$
while $i <= windows$ **do**
$\quad window \leftarrow GetWindow(wave_t, window_{size}, i)$
$\quad window_{std} \leftarrow STD(window)$
$\quad$ **if** $window_{std} > 0.3$ **then**
$\quad\quad Cmd_{detec} \leftarrow Cmd_{detection} \cup ones(length(window))$
$\quad\quad wave_{active} \leftarrow wave_{active} \cup window$
$\quad$ **else if**   **then**
$\quad\quad Cmd_{detec} \leftarrow Cmd_{detec} \cup zeros(length(window))$
$\quad$ **end if**
$\quad i \leftarrow i + 1$
end while

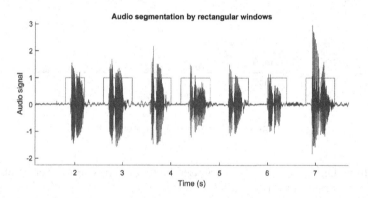

Fig. 3. Audio segmentation by rectangular audio windows.

confusion matrix, its precision, accuracy, sensitivity and specificity. Lastly, the developed application implements an interface allowing to present and verify the system results.

2.2 Machine Learning

Database. In order to collect the voice data, different voice commands were recorded on a voice recorded device using different tones from several subjects. To further increase the variety and amount of training examples, the Audacity software (Registered trademark) was used to modify the tone of the voice records, Fig. 5, regarding to use the same audio format for compatibility with the rest of the program in Matlab. Finally, the training examples were increased up to 4678 records.

Algorithm 3. Descriptor

---

while $Windows$ **do**
   $Window_f \leftarrow GetRealAbs(FFT(Window))$
   $a \leftarrow Hist(Window_f, n_{bins} = 25)$
   $a \leftarrow [a \cup CommLabel]$
   $dataset \leftarrow [dataset \cup a]$
end while

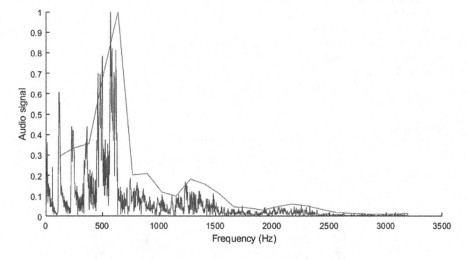

Fig. 4. Histogram of the audio signal.

Classifier. Different classifiers were used having into account several parameters for its own configuration.

The parametric setup for **k-Nearest Neighbor (KNN)** classifier is the number of nearest neighbors set to 4 and euclidean distance as a discriminant method to establish the categories classified as output, as is shown in [8].

Naive Bayes (NBC) It used a Gaussian distribution to perform the probabilistic classification. Also a **Neural networks(ANN)** was set up with 2 hidden layers of 12 neurons in the first and 8 in the second layer using a ReLU activation function.

Support vector machine (SVM) was trained based on a 1 vs methodology using different types of kernel functions such as linear and squared and cubic polynomials, having the best performance with the last of them.

2.3 User Interface

Interacting with the system is done thanks to the designed interface that allows the voice instructions to be captured through a button, and to visualize the corresponding command determined by the application out of the four predefined for this test: *Stop, Forward, Left, Right* and *Not recognized*. See Fig. 6.

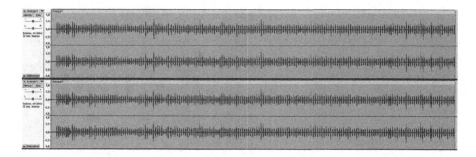

Fig. 5. Frequency display of data.

3 Results

The used descriptor in the voice recognition consists of a vector of 25 features, corresponding to the normalized histogram of a recognized voice command and a label (1 Stop, 2 move forward, 3 Right, 4 Left) indicating the command to which it belongs. The different classifiers were trained by means of the *Classification Learner* application in Matlab, which subsequently provided the different corresponding models. For training purposes, only 70% of the database was employed, and the remaining 30% was used as test set for the validation of the models.

The database used was treated with PCA (principal component analysis) for information visualization purposes, reducing the dimensionality of the data to three principal components and obtaining an approximation of visual representation, increasing its interpretability but, at the same time, minimizing the loss of information with an error of 42% measure from the proper values associated to transformation matrix PCA. Figure 7 shows a representation in 3D of the data set. Based on this data exploration is possible to conclude how complex is the classification process.

After the reduction procedure, it is evident that there is no clear separation of the data. Making it clear that the classification problem is rather complex, and data descriptors need as many features as possible for better classification performance. At first, our descriptor was a set of normalized peak values in the time domain, but it exhibited a low performance which maximum accuracy was around of 60%. Then we have chosen a normalized histogram built up from frequency spectrum of the audio signals showing already better results as a descriptor. In complement, it was selected an exact number of histogram bins for the descriptors testing with increasing size. As a result, the classification of histograms with more than 20 features yields within 90% of accuracy alike a bell-shaped behavior, where the best result occurred at 25 intervals.

Once training process was done, the performance of the generated classification models is verified using the accuracy, precision, sensitivity (Recall), specificity, and parameter f, all obtained from the confusion matrix.

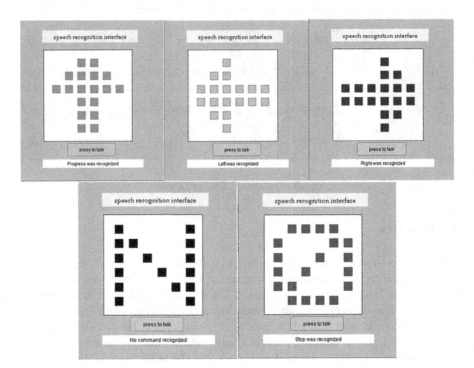

Fig. 6. Commands display interface.

Different classifiers were tested: **k-Nearest Neighbor (KNN), Naive Bayes (NBC), Neural Networks (ANN)** and **Support Vector Machines (SVM).**

The performance for **k-Nearest Neighbor (KNN)** shows an accuracy of 95.034%, a precision of 25%, a sensitivity of 92.588%, a specificity of 96.297% and an f value of 0.393. Figure 8 shows the corresponding confusion matrix. In which it is observed that for the stop command 364 tests were carried out with 359 successes, 4 prediction errors of the forward command and 1 error for the left command. With the forward command, 339 tests were performed with 307 hits, 28 prediction errors with the stop command, 1 error with the right command and 3 as the left command. With the command to the right, 358 tests were performed with 332 hits, 3 prediction errors with the forward command and 8 errors with the command to the left. And finally, with the command to the left, 342 tests were carried out with 335 hits, 1 error in the prediction of stopping, 5 prediction errors with the forward command and 1 error in the command to the right.

Likewise, the trained model **Naive Bayes (NBC)** exhibited an accuracy of 64.647%, a precision of 25%, a sensitivity of 50.996%, a specificity of 71.980% and an f value of 0.334. Figure 9 shows the corresponding confusion matrix. In which it is observed that for the stop command 364 tests were carried out with

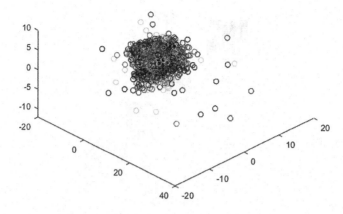

Fig. 7. Voice command database using three principal components.

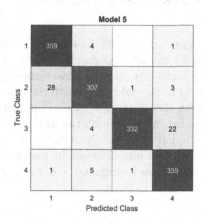

Fig. 8. Confusion matrix KNN.

306 hits, 25 prediction errors of the forward command, 6 prediction errors to the right and 27 errors for the left command. With the forward command, 339 tests were carried out with 135 hits, 81 prediction errors with the stop command, 24 errors with the command to the right and 99 with the command to the left. With the command to the right, 358 tests were performed with 232 hits, 61 prediction errors with the stop command, 12 errors with the forward command and 53 errors with the command to the left. And finally, with the command to the left, 342 tests were carried out with 233 hits, 41 errors in the prediction of stopping, 16 prediction errors with the forward command and 52 errors to the command to the right.

For the **Neural Networks (ANN)** classifier, it obtained an accuracy of 89.712%, a precision of 25%, a sensitivity of 88.953%, a specificity of 92.007% and an f value of 0.390. Figure 10 shows the corresponding confusion matrix. In which it is observed that for the stop command 364 tests were carried out with

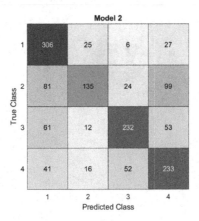

Fig. 9. Confusion matrix NBC.

332 successes, 23 prediction errors of the forward command, 4 prediction errors to the right and 5 errors for the left command. With the forward command, 339 tests were carried out with 298 hits, 31 prediction errors with the stop command, 6 errors with the command to the right and 4 with the command to the left. With the command to the right, 358 tests were carried out with 329 hits, 2 errors in the stop command, 7 prediction errors with the forward command and 20 errors with the command to the left. And finally, with the command to the left, 342 tests were carried out with 300 hits, 2 errors in the prediction of stopping, 13 prediction errors with the forward command and 27 errors to the command to the right.

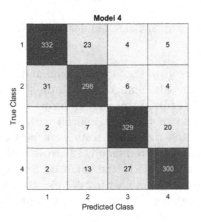

Fig. 10. Confusion matrix ANN.

Finally, for the **Support Vector Machines (SVM)** classifier, the trained model showed an accuracy of 95.465%, a precision of 25%, a sensitivity of

95.429%, a specificity of 96.816% and an f value of 0.396, as can be deduced from the confusion matrix shown in Fig. 11. In which it is observed that for the stop command 364 tests were carried out with 345 hits, 16 prediction errors of the forward command and 3 errors for the left command. With the forward command, 339 tests were carried out with 317 hits, 17 prediction errors with the stop command, 2 errors with the command to the right and 3 with the command to the left. With the command to the right, 358 tests were performed with 347 hits, 3 prediction errors with the forward command and 8 errors with the command to the left. And finally, with the command to the left, 342 tests were carried out with 329 hits, 4 prediction errors with the forward command and 9 errors with the command to the right.

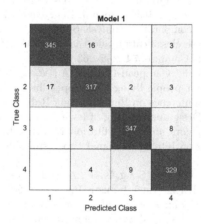

Fig. 11. Confusion matrix SVM.

4   Conclusions

In machine learning theory, there is not a definitive method to find suitable features to learn patterns and classify or predict data in a specific context. Defining valid description data as a set of features is a trial and error process guided by heuristics extracted from the data scientist experience. In the voice command recognition problem, the best strategy to describe data is to transform the information toward the frequency domain to achieve invariance to the tone and volume of the voice through normalizing power density histograms arranged in 25 frequency intervals.

As usual in machine learning, several classic and modern classifiers were tested for the discrimination of voice commands (up, down, right, left, forward, and stop), the minimum set to control the movement of a virtual or real mobile object. The classifiers that exhibited the best performance were the KNN and the SVM with 95.034% and 95.465% of accuracy, respectively.

Finally, the graphical interface shows a real-time user experience by displaying the command executed by voice on the screen with a prediction time of less than 1 s, suitable for video games or manipulation of robotic mechanisms.

In future work, we propose developing a voice control interface so that a cobot manipulator can execute high-level tasks in continuous interaction with the user and learn from its needs using AI paradigms such as reinforcement learning.

References

1. Alpaslan, D.K., Döven, G., Sezen, B.: Industry 5.0 and human-robot co-working. Procedia Comput. Sci. **158**, 688–695 (2019)
2. Laguarta, J., Hueto, F., Subirana, B.: COVID-19 artificial intelligence diagnosis using only cough recordings. IEEE Open J. Eng. Med. Biol. **1**, 275–281 (2020)
3. Okan, S.C., et al.: A comparative analysis of speech signal processing algorithms for Parkinson's disease classification and the use of the tunable Q-factor wavelet transform. Appl. Soft Comput. **74**, 255–263 (2019)
4. Samuel, P., Routhier, F., Campeau-Lecours, A.: Voice control interface prototype for assistive robots for people living with upper limb disabilities. In: 2019 IEEE 16th International Conference on Rehabilitation Robotics (ICORR). IEEE (2019)
5. Faeik, R.M., et al.: Design and testing of low cost three-modes of operation voice controller for wheelchairs and rehabilitation robotics. In: 2015 IEEE 9th International Symposium on Intelligent Signal Processing (WISP) Proceedings. IEEE (2015)
6. Zinchenko, K., Chien-Yu, W., Song, K.-T.: A study on speech recognition control for a surgical robot. IEEE Trans. Industr. Inf. **13**(2), 607–615 (2016)
7. Berdibayeva, G.K., et al.:: Features of Speech Commands Recognition Using an Artificial Neural Network. Ural Symposium on Biomedical Engineering, p. 2021. Radioelectronics and Information Technology (USBEREIT), IEEE (2021)
8. Precalculus, S.K.J.: A Functional Approach to Graphing and Problem Solving. Jones & Bartlett Publishers (2011)
9. Alibegović, B., Prljača, N., Kimmel, M., Schultalbers, M.: Speech recognition system for a service robot - a performance evaluation. In: 2020 16th International Conference on Control, Automation, Robotics and Vision (ICARCV), pp. 1171–1176 (2020). https://doi.org/10.1109/ICARCV50220.2020.9305342
10. HOY, Matthew B. Alexa, Siri, Cortana, and more: an introduction to voice assistants. Med. Ref. Serv. Quar. **37**(1) 81–88 (2018)

Photovoltaic Power Predictor Module Based on Historical Production and Weather Conditions Data

Elizabeth Martinez[2], Juan Cuadrado[2], and Juan C. Martinez-Santos[1]($\boxtimes$)

[1] Universidad Tenologica de Bolivar, Cartagena, Colombia
jcmartinezs@utb.edu.co
[2] EXIA Energía Inteligente, Cartagena, Colombia

Abstract. In recent years the demand for electrical energy has increased significantly. Usually, the electrical grid covers this demand. However, this fuel energy is known for its significant carbon footprint. For that reason, different mechanisms to bring cleaner energies have been explored, like hydraulic, wind, thermal, and one of the most popular solar energy. Although solar energy is abundant and environmentally friendly, the photovoltaic energy that comes from the sun, solar production is subject to different external perturbations, such as environmental conditions. Therefore it has been necessary to develop other methods based on statistics, machine learning, or deep learning to make solar forecasting and predict production and weather conditions. Specifically, this work proposes an evaluation of three different deep learning models to predict irradiance, temperature, and production of a photovoltaic system located in the city of Cartagena, Colombia. Those are irradiance and temperature using the historical data on production and weather conditions. This data has been registered on a web platform for seven months, from January 1, 2022, until June 28, 2022.

Keywords: Forecasting · Photo voltaic · Energy production · Condition monitoring · Deep learning

1 Introduction

In recent years, around the world, the demand for electrical energy has increased significantly [1]. Traditionally, the electrical power that comes from the grid supplies this demand. However, this energy source is obtained from fossil fuels [2], which leaves a significant carbon footprint on the earth [3]. For this reason, renewable sources, like hydraulic energy, wind energy, thermal solar energy, and photovoltaic (PV) solar energy, are designed and used to buck up, supply, or replace the energy demand from the electrical grid [4].

Specifically, solar energy is the most promising and popular renewable energy [5] since it is an environmentally friendly and abundant source considering solar

© The Author(s), under exclusive license to Springer Nature Switzerland AG 2022
J. C. Figueroa-García et al. (Eds.): WEA 2022, CCIS 1685, pp. 461–472, 2022.
https://doi.org/10.1007/978-3-031-20611-5_38

incidence over the earth's surface. It is around, $1.5 \times 1018[\frac{kWh}{year}]$, so it can cover 10,000 times the current world annually energy demand [6].

Even though a PV system efficiently converts energy from sunlight to produce electricity using photovoltaic cell arrays, the performance of the production of any PV system is mainly subject to uncontrollable meteorological and environmental variables and external factors. Examples in the first set are atmospheric temperature, wind, pressure, humidity, and solar irradiance. On the other hand, external factors such as unclean panels and growing vegetation shading may impact the system operation like low performance or failure risk. Therefore to mitigate risks and prevent unnecessary management costs, it is essential to continuous monitoring and forecasting to assess system performance, predict the power generation, and identify anomaly detection and the need for a PV system intervention.

Therefore, this work proposes different numerical, statistical, machine learning, and deep learning approaches to monitor and forecast a PV system's performance using usually historical data of energy production and weather parameters. Specifically, for PV forecasting, it is used numerical methods that include analytical approaches like exploratory data analysis (EDA) [7], statistical models like fuzzy logic(FL) [8], Markov chain, and autoregressive, among other regression models. For artificial intelligence models, there are machine learning models like support vector machine (SVM), and k-nearest neighbors [9], artificial neural network (ANN), naive Bayes, and random forest, genetic algorithm(GA) [10], and neural networks(NN) [11].

However, traditional numerical methods and machine learning cannot process the huge amount of historical data and often stop their learning increase at a certain data threshold. Fortunately, deep learning models have shown a strong relationship between the increased accuracy of predictions and the amount of data they fed or trained. Hence, deep, because PV solar systems gather huge amounts of sequential data, there are used time series specialized deep learning models for PV forecasting, such as recurrent neural network (RNN) [12], long short-term memory (LSTM) [13], gated recurrent unit (GRU) [14], and convolutional neural network-LSTM (CNN-LSTM) models are typical [15].

Specifically, this work proposes to evaluate to predict the irradiance, the temperature, and the power production of a photovoltaic system using historical data imported from the Fronius inverter web platform logged to a Photovoltaic system installed on the roof of a building located in the city of Cartagena, Colombia. This data is from January 1, 2022 - to July 28, 2022. We divide the data set into three-time period groups using 25% of each data set to train three deep learning models, CNN, LSTM, and GRU, and the percentage left to test the model predictions. Next, we evaluate the performance of each data period (one week, one month, and 2-month training to predict one month, four months, and five months) with MSE, MEAE, and R^2 metrics. The total evaluation results show that GRU, LSTM, and models have an accuracy up to 95% for each variable prediction.

Results also showed that the GRU method is the most accurate and fastest to train in an overall analysis of all the metrics evaluated. Being its performance 96%–97.1%, for Production prediction, 96%–97.8% for irradiance prediction, and 98.1%–98.3% for temperature prediction. The previous results analysis leads to an extender work focused on exploiting the different system sensed variables from both the inverter and the meteorological station to obtain a robust module for better forecasting, monitoring, and preventing management and failure detection.

2 Related Work

Time series-based methods are known to search data features and regular patterns in the historical data of a system. Different statistical machine learning (ML) and deep learning models are commonly used for PV solar forecasting since solar forecasting is based on sequential data time series. For example, a review of ML and statistical models based on historical data [16]. However, due to their fast adaptive property to environmental conditions change, ANNs and Support-Vector Machines (SVMs) are the best-performing models for forecasting.

Genetic Algorithms (GAs) are best for optimizing forecasting models' hyperparameters [17]. This work introduced a hybrid forecasting model for the DKASC weather data set. The hybrid method merges an improved K-means clustering algorithm, the grey relational analysis, and the Elman neural network for short-term prediction [18].

Another work, a review focused only on DL methods for renewable energy forecasting, shows Some notes on data pre-processing techniques for Forecasting data sets [19]. A comprehensive review of papers from 2008 till 2019 on ML, DL, and hybrid models to forecast power production from PV. Interesting concluding remarks. Mainly focused on methods for point forecasting [20]. A comparison of state-of-the-art models to predict PV power production focused on testing many simple linear regression models (also Ridge, Lasso, and Elastic Net) to the DT and ensemble models, both bagging (RF) and boosting (eXtreme Gradient Boosting).

A review focused only on three DL methods; LSTM, RNN, Gated Recurrent Unit (GRU), and a hybrid Convolutional Neural Network + LSTM (CNN+LSTM) to forecast solar irradiance and PV power production. Generally, LSTM performs overall until it deals with massive data set [21] and proposes a CNN+LSTM to solve this issue. This paper highlights using RMSE as the most helpful metric, allowing easy comparison of results [22]. And finally, the work a review of various reinforcement learning methods, both classical (multi-agent RL, etc.) and deep (Deep Q-network, etc.), shows prediction parameters for sustainable energy and electric systems [23].

3   Methodology

This section contains the steps required to make the historical data suitable to evaluate three prediction deep learning models. The deep learning models implemented for the predicted module are LSTM, GRU, and CNN.

3.1   Data General Description

Table 1. Historical data registered on fronuis web-platform

Variable	Unit
Date	[dd.MM.yyyy HH:mm]
Irradiation	[W/m^2]
Ambient temperature	[°C]
Module temperature	[°C]
Apparent power (S)	[VA]
Reactive power (Q)	[VAr]
PV Production	[Wh]

The data used to evaluate this method corresponds to a seven-month data imported from the Fronius Web Platform that had been registered information from the data captured by a three-phase inverter (AC) that is part of a 60.8 [kW] (DC) photovoltaic solar system. It is on the roof of a building located at (10.405139, −75.502959) at an inclination of 12° and azimuth of 192.2°. The installed system maximizes the available space's use and minimizes the effects of shadows, and it comes with a centralized monitoring system. This system allows hourly monitoring of the entire system's operation, accessible locally, on-site, or remotely, via the internet. The system supplies detailed information about the energy produced and the production status of the system. Additionally, it is equipped with a weather station, as shown in Table 1.

3.2   Data Flux and Pre-processing

As seen in Fig. 1 historical data of PV system and environment is first captured using an inverter and a weather station connected to a Web monitoring system provided by the inverter provider. However, the 100% of raw data stored can not be processed immediately because subject to the stability of the electrical grid and internet connection. Therefore, the first step to standardizing the data is pre-processing raw data to eliminate *null* and *nan* cells. Then normalize the remaining data in the [0, 1] range so that all the cells are either integral or float type and can help fill an empty data-set that feeds a prediction module.

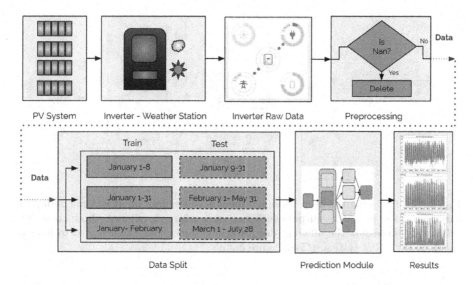

Fig. 1. This figure shows the flux of historical data obtained from the PV system, the inverter machine, and the weather station, following the pre-processing steps to final evaluation and predictions.

3.3 Data Set Split

As mentioned in the previous sections, historical data covers seven months. So, to evaluate the model, we decided to group the pre-processed data-set into three different period time groups to feed the block with three deep learning algorithms(LSTM, GRU, and CNN). Those periods are divided as follows in Table 2.

Table 2. List of time period groups

Train	Test
January 1–January 8	January 9–January 31
January 1–January 31	February 1–May 31
January 1–February 28	March 1–July 28

Note that we selected all three groups to evaluate each case if the training data-set is not enough to predict the test time accurately.

4 Prediction Module

This work aims to predict temperature, irradiance, and PV production using historical data, i.e., time series format data. We propose a prediction module that first takes one of the processed normalized data sets separated on the split

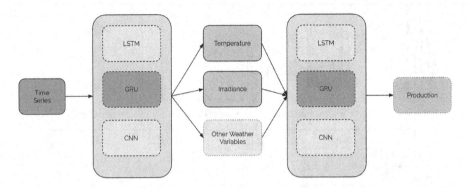

Fig. 2. Illustration of the deep learning pipeline, where data input is Time Series and variables in red boxes are outputs such as Temperature, Irradiance, Production. The yellow box represents the different deep learning approaches implemented to forecast the data of the PV system. (Color figure online)

process to follow the steps shown in Fig. 2. Those steps indicate that each data-time set goes first through an evaluation block composed of an LSTM network, a GRU network, and a CNN, used to predict the chosen period defined temperature, irradiance, and production variables over the selected period. Then each predicted variable is used to train another block again with the same three networks to estimate production using weather variables, temperature, and irradiance.

4.1 Long Short-Term Memory (LSTM)

LSTM is a developed artificial neural network proposed by Hochreiter et al. [24]. That was proposed to be used as a long-term information dependence, particularly this LSTM network has feedback connections that solve the vanishing gradient problem that commonly has the (RNN). As RNNs, LSTM helps classify tasks, processing images, video, sequences of data, and time series to predict any variable of a historical data-set, like PV solar historical data.

4.2 Gated Recurrent Unit (GRU)

The GRU network is another option to solve the vanishing gradient problem from de RNN [25]. GRU network has a similar architecture as the LSTM network. However, the GRU network has fewer learning parameters, which means that it is less complex than the LSTM network, leading to a more efficient network. As LSTM, this network helps for long traces of data signals, like language processing, audio processing, and time series predictions.

4.3 CNN

CNN is deep learning is a feedforward network that mainly has the property of learning network weights and biases. Although it is primarily for processing data with a grid topology, the CNN network layer convolution1D helps in applications like image and video recognition, classification and segmentation, image classification, natural language processing, and time like financial series or forecasting series.

4.4 Metrics

Defining some evaluation metrics for each of the forecast deep learning models used to train each data group is necessary to evaluate the performance of the prediction module. However, despite many metrics, specifically for forecasting is okay to evaluate prediction performance just by defining the variables shown in Table 3.

Table 3. Evaluation metrics.

Metric	Equation	Desired value
Coefficient of determination R^2	$1 - \frac{RSS}{TSS}$	$R^2 = 1$
Mean squared error (MSE)	$\sum_{i=1}^{D}(x_i - y_i)^2$	$MSE = 0$
Mean absolute error (MAE)	$\sum_{i=1}^{D} |x_i - y_i|$	$MAE = 0$

Specifically, the correlation coefficient R^2 is the proportion of the variation in the dependent variable that is predictable from the independent variable. R^2 coefficient typically takes a value between $[0-1]$ being $R^2 = 1$ the desired value. For mean square error (MSE) metric measures the average of the square error between the estimated value and the actual value. Its desired value is $MSE = 0$. And finally, the Mean absolute error (MAE) metric measures the average error magnitude in a set of predictions, and its desired value is $MAE = 0$.

5   Results

This section below shows the prediction metrics results for the predictions made on temperature, irradiance, and PV production obtained by implementing the prediction module. Each one of the Tables 4, 5, and 6 shows the prediction obtained at the output of the first three deep learning networks block. The period to evaluate those predictions was: January 9–January 31; and February 1–May 31. Table 6 shows an extra period prediction for PV production from January 9–January 31 and February 1–May 31. We evaluate these periods using the previous weather and production predictions as input for a second prediction block. This section also shows a compilation of images that visually displays the actual data in color blue vs. the predicted data in color orange for each indicated variable, temperature, irradiance, and PV production.

5.1   Temperature

Figure 3 shows an accurate temperature prediction in both periods (January 9–January 31 and February 1–May 31), being the Real value the one in blue color and the predicted value the one in orange color.

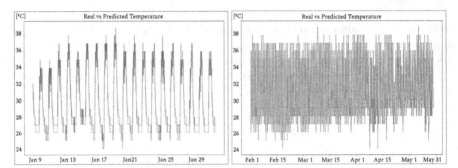

(a) Temperature prediction of three weeks. (b) Temperature prediction of four months.

Fig. 3. Temperature prediction (Orange) vs Real value (Blue) after first prediction module. (Color figure online)

Table 4. Temperature prediction Metrics.

	January 9–January 31			February 1–May 31		
	R^2	MSE	MAE	R^2	MSE	MAE
LSTM	0.98381	**0.0001**	0.0051	0.98089	0.00108	0.01867
GRU	**0.98389**	**0.0001**	**0.0048**	**0.98109**	**0.00107**	0.01842
CNN	0.98306	**0.0001**	0.0064	0.98107	0.00107	**0.01800**

Table 4 shows on the R^2 score is at least 0.98 which is near to the desirable value $R^2 = 1$. The MSE and MAE metrics also show that both are near to their desired value $MSE = MAE = 0$. It shows that all three methods, LSTM, GRU, and CNN, perform well for every prediction. However, it shows that GRU performs slightly better than the other two methods.

5.2   Irradiance

Figure 4 shows a most accurate prediction compared to the Temperature accuracy, in both periods of time. Results in Table 5 show that on this occasion, the LSTM network had better performance on the irradiance prediction for both periods for all metrics $R^2, MSE, and MAE$ being the predictions between 96.316%–97.801.

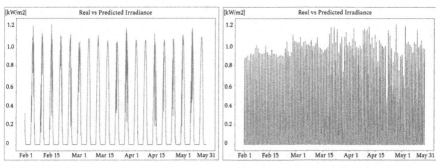

(a) Irradiance prediction of three weeks.   (b) Irradiance prediction of four months.

Fig. 4. Irradiance prediction (Orange) vs Real value (Blue) after first prediction module.. (Color figure online)

Table 5. Irradiance prediction metrics.

	January 9–January 31			February 1–May 31		
	R^2	MSE	MAE	R^2	MSE	MAE
LSTM	**0.97801**	**0.00116**	**0.01096**	0.96314	**0.00373**	**0.02301**
GRU	0.97783	0.00117	0.01165	**0.96316**	**0.00373**	0.023198
CNN	0.97749	0.00119	0.01238	0.96240	0.00380	0.02401

5.3 Production

Finally, we found that the GRU network obtained the best performance on all metrics evaluation for PV Production prediction. In addition, for both periods, it has an accuracy between 95.234%–97.143 (Figs. 5 and 6).

Table 6. Photovoltaic production prediction metrics.

	January 9–January 31			February 1–May 31			March 1–July 28		
	R^2	MSE	MAE	R^2	MSE	MAE	R^2	MSE	MAE
LSTM	0.97141	**0.00182**	0.01875	0.96239	0.00228	0.02084	0.95221	0.00274	0.02115
GRU	**0.97143**	**0.00182**	**0.01830**	0.96254	0.00227	**0.02008**	**0.95234**	**0.00273**	**0.02082**
CNN	0.97075	0.00187	0.01900	**0.96262**	**0.00226**	0.02037	0.95155	0.00277	0.02111

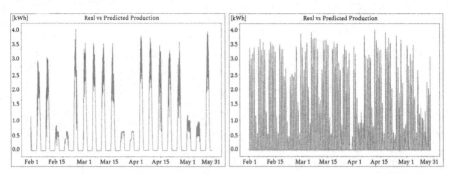

(a) Production prediction of three weeks.   (b) Production prediction of four months.

Fig. 5. Prediction (Orange) vs Real value (Blue) after first prediction module. (Color figure online)

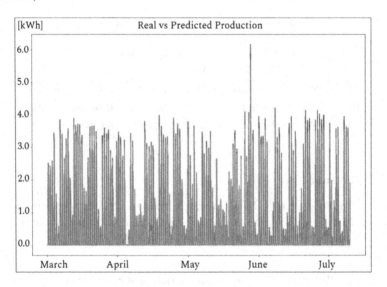

Fig. 6. Production prediction of five months shows prediction (Orange) vs Real value (Blue) using both historical production and weather data. (Color figure online)

6   Conclusion

The evaluation of the deep learning models implementing the methodology proposed shows that the prediction module achieved the expected value for each evaluation metric, that is, $MSE = MEAE = 0$ and $R^2 = 1$. Furthermore, we evaluated each metric using three different periods of data. These periods are (January 1–8 to predict January 9–31; January to predict February to May, and January to forecast March to July).

Specifically, GRU and LSTM methods had an accuracy up to 95% for each variable predicted. We also found that GRU has the best performance on each evaluated metric and is the fastest training method implemented. Also, the overall results has the best performance, that is, 96%–97.1% for Production prediction, 96%–97.8% for irradiance prediction, and 98.1%–98.3% for temperature prediction.

Finally, an extension of this work would focus on developing a robust prediction model that includes other sensed variables from the inverter monitoring system and the meteorological station. This extension may lead to a more detailed forecast and continuous system monitoring, including preventive management and failure prediction.

References

1. Dincer, F.: The analysis on wind energy electricity generation status, potential and policies in the world. Renew. Sustain. Energy Rev. **15**(9), 5135–5142 (2011)
2. Brockway, P.E., Owen, A., Brand-Correa, L.I., Hardt, L.: Estimation of global final-stage energy-return-on-investment for fossil fuels with comparison to renewable energy sources. Nat. Energy **4**(7), 612–621 (2019)
3. Aichele, R., Felbermayr, G.: Kyoto and the carbon footprint of nations. J. Environ. Econ. Manag. **63**(3), 336–354 (2012)
4. Li, K., Bian, H., Liu, C., Zhang, D., Yang, Y.: Comparison of geothermal with solar and wind power generation systems. Renew. Sustain. Energy Rev. **42**, 1464–1474 (2015)
5. Li, G., Li, M., Taylor, R., Hao, Y., Besagni, G., Markides, C.: Solar energy utilisation: current status and roll-out potential. Appl. Thermal Eng. **209**, 118285 (2022)
6. Hafezi, R., Alipour, M.: Renewable energy sources: traditional and modern-age technologies. In: Affordable and Clean Energy, pp. 1085–1099. Springer, Heidelberg (2021). https://doi.org/10.1007/978-3-319-95864-4_18
7. Amant, R.S., Cohen, P.R.: Intelligent support for exploratory data analysis. J. Comput. Graph. Stat. **7**(4), 545–558 (1998)
8. Pezeshki, Z., Mazinani, S.M.: Comparison of artificial neural networks, fuzzy logic and neuro fuzzy for predicting optimization of building thermal consumption: a survey. Artif. Intell. Rev. **52**(1), 495–525 (2019)
9. Li, R., Wang, H.-N., He, H., Cui, Y.-M., Du, Z.-L.: Support vector machine combined with k-nearest neighbors for solar flare forecasting. Chin. J. Astron. Astrophys. **7**(3), 441 (2007)
10. Zhou, Y., Zhou, N., Gong, L., Jiang, M.: Prediction of photovoltaic power output based on similar day analysis, genetic algorithm and extreme learning machine. Energy **204**, 117894 (2020)
11. Hocaoğlu, F.O., Gerek, Ö.N., Kurban, M.: Hourly solar radiation forecasting using optimal coefficient 2-d linear filters and feed-forward neural networks. Solar Energy **82**(8), 714–726 (2008)
12. Pang, Z., Niu, F., O'Neill, Z.: Solar radiation prediction using recurrent neural network and artificial neural network: a case study with comparisons. Renew. Energy **156**, 279–289 (2020)
13. Jung, Y., Jung, J., Kim, B., Han, S.: Long short-term memory recurrent neural network for modeling temporal patterns in long-term power forecasting for solar pv facilities: case study of South Korea. J. Cleaner Prod. **250**, 119476 (2020)

14. de Melo, G.A., Sugimoto, D.N., Tasinaffo, P.M., Santos, A.H.M., Cunha, A.M., Dias, L.A.V.: A new approach to river flow forecasting: LSTM and GRU multivariate models. IEEE Latin Am. Trans. **17**(12), 1978–1986 (2019)
15. Gao, B., Huang, X., Shi, J., Tai, Y., Zhang, J.: Hourly forecasting of solar irradiance based on ceemdan and multi-strategy CNN-LSTM neural networks. Renew. Energy **162**, 1665–1683 (2020)
16. Ajith, M., Martínez-Ramón, M.: Deep learning based solar radiation micro forecast by fusion of infrared cloud images and radiation data. Appl. Energy **294**, 117014 (2021)
17. Das, U.K., et al.: Forecasting of photovoltaic power generation and model optimization: a review. Renew. Sustain. Energy Rev. **81**, 912–928 (2018)
18. Lin, P., Peng, Z., Lai, Y., Cheng, S., Chen, Z., Wu, L.: Short-term power prediction for photovoltaic power plants using a hybrid improved kmeans-gra-elman model based on multivariate meteorological factors and historical power datasets. Energy Conv. Manag. **177**, 704–717 (2018)
19. Wang, H., Lei, Z., Zhang, X., Zhou, B., Peng, J.: A review of deep learning for renewable energy forecasting. Energy Conv. Manag. **198**, 111799 (2019)
20. Mellit, A., Pavan, A.M., Ogliari, E., Leva, S., Lughi, V.: Advanced methods for photovoltaic output power forecasting: a review. Appl. Sci. **10**(2), 487 (2020)
21. Li, W., Wu, H., Zhu, N., Jiang, Y., Tan, J., Guo, Y.: Prediction of dissolved oxygen in a fishery pond based on gated recurrent unit (GRU). Inf. Process. Agric. **8**(1), 185–193 (2021)
22. Rajagukguk, R.A., Ramadhan, R.A., Lee, H.-J.: A review on deep learning models for forecasting time series data of solar irradiance and photovoltaic power. Energies **13**(24), 6623 (2020)
23. Yang, T., Zhao, L., Li, W., Zomaya, A.Y.: Reinforcement learning in sustainable energy and electric systems: a survey. Ann. Rev. Control **49**, 145–163 (2020)
24. Liu, Y., et al.: Wind power short-term prediction based on LSTM and discrete wavelet transform. Appl. Sci. **9**(6), 1108 (2019)
25. Cho, K., et al.: Learning phrase representations using rnn encoder-decoder for statistical machine translation. arXiv preprint arXiv:1406.1078 (2014)

Vehicle Detection and Counting Framework in Aerial Images Based on SoC-FPGA

Julian Uribe-Rios[✉][iD], Luis Castano-Londono[iD], David Marquez-Viloria[iD], and Luis Morantes-Guzman[iD]

Department of Electronics and Telecommunication Engineering, Instituto Tecnológico Metropolitano ITM, Medellín, Colombia
julianuribe209085@correo.itm.edu.co,
{luiscastano,davidmarquez,luismorantes}@itm.edu.co

Abstract. The use of smart cameras on highways has increased to monitor traffic variables such as density, speed, and flow of vehicles and to prevent car accidents. Many current systems can become expensive due to the high demand for resources since large amounts of data must be processed. Other systems only store the video and perform the processing offline. In this work, it is presented the development of a system that performs the processing using a heterogeneous architecture based on FPGA to achieve a real-time implementation due to hardware acceleration and low power consumption. The implementation of the model obtained with SSD MobilenetV2 in the Ultra96V2 achieved a rate of 23 FPS only in detection and 18 FPS adding vehicle counting, tracking, and display on a monitor.

Keywords: CNN · Field programmable gate array (FPGA) · System-on-a-chip (SoC) · Deep Learning Processing Unit (DPU)

1 Introduction

In recent years, there has been growing interest in object detection models [1]. These models have prompted an advancement in smart video analytics and their applications have increased in the real world. For instance, Intelligent transportation systems (ITS) [2] take advantage of rapid growth of video surveillance systems [3] to boost solutions to problems of traffic parameters measurement [4] and traffic monitoring and analysis [5] based on computer vision algorithms. Furthermore, vision-based vehicle detection and counting [6] are key tasks for ITS. The number of vehicles is computed by analyzing videos acquired by a fixed camera [7] or by unmanned aerial vehicles (UAVs) [8].

Supported by investigation group AE&CC COL0053581.

© The Author(s), under exclusive license to Springer Nature Switzerland AG 2022
J. C. Figueroa-García et al. (Eds.): WEA 2022, CCIS 1685, pp. 473–484, 2022.
https://doi.org/10.1007/978-3-031-20611-5_39

Many of the current object detection approaches can be costly due to their high demand for resources and maintenance. One of the options to reduce this impact is FPGAs (field-programmable gate arrays), which reduce computational processes and energy expenditure. As far as we know, only a few studies have shown object detection on embedded systems. Li et al. [12] demonstrate that by using an FPGA for real-time object detection, an energy efficiency 3.3 times better than a GPU and up to 418 times better than a CPU is achieved. Chen et al. [11] use an FPGA because of its high computing power and low resource requirements. Because of this, he can stitch together images in real-time and generate panoramic videos in conjunction with a special camera.

This work presents a system for edge traffic monitoring using a heterogeneous FPGA-based architecture. The main contributions of this work are summarized as follows.

- A vehicle detection and counting framework using a heterogeneous architecture based on FPGA to achieve a real-time implementation at low power consumption is proposed.
- The Mobilenetv2 SSD architecture is selected to perform the transfer learning process achieving adequate results in terms of detection speed.
- The performance of our framework using the Ultra96V2 SoC-FPGA is demonstrated. Experimental results show a speed of 23 FPS for the detection system and 18 FPS testing the whole system with a power consumption lower than 3.5 W.

The rest of the paper is organized as follows: the proposed method is further discussed in section Sect. 2, experimental results are presented in section Sect. 3 to analyze the prototype's performance. Finally, conclusions are detailed in section Sect. 4.

2   Materials and Methods

The objective of this work is to implement a system that performs vehicular traffic detection considering cars, motorcycles, and trucks on edge in order to perform vehicle counting. The implementation is developed in a heterogeneous architecture based on FPGA, taking advantage of its multiple parallel operations and low power consumption. For this work, the Ultra96v2 from Xilinx was used, which allows working with convolutional neural networks and has a good price/performance ratio. The Ultra96V2 has a 2GB RAM LPDDR4 memory, and the chip is a Zynq UltraScale+ MPSoC ZU3EG A484 equipped with a 1.5 GHz ARM Cortex-A53 Quad Core.

Current object detection algorithms use deep learning models and are divided into two categories, two-stage detection algorithms such as R-CNN, Fast R-CNN, and Faster R-CNN; and one-stage detection algorithms such as YOLO and SSD. Among the performance indicators in object detection models is accuracy, where the object's positioning is considered in addition to its classification. Another important indicator is detection speed, where single-stage algorithms usually have an advantage [10].

Vitis AI is a development environment created by Xilinx which allows using Frameworks such as Tensorflow, Caffe, and PyTorch to develop applications using deep learning and allows users to use the hardware acceleration potential of FPGAs for processing and inference.

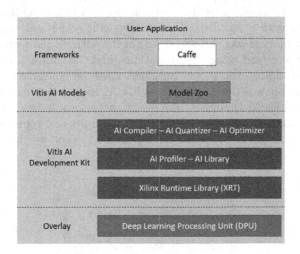

Fig. 1. Vitis AI platform

This development platform offers several pre-optimized models of convolutional neural networks, which can be implemented in Xilinx devices, as well as tools such as AI Quantizer, AI Optimizer, and AI Compiler to quantize, prune and compile the models. Vitis AI also provides different Deep Learning Processing Unit (DPU) configurations which are hardware overlays where inference is performed and can be configured depending on the workload and application. Figure 1 shows the tools used in this work from the Vitis AI platform.

2.1   Model Construction

When counting vehicles, it is essential to have an aerial view of the scene to avoid inconveniences such as occlusion and shadows, which affect the counting process. The available models cannot detect this aerial view due to the data set with which they are trained, so transfer learning was performed using a proprietary dataset obtained from videos of vehicular traffic captured from a drone to train the neural network.

The dataset was tagged with a semi-automatic labeling tool developed to generate files with XML extension containing the locations in each image of the objects to be detected and their respective class. The classes car, motorcycle, and truck were the three classes to be detected. A model with a Xilinx Mobilenetv2

SSD architecture available in the Vitis AI Model Zoo was chosen to perform the transfer learning process since this architecture is known for its good results in terms of detection speed. The model available in the Vitis AI Model Zoo was pre-trained with the BDD database in the Caffe Framework, had 11 classes, including the background, and had an input size of 480 × 360. The network was modified to change the number of classes to 4, including the background, as required by Caffe. Also, the path to the new training and validation dataset was modified. Only 31 images were used for training and 10 for validation to achieve good detection with a small dataset for a specific scene and application. The entire training process was performed within the Vitis AI platform on an Nvidia Gtx 1650 graphics card using 4000 iterations, and the training took 9 h.

After the training, the model obtained must be converted to run on the Ultra96 DPU; this was done using the Vitis AI tools following the flow shown in Fig. 2. Using the AI Quantizer, the quantization process was performed; this quantization allows using integer computational units and representing weights and activations in fewer bits since 32-bit floating point weights are generally used in neural network training.

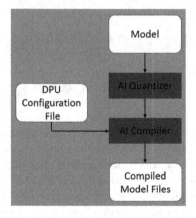

Fig. 2. Development flow for the model to implement

By converting 32-bit floating-point weights and activations to an 8-bit integer format, the Vitis AI quantizer can reduce computational complexity and minimize accuracy loss. The conversion is done since the fixed-point network model requires less memory bandwidth, which provides faster speed and higher energy efficiency than the floating-point model.

Vitis AI has another tool called AI Optimizer that can reduce the number of computations in neural networks by increasing the speed of inference. This tool performs model pruning by reducing complexity, aiming to arrive at smaller, more efficient neural networks. The compressed neural network runs faster and reduces the computational cost. This tool requires a license, so it was not used in this work.

After quantizing the model, the Vitis AI Compiler was used, where the model is compiled specifically for a DPU version. In this step, it is necessary to provide a configuration file containing a series of parameters. This DPU is an intellectual property (IP) core that is implemented in the programmable logic (PL) of the Ultra96V2 and connects directly to the processing system (PS) through the advanced extensible interface (AXI4) for data transfer. The DPU accelerates the execution of many operations in convolutional neural networks, such as convolution, deconvolution, and maximum clustering, as well as trigger functions such as ReLU, LeakyReLU, or softmax. The DPU can be configured by adjusting several parameters to optimize resource utilization and select the features needed for a given implementation scenario. One of these parameters is the DPU architecture, where each value can be selected from B512, B800, B1024, B1152, B1600, B2304, B3136, and B4096 representing the maximum number of operations per clock cycle that the DPU can achieve. Other parameters allow the configuration of the memory and use of DSP resources. This DPU configuration setting is important because it can be adapted to the application's requirements, taking into account the restrictions in terms of resources available on the chip being used. The parameters used in the DPU configuration file for this work are shown in Table 1.

Table 1. DPU's parameters used.

DPU's parameters	Setting
Architecture	B2304
URAM	Disable URAM
DRAM	Disable DRAM
RAM usage configuration	RAM usage low
Channel augmentation configuration	Enable
DepthWiseConv configuration	Enable
Pool average configuration	Enable
Support multiplication of two feature maps	Disable
RELU type configuration	RELU LEAKYRELU RELU6
DSP48 usage configuration	DSP48 USAGE LOW
Power configuration	LOW POWER DISABLE
Device configuration	MPSOC

For this DPU configuration in the Ultra96V2, the amount of resources used in the FPGA is shown in Table 2.

Table 2. Resources used.

Resource	Utilization	Available	Utilization%
LUT	56274	70560	79.75
LUTRAM	4295	28800	14.91
FF	90638	141120	64.23
BRAM	171	216	79.17
DSP	326	360	90.56

2.2 Tracking and Counting Application

The compiled model was copied to the Ultra96V2 micro SD card, where a Linux image is used in the PS built with Petalinux and has the Vitis AI tools to use the model. An executable file was generated, as shown in Fig. 3, developing an application in C++ language and using Vitis AI Library to perform the inference in the DPU and vehicle counting and tracking.

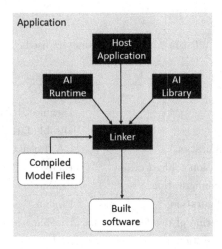

Fig. 3. Development flow for the application

Figure 4 shows the flowchart of the application created where the detection of vehicles is performed by obtaining from each of them the coordinates where they are in the image, the class to which they belong, and the probability. Then the coordinates obtained are passed to the tracker, which is in charge of verifying if the vehicle already has an identification number (ID) assigned or if it must be registered.

After a vehicle registered in the tracker is not found during the subsequent N frames, it is deleted. Figure 5 illustrates step by step the operation mode of the tracker, which works as follow:

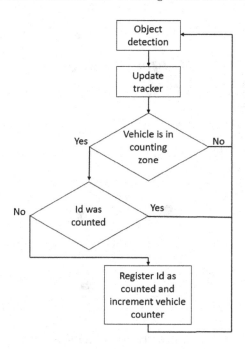

Fig. 4. Application flow chart

(a) The tracker receives the coordinates and calculates the centroids for each bounding box using the Eqs. 1 and 2 where X and Y are the positions of the vehicle on the axes, and W and H are the width and height of the bounding box.

$$Cx = X + W/2 \tag{1}$$

$$Cy = Y + H/2 \tag{2}$$

(b) The Euclidean distance between each centroid of the vehicles existing in the tracker concerning the input centroids just calculated is calculated.
(c) Associate input centroids with the existing ones according to the minimum distance between them.
(d) Register with an ID the new centroids that were not associated with an existing one.

A region was defined for vehicle counting; each vehicle passing through was counted, and its ID was recorded to avoid re-counting.

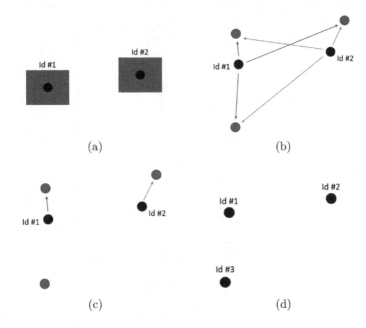

Fig. 5. Tracker operation

3   Results

Tests were performed on a video acquired with a drone on a road where vehicles circulate in two directions to obtain the results, as shown in Fig. 6. There, it can be seen that the counting zones for each lane are denoted with a green line in addition to each ID, class, and bounding box assigned to each detected vehicle.

Fig. 6. Detection results.

The detection rate obtained was 23 frames per second (FPS); however, with the addition of tracking, counting, and display on a screen through the Mini DisplayPort port of the Ultra96V2, the FPS decreases to 18.

To evaluate the vehicle detection model we use precision, recall and F1 score defined respectively by their equations in 3, 4 and 5. Where TP is truly positive, FP is a false positive, and FN is a false negative.

$$Precision = \frac{TP}{TP + FP} \tag{3}$$

$$Recall = \frac{TP}{TP + FN} \tag{4}$$

$$F1 = \frac{2TP}{2TP + FP + FN} \tag{5}$$

The results shown in Fig. 7 correspond to the evaluation in 10 test images of the three metrics mentioned above, using the neural network with transfer learning. False positives were not founded in any of these images. Therefore the metric precision for each image gives a value of 1.0. Most of the false negatives corresponded to the motorcycle class, which may be due to their smaller size or smaller presence in the training images.

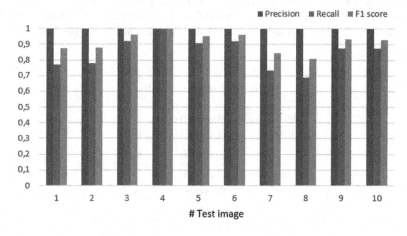

Fig. 7. Precision, Recall and F1 Score in neural network with transfer learning.

The values obtained for the precision, recall and f1 score metrics in the original neural network without transfer learning are shown in Fig. 8. The Mobilenetv2 SSD network although trained on the BDD database which is used to perform detection in vehicular traffic, is not useful for vehicle detection with an aerial view and this is reflected in the values obtained in the recall and f1 score metrics, which demonstrates the need for transfer learning.

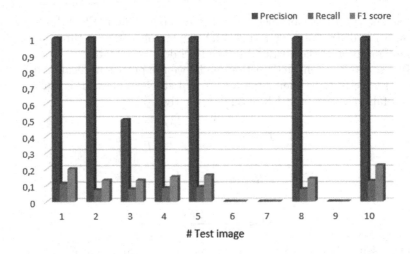

Fig. 8. Precision, Recall and F1 Score in the original neural network.

Table 3 shows the results for the vehicle count, showing the number of vehicles counted and the number lost for both lanes in the test video, taking into account that Direction A corresponds to vehicles going to the left and Direction B to those going to the right. The results show that the counting errors are not due to detecting objects with the model or the counting algorithm, but they are generated by the tracker in the ID assignment, which is an element to be improved.

Table 3. Counting results.

Direction A	Miss detection	4
	Detected	18
	Precision	81.81
Direction B	Miss detection	1
	Detected	20
	Precision	95.23

The Ultra96V2 has a power management bus (PMBus) connected to the chip rails and is accessible through a software tool on the Linux operating system running on the PS. The power was measured on the ten rails available before and during the application execution to observe its variation. Figure 9 shows that around second 20, the application starts to run, and the power is increased in the rails with VCCO 1.1V, PSINT_FP. Significantly VCCINT labels increase from 1.5 W with a series of oscillations that reach a maximum of 3.5 W because the DPU is used in the PL to perform inference with the neural network.

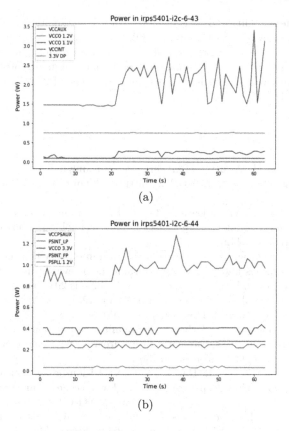

Fig. 9. Power consumption.

4   Conclusions

This work presents a system for edge traffic monitoring using a heterogeneous FPGA-based architecture. In this first application, it is presented the detection of cars, motorcycles, and trucks as well as counting and tracking of these vehicles. One of the characteristics sought in the system is to achieve good processing times and low power consumption. For this reason, it is used a heterogeneous architecture based on SoC-FPGA to achieve an acceleration in the implementation of convolutional neural networks using the DPU and without a significant increase in power consumption.

The FPS obtained with MobilenetV2 SSD shows that a real-time application can be achieved on the Ultra96V2, which performs all the inference and post-processing parts in the same device facilitating all the data sending parts.

In future work, it is proposed to improve the algorithm that performs the tracking, add speed estimation to the application and integrate the IoT system to send the necessary data.

Acknowledgment. This study was supported by the Automática, Electrónica y Ciencias Computacionales (AE&CC) Group COL0053581, at the Sistemas de Control y Robótica Laboratory, attached to the Instituto Tecnológico Metropolitano (ITM). The work was developed in project "Sistema de visión artificial inteligente con aceleración por hardware para aplicaciones IoT industriales" with code P20223 co-funded by ITM and FLY NORTH SAS.

References

1. Zaidi, S.S.A., et al.: A survey of modern deep learning based object detection models. Dig. Signal Process. **126** (2022). https://doi.org/10.1016/j.dsp.2022.103514. 226

2. Yuan, T., et al.: Machine learning for next-generation intelligent transportation systems: a survey. Trans. Emerg. Telecommun. Technol. **33**, e4427 (2022). https://doi.org/10.1002/ett.4427

3. Yang, Z., Pun-Cheng, L.S.: Vehicle detection in intelligent transportation systems and its applications under varying environments: a review. Image Vision Comput. **69**, 143–154 (2018). https://doi.org/10.1016/j.imavis.2017.09.008

4. Khazukov, K., et al.: Real-time monitoring of traffic parameters. J. Big Data **7** (2020). https://doi.org/10.1186/s40537-020-00358-x.158

5. Butilă, E.V., Boboc, R.G.: Urban traffic monitoring and analysis using unmanned aerial vehicles (uavs): a systematic literature review. Remote Sens. **14** (2022). https://doi.org/10.3390/rs14030620.130

6. Song, H., Liang, H., Li, H., Dai, Z., Yun, X.: Vision-based vehicle detection and counting system using deep learning in highway scenes. Eur. Transp. Res. Rev. **11**(1), 1–16 (2019). https://doi.org/10.1186/s12544-019-0390-4

7. Gomaa, A., et al.: Faster cnn-based vehicle detection and counting strategy for fixed camera scenes. Multimedia Tools Appl. (2022). https://doi.org/10.1007/s11042-022-12370-9.148

8. Srivastava, S., et al.: A survey of deep learning techniques for vehicle detection from uav images. J. Syst. Arch. **117** (2021). https://doi.org/10.1016/j.sysarc.2021.102152.206

9. Tayara, H., et al.: Vehicle detection and counting in high-resolution aerial images using convolutional regression neural network. IEEE Access 6, 2220–2230 (2018). https://doi.org/10.1109/ACCESS.2017.2782260

10. Wang, J., Gu, S.: FPGA implementation of object detection accelerator based on Vitis-AI. In: 2021 11th International Conference on Information Science and Technology (ICIST), pp. 571–577 (2021). https://doi.org/10.1109/ICIST52614.2021.9440554

11. Chen, L., et al.: Surrounding vehicle detection using an fpga panoramic camera and deep cnns. IEEE Trans. Intell. Transp. Syst. **21**(12), 5110–5122 (2020). https://doi.org/10.1109/TITS.2019.2949005

12. Li, S., Luo, Y., Sun, K., Yadav, N., Choi, K.K.: A novel fpga accelerator design for real-time and ultra-low power deep convolutional neural networks compared with titan x gpu. IEEE Access **8**, 105455–105471 (2020). https://doi.org/10.1109/ACCESS.2020.3000009

Correction to: Effect of Speckle Filtering in the Performance of Segmentation of Ultrasound Images Using CNNs

Caleb D. Romero-Mercado ⓘ, Sonia H. Contreras-Ortiz ⓘ,
and Andres G. Marrugo ⓘ

Correction to:
Chapter "Effect of Speckle Filtering in the Performance of Segmentation of Ultrasound Images Using CNNs" in:
J. C. Figueroa-García et al. (Eds.): *Applied Computer Sciences in Engineering*, CCIS 1685,
https://doi.org/10.1007/978-3-031-20611-5_13

In the originally published version of chapter 13, the author name Sonia H. Contreras-Ortiz was incorrectly written as Sonia H. Contreraz-Ortiz. This has been corrected.

The updated original version of this chapter can be found at
https://doi.org/10.1007/978-3-031-20611-5_13

© The Author(s), under exclusive license to Springer Nature Switzerland AG 2022
J. C. Figueroa-García et al. (Eds.): WEA 2022, CCIS 1685, p. C1, 2022.
https://doi.org/10.1007/978-3-031-20611-5_40

Author Index

Printed in the United States
by Baker & Taylor Publisher Services